What's New in this Edition

In this edition of the *Microsoft BackOffice Administrator's Survival Guide*, you will find many new additions, ranging from new notes and tips to completely new chapters. For the most part these additions focus on the Microsoft Internet Information Server, Microsoft Exchange Server, and Microsoft SQL Server 6.5. Here are some examples:

- Chapter 1 discusses some of the differences between publishing information internally on your LAN (intranet) and externally on the Internet. It points out several important uses of an intranet.

- Chapter 2 explains what the Microsoft Internet Information Server is and what it can do for you. It looks at some of the ways you can extend your Web server's functionality and describes some of the differences between using ISAPI or CGI extensions.

- Chapter 9 now includes installation and configuration of the Microsoft Domain Name System (DNS) service. This service is WINS-aware and can be quite useful for Internet connectivity and interoperability with UNIX-based systems.

- Chapter 10 is a completely new chapter and covers the Microsoft Internet Information Server from installation to configuration of the WWW, FTP, and Gopher publishing services.

- Chapter 11 is a completely new chapter and examines the dangers of Internet connectivity. It points out solutions to several possible problems that you may encounter once you have connected your network to the Internet.

- Chapters 14 to 19 include additional information on SQL Server 6.5, including how to use the Web Assistant to generate HTML documents suitable for publishing on the your intranet or on the Internet.

- Chapter 22 has been updated to include information on how to inventory your SMS network clients and how to build queries to view the installed applications on your SMS clients.

- Chapters 24 to 28 have been enhanced to cover the day-to-day administration duties of an Exchange Server mail administrator. These chapters have information on configuring the various connectors so that you can connect your Exchange Server installation to foreign mail servers, and they describe how to configure Exchange Server as an SMTP mail server so you can exchange e-mail over the Internet.

- Appendix B (on CD-ROM) has been updated to include relevant registry keys for the Internet Information Server.

- Appendix C (on CD-ROM) has been updated to include performance counters for the Internet Information Server and Exchange Server.

MICROSOFT® BACKOFFICE™ 2

ADMINISTRATOR'S SURVIVAL GUIDE

Second Edition

Arthur E. Knowles

SAMS
PUBLISHING

201 West 103rd Street
Indianapolis, Indiana 46290

International Standard Book Number: 0-672-30977-7

Library of Congress Catalog Card Number: 96-69394

99 98 97 96   4 3 2 1

Interpretation of the printing code: the rightmost double-digit number is the year of the book's printing; the rightmost single-digit, the number of the book's printing. For example, a printing code of 96-1 shows that the first printing of the book occurred in 1996.

Composed in New Century Schoolbook and MCPdigital by Macmillan Computer Publishing

Printed in the United States of America

Trademarks

PUBLISHER AND PRESIDENT:	*Richard K. Swadley*
PUBLISHING TEAM LEADER:	*Rosemarie Graham*
MANAGING EDITOR:	*Cindy Morrow*
DIRECTOR OF MARKETING:	*John Pierce*
ASSISTANT MARKETING MANAGERS:	*Kristina Perry*
	Rachel Wolfe

ACQUISITIONS EDITOR
Grace Buechlein

DEVELOPMENT EDITOR
Todd Bumbalough

SOFTWARE DEVELOPMENT SPECIALIST
John Warriner

PRODUCTION EDITOR
Mary Ann Faughnan

INDEXER
Chris Barrick

TECHNICAL REVIEWER
Robert Bogue
Michelle Friend
Blake Hall

EDITORIAL COORDINATOR
Bill Whitmer

TECHNICAL EDIT COORDINATOR
Lorraine Schaffer

RESOURCE COORDINATOR
Deborah Frisby

EDITORIAL ASSISTANTS
Carol Ackerman, Andi Richter, Rhonda Tinch-Mize

COVER DESIGNER
Tim Amrhein

BOOK DESIGNER
Alyssa Yesh

COPY WRITER
Peter Fuller

PRODUCTION TEAM SUPERVISOR
Brad Chinn

PRODUCTION
Debra Bolhuis, Jeanne Clark, Kevin Cliburn, Jason Hand, Louisa Klucznik, Clint Lahnen, Carl Pierce, Casey Price, Shawn Ring, Laura Robbins, Bobbi Satterfield, M. Anne Sipahimalani, Ian Smith

Overview

On the Companion CD-ROM

Contents

Acknowledgments

A project of this scope is a tremendous effort. So I want to thank my agent, Valda Hilley, for getting me involved, for her support along the way, and for her continuing faith that I could complete it. Special thanks go to Grace Buechlein, acquisitions editor, for staying the course. And thanks to development editor, Todd Bumbalough, and production editor, Mary Ann Faughnan for their editing expertise. And last, but not least, thanks to Sams Publishing for providing the opportunity. I would also like to thank the technical editors, and John Warriner for providing all those great shareware and evaluation products on the CD-ROM.

Thanks to Greg Todd of Compaq Computer Corp. for his help with Part V of this book. Eric Beauchamp and Alex Sampera of WinBook Computer Corporation deserve a heartfelt thank-you for providing the WinBook XP and WinBook XP5 notebook computers. Both models held up under the demanding load of Microsoft BackOffice.

I would also like to share my appreciation for the Windows NT bug reproduction team—Sam White, Todd Fredericksen, Chris Smith, Timothy Benham, John Hazen, Paul Bronowski, and Paul Donnelly. This special group is dedicated to reproducing bugs in the operating system so that they may be resolved. Their efforts provide you and me with a much better product. And lest we forget, all the other members of the Microsoft development teams who provide us with such excellent products deserve a nod of gratitude, too.

For those of you who are also considering authoring a book, all I would like to say is, I hope you have many friends and an understanding family. The one thing I have really learned during this project is that you cannot write a book without the support of friends and family. So thanks to my family, especially my mother, Antoinette Knowles, who put up with me while I was writing this book. And thanks to my cats (Kit and Kat) for amusing me in the wee hours of the morning.

About the Author

Arthur E. Knowles is president and founder of Knowles Consulting, a firm specializing in systems integration, training, and software development. Art is a Microsoft Certified Systems Engineer. His specialties include Microsoft Windows NT Server, Windows NT Workstation, SQL Server, Systems Management Server, Windows 95, and Windows for Workgroups. Art is the author of *Internet Information Server 2 Unleashed*, and has served as a contributing author for several books, including *Designing and Implementing Microsoft Internet Information Server 2*, *Windows 3.1 Configuration Secrets*, *Windows NT Unleashed*, and *Mastering Windows 95*. He is the forum manager of the Portable Computers Forum on the Microsoft Network. You can reach Art on the Internet at his address webmaster@nt-guru.com or on his Web site at http://www.nt-guru.com.

Tell Us What You Think!

As a reader, you are the most important critic and commentator of our books. We value your opinion and want to know what we're doing right, what we could do better, what areas you'd like to see us publish in, and any other words of wisdom you're willing to send our way. You can help us make strong books that meet your needs and give you the computer guidance you require. Do you have access to CompuServe or the World Wide Web? If so, check out our CompuServe forum by typing GO SAMS at any prompt. If you prefer the World Wide Web, check out our site at http://www.mcp.com.

Note

If you have a technical question about this book, call the technical support line at (800) 571-5840, ext. 3668.

As the team leader of the group that created this book, I welcome your comments. You can fax, e-mail, or write me directly to let me know what you did or didn't like about this book—as well as what we can do to make our books stronger. Here's the information:

FAX: 317/581-4669

E-mail: enterprise_mgr@sams.mcp.com

Mail: Rosemarie Graham
            Sams Publishing
            201 W. 103rd Street
            Indianapolis, IN 46290

Introduction

This book focuses on what Microsoft BackOffice is and how it is used in the real world. This book is designed for the intermediate-to-advanced reader and includes the basic concepts that must be understood to perform daily maintenance, trouble-shooting and/or problem solving, and it specializes in explaining some of the more arcane areas. Special emphasis is placed on integrating the Microsoft Network with existing networks like Novell NetWare, Banyan VINES, TCP/IP-based (UNIX) networks, and mainframe (IBM) integration.

This book aims to fulfill the following needs of readers (network administrators, network supervisors, upper management):

◆ Introduces Microsoft's new flagship product, System Management Server, and demonstrates how you can use it to manage your network.

◆ Introduces Microsoft's new enterprise mail product, Exchange Server, and demonstrates how you can use it to build a corporate e-mail system.

◆ Introduces Microsoft's Internet Publishing services and demonstrates how you can use them to build a presence on the Internet.

◆ Prepares you to be introduced to the client/server world. I estimate that over 80 percent of my consulting practice revenue has been based on installing Windows NT and SQL Server in existing networks. As a SQL Server platform, Windows NT cannot be beat, and for this reason the integration of Windows NT with existing networks is of major importance.

◆ The information contained in the overview and relevant product sections will help prepare you pass your Microsoft certification exam.

This book demonstrates through the use of step-by-step written procedures inter-spersed with figures captured from the actual tools. Icons point out information that impacts readers' day-to-day responsibilities. And technical sidebars look "under the hood" of the operating and file systems, giving you a better understanding of the products you are responsible for maintaining.

- Network Concepts

- Planning Your
  Network Installation

PART I

Overview

- The OSI Network Model

- The Windows NT Network Model

- Network Topologies and Segments

- Routers and Bridges

- Network Technology

- Transport Protocols

- Windows NT Server Concepts

- Systems Management Server Sites

- Internet and Intranet Publishing

- Basic E-Mail Concepts

CHAPTER 1

Network Concepts

This chapter discusses some of the underlying network concepts that affect your network design. A thorough understanding of these concepts is helpful in determining how to efficiently build your network and maximize your usage of the BackOffice products. The discussion begins with an introduction to the International Organization for Standardization (ISO) Open System Interconnect (OSI) network model. Then you'll learn about the Windows NT architectural network model and see how it differs from the OSI model. This information will help you better understand how your network actually works and will aid you later in your administrative duties when you need to troubleshoot your client connectivity problems.

You then will learn about the various network protocols that Windows NT supports. You can think of a protocol as the language a computer uses to communicate over a network. One thing to keep in mind is that in order for one computer to communicate with another computer, they must use the same protocol or language. This book communicates using the English language, for example, but it just as easily could use German or Spanish. In the same way, two computers must use the same protocol, such as NetBEUI, IPX/SPX, or TCP/IP to communicate. After you learn about the various network protocols, you will spend a little time looking at the various network topologies and technologies involved.

Next, you will look at the different domain models supported by Windows NT Server and the different site models supported by Systems Management Server (SMS). In my opinion, nothing is more important to an administrator than a complete understanding of the various domain models. Domains are the heart and soul of a Windows NT network, and SMS sites rely on this principle as well. The domain model you choose is the limiting factor in determining how large your network can be and how well it will perform. Then, you will get a chance to look into some of the possibilities for using the Internet Information Server to publish information on the Internet or intranet. Finally, you'll be introduced to a few basic e-mail system concepts.

If you're installing BackOffice as an upgrade to an existing network operating system (NOS), you might not need to read the initial sections of this chapter concerning the OSI and Windows NT network models (although I recommend that you do, as a refresher). This also applies to network topologies, technologies, and protocols because most of these decisions already have been made. You definitely should read the sections on domain and site concepts, however, before you install Windows NT Server or Systems Management Server. If you need to sway your managers toward the best way to implement Windows NT Server and SMS, these sections definitely will give you the ammunition you need.

THE OSI NETWORK MODEL

The OSI network model is a theoretically perfect model that few manufacturers actually follow. I have included it here because it's a good place to start this discussion and will be helpful when you look at the implementation of the Windows NT network model. The OSI model breaks the actions required by a computer network into seven separate layers, or modules, as shown in Figure 1.1. The top layer, called the application layer, defines how individual programs interact with the network. The bottom layer, called the physical layer, defines the network cable and other physical attributes of the network. The model's design requires that each module communicate only with the module directly above or below it. This gives you the capability to replace an individual module as long as the module's exported functions remain the same.

Figure 1.1.
The seven layers
of the OSI
network model.

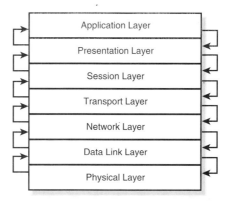

One other interesting concept defined by the OSI model is that each layer assumes that it's communicating with an identical layer on another computer. If you have two computers on a network, for example, when you connect to the other computer from your computer, you establish a session. The session layer on your computer then assumes that it's communicating directly with the session layer on the other computer, as shown in Figure 1.2. In reality, the data requests move up and down the various layers on each computer but, logically, these individual modules assume that they're communicating with their counterparts on the other computer. As each layer moves data up or down the layers on your computer, the data is encapsulated in a wrapper. This wrapper is removed when the data reaches the same layer on the destination computer. Now you'll take a closer look at the various layers of the OSI model and see exactly what they do.

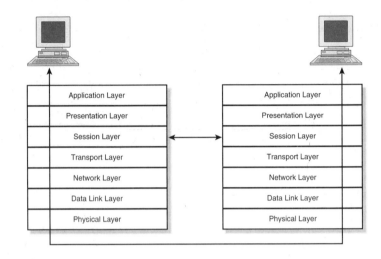

Figure 1.2.
An example of
two computers
establishing a
session in relation
to the seven layers
of the OSI
network model.

THE APPLICATION LAYER

The application layer is the beginning of the OSI model, and it's where your applications begin their communication across the network. This is the interface that your applications can use to access network resources. File Manager, Printer Manager, and Microsoft Mail, for example, are all instances of applications that use network resources and interface with the application layer. If you're using Microsoft Word for Windows and you save your file on a networked drive, this too is an example of an application interfacing with the OSI model's application layer.

THE PRESENTATION LAYER

The presentation layer takes the data passed to it from the application layer and converts it to an intermediate format that the presentation layer understands, compresses the data, and encrypts it (if required) before passing it down to the session layer. On the way back up from the session layer, this process is reversed. The data is converted from an intermediate format to a format that the application layer can use; it is uncompressed and decrypted, if necessary.

THE SESSION LAYER

The session layer is responsible for establishing and ending a communications linkage between two computers. It also regulates which computer can transmit data and how long this one-way transmission can occur before the other computer gets a chance to transmit data.

THE TRANSPORT LAYER

The transport layer ensures that the data is reliably sent across the network. It supplies error-recovery and recognition features. When data is transmitted across the network, the receiving transport layer sends an acknowledgment to the transmitting transport layer to assure it that the data was received. If no acknowledgment is received, the data is retransmitted. The transport layer also is responsible for repackaging messages by breaking large messages into smaller messages as required by the lower layer, or by building a large message from a series of smaller messages provided by a lower layer.

THE NETWORK LAYER

The network layer's primary purpose is to move your data across the network and to determine the best way to accomplish this task. It also performs logical-to-physical address translation. In addition to these tasks, the network layer acts as a traffic cop by managing the switching, routing, and congestion control of data packets on the network.

This layer also converts the data into a network packet and places a wrapper around the data. As part of this conversion process, an error-correction code (ECC) is inserted. If the network packet is too large for the data link layer to handle, the network layer reassembles the single large packet into several smaller packets that the data link layer can handle. On the way back up the layers, this process is reversed, and smaller packets are reassembled into larger packets before being passed to the transport layer.

THE DATA LINK LAYER

The data link layer takes the network packet provided by the network layer and converts it into data frames. A frame is basically another wrapper around the data that may be broken into smaller pieces. It includes additional network addresses. Data frames are network-dependent, so if a data frame is sent to a NetWare server, it might differ from a data frame sent to a Windows NT Server, even though they contain the same data. Like the network layer, the data link layer includes additional error-correction codes to ensure reliable frame transmission and reception. If the ECC code doesn't match, the data frame is discarded. This prevents upper layers from receiving bad data. If a frame is discarded, not received, or not acknowledged, it is retransmitted from the source data link layer.

The data link layer is further subdivided by some implementations into the logical link control (LLC) and media access control (MAC) layers. In this model, the LLC layer provides access to the services, and the MAC layer implements the addressing and error-correction arrangement.

THE PHYSICAL LAYER

The physical layer is responsible for moving the data frames supplied by the data link layer across the network cables. It performs this task much as a serial port does. Data is received in small fragments and is sent across the cable one bit at a time. This process includes the encoding and synchronization of the data bits sent across the cable. The physical layer also defines the characteristics of the network media, including how the data is sent, the network cabling, how the cable is attached, and even the electrical characteristics of the cable.

THE WINDOWS NT NETWORK MODEL

The Windows NT network functionality is fully integrated with the operating system, unlike its predecessors, such as MS-DOS, Windows 3.x, and OS/2 1.x, which had network functionality hacked in afterward. Because this network functionality was built into the original design of Windows NT, it's more efficient, and the network implementation is transparent to the user. Adding support for multiple network adapter cards or transport protocols is as simple as adding the adapter card and installing the drivers in the Control Panel's Network applet.

Using the OSI model as a basis for the Windows NT network model, the Microsoft engineers also used a modularized architectural design. Although it doesn't follow the OSI model exactly, it's pretty close, as Figure 1.3 illustrates. In this implementation, the application layer performs the same basic functionality as the application layer in the OSI model. The Windows NT network model then begins to digress from the OSI model. The presentation layer is so thin that it is almost nonexistent. The real work occurs below this layer, so that is where this discussion continues.

REDIRECTORS AND SERVERS

The session layer of the OSI model is subdivided into separate entities in the Windows NT network model. This includes the provider interface, the redirector subcomponent, and the server subcomponent. The provider interface includes the Multiple UNC Provider (MUP) and the Multiple UNC Router (MUR). The MUP is used to locate and resolve UNC (Universal Naming Convention) names and to route the UNC request to the appropriate provider, such as the Lanman Workstation provider. A UNC name is a means of specifying a resource based on the computer and share name. The UNC name \\ROADTRIP\C, for example, designates the share to the C drive on my laptop computer, called ROADTRIP. The MUR is used to provide a standard interface to Win32 applications to access resources on multiple networks. When the application programming interface (API) called is used to access a resource on the network, the API in turn calls a proprietary dynamic link library (DLL), which in turn calls the appropriate network provider to support the network request.

Figure 1.3.
The Windows NT
network model
compared to the
OSI network
model.

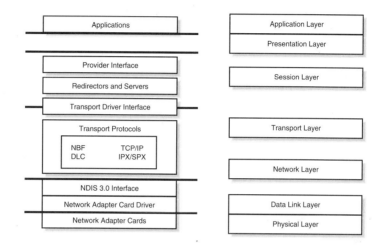

The redirector subcomponent accesses resources on another computer, and the server subcomponent shares resources on your computer. Both these subcomponents are implemented as Windows NT file system drivers. There are several benefits to having these network drivers written as a file system driver. These benefits include the capability to cache the network requests for improved system performance, the provision for dynamically loading and unloading the file system driver for improved memory management, and the capability of network drivers to coexist with other file system drivers.

THE TRANSPORT DRIVER INTERFACE

The transport driver interface is a boundary layer protocol that provides a single entry point from the network redirectors to the various network protocols. This gives you the capability to use any redirector but doesn't tie you to a specific protocol implementation. As you can see in Figure 1.3, the TDI layer straddles the session and transport layers when compared to the OSI network model. The Windows NT network model transport protocol layer combines the functionality of the OSI model transport and network layers. Later in this chapter, in the section "Transport Protocols," you will look at the specific transport protocols that Windows NT supports.

THE NETWORK DEVICE INTERFACE SPECIFICATION

The Network Device Interface Specification (NDIS) is where the big benefits occur in Windows NT. Although early network device drivers were designed to include the network transport protocol and bind this protocol to a single network adapter driver, NDIS drivers are designed to support multiple network protocols to access a single adapter or multiple network adapters.

The Microsoft implementation of the OSI data link layer is divided into two separate components. The NDIS 3.0 interface is included in the LLC layer, and the network adapter driver is included in the MAC layer. One of the really nice features of NDIS 3.0 is that it includes a C-callable interface, which makes the components easier to write. The components also are true 32-bit implementations that are safe for use in a multiprocessor system.

NETWORK TOPOLOGIES

Your network topology defines the physical layout of your network cables as well as how your network clients physically connect to the network. Three implementations are in use in today's networks: bus, star, and ring. Each has different strengths and weaknesses.

BUS

The low-end market uses a bus topology, in which each network adapter connects directly to the main network cable. Both thin Ethernet (coaxial) and thick Ethernet are bus network design implementations. The basic layout of a bus network, as shown in Figure 1.4, is a single network cable that is connected from the first computer, through each computer, to the last in a single line. The first and last computers in the chain must be terminated. A terminator is nothing more than a resistor to absorb the signal when it reaches the end of the network to prevent signal interference. Furthermore, one—and only one—end of the bus must be grounded in order to prevent ground loops.

Figure 1.4.
A network
implemented on a
bus topology.

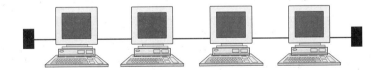

The primary flaw of the bus topology is that if one piece of the network cable is faulty, the entire network fails. Isolating the fault requires that you perform a binary test by splitting the bus into two separate sections to determine which half has the cable break. After you determine which half has the break, you must split that segment into two equal parts, and then continue this process until you find the cable break. This can be a time-consuming task, but don't let this discourage you from using a bus topology-based network. It's still quite useful for setting up training rooms and small networks in which the cables are easily accessible. In fact, I used a bus topology-based network while writing this book.

STAR

The majority of the network market uses the star topology because it overcomes the single-line-break problem associated with the bus topology by giving each computer its own connection to the main network cable. Each workstation is connected to a multiport repeater, which often is referred to as a hub or concentrator. The hub, in turn, connects to the main network cable. The basic purpose of the hub is to retransmit the signals from the main network cable to the individual workstations, as shown in Figure 1.5. If a single cable fails between the hub and the workstation, only that workstation is affected. The other workstations continue their network activity without experiencing any problems. If a hub fails, however, all the workstations connected to that hub fail. Of course, this problem is easily diagnosed because all the users connected to that failed hub are clamoring for your attention, and it is like sending up a signal flare. This situation is unlike a broken cable in a bus topology, which requires you to manually run around to each workstation in an attempt to isolate the broken cable.

Figure 1.5.
A network
implemented on a
star topology.

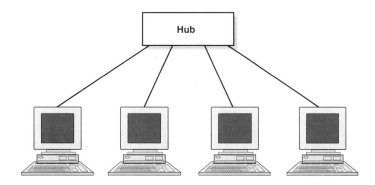

Planning for this type of disaster requires that you have a spare hub available to replace a failed hub. This is one reason why it makes sense to use the same type of hub throughout your network installation. It's also a good idea to use smart hubs. A smart hub supports the Simple Network Management Protocol (SNMP), which can be used to query the hub as to its performance and, in many cases, reboot it without walking over to the hub and cycling the power.

RING

A ring topology is used primarily in IBM shops to support token ring networks. The physical layout is identical to the star topology network shown in Figure 1.5. Instead of a hub, however, the workstations connect to a Multiple Access Unit (MAU), which logically connects the network workstations into a ring, as shown in Figure 1.6. A ring topology offers the same benefits as a star topology because its physical layout is the same, but it too suffers from the same problems because the MAU is a central point of failure.

Figure 1.6.
A network
implemented on a
ring topology.

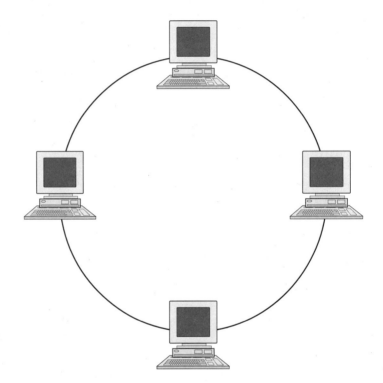

NETWORK SEGMENTS

Almost every production network must be split into multiple physical segments because of the limitations imposed by the technical specification of your network implementation. A network also can be split into separate segments to improve performance. Of course, after you physically split a segment, your networked workstations can't access any resources outside their local segment. This is where routers and bridges come into play.

ROUTERS

A router is used to physically combine multiple segments into one logical segment. You can use a router to combine two local area network segments, or to connect your local area network to the Internet. Routers work at the transport or protocol layer and retransmit data packets from one segment to another based on unique network addresses. Routers use an algorithm to build a list of network addresses in their local segments to provide the capability to route only data packets that require their intervention. If your network has multiple routers and one fails, the other routers often can manage to find an alternative path to make sure that the data packets reach their destinations.

Of course, this performance doesn't come without cost; routers often are expensive. Many routers are based on Intel 80386 or 80486 CPUs, although some use proprietary CPUs. A router requires quite a bit of processing power because of the time limit imposed by the network implementation. It does no good to route a data packet to another computer, for example, if the time-out limit for an acknowledgment has been reached. By the time the packet does reach the computer, the computer already has requested that the packet be re-sent from the host computer. If you have a small network, one less expensive alternative to a dedicated router is to use Windows NT's routing capabilities to route IPX/SPX and TCP/IP data packets. It is not a full-service router, but it does the job in most cases. Another point to consider with routers is that if they can't identify a particular packet type, they discard it. Discarding a packet can cause you numerous problems.

BRIDGES

Not all network protocols (such as NetBEUI) are capable of being routed, so an alternative method of combining segments is required. This is what a bridge is designed to accomplish. A bridge works at the MAC layer and either routes all packets regardless of their network addresses (transparent routing) or based on a specific network address (source routing). Some bridges combine both these capabilities into a single box. This commonly is referred to as a transparent source-routing bridge. Bridges most commonly are used in LAN Manager-based networks and still might be used when the network is upgraded to Windows NT Server.

I had an interesting problem caused by a bridge with Windows NT Server 3.1 and Windows for Workgroups 3.11 clients. This particular implementation used a transparent source-routing bridge to combine the network segments. When the WFW client attempted to establish a session with the Windows NT Server, the bridge intervened and issued both a source-routed packet and a transparent packet across the network segment. The Windows NT Server received both packets, issued an acknowledgment, and began its communication with the WFW client based on source-routed packets. When the NT Server realized that it didn't need to include the source-routing information, however, it switched to transparent routing. This caused the WFW computer to terminate the session it had established with the NT Server. Essentially, this meant that no resources on the NT Server could be accessed by the Windows NT client.

This particular problem was fixed in a service pack, although it was not specifically mentioned in the bug fix list. I'm only mentioning it here so that you'll be aware of the problem in case it creeps in again.

Note

If you use a bridge, you can eliminate this type of problem by using either source routing or transparent routing, but not both simultaneously.

NETWORK TECHNOLOGY

This section looks at the various technologies available to implement your network. The primary purpose here is to give you a full understanding of the possibilities so that you can design your network to fulfill your real-world requirements. Keep in mind that network technology is a rapidly changing environment, which means that the fastest technology today might not be the fastest tomorrow. It pays to plan ahead in order to pave the way for future technologies that can benefit you down the road.

NETWORK CABLE TYPES

Five types of network cable are in use today. Each cable type is designed for a specific network configuration and has its own associated strengths and weaknesses. These cable types follow:

◆ Thick Ethernet: This cable type was introduced by Xerox as a means of connecting multiple computers on their campus network. This cable is approximately 15mm thick and is quite rigid. It also is heavily shielded to prevent electrical interference. Thick Ethernet cables rarely are used in today's networks because of the expense involved.

◆ Thin Ethernet (coaxial or Thinnet): This cable is almost identical to the one used by your cable TV contractor. It has a core cable constructed of copper wire embedded in a plastic insulator surrounded by two layers of shielding material and a final plastic insulator. It is very inexpensive compared to

Thick Ethernet but rarely is used in today's production environments. It is, however, widely used in simple home, lab, and testing networks.

◆ Unshielded twisted pair (UTP): This cable uses two pairs of wire twisted around each other to provide a resonant magnetic field to increase signal quality (the more twists, the better the signaling capability). It looks just like a phone cable.

Note

There are actually five categories of UTP cabling. Levels 1 and 2 are low-grade cables designed for voice-only transmissions. Level 3 is the minimum required level for 10Mb networks. Level 4 supports up to 16Mb networks, and level 5 supports up to 100Mb networks. I recommend that you purchase level 5 UTP cable because approximately 75 percent of your installation cost is based on the labor of pulling the cables. If you choose to install level 5 cable, it will provide the longest service life and make your network cabling Fast Ethernet-ready if you decide to migrate to this medium later.

◆ Shielded twisted pair (STP): Like UTP cable, STP cable includes two pairs of wire twisted around each other. It differs from UTP in the shielding wrapped around each individual pair as well as the layer of shielding around both pairs. This shielding provides better signaling capabilities than UTP and should be used in electrically noisier environments.

◆ Fiber optic: This is the best cable for electrically noisy environments because it carries pulses of light rather than electrical pulses. It should be used as the backbone of computer networks to provide the fastest and most error-free data path between servers. Like a coaxial cable, a fiber-optic cable has a core made of glass rather than copper, surrounded by several layers to protect the glass core. Instead of a single cable that you can use to send and receive, however, you are required to use two separate fiber-optic cables—one to send data and one to receive it.

Note

Another use of fiber-optic cables is to provide an electrically isolated method of joining two physical segments. Instead of using electrical cables to span two segments in different buildings, for example, use a pair of fiber-optic cables. That way, you isolate the two networks from electrical interference rather than joining them with a lightning rod. I've actually seen the results of a lightning strike that destroyed several network servers connected with wire rather than fiber. After the incident, when the new hardware was installed, the choice to connect these two buildings was fiber-optic cable.

NETWORK CONFIGURATIONS

This is the real meat of your network design because it includes the specifications for your network topology, cabling, and, to some extent, your choice of network adapters. Ethernet networks (10BASE5, 10BASE2, and 10BASE-T) all use a Carrier Sense Multiple Access with Collision Detection (CSMA/CD) algorithm to send data across the wire. In this algorithm, the network adapter is required to listen (carrier sense) before sending data. If two or more computers (multiple access) send data at the same time, a data collision occurs and is detected by the computer (collision detection). When a collision occurs, the computers pause for a random time before retransmitting their data. Token ring networks use a token-passing algorithm. Only one computer will have the token that permits data to be sent on the network. After the data is sent, the token is released for the next computer to use in order to send data. Think of a token as the light at a crossroads. If the light is green, you can continue driving. If it is red, you must stop. Basically, the same process occurs on a token ring network. If you have the token, you can transmit on the network. If you do not have the token, you must wait.

THICK ETHERNET (10BASE5)

Thick Ethernet networks use a bus topology with a maximum segment length of 500 meters, a maximum of 100 workstations per segment, and a minimum distance of 2.5 meters between workstations. Thick Ethernet workstations use a drop cable with a maximum length of 50 meters to attach to the network trunk. The network trunk is the base cable that defines the network segment. It is a continuous length of cable. The drop cable is a connection between the workstation and the trunk. It connects like a T-connector to the network trunk. Thick Ethernet networks operate at speeds of up to 10Mbps.

THIN ETHERNET (10BASE2)

A Thin Ethernet implementation also uses a bus topology, but with a maximum segment length of 185 meters, a maximum of 30 workstations per segment, and a minimum 0.5 meter distance between workstations. Unlike a Think Ethernet network, Thin Ethernet networks don't use a drop cable. Instead, the network trunk is brought right up to the workstation and is connected to a bayonet nut connector, which resembles a T-connector. The T-connector then attaches directly to the network adapter. Thin Ethernet networks operate at speeds of up to 10Mbps.

ETHERNET (10BASE-T)

This is the most common network implementation in use today. It uses UTP/STP cables configured in a star topology with a maximum segment length of 100 meters. You can continue to add workstations to your network by adding more hubs and routers. Network performance is the limiting factor when determining the number of workstations you can add to a single segment. Ethernet networks operate at speeds of up to 10Mbps.

I find that more than 30 workstations on a single segment causes network congestion in a day-to-day work environment. Therefore, I recommend that you break up your segments with a router when you reach this limit. But you might want to break up your segments whenever you reach 20 to 30 percent of your network bandwidth or carrying capacity. At 50 percent of your bandwidth, you begin to encounter numerous data collisions that slow down your network or, in extreme cases, make it completely unusable.

TOKEN RING

Token ring networks use a ring topology and generally are used in IBM shops because they are the easiest networks to connect to IBM mainframes. Token ring networks can operate at either 4Mbps or 16Mbps.

Warning

You can't mix and match transmission rates in a single ring. A ring must be all 4Mbps or all 16Mbps. Mixing transmission speeds in a single ring can bring down the entire ring.

When you use STP cable, a single MAU can support up to 260 workstations with a maximum length of 100 meters between the MAU and the workstation. When you use UTP cable, this drops to 72 workstations with a maximum length of 45 meters between the MAU and the workstation. You should consider breaking up your segments whenever you reach 40 to 60 percent of your network bandwidth.

100MB OPTIONS

If you're considering implementing multimedia or video conferencing in your network, you'll need a high-performance medium. This means either fiber optic or

Fast Ethernet. But there are a few points to consider before you make the move to either of these:

◆ A fiber-optic network requires that you completely redesign your network. You must replace all your current network cables with fiber optic, which can be a costly proposition. You also have to replace all your hubs and routers. I don't recommend this unless you really need the electrical isolation that fiber optic provides.

◆ Fast Ethernet is a good alternative to replacing your network cables with fiber-optic cables because you have two choices, depending on your network cables. If you're using category 3 UTP cabling and aren't using the additional two pairs of wires for voice (never a recommended choice), you can use the 100BASE-VG Fast Ethernet adapters. These adapters provide 100Mbps transmission speeds by using all four pairs of wires in the standard RJ-45 cables. If you have category 5 UTP (the recommended choice), you can use the 100BASE-T network adapters. These network adapters use the same two pairs of wire in your UTP cable but provide 100Mb throughput.

TRANSPORT PROTOCOLS

Right out of the box, Windows NT gives you several choices of transport protocols to use with your network. Each of these choices has good and bad aspects that you should consider carefully before deciding which protocol to implement. Of course, if you're planning to integrate Windows NT into an existing network, your choices might already be made.

APPLETALK

The AppleTalk protocol is the native network transport for Macintosh computers. The AppleTalk protocol originated with many of the older Macintosh computers that included a built-in serial port which could be used to daisy-chain multiple Macintosh computers. You could build a slow (the maximum transmission speed for the serial port included with these models was 115,200bps) but workable network in this fashion. Many of today's Macintosh computers, however, include a built-in Ethernet adapter. With these newer computers you can directly connect them to your Ethernet network at 10Mbps. If you use a third-party network adapter, you can achieve speeds up to 100Mbps—a huge improvement over the original serial implementation.

When you install the Services for Macintosh service on your Windows NT Server installation, you are providing a means for your Macintosh computers to communicate with your server as a file, print, or application server. You are also providing a means for your Windows NT Server installations, which must also have the Services for Macintosh service installed, to use the Macintosh computers as file and print servers. Your Windows NT Server installations can then share a connection they have established on the Macintosh network to network clients on the Windows NT network. This means that all of your network clients can use resources on both sides of the AppleTalk connection.

NETBEUI

The NetBIOS Extended User Interface (NetBEUI) protocol is the fastest protocol, but it has a few limitations. Specifically, it can't be routed (but it can be bridged). It also can flood the network with broadcast messages that can eat up a considerable amount of network bandwidth. It's also a poor performer over wide-area networks (WANs). Nevertheless, I always include this protocol when I install Windows NT Server. I install NetBEUI for the following reasons:

- It's the most efficient protocol for use within a local subnet.
- It offers good error-recovery options.
- It has a small memory footprint.
- It's completely self-tuning.
- It provides network connectivity with legacy platforms, such as LAN Manager or the Windows for Workgroups 3.11 Remote Access Software implementation.
- It provides an alternative protocol if one of the other installed protocols fails.

IPX/SPX

If you have a Novell NetWare server, it's a no-brainer decision when looking at which network protocol to use. You will want to install the IPX/SPX protocol so that you can connect to your NetWare server. The IPX/SPX protocol also is quite useful for integrating the Microsoft SQL Server for Windows NT in a Novell environment. With IPX/SPX installed, your Novell clients can access SQL Server databases without major modifications. And it's a much safer and faster solution than implementing a SQL Server NetWare Loadable Module (NLM) because if an NLM is running in ring 0 for maximum performance and it fails, it can take down your entire server.

IPX/SPX also is a good choice for small-to-medium networks because it is a routable protocol. This protocol enables you to physically split network segments while maintaining a single logical network segment. On the down side, IPX/SPX also sends broadcast messages periodically, which can eat up network bandwidth. And, although it's a routable protocol, it's not the best choice for a WAN.

Note

> Microsoft recently introduced the File and Print Services for NetWare. This software lets your current NetWare clients access a Windows NT Server without changing the client drivers. If you use this with the Novell migration tools, you can just drop in Windows NT Server as a replacement for your Novell server.

TCP/IP

Transmission Control Protocol/Internet Protocol (TCP/IP) isn't a single protocol. It's a collection of protocols that include TCP, UDP, ARP, and many others. It's the most widely used protocol. And although it's not the most efficient protocol to use for a LAN, it is the best protocol to use for a WAN. Here are some of the reasons I find TCP/IP so useful and recommend it heartily:

◆ It provides the best integration with existing UNIX or UNIX derivatives (such as VMS) implementations. This includes Windows NT clients, such as Telnet, ftp, rsh, and rexec. It also provides network printer connectivity to and from UNIX printers.

◆ It provides easy integration with and access to the Internet via a dedicated connection or when used with the Remote Access Service and a supported modem.

◆ It can be used to support the Windows NT Socket implementation for access to SQL Server databases.

◆ It is fully routable.

◆ With the introduction of DHCP and WINS, TCP/IP administration is severely lessened. DHCP and WINS completely automate the assignment of IP addresses and NetBIOS computer name resolution.

DATA LINK CONTROL

The data link control protocol is used primarily to provide a connectivity solution (i.e., SNA Server) for IBM mainframes on a token ring network. It also is used to communicate with network printers such as the HP LaserJet 4 with the Jet Direct network card installed.

A trust relationship enables you to use the user accounts and global groups defined in the one domain (the trusted domain) in a completely different domain (the trusting domain). If this seems a bit fuzzy, don't worry. It even confuses me on some days. This is why you will look at this concept in a bit more detail in the section called "Domain Models," and in much more detail in the next chapter.

CONTROLLERS VERSUS SERVERS

As I mentioned earlier, you have three choices when installing Windows NT Server. Each choice basically defines a specific mode of operation, and each operating mode provides different functional capabilities and performance options. The choices are:

◆ Primary domain controller: This contains the master copy of the user database, which includes all your global groups, user accounts, and computer accounts. In addition, your PDC is used to authenticate your users when they logon to the network or access a shared resource. Your PDC also includes the tools you will use for centralized administration, such as User Manager for Domains, Server Manager for Domains, Dynamic Host Configuration Protocol server, and Windows Internet Name Service server, as well as a host of additional tools.

◆ Backup domain controller: This is similar in functionality to a primary domain controller, with one significant difference. It doesn't contain the master copy of the user database. Instead, the master database is replicated from the PDC. This means that you can't make any account changes (global groups, user accounts, or computer accounts) if the PDC is unavailable. The primary reason for using a backup domain controller is to balance the load for authenticating users on the network. In addition, if a PDC goes down (either inadvertently due to a hardware fault or intentionally for a hardware upgrade), you can promote a BDC to a PDC. Then you can continue to authenticate your users and carry out your network administration responsibilities.

◆ Server: A server's primary purpose is to provide optimum resource sharing. Because it doesn't authenticate users logging on to the network or participate in user database replication, it can devote all its resources to supporting your network clients. There is a trade-off for this increased performance, however: You lose the domain administration tools. Instead of having User Manager for Domains, for example, you get a copy of User Manager.

Tip

You can use Windows NT Server operating in server mode to bypass the hard-coded Windows NT workstation limit of 10 simultaneous client user connections.

One major point to consider is that in order to create a domain, you must have at least a primary domain controller on your network. You can have one or more backup domain controllers if you want, but they're not required. Keep in mind that a BDC can be very useful if you have a PDC failure—particularly because only a primary or backup controller can authenticate your Windows NT client.

DOMAIN MODELS

Microsoft has defined four basic domain models: the single domain model, the master domain model, the multiple master model, and the complete trust model. You should consider this a starting point when it's time to plan your network implementation. (This is discussed in more detail in the next chapter.) You don't have to limit yourself to a specific domain implementation. Instead, you can stretch the basic domain model to fit your specific needs. Take a look at these different models so that you can plan the best network design possible.

THE SINGLE DOMAIN MODEL

The single domain model shown in Figure 1.7 includes a primary domain controller and, optionally, one or more backup domain controllers and servers. It is the basis for all the other domain models. It is the simplest model that Microsoft offers, and it can perform well for you if you meet the following criteria:

- ◆ You have a small network with fewer than 300 users.
- ◆ You have fewer than 15 servers.
- ◆ You have an administrative group, such as an MIS department, that can administer the network.
- ◆ You do not have a WAN.

These criteria aren't hard-and-fast rules. Instead, they are based on my experience. You can play with these numbers for the maximum number of users and servers, as long as you keep in mind that the real issue is acceptable performance. If you have fast servers (single- or dual-CPU Pentiums, for example) and a high-performance backbone (100Mbps fiber optic, for example), you won't see the same performance limitation as a company that has 80386-based servers on a 10Mbps backbone.

Figure 1.7.
The single
domain model.

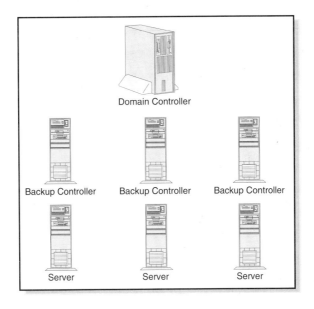

The single domain model does provide several benefits. It allows any network administrator to administer all the servers from any server or workstation on the network. Because only one user database is defined that contains all the user accounts and local and global groups, resource administration is completely central-ized. Because there is only a single domain, no trust relationships must be created in order to access resources in other domains.

Of course, the single domain model has some limitations as well. Browsing for resources is based on the domain, for example, and as the number of computers in your domain increases, performance problems might occur. As the number of users in your domain grows, so does the list you must search through in order to find an individual user account. And as you make changes to your accounts, either by creating or modifying user accounts and groups, you have to replicate these changes to every backup domain controller on the network, which can eat up much of your network bandwidth. Finally, if your company has multiple departments that don't want you to administer their network or have access to confidential files, you'll have to split up your domain and choose another domain model.

THE MASTER DOMAIN MODEL

The master domain model shown in Figure 1.8 includes a single master domain with one or more resource domains that trust the master domain. The master domain contains all the user accounts and global groups. No user accounts or global groups are defined in the resource domains. Because no user accounts exist on the resource domains, all logons and authentications are referred to the master domain.

Figure 1.8.
The master
domain model.

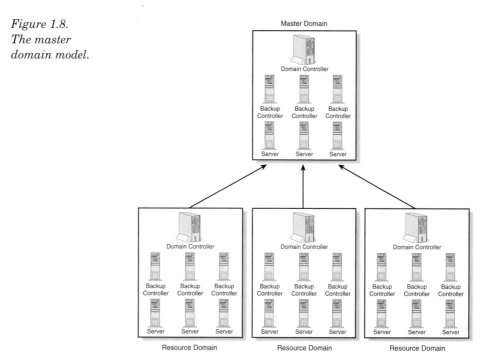

Warning

Because all user logons and authentications are processed by the master domain, if you don't include at least one backup domain controller in the master domain and the primary domain controller fails, no users will be able to logon to the network or to access shared resources.

The master domain model lets you split your network based on departmental resource allocations, yet it still provides for centralized administration of your network. The master domain model is well suited for your organization if it meets the following criteria:

◆ It has fewer than 1,000 users.

◆ It has fewer than 50 servers.

◆ It has an administrative group, such as an MIS department, that can administer the network.

Notice, however, that although each resource domain trusts the master domain, they do not trust each other. This is because all the user accounts and groups are defined in the master domain, and because each resource domain trusts the master domain, any user or group can be granted access to the resource domain, so no additional trust relationships are required. One other interesting capability of this model is that the central administration group can be limited to just creating user accounts in the master domain. The resource domain administrators then can determine who is granted access to the resources in their domain by creating global groups that include user accounts from the master domain.

You might want to keep in mind a couple of disadvantages of this model. A user list with 1,000 users can be pretty intimidating and slow to browse, for example. And replicating the entire user list to your backup controllers can generate enough network traffic to make your users scream, which is why I recommend that you do this after normal working hours. The limiting factor here is your network bandwidth and the speed of your servers. If your network bandwidth is insufficient to carry the user logon and authentication requests provided by your servers, or your servers can't process the logon requests quickly enough, your network performance as a whole will suffer. Consider a resource domain situated on a wide area network, for example. All user logons and authentications must travel across the slow WAN link to the master domain, even when they're accessing resources on servers in their local resource domain.

THE MULTIPLE MASTER DOMAIN MODEL

If you have more than 1,000 users or 50 servers, you really need to think about how you can lessen your administrative burden and provide additional fault-tolerance capabilities. The multiple master domain model might just fit the bill. Like the master domain model, it includes resource domains. But instead of a single domain with all the user accounts defined in it, you have two or more domains that contain all the user accounts, as shown in Figure 1.9. Your MIS department still can administer the entire network as long as it has accounts defined in either of the master domains.

In Figure 1.9, two domains have split the user accounts between them. The master domain on the left includes all the user accounts from A through K, and one on the right includes user accounts from L through Z. Each of these master domains trusts the other, which essentially provides you with one user database, much like the master domain model provides. Continuing this concept requires that each resource domain trust each master domain to give all users access to all resources in the resource domains.

Figure 1.9.
The multiple
master domain
model.

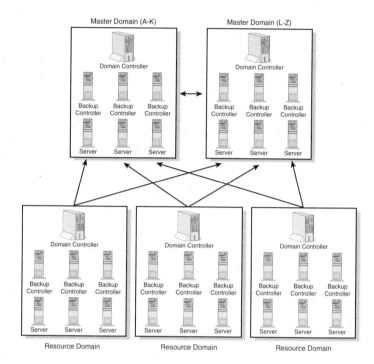

This increases your logon and user-authentication capabilities, because a single failure of a primary domain controller (assuming that you don't have backup domain controllers) only prevents half of your network users from logging on to the domain or being authenticated for resource access. If you have a WAN, you also can include a master domain on each side of the wire to give local users fast access to their local resources and still give them the capability to access resources anywhere on the network.

Although I've used this example to split user accounts alphabetically, this model works better for large organizations if you split the user accounts by department or division. Each department would have a master domain with all the departmental user accounts. Departmental resource domains then would trust this departmental master domain. This would give you (the administrator) the ability to create a global group containing all your users that could access a particular resource in only one domain rather than in two or more domains.

Suppose that you want to create a global group called OFFICE that includes all the users to be granted access to the MSOFFICE share (which contains the Office installation files). If all your departmental users are included in the departmental domain, it's a simple matter of creating the group and including your users. But if you have multiple master domains that split up user accounts alphabetically, you must create an OFFICE global group in each of the master domains. Then, in your resource domain, you must create a local group that contains the global groups defined in the master domain in order to accomplish the same task.

THE COMPLETE TRUST DOMAIN MODEL

The last domain model is the complete trust model. All the domains trust each other, as Figure 1.10 demonstrates, and each domain has its own user database. This particular model is designed for corporations that don't have a centralized administration group or don't want to have a centralized group dictate who has access to their network resources.

Figure 1.10.
The complete
trust domain
model.

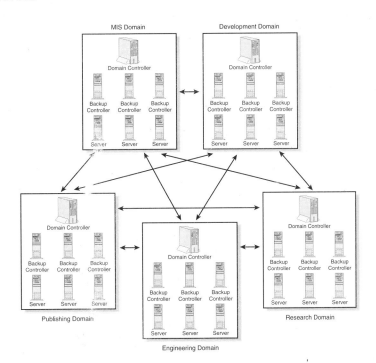

In some cases, corporations wind up with this model from lack of planning rather than any specific need. Although it works fine, it's much more difficult to administer. As your network grows, it becomes very time-consuming to create additional trust relationships. You can express the number of trust relationships mathematically as $n(n-1)$, where n is the number of domains on the network. If you have five domains, as shown in Figure 1.10, and you decide to add another domain, you must create 6 * 5 (30) trust relationships. If you have 20 domains, adding the twenty-first requires 420 trust relationships. And you thought your life as an administrator was difficult now!

SYSTEMS MANAGEMENT SERVER SITES

Systems Management Server (SMS) sites is a much easier concept than your domain model. SMS uses a hierarchical structure to determine how your sites will be installed. There are three site types:

◆ Central site: This is the top of the food chain. All other sites can be managed from here. A central site must have a copy of SQL Server available to store the SMS inventory for itself and all its clients or subsites. The SMS database is referred to as a site database. The central site is also a primary site because it includes full administration of all the subsites and contains its own SMS database.

◆ Primary site: This also has a copy of SQL Server available to store the site database for itself and its subsites. A subsite can be another primary site or a secondary site. A primary site also includes the tools to administer the site, as well as any subsites.

◆ Secondary site: This doesn't have a site database. It places all the information it collects into the primary site's SMS database. A secondary site doesn't include any administrative capabilities. It's only a collection point.

After you create the central site, you can add subsites. To add a primary site to a central site, you create the primary site and then attach it to the central site. To add a primary site to another primary site as a subsite, you install the primary site and then attach it to the other primary site. Secondary sites can be installed only from a primary site.

INTERNET AND INTRANET PUBLISHING

The Internet is taking the corporate and home markets by storm. People everywhere are looking to leverage it. The most commonly used Internet services include the World Wide Web (WWW) and File Transfer Protocol (FTP) services. For the most part these services have been used externally, or to be more specific, these services have been provided by sources outside of the local area network. Even when a corporation begins to provide these services, they are used to supply information to external users, sell products, or possibly even to provide technical support to customers—in other words, they have only been used to provide a means for external users, or Internet clients, to access these resources. This policy is slowly changing as third-party manufacturers add Internet capabilities to their products. One such application is Lotus Notes. It started as a groupware product used internally on the corporate LAN to facilitate user collaboration; it is now being enhanced to provide Internet support as well.

You may be wondering why. The bottom line is that the Internet has become such a rich source of materials that it is becoming difficult to live without. If a tool does not provide Internet support, it is seen as not nearly as useful as tools that do. Again, take Lotus Notes as an example. Your version of Lotus Notes may have a great deal of corporate information in its proprietary database, but now that you plan to connect to the Internet, you want to share some of this information with your Internet customers. The current version of Lotus Notes gives you the ability to use this information within your corporate LAN or to provide it externally as well.

While Lotus Notes is a powerful tool, not everyone has embraced it. One good reason for this is the expense involved; another is that the functionality provided by Notes doesn't suit everyone's needs. This is where Internet tools, such as a WWW browser, can be used on your local area network to provide similar functionality. These tools, while less developed than the current market of groupware products, are less expensive. More important, however, they are also much easier to maintain, configure, and access from various operating system platforms. Almost every operating system in existence today provides a TCP/IP stack and associated tools. With the Internet Information Server and the current crop of Web browsers you can create:

◆ Corporate Directories: It is really very simple to create a static Web page with links to specific sections within a document. It is possible to put your entire office directory (user name, office location, phone number, and so on) on your Web server to provide access to the most up-to-date information.

◆ Corporate Documentation: Most corporations maintain company documentation, such as employee handbooks, accounting procedures, EEO guidelines, and so on, that could be placed on a Web server to provide instant access to these materials. For the ecologically minded, just think of how many trees you could save by placing such material on your LAN's Web server rather than printing copies for all employees.

◆ Help Desks: Many companies use proprietary software to support customer relations. Such software is usually used to track individual customer problems as the solutions for the problems are worked out. Yet the cost of such software is often high, and even when a company can afford it, the software is typically difficult to use and is not customizable. One alternative would be a forms-based Web page, which you can customize to your heart's content.

A forms-based Web page could be used internally to provide a complete tracking mechanism just like a proprietary implementation. It could even be made available externally to customers who have Internet access, so that they can avoid the (sometimes) long delays while waiting for a customer representative to answer the phone. Customers can obtain up-to-the minute information by submitting a simple form with their customer tracking number. It's even possible to provide hooks to an FTP site within the customer response form so that customers can download the latest software patch created specifically to solve their problem.

◆ Online Inventory/Order Entry Access: Many corporations have internal and external sales forces that utilize an online database of information on current inventory and customer orders. To access this information, a database front end, such as Microsoft Access or a custom application, may be used. It is possible, however, to use a Web-based form to query the database or place an order. In essence you could use your Web browser to replace your current front end both for internal and external use.

When Sales representatives arrive at a client's office they could either dial up your server directly, or connect to the Internet through a local number, and access your Web server. By so doing, they could access the company database and check that items are in stock before placing an order via a form on your Web page. If the items are in stock, the order could be passed to the appropriate department and shipped out to the client. If the items are not in stock, an order could be sent to the supplier to obtain it. This entire process could happen in real time, right at the customer's office.

◆ Database Integration: There are many more possibilities for integrating your Web server and your online databases besides inventory or order entry systems. It is also possible to create forms for on-the-fly queries, dynamic Web pages that present database information in a standard HTML format, or high-performance search engines. The possibilities are limited only by your imagination, and your ability to write custom applications.

To be perfectly frank, intranet publishing is not suitable for every task. Nor is it for everyone. To publish data internally requires additional resources, and as with most products, there are pros and cons that you should be aware of before you commit these resources. These pros and cons are summarized in Table 1.1.

TABLE 1.1. THE PROS AND CONS OF INTRANET PUBLISHING.

Pro	Con
An intranet is an excellent platform for publishing information internally.	Collaborative applications for intranets are not nearly as powerful as those offered by traditional groupware products such as Lotus Notes.

Pro	Con
A Web browser is available for almost any operating system, unlike the proprietary clients used for traditional groupware applications.	Unlike a groupware product which has all of the applications integrated into a single product, you will need to install separate clients for Web browsing, e-mail, and so on.
Web servers, especially IIS, do not require as much raw processing power or hard disk space as compared to traditional groupware products.	While it is quite easy to link an ODBC-compliant database to your IIS Web server, there are few tools available to link other back-end components. It is possible to use the SDKs provided with the BackOffice components, including IIS, to integrate your Web server. But, if your third-party product does not have such a development kit, you will be unable to link the information.
There are numerous Internet products that you can use to access your data. These products generally interoperate quite well.	Intranet publishing requires the TCP/IP protocol to utilize these tools. If your LAN utilizes another protocol, you may be forced to change to TCP/IP, or install a gateway, before these products will function properly. If you plan to access the Internet as well, you will also need to obtain routable IP addresses.
IIS is a scaleable platform. As you need additional horsepower, you can migrate your system to another processor platform, or even add additional processors, to increase performance.	There are no built-in replication services to distribute your data.

continues

TABLE 1.1.   CONTINUED

Pro	Con
With the availability of new HTML authoring tools, such as Front Page, Hot Dog, and HotMetal, it is quite simple to create Web pages.	HTML, by itself, is not powerful enough to create client/server applications. While new standards, such as ActiveX, Visual Basic Scripting, Java Scripts, and so on are available, these are still in their infancy. Using these tools requires custom development.

To sum up this discussion on intranet versus Internet publishing, I would like to point out one major benefit of intranets. If you start with an intranet publishing site, when the time comes for you to enter the world of Internet publishing, you will be ready. It takes very little to actually convert an intranet site to an Internet site. Specifically you will need to consider the following:

◆ Routable IP addresses: These can be obtained from your Internet service provider, or from the InterNIC. In fact, if you think you may migrate to the Internet some day, you should follow the guidelines for intranets provided by the InterNIC. There is a wealth of information on this subject, which can be found at `http://www.internic.net` on the Web.

◆ A domain name: If you plan to let users find your site using the form `www.yourcompanyname.com`, you will need to register your domain name with the InterNIC. Your ISP may be able to perform this task for you.

◆ Security: The Internet is like a jungle—there are wild animals out there. To protect yourself, you will need to consider some possible hardware or software tools that you can use to prevent possible damage to your system. These include products such as routers, firewalls, network isolation, and just common sense.

BASIC E-MAIL CONCEPTS

When you buy a car, you are usually given a choice to purchase the car with an automatic or a manual transmission. The transmission is used to take the engine's energy output and turn the wheels of your car which in turn move you down the road. An automatic transmission requires little interaction from the driver, but is slightly less efficient than a manual transmission. When you purchase a car, it is your choice as to which transmission type to purchase. With an e-mail system, however, this choice is often made for you. Like a car's transmission, an e-mail system comes in two flavors: It is either client based or client/server based.

Microsoft Mail is client based, while Microsoft Exchange Server is client/server based. The Microsoft Mail client is responsible for processing the message and placing it in its stored location (a directory on the mail server). A Microsoft Mail client application periodically scans the directories looking for mail to forward to its final destination. This is called a store-and-forward e-mail system. Microsoft Exchange Server is another type of store-and-forward mail system, but here the mail server processes the message and forwards it to its final destination.

Store-and-forward is a term that is fundamental to understanding how e-mail systems work in general. It is also fundamental to understanding how a mail system works. The basic idea is

- Mail is sent from a mail client application to an e-mail recipient.
- The mail is stored in a local location until it is determined when and if it should be forwarded to another storage location on the way to its destination.
- If the mail doesn't need to be forwarded any further, it stays where it is until someone comes to get it.

This is a pretty simple concept. In fact, you deal with it every day with your own U.S. postal system. If you send a letter, for example, you place it in a mailbox at the Post Office. If the letter is addressed to a local resident, the letter is dropped in the local mailbox for final delivery. If the letter is addressed to a non-local resident (say someone in another city), it is forwarded to the non-local Post Office from your local Post Office. The letter may be routed to additional Post Offices along the way, but it eventually winds up in the mailbox of the recipient.

SUMMARY

This chapter looked at the OSI network model and compared it to the Windows NT architectural model to give you a better understanding of some of the concepts you'll see in later chapters and to help you troubleshoot your network. It also delved into the network topologies and technologies available to help you design your network. You learned about some concepts that might not be familiar to some Administrators who are new to Windows NT Server, Systems Management Server (SMS), Internet Information Server, and Microsoft Exchange Server, such as the various domain models, SMS sites, Internet versus intranet publishing, and store-and-forward e-mail systems.

The next chapter looks at how you can take these concepts a step further and actually build your network.

CHAPTER 2

Planning Your Network Installation

Planning your network installation before you actually begin installing the software can help you design a better network. The first step in this process is understanding what the network software you will be using has to offer. This chapter looks at some of these features and builds on the concepts introduced in Chapter 1, "Network Concepts," to help you prepare for your network software installation. As you look at the individual BackOffice components in future chapters, you also will learn about the specific requirements of each component so that you can better plan the installation of the software. But for now, I'll discuss the general principles involved to better prepare you for the installation.

Part of this preparation process is to help you build on your current network configuration. And that is where you will start—with a look at the workgroup configurations and options you have in order to continue using a workgroup or to convert your workgroup to a domain. Next, you will move to the concept of trust, which was introduced in Windows NT Server 3.1, and trust relationships. This will help you better understand the various domain models introduced in Chapter 1 and help you plan your network domain model. You might want to keep in mind that the domain models specified by Microsoft might not be the best models for you to use. Instead, you might want to consider a modified domain model. That's the focus of this discussion.

After the discussion of domain models, you will explore some of the features of Systems Management Server and SQL Server that you should consider before you install these products. The next topic looks at gateways—from the generic concept to the specific implementations offered with the Microsoft BackOffice products. Then I'll introduce you to the wide area network (WAN) facilities provided by the Remote Access Service (RAS). Using the RAS software enables you to link one or more servers or give your remote network clients access to the network while they travel or work from home.

After you've considered all these options, it's time to think about what you can do to implement policies to protect yourself in case a disaster occurs. And disaster planning shouldn't be taken lightly. For one thing, I can guarantee you that everyone experiences a network disaster at one time or another. No one escapes Murphy's law: "Whatever can go wrong, will." But if you plan accordingly, you'll be able to recover from such a situation and make your employer extremely thankful that *you* were hired and not someone else. Who knows—you could even get that raise you deserve!

WORKGROUPS

If your current network is using the peer-to-peer services of Windows 95, Windows for Workgroups, or Windows NT Workstation, you have a workgroup-based network model. Depending on the server model you implemented, your network has several advantages and disadvantages. To help you fully understand what I mean, this section takes a look at them.

Note

You also could be using Windows NT Server (operating in server mode) and a workgroup-based network. I don't discuss this here because you'll look at this topic in detail in the next section.

If you're using Windows for Workgroups or Windows 95 to provide your network services, your network model can be one of three models:

- ◆ A dedicated Windows for Workgroups or Windows 95 computer that functions as a standalone server that all your clients connect to for shared applications and data.
- ◆ A peer-to-peer network in which every computer shares applications and data on every other computer.
- ◆ A mixture of the preceding two models.

If you're using WFW as a dedicated computer used as a standalone server, your network server provides all the resource allocation, and all your client data is stored on it as well. This provides the capability to back up one computer to tape. In case of a problem, it easily is restored. This also provides a single point of failure. WFW isn't really designed to handle the high traffic loads imposed on it as a network server. It can work well for a small network in the 15-or-fewer client range, but above that it begins to show its limitations. These limitations include the inability to provide reliable network transmissions from multiple data sources to multiple clients. If you've ever tried to share two or three CD-ROMs and 25 to 50 network shares for your WFW clients to access on a WFW server with 8 to 16MB of RAM, you know what I mean. Performance is ragged, and some network connections seem unbearably slow.

For every user who does connect to shares on your WFW server, you have to choose to provide one of the following:

- ◆ No share-level password, which is a real nightmare, because any person with access to the network can connect to and delete the entire shared directory.
- ◆ A read-only password, which provides some network security and can prevent users from deleting the directory but also prevents some applications from running.

◆ A full-access password. This provides some security because if a user does not know the password, he cannot connect to the share. If the user knows the share password, he can completely demolish the directory if he chooses, however.

What makes this even more of a problem is that you (the administrator) have to create share-level passwords for each share and then distribute them to your users. If you change one of these passwords, you must inform all your users. Informing all your users of the change can be a major chore in itself. Still, this is the best model to choose in a standalone Windows for Workgroups network.

Perhaps you're wondering why I claim that using a WFW computer as a server with several WFW clients is a better alternative than using several WFW computers that all use peer-to-peer services. Well, the basic reason boils down to the administration of the network. With each user providing his own shared directory (which may contain shared applications), you have problems associated with a user changing a password without notifying the users who connect to that directory. The user could delete this same shared resource either accidentally or on purpose, which would cause your clients who rely on that resource to scream bloody murder. Or what happens when a user is connected to a resource, has open data files, and the peer-to-peer server crashes? You know that WFW still relies on MS-DOS for some system services and that this interrelationship can cause system failures. And this doesn't even take into consideration the memory resource leaks that occur with every Windows application you run. Over time, this loss of system resources also can cause a system failure. So the bottom line is that you can create a more robust WFW server by not running any applications on it.

Note

Another administrative consideration that might have escaped this mainstream discussion is that for every application you share, you must have a legal client license. If your peer-to-peer clients are arbitrarily sharing applications without a legal license, this could spell trouble for you down the road. If you are caught sharing applications for which you do not have a legal license, you could be sued for restitution. At a minimum, you could be forced to purchase additional licenses.

Robustness is the better reason to consider using Windows NT Workstation as your network server. Windows NT Workstation is less likely to crash and supports the NTFS file system. Windows NT Workstation offers a less expensive alternative to Windows NT Server, and it provides you with the network client licenses you're required to purchase in order to maintain a legal status. Because Windows NT

Workstation doesn't require a network client license and offers a more robust operating system, it seems like a good alternative. Windows NT Workstation also can run Microsoft SQL Server and other Windows NT–specific applications. So it has a lot to offer.

Windows NT Workstation is a true 32-bit operating system with no reliance on MS-DOS. It includes the NTFS file system, which offers greater data integrity at the file system level in case of a power failure. You also can create user accounts and groups and apply these to your shares to specify no access, read-only, change, or full control access at the share level. On an NTFS partition, you can even specify user and group level access to protect your shared data at the file system level. It even includes a backup application to back up your shared data to tape. So where's the catch, you ask? It's in the maximum client connections. Windows NT Workstation 3.5 and higher restricts you to a maximum of 10 user connections. If you have more than 10 network clients, you need more than one Windows NT Workstation to use as file servers.

Tip

> If you still have a copy of Windows NT 3.1 or Windows NT Server 3.1, you will realize that neither of these operating systems has a 10-user connection limit. Also, neither of them requires network client licenses. You might consider this as an alternative to upgrading to Windows NT Server 3.5, or higher, if all you need are file and print services for a small network.

For every Windows NT Workstation you use as a file server, you must create the same user accounts and groups. This defeats the concept of centralized administration. That's where Windows NT Server comes into play.

KEEPING YOUR EXISTING WORKGROUP MODEL

If you decide to keep your workgroup model and you have more than 10 network clients, you really should upgrade to Windows NT Server. You can even upgrade an existing Windows NT Workstation to Windows NT Server, as long as you install Windows NT Server and choose to operate it in server mode. This option keeps all your existing user accounts, groups, shares, and software configurations intact. It also enables more network clients to connect and, even better, provides for centralized administration of the network—at least as far as your file, print, and application server is concerned.

You still can't administer other Windows NT Workstation network clients remotely, as you can with Windows NT Server in a domain model, not unless you know all the

Windows NT Workstation Administrator accounts, anyway. So why do I suggest that you upgrade to Windows NT Server? Simply because it offers a network model that is easier to maintain when compared to a peer-to-peer model. It also offers you increased client connectivity, as well as the capability to use SQL Server and other Windows NT application servers. It even includes the capability to exceed the one-user RAS limitation, so you can support multiple remote client connections. It includes the capability to create a stripe set with parity and other fault-tolerant capabilities not included in Windows NT Workstation.

Note

A stripe set is a means of using two or more physical disk drives as a single logical drive. Each drive is divided into blocks, which, when combined, create a stripe. Multiple stripes then are combined to create a single logical drive. Any data read from or written to this logical drive also is divided into blocks and read from or written to simultaneously, increasing disk throughput.

Windows NT Server is a good match for small networks that are based on the workgroup model because it provides increased connectivity options, but it's not the perfect match if you need more than one server. Once you add another server, you lose what little centralized administration capabilities you had. Also, you can't run applications such as Systems Management Server, which requires the domain model. That is why you might want to consider migrating to a domain model.

MIGRATING TO A DOMAIN MODEL

The domain model offers several advantages when compared to a workgroup model. First, it provides the centralized administration you want. With a domain model, you can remotely administer any Windows NT domain client. You can create one user account that can be used by any network client. These network clients can include MS-DOS, Windows for Workgroups, Windows 95 LAN Manager, or Windows NT clients. You can further group these user accounts into local groups (which are accessible only on the local domain) or global accounts (which are accessible on any domain). If you decide to use global accounts from multiple domains, you have two choices. You can import global accounts from any domain you have administrative access to (which requires that you have multiple administrative accounts), or you can establish a trust relationship to share a user account and a global account database among one or more domains. Trust relationships are discussed in more detail in the next section.

Another benefit of a domain model is the Directory Replicator Service, which enables you to automate the copying of your logon scripts to your backup domain controllers. This method prevents a bottleneck in user authentication because the domain controller (backup or primary) with the fastest response time is used to authenticate the user. Because each domain controller also includes a copy of the user logon script (courtesy of the Directory Replicator Service), any domain controller can perform user authentication. The Directory Replication Service configuration is covered in Chapter 6, "Basic Administrative Tools."

Note

Directory replication is a two-part process. There must be an export directory (the directory to be duplicated) and an import directory. Any Windows NT configuration can import a directory tree (which can include subdirectories), but only a Windows NT Server can export a directory tree.

Of course, the major benefit of domains is that you can install software that requires the domain model to operate. This includes Systems Management Server, which you can use to automate the installation of shared applications and network client operating systems, and even to provide centralized inventory capabilities. These topics are discussed in more detail in Chapters 20, "An Introduction to Systems Management Server," and 21, "Planning and Installing Systems Management Server."

If you're using as your server a Windows for Workgroups computer, Windows NT computer, or Windows NT Server computer operating in server mode, you can install Windows NT Server as a primary domain controller on a new computer (basically, a cloning process), or you can upgrade the existing computer if the hardware platform supports Windows NT Server. LAN Manager and Novell NetWare upgrades are discussed in the next chapter. Integrating Windows NT Server domains with other networks is discussed in Chapter 6.

Note

Although you could leave your current workgroup server online during the upgrading process, I don't recommend it. If you leave it online, a user could change a data file, causing your replacement server's copied data files to be out of sync. Also, if you have connected users and you attempt to change the computer name, you will have to disconnect all your connected users, possibly causing data loss.

This cloned or upgraded computer becomes your replacement server, but you need to consider a few complications in this process:

◆ If you plan to completely replace your current workgroup server as transparently as possible with a new computer, both computers must have their names changed. This is required because computer names must be unique within a domain. Therefore, if your workgroup computer is called Server and your new replacement server is called NTServer, after the installation, you must give the workgroup server a new name (perhaps OldServer) and rename the replacement server to Server. The domain name of your new server should be the same as your current workgroup server name.

◆ After you create a new server with the appropriate computer and domain names, you must copy the shared data and applications. You can do this easily by connecting from your new domain controller to the workgroup computer and copying all the shared data. If you upgrade an existing workgroup computer, all the data already resides on the server.

◆ This shared data is where the major complication can arise. If you have a Windows for Workgroups computer, all you need to do is re-create the shared directories. If you have a Windows NT–based server, things can get a bit more complicated if you're using more than the share-level permissions provided by Windows for Workgroups. If you have your data on an NTFS partition and you assign directory or file permissions, for example, all this permission information is lost as part of the upgrade and must be re-created manually.

◆ All the directory and file permission information will be lost because when you upgrade a Windows NT Workstation—or a Windows NT Server operating in server mode—you can't upgrade and use the user account database. In fact, when you upgrade any of the platforms just mentioned, you have to replace all the configuration information. It's not a software upgrade but a replacement.

Note

Not only do you lose the user account database, but you also lose access to any striped sets, volume sets, or fault-tolerant partitions. This occurs because the existing NT operating system files and all the Registry files are deleted prior to the installation of Windows NT Server. The Registry files contain the user accounts, the system partition information, and any security information.

◆ The only other item to consider is related to network protocols and configuration. You need to install the same protocols that your clients currently are configured to use. If one of these is TCP/IP, your new server needs to use the old server's IP address and import any LMHOST files it was using. Your old server must, of course, have a new IP address allocated for its use.

After you create your new server, you must complete the following actions on the server:

♦ Create new user accounts and local and global groups on the server. This is required because during the installation, all your user account information is lost.

♦ Create your new shared directories and assign new user level or group level permissions for the new sharepoints.

♦ Take ownership of any directories and files if you upgraded a Windows NT Workstation or a Windows NT Server operating in server mode. Then reassign the directory and file permissions based on your new user accounts.

After you've done these things, you need to complete the following tasks on your network client computers:

♦ Change from a workgroup to a domain. You do this on a Windows for Workgroups, Windows 95, or Windows NT Workstation computer by running the Control Panel Network applet. On a Windows for Workgroups computer, you also should specify that the computer will be logging onto a domain. You access this option by clicking the Startup button.

Note

You don't have to change from a workgroup to a domain immediately. Your current clients will be able to connect to existing shared resources as long as they have current user IDs and passwords. Because you'll be changing all your network passwords (probably to your users' user names) and requiring that your users change their passwords at first logon, this could cause a bit of user anxiety. You should plan for this by distributing a mail message to all your users before you upgrade your server.

♦ For your Windows NT clients, you should change any shared directory permissions to use the accounts from the domain rather than the local database. This action prevents a user from requiring two separate passwords—one for the domain account and one for the shared directories on the NT Workstation. You don't have to do this immediately. As long as users have valid user IDs and passwords on the NT Workstation, they still can continue to supply them when prompted, or they can use the Connect As option in the Connect to Network Drive dialog box.

TRUST RELATIONSHIPS

A trust relationship is a means of sharing a domain database on one domain with another domain. This domain database includes your user and group accounts. It provides a means of authenticating a user of a foreign domain (where the user account or group is defined) to access a network resource on a local domain. Suppose that I'm a member of the Admin domain and you're a member of the User domain, and the User domain trusts the Admin domain. I can access resources on the User domain, but you cannot access resources on the Admin domain. The way trust works is that the local domain (which is called the trusting domain) requests authentication of my user account from the foreign domain (the trusted domain). After this authentication occurs, it may be applied or denied to a resource on the local domain. In order to actually gain access to a resource, my user account, or a global group that my user account is a member of, must be granted access on the local domain.

Note

> By using trust relationships, you can create an extremely large logical network server that can be used to authenticate all your users and shared resources. You can think of a domain as a single logical super server. By creating multiple authentication and resource domains, you can extend this capability to build a network that will serve an almost unlimited number of users. The only real limitation to the number of users you can support is determined by your network bandwidth.

Now look at this scenario one step at a time. Suppose that I'm a member of the Domain Admins group on the domain called Admins. And there is a share on the local domain, UserDomain, called AdminShare that has the share-level privileges assigned to the local Administrator group. The local Administrator group includes the global Domain Admins group by default. When you set up a trust relationship, the Admins\Domain Admins global group will be applied to the shared directory just as if I were a local member of the Administrator group. This provides me with administrative privileges to the share. This is an example of a one-way trust relationship.

But you also can set up a two-way trust relationship in which the Admins domain is trusted by the User domain as before and the Admins domain also trusts the User domain. Sound confusing? Well, it's not really that bad. Now stretch this example a bit further. Start again with the User domain trusting the Admins domain to give me administrative privileges to the User domain. And then set up a trust relationship in which the Admins domain trusts the User domain and you're a member of Users\Domain Users. I can give you user privileges to shared network resources in the Admins domain. Setting up such a trust relationship is covered in Chapter 6.

Although this capability to share an account database is a really nifty feature because it provides the capability to access networked resources as if you were a local member, it does have a minor (or major) problem (depending on how you set up your trust relationships). To be specific, it eats up a lot of network bandwidth. First, you must consider how the authentication process occurs. Whenever a trusted account is used, the request is passed from the trusting domain to the trusted domain. The more trusted users connect, the more network bandwidth is used. Trusting domains also periodically change their passwords. This process of passthrough authentication and periodic password changes can eat up a lot of network bandwidth quite quickly.

Obviously, if you have all your servers on a 100Mbps backbone, this isn't much of a problem. But, if you have domains located across routers, bridges, or RAS connections, the available bandwidth might not be sufficient to simultaneously support your passthrough authentications and your network client data access. So how do you get around this limitation? Well, you have a couple of possibilities. First, you can increase your network bandwidth on the slower network segments. Or you can manually include global groups from a foreign domain in a local group on the local domain. To do this, though, you need administrative access to both domains.

You can follow these basic steps to add a global group from a foreign domain to a local group on your local domain:

1. Use File Manager to connect to a sharepoint on the nonlocal domain (the one you aren't a member of) and use the Connect As option in the Network Connection dialog box to specify an administrative user account (in the form of *DomainName\UserName*).

2. After you've connected to the sharepoint, you have administrative privileges on the nonlocal domain.

3. You now can run User Manager for Domains on your local domain.

4. Double-click on the local group to which you want to add the foreign global group. Alternatively create a new local group first. (See Chapter 6 for more specifics on how to create and manage groups.)

5. In the Local Group Properties dialog box, click the Add button. The Add Users and Groups dialog box appears.

6. In the List Names From field, select the foreign domain. All the groups are displayed in the Names field.

7. Select the global group and click the Add button. Or just double-click the global group. This places the group in the Add Names field.

8. Now it's just a matter of clicking the OK buttons to return you to the User Manager for Domains main window.

As soon as you've added these global groups, you can assign permissions to local resources based on the local group you modified in these steps. When foreign users attempt to access the resource, they are granted access. These steps perform essentially the same action as a one-way trust relationship but without all the overhead involved in the passthrough authentication process. If you want to create a two-way relationship, just repeat steps 4 through 8 of the preceding process on the foreign domain with User Manager for Domains. Instead of selecting your domain (which is the default), choose User | Select Domain and, in the Select Domain dialog box, choose the foreign domain and then import your global group to a local group on the foreign domain.

BUILDING YOUR FIRST DOMAIN

In Chapter 1, you learned about the basic Microsoft domain models. These domain models are a good start for your network, but you might want to consider modifying one of them to best fit your physical network layout. You also should consider what will happen to your domain model as your network grows. This discussion will start with your choice for your first domain model. It will cover situations that will limit your growth potential or cause you severe administration headaches. Planning your network design before you actually implement it can make quite a difference in your growth potential and administrative burden.

Your choice of a first domain is the most important choice you make when you install Windows NT Server as your network operating system. You should plan it as carefully as possible and consider your future upgrade options. Although it's possible to expand any domain model to increase the number of users your network can support, some choices cause more of an administrative burden. If, during this discussion, you find yourself a little confused about the basic domain models, refer to Chapter 1 to get a better grasp of the basics.

THE SINGLE DOMAIN MODEL

If you have a small domain with about 100 users and you have no plans to support more than 300 users, the single domain model will serve you well. This model offers simplicity in its design because you have only one domain. Within this domain, you will have one primary domain controller and optionally one or more backup domain controllers and servers. You can increase the maximum number of users, but you will sacrifice a loss of performance, depending on the hardware platform you choose and your available network bandwidth. As you add more users, your administrative burden increases because you have to search through large lists of users for routine maintenance.

If you plan on simply adding more backup domain controllers or servers to your network to support additional users, you will see further performance degradation as your network clogs from user authentication on resource servers. Eventually, this domain model will collapse as the number of network clients increases. If you decide to create a WAN by just adding another backup domain controller or server supported by a Remote Access Service link or router, the available bandwidth will decrease because you are using it for synchronization or user authentication.

The single domain model is really a good choice for your first domain because it is readily expandable. You can upgrade it to a master domain model quite easily by using your current primary domain and backup domain controllers as your master domain and moving all your resource servers to a new domain. This can increase the supported number of users to at least 1,000 users. It could be more, depending on the number of backup controllers you have to distribute the authentication load, but I find that a single domain with 1,000 users is about the most I can deal with in my administrative duties.

THE MASTER DOMAIN MODEL

This domain model is generally my first choice for a corporate domain because it provides for centralized administration by an MIS department while still allowing your individual departments to administer their own resource domains if desired. In an unmodified master domain, you have one domain that contains all the user accounts and resource domains that contain only shared resources. All resource domains trust the master domain and refer all user authentication to the master domain. Within the resource domains, the local administrators (who really only have to be account operators) can assign permissions to locally shared resources.

By dividing your resource domains on a departmental basis, you can provide better performance to the users of that domain. This is possible because all the resources the department will use are contained in their domain. Therefore, they won't have to contend with other users for network bandwidth as single-domain model users will. This domain is also a good choice for a WAN because you can create a new server in a new domain on the other side of the WAN link. This new domain then trusts the master domain, as does every other domain, so that only user authentication must be performed by the master domain and sent across the WAN link. All resource access occurs locally within the resource domain. The network bottleneck eventually becomes the speed at which you can authenticate users in order to access their network resources on their local domain, both for domains on the LAN and domains on the WAN.

But, this still isn't the best choice for maximum performance because all user authentication still must be performed by the master domain. It's better to modify the domain model to include user accounts on the resource domains, particularly for domains on the other side of a WAN link. These user accounts still can be created by the administrators of the master domain (generally, your MIS department), but because the user accounts are contained locally on the resource domain, no user authentication must be referred to the master domain to access the local resources. This increases your potential to add more users by adding more domains while still performing adequately. You can think of this modified model as a hybrid between the master domain model and the multiple master model.

The down side of placing user accounts on the local resource domains is that once this has occurred, the users of a local domain can't access any resources outside their own domain. You can still provide this capability, however. You can create trust relationships, which eventually will place you in a complete trust model and therefore is not recommended. The preferred method is to place users who need access to external resources in a global account on their local domain and, on the foreign domain, to create a local account that includes these global accounts. Because all your master domain administrators have administrative privileges to all your resource domains, it's quite easy for them to perform group management tasks on behalf of the local resource domain administrators.

THE MULTIPLE MASTER DOMAIN MODEL

In the multiple master domain model, you have multiple master domains with your user accounts defined on them. Each of these master domains trusts the others, and all your resource domains trust each master domain. This model distributes the authentication load among many domains to provide a better base for supporting a large number of users. You can choose to split up your user base alphabetically, by department, or by division. The divisional choice will lead to better network management because it easily can be expanded to encompass your entire company, whereas the alphabetical method can lead to unbalanced loads as your network grows in size.

Like the hybrid master model mentioned earlier, you can include local administrator accounts on the resource domains to allow the departmental administrators to administer their own domains and user accounts to provide increased performance and better utilization of network bandwidth. This domain model is also an excellent choice for your wide area network.

I find that the multiple master domain model offers the best expansion options of all the domain models, while still providing centralized administration and resource access—as long as you plan its growth accordingly. The secret to excellent performance is to segment your design as much as possible. Create domains based on the highest level in your company, such as a division; then, within your division domains, create additional departmental domains. Finally, within the departmental domains, create your resource domains.

THE COMPLETE TRUST MODEL

You should avoid the complete trust model if at all possible. This model provides two capabilities that sound promising at first. For one thing, your network clients can access any network resource from any client workstation. Second, your network administrators can fully administer the network from any workstation. So what's bad about complete access to your network resources? Well, I'll tell you. It basically amounts to two words: complete chaos.

When you implement a complete trust domain, you have to trust every network administrator. But not all network administrators are created equal. Some of them are definitely better than others. And a poorly trained administrator can completely demolish your network. So how can you avoid this potential disaster? Well, you have two choices. You can choose another domain model, which is the best choice. Or you can remove all of the Domain Admins global groups from every foreign domain that you don't want to have administrative functions on your domain.

Suppose that you have three domains: Admins, Marketing, and Research. Each of these domains completely trusts the others (which just means that each domain has a two-way trust relationship with the other domains). If you look in the local Administrators group on each domain, you'll find that each domain has its global Domain Admins group included. To remove all administrative privileges from all domains but the Admins domain, you can use User Manager for Domains. Just follow these steps:

- Select the Marketing domain, select the Administrators group, and then remove the Research\Domain Admins group.
- For the Research domain, remove the Marketing\Domain Admins global group from the local Administrators group.
- In the Admins domain, remove the Marketing\Domain Admins and Research\Domain Admins global groups from the local Administrators group.

This leaves the local Administrators group for the Marketing and Research domains with the Admins\Domain Admins group. This gives the administrators of the Admins domain full administrative privileges on all domains but prevents any administrators of the Marketing or Research domains from administering any domain, other than their own domain, while still providing user-level access to each domain.

Note

If you want to further restrict access to your servers, you should perform the same actions for the other local groups: Account Operators, Server Operators, and Backup Operators.

The only way to completely prevent any administrator of these domains from making any changes is to revoke his administrative privileges. You can do this by removing the global Domain Admins group from the domain's local Administrators group. You also should change the password on the local Administrator user account. To be absolutely sure, remove any individual user accounts that might have been placed in the local Administrators group.

Although it's possible to continually add domains to your network in order to support additional users, each time you do, you have to create n(n - 1) trust connections, where n is the number of domains. If you have five existing domains, for example, and you decide to add a new domain, you must create 30 (6 * 5) trust connections. If you have 49 domains, you have to create 2,450 trust connections in order to add a fiftieth domain. This would be an awful lot of work—probably more than it's worth.

THE INTERNET INFORMATION SERVER

While there are currently other products available (such those included with the Windows NT Resource Kit) to allow you to publish content on the Internet using Windows NT, none of them offers the same range of features as the Microsoft Internet Information Server (IIS). After reading this, you may be wondering if I work for Microsoft. Well, I'm not a Microsoft employee; however, I do like what the Internet Information Server can do. I think you will, too.

WHAT IS THE INTERNET INFORMATION SERVER?

This question is not really as easy to answer as it seems. The Internet Information Server is more than just a port of a couple of Internet services to Windows NT Server. But since IIS does provide these services, a complete description practically requires that we describe them. So this is where you will start to learn just what the Internet Information Server is. Then you will learn more about what makes IIS different. The difference can really be summed up by just saying that IIS is an extensible platform. It provides many different methods for customizing IIS to suit your individual requirements.

A Collection of Windows NT Services

To begin, the Internet Information Server consists of three specific Windows NT Services that are used to publish content (data) using the TCP/IP protocol as the underlying transmission mechanism. This includes a World Wide Web (WWW) server, a File Transfer Protocol (FTP) server, and a Gopher server. The key to understanding just how this works is to realize that IIS provides the servers of a client/server product. Without a client application, such as a Web browser like the Internet Explorer, the server really doesn't do much good.

One reason why the Internet services use a client/server model is to lower the bandwidth requirements. You can think of the Internet, if you'd like, as a very large Wide Area Network (WAN), because in essence that's what it is. A WAN is a collection of computers that are not physically located in the same location as your network (or local area network). Most WANs use very slow (56Kbps) connections to connect them to your LAN. Some use higher-speed (up to 45Mbps) connections. The connection speed determines how much information can be passed between the server application and the client application. Considering that most Internet connections by clients occur using 14400–28800bps (57600–11520bps with compression), you can see the need to lower the bandwidth requirements as much as possible.

WWW Publishing Service

The Microsoft WWW Publishing Service is a WWW server. It uses the HyperText Transmission Protocol (HTTP) to communicate with its client application (a Web browser). This can be confusing sometimes as people might refer to your WWW Publishing Service as a WWW server or an HTTP server. It really doesn't matter as all of them perform the same task. Each responds to client application requests. These requests are the basis for publishing information on the World Wide Web.

The World Wide Web is a content-rich environment. It encompasses the majority of network traffic on the Internet. It can be used to display (on your Web browser) text, static graphic images, animated graphic images, 3D worlds, audio/video files, or to play audio files. And this is just the tip of the iceberg. New features are being added to Web browsers almost constantly, which in turn means adding additional extensions to your Web server in order to support them.

Web browsers are no longer tied specifically to supporting Web servers, either. Today's Web browsers can be used to connect to FTP sites, GOPHER sites, and even to access newsgroups. Future versions may encompass other Internet services as well. These services could include e-mail, telnet, remote shells, and so on. There's no telling what the future will bring in the World Wide Web client/server arena.

FTP PUBLISHING SERVICE

While the WWW Publishing Service is an HTTP server, the FTP Publishing Service is a File Transfer Protocol, or FTP, server. The FTP Publishing Service is much less complex than the WWW Publishing Service. The FTP Publishing Service is used primarily as a data repository. This repository can contain various types of files that users can upload or download to their systems using an FTP client application. It is similar to a communications program, such as Procomm for Windows, that you would use to access a bulletin board system (BBS). When you decide to download a file from the BBS, you have to specify a download protocol. Most often this is the ZMODEM protocol.

GOPHER PUBLISHING SERVICE

The Gopher Publishing Service is used much less frequently than either the WWW or FTP publishing services. It is used primarily to publish very large amounts of textual data. If you had an encyclopedia to publish, for example, the Gopher Publishing Service would be a good choice to use as your publishing medium. The biggest benefits of the Gopher Publishing Service are that it can be searched and that the data can actually span multiple servers. It is possible to perform similar processes with either the WWW or FTP publishing services, but you will need to do more work.

AN EXTENSIBLE PLATFORM

The key to any, and I do mean *any*, project is the ability to extend the capabilities of the project based on user demands. Every project either grows to encompass new features and keep the customer satisfied, or it stagnates and dies. This is true of the Information Server as well. The good news is that IIS is so extensible you might be overwhelmed by the possibilities. Of course, the bad news is that there is something for everyone. The software development kits available for IIS include legacy support, such as the Common Gateway Interface (CGI), as well as brand new APIs that bring the power of OLE (ActiveX) to the World Wide Web. While this chapter cannot cover all of these possibilities in depth, it can give you a brief taste of them.

INTERNET INFORMATION SERVER SOFTWARE DEVELOPMENT KIT

Depending on who you talk to, and when you talk to them, you may have heard of the Internet Server Application Programming Interface (ISAPI). This is a proprietary programming interface introduced with IIS as a replacement for CGI development tasks. You can create ISAPI applications that extend the functionality of the Internet Information Server just as you would a CGI application. The biggest difference between a CGI application and an ISAPI application is that a CGI application executes in a separate process, whereas an ISAPI application is really a dynamic link library (DLL) that executes in the same address space as the WWW Publishing Service. An ISAPI DLL is much faster than a CGI application that performs the same task. It also consumes fewer resources, which means you can service many more users.

Caution

There is a downside to ISAPI DLLs. Since they share the same address space as the HTTP server, it is possible that an errant ISAPI application could crash the WWW Publishing Server. Before you implement any new ISAPI application, be sure that it is thoroughly tested first.

So just what can you do with an ISAPI application? Well, you could create an online calculator, for example, where the user would see an interactive calculator screen on his Web browser. The actual calculations would be performed on the WWW server, with the result being returned for display on the client's Web browser. This is a very simple task, which may not be challenging enough for you, so perhaps you should consider these possibilities:

◆ The Internet Information Server includes the ISAPI Internet Connector. This is a DLL that provides access to ODBC (Open Database Connectivity) drivers. This means that your ISAPI applications can access any ODBC-compliant database, such as SQL Server, Oracle, RBase, Access, Paradox, dBase, and many more. Anything you can store in such a database can be displayed, or downloaded, on the client's Web browser.

◆ You could create an ISAPI filter that would be called whenever the WWW Publishing Service received an HTTP request. You could use this in much the same way that you would when you hook into the Windows operating system to control the behavior of the mouse to trap mouse messages, except in this case you would trap HTTP messages. You could use such a process to perform data encryption, data compression, user logging, or similar tasks.

ACTIVEX

ActiveX, formerly code-named Sweeper, is where the real heart-and-soul changes are going to be occurring in future products. ActiveX basically brings the power of OLE objects to the Internet. With ActiveX you will be able to create custom controls for Web browsers to enhance their functionality. If you currently have a custom control you have developed, it should not be too difficult to migrate it to ActiveX.

Custom controls will be insertable into Visual Basic applications, which implies the possibility of inserting them into Visual C++ applications, or any application environment that supports the OLE custom controls.

As another sideline benefit, ActiveX introduces the concept of OLE document objects, which enable you to create or host documents in a frame within a Web browser (a document in this context can be any object for which you have developed a custom control). You could view a Word document, for example, inside a frame of your Web browser. Or you could go so far as to turn your Web browser into a full-fledged word processor as you do today with OLE automation. This technology is going to revolutionize the Web, and you can be a part of it.

There is still more to talk about with ActiveX—in fact I could go on and on, but ActiveX is really so huge a topic that it requires its own book. However, I would like to point out two more items of potential interest to you. First, ActiveX supports two new scripting languages. The first is JScript which is based on SUN Microsystems Java language. Java is based on C++ and is used to provide interactive applications, commonly called applets, that can be integrated into your Web browser. The second scripting language is VBScript which is based on Microsoft's Visual Basic and performs a function similar to that of JScript. Both of these scripting languages have had been trimmed down to remove potentially dangerous functions—such as the ability to directly access the hard disk drive.

COMMON GATEWAY INTERFACE

The Common Gateway Interface, or CGI, has been around on the World Wide Web for quite some time. If you already have CGI applications, you can continue to use them. If not, you may want to consider writing some. The biggest question you should have if you are new to WWW development is which applications you should choose to develop: CGI or ISAPI applications? If your development skills are up to snuff, and you have been writing Windows applications in C++ for quite some time, there is really no contest. Choose ISAPI, and start coding today.

On the other hand, if you are new to application development using C++, or you prefer C, FORTRAN, PASCAL, or whatever, you may want to consider developing CGI applications. A CGI application is any application that supports the stdin (standard input), stdout (standard output) interface, and can access environment variables. This can cover a lot of ground and can provide you with an easier transition. You can also use CGI in conjunction with the Perl scripting language instead of a compiled application to rapidly develop HTTP server extensions.

SYSTEMS MANAGEMENT SERVER

Systems Management Server is based on a hierarchical design, so you should plan your installation accordingly. You should install your SMS central site to your highest-level domain, or at least a domain that is accessible by your domain administrators. This central site, of which there can be only one, will be used to manage all your primary and secondary sites. The whole idea behind SMS is that you can manage your entire network from one workstation. And this really is possible, to a degree, if you plan your installation properly. For information on the actual implementation for design, see Chapter 21.

There is more to your SMS installation than just dividing up your sites, however. For each central or primary site, you should consider the following:

◆ If at all possible, don't install Systems Management Server and SQL Server on the same server. Instead, spread this load among at least two servers.

◆ Systems Management Server places a heavy load on your network server. If you have several servers or workstations in your domains, you can spread some of the SMS worker services among them. This can lessen the load produced by SMS on a single server and achieve better performance.

◆ If you will be installing SMS sites on servers located on the other side of a WAN link for increased performance, you should install SMS as a primary site. This requires that the primary site also have a copy of SQL Server. The reason behind this philosophy is that you want to limit the amount of network traffic sent across the WAN link.

◆ To support your NetWare servers, you must install the Gateway Services for NetWare on the site server. Installation of the Gateway Services for NetWare is covered in Chapter 5, "Integrating Windows NT Server with Other Networks."

◆ Supporting your Macintosh clients requires that you have Services for Macintosh installed on your site server. Installation of Services for Macintosh is covered in Chapter 5.

◆ For all your Windows NT Server, Windows NT Workstation, and Windows 95 clients, you should install the Network Monitor Agent software. This software enables you to view additional performance counters with the Performance Monitor, but more importantly, it can be used by the SMS Network Monitor to remotely capture packets from the client computer rather than the computer running the SMS Network Monitor. This is very useful when diagnosing WAN clients and computers on subsegments of your LAN because it causes less network overhead.

Note

On a Windows NT–based computer, the Network Monitor Agent is installed via the Control Panel Network applet (the Add Software option). On a Windows 95 client, you have to install it manually from the Control Panel Network applet. Select Add, followed by Service, for the type of component to install. Click the Have Disk button. When prompted, select the `Admin\Nettools\Netmon` subdirectory on your Windows 95 CD-ROM.

SQL SERVER

When it comes to database management, Microsoft SQL Server is an excellent choice. It performs well and is integrated quite closely with Windows NT. It also is required as a subcomponent for all of Systems Management Server, because this is where it stores all its inventory data. Because it is required by your SMS installation, you should consider a few items beforehand.

The first thing to consider is your platform for SQL Server, because it won't perform well if you install it to a computer with limited resources. My preference is to use a dual Pentium server with at least 64MB of RAM. You should allocate at least 32MB of RAM to SQL Server for best SQL Server performance. Performance considerations for SQL Server are discussed in Chapter 18, "Optimizing SQL Server." For now, I just want you to consider that SQL Server should have its own dedicated computer (preferably a Windows NT Server operating in server mode) with as much hardware as you can budget.

Tip

If you have sufficient RAM in your server, you might also use it for the SQL Server temporary database (`tempdb`), which can vastly speed up your queries and sorts. I've seen SQL Servers with more than 256MB of RAM, and I have to admit that when properly configured, they perform exceedingly well.

The next thing to think about is your databases. When you install SQL Server, it creates the master database. This database contains system stored procedures and the model database. You can't expand the master database without losing all your modifications. This can cause complications down the road. So, although you'll find the minimum recommended database size set to 15MB, my recommendation is to set it for a minimum of 35MB or possibly even 50MB, depending on how much customization you plan on performing.

You also will find that you must preallocate your SQL Server devices used to contain your databases—much like an MS-DOS file is used to create a compressed drive. As part of this process of creating a database, you can create both your database and transaction logs (the logs provide data integrity and atomic operations for SQL Server data transactions) on the same device, but you should avoid this process. This is because you can't dump or restore a transaction log stored on the same device as the database. And working with transaction logs in this fashion is highly desirable, as you will see in future chapters.

Because you must allocate space in advance, you might want to plan on using a compressed NTFS partition to store your SQL Server databases. This gives you the capability to create larger devices and therefore larger databases. These databases and devices will compress extremely well because most of these components include null pages. An NTFS partition also offers you increased fault tolerance. If you're really looking for maximum performance, however, you should not use a compressed drive because this option is a trade-off of performance versus storage requirement. The best I/O performance can be achieved by installing the SQL Server devices on an uncompressed NTFS partition created on a stripe set.

GATEWAYS

If you've been working as a network administrator for a while, you're probably familiar with the concept of a gateway. But for the uninitiated, I should mention that a gateway is used to pass information from one source to another. During this passing process, the data may be converted from one data format to another. The Microsoft BackOffice products include several gateways you can use to provide services to your network clients:

◆ Gateway Services for NetWare: This is a gateway to a Novell NetWare server from your network clients. You can use this service to access a shared resource on your Novell server and then share it from your Windows NT Server. Then, all your network clients can access this resource even without a Novell user account. In effect, the Windows NT Server is a gateway to the shared Novell resources because the client must go through the Windows NT Server to access the Novell resource. In the process, the client network data request must be converted from the Microsoft network data request format to the Novell network data format.

◆ Services for Macintosh: This is installed on your Windows NT Server. It acts as a gateway between Windows NT Workstation clients and Macintosh clients to enable them to share data over the AppleTalk protocol. More important is the fact that this service provides the means for your Macintosh clients to access your Windows NT Server as a file, print, and application server just as if it were a native Macintosh network server.

◆ Microsoft Mail gateways: Microsoft Mail performs a similar function of routing data between different platforms; it routes mail messages from one source format to another source format. The base package includes a gateway to AT&T Easymail, but other options are available for access to the Internet, CompuServe, MCI mail, and others. All these gateways provide the capability to convert a Microsoft Mail message to the appropriate format for the final destination source.

◆ Microsoft Exchange Server mail gateways: The enterprise edition of Microsoft Exchange Server includes similar capabilities as Microsoft Mail. With Exchange Server these gateways are called connectors. There is an X.400, an SMTP, and a Microsoft Mail connector with third parties providing additional gateways to their proprietary mail systems.

◆ SNA Server gateways: Just like the gateways mentioned, SNA Server acts as a gateway between your network clients and your IBM mainframes. SNA Server establishes the connection to your mainframe, and then your network clients connect to SNA Server. Depending on your SNA Server connection to your mainframe and your SNA Link, you will have various types of data and transport conversions.

◆ TCP/IP gateways: A TCP/IP gateway is a bit different than the gateways just mentioned. This type of gateway is used to pass data between one network data segment and another network data segment. Each data segment has a different base IP address, and in order for data to pass between these two data segments, a gateway must be used. This type of gateway often is called a router.

WIDE AREA NETWORKS

Creating a wide area network (WAN) with Windows NT Server is extremely easy. You can follow the conventional method of using a router or bridge to connect two networks located at physically different locations, or you can use the Remote Access Service. Both of these methods have different strengths and weaknesses, which is the subject of this section.

USING REMOTE ACCESS SERVICE

For your first wide area network, I suggest that you use the Remote Access Service software. This service is included with Windows NT Server and therefore is the least expensive alternative for creating a WAN. It can support up to 256 simultaneous client connections, but supporting this requires you to have a third-party adapter from a manufacturer such as DigiBoard. If you do plan to support 256 simultaneous connections, this server shouldn't perform any other network action. With the

Remote Access Service, you can use an X.25 adapter card to connect to an X.25 source, which provides low speed but worldwide connectivity from a local phone number. Or, you can use a pair of modems, which, just like your bulletin board access, requires calling a standard phone number. Still another option is to use a pair of ISDN adapters. Chapter 5 covers installation of the Remote Access Service.

USING AN X.25 NETWORK

An X.25 RAS connection is a low-speed (about 9,600bps), packet-based connection (just like your LAN). The primary advantage of an X.25 network is that it's cheaper to implement than the regular modem-to-modem or ISDN-to-ISDN connection when supporting a large number of RAS clients. This is because you can use an X.25 connection from just about anywhere in the world just by dialing a local access number.

There are two parts to this process and two ways to implement an X.25 RAS connection. You can use an X.25-network-adapter-to-X.25-network-adapter connection, such as the one manufactured by Eicon. Or you can use an X.25 network adapter on the server and a modem on the client. The client dials up a local access number to gain access to the X.25 network. These network packets then are routed to your network server. After this occurs, a two-way communication linkage is established and the user can perform any desired network action, such as printing a file or running an application.

An X.25 network also is a good choice for a network that must maintain a low-cost and low-usage (particularly at 9,600bps) communication linkage between two remote locations. But this isn't for the security-minded, because the X.25 network easily can be tapped by potential hackers.

HIGH-SPEED MODEMS

The most common RAS connection is based on high-speed modems. You can use your standard 14,400 or 28,800bps modems to provide data transfers in the 57,600bps–115,200bps range. Although these aren't the fastest data-transfer rates, they are acceptable rates for infrequent network usage, and they work extremely well for distributed applications (such as SQL Server). However, as in most software packages, there are issues to consider:

◆ The first thing you should be aware of is that a reliable modem connection is based on the quality of the phone line. The faster the baud rate, the cleaner the line must be in order to obtain error-free data transmissions. Reliable 28,800 connections are almost impossible to achieve with local phone lines. Long-distance connections seem to perform better, probably because many of them are based on fiber-optic phone lines. If you do decide to go this route, talk to your phone-line provider and request a conditioned line. This generally requires a small, one-time fee, but you will get a cleaner data line.

◆ Next, you have to consider the UART (Universal Asynchronous Receiver Transmitter) on which your COM port is based. If you have the standard 16450, the best you can achieve is a 38,400bps data transmission. If you have a 16550 UART, the best you can achieve is a 57,600bps data-transfer rate. To obtain a higher data-transfer rate, you must use an internal modem with a buffered 16550 UART or another buffered UART supported by Windows NT Server. The best solution I have found is to use a DigiBoard adapter that supports from 2 to 256 UARTs and that includes a dedicated CPU to offload the work from the CPU on your motherboard.

◆ To obtain the higher data-transfer rates, you must modify the SERIAL.INI file located in the SystemRoot\System32\RAS directory. The MAXCONNECTBPS and IntialBps parameters must be changed to the highest DTE rate (from 38,400 to 57,600 for a 14,400 modem, and from 57,600 to 115,200 for a 28,800 modem). Your client software must be configured similarly. Otherwise, you will only achieve the data-transfer rate of the slowest RAS configuration.

◆ You also will want to test your RAS configuration to determine whether the hardware or software compression performs better. This depends on the speed of your CPU. For most computers, the software compression outperforms the modem's hardware compression. But you will need to test this to be sure on your hardware platforms.

◆ You also must consider the cost associated with local and long-distance access. This varies from state to state and from phone company to phone company.

THE ISDN CONNECTION

An ISDN connection offers the best performance when compared to an X.25 or a modem connection. This is because ISDN is a digital-based connection; therefore, the quality of the connection is superior to the average modem connection and much faster than an X.25 connection. However, ISDN uses a proprietary phone connection and is therefore unacceptable for mobile computer users. It does perform well for sites where your local phone company supports ISDN phone lines. An ISDN connection can support one or two 64KB connections. (Some phone companies use 8KB as overhead, so you might get only 56KB.) In theory, this can give you up to a 128KB (possibly only 112KB) data-transfer rate.

And, as with an X.25 connection, you need a proprietary adapter, which increases your WAN expense. You also should consider the monthly fee and per-minute access fees when planning your budget. These fees vary from state to state. ISDN service in general is not available in every state, so check with your local phone company before deciding to use this alternative.

USING ROUTERS TO INCREASE PERFORMANCE

You can use a router or bridge to provide an additional benefit that a RAS connection can't: the capability to dial up and connect to a remote network node based on user demand. A RAS connection must be user-initiated or permanent. A router or bridge (depending on the manufacturer) automatically can dial up a remote node when it detects a request for an external server in its internal database. This can decrease your phone bill quite a bit over a dedicated connection to your remote server.

Some routers can use a regular phone line or a digital leased line. Regular phone lines offer a limited bandwidth and an increased cost based on whether you dial local or long-distance phone numbers. For a constant communication linkage, I recommend a leased line. Leased lines vary in cost from location to location, so you should check with your phone company for the specific cost associated with connecting your sites. Leased lines also come in various types and speeds, as shown in Table 2.1.

TABLE 2.1. TYPES OF LEASED LINES.

Line Type	Minimum Speed	Maximum Speed
DS-0	56Kbps	56Kbps
Fractional T-1	112Kbps	768Kbps
T-1	1.544Mbps	1.544Mbps
T3/Fractional T3	3Mbps	45Mbps
SMDS	56Kbps	45Mbps
ATM	1.5Mbps	45Mbps

PLANNING FOR DISASTER

The final point to consider before you install your network software is what to do in case disaster strikes. Disasters can be as simple as the loss of a file due to a power failure or as complex as a loss of your entire server due to a lighting strike. What would you do if this happened? If you think about the possibilities beforehand, you can be prepared with a solution. These are what I want to introduce you to—the possibilities.

Aside from the fault-tolerant capabilities provided in the disk subsystem, such as disk mirroring and striped sets with parity, you need to consider what you can do in case of a failure of the entire system (losing your server to an unexpected power surge, for example) or a corruption of the file system—particularly if you've installed Windows NT Server to an NTFS partition. Currently, there are no tools to access an NTFS partition, except for the CHKDSK utility included with Windows NT. This basically leaves three possibilities for data recovery:

◆ A dual NT installation: This is the preferred method of accessing a failed Windows NT installation to repair any data inconsistencies in the NTFS file system. For this process, you need to install the version of Windows NT Server you plan to use on a daily basis and then install another copy of Windows NT Server to use as a backup copy—on different drives, preferably. If you have any fault-tolerant partitions in your second copy of Windows NT Server, you need to use the Disk Administrator to import the existing configuration. This gives you the best chance of recovering your primary NT installation because you can boot the secondary installation to recover the primary installation. This works in most cases, but it won't help you recover from a failed data partition.

◆ The repair disk: This is a secondary alternative to recovering a failed Windows NT Server installation. This process can't recover all failed file system errors, however, and it can't recover a failed partition. This process also requires access to the three boot floppy disks used to install Windows NT and to access to the source media (either on floppy disks or CD-ROM). As part of the installation process, you are prompted to create a repair disk, and I suggest that you do so. Then, whenever you make any system or software changes, update this repair disk with the Repair Disk Utility (RDISK.EXE).

Tip

> If you don't have access to your boot floppy disks because you installed Windows NT Server using the WINNT.EXE program method, you can build your own. Run WINNT.EXE from MS-DOS or WINNT32.EXE using /OX (create boot floppies) and /S:\PathName, where PathName is a UNC path name to a shared directory containing the source media or local drive—for example, WINNT32/OX /S:E:\I386.

◆ Data backups: The final option for disaster preparation is backing up your data to tape. I suggest that you do this on a daily basis. In a worst case scenario, you will have to restore Windows NT Server (by reinstalling) and then use your tape backups to restore your data. You will have some data loss—generally any data since your last backup—but a small loss of data is better than losing all your data. One serious flaw in this option is that unless you have verified that your hardware and tapes are good by actually running a restore of your data, you might find yourself with many backups that will do you no good at all. It is a good practice to occasionally test your backups by restoring a system to a test server just to make sure that everything is working as expected.

Tip

> As part of the backup process, you should use the scheduler service provided with Windows NT Server to automate your backups. In the `MBADMIN\Projects\Appendix D` directory on the CD-ROM, I have included a few backup scripts for you to use in order to accomplish this task. These scripts are discussed in more depth in Chapter 8, "Additional Administrative Tools," and Appendix D, "Example Batch Files and Logon Scripts" (which is located on the CD-ROM).

SUMMARY

In this chapter, you learned about some of the basic concepts involved in planning your network installation. The primary focus was on what is needed to migrate your workgroup-based network to Windows NT Server. You also learned about migrating your workgroup to a domain and what issues should concern you.

The chapter then moved on to the various domain models offered by Windows NT Server and reviewed some of their strengths and weaknesses. In particular, the focus was on which domain model to choose and possible upgrade paths for the various domain models. You also learned how to modify some of these domain models to offer increased performance in specific circumstances.

To prepare for additional software product installations, you looked at the Internet Information Server, Systems Management Server, SQL Server, and the concept of gateways and what Windows NT Server has to offer in this regard. You also looked at some of the basics involved in using the Remote Access Service to create a wide area network. The final topic you explored was disaster planning options—points to consider and implement prior to a system-wide failure.

The next chapter discusses the actual installation of Windows NT Server and walks you through the installation process so that you won't have any surprises. You'll also look at the initial configuration you will need to perform after you successfully install the software.

2

PLANNING NETWORK INSTALLATION

P A R T II

Windows NT Server

CHAPTER 3

An Introduction to Windows NT Server

This chapter introduces you to the features of Windows NT Server, explains the NT buzzwords that Microsoft uses to sell the product, and prepares you for the following chapters, in which you will actually begin working with Windows NT Server. If you're already familiar with its features, you might want to skip this chapter and move on to Chapter 4, "Installing Windows NT Server." If you've already installed Windows NT Server, you can jump to Chapter 6, "Basic Administrative Tools," which looks at the available tools provided with Windows NT Server to configure and manage your network.

If you've never worked with Windows NT Server, this chapter has a lot to offer. You will learn why Windows NT Server is one of the best network file and print servers available. If you find some of the discussion a bit too confusing or technical, you might want to take another look at Chapter 1, "Network Concepts," and Chapter 2, "Planning Your Network Installation." These chapters include more in-depth discussions of some of the features covered in this chapter.

THE WINDOWS NT DESIGN

The current version of Windows NT Server, 3.51, includes some enhancements (which are discussed later in this chapter), but the basic component model has stayed the same in each release. If you've been reading any of the literature produced by Microsoft about Windows NT Server, you've probably looked at it and wondered just what they were talking about with their scattering of various buzzwords. And you might have wondered how these buzzwords relate to your day-to-day activities as a network administrator. Well, that's what we'll look at here. Although I haven't included all the buzzwords, I have included the ones I think will make a difference in your life:

◆ Robust: When you hear this word used with Windows NT, it simply means that Windows NT is designed not to crash when an application fails in some fashion. Windows NT accomplishes this by using two specific features. The first is that all applications execute in their own address space (with the exception of 16-bit Windows applications, although this can be user-selected, so that even 16-bit applications execute in separate address spaces). Second, all the operating system components operate in protected mode. Windows NT doesn't rely on any real-mode components to interact with your computer hardware (as Windows 3.x does). A real-mode application can access any memory or I/O location arbitrarily, which can lead to a system crash. This feature is both good and bad, but it's the price you must pay for an operating system that will not crash easily.

Note

Because Windows NT doesn't use the BIOS (a real-mode component) to access the hard disk controller, not all hard disk controllers will work with NT. If you want your unsupported hard disk and controller to work with NT, you need a Windows NT device driver to support them. And because NT prevents applications from accessing the hardware directly, not all MS-DOS and Windows 3.x applications work when running under NT. To support an MS-DOS or Windows 3.x application that directly accesses the system hardware, a virtual device driver (VDD) is required to support the hardware access.

◆ Fault-tolerant: This particular feature is so important that I cover it in more detail in a later section of this chapter. For now, you can just understand it to mean that Windows NT Server provides the means to protect your data and to keep the server running if at all possible. It does this by detecting various software and hardware failures. If a failure is detected, the redundant hardware continues to provide access to your network server by your network clients.

◆ Secure: The good news about this particular feature is that Windows NT provides reliable methods of limiting access to any computer resource. This includes not only access to the server and your data, but also access from one application to another. There are two aspects to consider. The first is related to limiting access to the network file server's shared resources and the server itself. This is accomplished through user identifications (user IDs) and passwords, or local or group identifiers. These topics are covered in more detail later in this chapter in the section, "Centralized Administration." The second aspect is related to keeping your data secure from unauthorized access and is covered in the section, "The New Technology File System (NTFS)."

◆ Scaleable: When people mention scalability and Windows NT Server in the same breath, they're generally referring to providing additional performance. Most people only consider adding more resources, such as another CPU or disk channel (a disk controller and disk drives). But this term really refers to Windows NT's capability to execute on different hardware platforms, such as the NEC MIPS processor, the DEC Alpha processor, and the IBM/Motorola PowerPC processor. Each of these platforms can provide additional performance gains over Intel processors.

◆ Symmetric multiprocessing (SMP): Windows NT's internal design uses a symmetric processing model, which simply means that all processors can

3

access system resources (memory, interrupts, and so on) and that any process/thread can execute on any processor. This is quite different from an asynchronous multiprocessing (AMP) model, in which one processor is responsible for the operating system functionality and another is responsible for executing applications. With Windows NT, any process can execute on any processor, providing the capability to make more efficient use of available processor resources.

◆ Multithreading: A thread is the minimum executable resource in Windows NT. The difference between a thread and a process is that a process is the container for an address space, and a thread executes within that address space. A process by itself isn't executable; it is the thread that is scheduled and executed. What is unique about threads is that a single process can have more than one thread of execution. A multithreaded application can have one thread for user input (keyboard and mouse), another for printing, and another for file access, for example. When you print a file, or even save a file, these threads run in the background and the user thread runs in the foreground. So, as far as you're concerned, your application continues to respond to your input and you never see the hourglass, as you do in Windows 3.x.

◆ Compatible: This refers to the capability to execute your legacy applications. These applications include your MS-DOS, 16-bit Windows, and OS/2 character-mode applications. Compatibility also refers to the capability to execute recompiled POSIX 1003.1–compliant applications. Each of these applications executes in a different environmental subsystem. These subsystems are covered in the next section, "The Windows NT System Design Model."

◆ Integratable: This is one of the joys of working with Windows NT Server, because it means that you don't have to tear up your existing network. Instead, Windows NT Server happily coexists with your UNIX, Novell, Banyan, and LAN Manager networks. It also includes the capability to migrate your existing Novell and LAN Manager networks to Windows NT networks over a period of time, or even to emulate an existing Novell server. You'll look at some of these features in more detail in Chapter 4, "Installing Windows NT Server," and Chapter 5, "Integrating Windows NT Server with Other Networks."

THE WINDOWS NT SYSTEM DESIGN MODEL

There is much more to the Windows NT design than can be explained in a few simple words. As you've probably heard, a picture is worth a thousand words. I'm going to put that theory to the test. Figure 3.1 is a basic diagram of the Windows NT system design model, which illustrates several of the more important features. I like to think of Windows NT as a mainframe operating system that has been scaled down a bit to run on your desktop. As such, it includes many of the features of a mainframe operating system. Specifically, you should note that, like a mainframe operating system, Windows NT incorporates a split in the process hierarchy. This split includes a user mode (ring 3 on Intel CPUs), where your applications, environmental subsystems, and services execute; and a kernel mode (ring 0 on Intel CPUs), where the core operating system executes.

Figure 3.1.
The Windows NT
system design
model.

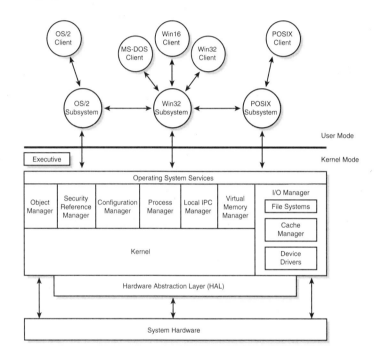

This split architecture keeps an errant application from bringing down the operating system. And, just like a mainframe operating system, it can't protect you from design flaws in the kernel. This includes poorly written device drivers. Any error in the kernel is trapped and, if possible, an error handler executes in order to maintain system integrity. If a device driver or another kernel component has an unrecoverable error, however, Windows NT displays a kernel core dump. I, and many others, often refer to this as the blue screen of death because the screen shows a blue background with white characters. This dump includes an error code, a device driver listing with an address location, and a stack dump of the offending driver(s). Just to ease your mind a bit, I'd like you to know that core dumps are very infrequent with Windows NT Server. If you use supported hardware and software, you might never see one. Chapter 4 lists some common blue-screen errors and some possible solutions in the section "Troubleshooting a Failed Installation."

Warning

Development tools such as Visual C++ interrelate with the operating system at very low levels during the build and debug stages. It's possible during one of these actions to hang the Win32 subsystem or the complete operating system. Therefore, if you will be developing applications for Windows NT Server, never do so on a production server. Always create a standalone network (server and workstations) for your development efforts to avoid any potential server down time.

To better understand kernel components, take a closer look at Figure 3.1. Notice that the core operating system component is called the executive and that it includes many subcomponents. These include the following:

◆ Object Manager: This component is responsible for basic object management, as the name implies. These objects include the object name space (used to resolve an object name to an object handle for use by an application), resource sharing, some security-related usage, and user-visible events (such as windows, processes, events, and files). Everything in Windows NT is an object, even though Windows NT isn't an object-oriented operating system. And the object is the key to all the security features provided by Windows NT.

◆ Security Reference Manager: This component is used with the Object Manager to determine whether a user or process has sufficient privileges to access or create an object. As an object is created, it is assigned a security descriptor that can be used later to limit access to the object. If no security descriptor is explicitly assigned, the owner's (the person who created the object) security descriptor is applied.

◆ Configuration Manager: This component is used to access the Registry. The Registry is explained in Appendix B, "The Registry Editor and Registry Keys." For now, you can consider the Registry the INI file replacement for Windows 3.x. It's the storehouse for all configuration data for Windows NT.

◆ Process Manager: This component is responsible for managing (creating, terminating, suspending, and resuming) processes and threads executing on the system.

◆ Local IPC Manager: This component is the heart of the message-passing mechanism that enables Windows NT to be such a good distributed computing operating system. It includes a fast and efficient mechanism based on the industry-standard remote procedure call (RPC) interface, which facilitates interprocess communication (IPC). This IPC mechanism is used to pass messages between the various clients (MS-DOS, Win16, Win32,

POSIX, and OS/2) and the environmental subsystem servers (Win32, POSIX, and OS/2), as well as between the environmental subsystems and the executive. Building on this same interface provides the capability to communicate between remote computers and to provide full client/server functionality across the entire network.

Note

One interesting feature provided by the Local IPC Manager is the capability to convert an RPC-enabled application to an LPC-enabled application. In an LPC application, both the client and the server applications execute on the same computer instead of on two computers. Simply changing the server name in the communication linkage to a single period enables LPC instead of RPC for the transport mechanism. LPC is faster than RPC for the same action. If you're using SQL Server on your computer for testing a new database design before you implement it on the server, for example, you can create a named pipe with the format

```
\\ServerName\Pipe\SQL\Query
```

and use RPC. Or you can use a pipe with the format

```
\\.\Pipe\SQL\Query
```

- ◆ **Virtual Memory Manager:** This is responsible for all memory manipulation, including, but not limited to, virtual-to-logical-to-physical memory address translation, shared memory between processes, and memory-mapped files. It also includes the management of your paging files, because this is where your virtual memory, memory-mapped files (by default, although memory-mapped files can use a different filename if the application supports it), and stop-event debugging information are read and written.

- ◆ **I/O Manager:** This component is special because it contains several subcomponents, unlike all the other components, which manage only one object type. These subcomponents are all I/O (input/output)-related, but they have different tasks to accomplish. These subcomponents include the file system drivers (NTFS, FAT, HPFS, CDFS, and any third-party additions), the cache manager (which hooks in the file systems to cache all file access, including network access), the device drivers (used to access system resources), and network device drivers.

- ◆ **Kernel:** This small component (about 60KB) is responsible for all process and thread scheduling, multiprocessor synchronization, and managing all exceptions (software-generated) and interrupts (hardware-generated). It is nonpageable (it's always resident in physical memory), nonpreemptive (no other thread of execution has a higher priority), and interruptible (it stops its current processing to service hardware-generated interrupts).

◆ Hardware Abstraction Layer (HAL): The HAL is the major interface to the hardware on the computer system. It is designed to isolate hardware-dependent code and is written in assembly language for maximum performance (unlike the other components, which are written in C). Most executive components access the system hardware through interfaces provided by the HAL, but the kernel and I/O manager can access some hardware resources directly.

That pretty much takes care of the kernel-mode components. The user-mode components include everything else, including services (such as the LanMan Server service, which is used to share resources on the network, the LanMan Workstation service, which is used to access shared resources, and many others) and the environmental subsystems (such as the OS/2, POSIX, and Win32 subsystems). These components are called environmental subsystems because each subsystem creates an emulation of a particular operating system (the environment), under which the applications (MS-DOS, Win16, Win32, and so on) execute. What is important here is that each of these environmental subsystems executes in an entirely different process address space and therefore is protected from the others. This means that if a POSIX application crashes, it has no effect on the other applications you're running.

All these subsystems are completely isolated from each other and have no communications facilities between each other except through supported RPC functions, such as named pipes or sockets. But there are two exceptions. First, the Win32 subsystem is responsible for all I/O interaction. This includes the mouse, the keyboard, and all on-screen rendering. Every subsystem must request such support from the Win32 subsystem (by using local procedure calls), which is why if the Win32 subsystem hangs, the entire system becomes unusable unless the Win32 subsystem can be restarted (which is possible, but very unlikely). Second, the Win32 subsystem also contains the support for your MS-DOS and 16-bit Windows applications. Both 16-bit and 32-bit Windows applications can pass messages back and forth, as well as make use of the standard OLE and DDE facilities.

The 16-bit Windows subcomponent is referred to as the Windows on Win32 (WOW) layer and can be restarted without complications (as far as I have seen to date). What's interesting about this particular subcomponent is that it uses the Virtual 8086 mode of the Intel processor's hardware support to emulate an Intel 8086 (on RISC processors, this emulation is entirely in software) and to provide completely independent address spaces for MS-DOS and 16-bit applications (if desired) under which to execute. Figure 3.2 illustrates the MS-DOS virtual DOS machine (VDM) architecture and Figure 3.3 illustrates the WOW architecture.

Figure 3.2.
The virtual DOS
machine (VDM)
architectural
model.

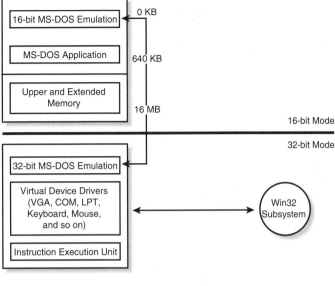

Figure 3.3.
The Windows on
Win32 (WOW)
architectural
model.

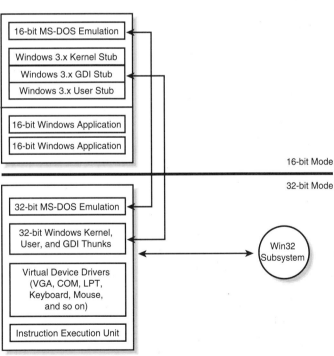

The OS/2 and POSIX subsystems are similar, but they're less complicated because they aren't built on the VDM concept. Instead, they just use the subsystem to directly support the application environment. What is important about the MS-DOS and WOW emulation is that, in order to directly support hardware access by an application, a virtual device driver must be available to support the emulation of the device and to control access to it. This is why many MS-DOS disk utilities fail under Windows NT, and why many Windows fax applications that use virtual device drivers in enhanced mode fail to execute under NT. It also explains why protected applications that use a dongle hanging off the parallel port fail: The standard NT parallel port driver doesn't support access to the required I/O ports in the way that the protected application expects. Another interesting concept for WOW applications is that, by default, they all run in a shared VDM. This provides the greatest level of compatibility, but if one WOW application fails, it can crash the entire WOW layer. In order to provide additional robustness (at the cost of compatibility) each 16-bit application can run in its own VDM. This gives you the capability to preemptively multitask your 16-bit Windows applications but prevents these same applications from making use of any shared memory (because they run in their own address spaces). This is one reason why you can't execute the 16-bit versions of Microsoft Mail and Schedule Plus in separate address spaces (they make use of shared memory).

THE NEW TECHNOLOGY FILE SYSTEM (NTFS)

Windows NT includes a new file system called, appropriately enough, the New Technology File System (NTFS). This file system has several enhancements over existing file systems currently in use on most network file servers. To begin with, it's entirely transaction-based. Much as SQL Server uses a transaction log to maintain data integrity, the NTFS file system uses a transaction log to maintain file system integrity. This doesn't mean that you can't lose data, but it does mean that you have a much greater chance of accessing your file system even if a system crash occurs. This capability stems from the use of the transaction log to roll back outstanding disk writes the next time Windows NT is booted. NTFS also uses this log to check the disk for errors instead of scanning each file allocation table entry, as the FAT file system does.

NTFS also has several other beneficial features:

◆ Security: The NTFS file system includes the capability to assign access control entries (ACEs) to an access control list (ACL). The ACE contains either a group identifier or a user identifier encapsulated in a security descriptor, which can be used to limit access to a particular directory or file. This access can include such capabilities as read, write, delete, execute, and even ownership. An ACL, on the other hand, is the container that encapsulates one or more ACE entries. When you apply permissions to a directory or file, you are creating an ACL that contains the user's security identifiers, which define who may access the directory or file.

◆ Long filenames: Long filenames exceed the normal MS-DOS 8.3 limitation. These names can contain up to 255 characters, can be any mix of uppercase or lowercase letters (although access to the file is not case-sensitive, except for applications executing in the POSIX subsystem), and can include UNICODE characters if you want. One of the key features of NTFS is that it automatically generates an equivalent MS-DOS–compatible filename. It does this by using the first characters of the long filename as the base, adding a tilde (~), adding a sequence number, and using the first three characters of the last file extension (the letters following the last period). For example, if you had a long filename such as `Accounts Payable.July.1995.XLS`, the equivalent MS-DOS 8.3–compatible filename would be `ACCOUN~1.XLS`.

◆ Compression support: This feature was introduced in Windows NT 3.51. It gives you the capability to compress any NTFS file, directory, or volume. Unlike MS-DOS compression packages, which create a virtual disk as a hidden file on your uncompressed host drive and require you to compress all the data on the compressed drive, Windows NT uses an additional layer in the file system to compress/uncompress files on demand without creating a virtual disk. This is particularly useful for compressing part of a disk (such as the user directories) or specific file types on a disk (such as graphics files). It's even more beneficial for users of portable computers who want to run NT. But I like it because I can compress SQL Server devices, which in turn means that my SQL Server databases also get compressed automatically. One thing you'll find with NTFS compression is that it isn't designed for maximum compression, as are the MS-DOS compression schemes; instead, it's designed for reliability and performance.

Fault-Tolerant Capabilities

The primary purpose of a file server is to provide the capability to share resources. This can include CPU, file, and print resources. But what happens if you have a hardware failure? In many cases, this means that your entire server goes down, along with all the resources you share with it. And if you can't get the server back on-line quickly enough, your job might go with it. This is where fault-tolerant capabilities come into play—to protect both your data and your job.

In the preceding section, you learned how an NTFS partition can provide data integrity at the file system level, but this might not be enough for mission-critical data. I define mission-critical data as any data required to continue your business practice. This could be a SQL Server database, the source code to build the applications you sell, or just everyday applications (such as Microsoft Word for Windows) that everyone at the office uses to perform their day-to-day jobs.

Windows NT Server provides three options that can be used separately or with each other to safeguard your data:

◆ Disk mirroring: This method works at the partition level to make a duplicate copy of your data. For every write to the primary partition, a second write is made to the secondary partition. If the fault-tolerant driver detects a device failure while accessing the primary partition, it can switch automatically to the secondary partition and continue providing access to your data.

◆ Disk duplexing: This method works at the partition level as well, but it also includes the capability to detect disk controller errors. It does this by using two separate disk controllers with separate disk subsystems. If you have a failure to access data on the primary partition or a hardware failure of the primary disk controller, access to your data can be maintained by using the redundant copy on the secondary controller and disk subsystem.

◆ Disk striping with parity: This option works by combining equally sized disk partitions on separate physical drives (from 3 to 32 disk drives) to create one logical partition. Data is written to the disk in discrete blocks. These blocks, when combined, are referred to as a stripe. When data is written to the disk, an error correction code (ECC) block is written as well. In the case of a disk failure, the data blocks can be combined with the ECC block to rebuild the missing data block. This is discussed in more detail in Chapter 8, "Additional Administrative Tools."

Tip

The best type of disk subsystem to use is SCSI-based, because this type of subsystem supports several important features. First, most SCSI controllers are bus masters, which means that they have their own dedicated controller to transfer data to and from the disk and to and from system memory. Second, most SCSI drives support command queuing (used to issue several commands to a disk) and bus detachment (which means that while the disk is processing the request, it detaches from the SCSI bus so that another SCSI peripheral can connect to the bus and possibly transfer data). Most SCSI controllers also include a dedicated CPU so that your system CPU doesn't have to watch over each byte of data transferred from the

SCSI controller, as do most IDE disk controllers. This means that your CPU can continue processing data and enhancing system throughput. One other important feature is that SCSI drives have spare sectors that can be mapped to a failing sector (IDE drives have a similar feature but don't support a specific command to replace a failing sector). The NTFS file system driver can take advantage of this.

The question is, when do you use each of these techniques? Each technique provides increased data integrity, but at a cost. You can use disk mirroring, for example, to split a single disk into two partitions. You can use one of these partitions to contain the primary data and the other to contain the copy (the mirror) of the primary partition's data. In order to create this copy, however, your disk controller must make two physical writes—one to each disk partition. If the entire disk becomes defective, all your data is lost. To offset this problem, you might use two separate disk drives, but if the disk controller becomes defective, you again lose access to your data. Table 3.1 summarizes the capabilities of fault-tolerant drivers.

TABLE 3.1. CAPABILITIES OF A FAULT-TOLERANT DRIVER.

Fault-Tolerant Driver	Pro	Con
Disk mirroring	Can be used on a single physical disk with at least two equally sized partitions. Can be used to mirror separate physical disks on a single disk controller as well.	Does not protect against disk failure if a single disk is used. Does not protect against controller errors. Limits disk storage to half of system capacity. Performance hit for disk writes.
Disk duplexing	Used to mirror separate physical disks on separate physical disk controllers. Protects against disk failures and disk controller errors.	Requires twice the hardware (two disk drives, two disk controllers) to provide half the storage capacity.

continues

TABLE 3.1. CONTINUED

Fault-Tolerant Driver	Pro	Con
Stripe set with parity	Provides fault tolerance for single-drive failure. Increased disk read performance.	Does not provide protection from disk controller errors. Does not protect against multiple disk failures. Requires a percentage of the disk partition to contain an ECC stripe. Slight CPU performance degradation for disk writes to calculate the ECC stripe.

My preference is to use striping with parity because it provides fault tolerance and increased performance (your paging file should be placed on a stripe set, not a stripe set with parity, because you do not need—or want—the overhead of the ECC stripe for your paging file). But if you need maximum data protection, use the disk duplexing option. Continuing this basic premise of keeping your server functional during hardware failures, you might want to consider using one of these optional techniques:

◆ Uninterruptible power supply: A UPS is used for two purposes. First, it protects against temporary power outages by providing a battery to supply AC power to the computer. In case of a long-term power outage, the UPS service shuts down the server in a graceful fashion. Second, a UPS also is used to filter your AC power. In my opinion, this is the most important feature, because poor power (spikes, surges, and low-line conditions) can cause more damage to your server's peripherals than anything else.

◆ Symmetric multiprocessing: When installed on a platform with multiple CPUs, not only is the performance of your server increased, but its fault tolerance increases as well. If one CPU fails, it is disabled, but processing continues on the other CPUs. If the CPU fails on a uniprocessor computer, the entire server goes down.

◆ Multiple network adapters: Installing multiple network adapters provides several advantages. First, these can be used to increase network performance by providing several channels among which to spread the network load. Second, these can increase performance of a specific network transport by binding that transport to a single adapter. Conversely, binding all the transports to all the network adapters increases fault tolerance. If a single adapter fails, it is disabled and the load spreads among the additional adapters.

CENTRALIZED ADMINISTRATION

One of the major benefits of using Windows NT is the capability to manage your entire network from any NT Server, NT Workstation, Windows 95, or Windows 3.x workstation running in enhanced mode. I have divided these management tools into two sections: "Computer Management" and "User Management." Specifics of how to use these tools appear in Chapter 6. For now, I just want to discuss what's available and why you'll want to use these options for your day-to-day system management.

Note

In order to use an NT Workstation or a Windows 3.x workstation to manage your network, you must install the client-based administration tools. You can do this by running the SETUP.BAT program located in the CLIENTS\SRVTOOLS\WINNT directory for an NT Workstation or the SETUP.EXE program located in the CLIENTS\SRVTOOLS\WINDOWS directory for a Windows 3.x workstation. The Windows 95 tools can be downloaded from the ftp site ftp.microsoft.com.

COMPUTER MANAGEMENT

Computer management includes all the administrative tools used to configure your local computer or a remote client computer. Although I won't mention all the tools, I will point out the more useful ones:

◆ Event Viewer: This tool is seriously underrated, in my opinion. It's the first tool you should use to determine NT Workstation client problems. It provides the capability to look at any NT computer and to determine whether any system, application, or security problems have occurred in the past.

Note

Every administrator should review all three logs on a daily basis to determine what type of problems might be accumulating. Not all problems are immediately flagged and sent to the administrator in an alert. Monitoring your system log can warn you of imminent failures (such as the SCSIDISK bad partition warnings on a SCSI drive, which

I have been receiving on my portable computer, indicating that this drive is getting ready to fail completely) or security breaches (hackers attempting to gain access to your system, for example) in the security log.

◆ File Manager: As you might expect from the name, File Manager is responsible for creating network sharepoints (a shared directory) as well as manipulating your own files and directories, as you might have done with the Windows 3.x File Manager. It also includes two new features for creating remote sharepoints (you'll read more about this in Chapter 7, "Resource Management Tools"), and it is your only interface at the moment for assigning permissions to directories and files and taking ownership of existing directories or files. You also can use it to enable auditing of directories and files on a per-user basis. One other feature that isn't included in any other tool is the capability to view who currently has a specific file open.

◆ Network Client Administrator: This tool can be used to do the following things:

> To create installation disks to install MS-DOS, Windows 3.x, or Windows for Workgroups from a network sharepoint;

> To create an installation disk set to install the MS-DOS 3.x client-based network drivers, TCP/IP-32 for Windows for Workgroups, the Remote Access client for MS-DOS, or the LAN Manager network client for MS-DOS or OS/2 1.x;

> To copy the client-based network tools to a network sharepoint for later installation.

◆ Print Manager: You can use this tool to create new printers, to connect to existing printers on the network, and to manage your local and remote print queues. It also is used to assign permissions and to take ownership of existing printers on the network, as well as to enable auditing of your printers.

◆ Remote Boot Manager: Use this tool to install and configure the software for your diskless workstations. It also is used to add network clients' network card addresses to the remote boot database to authorize their remote boot connectivity.

◆ Remote Access Server Administrator: This tool is used to completely control the Remote Access Service on a local or a remote NT computer. It includes the capability to start the service, to authorize users to make use of the RAS connectivity features, and to send messages to connected RAS clients on a per-port basis. The Remote Access Service also can be used to provide a cost-effective wide-area network solution, particularly if you make use of either a 28,800 baud modem or an ISDN connection.

Tip

> Until you authorize a user to use the RAS service, he won't be authenticated if he connects, and he won't be able to access any network resource.

◆ Server Manager for Domains: This tool is the beginning of limiting access to your domain. I say this because this tool is responsible for creating the computer account that your NT Workstation clients will use to gain a trusted connection to your server. Without a computer account, a domain network client computer can't be authenticated even if the user attempting to log onto the domain from the workstation has a valid user ID. It also can be used to control the services on a remote client, as well as to determine who is connected and what resources they have in use. You can even disconnect such users, if desired. If the FTP service is installed, you can monitor it from here as well. A few additional capabilities are included to provide the configuration of the replication service and alerts.

◆ Dynamic Host Configuration Protocol (DHCP) Manager: This tool is used to create and configure DHCP scopes (subnets) on your TCP/IP network. DHCP can be used to automate the assignment of IP addresses to network clients and, when their lease (or time-out) expires, to retrieve the IP address for allocation to a new user. You also can create IP address reservations (a reassignment mechanism) with this tool.

Windows Internet Naming Service (WINS) Manager: This tool manages all NetBIOS-computer-name-to-IP-name resolution. It effectively performs the same task that a UNIX Domain Name Server (DNS) performs. A useful feature of WINS is the capability to automatically replicate the database among several other WINS servers on the network.

Tip

> WINS isn't designed to work with network clients that aren't WINS-aware, such as UNIX clients. A solution does exist in the form of a WINS Proxy Agent, however. A WINS Proxy Agent is a Windows for Workgroups 3.11 or Windows NT computer that acts as an intermediary between the WINS server and the non-WINS-aware client and forwards the IP address to the client based on the NetBIOS name that

the client is attempting to find. To enable the WINS Proxy Agent feature, check the WINS Proxy Agent checkbox in the TCP/IP-32 configuration dialog box on a Windows for Workgroups 3.11 computer, or enable the WINS Proxy Agent feature in the Advanced Microsoft TCP/IP Configuration dialog box of a Windows NT computer.

USER MANAGEMENT

User management includes adding new users to the network and manipulating current user characteristics. Most of this is accomplished with User Manager for Domains, which is covered in Chapter 6. For now, I just want to introduce you to some of the features provided in the basic user-management area. The tools you will be using follow:

◆ User Manager for Domains: This is the heart of all user management. It's used to do the following:

> Enable system auditing on a global level.

> Create and manipulate local and global groups (local groups are unique to the computer they are created on, whereas global groups are domain-wide).

> Create and manipulate user accounts.

> Configure system user policies (such as the minimum password length, the maximum password age, account lockout features, and so on).

> Specify which computers the user can log on from and the time the user can be logged onto the system. You also can use User Manager to set up the user's profile, logon script, and any home directory.

Note

Unlike Novell NetWare and other network operating systems, Windows NT Server doesn't provide the capability to limit the amount of file space a user can access. So be prepared to implement a system policy of notifying users who exceed your maximum disk quotas, backing up their data, and then deleting it when file space runs low. Or, you can purchase a third-party add-on like DiskQuota from New Technology Partners to limit a user's maximum disk quota.

◆ User Profile Editor: This tool is used to create the initial user profile. A user profile is the environment in which the user works. It includes all File Manager, Print Manager, and other user-specific settings. A profile can be user-specific and non-sharable or sharable and nonuser-specific. It can't be both. A sharable profile is called a mandatory profile and is used to restrict a group of users who all use the same profile for changing their user environment, such as the desktop configuration, Program Manager groups, and display resolution.

Note

One interesting concept involved with profiles is the capability to use the same profile on more than one computer. As the user logs on from a different computer, his profile is used to configure the computer. He will see the same desktop and can use the same applications that he uses on his primary computer (as long as he is installed in the same directories on the local computer or is on a network sharepoint). But this occurs only if the user profile has been created and is available (shared) from a server that is accessible from the new location. Profiles also are server-specific, unlike logon scripts, which can be replicated from server to server and can be executed from the server that authenticates the user.

◆ Logon scripts: Logon scripts aren't really managed through a specific tool, although they are assigned (named) in User Manager for Domains. Basically, a logon script is a batch program that is executed when the user logs onto the domain. It can include such features as mapping sharepoints or printers, automatically checking the hard disk, running programs to keep track of a user's time on a project, or running any other program that can be run from the command line.

SUMMARY

This chapter looked at some of the features Windows NT Server provides. You also briefly looked at the system architecture to prepare for actually working with Windows NT Server. Hopefully, this chapter gave you the capability to answer some of your users' questions about software compatibility. You also learned about some of the more important features of Windows NT, such as the NTFS file system and what it can and can't do, along with fault-tolerant features. These features can be implemented as part of your normal configuration, depending on your needs, available hardware, and budget. Finally, you looked at some of the tools available to help you manage your network on a day-to-day basis.

In the next chapter, you will actually step through the Window NT Server installation process. You will learn about the various installation methods (floppy disks, CD-ROM, MS-DOS, or network) available to you to install Windows NT

Server. You will also learn a bit about troubleshooting the installation process, how to clone an installation to be used on other computers, and some of the migration capabilities from LAN Manager or Novell Netware.

- Performing the Installation

- Setting the Initial Configuration

- Troubleshooting a Failed Installation

- Cloning an Installation

- Migrating Your LAN Manager or Novell NetWare Servers to Windows NT Servers

CHAPTER 4

Installing Windows NT Server

This chapter will familiarize you with the installation options for Windows NT Server so that there will be no surprises when you finally install it. If you have not reviewed Chapter 1, "Network Concepts," and Chapter 2, "Planning Your Network Installation," you might want to check them out because they contain discussions of the various operating modes of Windows NT Server. And although I mention these operating modes briefly, I do not discuss them in depth in this chapter.

This chapter is basically broken down into five sections. The first is a discussion of the actual methods of installation and a walk-through of the CD-ROM installation method. The next section deals with your initial configuration of Windows NT Server after you have installed the product. The following section deals with any troubleshooting you might need to perform if you have problems with your installation. After you succeed with one installation, you will take a look at how you can use this installation as a pattern to clone Windows NT Server on as many identical hardware platforms as you want. Finally, you will look at the tools available for migrating your Microsoft LAN Manager (1.x) and Novell NetWare servers to Windows NT Server.

PERFORMING THE INSTALLATION

You can use one of several methods to install Windows NT Server to a new computer. For an Intel-based computer, you can install Windows NT Server by using floppy disks, by using the three boot floppies and CD-ROM, or from a network sharepoint by using MS-DOS and the WINNT.EXE installation program. All these methods eventually execute the same installation program. They differ only in their initial methodology of copying the source files to the computer. There is also a slight difference in installation for RISC-based computers because these computers are limited to installation from the CD-ROM only. You can upgrade a Windows NT Server installation using any of these methodologies, or you can run a Windows NT version of WINNT.EXE called WINNT32.EXE.

In this section, you will look at all these available methodologies to help you choose the best method to get Windows NT Server up and running. Before you begin to learn about the actual installation process, however, you should consider a few things. There are certain requirements for a successful Windows NT installation. After you look at these requirements, you can move on to the installation discussion. You'll start with the Intel processor platform. Then you'll move on to the difference in the installation process for the various RISC platforms. Finally, you'll take a look at the upgrading process.

PREPARING TO BEGIN THE INSTALLATION

Generally, the installation process is pretty straightforward. It is rare, but not unheard of, to encounter a problem with the installation. You can avoid severe problems and surprises by following a few basic rules:

◆ Check the Hardware Compatibility List (HCL). This booklet is included with your source media package and includes a listing of every hardware platform that Microsoft has tested to ensure compatibility with Windows NT Server. In this document, you might find specific BIOS requirements for your particular hardware platform or even specific BIOS requirements for peripherals (such as video or SCSI adapters). If your hardware platform is not listed by name, don't despair; it only means that the platform has not been tested for complete compatibility. In this case, look through the list of peripherals to see whether you can identify any problem areas (such as an unsupported network adapter) that you should consider before installation.

Tip

If you plan on installing Windows NT Server from your CD-ROM, check to see whether it is listed in the HCL. If it is a SCSI CD-ROM, see whether your SCSI controller is listed. If it is an IDE CD-ROM, then Windows NT Server does support the ATAPI interface and proprietary CD-ROM controllers from Sony, Panasonic, and Mitsumi. If the installation process does not autodetect your CD-ROM controller, try to manually install the controllers one at a time. If they all fail, you will be required to use the MS-DOS installation method (WINNT.EXE), which is discussed in the next section.

◆ Read SETUP.TXT and README.WRI. These files contain specific information about various hardware platforms and peripherals that often are not mentioned in the Hardware Compatibility List. You can find SETUP.TXT in the root directory of the CD-ROM drive, whereas README.WRI is a compressed file and is located in your installation subdirectory (I386 for Intel processors), which must be expanded manually prior to being read.

Tip

You can manually expand the README.WRI file by locating the file README.WR_ on your CD-ROM or installation disks and running the MS-DOS expand program (located in your MS-DOS or Windows 3.x installation directory). For example, you can type this line:

```
expand E:\I386\README.WR_ C:\TEMP\README.WRI
```

E: is the drive letter of your CD-ROM drive.

◆ Check your free space. Windows NT Server requires about 90MB for a complete installation (which includes the minimum paging file requirement). If this amount of free space cannot be located on a single disk drive, the installation program requires that you reformat your disk drive in order to continue the installation. Of course, you always can exit the installation by pressing the F3 key, deleting some files, and then restarting the installation process, but it is better to have sufficient free space before you start.

Tip

Check for unsupported partition schemes as well, as long as you are looking at your disk drive. Currently, only the OnTrack Disk Manager partition format is supported for accessing Enhanced IDE drives greater than 512MB. If you have a different manufacturer's third-party partitioning program, it is possible that setup will fail to detect your drive or that you will need to repartition and reformat it as part of the installation process.

◆ Check your hardware settings. Unlike MS-DOS, Windows NT does not support the sharing of interrupts on the ISA expansion bus. Only EISA, MCA, and PCI adapters can share interrupts. Make sure that you have no I/O, DMA, or upper memory conflicts before you start the installation.

Warning

If a network card cannot be found during the installation process, you might be unable to install Windows NT Server. A resource conflict, such as using IRQ 3 for your network adapter when you also have your second communication (COM2) port using IRQ 3, might cause the installation to fail. You can avoid this by selecting a different IRQ for your network card before you begin the installation. There are other options as well, which you will review as part of the installation process a little later in this chapter.

◆ Obtain your OEM drivers. If you have proprietary or unsupported hardware such as a network or SCSI adapter, you should assemble these driver disks before you begin your installation. During the installation, you are given a chance to install these OEM (Original Equipment Manufacturer) drivers.

Tip

You can find many OEM drivers for Windows NT Server in the DRIVLIB subdirectory (which includes disk controller drivers, video drivers, printer drivers, and so on) on the CD-ROM. And even if you have an OEM disk, you should look here to see whether a newer version is available. Don't despair if you cannot find a driver there, because Microsoft also maintains online areas that contain drivers as well. These are located on the Internet at ftp.microsoft.com and in the Windows Driver Library (GO WDL) on CompuServe; on the Microsoft network, choose Go Microsoft to access the Microsoft forum.

◆ Select a file system. Determine what file system you want to use before you install Windows NT Server. Currently, you can install Windows NT Server to a partition formatted as FAT, HPFS, or NTFS. Generally speaking, HPFS is used only for LAN-Manager-to-Windows-NT-Server upgrades, but you can keep that file system if you want. I recommend that you always use the FAT file system for the initial system partition. This partition always can be converted to NTFS later, using the CONVERT.EXE program. Installing Windows NT to the FAT file system guarantees that you will be able to access it from an MS-DOS boot disk if you have any unforeseen problems.

◆ Select an operating mode. Before you install Windows NT Server, decide in what mode of operation you want the installation to operate. Will it be a controller (either primary or backup), or will it be an application server operating in server mode? You must make this determination at install time. After you make this decision, the only way to change this mode is by reinstalling Windows NT Server. If you are unfamiliar with the various modes of operation for Windows NT Server, review the section titled "Controllers versus Servers" in Chapter 1.

PERFORMING AN INTEL PROCESSOR INSTALLATION

Installing Windows NT Server is no trivial task. Depending on your installation option and the performance of your floppy drive, CD-ROM drive, or network adapter, a base installation may take you as little as 30 minutes or as much as two hours. In this section, you explore these installation options to help you make the best decision about which method to use.

FLOPPY OR CD-ROM

There is very little difference between the floppy and CD-ROM installation, aside from the time it takes to perform the basic installation. The only real difference is that you do not have access to the additional support files on the CD-ROM (such as the DRVLIB and SUPPORT subdirectories). Both of the installs run you through the same three boot floppy disks to install the mini-kernel, which runs the text mode Setup program. This is phase 1 of the Setup process, which installs the core system files, installs the NT boot sector, and then reboots the computer. Phase 2 then starts the graphical Setup program to complete the installation.

PHASE 1: THE TEXT MODE SETUP

The first part of the Setup process is completely text-based. This part of the install process follows:

1. Insert the first setup boot floppy disk and restart the computer.

Note

If you are using Ontrack's Disk Manager to support an EIDE drive on a system that does not have BIOS support for EIDE drives, you need to take a slightly different approach than that mentioned in step 1. Instead of restarting the system with the setup boot disk in the floppy drive, you need to restart the system, then wait for the Disk Manager prompt, and press the space bar to boot from a floppy. When the prompt appears, press the space bar, then insert the setup boot disk and continue the installation. Otherwise the setup program will be unable to access the EIDE drive.

2. After the computer restarts, a white-on-black text message appears, stating that Setup is examining your hardware configuration. Next, the Windows NT Setup screen appears (white text on a blue background). If you look closely at the bottom status line, you will see each file by name as it is loaded. These files constitute what I refer to as the mini-kernel. After the files load, you are prompted to insert the second disk.

Caution

Because this hardware-detection process scans your serial ports, you should disconnect any serial cable attached to a UPS. Otherwise, the UPS could go into a self test, switch to battery-only operation, or even reboot the computer. None of these is a desirable action.

3. The second disk continues to load specific device drivers. After all these drivers are loaded, the disk actually starts the multiprocessing kernel. If you look closely at the top of the screen at this point, you will see how much memory the kernel was able to detect and use. If this differs drastically (by

more than 384KB) from your installed memory, you should check your BIOS and EISA memory settings.

4. After the multiprocessing kernel loads successfully, the Setup Welcome screen appears. At this point, you can press F1 for more information about the Setup process, press Enter to continue the Setup process, press R to repair a damaged installation, or press F3 to quit the install process.

Note

Remember the sequence mentioned in step 4 because this is the beginning of the process you will use to repair a damaged installation of Windows NT Server. You will use the repair disk (which you will create as part of the install process, or which you can create by running the RDISK.EXE program after you install Windows NT). The repair process uses copies of the Registry to replace a damaged Registry component and can repair or replace missing boot or system files.

5. After you press Enter to continue the installation, you are given a choice between performing an Express (press Enter) or a Custom (press C) installation. The Express option lets the Setup program do your thinking for you and is quicker than a Custom installation but not as desirable. The Custom installation lets you make the decisions for the install process. And I never ever recommend the Express option! I do not believe that the Setup program is as gifted as I am, and it cannot recover from certain misconceptions about my installed hardware. The rest of this discussion assumes that you have selected a Custom installation.

Tip

The other reason for selecting the Custom installation option is that it gives you more choices for selecting network adapters. The Express option only installs a driver for the first network adapter it detects. The Custom option lets you install multiple network adapter drivers. I also use the Custom option to install the MS Loopback adapter (this is just a piece of software that emulates a network adapter so that the services that rely on network connectivity will function) on new installations because Windows NT Server must have a network adapter driver in order to authenticate you with the winlogon service. If your network adapter fails to load and you do not have the MS Loopback adapter installed, you will have to reinstall Windows NT Server. Except this time, you'll remember to run through the Custom installation and install the MS Loopback adapter.

6. The next screen requests confirmation to perform the detection process for floppy and hard disk controllers. In some cases, this process can cause your computer to hang or even reboot. But these are very rare cases and, to be honest, I have never had them occur—although I know a few people who have. So if you press Enter, the various device drivers load and search for their supported adapters, and if the adapters are found, they appear in the next screen. I normally recommend the autodetection process, particularly if you do not know which SCSI disk or proprietary CD-ROM controller you have installed. If you know which devices you have installed, you can bypass this autodetection by pressing the S key (to skip).

Note

There are a few cases in which you should not use the autodetection process. I have a Media Vision Pro Audio Spectrum 16 sound card with a built-in SCSI controller, for example. However, on my installation, I have the CD-ROM drive connected to my Adaptec 1742a SCSI controller. If I let the autodetection continue, the Media Vision SCSI driver will later cause the sound card driver to fail to load because the SCSI device driver will fail to find any SCSI devices attached to the controller. You may have a similar situation in cases in which you have hardware installed but nothing connected to it; in these cases, you should follow the manual installation method.

7. This screen displays any detected SCSI disk controllers or proprietary CD-ROM drives that were found as part of the autodetection process.

8. Assume that either your adapter was not found or that you have an OEM driver that you want to install. Press the S key to specify the device driver manually. You are greeted with a list of supported SCSI and CD-ROM disk controllers, along with the default entry of Other. You use the Other entry to specify an OEM disk. After you select this entry, you are prompted to insert the OEM disk into drive A to continue the installation process. To manually install a device driver from the list, just scroll up the list with the up-arrow key until your entry is highlighted, and then press Enter. If your device driver is on disk 2, it loads to verify that the peripheral exists; otherwise, you are prompted for disk 3. In any case, after the driver loads, you are returned to the screen discussed in step 7.

9. Press Enter to continue the installation. The additional device drivers load (such as the standard IDE/ESDI, floppy, file system, and so on). After the file system drivers load, you might be greeted with a message about any unusual hard disk configuration information. I have a SCSI disk drive with more than 1,024 cylinders, for example, and the Setup program dutifully

informs me that MS-DOS might not be able to see a partition created on this disk if I use any of the cylinders above 1,024. This serves as a warning about properly configuring the disk to obtain maximum usage from it.

10. After the additional device drivers load, the Setup program scans for attached CD-ROM drives. If it finds one, it includes it in the list of installation media. If it does not find one, it just prompts you for disk 4 of the installation floppy disks.

Note

If the Setup program did not detect your attached CD-ROM drive, one of two things has occurred. Either the CD-ROM drive is non-SCSI and you did not install the appropriate device driver, or it is unsupported. In very rare cases, however, you may have a supported non-SCSI CD-ROM and have installed the appropriate device driver, but it still may not work. If this occurs, check for possible resource conflicts (you might need to configure the device to use a specific I/O address, DMA channel, or interrupt, as described in the HCL), or contact the manufacturer for an updated device driver. If you are using Ontrack Disk Manager to support an EIDE disk drive on the primary EIDE channel with an ATAPI CD-ROM attached to the secondary EIDE channel, and if you encounter problems, you may need to choose an alternate installation method such as that described in the sidebar titled "Ontrack Disk Manager and ATAPI CD-ROM Drives" in the section titled "MS-DOS and WINNT.EXE."

Note

If the Setup program did not detect your attached SCSI CD-ROM drive, the problem may be improper termination of the SCSI bus, the fact that no termination power is being supplied to the SCSI bus, there is an interrupt conflict with the SCSI adapter, or that you have an older SCSI-I CD-ROM. In some cases, the CD-ROM drive can be configured to support the SCSI-I or SCSI-II command set. If your CD-ROM supports this option, it should be set to SCSI-II for maximum compatibility. The other options you might want to look at are related to your SCSI controller. Many SCSI controllers support the capability to enable and disable synchronous negotiation with the SCSI device and support transfer rates of more than 5Mbps. If you are having problems, disable synchronous negotiation and set the transfer rate to a maximum of 5Mbps. If you still have problems, contact the manufacturer of the CD-ROM drive.

11. Assuming that the Setup program found your CD-ROM drive and that you pressed Enter to continue the installation, the Setup program scans your hard disk for locations in which to install Windows NT Server. If it found one or more existing versions of Windows NT, each of them is listed as possible upgrade options. If one or more prior versions are found, select the installation you want to install to or upgrade. Press Enter to begin the installation or press N to pick a new installation directory.

12. The next screen gives you a chance to verify your hardware configuration. It includes information and choices about your computer, display adapter, keyboard, keyboard layout, and pointing device. All these are user select-able by moving the highlighted bar to the appropriate entry with the up-arrow key and then pressing Enter.

Tip

If you have any of the following, you need to select the Computer entry and manually select the appropriate option to install the correct HAL (Hardware Abstraction Layer) for your installation if it was not detected properly:

AST Manhattan SMP
Compaq SystemPro Multiprocessor or 100-percent compatible
Corollary C-Bus Architecture
IBM PS/2 or Microchannel Architecture
MPS Uniprocessor/Multiprocessor PC
NCR System 3000 (Model 3360/3450/3550)
Olivetti LSX5030/40
C-Step I486 CPU motherboard
Wyse Series 70001 (Model 740MP/760MP)
OEM disk with an OEM HAL driver

13. After you make any changes to your system configuration, move the high-lighted bar back to the No Changes entry and press Enter.

14. Setup now scans for an alternate location in which to install Windows NT Server. If you have a version of Windows 3.x on your system, that will be the suggested location. Once more, you can press Enter to accept the default or press N to suggest a new location.

Tip

If you have a version of Windows 3.x (preferably Windows for Workgroups 3.x) installed on your computer, you can install Windows NT Server to the same directory and make use of the dual-boot characteristics to share the 16-bit system directory. Then you can migrate all your existing INI entries to the Windows NT Registry. That way, you do not have to reinstall your 16-bit applications, and you don't need to have duplicate copies of these files on your computer.

15. If you selected a different directory to install Windows NT Server to (you pressed N), the next screen gives you a choice of on what partition you want to install Windows NT Server. If the disk has been previously partitioned and assigned a drive letter, this information is displayed. If it has not been previously partitioned, instead of a drive letter, it is labeled as unknown. This screen also provides you with the option to create (press C on the highlighted drive/partition) or delete (press D on the highlighted drive/partition) a partition. If, during one of the previous location prompts, Setup could not find a drive with enough free space or could not find a supported partition, it may display this same screen and request that you repartition and/or reformat a drive. In any case, you eventually come back to this screen. Here, you can select the appropriate partition by pressing your up- or down-arrow keys to highlight the appropriate partition and then pressing Enter.

16. The next screen prompts you for the file system you want for the installation partition. The choices are to format it as FAT or NTFS, to convert the file system to NTFS, or to leave it as is. If the partition you selected does not have enough free space, you see this screen with a slightly modified description. Instead of a request for converting the file system or leaving it intact, it requests that you reformat it only.

17. After you select an appropriate partition, you have the choice to override the default installation directory of \WINNT35. If you want to make a change, just press the backspace key to delete the directory name and enter your own directory name. When you are finished, press Enter.

Note

The name you select is limited to MS-DOS filenames. It cannot exceed the 8.3 rule (an eight-character name, followed by a period, and a three-character file extension), and it can't include subdirectories.

4

18. The next screen prompts you to perform an exhaustive check of your hard disk drive. Actually, this really is not a very time-consuming process, and it isn't what I would call an exhaustive disk check. Instead, it is just a CHKDSK of your hard drive to look for possibly cross-linked files or bad long filenames. I recommend that you let the Setup program perform this check of your hard disk to verify file system integrity. You press Enter to begin the hard disk scan and press Escape to bypass it.

19. When the scan is complete, the file copy process begins. At this point, the core system files are being copied to your system to allow the graphical portion of the Setup process to continue the installation.

20. The next screen flashes by pretty quickly. It states that the setup process is completing its installation and that the Windows NT boot sector is being placed on your boot drive, the boot.ini file is being created, and the NTLDR and NTDETECT.COM files are being placed in the root directory of your boot drive. These support files are marked as read-only, system, and hidden to prevent accidental deletion.

Warning

Never delete the files BOOT.INI, NTLDR, or NTDETECT.COM from the root directory of your boot drive. If any of these files are missing or damaged, Windows NT Server fails to boot. This requires you to run through the repair process to replace the files.

21. The final screen of the text mode Setup process is a prompt to remove any Setup floppy disk left in your floppy disk drive and to press Enter to restart your computer and begin the graphical setup application.

Phase 2: The Graphical Mode Setup

After your computer restarts, it loads the standard kernel instead of the multiprocessor kernel, unless you specified a different computer during the Custom installation process. Then, the SCSI, video, and other device drivers load and the Windows NT Setup dialog box appears so that you can continue your installation as outlined in the following steps:

1. In the Windows NT Setup dialog box, specify your name and your company name. Fill in these fields and click the Continue button. You then are presented with a Confirmation dialog box. If any information displayed is incorrect, click the Change button; otherwise, click the Continue button.

2. A screen appears in which you are asked to enter your product identification number. You can find this number on the inside cover of your

installation guide or on the product registration card or on the back of the CD-ROM jewel case. You need it if you are going to use the Microsoft technical support options. After you enter the number, click the Continue button. A Confirmation dialog box appears. Click the Change button if any information is incorrect; otherwise, click the Continue button.

3. The Windows NT Server Security Role dialog box appears next. Here you have the choice of selecting this installation to be a domain controller (primary or backup) or a server. A domain controller is used to interact with the domain by supplying user authentication and includes all the administrative tools required to manipulate the user and computer accounts for the domain. A server is just a pumped-up version of Windows NT Workstation. It includes no user or computer database (as a domain controller does) or domain-based administrative tools. Unlike Windows NT Workstation, it does not include a 10-user connection limit. Make this the right choice the first time around, because if you choose the wrong choice, you must reinstall Windows NT Server in order to change it. For this sample installation, assume that you are installing Windows NT as a primary domain controller (PDC) and then click the Continue button.

4. The next option is to select a license mode. It can be Per Server or Per Seat. If you select Per Server, you also must indicate the maximum number of simultaneous connections to the server. The Per Server option generally is used when a user will use a particular server, whereas the Per Seat option is used when a user may access more than one server. If you are in doubt about which licensing method to use, you should pick the Per Server option at this time, because you are given a one-time chance to change this to a Per Seat option through the Control Panel Licensing applet. After it is changed, however, you can't convert back to a Per Server licensing model. After you select your mode of operation, click the Continue button. You then are prompted to agree to the licensing agreement before you can continue. Just enable the I Agree That checkbox and click the OK button.

Caution

Although you can indicate more licenses than you really have in the Choose Licensing Mode dialog box, it is a violation of a legal agreement between you and Microsoft. And this could cause you legal problems down the road. It is a much safer proposition to actually purchase the required number of client licenses and avoid any potential legal trouble.

4

INSTALLING WINDOWS NT SERVER

5. You next must supply a unique computer name for your server in the Windows NT Setup dialog box. It cannot be the same name as any other computer in the domain, and it cannot be the same as your domain name. The name can contain up to 15 characters. It cannot include a bullet (◆), broken vertical bar (¦), section symbol (§), or paragraph symbol (¶). If you plan to use logon scripts for your users, as most people do, you should not include any spaces in your computer name because this can prevent a client from accessing the NETLOGON share and finding his logon script. After entering a unique name, click the Continue button. You then are presented with a Confirmation dialog box. If the name displayed is incorrect, click the Change button; otherwise, click the Continue button.

6. Setup then examines your computer based on the keyboard layout you specified during the installation process and prompts you to pick a language in the Language (Locale) dialog box. If the default language is not the one you want, select the appropriate one from the drop-down list. Then click the Continue button.

7. Next, another Windows NT Setup dialog box appears, giving you the option of specifying that Setup should set up only the windows components you select (these are the accessory applications, games, screen savers, media files, and background bitmaps), locally connected printers, and any applications on the hard disk. I rarely make any changes here unless I am installing on a portable computer or a computer with limited free space on the disk. After you make your selection, click the Continue button.

8. If you didn't make any changes to the last dialog box, then this Optional Windows Components dialog box offers you the chance to install optional files. These files include the README files, accessories, games, screen savers, background, and media files. After you make your selection, click the Continue button.

9. Next, the Set up Local Printer dialog box appears, enabling you to specify your locally attached printer. Specify a name for the printer, select the printer driver to be installed, and select the port to which the printer is connected. Click the Continue button to move to the next part of the install.

10. Now you've come to the fun part: the network adapter-detection process. The Network Adapter Card Detection dialog box offers you two choices: Continue attempts to automatically detect your network adapter, and Do Not Detect requires you to manually select a network adapter. Normally, I recommend that you use the Continue option and let Setup attempt to detect your network adapter, but if your network adapter is not on the HCL

and you have an OEM disk, or if you've had problems before with autodetection (sometimes this can cause strange results), then select the Do Not Detect option.

11. If you selected the autodetection feature, the next dialog box displays the network adapter that was found by Setup. If the adapter listed is correct, you can click the Continue button and continue the installation. Otherwise, you can click the Find Next button to have Setup continue to search for network adapters, or you can click the Do Not Detect button and manually specify an adapter.

Tip

If autodetection fails to find your network adapter, I recommend that you play it safe and install the MS Loopback adapter, even if you manually specify a network adapter. This is because Windows NT Server must have a network adapter that is functioning in order to log you on locally. You will need to log on locally later so that you can make configuration changes.

12. If autodetection failed, or you requested to not have Setup perform the autodetection, the Network Adapter Card Detection dialog box appears, specifying that no network adapter was found. It prompts you to click the Continue button to manually pick your network adapter, or to click the Remote button to install the Remote Access Service.

13. If you specified to manually install a network adapter, the Add Network Adapter dialog box appears. Select your network adapter or the other option from the drop-down listbox and then click the Continue button.

Warning

Even though you will see an option in the Add Network Adapter dialog box that specifies <None> Network Interface To Be Chosen Later, do not use it. If you do use it, you will be unable to log onto the system and will have to reinstall Windows NT Server to correct the problem. Instead, specify the MS Loopback adapter. This gives you a chance to log on after the installation has completed and to add a network adapter.

14. After specifying your network adapter, you might have to configure the device driver by specifying what I/O port, interrupt, memory base, or transceiver type to use. After all this configuration information has been entered, you can click the Continue button. If the driver failed to load

4

INSTALLING WINDOWS NT SERVER

because it could not find the network adapter, a resource conflict exists, or you supplied the wrong configuration information, you are prompted to reselect the network adapter. If errors continue, select the MS Loopback adapter. You always can change this later, after you install Windows NT Server.

15. Your next choice is to determine the network transport protocols you want to install in the Windows NT Setup dialog box. You have a choice of NetBEUI, TCP/IP (the default), or IPX/SPX. Of course, you can install all of them, but you will obtain better performance if you only use one of them. For more information on the available protocols, refer to Chapters 1 and 2. For this example, select all three transport protocols for installation. After you make your choice, click the Continue button.

Note

As a quick summary, NetBEUI is the default protocol for LAN Manager and Windows for Workgroups clients, TCP/IP is the default for UNIX clients, and IPX/SPX is the default for Novell NetWare clients. If you will be interacting with any of these operating systems, you will have to install the appropriate protocol.

16. The various protocols then are installed and you may see additional installation options. For TCP/IP, for example, you are prompted to select such optional components as the following:

Connectivity Utilities (the default that includes utilities like `ping`, `nbtstat`, and so on)

SNMP Service

TCP/IP Networking Printing Support (used to support UNIX clients printing to your shared printers and to enable you to print to shared UNIX printers)

FTP Server Service

Simple TCP/IP Services

DHCP Server Service

WINS Server Service

At the bottom of this dialog box is a checkbox to enable automatic DHCP configuration. This option can be used only if there already is an existing DHCP Server on the network. If this option is selected, an IP address automatically is provided by the DHCP Server. After you make your selection, click the Continue button.

DHCP and WINS are covered in detail in Chapter 9, "Using DHCP, WINS, and DNS," and the other TCP/IP utilities are covered in Chapter 5, "Integrating Windows NT Server with Other Networks."

17. At this point, you finally see the rest of the Windows NT system files being copied to your computer. When this process is completed, you are prompted to install any additional network components. You can install additional network adapters by clicking the Add Adapter button or additional network software by clicking the Add Software button. After you complete your software and hardware choices, click the OK button to continue.

Note

Normally, I will install all the network software—such as the Remote Access Service, Gateway Service for NetWare, Services for Macintosh, and Remoteboot software—if I plan to use it. These components are not covered here; they are covered in Chapter 5.

18. You next are prompted to choose your IPX/SPX frame type. Normally, I choose the autodetection (the default). If your Novell network is using an 802.2, 802.3, Ethernet II, or Ethernet SNAP frame type, however, you will want to select the Manual Frame Type Selection option and choose the appropriate frame type. Then click the OK button to continue.

19. The TCP/IP Configuration dialog box appears next. At this point, you need to specify the IP address, subnet mask, default gateway (if any), and the address of your primary and secondary WINS servers (if available). You also have the choice of specifying your domain name servers by clicking the DNS button. If you click the Advanced button, you also can specify such additional configuration choices as adding default gateways, enabling DNS for Windows name resolution, enabling LMHOST lookups (and importing an existing LMHOST file), enabling IP routing (if you have multiple network cards), and enabling the WINS Proxy Agent (if you have existing WINS servers on your network). After you complete all your selections, click the OK button to continue.

Note

A WINS Proxy Agent is an intermediary between non-WINS clients (such as a UNIX client) and the WINS service. In effect, this machine then acts as a gateway to your WINS server to provide an IP address for a broadcast NETBIOS name.

20. After you complete the information in all the configuration dialog boxes, Setup attempts to start the network. After this is completed, you are prompted to select the settings for your domain controller in the Domain Settings dialog box. It must be a primary domain controller, which includes the master copy of the user and computer database, or a backup domain controller. If you specify a backup domain controller (the default), you also must specify an Administrator user identification and password (this is used to create the computer account on the primary domain controller for the backup domain controller). After you enter the appropriate information, click the OK button to continue. Setup browses the network to make sure that no other primary domain controller for the domain name you selected already exists. If you selected a backup domain controller, Setup attempts to add your computer to the domain. If either of these attempts fail, you are returned to the Domain Settings dialog box.

21. The next step is the creation of your Program Manager groups, followed by a dialog box to specify your Administrator password. After you enter the password twice (once to enter it and once to confirm it), click the OK button to continue.

Warning

Be sure to manually enter your password. Never cut and paste it. Otherwise, if you make a typo, you will be unable to log onto the computer using the Administrator account, which means that you will have to reinstall to correct the problem. Also be sure to write this password down somewhere and keep it in a secure place.

22. Your next choice is to specify your initial paging file size and location. After you make these selections, click the Continue button.

Note

I suggest at this time that you accept the default paging file size. After you have finished your installation and installed any optional services, you can turn to choosing an optimal location and paging file size for your server as described in Chapters 12, "Getting the Most from Your Microsoft Network" and 13, "Tuning Your Server."

23. You then are offered a chance to search your disk drives for applications that Windows NT recognizes (just as Windows 3.x Setup does). After Setup detects the applications, you can make any changes and select the applications you want to include in your Program Manager groups.

24. Next, you are given the choice of selecting your date, time, and time zone. Select the appropriate choices and then click the OK button to continue.

25. Your display then will go blank as Windows NT detects your video adapter. You then can make changes to your desktop area (resolution), refresh frequency, color palette, and font size. You cannot change the display type at this point, however. You can do that only after the initial installation. After you make any changes, click the Test button. This displays a test bitmap pattern. After answering the message box about whether you saw the bitmap okay, click the OK button to continue.

26. At this point, your system configuration is saved to your repair directory located in your `SystemRoot\Repair` subdirectory. You then are offered the chance to create an emergency repair disk. And if you consider what you just went through to get Windows NT Server installed, you will understand when I suggest that you do so now.

27. After you complete your repair disk, you see your final Setup dialog box, which prompts you to reboot your computer. And I suggest that you do so to make sure that the system is functioning and so that you can continue with the system configuration, as outlined later in the section "Setting the Initial Configuration."

MS-DOS AND WINNT.EXE

If you have an unsupported CD-ROM drive or no CD-ROM drive at all, or if you encounter problems with the installation process and a supported CD-ROM drive, you still can install Windows NT Server without using floppy disks by booting MS-DOS and running the WINNT.EXE program. You can run this program from a local CD-ROM drive supported by MS-DOS, or from a network sharepoint from MS-DOS, Windows 3.x in standard mode, Windows for Workgroups 3.11 (which must be started with the WIN/T switch and must have an NDIS 2.0 or other real-mode network driver loaded), or Windows 95 (which must have the MS-DOS session's advanced properties configured to prevent an MS-DOS program from detecting Windows). All these methods copy the entire source media for the Windows NT Server installation to the local hard disk and then run the same install program as mentioned earlier, but they use this local copy as the source media instead of a CD-ROM.

Note

If you are going to install Windows NT Server from a network sharepoint, you first must copy the entire installation directory to this sharepoint and share it (preferably as read-only). To prepare for an Intel installation, for example, copy the entire I386 subdirectory on

4

the CD-ROM to a directory on a server, and then share that subdirectory.

The command line for WINNT.EXE follows:

WINNT /s:*SourceMediaPath* /t:TempDrive /i:*InfFile* [/o ¦ /ox] /x /f /c /b

Descriptions for the syntax of this command follow:

/s:*SourceMediaPath*: Source path for the installation files in the form of a UNC filename (such as \\SRV\CD-ROM\I386) or a local drive letter (such as E:\I386).

/t:TempDrive: Temporary drive to which the source media will be copied. The temporary directory is always WIN_NT.~LT.

/i:*InfFile*: Specifies a different inf file for the text Setup program to use. The default is DOSNET.INF.

/o: Creates the three boot floppy disks that specify the temporary directory as the source media.

/ox: Creates the three boot floppy disks that can use the CD-ROM or additional floppy disks for installation. These floppy disks are an exact copy of the floppy disks that ship with Windows NT Server.

/x: Overrides the creation of any boot floppy disks.

/f: Overrides the verification of files as they are copied from the source media to your local hard disk.

/c: Skips the free space check (to make sure that you have enough free space to contain the copied files) on your local hard disk drive.

/b: Skips the creation of boot floppy disks, but creates a new directory on your hard disk called WIN_NT.~BT that contains a complete copy of the boot files.

Warning

Because Windows NT Server does not support any MS-DOS compression schemes, you must make sure that the local files are copied to a directory that is accessible from the Windows NT Setup program. You can use the /t:TempDrive switch to override the WINNT drive selection for the temporary files.

Tip

Use the /ox switch to create boot floppy disks that can be used for the repair disk process. I suggest this switch because this version can use floppy disks (or a portable CD-ROM drive) for the source media comparison, whereas floppies created with the /o switch attempt to find files in the WIN_NT.~LT directory on your hard disk and, after the install, this directory is deleted. After the directory is deleted, it is no longer available for a source-media-to-local-copy comparison.

Tip

My favorite installation method (compared to a floppy disk installation) is to use the

```
WINNT /S:SourceMediaPath /B
```

option. This provides the fastest installation method when you have no supported CD-ROM drive.

After the installation process starts, files are moved from the temporary directory to the SystemRoot directory. This means that you do not need twice the free space to install Windows NT Server in this fashion. And if, for any reason, the temporary directories (WIN_NT.~LT and WIN_NT.~BT) are not deleted automatically after the installation, you can delete them. If you want to add drivers later, you can specify the network sharepoint (in UNC format) as the source media path.

ONTRACK DISK MANAGER AND ATAPI CD-ROM DRIVES

Recently I tried to install Windows NT Server 3.51 on a computer with an EIDE disk connected to the primary EIDE channel and an ATAPI CD-ROM connected to the secondary EIDE channel. As this is a fairly common situation, I didn't really expect to have any problems. Boy, was I surprised! This particular computer is a slightly older computer. The motherboard BIOS does not support EIDE disk controllers. The EIDE disk controller does not include a built-in BIOS to resolve this situation, so I used Ontrack Disk Manager to provide EIDE drive support.

During the installation I encountered repeated failures. I started, of course, with the normal installation process using the three setup floppies and the BackOffice CD-ROM, but the setup program locked up when it tried to install the ATAPI CD-ROM driver. I then tried a floppyless WINNT install (using the /b switch) so I did not need to load the ATAPI CD-ROM driver, but this failed to find the disk partition on the EIDE drive. This was pretty weird, especially when you consider that it booted from this same disk. I was almost ready to give up, when I decided to try the only other option left to me—a regular WINNT install using the three boot disks created by WINNT.

Once more, I had to skip installing the ATAPI CD-ROM driver or the setup program would lock up, but I was able to install Windows NT Server. After a successful installation I added the ATAPI CD-ROM driver using the Windows NT Setup applet located in the Main program group. Once more NT locked up. Luckily I could use the Last Known Good option to return to my previous system configuration so I did not have to reinstall Windows NT Server. As I needed the CD-ROM to work under Windows NT Server, I was not ready to give up. I tried various hardware and software configurations, but nothing really worked. Finally I decided to download and install Service Pack 4. That did the trick. After the service pack was installed I was able to install the ATAPI CD-ROM driver and access the CD-ROM drive.

The moral to this story is simple: If at first you do not succeed, try again. And again. And again, if necessary. Perseverance, or downright stubbornness, sometimes pays off. You may encounter similar problems with the BackOffice 2.0 CD-ROM set because the master copy is based on the original product. It doesn't include the latest patches that are included in the service packs, as you might think. Instead, you will have to install Service Pack 4 for Windows NT Server after your installation to be up to date. The service packs for Windows NT Server can be found on disc 1 of your CD-ROM set in the WINNT351.QFE subdirectory. The other BackOffice component service packs can be found on the Microsoft Web site at http://www.microsoft.com/msdownload.

PERFORMING A RISC PROCESSOR INSTALLATION

Installation on a RISC processor follows the same basic format as installation on an Intel processor, with a few minor differences. The first gotcha is that each RISC-based computer is a bit different in how you run a program from the CD-ROM drive, so I have to refer you to your operating manual to determine that particular process. The basic process follows:

1. Insert the Windows NT Server CD-ROM into your CD-ROM drive.
2. Restart the computer.

3. When the ARC menu appears, choose to run a program from the menu.

4. Type CD:\System\SETUPLDR (where System is the RISC computer type Alpha, MIPS, or PPC). Then press Enter. Note that this varies from RISC computer to RISC computer, and in some cases you must supply a full qualified device name. Your documentation will include the specifics. The goal here, however, is to run the SETUPLDR program, which is the same program that the normal install process executes.

5. At this point, the installation process is exactly the same as the process for installation on an Intel processor.

Note

In order to install Windows NT Server, you must have a system partition of at least 2MB. This partition must be formatted as FAT.

Tip

If you are upgrading an existing version of Windows NT Server or converting a Windows NT Workstation to Windows NT Server, you can run the WINNT32.EXE program instead of these steps. WINNT32.EXE is discussed in the next section.

UPGRADING AN EXISTING INSTALLATION

You can upgrade an existing Windows NT Server installation by running any of the normal installation methods mentioned earlier, or you can run the Windows NT-specific Setup program called WINNT32.EXE. The process for an upgrade follows the same basic procedure as previously mentioned, with one difference. You are not required to select any network adapter, printer, video adapter, and so on. Instead, the install process makes all those determinations for you. WINNT32.EXE has the following syntax:

WINNT /s:SourceMediaPath /t:TempDrive /i:IniFile [/o ¦ /ox] /x /b

Explanations of the syntax used in this command line follow:

/s:SourceMediaPath: Source path for the installation files in the form of a UNC filename (such as \\SRV\CD-ROM\I386) or a local drive letter (such as E:\I386).

/t:TempDrive: Temporary drive to which the source media will be copied. The temporary directory is always WIN_NT.~LT.

/i: *InfFile*: Specifies a different inf file for the text Setup program to use. The default is DOSNET.INF.

/o: Creates the three boot floppy disks that specify the temporary directory as the source media.

/ox: Creates the three boot floppy disks that can use the CD-ROM or additional floppy disks for installation. These floppy disks are an exact copy of the floppy disks that ship with Windows NT Server.

/x: Overrides the creation of any boot floppy disks.

/b: Skips the creation of boot floppy disks but creates a new directory on your hard disk called WIN_NT.~BT that contains a complete copy of the boot files.

SETTING THE INITIAL CONFIGURATION

After you complete the base installation of Windows NT Server, it's time to work on it a bit more. Specifically, you will want to set various options and complete the installation of any accessory software. Some of the items you will want to complete follow:

- ◆ Using User Manager for Domains (which is covered in detail in Chapter 6, "Basic Administrative Tools"), add an administrative user account for yourself and any other network Administrators. While you are there, configure the system policies and select the auditing features you want to enable.

- ◆ Using Windows NT Setup, add a tape device driver to support your tape backup device. Currently, device drivers exist to support most 4mm DAT drives, some 8mm DAT drives, and some QIC tape drives.

- ◆ In the Control Panel System applet, configure your virtual memory (paging files) and tasking options. These items are covered in Chapter 7, "Resource Management Tools," as performance enhancements.

- ◆ Use the Control Panel UPS applet to install and configure your uninterruptable power supply (UPS). This will protect your server against power outages and poor line conditions. This is covered in Chapter 8, "Additional Administrative Tools," in the section "UPS Service."

- ◆ Install any additional printers with Print Manager. This is covered in Chapter 6.

- ◆ Install any additional network software, such as the Gateway Service for NetWare, the Macintosh Services, Remote Access Service, or additional services. This is discussed in Chapter 5.

- Create any additional partitions, striped sets, stripe sets with parity, or other fault-tolerant partitions with Disk Administrator. This is discussed in Chapter 8, in the section titled "Disk Administrator."
- Add the Registry Editor (REGEDT32.EXE) and the Repair Disk Utility (RDISK.EXE) to the Administrative Tools group. This is discussed in Appendix B, "The Registry Editor and Registry Keys," which is located on the accompanying CD-ROM.
- Add any multimedia device drivers with the Control Panel Devices applet.
- Add a computer description in the Control Panel Server applet. And while you are there, configure the system alerts and possibly the replication service as well.
- Compress any directories or drives (must be on NTFS drives only) with the COMPACT.EXE or File Manager.
- Install and configure the DHCP and WINS services. These items are covered in Chapter 9.
- Review the event logs with the Event Viewer to check for any installation-related problems as described in Chapter 6.

After you complete all the basic system modifications and restart the system (so that all your changes are applied), make sure that you run through the Repair Disk Utility to create a new repair disk and update the local repair information. That way, you can restore the system to this same state at a later date if you have any problems. I would even recommend that you make a complete system backup at this point, just in case. You should test out the reliability of your tape backup hardware anyway.

TROUBLESHOOTING A FAILED INSTALLATION

A Windows NT Server installation may fail for several reasons. Most of them are related to incompatible hardware. The first thing I suggest that you do is check to see what the error code (at the top-left corner of your screen) is if you received a blue screen core dump. If the error code is not listed here, you can use the Windows NT Message database to search for the code for an explanation. The Setup application for this tool is contained in the SUPPORT\WINNTMSG subdirectory. You also should look in the Event Viewer logs for any additional information that might be contained there about the error.

Table 4.1 shows some of the more common error codes.

TABLE 4.1. COMMON FATAL EXCEPTION ERROR CODES.

Error Code	Description
F002	Indicates that a parity error or non-maskable interrupt occurred. In most cases, this error is memory-related, although some network and video adapters also can generate this error. If you receive this error, you should run a system diagnostic on the computer, check your BIOS memory refresh rates, and check your cache settings. In some cases, this error is caused by a poorly seated SIMM. You might want to remove each SIMM, clean it with an eraser, and then reinstall it.
0000001E	Most of the time, this unhandled kernel exception indicates a problem with the file system. If you receive this error, look at the bottom right of the blue screen for the stack dump and look for possible causes. If you see RDR.SYS listed, for example, it indicates a problem with the network redirector, so check your network adapter settings. If you see NTFS.SYS or FASTFAT.SYS, that is an indication that you have an error in your NTFS or FAT partitions and you should run the CHKDSK.EXE program on all your drives with the /F option (to fix any errors).
0000000A	This is a catastrophic hardware error and generally indicates an interrupt, I/O, or DMA conflict. Check your hardware to make sure that you are not sharing any IRQs and that you have no other resource conflicts.
0x0000007B	This is an indication that your boot drive is inaccessible. Possible causes are disk drives with greater than 1,024 cylinders, unsupported disk-partitioning schemes, accidentally compressing the boot drive with an MS-DOS compression program in a dual-boot environment, or a boot sector virus.

Tip

The Windows NT Diagnostics program (WINMSD.EXE) can help you identify resource-related problems. This tool is located in the Administrative Tools group.

Note

LAN Manager for UNIX is not a supported upgrade or cloning platform. However, if you install a Microsoft LAN Manager 1.x server to your LAN Manager for UNIX domain and make it a server, that computer can be used to migrate all the user accounts. You then can just copy the user directories from the LAN Manager for UNIX servers to your new Windows NT Server and, in effect, clone that system.

The basic process for upgrading a LAN Manager follows:

1. Install Windows NT Server on the platform of your choice.

2. Change to the UPGRADE.LM2 directory on your installation CD-ROM.

3. For a clone on an MIPS computer, change to the MIPS subdirectory; for an Alpha, change to the ALPHA subdirectory; and for an Intel processor, change to the X86 subdirectory.

4. Run the SETUP.CMD batch file. It takes one parameter—a drive letter specifying where to install the upgrade files. It stores these files in an UPGRADE subdirectory on the specified drive.

5. Run LMUPMGR.EXE on your LAN Manager server. This is a graphical shell that runs other LAN Manager utilities and captures the requisite information.

6. Run WNTUPMGR.EXE on your Windows NT Server. This graphical shell restores the information captured on the LAN Manager server to your Windows NT Server.

Novell NetWare

Novell NetWare migration is similar to the LAN Manager cloning process. It can be used to capture user accounts, directories, and file information. After these have been captured, you can move the data files from your Novell server, but your clients will need to have changes made to their network protocols in order to function with Windows NT Server. You can avoid any changes to your client configuration by using the Microsoft emulation of the NetWare file and print services, which is called the File and Print Service for NetWare.

Currently, the basic migration process follows:

1. Install Windows NT Server on the platform of your choice.

2. Install and configure the Gateway Services for NetWare on your Windows NT Server.

3. Run the NWCONV.EXE program.

4. Select your NetWare and Windows NT Servers for the migration.

5. Begin the migration process.

6. Check for possible errors.

SUMMARY

This chapter included information and a step-by-step guide for the basic installation process. You also looked at the various installation methods. By now, you should be familiar with the various installation options and be prepared for your own Windows NT installation. You also looked at unsupported (by Microsoft) methods for cloning your Windows NT Server installation to speed up the install process. You took a brief look at some of the troubleshooting errors and looked at the basic migration process for LAN Manager and Novell NetWare.

In the next chapter, you will look a bit more into integrating Windows NT Server with your UNIX, Novell, and LAN Manager networks.

- LAN Manager

- Novell NetWare

- UNIX

- Macintosh

- Remote Access Service

CHAPTER 5

Integrating Windows NT Server with Other Networks

One of the features I really like about Windows NT Server is that it can be added to almost any network. I have not actually found a network that I could not integrate Windows NT Server with, but I'm sure that if I searched long enough I could find one. It probably would be an antique network operating system, but one thing I've found is that there are some real antiques out there in the market. The only reason I would be unable to integrate Windows NT Server with one of these antiques would be because I would not be able obtain an updated network protocol stack for its existing server.

That is not a problem for today's network operating systems. If your network is based on NetBEUI, IPX/SPX, or TCP/IP, you can plug Windows NT Server into your existing network and start playing immediately. In some cases, you will need additional software from the manufacturer or a third-party add-on package to implement a complete solution, but in many cases, you can just install the optional software components provided with Windows NT Server or available from Microsoft to gain this functionality. That is what this chapter is all about: finding these components, installing them, and then configuring them to provide the additional services you need to integrate Windows NT Server with your existing network.

This chapter begins by showing you the available options that Microsoft LAN Manager and LAN Manager for UNIX offer. Next, you'll learn about integration with Novell NetWare networks. The NetWare discussion also includes a look at the File and Print Services for NetWare you can use to make your Windows NT Server emulate a Novell server, and includes a look at the NetWare Directory Service for Windows NT Server. You'll learn about the available options for UNIX interoperability and how to connect your AppleTalk (Macintosh) network clients. Finally, you'll explore the Remote Access Service.

LAN MANAGER

Integrating your LAN Manager or LAN Manager for UNIX networks with Windows NT is one of the easiest processes you will encounter, but there are a few differences and quirks, particularly with LAN Manager for UNIX. The best way to obtain full functionality is to upgrade your LAN Manager servers to Windows NT Server as soon as possible. The primary reasons to upgrade your servers are to provide logon authentication for your Windows NT clients and to avoid the pitfalls mentioned in the next section. Only a Windows NT Server can authenticate your Windows NT clients, although your LAN Manager servers can authenticate your MS-DOS, Windows 3.x, Windows 95, and OS/2 1.x clients.

INTEGRATION OF A MIXED DOMAIN

The first item on your list in order to accomplish this integration of LAN Manager and Windows NT Server is to create a new Windows NT Server primary domain controller and to run through the migration process, as outlined in Chapter 4, "Installing Windows NT Server." This process migrates all your user accounts, global group accounts, sharepoints, directory replication configurations, and other settings. The only hitch with this process is that you cannot use the migration tools on a LAN Manager for UNIX server. To migrate your settings on a LAN Manager for UNIX server, you must install Microsoft LAN Manager on a spare computer and create another LAN Manager server. You can use this server with the migration tools. After you complete the migration, you should be aware of the differences between a Windows NT Server domain and a LAN Manager domain:

◆ Your Windows NT Server must be a primary domain controller (PDC) and your LAN Manager servers must be backup domain or member servers. If you have a LAN Manager PDC, the users of that server will be unable to log onto the network.

Warning

Not only will the users of the LAN Manager PDC not be able to log onto the network, but it is possible that having a LAN Manager PDC in your Windows NT domain could bring down the entire network.

◆ Always use your Windows NT Server primary domain controller to make any changes to your account database. Any change you make on the Windows NT Server is replicated to your LAN Manager domains, but changes you make on your LAN Manager server are not replicated to your Windows NT Server.

Warning

If you change an administrative account on your LAN Manager server, that account loses the capability to modify user accounts in the domain. Always use User Manager for Domains to modify the account on the Windows NT Server to avoid such a possibility.

◆ LAN Manager does not support the Windows NT Server trust relationship concept. Therefore, if you have a LAN Manager server in a Windows NT domain with a trust relationship, no users of the trusted domain are able to access shared resources on the LAN Manager domain because they cannot be authenticated. Users of trusted domains who need to access a LAN Manager resource must have a local account created on the Windows NT Server domain. This local account then can be placed in a global group that can be used to grant permission to a shared resource on the LAN Manager server.

Note

Local accounts are created with User Manager for Domains. Just select the user account and choose User | Properties to display the User Properties dialog box. Then you only need to click the Account button, which displays the Account dialog box. For the account type, specify that the account is a local account for users from untrusted domains.

◆ LAN Manager servers do not support Windows NT Server local groups. You therefore cannot assign permissions on a LAN Manager resource based on a local group. Instead, you must create a global group to contain the user accounts to which you want to provide access to the shared resource on the LAN Manager server.

◆ LAN Manager servers can support only a maximum of 252 global groups. Exceeding this limit on your Windows NT Server domain can cause replication problems. So, in effect, in a mixed domain, you also are limited to a maximum of 252 global groups.

◆ LAN Manager only supports a maximum of 254 domains, whereas a Windows NT network can support up to 4,096 domains. To avoid problems in this area, you should use a master domain (or multiple master domain) in which all your user accounts reside, and then you can have mixed domains that trust the master domain.

INTEROPERABILITY WITH FOREIGN LAN MANAGER DOMAINS

After you perform a successful migration, things should be in good shape, aside from any inconsistencies mentioned earlier. On the other hand, if you decided to install Windows NT Server as a new domain and leave your existing LAN Manager domains as standalone domains, then you have a few additional modifications to make to your Windows NT Server configuration.

These modifications follow:

◆ If you want your Windows NT domain and your LAN Manager domain to provide resource sharing with the same user accounts, you need to add the LAN Manager global groups to your Windows NT local groups and then use these local groups to apply permissions on your Windows NT Server. If you have a LAN Manager domain called LanMan and a Windows NT domain called NTDomain, for example, you should add the global LanMan\Users group to the local Users group on the NTDomain server. Then when you share a directory on your NTDomain server, set the share permissions to the local Users group. Because LanMan\Users is a member of the local Users group, these LAN Manager members are able to access the sharepoint.

Note

You want to add the LAN Manager global groups to your Windows NT Server local groups instead of running the LAN-Manager-to-Windows-NT upgrade utilities. These utilities include backat, which backs up the LAN Manager user accounts, and portuas, which merges a LAN Manager user account database with the Windows NT Server account database. If you modify the LAN Manager user account database, these changes are not reflected on the Windows NT Server domain. If you did not use the group method, every time you added a user on the LAN Manager domain, you would have to rerun the utilities to keep a consistent account database.

◆ If you want to copy directories and files from your LAN Manager server to your new Windows NT Server, you should use the hcopy program included in the LAN-Manager-to-Windows-NT upgrade process. This program copies hidden directories and maintains the extended attribute information (such as the file type, creator/owner, and so on), which might be lost if you copy the files with the xcopy command.

Note

If you are migrating directories and data that were used by the LAN Manager Services for Macintosh, you should back up your data files with the Sytos Plus backup utility and then use the NTBACKUP program to restore them on your Windows NT Server. This is required because the hcopy program does not copy noncontiguous extended attributes, but the Sytos Plus backup utility does.

◆ If you want your Windows NT domain to be able to view shared resources on a LAN Manager domain, you need to configure the Computer Browser service.

If your LAN Manager domain has a Windows for Workgroup or Windows NT Workstation client, you do not need to manually add the LAN Manager domain to the list of domains to browse, unless you also have set the MaintainServerList=NO entry in your Windows for Workgroup client's system.ini file or have set this option in the Registry of your Windows NT clients in the following key:

HKEY_LOCAL_MACHINE\System\CurrentControlSet\Services\LanmanWorkstation\Parameters

To configure the Computer Browser service, follow these steps:

1. Open the Control Panel Network applet to display the Network Settings dialog box.

2. In the Installed Network Software field, select the Computer Browser. Then click the Configure button. The Browser Configuration dialog box appears (see Figure 5.1).

Figure 5.1.
The Browser
Configuration
dialog box.

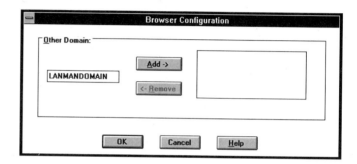

3. Enter the name of the LAN Manager domain in the entry box to the left (where you'll see my LANMANDOMAIN). Then click the Add button. This moves the domain name to the left field, which is used to indicate additional domains to be browsed. To remove a domain, select it in the list on the right and click the Remove button. To exit the dialog box, click the OK button.

4. Click the OK button to exit the Network Settings dialog box.

Caution

> Before you migrate any of the LAN Manager servers you have added to the browse list, you should remove them from the list in the Computer Browser. Then stop the Browser service and restart it to flush the browse list cache. After this, you can migrate the server as usual.

If your LAN Manager servers and clients cannot see any resources on your Windows NT domain, you should make sure that the Make Browser Broadcasts to LAN Manager 2.x Clients option is enabled in the Server service. Follow these steps:

1. Open the Control Panel Network applet to display the Network Settings dialog box.

2. In the Installed Network Software field, select Server. Then click the Configure button. The Server dialog box appears. Enable the Make Browser

Broadcasts to LAN Manager 2.x Clients option. Then click the OK button to exit the Server dialog box.

3. Click the OK button to exit the Network Settings dialog box.

LAN MANAGER FOR UNIX ISSUES

You should be aware of a few other problems with Windows NT Server and LAN Manager for UNIX. These problems occur because LAN Manager for UNIX is an emulation of LAN Manager running on top of the UNIX operating system. This emulation does not properly implement all the functionality for the LAN Manager APIs.

Some of these problems follow:

◆ The Microsoft Mail and Schedule Plus 32-bit clients run very slowly on postoffices that are installed on the LAN Manager for UNIX server. In some cases, you can corrupt your Microsoft Mail file (.MMF) on the LAN Manager server. You can solve the data corruption by using the 16-bit mail clients; however, the performance still will be quite poor. The better alternative is to move the postoffice to a Windows NT Server computer and to change your client postoffice directory mapping.

Note

The mapping information is contained in the Registry under the key

`HKEY_CURRENT_USER\Software\Microsoft\Mail\Microsoft Mail`

Change the ServerPath value to point to the new sharepoint if a UNC filename was used, or if you migrated an existing 16-bit mail implementation, map the mail drive (usually M) with File Manager or in their logon script to point to the new location of the postoffice.

◆ Directory and File permissions are not properly applied from File Manager on a shared directory on a LAN Manager for UNIX server. Although File Manager displays the permissions on the directories and files as if they were applied, a refresh shows that the permissions have not been applied successfully. The only directory or file properties you can apply are the standard read-only, archive, hidden, or system properties.

◆ Other problems include repeated errors listed in the Event Viewer concerning failed network connections and improperly formatted Server Message Block (SMB) notifications.

The only permanent resolution to these problems is a planned migration to Windows NT Server.

NOVELL NETWARE

The Gateway Services for NetWare included with Windows NT Server gives you the capability to connect to a Novell Server's shared resources and share them among your Microsoft network clients. These clients do not need to have the IPX/SPX protocol installed, and they do not need any NetWare network client drivers installed. Instead, a request from a network client is passed to the Windows NT Server, which reformats the data request and passes it onto the NetWare server. After the NetWare server services the data request, it is passed back to the Windows NT Server and then onto the network client.

Note

The Gateway Services for NetWare also is required in order for Systems Management Server to manage a NetWare server.

GATEWAY SERVICES FOR NETWARE

Installing the Gateway Services for NetWare follows the same basic principles as all other network software installation. Follow these steps:

1. Open the Control Panel Network applet to display the Network Settings dialog box.
2. Click the Add Software button. The Add Network Software dialog box appears.
3. In the Network Software drop-down list, select Gateway Service for Novell NetWare. When prompted, enter the source path for the distribution files. Then click the OK button.
4. After the files are copied to your server, click the OK button in the Network Settings dialog box. The Configuring Network dialog box appears, informing you that it is analyzing your network bindings. You then see messages about the various transport protocols as each item is configured.
5. You are prompted to restart your computer by the Network Settings Change dialog box. Click the Restart Now button to restart your server.
6. After your system restarts, the Logon dialog box appears. Log on as you normally do. The Select Preferred Server for NetWare dialog box appears.
7. In the drop-down listbox, choose the NetWare server you want to use as your preferred (default) server or choose <none>. If you do not choose a server, the closest server is used as your preferred server. Then click the OK button.

Note

> In order for this account to connect to your NetWare server, you need to create a user account on your NetWare server. You also have to create a group called NTGATEWAY, of which this user account is a member. This group must have sufficient privileges to access any shared NetWare resource that you want to share on your Microsoft network.

8. Rerun the Control Panel Network applet. In the Network Settings dialog box, click the Networks button to display the Network Provider Search Order dialog box.

9. Select the Network Provider entry in the Show Providers For field. Then, in the Access Providers in This Order field, select the network provider you want to be first in the browse list. The default after installing the Gateway Services for NetWare is the NetWare or Compatible Provider. If you have more Microsoft network servers than Novell NetWare Servers, select the Microsoft Windows Network entry and click the up arrow to move the entry to the top of the list.

10. Select the Print Provider entry in the Show Providers For field. Then, in the Access Providers in This Order field, select NetWare or Compatible Network (the default) or LanMan Print Services. Once more, you should choose the entry that contains the most shared resources.

11. Click the OK button when you finish your modifications to exit the Network Provider Search Order dialog box. Then click the OK button in the Network Settings dialog box to exit that box. When prompted to restart your server, click the Restart Now button for the changes to take place immediately, or you can click the Don't Restart Now button for your changes to take place the next time the server is restarted.

After you install the Services for NetWare, you need to configure it in order to share the NetWare resources. This is accomplished by first activating a gateway. Then you need to add file or print shares. To enable a gateway, follow these steps:

Note

> A gateway is used instead of File Manager or the NET USE command because these types of access to the NetWare server are user specific. If the user logs off the server, these shared resources no longer will be accessible by Microsoft Network clients.

1. Open the Control Panel and select the GSNW (Gateway Service for
   NetWare) applet. The Gateway Service for NetWare dialog box appears (see
   Figure 5.2).

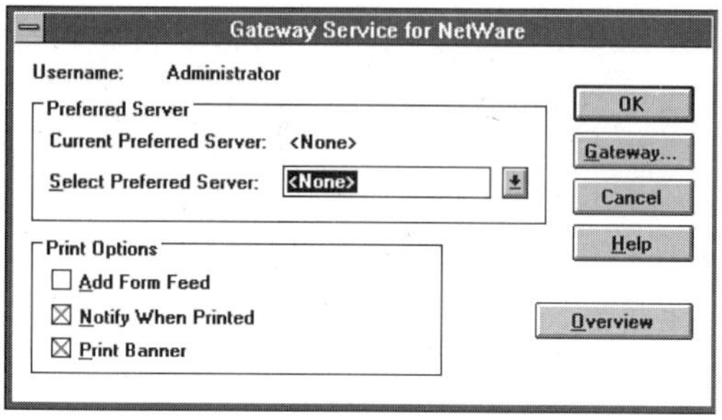

Figure 5.2.
The Gateway
Service for
NetWare
dialog box.

2. If you want to change your preferred server, select it in the Select Preferred
   Server drop-down listbox.

3. Click the Gateway button. The Configure Gateway dialog box appears, as
   shown in Figure 5.3.

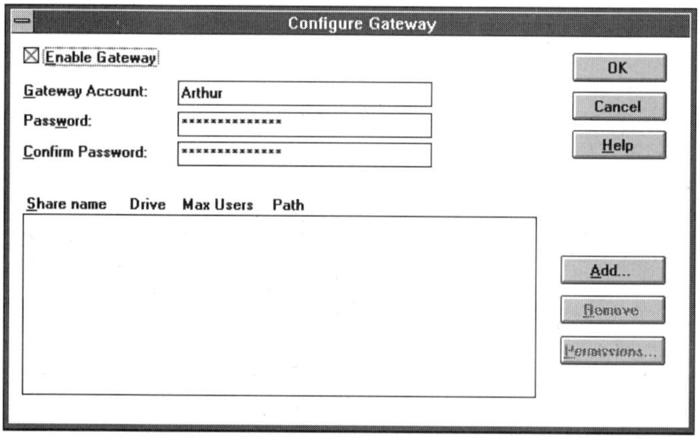

Figure 5.3.
The Configure
Gateway
dialog box.

4. Place an X in the Enable Gateway checkbox to enable your gateway. Then
   enter a Novell NetWare user account, password, and confirmation of the
   password in the appropriate fields.

Note

The user account specified must be a member of the NTGATEWAY group. This group must be created on your NetWare server prior to accessing any shared resources. This group also must have sufficient privileges on the Novell NetWare server in order to access the resources to be shared.

5. Click the OK button to return to the Gateway Service for NetWare dialog box. Then click OK to exit the dialog box and return to the Control Panel.

To share a NetWare directory, follow these steps:

1. Repeat steps 1 through 4 of the process for enabling a gateway.

2. Click the Add button in the Configure Gateway dialog box to display the New Share dialog box, as shown in Figure 5.4.

Figure 5.4.
The New Share
dialog box.

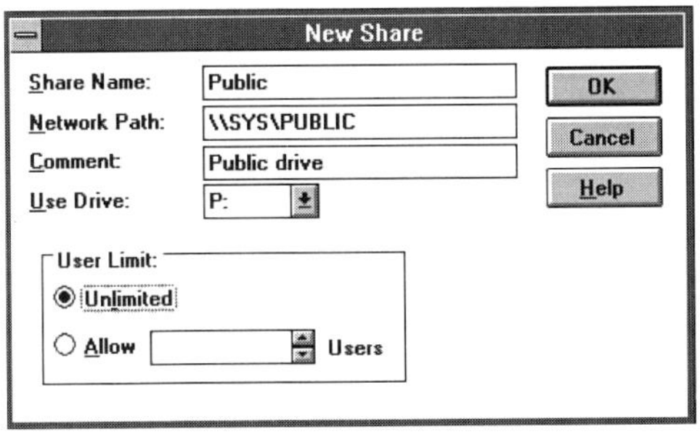

3. In the Share Name field, enter the name for your Microsoft clients to use to connect to the sharepoint.

4. In the Network Path field, enter the path to the sharepoint.

5. In the Comment field, enter a comment for your Microsoft clients to view when they browse the network for shared resources.

6. In the Use Drive field, select the local drive letter to be used on your Windows NT Server to map the shared directory to.

7. In the User Limit section, enter a maximum number of users to allow a connection to this sharepoint in the Allow Users box.

8. Click the OK button to return to the Configure Gateway dialog box.

9. If you want to limit access to the gateway share, select the share in the box at the bottom of the Configure Gateway dialog box and click the Permissions button. The Access Though Share Permissions dialog box appears.

This dialog box is explained in depth in Chapter 7, "Resource Management Tools," in the section "Setting Share Level Permissions on a Network Sharepoint."

Tip

To remove a gateway share, access the Configure Gateway dialog box. In the Share Name box, select the shared directory and click the Remove button.

10. After you set any permissions for the share, click the OK button to return to the Configure Gateway dialog box. When you finish setting your permissions, click the OK button to return to the Control Panel.

To share a NetWare printer, follow these basic steps:

1. Use Print Manager to connect to the NetWare printer. You follow the same basic principles as outlined in Chapter 7 for connecting to a shared printer, except that you need to browse the NetWare or compatible network instead of the Microsoft Windows network.

2. Share the printer, as outlined in Chapter 7.

Note

If you want your MS-DOS clients to be able to access this printer, be sure to set the share name to less than 12 characters and follow the basic MS-DOS naming conventions.

3. If you want to set permissions, select the printer in Print Manager and choose Security | Permissions. This process is covered in Chapter 7.

EXAMINING MICROSOFT FILE AND PRINT SERVICES FOR NETWARE

The File and Print Services for NetWare service gives a Windows NT Server the capability to emulate a Novell NetWare server. This means that your NetWare clients do not have to have any modifications to their configurations in order to use the shared resources on the Windows NT Server. This gives you the capability to plan a slower migration from Novell NetWare to Windows NT Server, and you will want to migrate your clients' network drivers just because you can obtain increased performance and reliability when compared to the Novell NetWare client drivers. I'm sure that at one time or another you have had a network client lose his connection to the NetWare server; when this happens, the network client computer generally hangs, requiring you to reboot the system and resulting in lost data for the client. The Microsoft network drivers are more forgiving; they give you the chance to reestablish a connection and then to proceed as usual.

So why would you want to use File and Print Services for NetWare and Windows NT Server if you already have a well-established Novell network? In addition to the features just described, you get the following benefits:

◆ Windows NT Server is an excellent application server. You can add Microsoft SQL Server and provide robust database capabilities to your network without running it as a NetWare Loadable Module (NLM) and taking the chance that the NLM will crash the server.

◆ Windows NT Server is required to support Systems Management Server. With SMS, you can automate the installation of software upgrades, determine which hardware platforms are available, which hardware platforms need to be upgraded, and even whether you have software that should not be installed on your client computers—all from a single console.

◆ Windows NT Server includes the Services for Macintosh service as part of the operating system. It provides complete file and print sharing with a common user account on the server for your Macintosh clients.

◆ You can install SNA Server to provide access to your IBM mainframes or Digital Equipment Corporation's PathWorks for Windows NT to connect to your DEC mainframes.

◆ You can use Microsoft Mail to provide e-mail services for your network clients. With the addition of some of the optional gateways for Microsoft Mail, you can provide e-mail services to almost any e-mail service, including CompuServe, the Internet, MCI Mail, and many others.

◆ You can build extremely large networks—all with a common user logon—so that your network clients can access any resource on the network.

Note

The common user logon capability requires that the Microsoft Directory Services for NetWare service be installed on your Windows NT Server. This is another add-on product (like the File and Print Services for Netware) that provides the capability to use one user logon to access your Windows NT network resources as well as your Netware resources.

◆ Windows NT Server includes the Remote Access Service so that you can support your dial-in clients and provide seamless access to your entire network. You can even use the Remote Access Service to connect to the

Internet and use your Windows NT Server as a gateway to Internet services for your network clients.

This list goes on and on. The bottom line is that you can integrate Windows NT Server into your existing Novell NetWare–based network and provide seamless connectivity. With the addition of some third-party software, you can even integrate Windows NT Server with your UNIX-based networks.

UNIX

Integrating Windows NT Server with your UNIX networks is possible with Windows NT Server. But there are some limitations to what can be accomplished with the base product. Most of these limitations can be overcome by installing third-party software to provide the missing functionality not included with Windows NT Server. Before you look at the limitations, however, look at what Windows NT Server provides for your UNIX network:

◆ A complete implementation of the TCP/IP protocol, including an implementation of TCP/IP sockets.

◆ A File Transfer Protocol server and client.

◆ A printer server that supports sharing your Microsoft Network shared printers with your UNIX clients. You also get a print client used to connect to your shared UNIX printers. You also have the command-line utilities lpq (line printer queue) and lpr (line printer remote) for managing your UNIX print queues and command-line printing to your UNIX printers.

Tip

> By using the TCP/IP printer connectivity, you can connect a Windows NT computer to a shared UNIX printer. After you install the appropriate printer driver, you can share this printer on the network. This provides access to the printer for your Microsoft network clients—even for those clients without the TCP/IP protocol installed. This basically creates a printer gateway through which your Microsoft clients connect to your server, and your server then routes the data to the appropriate UNIX printer. Connecting a printer to a UNIX print queue is covered in Chapter 7.

◆ Several client utilities, including Telnet (terminal emulation), remote shells (rsh and rexec), remote copy (rcp), and the trivial file protocol (tftp).

◆ Configuration and connection utilities such as arp, hostname, nbstat, netstat, tracert, ping, and ipconfig.

So with all of this, you might ask what is missing. Well, there is no support for the Network File System (NFS) and there are several UNIX daemons missing that provide the server service for Telnet, rsh, rexec, wais, gopher, www, and others. Without these, it is difficult to provide a complete UNIX replacement or offer total UNIX integration. The good news is that many of these missing utilities are available from third parties or on the Internet.

Tip

The Windows NT Resource Kit, the Microsoft Developer Network CD-ROM, or the Microsoft TechNet CD-ROM contains additional UNIX tools, including the following:

ar	grep	rm
cc	ld	rmdir
chmod	ls	sh
chown	lstlib	term
cp	make	touch
elvis	makdir	vi
find	mv	wc

You also can find these utilities in the Microsoft FTP site (ftp.microsoft.com).

Note

You can download the Microsoft Internet Information Server from the Microsoft Web page (http://www.microsoft.com/msdownload), which includes a World Wide Web, FTP, and Gopher server. A more detailed description of the Internet Information Server is covered in Chapter 10, "Using the Internet Information Server."

INSTALLING THE TCP/IP PROTOCOL AND UTILITIES

If you did not install all the TCP/IP utilities during your initial Windows NT Server installation, you can add them through the Control Panel Network applet. Just follow these steps:

1. Open the Control Panel Network applet to display the Network Settings dialog box.

2. Click the Add Software button to display the Add Network Software dialog box.

3. In the Network Software listbox, select TCP/IP Protocol and Related Components and click the OK button to display the Windows NT TCP/IP Installation Options dialog box. If an option is grayed out, it means that you already have installed the component. The components you can install include the Connectivity Utilities (Telnet, rsh, rexec, and so on), SNMP (Simple Network Management Protocol) Service, TCP/IP Printing Support, FTP (File Transfer Protocol) Server Service, Simple TCP/IP Services, DHCP Service, and WINS Server Service.

4. After selecting the components you want to install, click the OK button. When prompted, enter the source path for the distribution files. Then click the OK button.

5. After the files are copied to your server, click the OK button in the Network Settings dialog box. The Configuring Network dialog box appears, which tells you that it is analyzing your network bindings. You then see messages about the various transport protocols as each item is configured.

6. If an item has not been configured, you are prompted to configure it. The FTP Service, for example, requires you to select a default home directory and prompts you to allow or disallow anonymous connections. The SNMP Service prompts you to configure it as well.

Caution

The FTP Server sends unencrypted passwords across the network. To prevent a possible security breach, you should allow only anonymous connections via an FTP connection.

7. After all the utilities have been configured, you are prompted to restart your computer for the changes to take effect. You should click the Don't Restart Now button.

8. You now have the chance to use the Control Panel Services applet to configure the TCP/IP Print Server. Change the startup value from Manual to Automatic. This enables your UNIX clients to connect to any shared printer whenever you start Windows NT Server. If you do not enable this setting, you must manually start the service to provide UNIX connectivity.

9. Now you can use Program Manager to restart your system to enable the changes you made to take effect. When you restart, you can connect to a UNIX printer, have your UNIX clients connect to any shared printers, and use any of the TCP/IP utilities included with Windows NT Server.

5

Examining Third-Party Enhancement Products

As I mentioned before, Windows NT Server does not include all the necessary TCP/IP components for your UNIX clients to connect to your Windows NT Server. You might want to look at some of these manufacturers for additional services:

◆ AGE Logic Inc.: XoftHost for Windows NT is an OSF/Motif and X Window development environment for Windows NT. XoftWare32 is a 32-bit implementation of an X Window Server. (619) 455-8600

◆ BGW Computers: UUtil adds many of the common UNIX shell commands and utilities. (612) 934-3986

◆ Congruent Corporation: NTNix allows X Window applications to be hosted on your Windows NT computer. (212) 431-5100

◆ Digital Equipment Corporation: eXcursion is another X Window host environment that enables you to run both your Windows NT and X Window applications on the same platform. (506) 486-2703

◆ Frontier Technologies Corporation: Provides VT320 and TN320 terminal emulation. Supports e-mail with the MIME binary format, SMTP, POP2, and 3. Includes NFS client/server support for access to and from your UNIX clients. (414) 241-4555, ext. 217

◆ Hamilton Laboratories: Hamilton C Shell creates the original UNIX C shell on Windows NT. It includes more than 130 commands, utilities, and functions. (508) 358-5715

◆ Hummingbird Communications, Ltd.: eXceed for Windows NT provides an X Window Server. (416) 470-1203

◆ Intergraph Corporation: DiskShare is an NFS server that provides for UNIX client connectivity. PC-NFS provides connectivity from a Windows NT Server to your UNIX servers. (800) 345-4856 or (205) 730-2000

◆ Mortice Kern Systems, Inc.: MKS Toolkit provides many of the more common UNIX development utilities and an implementation of the MKS Korn shell. (800) 265-2797 or (519) 884-2251

Macintosh

The Windows NT Server Services for Macintosh enables your Macintosh clients to connect to your Windows NT Server just as if it were a native AppleTalk server. With Services for Macintosh, you can share directories and printers with your Macintosh clients. This benefits you because you can place all your printers on your Microsoft network and let all your clients use the printers. You can even have your Macintosh clients print to non-PostScript printers because the Service for Macintosh service includes a PostScript emulator. Not only can you share printers, but you can share data files as well, if you share a directory, by creating a Macintosh volume and a Windows NT sharepoint on the same directory.

You should be aware of a couple of requirements before you implement the Service for Macintosh. Your Macintosh clients must be using version 6.0.7 or higher (including System 7) of the Macintosh operating system, and a version 6.x or later LaserWriter printer driver. You also must have an NTFS partition on your Windows NT Server in order to create Macintosh volumes. And, finally, if you want to make sure that your Macintosh clients do not send clear text passwords over the network, you must install the Microsoft UAM (User Authentication Module) in the Macintosh System folder.

INSTALLING SERVICES FOR MACINTOSH

Like every other network software module, you start your installation process from the Control Panel Network applet. After the Network Settings dialog box appears, you can follow these steps to install the Services for Macintosh service:

1. Click the Add Software button; the Add Network Software dialog box appears.
2. In the Network Software drop-down listbox, select Services for Macintosh. When prompted, enter the source path for the distribution files. Then click the Continue button.
3. After the files are copied to your server, click the OK button. The AppleTalk Protocol Configuration dialog box appears (see Figure 5.5).

Figure 5.5.
The AppleTalk
Protocol Configu-
ration dialog box.

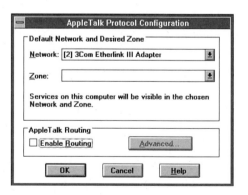

4. In the Zone drop-down list, select the zone you want the shared resources to appear in on the Macintosh clients.

5. If you have multiple network adapters on your server and want to support the routing of AppleTalk data packets, enable the Enable Routing check-box. This then enables the Advanced button. If you click the Advanced button, the AppleTalk routing Configuration dialog box appears so that you can seed (or initialize) the network and create additional zones for your AppleTalk network.

6. After you complete your configuration, click the OK button. When you are prompted to restart your computer, click the Restart Now button to restart your server. After your server restarts, your Macintosh clients can connect to your Microsoft network.

After you install the Services for Macintosh, you might want to create a few volumes or printer connections for your Macintosh clients to use.

REMOTE ACCESS SERVICE

The Remote Access Service is a powerful tool you can use to support your dial-in clients and to provide complete access to your network. You also can use the Remote Access Service to create a wide area network, or you can use it as an Internet gateway. Before you can use the software, however, you must install it. After installing the software, you have to grant access to your remote clients with the Remote Access Administrator. Otherwise, these clients will be able to connect, but they will be denied access to the network and forcibly disconnected. The Remote Access Administrator also is useful for managing your remote access clients, as you will see a little later in this section.

One of the most interesting and powerful aspects of the Windows NT Server Remote Access Service is that it can use any of the installed network transports (NetBEUI, IPX/SPX, or TCP/IP) for your connection. And it can support up to 256 simultaneous client connections on a single server. This can provide the means to create a serious communications server to support your entire sales force. It even works quite well with client/server applications because these applications do not send great amounts of data over the wire. Although it is possible to share applications over the wire, I do not recommend it due to the limited bandwidth. The Remote Access Service should be used to provide limited connectivity; you should share only data files—not applications. Instead of sharing Microsoft Word for Windows, for example, you should install the application directly on the remote user's computer so that it will execute quickly. The data files the user accesses may be on the server, however. This still provides adequate user performance.

Note

The Windows NT Workstation and Windows 95 Remote Access Service can support the NetBEUI, IPX/SPX, and TCP/IP protocols. MS-DOS and Windows 3.x Remote Access Service client software is limited to the NetBEUI protocol. If you want to use the IPX/SPX or TCP/IP transports with these clients, you need additional third-party software such as an Internet SLIP or PPP application to provide your client TCP/IP connection to your Windows NT Server.

INSTALLING THE REMOTE ACCESS SERVICE

Installing the Remote Access Service is a multipart process if you want to get the most out of it. This is because Microsoft has configured the default settings to provide more reliable data communications on slower UARTs. To obtain a minimum connection of 38400bps, you must have a 16450 or better UART. And in reality, a 16450 sometimes drops data, so a 19200 connection is a better selection. You will need a 16550 UART, which contains a 16-byte FIFO (First In First Out) buffer to obtain a speed of 57600. You will need a proprietary UART from DigiBoard, Hayes, or other manufacturers to obtain a reliable 115200 connection rate.

Obtaining these higher data rates requires modifications to the serial.ini file (a temporary modification) or to the modem.inf file (a permanent modification). These files are installed or created during your Remote Access installation. These modifications will be pointed out at the appropriate time during the installation discussion. Before you install the Remote Access Service, you should install your multiport adapter, X.25 adapter, or ISDN adapter. After the hardware is added to the system, you need to install the adapter device driver.

To install the adapter device driver, follow these steps:

1. Open the Control Panel Network applet and click the Add Adapter button. The Add Network Adapter dialog box appears.
2. Scroll down through the Network Adapter Card list to find your adapter. If it is not listed, choose <Other> Requires Disk from Manufacturer and insert the OEM disk into your drive A. Then choose the correct adapter from the list.
3. After installing the device driver and configuring it if required, click the OK button. When prompted to restart your computer, click the Restart Now button and restart the server.

After the server restarts, you can install the Remote Access Service software. This is performed, once again, from the Control Panel Network applet. Just follow these steps:

1. In the Network Settings dialog box, click the Add Software button to display the Add Network Software dialog box.

2. In the Network Software drop-down listbox, select Remote Access Service. When prompted, enter the source path for the distribution files. Click OK.

3. After the files are copied to your server, click Continue in the Network Settings dialog box.

Note

At this time, you will want to interrupt your Remote Access Software installation to modify the `modem.inf` file to permanently change the configuration for your installed modems. You execute Notepad and open the `SystemRoot\System32\ras\modem.inf` file. Then search for your modem. If you have a Supra v.32bis modem, for example, perform a search for Supra. When you find [Supra Fax Modem V.32bis], you have found the right entry. Then you should change the MAXCONNECTBPS parameter from its default of 38400 to 57600. If you have a 28800 modem, change this parameter from 57600 to 115200. Then save the file and continue your Remote Access Service configuration.

4. When the Add Ports dialog box appears, select your first port to use for a remote connection. Then click the OK button to continue.

5. The installation then offers to detect the modem. You can answer yes to this, and you should if you do not know what type of modem you have or cannot find it listed in the Hardware Compatibility List, but it will take some time to try to detect your modem. Clicking Cancel brings you to the Configure Port dialog box.

6. This dialog box offers you the capability to select your modem, pad, or ISDN connection from the Attached Device drop-down listbox. After you select the device, you need to choose a Port Usage entry. You can choose to support only dial in (Receive Calls Only), dial out (Dial Out only), or both (Dial Out and Receive Calls).

Tip

If you click the Settings button in the Configure Port dialog box, you can configure additional modem characteristics. These include enabling or disabling the modem speaker, enabling or disabling hardware flow control, and enabling or disabling error control. All these options are enabled by default. However, you also can choose to enable the hardware compression features (disabled by default) of the modem. In most cases, you should use the software compression because it can outperform the hardware compression (particularly if you do not set the DTE rate to four times your carrier rate—57600 for a 14400 modem). If you have a slower CPU, however, then enabling hardware compression sometimes can outperform software compression. For this feature, you will need to use the trial-and-error method to determine which is better for you and your clients. For what it's worth, when I connect with my laptop (a 486/33), I find that the hardware compression performs better than the software compression.

7. After configuring your modems, click the OK button to return to the Remote Access Setup dialog box. Then click the Network button to display the Network Configuration dialog box.

8. In this dialog box, you choose which protocols to support based on the protocols you have installed. You can choose to enable any protocol (NetBEUI, IPX/SPX, or TCP/IP), or only a single protocol for your dial-out and dial-in connections.

9. For each dial in (Server Settings field), you can choose to allow the clients access to your entire network or to only the server to which they connect. You additionally can set a static range of IP addresses for your TCP/IP clients to use, or you can use DHCP to assign IP addresses. I prefer to use DHCP to assign IP addresses. For your IPX/SPX clients, you can choose to allocate individual network numbers for each client or assign each IPX client the same network number. If you are integrating your Windows NT Server with a Novell NetWare network and will be providing access to it from your remote connections, you should allocate network numbers. Just pick a number that currently is not in use, and enter this in the From field. The To field is entered automatically based on the number of remote access ports you have installed. For both your TCP/IP and IPX/SPX connections, you can allow your dial-in clients to allocate a predetermined IP address or network address.

Tip

You also can set encryption settings for your dial-in clients in the Network Configuration dialog box. The default is to enable the Microsoft encrypted authentication checkbox. This setting may prevent PPP and SLIP connections from being authenticated if you are not using the Microsoft remote access client. To prevent this from happening, enable the Allow Any Authentication Including Clear Text option checkbox. This option still attempts to encrypt the password, but if all else fails, it supports a clear text password attempt.

Tip

If you are really concerned about the security of your data when it is sent over the remote access connection, you can enable the Require Data Encryption checkbox setting. This encrypts all data transmitted over the connection.

10. After clicking the OK button, you are returned to the Remote Access Setup dialog box. If you have additional ports to add, the quick and easy way is to click the Clone button. This copies your current configuration to the next available port. Repeat this step for each port you want to install. If you have a different modem on a port, just select it and click the Configure button. You then can pick out the correct modem for it. Just remember to change the modem settings if you choose another modem in order to configure it properly.

11. After all your modems have been installed and configured, click the Continue button in the Remote Access Setup dialog box. Then click OK in the Network Settings dialog box. You will then be prompted to restart your computer. At this point, be sure to click the Restart Now button.

CONFIGURING THE REMOTE ACCESS SERVICE

After you restart your computer as recommended in the preceding instructions, you can use the Remote Access application located in the Remote Access Service group in Program Manager to dial out and connect to other Remote Access Service servers. If you did not perform the modifications to the `modem.inf` file during the installation, you should modify the `serial.ini` file, located in the `SystemRoot\System32\ras` directory. For each COM port installed, change the `MAXCONNECTBPS` and IntialBps parameters to reflect your highest DTE rate (57600 for a 14400 modem, and 115200 for a 28800 modem).

After you make this change to your `serial.ini` file, you can run the Remote Access client. The first time you do, you are prompted to create a phone book entry. In the Edit Phone Book Entry dialog box, enter a name for your connection in the Entry Name field, a phone number to dial in the Phone Number field, and a comment for the entry in the Description field.

USING THE REMOTE ACCESS ADMINISTRATOR

The Remote Access Admin application is located in the Remote Access Service group of Program Manager. You use this application to grant access to your dial-in users, to check the status of the communications port, to send messages to your remotely connected users, and to stop or start the Remote Access Service on your computer or a remote computer.

PREPARING FOR CLIENT CONNECTIVITY

Before your dial-in clients can access your network through the Remote Access Service, you must grant these users permission to connect through a dial-in connection.

For each user you want to provide dial-in access to, follow these steps:

1. Choose Permissions from the Users menu. The Remote Access Permissions dialog box appears.
2. Select the user name in the Users field.
3. Enable the Grant Dialin Permission to User checkbox.

Tip

> To quickly grant permission to all users to dial into your network, click the Grant All button. To delete all user permissions, click the Revoke All button.

4. Specify a callback option of No Call Back, Set By Caller, or Preset To. If you specify Preset To, be sure to enter a complete phone number, including any dial-out codes, calling card codes, and so on. This option is used to provide one of two features. It can be used to enhance your system security by using the Preset To option to always call a user back at a specific phone number. Or it can be used to lower the bill of a remote user (such as a member of your sales department who travels a lot) by using the Set By Caller option. The user can specify a phone number at which to be called back, so that the client he is with will not have to pay long distance charges. If you specify Preset To, be sure to enter a complete phone number, including any dial out codes, calling card codes, and so on.

5. Click the OK button to exit the Remote Access Permissions dialog box, and you're done. Your remote access callers now can dial into your network.

MONITORING REMOTE ACCESS CONNECTIONS

To determine who is using your remote access connections, just double-click the server entry, or choose Server | Communications Ports to display the Communications Ports dialog box. If you have any connected users, the User field lists the connected user and the Started field lists the time the user connected to your server. If you have an active connection, the following buttons are enabled:

◆ Disconnect User: Disconnects the selected user.

◆ Send Message: Sends a message to the selected user.

◆ Send to All: Sends a message to all connected users. This is extremely useful when you are about to bring down the server or restart the Remote Access Server because you can warn your connected users beforehand.

Note

To send a message to a Windows 3.x or Windows 95 client, the Windows messaging utility (winpopup.exe) must be running on the client computer.

If you want to determine the compression ratios or errors that have occurred on the selected port, click the Port Status button.

USING REMOTE ACCESS AS A GATEWAY TO THE INTERNET

In order to use the Remote Access Service to connect to the Internet, you need a PPP (Point to Point Protocol) or SLIP (Serial Line Internet Protocol) account from an Internet provider. After you get an account, all you need to do is create a phone book entry with the Remote Access client.

Follow these steps:

1. Click the Edit button to display the Edit Phone Book Entry dialog box. Click the Advanced button to see more options in the dialog box. Click the Network button to display the Network Protocol Settings dialog box.

2. Disable the NetBEUI and IPX protocols in the PPP entry if you will be using a PPP connection to connect to the Internet service provider. If you have a preassigned IP address or DNS IP address from your Internet provider, click the TCP/IP Settings button to enter this information.

If you will be using a SLIP connection to connect to your Internet provider, enable the SLIP radio button instead of the default PPP radio button.

3. Click the OK button to return to the Edit Phone Book Entry dialog box. Then click OK to return to the Remote Access client main window.

After you complete these steps, just double-click your new entry to dial out and connect to your Internet provider. If you will be using your RAS connection as a gateway to the Internet so that your LAN clients can access the Internet through this same server, you have a bit of additional work to do. Specifically you need to add the following values to the following keys in the registry:

Key:

HKEY_LOCAL_MACHINE\System\CurrentControlSet\Services\RasArp\Parameters

Value:

DisableOtherSrcPackets

Key:

HKEY_LOCAL_MACHINE\System\CurrentControlSet\Services\RasMan\PPP\IPCP

Value:

PriorityBasedOnSubNetwork

These values are regular double-words (REG_DWORD). DisableOtherSrcPackets should be set to 0, and PriorityBasedOnSubNetwork should be set to 1. The first entry specifies that network packets should use the IP address of the LAN client for network traffic sent over the RAS link instead of the IP address of the computer providing the RAS connection. This will ensure that the data is routed to the proper client. The second entry specifies that the network packets should be sent to the appropriate destination and adapter, based on the individual subnet. This is usually required, for example, when your LAN has a subnet like 206.170.127.x and your RAS connection (or your ISP's subnet) is 206.170.126.x. If the PriorityBasedOnSubNetwork is not set to 1 (the default is assumed to be 0) then all network traffic would be routed through your network adapter. When you set this value, however, your LAN traffic will be passed over your network adapter, and your Internet traffic will be passed over your RAS connection.

Note

There is one other critical part to this process that must be completed before your clients can use your server as a gateway to the Internet. Your ISP must create a routing table, and your server and client IP addresses must be added to their DNS servers (or your DNS server could be a client of their DNS server and replicate the information). If you experience problems transmitting or receiving data over the Internet, and your ISP has performed the above steps, look at your routing table using the ROUTE PRINT command. You may need to modify this information, and your ISP should be able to help you through this step, in order to successfully use your computer as a gateway.

SUMMARY

The primary focus of this chapter was integration. You learned about your LAN Manager and LAN Manager for UNIX domains, Novell NetWare networks, UNIX networks, and Macintosh networks. You also looked at how to install and configure the various services to provide optimum connectivity for these networks. You then moved on to explore the Remote Access Service installation and basic configuration.

In the next chapter, you will use Server Manager to manage your servers and client computers. You also will look at managing your user accounts and groups with User Manager for Domains.

CHAPTER 6

Basic Administrative Tools

As a network administrator, your primary duties consist of constantly adding new computers and new users, or modifying existing user accounts. It seems that there is always at least one more person who requires network access. This requires that you install the network client software on his computer and create his user account on the server. Then there is the user who constantly forgets his password, which requires your interaction to correct. It's a never-ending story, but at least it provides job security.

The tools you use to perform these tasks are included in the Program Manager's Administrative Tools group. These tools include Server Manager and User Manager for Domains. In this chapter, you'll explore the capabilities of these tools for managing your network. You'll learn some of the command-line alternatives to managing your network in case you prefer to use the command line for your day-to-day activities.

USING SERVER MANAGER

Server Manager is a wonderful administrative tool. It encapsulates the manipulation of a remote computer's resource management into a single application. With it, you can manage your network client (Windows NT only) computer's shared resources and even determine what shared resources your other network clients are using. You also will use this tool to create computer accounts and to synchronize your backup domain controllers database with your primary domain controller. And you can perform all this from your own server or workstation.

Note

To use a Windows NT Workstation or a Windows client to perform these tasks, you first must install the software. You can find this software in the \CLIENTS\SRVTOOLS directory on the Windows NT Server CD-ROM. You also can install the software from a network sharepoint. You can create this sharepoint and copy the installation software by using the Network Client Administrator.

This discussion assumes that you are using the local domain for your administration. If you want to administer a different domain, just choose Select Domain from the Computer menu, and then choose the domain to administer in the Select Domain dialog box.

CREATING COMPUTER ACCOUNTS

The most important task of Server Manager is the creation of computer accounts. A computer account has to be the same as the computer name of a client computer.

A client can be a Windows NT Server backup domain controller, a Windows NT Server operating in server mode, or a Windows NT Workstation, for example. It is the beginning point of all access for domain members. This component is used to establish the trusted connection between your domain controller and your client. This trusted connection is the beginning of the network authentication process for domain members.

The major benefit of creating the computer account with Server Manager is that by creating the computer account in advance, you also can specify the computer name on the client. This can enable you to regulate the naming convention of client workstations on your network. So instead of having names like FRODO, SUPER-MAN, and JUNGLE JIM, you can have responsible and descriptive names like FRED WARD, ACCOUNTING, or MARKETING. Using Server Manager provides another important benefit: You don't have to give out an administrative password (which you would have to change afterward) to a user, and you don't have to physically go to the location of the client computer and enter your administrative account and password in the Control Panel Network applet's Domain/Workgroup Settings dialog box.

An additional administrative benefit provided by being a domain user is that a domain client computer automatically adds the Domain Admins global group to the client computer's local Administrators group. This provides you, the domain administrator, with administrative capabilities on the client machine locally or remotely.

Warning

On a network with two-way trust relationships, if you do not have a computer account, you are not a trusted member of the domain and you have no access to a domain controller. This means that even if you have a user account on the domain controller, without a computer account, you cannot be authenticated at the user level. And if you cannot be authenticated, you cannot access network resources. On a network with no trust relationships or with a one-way trust relationship, a user account can be mapped to a user account on the remote computer. This local-user-account-to-remote-user-account mapping provides limited access to network resources.

You also can use computer accounts to restrict access by a client to a specific set of workstations on your network. This possibility is discussed when you look at User Manager for Domains and the creation of user accounts later in this chapter in the section titled "Creating User Accounts."

To create a computer account, follow these steps:

1. Choose Add to Domain from the Computer menu. The Add Computer to Domain dialog box appears.
2. Select the computer type. A computer type can be a Windows NT Workstation or Windows NT Server operating in server mode, or a Windows NT backup domain controller. Enter the computer name in the Computer Name field.
3. Click the Add button.
4. Repeat steps 2 and 3 for each computer account you want to create. Then click the Close button.

Deleting a computer account with Server Manager is as simple as selecting the computer account and pressing the Delete key. Alternatively, you can choose the Remove from Domain command from the Computer menu.

Caution

Computer accounts have unique security identifiers. If you delete an account and then re-create it, your user must rejoin the domain. If your user changes from one domain to another domain and then attempts to rejoin the original domain using the original computer account, the attempt will fail. If the user changes from a domain to a workgroup and then attempts to rejoin the domain using the original computer account, the attempt will fail. If the user changes the computer name and then attempts to log on, the attempt will fail. If he then changes the name back to the original name, the attempt still will fail. In all these cases, a new computer account must be created for the user. The computer account can be the same name, but you have to delete the original account and then re-create it.

COMPUTER ACCOUNT MANAGEMENT FROM THE COMMAND LINE

Adding or deleting computer accounts from the command line is an easy task. As with most network-related commands, it begins with the NET command.

This version of the NET command is available only on Windows NT Server computers:

```
NET COMPUTER \\ComputerName /ADD /DEL
```

Explanations of the syntax follow:

> *ComputerName*: Name of the computer account you want to create.
>
> /ADD: Specifies that you want to create the computer account and add the computer to the domain.
>
> /DEL: Specifies that you want to delete the computer account and remove the computer from the domain.

SYNCHRONIZING THE DOMAIN DATABASE

As mentioned in earlier chapters, the domain database, which includes your computer and user accounts, physically resides on the primary domain controller. Changes to this database are replicated to your backup domain controllers every time you add a new computer or user account or modify existing accounts. Sometimes this replication process fails due to a poor network connection or other problems. You can use Server Manager to manually replicate this database to all controllers in the domain or to a specific controller in the domain.

To synchronize all the backup domain controllers with the primary domain controller, follow these steps:

1. Select the primary domain controller in the main window of Server Manager.

2. Choose Synchronize Entire Domain from the Computer menu.

   You receive a message telling you that the process may take several minutes to complete and a prompt telling you to continue.

   You receive this message because synchronizing the account database can use quite a bit of network bandwidth and can affect your network performance. So you should use this command during peak network usage hours only if you absolutely have to, particularly if you have a large number of accounts and users to replicate to the backup domain controller.

3. Click the OK button to proceed.

4. You are informed that you should check the event log of the primary and backup domain controllers to make sure that the replication process succeeded. The idea here is to make sure that the primary domain controller and the backup domain controller sent and received the same number of accounts. This information is contained in the system event log Net Logon.

To synchronize a specific backup domain controller with the primary domain controller, follow these steps:

1. Select the backup domain controller in the Server Manager main window.

2. Choose Synchronize with Primary Domain Controller from the Computer menu. You will see a message that the process may take several minutes to complete. Click the OK button to proceed.

3. You are informed that you should check the event log of the primary and backup domain controller to make sure that the replication process succeeded.

Because all computer accounts and user accounts have to be created on the primary domain controller's database, if the PDC fails and goes offline, you cannot make any account modifications. If this occurs, you can promote a backup domain controller (BDC) to a PDC temporarily to make account modifications. After you solve the problem with the PDC, you can bring it back online. There are several items to consider when a failed PDC is restored or when promoting a BDC to a PDC:

◆ When you promote a backup domain controller to a primary domain controller, all client connections on both domain controllers are terminated. This could cause a loss of data for your network users. Because of this possibility, you should warn your users to disconnect prior to promoting a backup domain controller.

◆ When you use a RAS connection to synchronize domains, you cannot use a RAS Server on the current primary domain controller or on the backup domain controller you want to promote. This is because the RAS connection will be terminated before the role change is completed. When the connection terminates, the request is rolled back and the backup domain controller is not promoted.

◆ When you bring a failed PDC back online and a BDC was promoted to a PDC, you now have two PDCs on the domain. This prevents you from making any changes to the account database. To correct the situation, you must demote one of the PDCs to a BDC.

◆ Before you bring your PDC back online, you should keep a few considerations in mind. Never use a domain controller that has stale data as a synchronization source. To prevent this from occurring, demote your failed PDC to a BDC. Then force the synchronization of the BDC with the current PDC. Then you can promote the BDC (the original PDC) back to a PDC and return to your original configuration. Synchronizing the database first ensures that the account database update will be successful (because you can check the event logs to make sure) and that any changes you made while the original PDC was down will be maintained. If you fail to synchronize the database prior to demoting the current PDC, you might overwrite your user databases on the backup controllers with an older copy (the one on your failed PDC) and lose any account modifications that occurred while the original PDC was down.

To promote a BDC to a PDC, follow these steps:

1. Select the backup domain controller in the Server Manager main window.

2. Choose Promote to Primary Domain Controller from the Computer menu. You see a message telling you that the process may take several minutes to complete. Click the OK button to proceed.

3. After the account synchronization finishes, the backup domain controller is displayed as a primary domain controller and the old primary domain controller is displayed as a backup domain controller in the main window.

SYNCHRONIZING THE ACCOUNT DATABASE FROM THE COMMAND LINE

You can synchronize the entire domain account database by running the following command from a command prompt:

```
NET ACCOUNTS /SYNC /DOMAIN
```

Descriptions of this syntax follow:

/SYNC: Synchronizes the entire domain if it is executed on a PDC, or it synchronizes just the BDC with the PDC if it is running on a BDC.

/DOMAIN: Synchronizes the entire domain regardless of where the application is executed. Normally, this switch is used only when the command is executed on a Windows NT Workstation or Windows NT Server operating in server mode.

MANAGING REMOTE COMPUTER RESOURCES

You can use Server Manager to manage your local or remote computer resources. I find this capability to manage remote computer resources highly useful in my day-to-day administrative activities because it does not require me to leave my desk. With Server Manager, you can stop, start, pause, continue, or configure system services on a remote computer. You use it to create new sharepoints or to delete existing sharepoints. You can use it to determine the users connected to or even to determine the sharepoints available or in use on the remote computer. And if that is not enough for you, you might consider that you also can use Server Manager to configure the Replication and Alert services on a remote computer. In this section, you will learn how to use each of these features to remotely manage your Windows NT servers and workstations.

MANAGING SERVICES

The normal method to access a Windows NT computer's service control manager database is to use the local computer's Control Panel Services applet. With this tool, you can stop, start, pause, or continue the execution of a service. You can use Server Manager to perform this same task; highlight the computer in the main window and choose Services from the Computer menu. The Services on *ComputerName* (SRV in this case) dialog box shown in Figure 6.1 appears.

Figure 6.1.
The Services on
SRV dialog box.

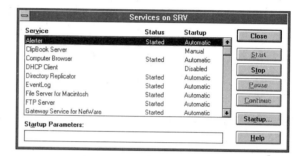

Tip

Before you stop a service that a client is using, you should pause it. This prevents any new clients from connecting to this service. You then can send a message (by choosing Send Message from the Computer menu) to the connected users to inform them of your intention to shut down the service. The clients then have the chance to save their data before you shut down the service.

The buttons you can click to perform selected functions follow:

◆ Start: Starts a service that is not executing. If you enter any command-line parameters in the Startup Parameters field, these parameters are passed to the service when it starts executing.

◆ Stop: Stops a service that is currently running.

◆ Pause: Prevents new connections to a service (if it is a network-aware service, such as the Server service), while still providing support to currently connected users.

◆ Continue: Continues the operation of a paused service.

◆ Startup: Changes the startup characteristics for a service. The available options provided in the Services dialog box are the Startup Type and Log On As fields. The Startup Type entry can be Automatic, Manual, or

Disabled. Log On As can specify that the service should use the default system account or a user account that you created with User Manager for Domains. If you specify a user account, you also have to specify a user password.

MANAGING SHAREPOINTS

Just as you can manipulate a remote computer's service control manager database with Server Manager, you also can manipulate a remote computer's network sharepoints.

First, select the computer in the Server Manager main window to highlight it. Then choose Shared Directories from the Computer menu. The Shared Directories dialog box appears, as shown in Figure 6.2.

Figure 6.2.
The Shared
Directories dia-
log box.

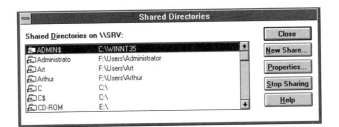

You can create a new network sharepoint by clicking the New Share button. The New Share dialog box appears, asking you to specify the share name, path, comment, and number of users that can connect to the share. By clicking the Permissions button, you can specify the share level permissions. The New Share dialog box is discussed in depth in the following chapter in the section "Creating Network Sharepoints."

You can modify an existing share by highlighting a shared directory and then clicking the Properties button. The Shared Directory dialog box appears, which is similar to the New Share dialog box. The Shared Directory dialog box also is discussed in detail in Chapter 7, "Resource Management Tools."

If you want to remove an existing network sharepoint, highlight the shared directory and click the Stop Sharing button.

Warning

Clicking the Stop Sharing button in the Shared Directories dialog box immediately stops sharing the directory. There is no confirmation message. Before you do this, you should check to see who is using the share. This is discussed in the next section.

PERFORMING RESOURCE ACCOUNTING

If you want to determine which users are connected to a computer, the network sharepoints available on a computer, or the sharepoints in use on a remote computer, you can do so by double-clicking a specific computer listed in the Server Manager's main window, or you can select a computer in the main window and choose Properties from the Computer menu. The Properties dialog box appears, as shown in Figure 6.3. This is the same dialog box displayed in the Control Panel Server applet.

Figure 6.3.
The Properties
dialog box.

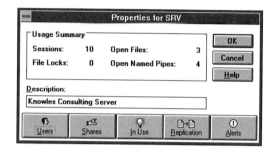

The Properties dialog box enables you to access the following functions:

◆ Usage Summary: Lists the number of sessions, file locks, open files, and named pipes in use on a computer. The number of sessions actually reflects the number of users connected to the computer because each connected computer uses one session.

◆ Users: Displays the User Sessions dialog box, shown in Figure 6.4, and determines which users are connected to the computer and what resources they have in use. The upper box lists the connected users, the connection to a specific computer, the number of open files, the total connection time, the total idle time, and whether the users have connected with guest privileges. The lower box lists the resource, number of open files, and total connection time in use by a selected user. To disconnect a specific user, highlight the user and click the Disconnect button. To disconnect all users from all resources, just click the Disconnect All button.

◆ Shares: Performs a similar action as the Users button. After you click this button, the Shared Resources dialog box appears, as shown in Figure 6.5. The emphasis here is on the sharepoints. The upper box lists the sharepoints, number of connections, and physical path of the shared directory. The lower box lists the connected users, total connection time, and whether the connection currently is active. To disconnect all users from a specific sharepoint, highlight the sharepoint and click the Disconnect button. To disconnect all users from all resources, just click the Disconnect All button.

Figure 6.4.
The User Sessions
dialog box.

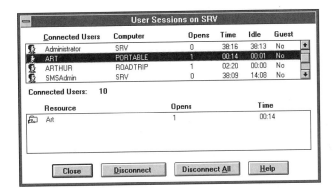

Figure 6.5.
The Shared
Resources dia-
log box.

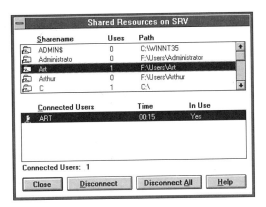

◆ In Use: Clicking In Use displays the Open Resources dialog box, as shown in Figure 6.6. This lists the resources that currently are open. This dialog box also displays named pipe connections (shown as a gray pipe), print jobs (a small printer icon), LAN Manager communications device queues (a small gray microphone), unrecognized types (a question mark), and files (a small document icon). It also includes information about the user who has opened the resource, the permission granted when the resource was opened, any locks, and the path name to the open resource. To disconnect all users from a specific resource, highlight the resource and click the Close Resource button. To disconnect all users from all resources, just click the Close All Resources button.

Figure 6.6.
The Open
Resources dia-
log box.

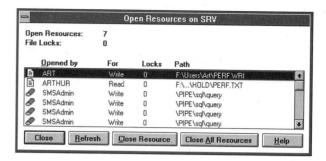

Note

Replication and alerts are discussed later in this chapter in the sections "Configuring the Directory Replicator Service" and "Configuring Alerts."

Caution

If you disconnect a user, any files that have been opened by the user will not be closed properly and the user might lose data. Disconnecting a user in this fashion also does not prevent him from reconnecting. If the user or the user's application attempts a reconnect, it will be granted.

CONFIGURING THE DIRECTORY REPLICATOR SERVICES

You use the Directory Replicator Service to copy directories and files from a Windows NT Server to another server or workstation. The service consists of an export component specifying the root directory to export and an import component used to copy directories and files from the export server. The export server is limited to a single directory tree, which consists of the root directory and a maximum of 32 nested subdirectories. To configure the replication service, you need to perform the following tasks:

◆ Create the logon account for the service. You can create this account with User Manager for Domains, and it must have the following properties:

    ◆ It must be a member of the Backup Operators group.

    ◆ It must have the Password Never Expires option enabled.

    ◆ It must have no logon hour restrictions.

For specific information on these settings and how to add user accounts to groups, refer to the section "Creating User Accounts," later in this chapter.

◆ Configure the replication service startup values. The Directory Replicator Service's startup values must be changed to start up automatically and to use the This Account option in the Log On As field. The account specified must be the account you created in the previous step.

◆ Set the logon script path. The replication service is really designed to copy your logon scripts from one domain controller to your other domain controllers. Generally, this directory is your SystemRoot\System32\REPL\Import\Scripts path, which is where your logon scripts are stored. If you want to import your scripts to a different directory path, just change the Logon Script Path entry in the Directory Replication dialog box to the directory path you want to use. (See Figure 6.7.) This path is used by your domain controller to locate your logon scripts during the user authentication process. Do not leave a blank entry in the Logon Script Path field or your logon scripts will not be found when your network clients log onto the network.

Figure 6.7.
The Directory
Replication
dialog box.

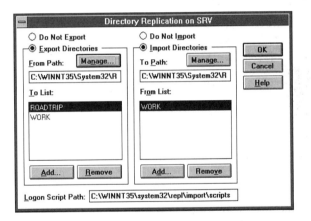

Note

When you configure the replication service to start, it creates a special share called REPL$ based on the directory you specify as the logon script path. Generally, this is SystemRoot\System32\REPL\Export.

◆ Configure the server to export a directory tree. This process is a bit complex and is covered in the following section.

◆ Configure the client to import a directory tree. This is similar to configuring for an export server. This is discussed later in this chapter in "Configuring the Import Server."

CONFIGURING THE EXPORT SERVER

To configure your Directory Replicator Service to export a directory tree, use Server Manager. Just double-click the name of the server to display the Properties dialog box, and then click the Replication button to display the Directory Replication dialog box. Then follow these steps:

1. Enable the replication service by enabling the Export Directories radio button.

2. Add computers to replicate to in the To listbox. You do this by clicking the Add button at the bottom left of the screen. The Select Domain dialog box appears.

3. Select the individual domains and computers to which you want to export. Then click the OK button. You are returned to the Directory Replication dialog box. To add additional computers, repeat steps 2 and 3.

Note

By default, the local domain is always included as an export partner, unless you add an entry in the To listbox. If you do add an entry, the local domain no longer is automatically included. To continue to export to the local domain, you need to add the domain name to the To listbox.

4. Specify the export path (if the default is not acceptable, although in most cases you will not need to change this entry) in the From Path field. Generally, this is the SystemRoot\System32\Repl\Export directory.

5. Add the subdirectories off the root export directory. Click the From Path Manage button, which displays the Manage Exported Directories dialog box. (See Figure 6.8.)

6. Specify the subdirectories to export by clicking the Add button. The Add Subdirectory dialog box appears, in which you can specify the subdirectories of the root export path to export. For each subdirectory you select, you must specify whether you want to wait until the files in the directory have been stable (no changes have been made for two minutes) by enabling or disabling the Wait Until Stabilized checkbox, and whether you want any subdirectories to be copied by enabling or disabling the Entire Subtree checkbox. Remember that you must repeat this step for each subdirectory you want to export.

For each subdirectory entry, you can see some status information by looking at the following columns:

◆ Locks: Specifies the number of active locks on the subdirectory.

◆ Stabilize: Indicates whether the files must be idle for two minutes before replication can occur (which can prevent partial replication changes if the files are very active).

◆ Subtree: Indicates that all subdirectories are to be replicated.

◆ Locked Since: Indicates that a subdirectory has been locked since a specific date/time.

Figure 6.8.
The Manage
Exported Directo-
ries dialog box.

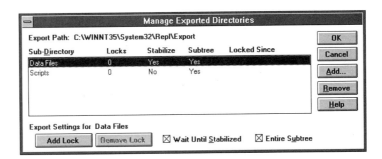

Tip

If you are going to be making a lot of changes to a subdirectory you have marked for export, use the Add Lock button to lock the directory. This prevents the directory from being replicated until all the locks are released.

CONFIGURING THE IMPORT SERVER

This process is quite similar to exporting a directory tree. From the Directory Replication dialog box, follow these steps:

1. Enable the replication service by enabling the Import Directories radio button.

2. Add computers to replicate to in the From listbox. You do this by clicking the Add button at the bottom right of the screen. The Select Domain dialog box appears.

Note

By default, the local domain is always included as an import partner unless you add an entry in the From listbox. If you do add an entry, the local domain no longer is automatically included. To continue to import from the local domain, you need to add the domain name in the From listbox.

3. Select the individual domains and computers to which you want to import. Then click the OK button. You are returned to the Directory Replication dialog box. To add additional computers, repeat steps 2 and 3.

4. Add the subdirectories off the root import directory. Click the To Path Manage button, which displays the Manage Imported Directories dialog box. (See Figure 6.9.)

Figure 6.9.
The Manage
Imported Directo-
ries dialog box

5. The only difference in the Manage Imported Directories dialog box is that the status information for each entry consists of the number of locks on the directory, the status (OK, which indicates that the directory is receiving regular updates; No Master, which indicates that no updates are being received; No Sync, which indicates that the directory has received updates, but the current data is outdated; and a blank entry, which indicates that replication has never occurred), the date/time the last update occurred, and the date/time of the oldest lock on the directory.

Tip

If you want to prevent an import directory from being updated, just select it and click the Add Lock button. An import directory with a lock will not be updated.

Caution

If you are importing directories from a domain or server located on the other side of a WAN connection, the import might fail from the local domain. To ensure that this does not occur, manually add the domain or computer name in the From field of the Manage Imported Directories dialog box.

Windows NT Workstation cannot act as a replication export server. It can be used only to import a directory tree from an export server. Also, Windows NT Workstation cannot change the default replication path from `SystemRoot\System32\Repl\Import\Scripts`.

CONFIGURING ALERTS

You use alerts to notify a domain administrator of a serious problem that has occurred on a Windows NT computer. You can send an alert to a particular domain user or to a specific computer monitored by several administrators or support personnel.

If you want to guarantee that the alert will be sent, you also should modify the client workstation to start the Alert and Messenger services at system startup. This ensures that the services are functioning and available to send administrative alerts. If the services are left in their default startup setting of Manual, the services will attempt to send the alert, but might fail due to unforeseen circumstances. If they fail, the alert is not sent. A Windows NT Server computer has a default startup setting of Automatic and does not have to be reconfigured. In order to receive an administrative alert, the messenger service must be running.

To configure the Alert service, use Server Manager. Just double-click the name of the server to display the Properties dialog box. Then, follow these steps:

1. Click the Alerts button in the Server dialog box. The Alerts dialog box shown in Figure 6.10 appears.

Figure 6.10.
The Alerts
dialog box.

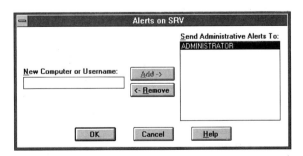

2. To add a new computer or user to be notified, enter the computer or user name in the New Computer or Username field and then click the Add button. The computer or user name then is moved to the Send Administrative Alerts To box.

3. To remove a computer or user, select the computer or user name in the Send Administrative Alerts To box and click the Remove button. This moves the computer or user name to the New Computer or Username field.

Note

You do not have to include the double backslashes (\\) for a computer name, as you do for just about every other usage involving a computer name. If you do, the double backslashes are dropped when the name is moved.

4. To add or remove additional computers or users, repeat step 2 or 3.

5. When you finish entering or removing computer and user names, click the OK button to return to the Server Manager main window.

MANAGING YOUR MACINTOSH CLIENTS

Just as you can use the Properties dialog box to manage the Microsoft clients connected to your computer, you can use the MacFile Properties dialog box to manage your Macintosh clients. To access this dialog box, as shown in Figure 6.11, choose Properties from the MacFile menu.

Figure 6.11.
The MacFile
Properties dia-
log box.

The MacFile Properties dialog box includes the following options:

◆ Usage Summary: Lists the active AppleTalk sessions (the total number of connected Macintosh users), open file forks (combined data and resource forks), and the number of locks on open file forks. It's a quick indication of resource usage on the selected computer.

◆ Users: Displays the Macintosh Users dialog box. It works just like the User Sessions dialog box mentioned earlier in the "Performing Resource Accounting" section, except that it displays connected Macintosh users. To disconnect an individual user from all connected resources, select the user in the upper edit field and click the Disconnect button. To disconnect all connected users, click the Disconnect All button.

◆ Volumes: Performs the same action as the Shares button for Microsoft clients, except in this case, it displays the Macintosh-Accessible Volumes dialog box. You use this box to display Macintosh users connected to a shared resource. The upper box lists the Macintosh volumes by name, the total number of connected users, and the system path to the shared resource. To disconnect a user, select the volume in the upper box. The lower entry then lists the individual users, the total time they have been connected to the resource, and whether it is currently in use. Just select a user and click the Disconnect button. To disconnect all users from the resource, click the Disconnect All button.

◆ Files: Performs the same basic functions as the In Use button in the Properties dialog box for Microsoft clients. The only real difference is that the Files Opened by Macintosh Users dialog box is displayed instead. And, instead of files, you'll see entries for file forks. To close an individual file, select the user and click the Close Fork button. To close all forks, just click the Close All Forks button. If your dialog box has been on-screen for a while, you can click the Refresh button to update the display.

Caution

If you disconnect a user, any files that have been opened by the user will not be closed properly and the user might lose data. Before you take such a drastic action, you should send the user a message warning him of the impending disconnection and giving him the chance to save his data. You can do this by selecting the user in the upper entry and clicking the Send Message button. A dialog box appears where you can specify the message to send.

◆ Attributes: Enables you to modify the behavior of the Macintosh service. After you click Attributes, the MacFile Attributes dialog box appears. Here, you can specify the name your Macintosh clients will see when they browse for resources on this computer by clicking the Change button in the Server Name for AppleTalk Workstations field. You can specify a message that the Macintosh user will see when he logs onto the server in the Logon Message field. This text field can contain up to four lines of text. The Security field enables you to specify whether guests can log onto the server, whether

Macintosh workstations can save their passwords locally, and whether the Microsoft UAM must be used to encrypt the user password at logon time. In the Sessions field, you can determine the maximum number of simultaneous Macintosh clients that can connect to this server.

For more details on the Microsoft UAM and how to install it on your Macintosh clients, refer to Chapter 5, "Integrating Windows NT Server with Other Networks."

Tip

> If you limit the number of simultaneous Macintosh connections to a single server, you can improve the performance of that server. An unlimited connection setting is limited only by the network bandwidth, but as with any server, the more connections you have, the poorer the server's performance will be. If you have multiple Windows NT Server computers, you should distribute the load evenly for best performance.

You can manage your Macintosh volumes locally with File Manager (as described in the next chapter), or by choosing MacFile | Volumes, which displays the Macintosh-Accessible Volumes dialog box, as shown in Figure 6.12. In this box, you can create a new volume, change the existing properties of a volume, or delete a volume.

*Figure 6.12.
The Macintosh-
Accessible
Volumes dia-
log box.*

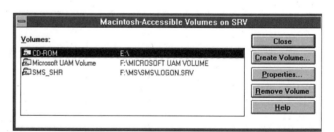

You can create a new Macintosh volume by clicking the Create Volume button to display the Create Macintosh-Accessible Volume dialog box. If you just want to share any other resource, you need to supply a name for the share, a physical path name, and a password (and confirm it too). If you want to further restrict access to the shared volume, you can specify the volume is read-only by enabling the This Volume is Read-Only checkbox, or you can restrict guests from accessing the volume by disabling the Guest Can Use This Volume checkbox in the Volume Security field. You can specify the number of simultaneous connections in the User Limit field.

Tip

> To really restrict the usage of the shared volume, click the Permissions button. The Directory Permissions dialog box appears, in which you can specify additional permission settings by group. This includes the capability to See Files (the same as the List Files permission), See Folders (the same as the List Directories permission), or Make Changes (the same as the Change permission). You can further specify to replace all permissions on all subdirectories of the parent directory (when you make a change to the permission settings), and you can specify that the user cannot move, rename, or delete existing files.

You can change the settings of an existing volume by clicking the Properties button. This displays the Properties of Macintosh-Accessible Volume dialog box; the name and physical path are preselected and cannot be changed. You can change all the other settings, however. Deleting a volume is as simple as selecting the shared volume and clicking the Remove Volume button. This displays a confirmation message box (unlike the Stop Sharing button of the Shared Directories dialog box for Microsoft clients), giving you the chance to confirm your selection before the sharepoint is deleted.

Using User Manager for Domains

User Manager for Domains, as shown in Figure 6.13, is the focal point for all user account manipulation. You can use User Manager for Domains to create or modify local and global groups, to manipulate user accounts, and to set system policies. You also use User Manager for Domains to enable auditing on your domain and to set up trust relationships. In this section, you will look at these features and explore the usage of each to get a better grasp of the user-management features provided in Windows NT Server.

Note

> This discussion assumes that you are using the local domain for your administration. If you want to administer a different domain, just choose Select Domain from the User menu and then select the domain to administer in the Select Domain dialog box.

Figure 6.13.
User Manager for
Domains.

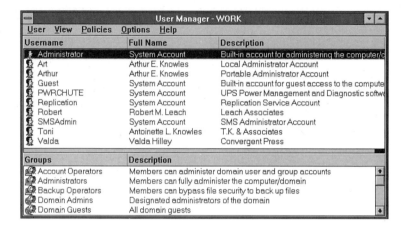

CREATING AND USING LOCAL AND GLOBAL GROUPS

A group is a named resource that includes one or more users. You can use these groups with any application that can assign permissions or auditing to make your job easier. Instead of assigning individual users to a resource to assign permissions or enabling auditing, you can use a group. The same principle applies to managing user rights (which are discussed in detail later, in the section "Assigning User Rights"). When you assign user rights to a group and then add users to the group, all users of the group obtain the same user rights.

You can use two types of groups with Windows NT Server. You can use local groups, which can contain user accounts or other global groups. You also can use global groups, which can contain only user accounts. Local groups apply only to the local domain. Global groups can be used across domains. When you look at a local group in User Manager for Domains, it has an icon associated with it that includes a computer with user profiles layered on it. A global group's icon is a picture of the world with user profiles layered on top of it.

Tip

You can use a global group from a foreign domain to assign user rights and permissions to a shared resource on a local domain without creating a trust relationship. This method has less overhead and does not use as much of your network bandwidth as a trust relationship between two domains.

Several built-in groups are included in User Manager for Domains. Each of these groups include different user rights and can be divided into local or global groups. Table 6.1 summarizes these groups.

TABLE 6.1. THE BUILT-IN USER MANAGER FOR DOMAINS GROUPS.

Name	Type	Enables Members of this Group to
Administrators	Local	Fully administer the local computer and any domain resources.
Account Operators	Local	Administer domain user and group accounts.
Backup Operators	Local	Bypass the security restrictions on directories and files in order to back them up.
Domain Admins	Global	Fully administer domain resources. These members are added automatically to the local Administrators group of all domain members.
Domain Guests	Global	Be added automatically to the Guests group.
Domain Users	Global	Be added automatically to the local Users group.
Guests	Local	Have limited access to the domain. In effect, these users can sign on if they know a guest account and password, but they cannot change any settings on the local computer.
Print Operators	Local	Administer the domain printers.
Replicator	Local	Be granted the appropriate privileges to replicate files in the domain. This group is used only to support the Directory Replicator Service.
Server Operators	Local	Administer the servers in the domain. This includes logging on locally, restarting the server, or shutting down the server.
Users	Local	Be normal users of the domain and have limited access to the domain and their own computer. They can make some configuration changes to their environment, but they have limited functionality. They cannot create new shared directories or stop and start services, for example.

6

BASIC ADMINISTRATIVE TOOLS

To create a local group, follow these steps:

1. Choose New Local Group from the User menu. The New Local Group dialog box appears. (See Figure 6.14.)

Figure 6.14.
The New Local
Group dialog box.

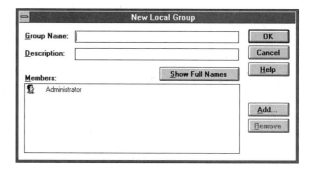

2. Enter a name for the group in the Group Name field.
3. Enter a description for the group in the Description field.
4. To add a user to the group, click the Add button. The Add Users and Groups dialog box shown in Figure 6.15 appears.

Tip

If you have cryptic user names, you can click the Show Full Names button in the New Local Group dialog box to display the account name and the full username in the Members box.

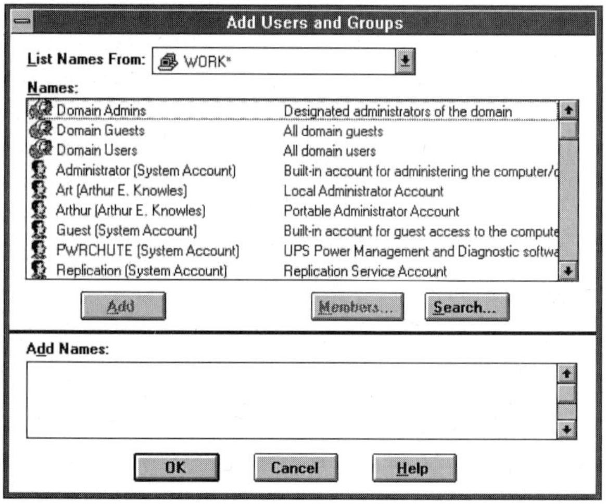

Figure 6.15.
The Add Users
and Groups
dialog box.

5. By default, the domain you logged onto is displayed in the List Names From drop-down listbox. However, you can use the domain user database from any domain with which you have established a trust relationship. You also can use the local database for a Windows NT Workstation or Windows NT Server computer operating in server mode.

6. To add an existing group or user, just double-click the group or user name displayed in the Names box or select a group or name and click the Add button. This copies the user account or group to the Add Names box.

Tip

> If you mistakenly add a name to the Add Names list, you can high-light the name with the mouse and then press the Delete key to remove it.

If you have a large user domain list, it might be easier to click the Search button to display the Find Account dialog box. In this dialog box, you can specify the local, global, or user account to locate. You also can specify the domains or computers to include in the search list by enabling the Search Only In radio button and selecting the domains and computers in the list. The default selection has the Search All radio button enabled and includes all domains and computers. After you enter the account, click the Search button. Any accounts that have been found are listed in the Search Results field. To add an account, highlight the account and click the Add button. The accounts you have added then appear in the Add Names box of the Add Users and Groups dialog box.

To display individual user accounts, select a group name in the Names box and click the Members button. If you select a local group and click the Members button, the Local Group Membership dialog box appears. This box includes local user accounts and global groups defined in the local group. If you then select a global group and click the Members button, the Global Group Membership dialog box appears, which includes a list of users defined in the global group. In either of these dialog boxes, you can select individual user accounts (or global groups in the Local Group Membership dialog box) and click the Add button to add users or global groups to the Add Names box of the Add Users and Groups dialog box.

7. Click the OK button to return to the New Local Group dialog box. All the user and group accounts now are displayed in the Members box of the dialog box. Click the OK button to assign the users you selected to the group and to return to the main window of User Manager for Domains. To remove a member from a group, highlight the account in the Members box and click the Remove button.

Tip

If you highlight the users prior to choosing the menu option, these users are added automatically to the Members box. To choose a contiguous range of users, select the first user and then, while holding down the Shift key, select the last user. To choose a noncontiguous series of users, hold down the Ctrl key while you select each user.

To create a global group, you follow the same basic steps outlined here with a few differences. First, the name of the dialog box you use is the New Global Group dialog box. Also, in this dialog box, you can add only user accounts.

CREATING GROUPS FROM THE COMMAND LINE

You can create both local and global groups from the command line by using the NET command. The syntax for creating a local group follows:

To modify an existing group, use this command:

```
NET LOCALGROUP GroupName /COMMENT:"Text Description" /DOMAIN
```

To create a new group, use this syntax:

```
NET LOCALGROUP GroupName /ADD /COMMENT:"Text Description" /DELETE /DOMAIN
```

To modify an existing group or create a new group and add users to the group, use this command:

```
NET LOCALGROUP GroupName UserName [...] /ADD /COMMENT:"Text Description"
/DELETE /DOMAIN
```

The syntax for creating a global group follows.

To modify an existing group, use this command:

```
NET GROUP GroupName /COMMENT:"Text Description" /DOMAIN
```

To create or modify a global group, use this command:

```
NET GROUP GroupName /ADD /COMMENT:"Text Description" /DELETE /DOMAIN
```

To create a new group, use this syntax:

```
NET GROUP GroupName /ADD /COMMENT:"Text Description" /DELETE /DOMAIN
```

To modify an existing group or create a new group and add users to the group, use this syntax:

```
NET GROUP GroupName UserName [...] /ADD /COMMENT:"Text Description"
/DELETE /DOMAIN
```

Explanations of the syntax for this command follow:

GroupName: Name of the group you want to create or modify.

UserName: Name of a user or users (specify multiple users with spaces between the user names) to add to a group.

/ADD: Creates a new group.

/COMMENT: Includes a description for the group.

/DELETE: Deletes a group or removes a user from an existing group.

/DOMAIN: Specifies that the action is to take place on the domain controller. Otherwise, the action occurs on the local computer.

SETTING DOMAIN POLICIES

Every network has certain rules for user accounts that can be used to provide additional security for your network. Windows NT Server is no exception. Choose Account from the Policies menu to display the Account Policy dialog box. (See Figure 6.16.)

In the Account Policy dialog box, you can set the following options:

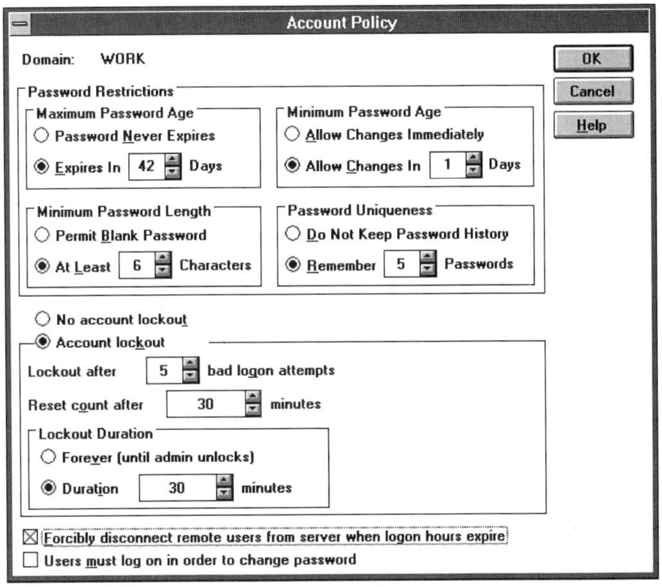

Figure 6.16.
The Account
Policy dialog box.

◆ Maximum Password Age: You can require that a user change his password every so often by specifying a number in the Expires in Days edit field. This is a good idea to implement because it requires that the user change his password and prevents a potential breach of network security.

◆ Minimum Password Age: By specifying a number in the Allow Changes In Days edit field, you can limit the time period during which the user can change his password. This provides two useful benefits. First, it provides some administrative relief by requiring that a user employ a specific password for a period of time. Second, it provides some network security by preventing a user from setting his password back to a previous password immediately if you have the Password Uniqueness option enabled.

◆ Minimum Password Length: This option has a trade-off that you need to consider before implementing. First, you need to consider that the smaller the password length, the easier it is for the user to remember. However, it also makes it easier for a network hacker to gain access to your network by repeatedly guessing the password for a particular user account. The larger password lengths offer increased network security, but probably will require more intervention from you because your network users will forget their passwords. To specify the minimum length of a password, enter a number in the At Least Characters edit field.

You probably should require a minimum password length of eight characters. This is a good balance between the ease of user management and potential security breaches.

◆ Password Uniqueness: Specifying a number in the Remember Passwords edit field prevents a user from using an older password based on the history list. The history list is a record of the user passwords. The number you enter here is used to specify the number of passwords that should be recorded. Any password included in this record cannot be employed by the user when it is time to choose a new password based on the maximum password age.

◆ Account Lockout: This is your best weapon to fight system hackers because it specifies how many times a user can enter the wrong password to access an account before the user account is disabled. This option prevents a hacker from repeatedly attempting to specify a password for a user account to gain access to your network. On the down side, it also can lock out your users who forget their passwords during a logon sequence.

You can specify the number of logon attempts before an account lockout occurs in the Lockout After Bad Logon Attempts edit field. This count is based on the Reset Count After Minutes edit field. This duration specifies the time frame to determine the count of bad logon attempts. If the number of attempts occurs within the time frame you specify here, the account is locked out. In the Lockout Duration group, you can specify whether the account is locked out for a specific period of time by entering a number in the Duration field, or until an administrator reactivates it by selecting the Forever radio button.

◆ Forcibly Disconnect Remote Users from Server When Logon Hours Expire: You can enable this checkbox to force any connected user off the network and close any shared network files (like a SQL Server database) so that you can make system backups.

◆ Users Must Log On in Order to Change Password: You can enable this checkbox to require that the user log on first, before he can change his password. This option can prevent a user from using an expired password to gain access to the network for an idle account.

The security of your network is only as good as the policies you implement on your network. You need to balance the aggravation your users encounter due to these policies with reasonable security measures. A good balance between the ease of user management and potential security breaches is to specify a value of 45 to 60 days for the maximum password age, for example. This requires that users change their passwords occasionally to help prevent a hacker from gaining access to your network by using an easily remembered password that never changes.

CONFIGURING ACCOUNT POLICIES FROM THE COMMAND LINE

Just as you can create local or global groups from the command line with the NET command, you can specify the domain account policies. The syntax follows:

```
NET ACCOUNTS [/FORCELOGOFF{Minutes¦NO}] [/MINPWLEN:Length] [/
MAXPWAGE:{Days¦UNLIMITED}] [/MINPWAGE:Days] [/UNIQUEPW:Number] [/DOMAIN]
```

Explanations for the syntax of this command follow:

/FORCELOGOFF{Minutes¦NO}: Specifies that a warning message is to be issued a certain number of minutes before a user is forcibly logged off the system. If you choose NO, users are not forced off the system.

/MINPWLEN:Length: Specifies the minimum password length. The default is 6, and valid ranges are from 0 to 14.

/MAXPWAGE{Days¦Unlimited}: Specifies the maximum time a user's password is valid. The default is 90 days, and valid ranges are from 1 to 49,710. (49,710 is the same as unlimited.)

/MINPWAGE:Days: Specifies the minimum time before a user can change his password. The default is 0, and the valid range is 0 through 49,710.

/UNIQUEPW:Number: Specifies that a user cannot reuse the same password for the number of changes defined. The default is 5, and the valid range is 0 through 8.

/DOMAIN: Specifies that the operation should be performed on the primary domain controller when the command is executed on a Windows NT Server operating in server mode or from a Windows NT Workstation.

ENABLING AUDITING

If you want to be able to determine who is using your shared network resources or even who is abusing their privileges on your network, you need to enable the auditing features provided in Windows NT Server. Auditing is divided into several categories, however, and is not enabled in a single application.

To audit a system event related to account usage or modification and the programs running on your server, choose Audit from the Policies menu to display the Audit Policy dialog box. (See Figure 6.17.)

Figure 6.17.
The Audit Policy
dialog box.

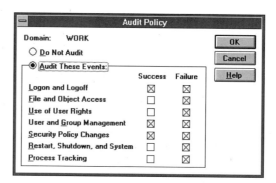

To audit any event, you first need to enable auditing by enabling the Audit These Events radio button in the Audit Policy dialog box (even if you select no options here to audit) and then choose the application's audit options. To audit the use of files, you use File Manager; for printer use, you use Print Manager; and for shared Clipbook pages, you use Clipbook Viewer. All these have an Auditing option on the

Security menu that displays a dialog box similar to the Audit Policy dialog box. There, you can specify the events to audit.

When you select an event to be audited, it is entered into the security log, which you can view with the Event Viewer. You can select to audit the successful use of a privilege, failure to obtain access (which indicates a security violation attempt), or both.

You can audit the following events:

◆ Logon and Logoff: Determines who has logged onto or off your network. I recommend that you enable both these checkboxes (Success and Failure) to determine who is using your network.

◆ File and Object Access: Works with other applications that have been used to specify auditing. You can use File Manager to enable auditing of a directory, for example. You can enable the Success or Failure events for the File and Object access in order to record any access to the audited directory.

Tip

If you plan to use the Internet Information Server services, it is a good idea to enable the File and Object Access event. This will let you use File Manager to enable auditing of your WWW, FTP, and Gopher root directories and tell if someone has been accessing data they shouldn't. Directory and file auditing is discussed in Chapter 7.

◆ Use of User Rights: Provides the capability to audit any use of a user right, other than logon and logoff, such as the capability to log on as a service.

◆ User and Group Management: Gives you the capability to track any user account or group management—whether a new user is added, an existing user password is enabled, or new users are added to a group, for example.

If you have constant problems with a particular user account or group being modified and cannot determine who is making these changes, you should enable both Success and Failure for this option. This can help you determine who may be making the changes. I've seen a few problems caused by personnel who have been granted administrative privileges, but who are not trained in their use, for example. By using this option, you can determine who needs additional training, or even who should have his administrative privileges revoked.

◆ Security Policy Changes: Helps you determine who may be making changes to your system audit policies, user right policies, or trust relationships. Enable this option for both Success and Failure to determine who is modifying your network policies. This is a good idea particularly if you have several Administrators and find that things have been changing without anyone admitting responsibility.

◆ Restart, Shutdown, and System: Enables you to determine who may be shutting down your servers or performing any event that affects system security or the security log.

◆ Process Tracking: Determines which applications are executing on your system.

Caution

Auditing the Success events for Process Tracking can fill up your security log in a matter of minutes. Only enable this event for Success when absolutely necessary.

MANAGING TRUST RELATIONSHIPS

You use a trust relationship to use the domain database of a foreign domain on a local domain. The foreign domain is referred to as the *trusted domain*, whereas the local domain is called the *trusting domain*. The way a trust relationship works in principle is that the domain database on the trusted domain is applied on the trusting domain for any user who does not have a local account on the trusting domain. This can provide you with the capability to create an administrative domain (the trusted domain) that contains all your administrative user accounts and still administers all your resource (the trusting) domains. These resource domains will contain shared network resources and local user accounts, but they will be administered by users who have accounts in the trusted domain.

Creating a trust relationship is a two-fold process. First, you have to specify which domain is permitted to trust your domain. Then, in the other domain, you have to establish a trust relationship with the domain that has permitted the trust relationship.

To establish a trust relationship, follow these steps:

1. Choose Trust Relationships from the Policies menu. The Trust Relationships dialog box appears, as shown in Figure 6.18.

2. Next to the Permitted to Trust This Domain box, click the Add button to display the Permitted Domain to Trust dialog box. This step must be completed on the domain controller that is to be the trusted domain.

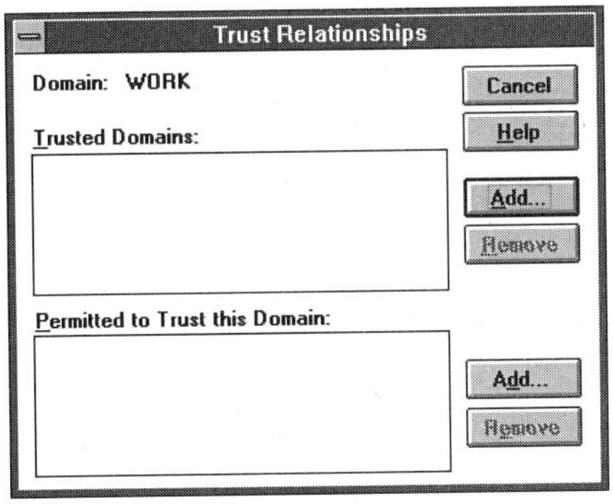

Figure 6.18.
The Trust
Relationships
dialog box.

3. Enter the name of the trusting domain with which you want to allow a trust relationship to be established. Enter a password and confirm it. Then click the OK button. You return to the Trust Relationships dialog box.

4. Go to the other computer domain controller and in the Trust Relationships dialog box, click the Add button beside the Trusted Domains box to display the Add Trusted Domain dialog box. Enter the name of the domain you want to trust (the name you entered in the Permitted to Trust this Domain field from the previous step) in the Domain field. Enter the password you set in the previous dialog box on the other computer in the Password field. Then click the OK button.

Note

This password you are setting will be used only to create the initial trust relationship. Immediately after the trust relationship is established, the two domains will create their own passwords. If, for any reason, a trust relationship fails, you will have to remove the trust relationship from both domains and re-create it.

Tip

If you have an administrative account on both domains, you can use this privilege to establish a trust relationship between two domains from a single computer. To do this, you will need to cheat a bit. First use File Manager to connect to the non-local domain (the one you are not a member of) and use the Connect As option in the Network Connection dialog box to specify an administrative user account (in the form of DomainName\UserName). After you connect to the sharepoint, you have administrative privileges on the non-local domain. You now can bring up another copy of User Manager for Domains, choose User | Select Domain, and pick the non-local domain. Then you can launch another copy of User Manager for Domains and use the local domain. In both copies of User Manager for Domains, access the Trust Relationship dialog box and follow the preceding steps to create the trust relationship.

CREATING USER ACCOUNTS

User accounts are unique resources. Each user account has a security identifier (SID) assigned to it when it is created. This security identifier is used by Windows NT Server for assigning permissions to directories, files, and shared network resources. This same identifier is used in the auditing process as well. If you delete a user account and then re-create it, any shared network resources that were owned by this user become inaccessible to the user. The only way he will be able to obtain access to the resource is if an administrator takes ownership and assigns the user the capability to take ownership, and then the user takes ownership of the resource.

To create a user account, follow these steps:

1. Choose New User from the User menu. The User Properties dialog box appears, as shown in Figure 6.19.

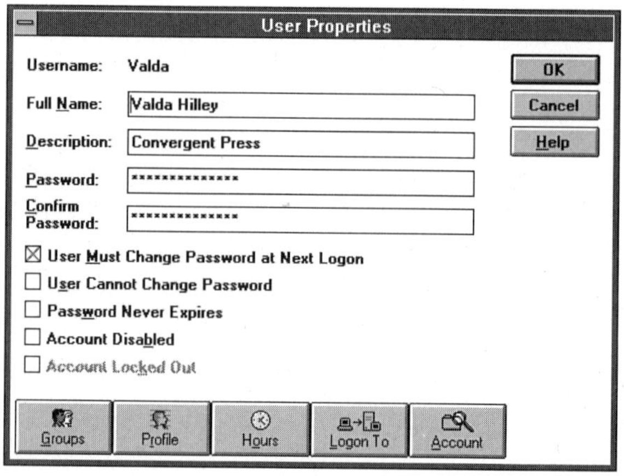

Figure 6.19.
The User Proper-
ties dialog box.

2. In the Username field, enter a name for the user account.
3. In the Full Name field, enter the user's complete name.
4. In the Description field, enter a comment for the user.

5. Enter and confirm the user's password in the Password and Confirm Password fields.

6. To specify additional user properties, enable the checkbox for the following options:

   ◆ User Must Change Password at Next Logon: Requires that the user change his password immediately after logging on the first time.

   ◆ User Cannot Change Password: Prevents the user from ever changing his password.

Tip

This is a good choice for users who always forget their passwords. Just don't enable this option for any user who has access to sensitive data.

   ◆ Password Never Expires: Bypasses the Maximum Password Age account policy.

   ◆ Account Disabled: Creates an account in an inactive state.

Tip

You also can use the Account Disabled option to temporarily disable an account prior to deleting it. As mentioned before, user accounts have unique security identifiers, and if you delete the account, you orphan all the user data files. This requires you (the administrator) to take ownership of the files in order to access them.

   ◆ Account Locked Out: This option is displayed only for existing user accounts. If it is enabled, it indicates that the account was locked due to an invalid number of invalid password attempts during a logon sequence.

7. If the user is to be just another domain user, there is no reason to use the Groups button. However, if the user will be a member of a different group, then click the Groups button to display the Group Memberships dialog box, where you can assign membership to local and global groups and select the primary group.

Tip

You can assign a user account to a group, as mentioned earlier, or you can just double-click the group listed in the Groups field of the main window of User Manager for Domains. This displays the Group Properties dialog box, in which you can add or remove accounts to the group.

8. To set the user's profile path, logon script name, and home directory, click the Profile button to display the User Environment Profile dialog box.

   Use the environment variable `%UserName%` for the logon script name and user profile. The `%UserName%` will be expanded to the name of the user during the logon process to build a fully qualified filename. The format for a logon script would appear as `%UserName%.CMD`, for example.

   The user profile must have a fully qualified UNC filename to specify the location of the profile. For example, you could use

   `\\ServerName\REPL\Import\Scripts\%UserName%.USR`

   Also, in order to use this method, you must explicitly create the `REPL` share by sharing the `SystemRoot\System32\REPL` subdirectory.

   If you have created a sharepoint as your base directory for your user home directories, when you enter the user's home directory with User Manager for Domains, it is created automatically. If you share the `\USERS` subdirectory as `User` on server SRV and you enter a home directory of `\\SRV\USERS\%UserName%`, for example, the user directory automatically is created and assigned the appropriate permissions for that user. The downside to this is that all users are mapped to the base directory and have to manually change to their own subdirectory. If you want to map the user home directory to `\\SRV\%UserName%`, you must manually create the directory, share the directory, and set the permissions on the directory with File Manager.

9. To limit the hours the user can be logged onto the network, click the Hours button to display the Logon Hours dialog box. In this dialog box, you can choose the days and times on a per-day basis that the user may log onto the network. To specify a time range, move the mouse to a day, click once under the minimum hour, and drag the mouse to the maximum hour. Then click the Allow button to allow the user to log on during this time frame. Or, click the Disallow button to prevent the user from logging on during this time frame.

10. Click the Logon To button to limit the user to a maximum of eight workstations he can log onto.

11. Click the Account button to specify a date that the account will expire and to specify the type of account. The type of account can be global for regular domain users or local for users from a foreign domain. The default expiration is to never expire, and the default account type is a global account, so no action is needed here for regular domain users.

12. Click the Add button to add the user to the domain database. Then repeat these steps for each new user. When you are done, click the Close button to return to the main window of User Manager for Domains.

Tip

> To remove the administrative capabilities of a domain administrator on your local computer, just remove the Domain Admins global group from your local computer's Administrator group. If you want to provide limited access to a select group of network administrators, just add these users to your local Administrators group.

PERFORMING USER ACCOUNT MANAGEMENT FROM THE COMMAND LINE

If you do not want to use User Manager for Domains, you can use the NET USER command-line option instead. With this option, you can add, modify, or delete a user account from the domain database.

To modify an existing account, use this syntax:

```
NET USER UserName [Password¦*] [Options] [/DOMAIN]
```

To add a new user account, use this command:

```
NET USER UserName [Password¦*] [/ADD] [Options] [/DOMAIN]
```

To delete an existing account, use this syntax:

```
NET USER UserName [Password¦*] [/DELETE] [/DOMAIN]
```

Explanations for the syntax of this command follow:

UserName: Name of the new user account.

Password¦*: Password for the user. Or, you can specify an asterisk (*) to prompt you for the password and then mask the characters you type.

/DOMAIN: Specifies that the action is to occur on the primary domain controller. This applies only when executing the command from a Windows NT Workstation or a Windows NT Server operating in server mode.

Options: Specifies one or more of the following options. Each option must be separated by at least one space.

/ACTIVE:{NO¦YES}: Enables or disables the user account. The default is to enable the account.

/COMMENT:"*User Description*": Provides a descriptive comment about the user. The maximum length is 48 characters.

/COUNTRYCODE:NNN: Specifies the user account country code. A value of 0 specifies to use the default system country code.

6

`/EXPIRES:{Date|NEVER}`: Specifies that the user account expires on the date set. The date is in the form of MM/DD/YY; DD/MM/YY; or MMM,DD,YY; depending on the country code.

`/FULLNAME:"UserName"`: Specifies the user's complete name.

`/HOMEDIR:"PathName"`: Specifies a path for the user's home directory. The specified path must exist or an error will be generated.

`/HOMEDIRREQ:{YES|NO}`: Selects whether or not a home directory is required.

`/PASSWORDCHG:{YES|NO}`: Enables or disables the user's capability to change his password.

`/PASSWORDREQ:{YES|NO}`: Specifies whether the user account must have a password. The default is to require a user password.

`/PROFILEPATH:PathName`: Specifies the path name for the user profile.

`/SCRIPTPATH:PathName`: Specifies the path name for the logon script. The path name specified is relative to the logon server's logon script path. Generally, you only need to specify the script filename and extension.

`/TIMES:{Times|ALL}`: Specifies the valid logon times for the user in the format `Day [-Day]...,Time [-Time]...` where the day can be spelled out or abbreviated and the time can be in 12- or 24-hour notation, for example, `M,6AM-6PM`, `T,0600-1800` (specifies only Monday and Tuesday from 6 a.m. to 6 p.m.) or `M-F, 6AM-6PM` (specifies from Monday to Friday from 6 a.m. to 6 p.m.).

`/USERCOMMENT:"User Description"`: Lets an administrator change the User Comment field.

`/WORKSTATION:{ComputerName|*}`: Lists up to eight workstations separated by commas from which the user can log onto the network. The * specifies that there are no restrictions.

`/Delete`: Deletes an existing account.

ASSIGNING USER RIGHTS

User rights provide the capability for a user account to perform a specific action on a computer. User rights are divided into basic and advanced user rights; many of these are listed in Table 6.2.

TABLE 6.2. USER RIGHTS.

User Right	Type	Description	Domain Controllers	Workstations
Access this computer from the network	Basic	Allows a user to access this computer from a remote computer.	x	x
Add work- stations to domain	Basic	Allows a user to create computer accounts and add work- stations to the domain. Members of the Administrators and Server Operators can always add workstations to the domain, even if they are not explicitly granted this right.	x	
Back up files and directories	Basic	Allows a user to back up directories and files on a computer regardless of the permissions that have been applied to the directories or files.	x	x

continues

TABLE 6.2. CONTINUED

User Right	Type	Description	Domain Controllers	Workstations
Change the system time	Basic	Allows the user to change the system date and time.	x	x
Force shutdown from a remote system		Allows a user to shut down a computer from another networked computer.	x	x
Load and unload device drivers	Basic	Allows a user to dynamically load or unload device drivers on the computer.	x	x
Log on locally	Basic	Allows a user to log onto the computer interactively.	x	x
Manage auditing and security log	Basic	Allows a user to manage the auditing of objects in a system. It does not affect the right of an administrator to use the Audit command in User Manager.	x	x
Restore files and directories	Basic	Allows a user to restore directories and files on a computer, regardless of the permissions	x	x

User Right	Type	Description	Domain Controllers	Workstations
		that have been applied to the directories or files.		
Shut down the system	Basic	Allows a user to shut down the computer when logged on interactively.	x	x
Take ownership of files or other objects	Basic	Allows a user to take ownership of directories, files, and other objects on the computer.	x	x
Create a pagefile	Advanced	Allows a user to create or modify the file used as a backing store for virtual memory.	x	x
Debug Programs	Advanced	Allows a user to debug a locally executing application.	x	x
Profile single process	Advanced	Allows a user to profile an application. Generally, this is used by developers during the development phase of an application.	x	x

continues

6

BASIC ADMINISTRATIVE TOOLS

TABLE 6.2. CONTINUED

User Right	Type	Description	Domain Controllers	Workstations
Profile system performance	Advanced	Allows a user to monitor the performance of the operating system.	x	x
Bypass traverse checking	Advanced	Allows a user to scan through a directory tree, even if the user does not usually have permission to view the directories.	x	x
Log on as a service	Advanced	Allows an application to log onto the system as a service.	x	x

To modify the user rights for a user or group, follow these steps:

1. Choose User Rights from the Policies menu. The User Rights Policy dialog box appears.

2. In the Right drop-down listbox, choose the right to grant or revoke. This displays a list of users with this right in the Grant To field.

Tip

> To display advanced rights in the Right listbox, enable the Show Advanced User Rights checkbox in the lower left corner of the User Rights Policy dialog box.

3. To add a user or group to the list, click the Add button. The Add Users and Groups dialog box appears, enabling you to select additional users or groups. Users and groups you select are added to the Grant To field.

4. To remove a user or group, select the user or group in the Grant To field and click the Remove button.

5. Repeat these steps for each user right you want to assign to specific users or groups. When you are done, click the OK button.

CREATING USER PROFILES WITH THE USER PROFILE EDITOR

The User Profile Editor, as shown in Figure 6.20, is included in the Administrative Tools group on every domain controller. With this tool, you can create the initial user profile for a user (choose File | Save As File), set the system default profile used by the operating system (choose File | Save As System Default), and create the default user profile used by all new users who log onto the computer (choose File | Save As User Default).

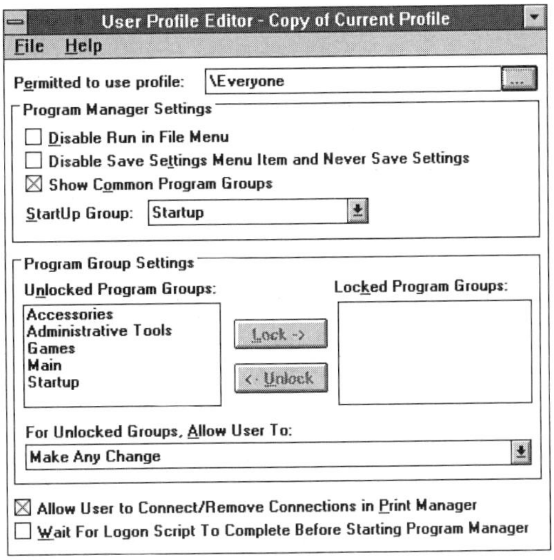

Figure 6.20.
The User Profile
Editor.

Note

The profile you will be saving is the current profile of the user who is logged on. This includes the placement of the Program Manager groups as well as their current states (opened, closed, and so on), so make sure that the default settings for all the applications (Program Manager, File Manager, Print Manger, and so on), and the custom settings for the screen saver, background, color scheme, and other options are what you want before saving the profile.

You can specify the following options in the User Profile Editor:

◆ Permitted to Use Profile: You can create two types of user profiles. You can create a shared profile, which will have a .MAN (mandatory) extension and a .USR (user) profile. A mandatory profile can be shared by more than one user, but no user of the profile can change his environment settings. In order to allow the user to customize his environment, you must employ a user profile. For each profile, you can specify which user or group of users can use it by clicking the button to the right of this field. This displays the User Browser dialog box, which is basically the same as the Add Users and Groups dialog box mentioned earlier.

◆ Disable Run in File Menu: By enabling this checkbox, you can prevent a user from running programs from the run line in the Program or File Manager. This does not prevent a user from running programs from an MS-DOS command prompt or from within any other application that has the capability to launch another application.

◆ Disable Save Settings Menu Item and Never Save Settings: By enabling these checkboxes, you can prevent the user from saving any changes he makes to customize the view and placement of Program Manager, File Manager, and Print Manager.

◆ Show Common Program Groups: If you disable this checkbox, only personal program groups are displayed in Program Manager.

◆ StartUp Group: You can use this drop-down list to specify the applications contained in the Program group that should be executed automatically at logon time by selecting the Program Manager group. You can even disable it completely by specifying (none).

◆ Program Group Settings: You can lock or unlock groups by selecting them in the Unlocked Program Groups box or the Locked Program Groups box and clicking the Lock or Unlock button to move them to the appropriate field.

Note

Only personal Program Manager groups appear in the StartUp Group and Lock/Unlock Program Group fields.

◆ For Unlocked Groups, Allow User To: For unlocked groups, you can specify whether the user can make any changes—such as adding new program groups; adding program items; deleting existing program items; or changing the description, command line, working directory, shortcut key, run minimized, run in separate address space, or icon of a program item. You can limit the user to just creating, deleting, and changing program item properties. You can allow him to just change program item properties. Or you can allow the user to change all program item properties but the command line that points to the executable application.

◆ Allow User to Connect/Remove Connections in Print Manager: You can disable this checkbox to prevent a user from connecting to or disconnecting from printers in Print Manager.

◆ Wait For Logon Script to Complete Before Starting Program Manager: You can enable this checkbox to force a user to wait until the logon script has completed before he can run any other applications.

CREATING USER LOGON SCRIPTS

Your user logon scripts are really nothing more than batch files that are run when the user logs onto the domain. If the network client is a Windows NT or OS/2 LAN Manager client, the file extension can be .CMD or .BAT. If the client is an MS-DOS client, however, the file extension must be .BAT; otherwise, the file will not be executed. For convenience, you always should use a .BAT file extension because this provides the maximum compatibility.

Note

By default, logon scripts are located in the SystemRoot\System32\Repl\ Import\Scripts subdirectory of the primary domain controller and any backup domain controllers.

The batch file can contain any Windows NT or MS-DOS command, as well as any executable program. This means that if you want, you can run another batch file, an MS-DOS application, a Windows application, or any other supported application. Here's what I think a minimum logon script should contain:

```
NET TIME \\SRV /SET /YES
NET USE LPT1: \\SRV\HPLJ4 /PERSISTENT:NO
NET USE D: \\SRV\C /PERSISTENT:NO
    NET USE H: \\SRV\Art /PERSISTENT:NO
```

The first line synchronizes the client workstation clock with the clock on the server. The second line connects to an HP LaserJet 4 printer and assigns it to the client's LPT1 parallel port. The third and forth lines assign sharepoints to local drive letters. All shares are nonpersistent shares in order to prevent an error from being reported during the logon process. If the share were a persistent share, the next time the user logged onto the network, there would be a device conflict because the share already would exist.

If the logon script is to be executed on a Windows for Workgroups or Windows 95 client computer, you also might want to create a network share to the local hard disk drives by including the following line in the logon script:

```
NET SHARE DriveC=C:\ /REMARK:"Administrative share for backups" /SAVESHARE:NO /
FULL:ShareAccessPassword /YES
```

Tip

I often include a disk-checking program, such as SCANDISK, and a virus-checking program, such as SCAN, on MS-DOS–based computers to check for possible disk errors and viruses that might be present on the client computer.

Note

I have included additional logon script examples and useful script commands in Appendix D, "Example Batch Files and Logon Scripts," which is located on the CD-ROM with this book.

USING THE EVENT VIEWER

You use the Event Viewer to display status events that occur on your computer. These events are divided into three categories. Each category is contained in a specific log. The system log includes events related to the operation of the operating system, the application log includes application-specific events, and the security log includes auditing events. These events are further divided into types that have specific icons associated with them. Table 6.3 summarizes the event types for each log category.

Note

You should use the Event Viewer to view your logs on a daily basis for your file servers, and at least once a week for a workstation. If you do not review your logs in this time frame, you might be unaware of system errors that could propagate to a system failure and you will not be aware of possible attempts to violate the security of your network.

TABLE 6.3. EVENT ICONS AND TYPES.

Icon	Type	Description
STOP	Error	Indicates a serious problem that prevents an application, system service, or device driver from functioning properly. Or a malfunction that has been noticed by an application, system service, or device driver.
(!)	Warning	Indicates a problem that is troublesome but noncritical to the operation of the operating system or application. Warnings often can propagate to errors over time, and therefore should not be ignored.
(i)	Informational	Does not indicate a problem. This is just a status code to inform you that an application, system service, or device driver is functioning properly.
(key)	Success Audit	Informational events to indicate the success of a security modification or usage of a security-related operation. These event entries are based on the audit events you have selected with User Manager for Domains, File Manager, Print Manager, Clipbook Viewer, Registry Editor, and any other application that supports auditing.
(lock)	Failure Audit	Informational events to indicate the failure of a security-related operation. These event entries are based on the audit events you have selected with User Manager for Domains, File Manager, Print Manager, Clipbook Viewer, Registry Editor, and any other application that supports auditing.

If you are trying to determine why your computer cannot connect to the network, you might want to start your search with the system event log. There, you might find that the problem is caused by the device driver for your network adapter. The event might mention something about not being able to find the adapter, which is usually an indication that the network adapter's configuration has changed or a resource conflict has occurred. These types of problems could occur, for example, if you just installed a plug-and-play sound card into the computer. These new resource demands could cause your network adapter to be configured with different resources than the ones you previously used to configure the device driver. If you need to isolate a problem with the DHCP service (or other system service) you should also start in the system event log. But if you want to track down an add-on Windows NT Server product such as Microsoft SQL Server, SNA Server, or Exchange Server, you should start with the application log. The application log also contains events from other Windows NT utilities, like CHKDSK or NTBACKUP. The application log is also used by most third-party manufacturers as well.

The only time to look at the security log is when you have that paranoid feeling that someone is out to get you. It's not a bad feeling for a network administrator, because most likely someone is out to get you! There always seems to be a least one person on any network who just likes to explore the possibilities. If you leave your network wide open, someone will surely step into the breach and create mayhem. They might not mean to cause any harm; they might just be inexperienced. On the other hand, if you are connected to the Internet, the mayhem might be deliberate. Some people on the Internet get a kick out of trying to break into computer systems. Some people get a kick out of successfully breaking in and causing as much grief as they can. Using the security event log can help you to isolate the individuals causing the problem as well as help to prevent a similar problem from reoccurring in the future. In Chapter 11, "Securing your Network from the Internet," you will learn more about security concerns and about the options available to combat security-related problems.

VIEWING EVENTS

In order to view the events that have occurred on your system, you first need to select the log to view. You access this information from the Log menu. You can select the application, security, or system log to view. Each event in a log is broken down into components that describe the event. Table 6.4 summarizes these event components. To get the details of an event, just double-click one and the Event Detail dialog box appears, as shown in Figure 6.21. What is important to note here is that the description contains a textual message in the Description box that describes the error condition, and if the event has any associated data with it, this is included in the Data box. This data list often contains information that you or Microsoft technical support can use to isolate and solve the problem.

TABLE 6.4. THE EVENT COMPONENTS.

Component	Description
Icon	A quick indicator to the type of event.
Date	The date the event occurred.
Time	The time the event occurred.

Component	Description
Source	The name of the application, system service, or device driver that reported the event.
Category	A general classification of an event type. In most cases, categories are used only in the security log.
Event ID	An event number specific to the event source and associated with a specific error message.
User	An event can be associated with a specific user that triggered the event. In most cases, this is used only in the security log.
Computer	An event can be associated with a specific computer that triggered the event. In most cases, this is the name of the host (the computer where the log resides) computer.

Figure 6.21.
The Event Detail
dialog box.

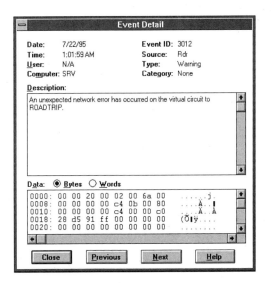

FILTERING EVENTS

One of the problems you will notice over time is that so many events occur on your system that finding the trouble spots can be quite time consuming. And if it takes too much of your time, you probably will stop checking for these problems. Eventually, a problem will grow into a system-related failure that could cause you to lose your job. And I would like to help you avoid that possibility. The easiest way to minimize the amount of data overload is to use the Event Viewer's filtering capabilities.

Follow these steps:

1. Choose Filter Events from the View menu to display the Filter dialog box shown in Figure 6.22.

Figure 6.22.
The Event Viewer
Filter dialog box.

2. In the View From section, select the Events On radio button. Then specify a date and time.

3. In the View Through section, select the Events On radio button. Then specify a date and time.

4. In the Types section, select the type of event to report. For a quick look, I suggest only looking for warning and error conditions.

5. In the Source drop-down listbox, select the event source to view. This is useful for limiting the report to a specific application, system service, or device driver to determine how often the error has occurred.

6. In the Category drop-down listbox, select the event categories to view. In most systems, there will be only security-related categories, or possibly no subcategories. If you have categories, you can further limit the report to a particular category by selecting it from the list.

7. In the User field, enter the user account you want to use to further limit the report. This can be useful when you are checking events in the security log and have noticed a potential violation. By limiting the report to just this user, you can determine how often the user has attempted to violate your system security.

8. Enter the computer name in the Computer field to further limit events to just events that have occurred on the specific computer.

9. If you are looking for a specific event, enter the event number in the Event ID field. This can be useful to determine how often a specific event has occurred in the past.

10. After you finish entering all your filtering characteristics, click the OK button to engage the filter. When a filter has been engaged, the title bar of the Event Viewer changes to include the word (Filtered).

Note

After a filter has been specified, it remains in effect until you change it. If you enabled the Save Settings on Exit option, the next time you launch Event Viewer, the filter also remains in effect.

To remove a filter that you have created using these steps, just choose the View I All Events menu option, and all the events are displayed in the logs.

ARCHIVING EVENTS

Instead of just throwing away the events in your event logs when you fill them up, you should archive them. This gives you the capability to load them at a later date for comparison with current logs to isolate any potential problems. You also can use these logs with Excel or any database that can import a comma-separated value or ASCII text file. You can use this imported data to spot trends that can indicate a potential network trouble spot or hardware-related failure. If you plan to connect your network to the Internet or just want to keep track of potential troublesome network clients, you can use archives of your security event logs to isolate possible breaches of network security.

Tip

You can set the maximum size of the log by choosing the Log I Log Settings menu option to display the Log Settings dialog box. In this dialog box, you also can specify that you want the log to automatically wrap and overwrite events on an as-needed basis, to overwrite events after a specific number of days, or to manually clear the log to free space for further events.

To archive a log, follow these steps:

1. Choose Log Type from the Log menu, where Log Type is the Application, Security, or System log.

2. Choose Save As from the Log menu to display the Save As dialog box. In the Save File As Type field, select Event Log Files (*.EVT) to save the event file as a binary file that can be reloaded later into the Event Viewer. Or, select Text Files (*.TXT), which is a standard ASCII text file, or Comma Delim Text (*.TXT), which is a comma-separated value text file.

3. Enter a filename in the File Name field and click the OK button. If the drive or directory is not the one you want, change it before clicking the OK button.

SUMMARY

This chapter covered many of the basic administrative duties you will be required to carry out on a day-to-day basis. You first learned about Server Manager, which you use to create your computer accounts, synchronize the domain account database, perform remote management of your network clients' shared directories, perform remote service configuration (which includes enabling the Directory Replicator Service to copy your logon scripts to other servers), and perform remote resource accounting of your network clients.

You also learned how to use User Manager for Domains to create your user accounts, enable system auditing, and set your system-wide user account policies. You took a quick look at creating and managing your local and global groups, user rights, and setting up a trust relationship with another domain. You even took a stab at the User Profile Editor and basic logon scripts.

Continuing the discussion of auditing system events that have occurred on your server, this chapter covered the Event Viewer, discussed the basic usage of the tool, and provided a means for you to archive the data for future reference.

In the next chapter, you will look at File Manager and Print Manager to learn the basics for sharing directories and printers and managing these resources.

- Using File Manager

- Managing Your
  Printers with Print
  Manager

CHAPTER 7

Resource Management
Tools

In this chapter, you will learn how to use File Manager and Print Manager to manipulate your shared network resources on your Microsoft network. This includes such topics as creating and deleting network sharepoints, connecting and disconnecting network sharepoints, setting permissions at the share level and directory or file level, and even enabling auditing of directories and files with File Manager. For Print Manager, you will look at creating your printers, sharing them on the network, connecting to shared network printers, limiting access to printers by applying share level permissions, and enabling auditing of your printers to determine who is using them as well as who may be attempting to misuse them.

Note

> A shared directory on your file server in Microsoft technospeak is referred to as a network sharepoint. This book also refers to this shared directory as a sharepoint.

For your Macintosh clients, you will learn how to create Macintosh volumes on your NTFS partitions with File Manager. And for your UNIX or TCP/IP-based network clients, you will look at how you can create printers that are accessible from these clients. You also will look at the flip side of this—how you can connect to a TCP/IP-based network printer and then share it for your non-TCP/IP-based clients to access.

USING FILE MANAGER

The heart of creating and accessing a shared directory on your network is File Manager. Although you can use command-line tools for some options (I will point out the alternatives where this is possible), in some cases (such as the security options) the only interface you can use is File Manager. This section looks at some of the more useful network administrative features. If you are completely unfamiliar with File Manager, you might want to look at *Windows NT 4 Server Unleashed*, published by Sams Publishing.

This discussion begins with the management capabilities provided by File Manager. You then learn how to create Macintosh volumes for your Macintosh clients to connect to just as if they were shared folders on a Macintosh computer. Next, you'll look at setting access permissions on directories and files. And if you are going to set permissions, you'll want to know how to enable auditing on directories and files so that you can use the Event Viewer to see who may be attempting to violate your security restrictions. Finally, you'll look at the compression options provided by Windows NT Server for NTFS partitions.

MANAGING NETWORK SHAREPOINTS

Managing your network sharepoints falls into five categories. First, you must create a sharepoint in order to allow your network clients to access a shared directory. To restrict access to a network sharepoint, you can set permissions on it. If you create a temporary sharepoint or if you decide to move the shared directory to another disk drive, you also need to be able to delete a sharepoint. In order to access a shared directory from a remote computer, you need to connect to it. And because you still are limited to 26 drive letters, when you are finished with a connection to a network sharepoint, you should disconnect from it.

Tip

Although you still are limited to 26 logical drive letters as a carry-over from MS-DOS, this does not mean that you are limited to 26 connections. Many Win32 applications are capable of using UNC (`\\Server\ShareName`) filenames to access data files. You can use Program Manager to specify `\\Server\ShareName\Path\ApplicationName` in the Command Line of the Program Items Properties dialog box to run an application. If you want to run Notepad from a different server, for example, and you have Admin privileges, you can use `\\Server\ADMIN$\System32\NOTEPAD.EXE` in Program Manager or from a command-line prompt.

CREATING NETWORK SHAREPOINTS

Before a network client can connect to a directory on your file server, you have to create the sharepoint. To create a sharepoint, follow these steps:

1. Choose Share As from the Disk menu to display the New Share dialog box shown in Figure 7.1.

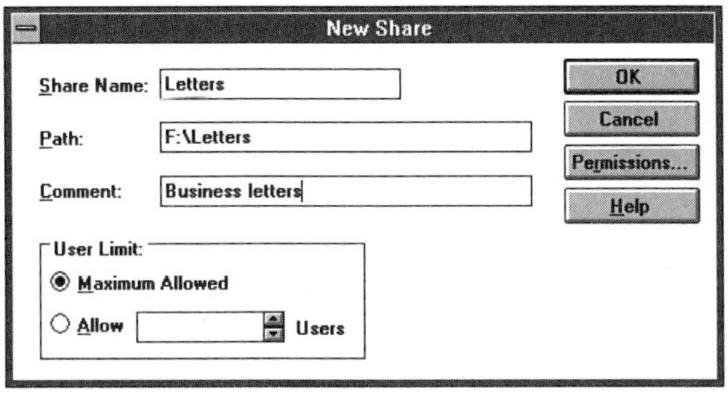

Figure 7.1.
The New
Share dialog
box.

Tip

As a shortcut to this menu option, you can click the Shares a Directory button on the toolbar.

2. In the Share Name field, enter the name that the network client will use to connect to the shared directory. This name also will be displayed in the browse list of shared resources for the computer.

RULES FOR SHARE NAMES FOR WINDOWS NT AND WINDOWS 95 COMPUTERS

The name cannot contain more than 12 characters. It can contain spaces.

The name cannot include the following special characters:

< > * , ? | : / \ "

ADDITIONAL RULES FOR ACCESSING A SHAREPOINT FROM AN MS-DOS APPLICATION

The name is limited to 12 characters (an eight-character name, a single period, and a three-character extension) and must follow the MS-DOS naming conventions.

The name cannot have embedded spaces, it cannot have more than one period (.), and it cannot include the following characters:

< > + * ? , = | ; : [ ] / \ "

The name cannot be one of the reserved MS-DOS names. These names include the following:

COM1	COM2	COM3	COM4	PRN	LPT1
LPT2	LPT3	LPT4	CON	AUX	NUL

Tip

You can create a hidden share simply by appending a dollar sign ($) to the end of the share name. These hidden shares will not show up in any browse list of available resources, but they can be used if you know the resource name.

3. The Path field specifies the directory path of the resource to be shared. If the entry displayed is not the correct path, change it.

Tip

> If you select the directory in File Manager prior to choosing Share As from the Disk menu or using the toolbar button, this path name automatically is entered in the Path field of the Shared Directory dialog box.

4. You can specify a description to be displayed in the browse list for the share by entering text in the Comment field.

   Many network Administrators skip this step because they do not consider it necessary. If you have a large network, however, or if you have users who routinely browse for network resources, this can avoid confusion and provide easier client access. I highly recommend that you use a Comment field whenever you create any shared resource.

5. You can limit the number of simultaneous connections to the share by selecting the Allow radio button in the User Limit group and specifying a maximum connection limit.

Tip

> You can use the Allow button to limit the connections to application software and abide by your license agreement for application software, which does not have any network licensing method.

6. To prevent unauthorized access to a sharepoint, you can click the Permissions button, which displays the Access Through Share Permissions dialog box. In this box, you can specify the users who can connect to the sharepoint. Because the topic of share permissions is very complex, it is covered in the following sidebar, "Creating or Modifying Sharepoints from the Command Line."

7. To actually create the sharepoint, click the OK button in the New Share dialog box. This creates the sharepoint and returns you to File Manager.

Modifying an existing sharepoint follows the same basic steps. You select the directory with File Manager and choose Share As from the Disk menu or click the Share a Directory toolbar button to access the Shared Directory dialog box, as shown in Figure 7.2.

7

RESOURCE MANAGEMENT TOOLS

Figure 7.2.
The Shared
Directory dialog
box.

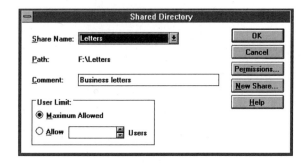

There are a few minor differences between this dialog box and the New Share dialog box:

◆ You cannot change the share name, although if you have more than one sharepoint to the same directory, you can select the sharepoint from the Share Name drop-down listbox.

◆ You cannot change the path name.

◆ You can click the New Share button to access the New Share dialog box. You can use this box to create a new sharepoint with a different name and later delete the other sharepoint, if desired.

CREATING OR MODIFYING SHAREPOINTS FROM THE COMMAND LINE

You can use the NET SHARE command to create network sharepoints from the command line. The syntax follows:

```
NET SHARE ShareName = Drive:PathName [/users:Nbr ¦ /unlimited]
[/remark:"Comment"]
```

Explanations for this syntax follow:

ShareName: Name to be displayed in the browse list, which users will use to connect to the sharepoint.

Drive: Logical drive letter.

PathName: Physical path to the directory.

/users: Includes the number of simultaneous connections to which you want to limit the share.

/unlimited: Specifies that there is no limit to the number of user connections to the sharepoint.

/remark: Description for the share. Must be enclosed in quotation marks.

Note that you can specify only /users or /unlimited—not both.

Tip

One of the interesting features of creating sharepoints with File Manager is that if you select a remote network drive and then bring up the New Share or Shared Directory dialog box, you can create remote sharepoints. This means that the sharepoint you create will not be created on your computer; instead, it will be created on the remote computer. This can be particularly useful for an Administrator because you can connect to a remote computer's root directory hidden share and then create a subdirectory that you then can share.

SETTING SHARE LEVEL PERMISSIONS ON A NETWORK SHAREPOINT

You can limit access to a network resource in two ways. You can set permissions on a directory or one or more files, as described in "Setting Permissions on Directories and Files," later in this chapter. Or, you can set share level permissions on an individual sharepoint. Share level permissions apply only to access from a remote computer.

Share level permissions are divided into four incremental possibilities:

◆ No Access: This permission level prevents any access to the data contained in a network sharepoint. This includes the parent directory, any subdirectories, and all the files. Although it does not prevent a user from connecting to a sharepoint, it does deny all access to files and subdirectories that it contains.

Caution

Use the No Access option with care because it is exclusive of all other privileges. If you set permissions for sharepoints with No Access permissions by user or group, then all users or group members are denied access. This occurs even if a different group, which includes selected users of the first group, provides access.

Suppose that you have a group called ReadAccess that includes the users Joe, Mary, and Bob; and another group called ExcludeAccess that includes Bob, Fred, and Sally. If you assign the No Access share privilege to the ExcludeAccess group and then assign read access to the ReadAccess group, Bob, Fred, and Sally will be denied access to the data in the sharepoint, whereas Joe and Mary will have read access to the sharepoint.

◆ Read: Provides read-only access to the parent directory and any subdirectories and files in a shared directory. Users can connect to the sharepoint, list the directory contents, change subdirectories, read files, and execute applications. But they cannot create subdirectories, add additional files, or make changes to any data files in the shared directory.

Tip

If you share a read-only resource such as a CD-ROM, make sure that you specify Read as the share level permission setting. This prevents any application from attempting to write to the medium and generating a fatal error. I have seen some MS-DOS applications crash because they attempted to write to read-only media.

◆ Change: This permission level includes all the functionality of read access. It also provides the capability to create subdirectories, add files, and make changes to data files. You also can delete subdirectories and files.

◆ Full Control: Not only does this level provide the capabilities of the Change share level permission, but it also enables users to change the subdirectory and file-level permissions on network sharepoints that have been created on NTFS partitions.

Table 7.1 summarizes the share level permissions. Table 7.2 explains the abbreviations for these permissions.

TABLE 7.1. SHARE LEVEL PERMISSIONS.

Permission Level	Directory/Subdirectory Access	File Access
No Access	None	None
Read	(L)(R)(E)	(L)(R)(E)
Change	(L)(R)(W)(E)(D)	(L)(R)(W)(E)(D)
Full Control	(L)(R)(W)(E)(D)(P)(O)	(L)(R)(W)(E)(D)(P)(O)

TABLE 7.2. PERMISSION ABBREVIATIONS.

Abbreviation	Permission
D	Delete subdirectories and files.
E	Execute applications.
L	List subdirectories and files.
O	Take ownership of subdirectories and files on NTFS partitions. In effect, this gives the user full control of the directory, subdirectories, and files, which can be extremely dangerous. Therefore, this privilege should be granted only to Administrators or the owner of the directory.
P	Change permissions on subdirectories and files on NTFS partitions.
R	Read files, but make no changes.
W	Create subdirectories and files as well as modify existing files.

After you click the Permissions button in the New Share or Shared Directory dialog box, the Access Through Share Permissions dialog box appears. (See Figure 7.3.) You can use this dialog box to assign new user or group share level permissions, or to modify the share level permissions for existing users or groups.

Figure 7.3.
The Access
Through Share
Permissions
dialog box.

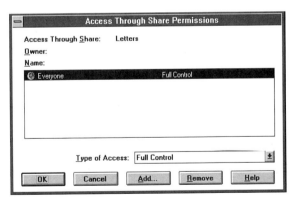

To assign new user or group share level permissions, follow these steps:

1. Click the Add button. The Add Users and Groups dialog box appears. (See Figure 7.4.)

Figure 7.4.
The Add Users
and Groups
dialog box.

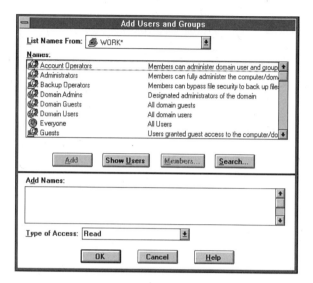

2. By default, the domain you logged onto is displayed in the List Names From drop-down listbox. However, you can use the domain user database from any domain with which you have established a trust relationship. You also can use the local database for a Windows NT Server computer operating in server mode.

Note

There is a distinct difference between using a domain database and using your local database on a Windows NT Server computer running in server mode or a Windows NT Workstation. The domain database is a global resource; all user and group (local or global) accounts are defined in the primary domain's security account manager database and can be shared among all members of the domain. A local database, however, is unique to the computer you are working on; user and local groups of a local database are distinctly different from a user account or group that also is defined in the domain (they have different security identifiers, or SIDs, and a SID is the basis for all security).

3. By default, only groups are listed in the Names box. If you want to include user accounts, click the Show Users button. This adds all your user accounts to the end of the list. To add an existing group or user, just double-click on the group or user name displayed in the Names box or select a group or name and click the Add button. This copies the user account or

group to the Add Names box. If you mistakenly add a name to the Add Names box, you can highlight the name with the mouse and then press the Delete key to remove it.

4. After the user accounts or groups are placed in the Add Names box, you need to select the share permission level from the Type of Access drop-down listbox. You can select No Access, Read, Change, or Full Control.

Tip

To display individual user accounts, select a group name in the Names box and click the Members button. If you select a local group and click the Members button, the Local Group Membership dialog box appears, which includes local user accounts and global groups defined in the local group. If you then select a global group and click the Members button, the Global Group Membership dialog box appears, which includes a list of users defined in the global group. In either of these dialog boxes, you can select an individual user account (or global group in the Local Group Membership dialog box) and click the Add button to add users or global groups to the Add Names box of the Add Users and Groups dialog box.

5. Click the OK button to return to the Access Through Share Permissions dialog box. All the user and group accounts now are displayed in the Name box of the dialog box. Click the OK button to assign the share level permissions you selected and return to the New Share or Shared Directory dialog box.

To modify an existing user or group share level permission, follow these steps:

1. In the Access Through Share Permissions dialog box, select the user account or group name listed in the Name box.

2. In the Type of Access drop-down listbox, select the share permission level. You can select No Access, Read, Change, or Full Control.

3. Repeat these steps for each user account or group for which you want to change the share level permission.

To delete an existing user or group share level permission, follow these steps:

1. In the Access Through Share Permissions dialog box, select the user account or group name listed in the Name box.

2. Click the Remove button.

3. Repeat these steps for each user account or group that you want to delete.

DELETING A NETWORK SHAREPOINT

If you are going to move a shared directory from one disk drive to another, you need to stop sharing the directory first. This ensures that users will not attempt to use a shared directory that no longer exists, thereby receiving an error message. After you stop sharing the directory, you can move it and then re-create the sharepoint.

To stop sharing a directory, follow these steps:

1. Choose Stop Sharing from the Disk menu. The Stop Sharing Directory dialog box appears, as shown in Figure 7.5.

Figure 7.5.
The Stop Sharing
Directory dialog
box.

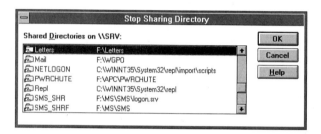

Tip

As a shortcut to this menu option, you can use the Stop Sharing a Directory toolbar button. Notice that this button is similar to the Share Directory button, but the folder is grayed out.

Tip

If you select the shared directory with File Manager prior to displaying the Stop Sharing Directory dialog box, all the sharepoints for that directory are preselected. This is both good and bad. It is good in the sense that you do not have to scroll down the list to find the entry to delete. It is bad in the sense that if you have multiple sharepoints (including your hidden sharepoints), you can accidentally delete them all with one click of the mouse button.

2. Select the network sharepoint and click the OK button to delete it. If you want to delete a contiguous range of sharepoints, select the first sharepoint and then, while pressing the Shift key, select the ending sharepoint. This highlights an entire range of sharepoints. To select multiple, noncontiguous

sharepoints, press the Control key while selecting each sharepoint. Any highlighted sharepoints are deleted after you click the OK button.

DELETING SHAREPOINTS FROM THE COMMAND LINE

You also can use the NET SHARE command to delete an existing network sharepoint. The syntax follows:

```
NET SHARE {ShareName ¦ Drive:PathName} /delete
```

Explanations of this syntax follow:

ShareName: Name to be displayed in the browse list that users use to connect to the sharepoint.

Drive: The logical drive letter.

PathName: The physical path to the directory.

/delete: Specifies that the sharepoint is to be deleted.

Note that only one of these options (ShareName or Drive and PathName) can be used to designate the shared directory to be deleted. You can refer to it by the ShareName, such as Mail, or by the logical drive mapping, such as M:\MS\MAIL, but not both.

CONNECTING TO A NETWORK SHAREPOINT

Connecting to a network sharepoint is an easy task with File Manager; it is a simple matter of pointing and clicking to connect to the appropriate resource. Or, at least it is if you have designed your network well. When you use File Manager to connect to a network by choosing Connect Network Drive from the Disk menu, the Connect Network Drive dialog box appears. (See Figure 7.6.) This dialog box includes the Shared Directories listbox, which displays a list of all shared directories for all the network providers (Microsoft Network, Novell Network, and so on) you have installed.

The Shared Directories listbox is basically a repository for the browse list and contains, by default, an expanded listing of the user's home domain. This expanded listing includes all computers that are members of the domain. To actually find the required network resource, the user has to double-click on the individual computer names to see which resources have been shared. This can be a tiresome task if you have many domain members.

Figure 7.6.
The Connect
Network Drive
dialog box.

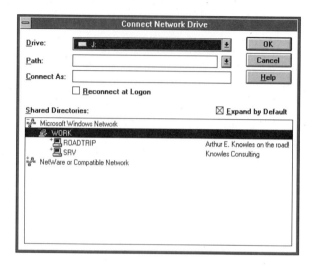

A couple of items that can make browsing for network resources more efficient follow:

◆ When you design your network, break up your servers in a hierarchical manner. If you have an accounting department, for example, then you should have an accounting domain. This accounting domain will contain all the shared network resources for the accounting department. This makes browsing for accounting resources quite easy for your users and gives you more efficient usage of network bandwidth. If your network is too small to contain multiple domains, just break up your resource sharing at the server level. Create an accounting server that contains all your shared resources for your accounting users.

◆ For each server that you create, create a logical name and include a description for it with the Control Panel Server applet. Or, you can use Server Manager, as described in Chapter 6, "Basic Administrative Tools," so that the users can find the appropriate resources quickly.

Note

Now take the accounting example a step further, and suppose that you have multiple accounting servers. You could name them ACCOUNT1, ACCOUNT2, or ACCOUNT3. But it would be better to choose names like ACCOUNT_ADMIN, ACCOUNT_PAY, and ACCOUNT_RECV for your administrative accounting server, your accounts payable server, and your accounts receivable server. Each of these should have a good description that defines the role of the particular server. This description is displayed in the browse list and can help the user find the resources he wants much more quickly than if he had to expand each server and browse through its resource list.

◆ When you create a network sharepoint, always include a description that explains the use of the shared directory. This is important because you can view the descriptions in the browse list just as you can view server descriptions. This too can be used to help the user find the right resource more efficiently.

◆ If you have a large network, disable the Expand by Default checkbox in the Connect Network Drive dialog box. This forces your users to manually browse the network but can provide more efficient and quicker access to network resources.

I think that is enough discussion on the pitfalls of browsing for network resources. To connect to a network sharepoint, follow these steps:

1. Choose Connect Network Drive from the Disk menu to display the Connect Network Drive dialog box.

Tip

As a shortcut to the Disk | Connect Network Drive option, you can click the Connects to a Network Drive toolbar button.

2. In the Drive drop-down list, select a logical drive letter to be used for this network connection. The default drive letter is the next sequential drive letter in use on your system.

3. Scroll through the browse list and then double-click on a domain name (such as WORK in the example in Figure 7.6) to display a list of all computers in the domain.

Tip

If you have a large number of domains in your network, you can enter a domain name (\\WORK, for example) in the Path drop-down listbox and click the OK button. This is faster than waiting for the browse list to appear and then double-clicking on a domain name to show the browse list for that domain.

If you have a large number of computers in your domain, you can enter a computer name (\\SRV, for example) in the Path drop-down listbox and click the OK button. This is faster than waiting for the browse list to appear and then double-clicking on a computer name to show the browse list for that computer.

4. Scroll through the browse list and double-click on a computer name to display a list of all network sharepoints on that computer.

5. Select a network resource by clicking on it once. This places the \\ComputerName\Sharename in the Path drop-down list. You can double-click on a network resource to instantly connect to a shared directory and close the dialog box.

Tip

The Path drop-down listbox displays your last 10 connections. You can use this listbox to quickly reconnect to a sharepoint you use frequently, but not on a permanent basis.

6. After you insert a path name in the Path drop-down listbox, click the OK button to connect to the sharepoint and close the dialog box.

A couple of other options in the Connect Network Drive dialog box may be of interest to you:

◆ Reconnect at Logon: If this checkbox is enabled, the next time you log onto your computer, the connection is reestablished automatically.

◆ Connect As: You can use this field to specify a different user account to use when connecting to the network sharepoint. It can be in the form of DomainName\UserName, where DomainName is assumed to be the current domain if not supplied. If you supply a domain name, however, the user account from that domain is used to supply the authentication. This can be very useful for an administrator who is on a user's computer and is using the user's logon account, but who needs to access an administrative-only sharepoint.

CONNECTING TO A SHAREPOINT FROM THE COMMAND LINE

You can connect to a network sharepoint from the command line with the NET USE command. The syntax follows:

```
NET USE [DeviceName ¦ *] [\\ComputerName\ShareName] [Password ¦ *]
[/user:DomainName\UserName] /persistent:{yes¦no}
```

Descriptions of this syntax follow:

DeviceName: Logical drive letter to be assigned to the sharepoint. Use an asterisk (*) to indicate that the next available drive letter should be used.

ComputerName: Name of the computer with the shared resource.

ShareName: Name of the network sharepoint.

/Password: Password to be used for the supplied user account. Use an asterisk (*) to mask the password when you type it to prevent the password from displaying on-screen.

/user: User name to be used to authenticate access to the sharepoint.

DomainName: Domain database containing the user account specified by UserName.

UserName: The user identification or account name associated with a particular network client.

/persistent: Specifies that the connection is to be reestablished automatically the next time you log on (if you specify Yes). If you specify No, the connection is only active for the current user session.

Deleting a Connection to a Network Sharepoint

Removing a connection from a network sharepoint is a simple task and can be accomplished by following these steps:

1. Choose Disconnect Network Drive from the Disk menu to display the Disconnect Network Drive dialog box, as shown in Figure 7.7.

Figure 7.7.
The Disconnect
Network Drive
dialog box.

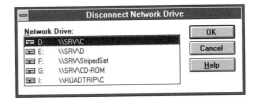

Tip

As a shortcut to the Disk | Disconnect Network Drive option, you can click the Disconnect From Network Drive toolbar button.

2. Select the network connection and click the OK button to delete it. If you want to delete a contiguous range of connections, select the first connection and then, while pressing the Shift key, select the last connection. This highlights an entire range of connections. To select multiple, noncontiguous connections, press the Control key while selecting each connection. Any highlighted connections are deleted after you click the OK button.

DELETING A CONNECTION TO A NETWORK SHAREPOINT FROM THE COMMAND LINE

You can connect to a network sharepoint from the command line with the NET USE command. The syntax follows:

NET USE [DeviceName] /delete

Explanations of this syntax follow:

DeviceName: Logical drive letter assigned to the sharepoint.

/delete: Specifies that the connection is to be deleted.

CREATING MACINTOSH VOLUMES

Macintosh volumes are quite similar to sharepoints for your Microsoft clients, but they differ in a couple of aspects. First, these volumes can be created only on an NTFS partition or CDFS. This is because every Macintosh file or folder has two components. It has a data fork and a resource fork. These individual components are stored in separate streams on an NTFS partition. A FAT or HPFS partition can contain only a single data stream, and therefore cannot be used to create Macintosh-accessible data files. Second, a Macintosh name is limited to 31 characters. If you create a name longer than this, it is truncated on the Macintosh client side.

To create a Macintosh-accessible volume, follow these steps:

1. Choose Create Volume from the MacFile menu to display the Create Macintosh-Accessible Volume dialog box, as shown in Figure 7.8.

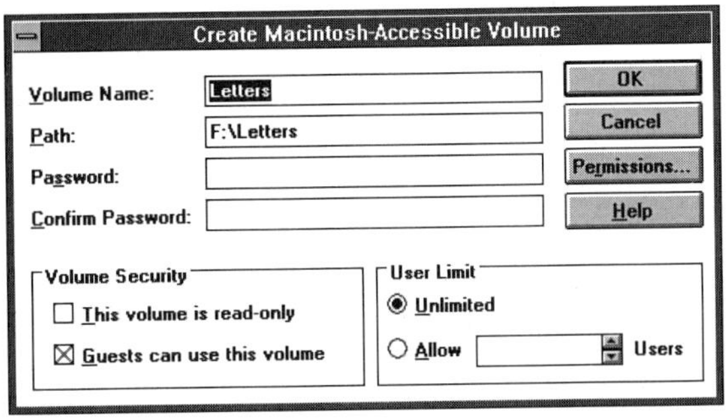

Figure 7.8.
The Create
Macintosh-
Accessible
Volume dialog
box.

2. Enter a name for the new shared directory in the Volume Name field.

3. Enter a physical path (if the selected path is incorrect), in the Path field.

Tip

If you select the directory you want to share as a volume in File Manger prior to choosing the MacFile | Volume menu option, the volume name and path are entered automatically for you in the Create Macintosh-Accessible Volume dialog box.

4. In the Password field, enter a password. Confirm it in the Confirm Password field.

5. To specify that the volume is read-only, enable the This Volume Is Read-Only checkbox in the Volume Security section. To prevent Macintosh guests from using this volume, disable the Guests Can Use This Volume checkbox.

6. To limit the number of simultaneous connections to this volume, select the Allow radio button and specify a maximum number of users to be able to access the volume in the Users box.

7. To specify additional restrictions, click the Permissions button. This enables you to specify additional restrictions based on a group account. This includes preventing the capability to see files (the same as the List Files permission), see folders (the same as the List Directories permission), or make changes (the same as the Change permission). You can further specify to replace all permissions on all subdirectories of the parent directory (when you make a change to the permissions settings); you also can specify that the user cannot move, rename, or delete existing files.

8. Click the OK button when you have completed your selections to create the Macintosh volume and return to the main window of File Manager. Repeat these steps for each directory you want to share with your Macintosh clients.

7

Tip

To share a directory for your Windows clients as well as your Macintosh clients, create two shares for the same directory. One should be shared with the Disk | Share As menu option (for your Microsoft clients) and the other with MacFile | Create Volume (for your Macintosh clients). Then both your clients can access the shared directory and share data between them. Keep in mind that your Windows NT and Windows 95 clients can view filenames of up to 255 characters, your Macintosh clients are limited to 31 characters, and your MS-DOS clients are limited to the old 8.3 rule. The client that saves the data with a smaller filename will truncate it, so you should limit your filenames to the lowest common denominator.

You can modify an existing share by choosing the MacFile | View/Modify Volumes option to display the View/Modify Macintosh-Accessible dialog box. In this dialog box, select the volume you want to modify and then click the Properties button. This displays the Properties of Macintosh-Accessible Volume dialog box, where you can change the configuration as well as the volume name and physical path.

To delete a Macintosh volume, choose MacFile | Remove Volume to display the Remove Macintosh-Accessible Volumes dialog box. Then select the volume to delete and click the OK button. This displays a confirmation message box before it actually deletes the shared volume.

To modify the permissions of a volume, choose the shared volume in File Manager and then the MacFile | Permissions menu option. Or, click the Permissions button in the Create Macintosh-Accessible Volume dialog box or the View/Modify Macintosh-Accessible Volume dialog box.

One other interesting option for Macintosh volumes is the capability to associate a file type for your Macintosh applications with an application just like you do for your Windows applications. The difference here is that you will be selecting an MS-DOS/Windows three-character file extension and providing an association for your Macintosh clients. You do this by choosing MacFile | Associate to display the Associate dialog box. In this dialog box, you choose the MS-DOS file extension in the Files with MS-DOS Extension field and then select the Macintosh application with which to associate it in the Associate Macintosh Document Creator and Type field. If you cannot find a corresponding Macintosh application, you can add it by clicking the Add button. After you select the appropriate types, click the Associate button to add the file association.

SETTING PERMISSIONS ON DIRECTORIES AND FILES

You can prevent unauthorized access to a network resource by setting permissions at the share level, as described in "Setting Share Level Permissions on a Network Sharepoint," earlier in this chapter. Or, you can set permissions on a directory on one or more files. You can even combine these permissions settings. The difference between share level and directory or file level permissions is that share level permissions apply only to remote access, whereas directory and file level permissions apply to local and remote access.

Tip

It is a good idea to set access permissions on your Internet Information Server root directories. You could, for example, set access permissions on the individual subdirectories of your FTP Publishing Service's root directory to allow only a domain administrator or a specific user to access a particular subdirectory. This would then restrict other FTP clients from viewing or modifying data in subdirectories other than their own. By setting permissions on individual subdirectories in this manner, you have in essence created a user directory on your FTP server that can be used in much the same fashion as a user's home directory on the network file server.

Directory and file level permissions are divided into the following incremental possibilities:

◆ No Access: This permission level prevents any access to the selected directory or files. This includes the parent directory, any subdirectories, and all the files.

Caution

Use the No Access option with care because it is exclusive of all other privileges. If you set permissions for directories or files with No Access permissions by user or group, then all users or group members are denied access. This occurs even if a different group, which includes selected users of the first group, provides access.

Suppose that you have a group called ChangeAccess that includes the users Bob, Valda, and Mary. You have another group called ExcludeAccess that includes Mary, Joe, and Sally. If you assign the No Access share privilege to the ExcludeAccess group and then assign

Change access to the ChangeAccess group, Joe, Sally, and Mary are denied access to the data in the directory, whereas Bob and Valda have change access to the sharepoint.

♦ Add: This is an interesting permission level because it denies the user the capability to list the contents of a directory or file. The only thing a user with this permission setting can do is create a subdirectory or file. After he creates the file or subdirectory, he cannot make any changes to it.

Tip

I have found two good reasons to use just the Add permission setting. The first is if you want to create an anonymous drop box. You might want to allow users to send you a data file but prevent all other users from seeing it, for example. The second good use for this setting is as a backup directory. You can let users drop confidential data files into this directory for backup but prevent any users (including the owner) from accessing it, for example. The only catch for this type of permission setting is that you have to delete directories or files after using them so that the users can add them again later. This is because the user has a one-time option to add a directory or file but cannot replace an existing one.

♦ Add and Read: This permission is similar to the Add permission, but it also includes the capability to list the directory contents, to open a data file, or to execute an application.

♦ Read: Provides read-only access to the parent directory, any subdirectories, and files in a shared directory. Users can connect to the sharepoint, list the directory contents, change subdirectories, read files, and execute applications. But they cannot create subdirectories, add additional files, or make changes to any data files in the shared directory.

♦ Change: This permission level includes all the functionality of read access. Users can create subdirectories, add files, and make changes to data files. They also can delete subdirectories and files.

♦ Full Control: Not only does this level provide the capabilities of the Change share level permission, but it also lets users change the subdirectory and file level permissions.

♦ Special Directory Access: This is a user-specified accumulation of the permissions specified from the list of Read, Write, Execute, Delete, Change Permissions, or Take Ownership and applies only to directories.

◆ Special File Access: This is a user specified accumulation of the permissions specified from the list of Read, Write, Execute, Delete, Change, or Take Ownership Permissions and applies only to files.

Note

The capability to change subdirectory and file level permissions applies only to network sharepoints that have been created on NTFS partitions.

Tip

Use the Special Directory Access or Special File Access permission if one of the default settings does not provide the restrictions you want. You might want to give someone the capability to use a source code revision program to which you assign the Read, Write, and Delete special file permissions, for example. This assignment lets users make changes to the source code but does not enable them to change any permission settings, to take ownership of the files, or to execute applications contained in the directory. If you combine this assignment with the special directory permissions, you can even restrict the user from listing or accessing subdirectories.

Table 7.3 summarizes the directory and file-level permissions. Table 7.4 contains explanations of these abbreviations.

TABLE 7.3. DIRECTORY AND FILE-LEVEL PERMISSIONS.

Permission Level	Directory/ Subdirectory Access	File Access
No Access	None	None
Add	(A)	(A)
Add and Read	(L)(R)(W)(E)	(L)(R)(W)(E)
Read	(L)(R)(E)	(L)(R)(E)
Change	(L)(R)(W)(E)(D)	(L)(R)(W)(E)(D)
Full Control	(L)(R)(W)(E)(D)(P)(O) (L)(R)(W)(E)(D)(P)(O)	

continues

TABLE 7.3. CONTINUED

Permission Level	Directory / Subdirectory Access	File Access
Special Directory Access	User Specified	Not Specified
Special File Access	Not Specified	User Specified
List	(L)	(L)

TABLE 7.4. DIRECTORY AND FILE PERMISSION ATTRIBUTES.

Attribute	Description
A	Creates a directory or a file once but you can't make any changes thereafter.
D	Deletes subdirectories and files.
E	Executes applications.
L	Lists subdirectories and files.
O	Takes ownership of subdirectories and files on NTFS partitions.
P	Changes permissions on subdirectories and files on NTFS partitions.
R	Reads files but makes no changes.
W	Creates subdirectories and files as well as modifies existing files.

To set permissions on directories, follow these steps:

1. Select the directories by using File Manager.
2. Choose Permissions from the Security menu to access the Directory Permissions dialog box. (See Figure 7.9.)

Figure 7.9.
The Directory
Permissions
dialog box.

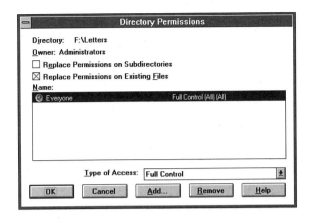

Tip

As a shortcut to the Security | Permissions menu option, you can click the Permissions toolbar button.

3. Click the Add button. The Add Users and Groups dialog box appears. (Refer to Figure 7.4.)

4. By default, the domain you logged onto is displayed in the List Names From drop-down listbox. You can use the domain user database from any domain with which you have established a trust relationship, however. You also can use the local database for a Windows NT Server computer operating in server mode.

5. By default, only groups are listed in the Names drop-down listbox. If you want to include user accounts, click the Show Users button. This adds all your user accounts to the end of the list. To add an existing group or user, just double-click on the group or user name displayed in the Names drop-down listbox, or select a group or name and click the Add button. This copies the user account or group to the Add Names box. If you mistakenly add a name to the Add Names box, you can highlight the name and then press the Delete key to remove it.

7

Tip

To display individual user accounts, select a group name in the Names box and click the Members button. If you select a local group and click the Members button, the Local Group Membership dialog box appears, which includes local user accounts and global groups defined in the local group. If you then select a global group and click the Members button, the Global Group Membership dialog appears, which includes a list of users defined in the global group. In either of these dialog boxes, you can select an individual user account (or global groups in the Local Group Membership dialog box) and click the Add button to add users or global groups to the Add Names box in the Add Users and Groups dialog box.

6. After you place the user accounts or groups in the Add Names box, you need to select the directory permission level from the Type of Access drop-down listbox. This can be No Access, Add, Add and Read, Read, Change, or Full Control.

7. Click the OK button to return to the Directory Permissions dialog box. All the user and group accounts now are displayed in the Name box of the dialog box.

8. If you want to replace the permissions on all subdirectories of the directory you are setting permissions on, make sure to enable the Replace Permissions on Subdirectories checkbox. If you do not want to replace the permissions on files currently contained in the directory, be sure to disable the Replace Permissions on Existing Files checkbox.

9. Click the OK button to assign the directory level permissions you selected.

10. After you see a confirmation dialog box, click the OK button to continue.

To modify an existing user or group directory level permission, follow these steps:

1. In the Directory Permissions dialog box, select the user account or group name listed in the Name box.

2. In the Type of Access drop-down listbox, select the Share permission level. This can be No Access, Add, Add and Read, Read, Change, Full Control, Special Directory Access, or Special File Access. If you specify Special Directory Access, the dialog box shown in Figure 7.10 appears. If you select Special File Access, the dialog box shown in Figure 7.11 is displayed. In these dialog boxes, you can specify the exact permission settings you want.

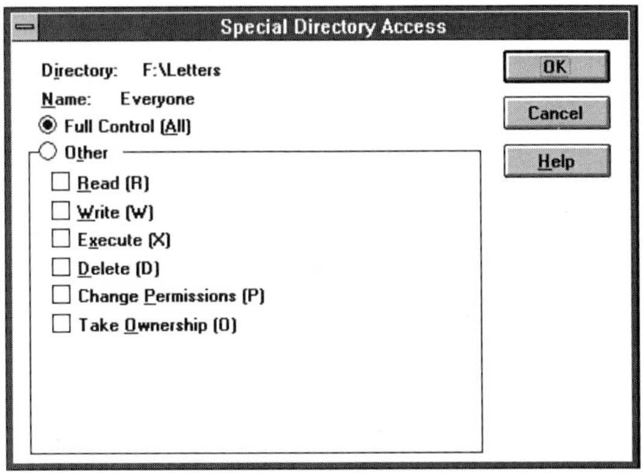

Figure 7.10.
The Special
Directory Access
dialog box.

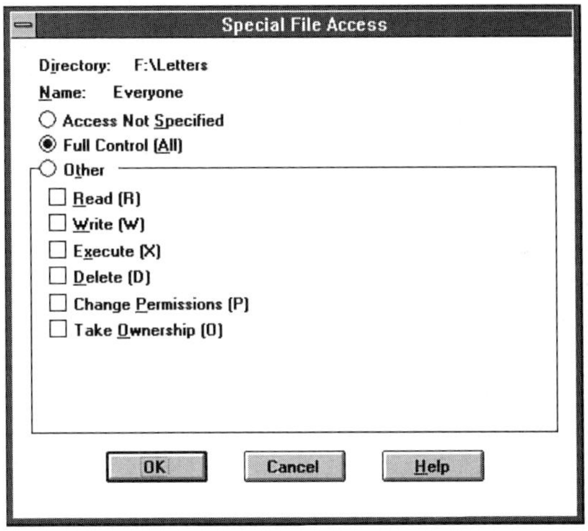

Figure 7.11.
The Special File
Access dialog box.

3. Repeat these steps for each user account or group for which you want to change the permissions.

To delete an existing user or group permission, follow these steps:

1. In the Directory Permissions dialog box, select the user account or group name listed in the Name box.

2. Click the Remove button.

3. Repeat these steps for each user account or group you want to delete.

To set file permissions, you follow the same basic steps as outlined earlier, with two basic differences. First, when you select files instead of directories, the File Permissions dialog box appears, as shown in Figure 7.12. If you select Special Access in the Type of Access drop-down listbox of the File Permissions dialog box, the Special Access dialog box shown in Figure 7.13 is displayed.

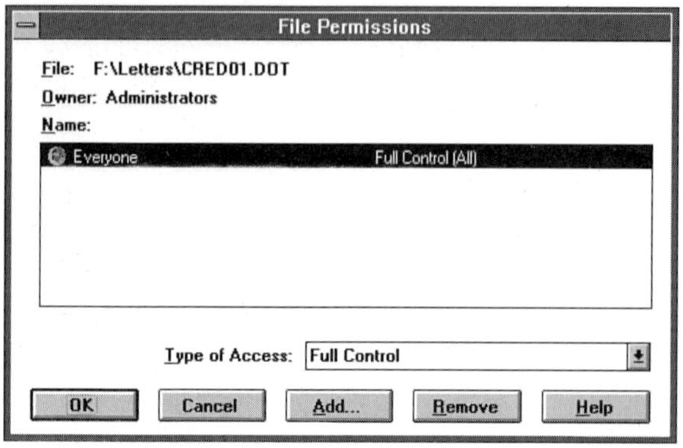

Figure 7.12.
The File Permis-
sions dialog box.

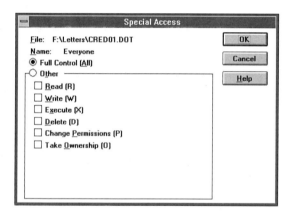

Figure 7.13.
The Special
Access dialog box.

One other interesting feature you can select from the Security menu is the Owner selection. If you select directories or files and then the Security | Owner menu option, you can take ownership of these directories or files. In essence, you replace all the permission settings with those from your current user account. This can be useful if you need to assume the ownership of orphaned directories or files so that you later can give this ownership back to another user. You can give ownership back to a user by assigning permissions for that user and specifying the Take Ownership permission setting. Then have the new user take ownership by using File Manager. After he takes ownership, only he will be able to access the directories or files. Or, you can just assign permissions using his user account.

AUDITING DIRECTORIES AND FILES

If you need to monitor who is using your network resources or you are concerned about users who consistently attempt to bypass your security restrictions, you can use the auditing features to determine who is doing what with your shared directories or files. Suppose that you have a Word document as a template on your server that is used by many users on your network. These users should save their copy of the data file under a different name. But suppose that someone inadvertently saves his version of the file and replaces the original. Then, to hide his mistake, he deletes the file. If you have enabled auditing of the file, you will know which user modified or even deleted it. You then can have a serious talk with him about network security.

Note

Auditing is available only on NTFS partitions.

You can view this auditing information by using the Event Viewer and examining the security log. This is covered in the section "Using the Event Viewer" in Chapter 6. For now, just take a look at what is required to enable auditing of directories and files with File Manager. The first thing to consider is that in order to enable auditing at the system level, you have to use User Manager for Domains and choose Policies | Auditing to turn on the auditing features. This is covered in Chapter 6 in the section "Enabling Auditing."

Tip

It is a good idea to enable auditing of the Internet Information Server root directories. This auditing information can be used to tell you if someone is trying to access data outside of your original intentions. These clients could be intranet (a local network client) or Internet clients.

After you enable system-wide auditing, you can follow these steps to audit your directories on your server:

1. Select the directories you want to audit with File Manager. Then choose Auditing from the Security menu. The Directory Auditing dialog box appears. (See Figure 7.14.)

Figure 7.14.
The Directory
Auditing dialog
box.

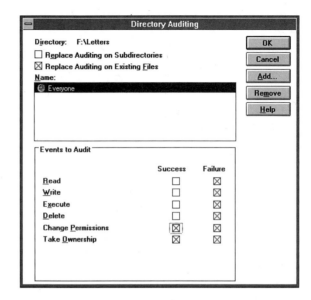

2. Select the users or groups you want to audit. To accomplish this task, click the Add button and the Add Users and Groups dialog box appears. (Refer to Figure 7.4.)

3. By default, the domain you logged onto is displayed in the List Names From drop-down listbox. You can use the domain user database from any domain with which you have established a trust relationship, however. You also can use the local database for a Windows NT Server computer operating in server mode or a Windows NT Workstation.

4. By default, only groups are listed in the Names box. If you want to include user accounts, click the Show Users button. This adds all your user accounts to the end of the list. To add an existing group or user, just double-click on the group or user name displayed in the Names list or select a group or name and click the Add button. This copies the user account or group to the Add Names listbox.

Tip

The easiest way to begin this process is to select the Everyone group. This enables the auditing of every user for the selected directories. If you are concerned only about network users who remotely connect to the resource, select the Network group instead.

5. After you complete your user and group selections, click the OK button to return to the Directory Auditing dialog box.

6. Now you have to make the determination of which events to audit. You do this by checking the boxes in the Success or Failure column. Normally, I audit all Failure audit events but only the Take Ownership and Change Permissions Success events (as shown in Figure 7.14).

7. If you want to replace the auditing information for all the subdirectories of the parent directory, make sure to enable the Replace Auditing on Subdirectories checkbox. If you do not want to replace auditing on the files in directories, clear the Replace Auditing on Existing Files checkbox.

8. Now click the OK button to change your current auditing settings.

9. After you receive a confirmation message box, just click the OK button to continue.

To audit files, you follow the same procedure as outlined here. The dialog box displayed will not have the Replace Auditing on Subdirectories or Replace Auditing on Existing Files checkboxes, however.

DATA COMPRESSION SUPPORT

Windows NT 3.51 includes compression support for NTFS partitions. It does not include the capability to compress FAT or HPFS partitions, and it cannot read any current MS-DOS compression schemes in today's market. What it does do works quite well, however. I find it extremely useful for compressing my SQL Server databases, and I think you will too. What is unique about NTFS compression is that it does not create a hidden file on your system and treat it as a logical drive. Instead, the compression driver is just another layer in the device driver chain. This gives you the capability to compress an entire drive, individual directories, or just individual file types.

Compressing your entire drive is as simple as selecting the root directory of your NTFS partition and then choosing the File | Compress menu option. You then see a confirmation dialog box asking you whether you want to compress all the subdirectories as well. Just click the Yes button to continue the process. The Compress File Progress dialog box appears, showing you the compression status in real time.

Uncompressing your drive with File Manager is just as easy. Just select the root directory and then choose the File | Uncompress menu option. Once more, a confirmation dialog box appears, to which you should answer Yes. The Uncompress File Progress dialog box is displayed.

You can use the same process mentioned earlier to compress or uncompress individual directories or files. Just select them with File Manager as if you were going to copy or move them and then choose the File | Compress or File | Uncompress menu option.

COMPRESSING/UNCOMPRESSING DATA FROM THE COMMAND LINE

You can compress or uncompress your data from the command line with the COMPACT.EXE application. This tool can be quite useful in automating the compression of specific file types because you can use wild cards in the filename specifier. The syntax for COMPACT follows:

```
COMPACT [/C ¦ /U] [/S[:dir]] [/A] [/I] [/F] [/Q] [Filename [...]]
```

Explanations of this syntax follow:

/C: Compresses the specified files. If a directory is specified, it is marked so that any files added afterward to the directory are compressed as well.

/U: Uncompresses the specified files. If a directory is specified, it is marked so that any files added afterward to the directory are not compressed either.

/S: Compresses/uncompresses files in the specified directory and all subdirectories. The default directory is the current directory.

/A: Displays files marked with the Hidden or System attributes. Normally, files marked with one of these attributes are omitted from the display.

/I: Continues processing even if an error is encountered.

/F: Forces the compression process even on files already marked as compressed.

/Q: Reports only significant information.

Filename: Specifies a wild-card pattern, one or more files, or one or more directories.

If COMPACT is used without parameters, it displays the compression state of the current directory and any files contained within it.

MANAGING YOUR PRINTERS WITH PRINT MANAGER

You can use Print Manager for several tasks. This section discusses the features most useful for network Administrators. First, you will learn about the basics of creating a shared network printer and creating a printer pool. Next, you learn how to connect to other printers on the network, and even how to connect to TCP/IP-based printers. Finally, you will look at setting share level permissions on your printers and enabling auditing for your printers.

CREATING A PRINTER

You need to create a printer only for printers that are physically connected to your server or controlled by your server through a network adapter installed in your printer (such as an HP Jet Direct card).

Note

One of the interesting features about NT print management is that all printers you create are really logical printers. You therefore can create multiple printers for a single physical printer. You might want one printer for you to use by an Administrator that has a higher priority than any user printer, for example. This ensures that your print jobs always print first. You can even create two printers—one with a portrait orientation and another with a landscape orientation—so that you can just pick the right printer in your application and not have to define any settings.

To create a printer, follow these steps:

1. Choose Create Printer from the Printer menu. The Create Printer dialog box appears, as shown in Figure 7.15.

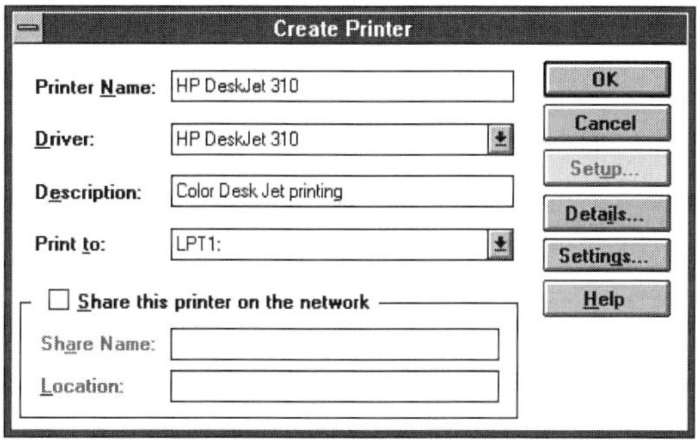

Figure 7.15.
The Create
Printer dialog
box.

2. In the Printer Name field, specify the local name for the printer. The printer name can contain a maximum of 32 characters.

3. Select a printer driver from the Driver drop-down listbox. If you do not find your printer listed but you have a printer driver from the manufacturer, select Other from the list.

4. For your user's convenience, add a textual description in the Description field.

5. In the Print To drop-down listbox, select the port to which the printer is connected. This can be an LPT port, a COM port, a file (if you want to create a binary file you can copy to a printer), or Other.

   If you select Other, you have the following options:

   ◆ Digital Network Port: Used to connect an HP printer with a Jet Direct card installed. You have to stipulate the HP Network Port address and a name for the port.

   ◆ Local Port: Specifies a parallel port greater than LPT3 or a COM port greater than COM4.

   ◆ LPR Port: Specifies a printer on a UNIX or TCP/IP-based network. You must supply the IP address or DNS name for the printer, as well as the actual name of the shared printer.

   ◆ Other: Installs an OEM print monitor. Generally used for third-party, network-capable printers.

6. If you want to share this printer over the network, enable the Share This Printer on the Network checkbox. Then, in the Share Name field, enter a name for the shared printer. In the Location field, enter a comment to describe the location of the printer.

7. Click the Details button. The Printer Details dialog box appears, as shown in Figure 7.16.

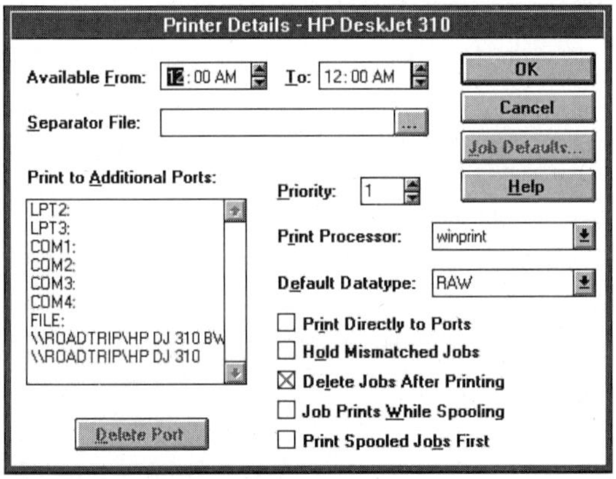

Figure 7.16.
The Printer
Details dialog
box.

In this dialog box, you can specify any of the following settings:

- ◆ Available From and To: Specify a time frame for which you can make the printer available.
- ◆ Separator File: Can be used to separate print jobs.
- ◆ Print to Additional Ports: If you specify additional ports to print to, you can create a printer pool. A printer pool is made up of identical printers physically connected to the same server. This provides the capability to share the print load by using several physical printers as one logical printer. When one printer is busy, the next printer in the chain is used to print the next job.
- ◆ Priority: A priority level from 1 to 99. Higher numbers have a higher priority. This is useful for creating two logical printers. Both these printers can be physically connected to the same printer port, but the print jobs in the logical printer with a higher priority print first.
- ◆ Print Processor: A print preprocessor that is always Winprint unless you have a third-party print processor to replace it.
- ◆ Default Datatype: Specify a datatype here. In most cases, you will not need to change this setting. However, if you have problems printing, such as your last page not ejecting, you can change the setting to RAW [FF Appended] to automatically add a form feed to the end of the print job.
- ◆ Print Directly to Ports: If you enable this checkbox, you will bypass the print spooler.
- ◆ Hold Mismatched Jobs: If you enable this checkbox, and you have a print failure, you can restart the print job without reprinting it from the application.
- ◆ Delete Jobs After Printing: This checkbox is enabled by default. If you disable this, you must manually clear the print queue.
- ◆ Job Prints While Spooling: This checkbox is enabled by default. However, if you experience poor-quality print jobs or see graphics characters in your printer output, disable this checkbox. This slows down printing somewhat but generally provides superior quality and less errors.
- ◆ Print Spooled Jobs First: Enable this checkbox to print jobs that already have been spooled to your server, instead of jobs that still are in the spool process. This can enhance printing performance.

8. After you select all your printer details, click the OK button to return to the Create Printer dialog box. Then click the OK button to actually create the logical printer.

To remove a printer you have created, just select the printer window to make it the active window, and then choose the Printer | Remove Printer menu option.

CONNECTING TO A PRINTER

Connecting to an existing network printer is much easier than creating a printer. After you choose the Printer | Connect to Printer menu option, the Connect to Printer dialog box appears. This dialog box is similar to the File Manager Connect Network Drive dialog box and basically functions the same way. The only real concern here is that if you connect to a non-Windows NT compatible printer queue (such as a NetWare print queue), you are asked to install a printer driver.

CONNECTING TO A PRINTER FROM THE COMMAND LINE

Connecting to a shared printer is quite similar to connecting to a shared directory, as shown in the following syntax:

```
NET USE [DeviceName ¦ *] [\\ComputerName\ShareName] [Password ¦ *]
[/user:DomainName\UserName] /persistent:{yes¦no}
```

Explanations of this syntax follow:

DeviceName: Logical port to be assigned to the sharepoint. Use an asterisk (*) to indicate that the next available port should be used.

ComputerName: Name of the computer with the shared resource.

ShareName: Name of the network sharepoint.

/Password: Password to be used for the supplied user account. Use an asterisk (*) to mask the password when you type it to prevent the password from displaying on-screen.

/user: User name to be used to authenticate access to the sharepoint.

DomainName: Domain database containing the user account specified by UserName.

UserName: The user identification or account name associated with a particular network client.

/persistent: Specifies that the connection is to be reestablished automatically the next time you log on (if you specify Yes), or only temporarily (if you specify No).

SETTING PERMISSIONS

Setting share level permissions for a printer is almost exactly the same as for setting share level permissions on network sharepoints. The only real difference here is the share level types.

These access types follow:

◆ No Access: This permission level prevents any access to the printer.

Caution

Use the No Access option with care because it is exclusive of all other privileges. It works just like the share level permissions for network sharepoints. If a user is a member of a group that has No Access defined for it but is also a member of a group that has a higher permission access, the user still is denied access to the printer.

◆ Print: Provides print-only access to the printer. Users can manage their own print jobs but not any other users' print jobs.

◆ Manage Documents: This permission level is basically the same as the Change share level permission. It allows the user to create print jobs, delete print jobs, pause the printer, and manage document priorities.

◆ Full Control: Not only does this level provide the capabilities of the Manage Documents share level permission, but it also allows users to change the permission level and to take ownership of print jobs and print queues.

Because this process duplicates the process for setting share level permissions with just a title change in the dialog box, I will not bore you with a copy of the dialog box or step you though the process of setting permissions. Instead, I will just mention that to set the permissions on a printer, just select the window for the printer you want to assign the permissions on and then choose the Security | Permissions menu option. This displays the Printer Permissions dialog box, where you can add or remove users and groups.

AUDITING PRINTER USAGE

Printer auditing also follows the same conventions as directory and file auditing, with one minor difference—and that is in the events you can audit. Print Manager auditing is limited to auditing the success or failure of the Print, Full Control, Delete, Take Ownership, and Change Permissions events. You can enable printer auditing by selecting the printer you want to audit and then choosing the Security | Auditing menu option. This displays the Printer Auditing dialog box, where you can add users and groups to audit, as well as the audit events.

Note

If you want to take ownership of a printer, you can do so by selecting the printer and then choosing the Security | Owner menu option.

SUMMARY

This chapter discussed the administrative features provided by File Manager and Print Manager, which you can use in your day-to-day activities. It encompassed the creation of shared resources and the connection of shared directory or print resources. It also discussed some of the security-related features, such as share level and directory or file level permissions, as well as auditing resource usage.

The goal here was not to step you through all the features provided by these tools, but to give you an understanding of the administrative functions. You also should have learned alternatives to the graphical tools provided with Windows NT Server so that you can automate some of these procedures in your logon scripts or for your less-initiated users.

In the next chapter, you will continue to learn about some of the tools you will use to administer your server and to provide additional functionality.

CHAPTER 8

Additional Administrative Tools

The primary focus of this chapter is to introduce you to some additional tools you will use to manage your Windows NT Server installation. These tools consist of applications divided into three categories. The first group includes management tools you can use to manage your hard disk. These include the Disk Administrator, which you use to manage your hard disk partitions, and NTBackup, which you use to back up your data to tape. The next category includes tools you can use to help ensure the integrity of your system. These include the Repair Disk Utility, the UPS service, and the UPS Monitor Service (a utility I developed to provide additional functionality; this is included on the CD-ROM that accompanies this book and is provided for your convenience and added safety). The final category revolves around user management. This includes creating and managing your Workgroup postoffice with Microsoft Mail32; the Network Client Administrator, which you use to create client installation disks; and the Remoteboot Manager, which helps you manage your diskless workstations.

USING THE DISK ADMINISTRATOR

With MS-DOS, you used FDISK.EXE to create or delete partitions on your hard disk and FORMAT.COM to format the partition. These functions have been incorporated into the Disk Administrator, which is located in your Administrative Tools Program Manager group. Disk Administrator has additional functionality not included in the MS-DOS tools. You can use Disk Administrator to change volume labels, assign drive letters to a partition, or change the drive letter for your CD-ROM drive, for example. You also can use Disk Administrator to create your fault-tolerant partitions, such as a mirrored set or stripe set with parity. Best of all, you can use Disk Administrator to save your current configuration before you make any changes to your partitions on your hard disks, and then to restore the original configuration if you made a mistake or change your mind.

This section begins by reviewing the basic functions provided by Disk Administrator for managing your partitions. Then it moves on to working with volume sets, mirrored sets, stripe sets, and stripe sets with parity. This discussion wraps up with the configuration options to save or restore a previous partition configuration.

MANAGING YOUR PARTITIONS

You use Disk Administrator to prepare your hard disk drive for use by the operating system.

Note

To use any of the following commands, first select the partition with the mouse and then choose the appropriate menu command.

You can use the following Disk Administrator commands to accomplish the following actions:

◆ Partition | Create: Creates a primary partition. Unlike MS-DOS, which can create only one primary partition (with FDISK.EXE), Disk Administrator can create up to four primary partitions on a single disk.

◆ Partition | Create Extended: Creates an extended partition. Extended partitions can be subdivided into additional logical drives.

◆ Partition | Delete: Deletes a partition.

◆ Partition | Mark Active: Marks a primary partition as the active partition. There must be one active primary partition on your disk drive. This partition is used to boot the operating system.

◆ Tools | Format: Formats a partition. You can format a partition as FAT or NTFS.

◆ Tools | Label: Creates a description for a drive or changes an existing description.

◆ Tools | Drive Letter: Changes the drive letter associated with a specific disk. You can use this command to change a disk drive from drive letter D to drive letter E, for example.

◆ Tools | CD-ROM Drive Letters: Changes drive letters (as in the Drive Letter option), but only works on CD-ROM drives.

Tip

If you want to move the order of your disk drives, you can do so with the Drive Letter and CD-ROM Drive Letters commands. My Toshiba laptop, for example, has a docking station with an internal drive (D). I installed Windows NT Workstation to an extended partition (drive E) on my internal disk. Yet when I removed the unit from the docking station, drive E became drive D and caused all my applications to fail to launch. I used Disk Administrator to reassign this volume to drive E, and after this, the drive was always drive E regardless of whether the laptop was docked or undocked.

You can use this same procedure to assign your CD-ROM drive letters to follow all your hard disk drive logical drives. Just assign your CD-ROM drives to high-order drive letters, and then you can change the drive letters on your hard disk partitions to the drive letters used by the CD-ROM drives.

8

ADDITIONAL ADMINISTRATIVE TOOLS

WORKING WITH SETS

I really like the capabilities provided with Windows NT Server to organize my disk drives. Specifically, I like the set feature. A set is a means of grouping two or more disk partitions into a single logical drive. With Windows NT Server, you can create a volume set, a mirrored set, a stripe set, or a stripe set with parity.

A volume set, as shown in Figure 8.1, combines small fragmented partitions into a larger usable unit. If you have 2MB of free space at the end of one drive, 10MB at the end of another drive, and 30MB at the end of a third drive, you can create a volume set using all these partitions and create a single logical drive of 42MB. One of the major benefits of a volume set is that it can be enlarged without deleting the partition and re-creating it. This is because data on a volume set is accessed at the beginning of the set and gradually added until all the space has been used. So adding additional space does not disturb the data that already has been written. The down side to a volume set is that if any portion of the set becomes inaccessible (because of a disk failure, perhaps), then all the data is lost. So a volume set should not be used for mission-critical data, and if you do use it, be sure to back up to tape often.

Figure 8.1.
A volume set.

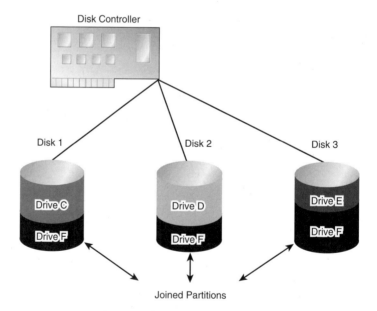

Note

You can combine from 1 to 32 drives into a single logical drive for a volume set.

A mirrored set, as shown in Figure 8.2, is used to copy one partition to another partition in case of a data failure. You can add an additional level of fault tolerance by using disk duplexing, as shown in Figure 8.3, by creating a mirrored set on two physical disk drives on two physical disk controllers. Then, if the primary disk fails or the primary disk controller fails, the secondary one is used.

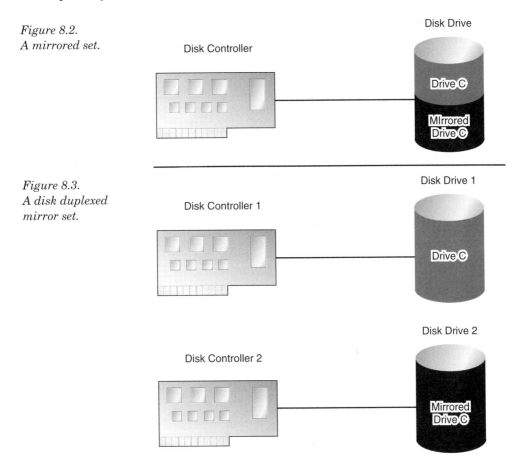

Figure 8.2.
A mirrored set.

Figure 8.3.
A disk duplexed mirror set.

A stripe set, as shown in Figure 8.4, increases the performance of your disk subsystem by breaking the data into blocks. These blocks then are striped across the multiple disk drives. In theory, a single read of a stripe set with five drives can read data five times as fast as a single large disk. In reality, you will not achieve a fivefold increase, but it will be close. When using a stripe set or stripe set with parity, additional memory is required to hold the stripe before it is written or read from the disk. Another consideration for using a stripe set is that if a stripe is damaged (due to a disk failure, for example), all data on the stripe is lost. If this possibility alarms you, you have three choices: back up to tape often (which you should do anyway), use the stripe set for non-critical data (such as the paging file), or use a stripe set with parity.

Figure 8.4.
A stripe set.

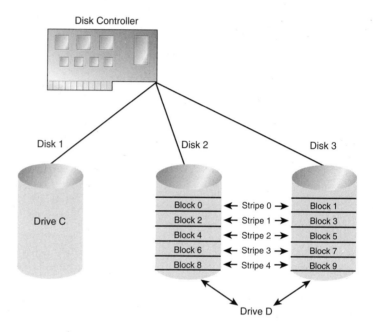

Note

You can combine from 2 to 32 drives into a single logical drive for a stripe set.

A stripe set with parity, as shown in Figure 8.5, is similar in principle to a stripe set, but it adds a parity block to each stripe. This parity block is not all placed on a single drive, but is instead migrated to multiple drives. The first parity block is placed on the last drive, the next parity block is placed on the first drive, and the following block is placed on the second drive, for example. This process continues until the parity block wraps around to the last disk drive once again to start a repeat scenario. If a single disk fails on a stripe set with parity, the data still can be read because the parity block can be used to generate the missing data block. If two disk drives fail, however, the entire logical drive is lost. If a single drive fails, you can power off the system, replace the drive, and then regenerate the missing data.

Figure 8.5.
A stripe set with
parity.

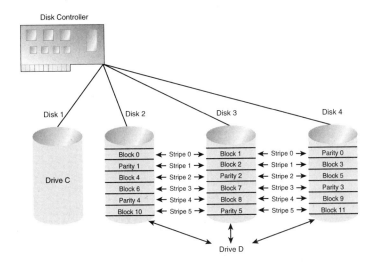

Note

You can combine from 3 to 32 drives into a single logical drive for a stripe set with parity.

Each of these sets has its own menu command, but all of them follow the same basic principles of creation. First, you must select one or more unused partitions. Press the Control key as you select each partition with the mouse. Then choose one of the following menu commands:

◆ Partition | Create Volume Set: Combines multiple blocks of free space into a single logical drive. Unlike stripe sets, a volume set can combine fragmented free space on a single physical disk into a larger partition. This option does not increase performance because data is written to the logical drive in contiguous blocks, beginning with the first free partition you used to create the volume set. When this first partition is full, data is written to the next free partition.

◆ Partition | Extend Volume Set: Extends a current volume set. You first must select the current volume set and then select the additional free space to add to it before executing the menu command.

◆ Partition | Create Stripe Set: Merges two or more partitions on two or more physical drives into a single logical partition and increases performance. The partitions must all be uniform in size, however. If they are not, then the smallest partition determines the unit of measure to be combined. If you have three disk drives with 150MB free, 200MB free, and 300MB free, for example, the maximum stripe set you can create is 450MB.

◆ Fault Tolerance | Establish Mirror: Duplicates the data on one disk onto another disk. If an error occurs, the second disk can be used as a replacement. However, when a failure occurs, you first have to break the mirror relationship. This then assigns the replacement partition as the primary partition and you can continue work as usual.

◆ Fault Tolerance | Break Mirror: Breaks the copying of data from a primary mirrored partition to a secondary mirrored partition. When you issue this command, the secondary drive is assigned its own drive letter and the data remains intact. If you issue this command after a primary mirrored partition failure, the secondary mirrored partition is assigned the primary mirrored partition's drive letter.

◆ Fault Tolerance | Create Stripe Set with Parity: Works just like the Create Stripe Set option, except that it is a fault-tolerant partition. It includes the same limitation as those when combining free space into a single partition. You also lose a portion of the total disk space, which is used for the parity blocks.

◆ Fault Tolerance | Regenerate: When a disk failure occurs on a stripe set with parity, the disk should be replaced as quickly as possible. After the disk is replaced, you can use this option to regenerate the data on the replacement disk. Just select the stripe set with parity and use this menu command to begin the regeneration.

Note

For more information on the fault-tolerant capabilities of Windows NT Server, see Chapter 3, "An Introduction to Windows NT Server."

WORKING WITH PARTITION CONFIGURATIONS

One of the more useful features of Disk Administrator is that it includes its own partition Save and Restore functions. Similar to the third-party MS-DOS partition utilities, Disk Administrator can save its partition information to a floppy disk, and you can use this floppy disk to restore the configuration. It cannot be used to restore a partition that has been reformatted, however. These commands are accessed through the Partition | Configuration option.

Tip

If you have more than one Windows NT Server installation and you have a fault-tolerant partition or a volume set, these partitions are not accessible from the secondary installation. To make them accessible, you can use the Partition | Configuration | Search option. This searches your disk drives for additional Windows NT installations. After the installation is found, you can migrate the partition configuration to your secondary installation. Then, after rebooting, both installations can access the partitions.

USING THE TAPE BACKUP UTILITY

There is nothing more important than the data you have on your server; without this data, you have no resources to share. Luckily, Microsoft takes this aspect seriously and has provided a tape backup utility, as shown in Figure 8.6. This utility supports most 4mm DAT drives, many 8mm DAT drives, and several other formats as well. There are some considerations to using this application. First, you have to install a tape device driver, and then you can back up your data or restore your data.

Figure 8.6.
The tape backup
application with
tiled windows.

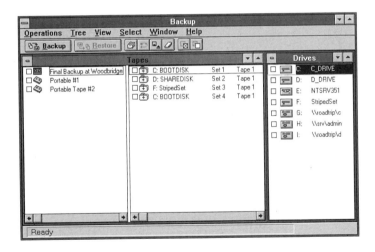

8

Note

Not only can you use the tape backup utility to backup the data on your disk drives, but you can use it to back up your Exchange Server information store and directory databases while Exchange Server is still running. Exchange Server includes a replacement to the tape backup utility (NTBACKUP.EXE) that provides this capability. For more information on how to back up your Exchange Server databases refer to Chapter 27, "Managing Your Postoffice."

You should be aware of some aspects of this application before using it. It does not support every tape drive on the market. You should refer to the Hardware Compatibility List to see whether your model is supported. If it is not supported, you should call your manufacturer to see whether it has a driver for it. It also cannot back up the Registry on a remote computer, although you can back up the data on remote computers as long as the files are not in use. And if you have a QIC 40/80 tape drive, it is supported only on a floppy disk controller. The proprietary accelerator adapters are not supported. Finally, the application does not support software compression, although it can enable hardware compression if your tape drive supports it. If you need software compression or remote Registry backup capabilities, you should look at the replacements from Arcada or Cheyenne.

INSTALLING A TAPE DEVICE DRIVER

You install your tape device driver from the Windows NT Setup application located in your Main Program Manager group. To install the driver, follow these steps:

1. Run the Windows NT Setup application.
2. Choose Options | Add/Remove Tape Devices. The Tape Device Setup dialog box appears.
3. Click the Add button to display the Select Tape Device Option dialog box.
4. In the Device drop-down listbox, select your tape device from the list. If you have a 4mm DAT drive, for example, select the 4 Millimeter DAT Drive entry. If your tape device is not listed but you have an OEM disk, select Other (Requires a Disk From a Hardware Manufacturer). Then click the Install button to copy the driver.
5. Click the Close button. Your changes do not go into effect until you restart the machine, so if you are in a hurry to try out the backup application, restart your computer.

Tip

If your tape drive is not powered up when your machine restarts, the tape driver will fail to load and you will be required to restart your computer before you can use the backup application. To avoid this problem, you can change the tape device driver to be started manually rather than automatically in the Control Panel Devices applet. I do this with my 4mm DAT drive to lower the wear and tear on the unit. If you do this, you might have to have the tape drive powered up for the SCSI controller to scan the logical unit number (LUN) before you can power off the unit. This is manufacturer-dependent, and my Adaptec 1742/a requires it. Otherwise, when I power up the tape drive and start the tape device driver, the driver cannot find my tape drive.

BACKING UP YOUR DATA

You can back up your data to tape interactively with the tape backup utility or by executing a batch process to start the tape backup utility. I actually use both methods in my day-to-day activities. But I generally use the scheduler service to automate my batch backup process. This frees me from the tedious task of remembering to perform the daily backups that everyone needs to perform. However, before you look at automating the backup process, take a look at the interactive process.

To back up your data, follow these steps:

1. Launch the Backup application located in your Administrative Tools Program Manager group.

2. Select the drive you want to back up from the Drives window by clicking on the square next to the drive icon. This places an X in the square, indicating that the entire drive will be backed up to tape. If you only want to back up a specific set of directories or files, double-click the drive icon. This displays a list of folders similar to the list in File Manager. Just click each square next to a directory folder to mark it, or double-click the directory folder to expand it. Mark each directory folder or file you want to back up.

Note

The square next to the drive icon is a solid white square with an X to indicate a complete drive backup. Otherwise, it is a gray square with an X to indicate a partial selection.

3. Repeat step 2 for each drive or directory you want to back up to tape. After you select all your files, click the Backup button to display the Backup Information dialog box.

8

ADDITIONAL ADMINISTRATIVE TOOLS

4. In this dialog box, you should make the following selections:

   ◆ Tape Name: Specifies the name to give a tape.

   ◆ Operation: Specifies the operation. You can choose Append to an existing tape, in which case you cannot specify a name for the tape. Or you can choose Replace, which overwrites any data on the tape.

   ◆ Verify After Backup: Verifies the data copied to the tape.

   ◆ Backup Registry: Copies the Registry files.

   ◆ Restrict Access to Owner or Administrator: Restricts access to the backup set on the tape to the owner (the person who created the data) or the administrator.

   ◆ Hardware Compression: Enables hardware compression if your tape device supports it.

   ◆ Description: Provides a description of the backup.

   ◆ Backup Type: Specifies the type of backup. You can choose from the following types:

     Normal: Copies the data to tape and sets the archive bit.

     Copy: Copies the data but does not change the archive bit.

     Differential: Copies only data files that have been modified but does not set the archive bit.

     Incremental: Copies the data that has been modified and sets the archive bit.

     Daily: Copies data files that have been modified on that day but does not set the archive bit.

   ◆ Log File: Specifies a file for the log. You can specify whether the log should contain a record of each file backed up to tape (Full Detail), just a summary that includes problems and totals (Summary Only), or no logging at all (Don't Log).

5. Click the OK button to begin the data backup. A backup status dialog box appears. If you want to stop the backup, click the Abort button.

And that is all it takes. To automate this process, you can run NTBACKUP.EXE (the tape backup program) from a batch file. The syntax follows:

```
NTBACKUP Operation PathName [/a] [/v] [/r] [/d"Comment"] [/b] [/hc:{on¦off}]
   [/t  {Option}] [/l"LogFileName"] [/e] [/tape:{TapeNbr}]
```

Explanations of this syntax follow:

Operation: Should be backup for a tape backup.

`PathName`: One or more fully qualified directory names, for example, C:\ D:\.

`/a`: Specifies that the data to be backed up is appended to the end of the tape.

`/v`: Verifies the data that has been backed up to the tape.

`/r`: Restricts access to the tape to the owner or administrator.

`/d"Comment"`: Specifies a description for the backup set, where `"Comment"` is your description.

`/b`: Backs up the local Registry files.

`/hc:{on¦off}`: Enables (On) or disables (Off) hardware compression.

`/t {Option}`: Specifies the backup type, where `Option` is `Normal`, `Copy`, `Incremental`, `Differential`, or `Daily`.

`/l"LogFileName"`: Specifies a name for the log, where `"LogFileName"` is the fully qualified path name.

`/e`: Specifies that the backup log only includes exceptions.

`/tape:{TapeNbr}`: Specifies the tape drive to use if you have more than one. Tape drive numbering starts at 0.

Note

If you install Exchange Server, you can specify a *ServerName DataBaseName* in place of `PathName` where *ServerName* is the name of the computer running Exchange Server and *DataBaseName* is DS for directory store or IS for information store. For example, to back up both the directory and information stores on a server called SRV, the command line would look like this:

```
NTBACKUP backup \\SRV DS \\SRV IS /a /v /d"Exchange Server Backup" /b
➡/t Daily /l  "SystemRoot%\Batch\Exchange.LOG" /e /tape:0
```

To completely automate the process, you can use the scheduler service to perform your backup at specific times. To back up your daily files on drive C after you have left work, for example, try this command:

```
AT 17:00 %SystemRoot%\Batch\Daily.CMD
```

Where `DAILY.CMD` contains

```
NTBACKUP backup C:\ /a /v /d"Daily Backup" /b /t Daily
➡/l  "SystemRoot%\Batch\Daily.LOG" /e /tape:0
```

8

Additional Administrative Tools

Tip

Notice that I did not hard code a path name to the files. Instead, I made use of the SystemRoot environment variable. This is because I often share my batch files with other users. For each installation (no matter what drive NT is installed on), I always create a Batch directory off of the root installation directory (generally, C:\WINNT35 or a similar directory). The SystemRoot environment variable is expanded to the physical drive and directory where NT was installed at runtime.

The command

```
AT 17:00 %SystemRoot%\Batch\Daily.CMD
```

runs the DAILY.CMD batch file at 5:00 p.m. DAILY.CMD includes the actual command line for the backup. This particular command appends all the changed data for the day on drive C to your first tape device, verifies the data, restricts access to the tape, backs up your local Registry, and puts all the log exceptions into the DAILY.LOG file. You could have specified the command line right on the AT command line, but I've found a few irregularities with multiple quotation marks in a scheduler command line. So I suggest that you do as I have done here and include such entries in a separate batch file. For more examples, refer to Appendix D, "Example Batch Files and Logon Scripts," which is located on the CD-ROM included with this book.

RESTORING YOUR DATA

Restoring your data follows a similar process to backing up your data. Instead of selecting items from the Drives window, however, you select them from the Tapes window. To restore your data, follow these steps:

1. To find the data you want on a backup set, you first must catalog the tape by double-clicking the tape icon. This displays a list of all the backup sets for the tape. Alternatively, you can choose Catalog from the Operations menu.

2. After the backup sets are displayed, you need to find the information to restore in the backup set. Backup sets are displayed on the right side of the Tapes window. You can do this by double-clicking on the backup set.

3. After the backup set is completely cataloged, a window is displayed with a directory tree. This window has the same characteristics as the drive backup listing mentioned earlier.

4. After you select all the directories and files to be restored, click the Restore button. The Restore Information dialog box appears, in which you can specify an alternate path to restore the data to, compare the data written to

the disk with the data on the tape, restore the local Registry, and specify your log file details.

5. Click the OK button to continue the restore process. If you want to stop the process, click the Abort button in the Restore Status dialog box.

USING THE REPAIR DISK UTILITY

The Repair Disk Utility is not automatically installed in any Program Manager group when you install Windows NT Server. However, I find this tool to be so useful that I immediately install it whenever I install Windows NT Workstation or Windows NT Server. And I suggest that you do so as well. This tool enables you to update your repair information, which is contained in your SystemRoot\Repair subdirectory, or even to create a new repair disk. If you were unable to create a repair disk during the installation process, this utility is your only alternative, aside from the tape backup application, to protect yourself from a system failure.

You can use the repair disk with the three installation disks to repair a failed installation of Windows NT. It is useful for restoring the Registry (which is what the repair information includes) when you make a mistake with the Registry Editor or install some software that prevents your system from functioning properly. If you have a recent copy of the repair disk, you can back out of the changes to your system just by running through the repair process. You'll be back up and running in minutes.

Tip

You can create the three boot disks by running

```
WINNT32.EXE /OX /S:SourcePath
```

from the CD-ROM in the \I386 directory. /OX specifies that you want to create the three installation disks that use floppy disks or the CD-ROM as the installation source medium. You can use /O instead of /OX to create the three boot floppy disks, which use the temporary copy of the installation directory (WIN_NT.~LS) that was copied to your hard disk from a WINNT.EXE (MS-DOS-based) installation. The /S:SourcePath should be a UNC name (such as \\SRV\CD-ROM\I386) or a local device name (such as E:\I386) for the installation media.

Warning

Before you make any system modifications, you should use the Repair Disk Utility to back up your Registry. At the very least, you should update the local repair information, although I recommend that you

8

ADDITIONAL ADMINISTRATIVE TOOLS

also make a new repair disk. In fact, you should keep at least three repair disks so that you will always have one you can use to restore your configuration. Much as you have multiple backup sets, if you have multiple repair disks, you can restore your system to a known good state. At least one of these repair disks should contain a valid Registry to restore your Registry configuration.

INSTALLING THE REPAIR DISK UTILITY

To install the Repair Disk Utility, follow these steps:

1. Open the Administrative Tools group in the Program Manager.
2. Choose New from the File menu and select Program Item. The Program Item Properties dialog box appears.
3. In the Description field, type Repair Disk Utility.
4. In the Command Line field, type RDISK.EXE.
5. Click the OK button to save the new program item.

USING THE REPAIR DISK UTILITY

After you create the program item for the Repair Disk Utility, it is a good idea to run it and back up your system configuration. When you run the application, the Repair Disk Utility dialog box appears, as shown in Figure 8.7.

Figure 8.7.
The Repair Disk
Utility dialog box.

The Repair Disk Utility dialog box has four buttons:

◆ Update Repair Info: Updates the Registry information contained in the SystemRoot\Repair directory. After you click this button, you are asked whether you want to create a new repair disk.

◆ Create Repair Disk: Formats a high-density floppy disk and copies the same repair information as described for the Update Repair Info button. This repair disk is used by the repair process to restore your Registry.

Tip

If you have a 2.88MB floppy drive and experience problems creating a repair disk, insert a 1.44MB floppy and use this to create your repair disk.

◆ Exit: Exits the application.

◆ Help: Displays brief descriptions of the Repair Disk Utility buttons' actions.

The information in the `SystemRoot\Repair` directory consists of uncompressed copies of your `autoexec.nt` and `config.nt` files and the compressed files listed in Table 8.1.

`SystemRoot\Repair`, however, does not include all your local profiles. If you want to back up these, you need to do so with the tape backup utility or by manually copying them from the `SystemRoot\System32\Config` subdirectory (where `SystemRoot` is the root directory where you installed NT Server—usually, `C:\WINNT35`).

Tip

If you have `compress.exe`, which is included with several of the Microsoft SDKs and development platforms, you can compress the files in a format that is compatible with the Microsoft expansion program. `Expand.exe` is included with Windows NT and is used to manually uncompress these files. You might want to use the same format because you will have this program (`expand.exe`) on every system you use.

TABLE 8.1. KEY COMPONENTS OF THE REGISTRY.

Filename	Registry Key	Description
default._	HKEY_USERS\DEFAULT	The default system profile
sam._	HKEY_LOCAL_MACHINE\SAM	Your Security Account Manager
security._	HKEY_LOCAL_MACHINE\Security	The security database
software._	HKEY_LOCAL_MACHINE\Software	The software configurable settings
system._	HKEY_LOCAL_MACHINE\System	System-specific configuration settings

You will see one additional file not mentioned in the SystemRoot\Repair directory if you enable the Show Hidden/System Files option with File Manager (this is accessed from the View | By File Type menu option). This file is called setup.log, and it should never be deleted. This file is used by the Setup program during an upgrade. If the Setup program cannot find enough free space during the upgrade, it prompts you to delete some files from your current installation. The files listed in setup.log are the files that will be deleted to make room for the upgrade. If this file is missing and you have insufficient disk space, the Setup program will be able to continue only if you format your hard disk. This is rarely an acceptable solution and could be quite dangerous to your continued health if this installation is your only domain controller (which contains all your account information), has critical data files, or contains similar nonrecoverable components. Your only other alternative is to exit the upgrade process and manually delete enough files for you to reinstall.

Using the UPS Service

The UPS Service is used with an Uninterruptible Power Supply (UPS) to provide electrical power to your system in case of a power failure. It also is used to filter your electrical power, which, in my opinion, is more important. Power failures occur infrequently, but surges, spikes, and brownouts occur much more often. In fact, the power is so poor where my server is connected that every time the air conditioner kicks in, I have a power spike of close to 130 volts and the lights dim. My American Power Conversion (APC) UPS protects my server and its installed peripherals from these potentially damaging line conditions. You can use a UPS to help protect your server as well. If you consider that a UPS costs less than 10 percent of the price of your server, it makes a more attractive option the longer you think about it.

Tip

You should try to purchase a UPS that uses a true sine wave for power output. A true sine wave is exactly what your normal AC power outlet supplies. Alternative sine waves include a modified step sine wave, which is a good alternative to square sine waves, which are not a very good choice. A square sine wave has the potential to damage delicate equipment. Even a modified sine wave can cause potential problems. On my server, the NEC 4Ds monitor would produce a high-pitched squeal and flicker uncontrollably on a stepped sine wave, which is why I quickly decided to replace it with a true sine wave output device from APC.

CONFIGURING THE UPS SERVICE

Just placing your UPS between your server and your AC power outlet provides you with power filtering and limited runtime when the power fails. But this is not enough. Before you can use your UPS effectively, you need to get it to communicate with Windows NT Server. Otherwise, when the battery in your UPS runs down, your server will be powered off, just as if you had pressed the Off switch. This can lead to lost data and corrupted file systems. It could even lead to an unbootable operating system and a pink slip from your employer.

The UPS Service provides the link between your UPS and Windows NT Server. The UPS Service communicates with your UPS through a proprietary cable connected to a serial port on your server and a serial port on your UPS. So the first item you must have in order to get the UPS Service working is a free serial port. Next, get the UPS cable from your UPS manufacturer. Make sure that when you order the cable from the manufacturer, you get the right one. My APC UPS uses a gray cable to work with the UPS Service provided with Windows NT Server but a black cable when used with the APC UPS Service (called PowerChute Plus). These two cables have different pin outs and can provide additional services when used with the APC UPS Service.

Note

The serial port you choose for the UPS Service does not have to be a high-end serial port (such as a 16550), but it does have to be completely conflict free. This means that you cannot share an IRQ or I/O port with any other device. This is because the UPS Service constantly polls the UPS, much as your serial mouse port constantly polls for mouse movement.

As soon as you have the right cable, just connect the cable to your UPS and your free serial port. Then open the Control Panel and launch the UPS applet. The UPS dialog box appears, as displayed in Figure 8.8.

Follow these steps to configure the UPS Service:

1. Enable the Uninterruptible Power Supply Is Installed On field and select the COM port the UPS cable is connected to from the drop-down listbox.
2. If your UPS supports a communications interface by raising a signal on the Clear To Send (CTS), Data Carrier Detect (DCD), or Data Terminal Ready (DTR) pin, you can select options from the UPS Configuration group. Options in this group follow:

◆ Power Failure Signal: Uses the CTS pin on your serial port to indicate that the AC power has failed.

◆ Low Battery Signal at Least 2 Minutes Before Shutdown: Uses the DCD pin on your serial port to indicate that the UPS battery is low and that power will be discontinued.

◆ Remote UPS Shutdown: Uses the DTR pin on your serial port to indicate that the UPS Service is shutting down the system.

Figure 8.8.
The UPS dialog box.

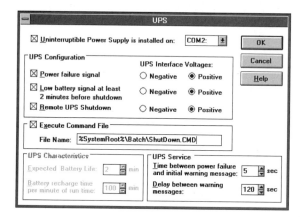

Warning

If you enable any of the options in the UPS Configuration group, you must indicate the correct UPS interface voltage for the Remote UPS Shutdown entry, even if you do not use this feature. This must be set because some UPSs shut down the system unexpectedly when a loss of AC power occurs if the correct voltage is not specified.

Tip

The American Power Conversion (APC) UPS uses all three of the UPS configuration signals. The UPS interface voltage should be set to all positive settings.

Note

The UPS interface voltage for supported UPSs is included the Hardware Compatibility List.

3. If you want to run a batch file or program before the server shuts down, enable the Execute Command File checkbox and specify a file to execute. This file can be any executable file, but it cannot wait for any user input (by displaying a dialog box, for example) and must complete within 30 seconds. If it runs longer than 30 seconds, the integrity of your system may be in jeopardy.

Note

A default message is broadcast automatically to members of your domain informing them of a power failure and impending shutdown. You might want to send a message to users of another domain, however. You can use the NET SEND command to do this. For example,

```
NET SEND /domain:WORK "Server SRV is shutting down in 30 seconds."
```

sends a message to all users of the Work domain.

4. If your UPS does not support the low battery signal, you can use the UPS Characteristics group settings to specify an estimated battery life by setting the number of minutes in the Expected Battery Life box. You can also specify the estimated number of minutes before the battery will be fully charged for every minute of run time (while on battery power). Do this after the AC power is restored by setting the number of minutes in the Battery Recharge Time per Minute of Run Time box.

5. You can specify the time that the first warning message is sent to your domain members after a power failure by specifying the number of seconds in the Time Between Power Failure and Initial Warning Message box. Set the time to repeat this message in the Delay Between Warning Messages box in the UPS Service group.

USING THE UPS MONITOR SERVICE

The UPS Service supplied with Windows NT Server works well with one exception. After a power failure occurs, the UPS battery is in a low battery condition. This means that when the UPS Service attempts to start, it notices this condition and fails to start. This is why I wrote the UPS Monitor service. This service monitors the status of the UPS Service. If the UPS Service is not running, then the UPS Monitor Service attempts to start it. After the UPS Service starts, the UPS Monitor Service stops automatically.

To install the UPS Monitor Service, follow these steps:

1. Open a command prompt (run CMD.EXE) and change to the TOOLS\UPS directory on the supplied CD-ROM.

8

ADDITIONAL ADMINISTRATIVE TOOLS

2. Run the UPSMNIST program with the /I switch to install the service. If you need to remove the service, use the /R switch. The UPSMON.EXE (the UPS Monitor Service) and the UPSMON.DLL (the event message dynamic link library) are copied to your SystemRoot\System32 subdirectory. It also installs the service.

3. Open the Control Panel Service applet. Scroll through the list until the UPS Monitor Service is viewable.

4. Select the service and click the Startup button. Set the service to start up automatically.

   In the Startup Parameters field, you can specify switches. You can use /q or /Q to specify that information messages should not be placed in the log (such as the service starting or stopping) and you can specify a /t:X or /T:X switch, where X is a time in milliseconds. This time value determines the polling interval at which to check whether the UPS Service is running. The default is to display all messages and to allot a period of one minute (60,000 milliseconds) to poll the UPS Service.

5. Click the Start button to start the service with the parameters you specified.

Note

These configuration parameters are stored in the Registry under the HKEY_LOCAL_MACHINE\Software\Knowles Consulting\UPS Monitor subkey. You will find a Display Message value and a Time value. The Display Message value can be 0 or 1. The Time field can be any value from 1 to 4 billion milliseconds. Both these values are stored in a REG_DWORD.

USING THIRD-PARTY UPS PRODUCTS

The UPS Service supplied with Windows NT Server does give you the capability to safely shut down your server in a graceful manner in case of a power failure. You still might want to purchase a replacement UPS Service from your UPS manufacturer, however. Perhaps this makes you wonder why you should consider spending additional money to replace what is working now? Well, I'll tell you. Some of these third-party replacements offer additional functionality. The APC UPS Service replacement includes an application to monitor and configure the operation of the UPS Service, for example (see Figure 8.9).

Figure 8.9.
The PowerChute
PLUS applica-
tion.

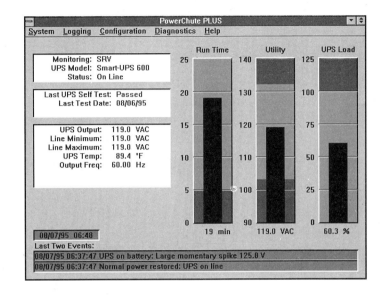

This replacement is called PowerChute PLUS and provides these additional benefits:

◆ Monitoring any APC UPSs on your network servers that use PowerChute PLUS as their UPS service. You can even shut down a server remotely or schedule UPS shutdowns to occur on these servers.

◆ Monitoring your power quality and problems that might have occurred in the past through the data logs. These logs contain the following information:

> Date the event occurred
>
> Time the event occurred
>
> Minimum voltage
>
> Maximum voltage
>
> UPS voltage output
>
> Battery voltage
>
> AC frequency
>
> UPS load (percentage)
>
> UPS temperature

If you have the optional temperature sensor, it includes the temperature and the humidity of the surrounding area. You can even import these logs into a spreadsheet for analysis of your AC power.

8

◆ Monitoring additional UPS events. These events include the following:

Power-failure messages (more than just the default UPS Service message that the UPS is being used or that power was restored)

UPS hardware failure messages

Battery diagnostic messages (including when to replace the UPS battery)

Other messages related to the operation of the UPS

◆ Modifying the UPS operating parameters without flipping dip switches on the UPS. These parameters include the following:

High and low transfer points (if the AC voltage is higher than or lower than these settings, the UPS uses the battery to supply AC power until the condition is resolved)

Sensitivity (determines how sensitive the UPS is to line disturbances)

UPS output voltage

Name of the UPS (my UPS is named SRV_UPS, for example)

Date of the last battery replacement

UPS serial number

Manufacturer date

Firmware revision number

◆ Modifying the UPS shutdown parameters, which include the following:

Remaining battery time the UPS must have before the low battery signal is sent (for many UPSs, the default is two minutes, but I set mine to five minutes)

UPS turn-off delay (how long the UPS stays online after receiving a shutdown signal)

UPS wake-up delay (how long to wait after AC power is restored before supplying power to the AC receptacles on the UPS)

Minimum UPS wake-up capacity (how much battery capacity must be available before the UPS goes online and supplies AC power to its receptacles)

When to enable the UPS alarm to notify you of a power failure

Whether to automatically reboot (this setting determines whether the UPS automatically restores power to its AC receptacles when power is restored or whether it requires an administrator to manually enable the power switch)

Note

In my opinion, the minimum UPS wake-up capacity is really a re-quirement for any UPS connected to a server. Power could be turned on and off repeatedly during a thunderstorm. And if your UPS does not offer this capability, your server will turn on and off repeatedly. During one of these periods, you can be sure that your UPS will no longer maintain enough battery capacity to safely shut down your system. This can lead to data loss or a corrupted file system.

◆ Performing routine diagnostics such as a self test, runtime calibration, simulating a power failure, and testing the UPS alarm. This can be useful to ensure that your UPS is operating properly, that the battery offers enough capacity to maintain your server during a power failure for a minimum length of time, that the UPS service is operating properly, and that the UPS alarm is functional.

◆ Scheduling UPS self tests and runtime calibrations at specific intervals to ensure that the UPS is continuing to run properly and that the battery capacity is still sufficient to operate your server in case of a power failure.

Your UPS manufacturer may offer similar options that you can use to provide long-term monitoring of your AC line conditions or to set your UPS characteristics as the APC UPS service replacement offers. Before you spend any additional money for this product, however, you should check with the manufacturer to see exactly what it is that you are buying. If it does not offer any additional functionality than that provided with the default UPS service, you should not bother to purchase it.

WORKING WITH A WORKGROUP POSTOFFICE

Windows NT Server (and Windows NT Workstation) includes a 32-bit Microsoft Mail client application. This application can be used to create a postoffice and then administer it, or you can just use it to connect to an existing postoffice. It does not offer all the functionality of the full-blown Microsoft Mail 3.x mail server, but if all you need is rudimentary e-mail services, it may be just the ticket for you. In later chapters, you will learn about the complete Microsoft Mail 3.x package and the upgrading possibilities.

CREATING A WORKGROUP POSTOFFICE

Creating a postoffice is easy, but you should keep a few considerations in mind. First, only the creator of the postoffice can administer it. Second, a workgroup postoffice

can display only personal or shared folders one at a time and not both simultaneously. Third, if you have more than 10 users, do not install the postoffice on a
Windows NT Workstation computer because a Windows NT Workstation is limited
to 10 simultaneous connections.

To create your workgroup postoffice, follow these steps.

1. The first time you run Mail (located in the Main Program Manager group)
   you are presented with a dialog box that enables you to connect to an
   existing postoffice or to create a new workgroup postoffice. You should
   choose to create a new workgroup postoffice.

2. You are warned about creating multiple postoffices. Click Yes to proceed.

   There should be only one workgroup postoffice in your workgroup/domain.
   If you create more than one postoffice, these users cannot send e-mail
   outside their local postoffice. You need the complete Microsoft Mail 3.x
   package in order to support multiple postoffices.

3. The next dialog box prompts you for the location of the WGPO (Work Group
   postoffice) directory. This should be installed on a partition with sufficient
   free space to handle all your client's mail data if you store the MMF
   (Microsoft Mail File) file on the server. If you will have 10 clients with a
   maximum of 10MB of mail per user, for example, you will need at least a
   100MB partition.

Warning

If you install your postoffice to a compressed NTFS volume, you may
gain a slight bit of additional storage space, but you will decrease the
performance of your mail server. This occurs because Microsoft Mail
Files (MMFs) are already compressed. The overhead of trying to
compress an already compressed file, or to uncompress these files as
they are used, is rarely worth the effort.

4. After the WGPO directory is created, you are prompted to enter your
   Administrator account detail information. In this dialog box, you should
   enter a name (such as Mail Administrator), a mailbox name (such as
   Admin) with a maximum length of 10 characters, a password with a maximum length of eight characters, and miscellaneous information (such as
   your phone numbers, office, department, and notes). Then click the OK
   button to create your account.

Note

If you create an account and do not assign a password, the default will be PASSWORD.

A confirmation dialog box appears, telling you of the location where the postoffice was created and reminding you to share the directory you just created.

And that's all there is to it. In addition to using File Manager to share the postoffice directory, be sure to create the share with at least Change permission or the users will not be able to use their mail clients without errors.

Tip

I prefer to create the share with Full Control permissions for the Everyone group and then to set directory and file-level permissions with File Manager. This way, I can set Change permissions for the Domain Users group, Read for Domain Guests (which provides very limited functionality and does prevent them from deleting the entire directory), and Full Control for Domain Admins, which gives the administrators the capability to run mail utility programs.

MANAGING YOUR WORKGROUP POSTOFFICE

Managing your workgroup postoffice does not consist of very many options. In fact, the primary option you will use is to just create mailboxes for your network clients. This is accomplished by choosing postoffice Manager from the Mail menu. The postoffice Manager dialog box appears, which you can use to display the details of a mailbox (click the Details button), create new mailboxes (click the Add User button), delete a mailbox (click the Remove User button), and look at the shared folders' usage summary (click the Shared Folders button).

Whenever you add a user, you must supply a mailbox name with a maximum length of 10 characters, a password with a maximum length of eight characters, and miscellaneous information (such as the phone numbers, office, department, and notes). This procedure is just like the one you followed when you created your own account earlier. If you do not create the accounts, the individual users can create their own accounts the first time they run the 32-bit Microsoft mail client.

There are a couple of ways that you can make your postoffice a little safer:

◆ You can specify that the user's MMF file be located locally on his computer or remotely on the server. To place the file on the server, each user must choose Options from the Mail menu. The Options dialog box appears. Click the Server button. The Server dialog box appears, in which the user can specify in the storage group that the MMF file should be stored in the postoffice or locally on the user's computer. If you store all your MMF files on the server, backing up these files becomes a relatively easy task.

Tip

You also can use the Options dialog box to specify that the inbox (where new messages are stored) be copied to the user's local MMF file when the user connects through remote access.

◆ If the MMF is stored locally, the individual users must back up their own MMF files by choosing Backup from the Mail menu.

◆ You can choose Export from the File menu to back up a single folder to a file, and you can choose Import from the File menu to restore a folder from a file.

◆ If you want to create shared folders to allow your mail users to share a single folder, you can choose New Folder from the File menu to create a shared folder. Shared folders can be limited to Read, Write, or Delete privileges for your connected users. And by using a shared folder, you can save space in your workgroup postoffice. You also can use this command to create a new personal folder.

USING THE NETWORK CLIENT ADMINISTRATOR

The Network Client Administrator provides two very useful functions for any network administrator to use. First, you can use it to create a network installation disk so that you can install the MS-DOS 3.0 network client for MS-DOS or Windows 3.x. Or you can install Windows for Workgroups 3.11 from a network sharepoint. And with some modification, you can use it to install Windows 3.x, Windows NT, or Windows NT Server. Second, you can use it to create an installation disk set to install the MS-DOS Remote Access Service 1.1 client, the MS-DOS 3.0 network client drivers, TCP/IP 32 for Windows for Workgroups 3.11, or the LAN Manager 2.2c network client drivers for MS-DOS or OS/2 clients.

The Network Client Administrator is located in your Network Administration Program Manager group. When you launch it, the dialog box shown in Figure 8.10 appears.

Figure 8.10.
The Network
Client Adminis-
trator dialog box.

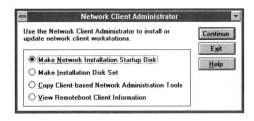

When you first use the application to create an installation disk, a dialog box appears, which you can use to determine the location of the data files (see Figure 8.11).

Figure 8.11.
The Share
Network Client
Installation Files
dialog box.

Note

If you install the client-based network administration tools (this includes versions of the Event Viewer, DHCP and WINS managers, RAS Administrator, Remoteboot Manager, User Profile Editor, User Manager for Domains, and Server Manager for your Windows NT or Windows 3.x clients), a dialog box similar to the Share Network Client Installation Files dialog box appears. In this box, you can decide to share the existing directory on the CD-ROM, copy the files to a new directory and then share it, or use an existing sharepoint.

8

ADDITIONAL ADMINISTRATIVE TOOLS

The Share Network Client Installation Files dialog box contains the following options:

◆ Use Existing Path: Uses a local path to access the required data files. This can be the path to the files on the CD-ROM or the path to a copy of the files that you manually copied to your server.

◆ Share Files: Creates a share name for you (although you can modify the name) that points to the path to the files on the CD-ROM or to a copy of the files that you copied manually to your server.

Tip

I prefer the Share Files method because it requires no space on your network server. Copying all the files requires more than 53MB of disk space. If you will be roaming the network and creating client installation disks, however, the Copy Files to a New Directory, and Then Share option is your best choice.

◆ Copy Files to a New Directory, and Then Share: Copies the data files to a directory on your server and then creates a sharepoint for it.

◆ Use Existing Shared Directory: Uses an existing sharepoint that contains the data files. It uses the sharepoint created earlier or one that you manually created.

Tip

If you also copy the NCADMIN.EXE, NCADMIN.HLP, and NCADMIN.CNT files to a shared directory, you can run the Network Client Administrator from any Windows NT computer to create your installation disks.

CREATING NETWORK INSTALLATION DISKS

After you configure the Network Client Administrator, you are ready to create your installation disks. Follow these steps:

1. Open the Network Client Administrator located in your Network Administration Program Manager group. Then select the Make Network Installation Startup Disk option and click the Continue button. The Share Network Client Installation Files dialog box appears.

2. If any information is incorrect, change it. (The application stores the location of the data files, but if you are running the application from a

client you might need to specify the sharepoint manually.) Then click the OK button.

3. Insert a freshly formatted MS-DOS system disk into your drive A. This can be a 3-1/2-inch or 5-1/4-inch floppy disk. Select the floppy drive type in the Floppy Drive group.

Tip

> Don't be concerned that step 3 is for drive A only. In the Network Startup Disk Configuration dialog box, you can specify the disk drive. It can be A, B, or any other relative path.

4. In the Network Client group, select the type of disk to create. This can be an installation disk for Windows for Workgroups 3.11 or the MS-DOS 3.0 network client.

5. Select the network adapter in the Network Adapter Card drop-down listbox.

6. Click the OK button. The Network Startup Disk Configuration dialog box appears. In this dialog box, you must specify a computer name, user name, domain name, and the network protocol to use. If you choose TCP/IP, you also can set the TCP/IP settings (such as to use DHCP to automatically allocate an IP address or manually set the IP address). You also can specify a destination path. Then click the OK button.

The installation disk then is created. But you are not finished yet. If your network adapter is not software configurable, then you also may have to change the default settings for the card. This information is stored in the `protocol.ini` file located in the NET subdirectory on the floppy disk. If necessary, change the IRQ, I/O address, DMA channel, or base memory address before you use the installation floppy disk.

Tip

> If you want to use this installation disk to install Windows NT, Windows NT Server, or other application software, you will need to edit the `autoexec.bat` file. Just change the mapped directory to the directory containing the installation files. And change the setup program name to the application's setup program. I use this to change the drive mapping to `USE Z: \\SRV\CD-ROM` and the `setup.exe` entry to `WINNT /B /S:\\SRV\CD-ROM\I386` to install Windows NT Workstation from a shared directory on my CD-ROM drive, for example.

CREATING INSTALLATION DISK SETS

Creating an installation disk set is quite similar to creating a network installation disk. The major differences are that the disks do not have to be bootable and that you might need more than one disk because the software to be installed is not stored on the network. Furthermore, the files are just copied to the installation floppy disks. The user is prompted for the information you supplied in the previous section. This information includes the user name, computer name, network adapter, and other miscellaneous items.

In order for the user to install the software, he must run the setup program (setup.exe) on the floppy disk. This begins the installation process and prompts users for all required information.

Tip

One of the features I find particularly useful with this installation process is that you can copy the entire CLIENTS\WDL\NETWORK directory to another floppy disk and use this (or an OEM floppy disk) to install network adapters that are not supported with the Network Installation Startup Disk option.

USING THE REMOTEBOOT SERVICE

The Remoteboot Service is used to support your network clients who boot their operating system from the server rather than from a local disk drive. This process uses a Remote Program Load (RPL) ROM located in the network adapter to load a boot block from the server. The boot block is the actual startup code for the operating system. After this boot block is loaded, the rest of the operating system is loaded. Most of these network clients do not contain a floppy drive or a hard disk and are referred to as diskless workstations.

A diskless workstation can offer a few advantages for you and your company:

◆ Diskless workstations can prevent the spreading of viruses because there is no mechanism to introduce them. Most viruses are spread from a bootable floppy disk inserted into a local disk drive on a user's computer.

◆ You can control the distribution of information and software on your network. This is because the network client does not have the capability to change its configuration because it cannot save any settings to the shared software installation. It can execute only the software you permit or save its configuration in a home directory that you provide. But as an administrator, you can control these options.

◆ Software upgrades are easier to perform because you only have to update the central configuration. The users automatically benefit from these changes.

◆ Computers without local floppy drives or hard disk drives are less expensive.

Of course, there are a few disadvantages to diskless workstations as well. They increase the traffic on the network because every user is accessing the same files. Windows performance suffers because any paging must be performed on the networked drive, and the loading of dynamic link libraries must be performed from this shared installation. You can offset some of these disadvantages by using a local hard disk. This hard disk can be used to create the paging file, and it contains the user's data files (and applications, if desired), while still giving you the benefits of easy operating system upgrades and the prevention of virus introductions.

INSTALLING THE REMOTEBOOT SERVICE

Installing the Remoteboot Service is a multipart process. First, you have to install the service. Then you have to copy the operating systems to the RPL root directories. And finally, you have to use the Remoteboot Manager to set the security on these files and check the configurations. All this before you can create a profile. A profile contains the user configuration. You might have a profile for MS-DOS 5.0 or MS-DOS 6.x, for example, with both of them being able to run Windows 3.x from the shared installation.

Note

Before you install the Remoteboot Service, you should be aware of two points. First, your server name cannot contain any spaces or your MS-DOS clients will not be able to connect to it. Second, you should install the remote boot files to an NTFS directory because the FAT file system cannot support more than 100 remote boot clients. Through such an installation, you can specify the correct permissions on the shared files.

To install the Remoteboot Service, follow these steps:

1. Open the Control Panel Network applet. The Network Settings dialog box appears.
2. Click the Add Software button to display the Add Network Software dialog box.
3. Select the Remoteboot Service and click the Continue button.

Note

> You also need the DLC (Data Link Control) and NetBEUI transport protocols on your server. If you have not installed them already, add them now. Just repeat steps 2 and 3 for the DLC Protocol and NetBEUI Protocol. This is required because the Remoteboot Service uses these transport protocols to operate.

4. When prompted, enter a path to specify where you want to install the remote boot files. This should be an NTFS partition.

5. When prompted, enter a path to the location of the remote boot client files. These are stored in the \CLIENTS\RPL directory on your CD-ROM.

6. Click the OK button to exit the Network Settings dialog box.

7. Reboot when prompted.

The next step involves copying the client files to your remote boot directory that you created in step 4 to install the Remoteboot Service so that you can create a client profile. You can copy the MS-DOS system files and Windows 3.x system files to support an MS-DOS client and allow it to run the shared copy of Windows 3.x, for example.

To set up a client, follow these steps:

1. Find a copy of the version of MS-DOS you want to support. On the client workstation, log onto the network, and then connect to the remote boot shared directory (USE X: \\ServerName\RPLFILES, where ServerName is the name of your server and x is the drive letter you choose to use for the mapped drive).

2. Remove the attributes on the MS-DOS boot files. These files are IO.SYS and MS-DOS.SYS. Use these commands:

```
ATTRIB -h -s IO.SYS
ATTRIB -h -s MS-DOS.SYS
```

3. Copy these files to the appropriate subdirectory. If you are copying an MS-DOS 5.0 installation, copy these files to the BINFILES\DOS500 sub-directory, for example:

```
COPY IO.SYS X:\BINFILES\DOS500
COPY MS-DOS.SYS X:\BINFILES\DOS500
COPY COMMAND.COM X:\BINFILES\DOS500
```

Note

> Do not create any additional subdirectories in the BINFILES root directory. If you are installing any version of MS-DOS 6.2x, for example, it

must be placed in the BINFILES\622 subdirectory. This means that you can support only one version of MS-DOS in a particular directory. You cannot install MS-DOS 6.2, 6.21, and 6.22 in the same directory.

Note

If you are copying files from an IBM version of PC-DOS, rename the files on the server from IBMDOS.COM to MSDOS.SYS and from IBMIO.COM to IO.SYS.

4. Replace the attributes on the MS-DOS boot files. These files are IO.SYS and MS-DOS.SYS. Use these commands:

```
ATTRIB +h +s IO.SYS
ATTRIB +h +s MS-DOS.SYS
```

5. Repeat steps 1 through 4 for each version of MS-DOS that you want to support.

The next step requires that you choose the Configure | Fix Security and Configure | Check Configurations menu options to set the appropriate permissions on the files and to verify that all the required boot files are present. These boot files include BOOTSECT.COM, IO.SYS, MS-DOS.SYS, and COMMAND.COM. If any of these files are missing, you will be unable to create a profile.

To create a profile, follow these steps:

1. Choose New Profile from the Remoteboot menu. The New Profile dialog box appears.
2. In the Profile Name field, enter a unique name containing up to 16 characters. This name cannot contain any spaces or backslashes (\).
3. In the Configuration field, select the operating system and network adapter. Select DOS 6.22 3Com Etherlink III to support clients with Etherlink III network adapters and to provide MS-DOS 6.22 as the operating system, for example.
4. In the Description field, enter a description for this profile if the default is not acceptable.

Note

If you enter a description before selecting the configuration, your description is overwritten with the default description. The default description is the same as the configuration you choose.

5. Click the OK button and your profile is displayed in the Profile Name field.

6. Repeat these steps for each profile you want to create.

MANAGING YOUR REMOTEBOOT CLIENTS

Now that you have created your profiles, it is time to add workstations to the Remoteboot Service. This is accomplished with the Remoteboot Manager. There are two ways to create a new workstation record. You can create a new workstation record manually, or you can automate the process a bit.

Note

You must have the network client for which you want to create a workstation record turned on and available to be queried by the Remoteboot Manager. Otherwise, the process will fail.

To create a new workstation record manually, follow these steps:

1. Choose New Workstation from the Remoteboot menu. The New Remoteboot Workstation dialog box appears, as shown in Figure 8.12.

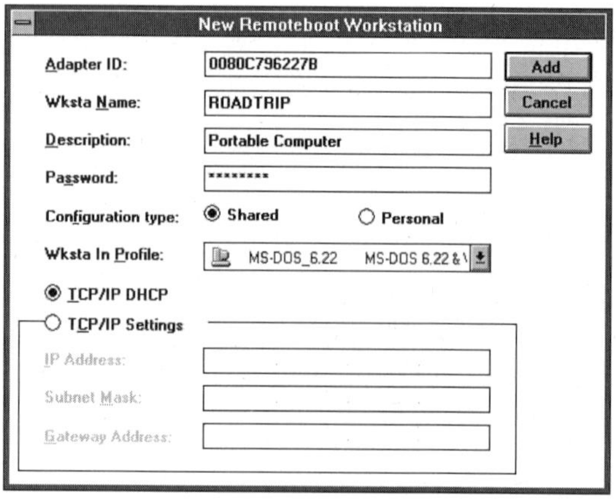

Figure 8.12.
The New
Remoteboot
Workstation
dialog box.

New Remoteboot Workstation	
Adapter ID:	0080C796227B
Wksta Name:	ROADTRIP
Description:	Portable Computer
Password:	••••••••
Configuration type:	◉ Shared ○ Personal
Wksta In Profile:	MS-DOS_6.22 MS-DOS 6.22 & \
◉ TCP/IP DHCP	
○ TCP/IP Settings	
IP Address:	
Subnet Mask:	
Gateway Address:	

Buttons: Add, Cancel, Help

2. In the Adapter ID field, enter the 12-digit hexadecimal adapter identification number of the network adapter. If you do not know this number, use the automatic installation procedure.

3. In the Wksta Name field, enter the computer name of the workstation.

4. In the Description field, enter a comment for the workstation.

5. In the Password field, enter a password.

Note

> This password is not the user account password you created with User Manager for Domains. Instead, it is used by the Remoteboot Service to authenticate the workstation and to enable users to set the permissions for the user configuration maintained by the Remoteboot Service. In fact, a user account is created based on the workstation name you supply, and the password for this account is the password you supplied in the Password field in the New Remoteboot Workstation dialog box.

6. Select a Configuration type option. This can be Shared or Personal. A shared configuration can be used by multiple users, although they cannot make any changes. A personal configuration is user-specific and can have user-customizable settings.

7. From the Wksta In Profile drop-down listbox, select a profile for the account. This will be one of the profiles you created earlier.

8. If you are using TCP/IP as your network protocol, select TCP/IP DHCP to use your DHCP server to provide an IP address (the preferred method). Or, to manually assign an IP address, a subnet mask, and a gateway address, enable the TCP/IP Settings option instead.

9. Click the Add button to add the workstation record.

10. Repeat these steps for each new workstation record.

To create a new workstation record automatically, follow these steps:

1. Boot the workstation client. When the workstation starts, it attempts to find an RPL server that will create an adapter record.

Note

> An adapter record appears just like a workstation record in the Remoteboot Manager main window, but it doesn't have a workstation name associated with it. Instead, it has the 12-digit hexadecimal adapter identification number listed.

2. Select the adapter record. Then choose `Convert Adapters` from the Remoteboot menu. The New Remoteboot Workstation dialog box appears.

3. Repeat steps 3 through 10 of the preceding procedure to create a new workstation record manually.

8

ADDITIONAL ADMINISTRATIVE TOOLS

> ## Tip
>
> To convert multiple adapter records one at a time, select each adapter record while pressing and continuing to hold down the Control key. Then choose Remoteboot¦Convert Adapters. To convert all adapter records, just choose Remoteboot¦Convert Adapters.

Now that you have created these configuration programs, you probably will want to install some software for them to use—maybe Windows 3.x or Microsoft Office.

First, you need to install the application files on the server. For this example, use Windows 3.x. Follow these steps:

1. Boot the client workstation and sign on with an Administrator account.
2. Insert the Windows installation disk (or other application disk) and run the network version of the setup program. To run the Windows network installation program, for example, type setup /a.
3. When prompted for an installation directory, specify C:\WIN. This copies the expanded files into the RPLFILES\BINFILES\WIN subdirectory. For an application, specify C:\WIN\AppName, where AppName is a unique name.

> ## Tip
>
> If you are installing an application that is already expanded and does not require any network-configurable parameters, you can just copy the files without running through the network installation process.

Second, you need to install the files in the client profile configuration. This configuration can be a shared configuration profile, in which case all users of the configuration profile benefit, or a personal configuration profile, which is unique to that individual. Follow these steps:

1. Boot the client workstation and sign on with an Administrator account.
2. Change to the Windows directory (type CD C:\WIN).
3. Type setup /n and press Enter to run the network client installation. Do not upgrade the installation; instead, just choose the Express installation.
4. Install Windows in the C:\WINDOWS directory.
5. Copy all the files in the C:\WINDOWS directory to the C:\WKSTA.PRO\WIN directory by using the following command:

```
XCOPY C:\WINDOWS C:\WKSTA.PRO\WIN /E
```

This copies the files to the configuration profile and gives all users of this profile the capability to run the application.

Tip

To install additional applications, perform the same steps, but install to a subdirectory of the `c:\WINDOWS` directory. If you performed a network setup for Microsoft Office to the `c:\WIN\OFFICE` directory, for example, when you run Setup, specify `c:\WINDOWS\OFFICE` as the destination directory. Then copy the `OFFICE` subdirectory files to the `c:\WKSTA.PRO\WIN\OFFICE` subdirectory.

SUMMARY

This chapter discussed some of the tools you will use on a daily basis to manage your server. Specifically, you took a look at the Disk Administrator for managing your disk partitions and creating and deleting volume sets, stripe sets, stripe sets with parity, and mirrored sets. You then spent some time learning about the NTBACKUP application so that you can back up your data to tape and automate the process with batch files and the scheduler service.

Next, you looked at some tools to help you maintain the integrity of your server. These tools include the Repair Disk Utility, UPS Service, UPS Monitor Service, and third-party UPS service replacements.

Your final stop was a look at managing your workgroup postoffice, using the Network Client Administrator to create installation disks, and using the Remoteboot Service to support your diskless workstations.

In the next chapter, you will look at installing and configuring the Dynamic Host Configuration Protocol (DHCP) and Windows Internet Naming Service (WINS) to aid you in managing your TCP/IP-based network.

CHAPTER 9

Using DHCP, WINS, and DNS

If you have a TCP/IP-based network and want to make your administrative life a little easier, there is nothing more important than the Dynamic Host Configuration Protocol (DHCP) and the Windows Internet Naming Service (WINS). These two services give you the capability to automatically manage your client TCP/IP IP address allocations and NetBIOS name resolution, respectively. These services can even interoperate with existing third-party DHCP servers and UNIX Domain Name System (DNS), with some reservations, which are discussed in this chapter. If you want to connect your network to the Internet, or support clients that do not support the Microsoft implementation of DHCP and WINS, you will also be interested in the Microsoft Domain Name System (DNS). This version of DNS is WINS aware, and is included on the Windows NT Resource Kit CD-ROM. Using the Microsoft version of DNS provides you the ability to have your DNS service query the WINS service for name resolution of any names not included in the static configuration files. You could also use the DNS service instead of DHCP and WINS, but I would not recommend it unless this was for a stand-alone server or Internet firewall, because DHCP and WINS are much easier to administer.

All of these services are client server applications. This means that you have a service running on your Windows NT Server domain controller (which is the server side of the component) and a service running on a network client (which is, of course, the client component). Currently supported DHCP and WINS clients include Windows NT Workstations, Windows 95, Windows for Workgroups, and MS-DOS (including Windows 3.1) clients using the Microsoft Network Client 3.0 as their network interface.

The basic goal of this chapter is to provide you with an understanding of these services so that you can properly implement the DHCP, WINS, and DNS services on your network. This chapter discusses design goals, installation, configuration, and management of these services; this covers most of the administrative issues. Specific discussions concerning interoperability with existing UNIX services, tips to get the maximum mileage from these services, and some of the possible problems (gotchas) to avoid also are included.

THE DYNAMIC HOST CONFIGURATION PROTOCOL

The DHCP service is based on the Request for Comment (RFC) 1541; it is not a newly invented mechanism by Microsoft for managing your TCP/IP IP address allocations. The Microsoft implementation varies a bit from the actual design goals, as specified in RFC 1541, but it fulfills the basic design functionality quite well for your Microsoft network clients. You should keep a few concerns in mind for interoperation with your existing TCP/IP-based clients that do not support DHCP, as well as some specific times not to use DHCP. Both these considerations require that you maintain an LMHOST file on your Windows NT Server domain controllers, and I will point out these issues throughout the chapter as they arise.

Note

RFC 1541 (and other RFCs mentioned in this chapter) is installed from the accompanying CD-ROM to the MBADMIN\Projects\ Requests for Comments (RFC) subdirectory as RFC1541.TXT. It is a rather interesting document, and I highly recommend that you read it for a fuller understanding of the DHCP service. You can find information on these RFCs and much more on the Web site

http://www.cis.ohio-state.edu/hypertext/information/rfc.html

Or, you can use ftp directly from the InterNIC Directory and Database Service (ds.internic.net) as rfc/rfc####.txt, where #### is replaced by the RFC number without leading zeroes.

This discussion of the DHCP service begins with some of the design goals of the service and then moves on to planning your installation, installing the service, and using the DHCP Manager to administer the DHCP service. Administering your DHCP service consists of creating or deleting scopes and configuring individual scope properties. A scope is nothing more than a collection of IP addresses grouped into a single component for ease of administration. A scope can include all the IP addresses in a single subnet if desired, or you can subdivide a subnet into multiple scopes. Finally, this section looks at the DHCP database management required from time to time to improve performance. You also will learn about some of the Registry keys that cannot be configured directly using the DHCP Manager.

LOOKING AT DESIGN GOALS FOR THE MICROSOFT DHCP PROTOCOL

All companies have definite goals they must reach prior to releasing their products into the market. And Microsoft had definite goals in mind for implementing DHCP for its operating systems. The primary concern was making administration of a TCP/IP-based network easier to implement and maintain, which incidentally makes it easier for the Microsoft Product Service Support (PSS) technical support groups as well, because TCP/IP is one of the most widely implemented protocols. The TCP/IP protocol is recommended for medium to large local area networks, it is the preferred protocol to use for wide area networks, and it is required for integration with a UNIX network or the Internet.

Some of the goals for the Microsoft DHCP implementation follow:

◆ Centralized administration of your TCP/IP IP subnets. All of your IP addresses, along with the configuration parameters for each, are stored in a central database located on your server.

◆ Automatic TCP/IP IP address assignment and configuration. As a client computer starts up and accesses the network for the first time, it is automatically assigned an IP address, subnet mask, default gateway, and WINS server IP address. If the client computer then moves between subnets, such as a portable computer user, the original IP address and related configuration information are released back to the original pool of available IP addresses, and the client is assigned a new IP address and related configuration information at system startup.

◆ The return of unused IP addresses to the available pool of IP addresses. Normally, IP addresses are allocated statically by a network administrator, and these IP addresses are stored on a piece of paper or a local database. But often this list can become out of date as clients move between subnets or as new IP addresses are allocated without updating the list of IP addresses. This means that some IP addresses will be lost, so they will not be able to be reused. DHCP uses a time-based mechanism, called a lease, which a client must renew at regular intervals. If the lease expires and the client does not renew it, the IP address is returned to the pool of available IP addresses.

UNDERSTANDING HOW A DHCP LEASE WORKS

A DHCP client computer steps through one of six transition states in the process of establishing a valid IP address for use by the client computer (see Figure 9.1).

Figure 9.1.
The six transition states of a DHCP client.

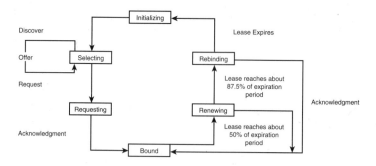

The six transition states follow:

♦ Initializing: As the operating system starts, a DHCP client broadcasts a discover message on the network. This message may be received by all DHCP Servers on the network. For each DHCP Server that receives the discover message, an offer message is returned to the clients. Each offer message includes a valid IP address and relevant configuration information.

♦ Selecting: At this point, each of the offer messages is collected by the client.

♦ Requesting: The client selects an offer message and sends a request message that identifies the DHCP Server for the selected configuration. The DHCP server, in turn, sends an acknowledgment message to the client, which contains the IP address initially sent in the offer message along with a valid lease.

♦ Bound: When the client receives the acknowledgment message, it stores the information locally on the computer (if a local storage mechanism, such as a hard disk, is available), completes the operating system startup, and then can participate as a network member with a valid IP address. This locally stored information then is used during subsequent system startups.

♦ Renewing: When the lease reaches approximately 50 percent of its expiration time, the client attempts to renew the lease. If the lease is renewed via an acknowledgment message from the DHCP Server, the client enters the bound state once again.

♦ Rebinding: When the lease reaches approximately 87.5 percent of its expiration time, the client attempts to renew the lease once again if it could not be renewed in the preceding attempt. If this fails, the client then is assigned a new IP address from the DHCP server and enters the bound state once again. The client enters the initializing state to repeat the entire process only if the original DHCP server could not provide a valid IP address and lease.

PLANNING YOUR DHCP INSTALLATION

If you have a small network with no UNIX-based interoperation required, then you have a fairly easy DHCP Server installation. But this does not mean that you can just install the DHCP Server components and forget about it. Instead, it just means that there are fewer issues to contend with in your network installation. When you begin your planning, there are two types of network configurations to consider. The first, as shown in Figure 9.2, is a simple network with only one subnet. The second, as depicted in Figure 9.3, is a network with multiple subnets. The most common configuration is one with multiple subnets, and that is the focus of this discussion.

Figure 9.2.
A network with a
single subnet.

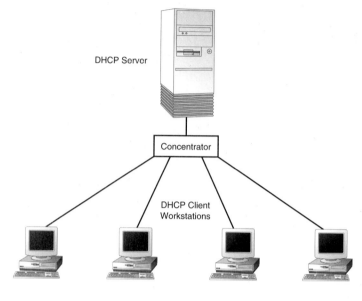

Figure 9.3.
A network with
multiple subnets.

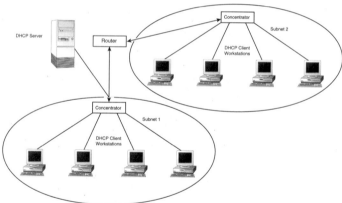

A single subnet is the easiest type of subnet to work with. All the DHCP and WINS servers are located on the same subnet, so very little maintenance is required. Maintaining the LMHOST files is not difficult unless you use many MS-DOS or Windows 3.x clients that use the Microsoft Network Client 3.0 software. Because these computers are all on a single subnet, you can use the B-node node type for name resolution and bypass WINS configuration and LMHOST file maintenance altogether. But it pays, in performance, to use the same techniques that will be described for your network just as if you did have multiple segments. It also pays off if your network grows and must be divided into separate segments.

For a multiple-segmented (subnets) network, you must do some planning before installing DHCP on your server and implementing DHCP on your clients. Some of the issues you need to think about follow:

♦ Routers: Your routers must support RFCs 1532, 1533, 1541, and 1542. These RFCs deal with the forwarding of packets required by the DHCP service. If your routers do not support these RFCs, then your routers may discard the network packets required for DHCP operation. In this case, you may need a firmware upgrade. Consult your documentation to determine whether your routers support these specifications. If your routers do support these RFCs but you have connectivity problems, check your documentation to see whether the default configuration passes or drops these packet types.

♦ WINS Configuration: If you are planning to use DHCP to configure your WINS clients automatically, be sure to set options 44 and 46 (these options are discussed later in this chapter in "Working with DHCP Scopes"). Option 44 specifies the WINS Server IP addresses to be assigned to the WINS client, whereas option 46 specifies the TCP/IP node type to be used. A node type specifies the mechanism the TCP/IP protocol uses to resolve NetBIOS name requests or to convert a NetBIOS name to a TCP/IP IP address.

Supported node types follow:

B-node: Resolves names using broadcast messages. This option is the worst possible option to use because it can flood your network segment with broadcast messages, lowering your network's capability to carry data over the network and effectively lowering your network bandwidth on the segment. Broadcasts also are not forwarded by routers, so if the requested resource is on the other side of a router, it will not be found. I recommend this type for a very small network with a single subnet, and one that does not have a dedicated network administrator to maintain the network. (Using broadcasts can essentially eliminate the need to maintain an LMHOST file or WINS database, and for a small network, very little network bandwidth is eaten by the broadcasts.) Another good reason to use B-node is that computers located on the same segment still can find each other even if the WINS server or DNS server is down or unavailable.

P-node: Resolves names with a name server (WINS or DNS) using point-to-point communications. Point-to-point communications are based on IP- address-to-IP-address as the communication linkage. This is the most efficient mechanism, but should be used only on networks with a dedicated administrator, and one that will religiously update the various LMHOST files on the network. (If these files are not updated, the client may not be able to find a resource by name, or the resource computer may not be able to find the client.) If you are using WINS, the updates should occur automatically, except for network clients using the Microsoft Network Client 3.0 software. These clients will need their IP addresses added to the LMHOST files of the DHCP servers. The domain controller TCP/IP configuration also must be configured to use the LMHOST file.

M-node: Uses B-node first (broadcasts) to resolve the name and then uses P-node (name queries) if the broadcast fails to resolve a name. This method works, but it has the same problem as a B-node because it can flood the network with broadcasts.

H-node: This is the default node type when configuring TCP/IP manually, unless the WINS IP address field is left empty. It uses P-node first (name queries) to resolve the name and then B-node (broadcasts) if the name service is unavailable or if the name is not registered in the WINS Server's database. This is my recommended node type because it first uses a point-to-point connection to find a resource's IP address; it uses a broadcast to find the resource only if that fails. This is the most efficient node type to use, and it practically guarantees that the resource will be found even if the LMHOST file or WINS database does not contain the requested resource's IP address.

◆ Multiple DHCP Servers: If you are planning to implement multiple DHCP Servers, which is a good idea to distribute the load on a large network, each DHCP Server must have a statically assigned IP address. These IP addresses must be excluded from the DHCP scope that you create. You do not necessarily have to have a DHCP Server on each subnet. Your router should be capable of forwarding DHCP requests across subnets, unless your router does not support the RFCs mentioned previously, in which case you should not use DHCP until you update your router firmware.

◆ Static IP Addresses: Any static IP addresses—such as those used by other DHCP Servers, non-DHCP computers, routers, and non-Microsoft Remote Access Software (RAS) clients that do not support a dynamically assigned IP address and are using PPP (Point-to-Point Protocol) to connect to your network—must be excluded from the DHCP scope. If you forget to exclude these IP addresses, a name/address conflict probably will occur and could prevent your clients from communicating or even cause your network to crash (in the case of a router).

◆ DHCP Server Database Replication: This feature doesn't exist in the current implementation, so if you install multiple DHCP Servers to support a single segment, you also must split the DHCP scope into distinct IP ranges.

◆ DHCP Server Database Backup: Because the DHCP database contains all the DHCP scopes for the server and the configuration parameters, it is a good idea to implement a backup policy. Normally, the DHCP database is backed up automatically, and this backup is used if the original is corrupted. You should not rely on this mechanism as your only backup, however. Instead, back up the database regularly and then copy the files from the `SystemRoot\System32\DHCP\Backup\Jet` directory.

Tip

> If you have a corrupted primary database file and this is not detected by the DHCP service, you can force the backup copy to be used by editing the Registry. Set the Registry key `HKEY_LOCAL_MACHINE\SYSTEM\ CurrentControlSet\Services\DHCPServer\Parameters\RestoreFlag` to 1. Then restart the DHCP service by using the following commands:
>
> ```
> net stop dhcpserver
> net start dhcpserver
> ```

◆ Lease Expiration: The minimum lease expiration should be twice the maximum expected server down time. If you plan to upgrade the server over the weekend, for example, the expiration time should be at least four days. This prevents a client from losing his lease and his IP address, which would prevent the computer from communicating on the network.

Tip

> A good lease minimum should be based on your network turnaround. If you have many portable computer users, frequent computer upgrades, or many users passing between subnets, then you want a lease time of about two weeks. This will return the unused IP addresses back to the pool of IP addresses, quickly making them available for reassignment. On the other hand, if you have a pretty static network, lease times of six months could be used. The one lease to avoid is an unlimited lease because these addresses will never be released automatically and returned to the IP address pool.

If you are planning to implement your Microsoft DHCP Server service in a mixed environment, such as with a third-party UNIX DHCP Server service, then you should be aware that not all the DHCP configuration options are supported by the Microsoft client. Specifically, the Microsoft DHCP clients only use the configuration options as specified in Table 9.1. Any other options received by the client are ignored and discarded.

TABLE 9.1. MICROSOFT DHCP CLIENT CONFIGURATION OPTIONS.

Number	Name	Data Type	Description
1	Subnet Mask	Subnet Address	Specifies the TCP/IP subnet mask to be used by DHCP clients. Note: This value can be set only when you create a scope or when accessed from the DHCP options | Scope Properties menu option.
3	Router	IP Address Array	Specifies a list, in order of preference, of router IP addresses to be used by the client. A locally defined gateway can override this value.
6	DNS Servers	IP Address Array	Specifies a list, in order of preference, for DNS name servers for the client. Note: A multihomed computer (a computer with more than one installed network adapter) can include only one IP address, not one IP address per adapter.
15	Domain Name	String	Specifies the DNS domain name the client should use for DNS host name resolution.
44	WINS/NBNS	IP Address Array	Specifies a list, in order of preference, of NetBIOS Name Servers (NBNS).
46	WINS/NBT Node Type	Byte	Specifies the node type for configurable NetBIOS clients (as defined in RFC 1001/1002). A value of 1 specifies B-node, 2 specifies P-node, 4

Number	Name	Data Type	Description
			specifies M-node, and 8 specifies H-node. Note: On a multihomed computer, the node type is assigned to the computer as a whole—not to individual network adapters.
47	NetBIOS Scope ID	String	Specifies the scope ID for NetBIOS over TCP/IP (NBT) as defined in RFC 1001/1002. Note: On a multihomed computer, the scope ID is a global resource and is not allocated on a per network adapter basis.
50	Requested Address	IP Address	Specifies that a client's preset IP address be used.
51	Lease Time	IP Address	Specifies the time, in seconds, from the initial IP address allocation to the expiration of the client lease on the IP address. Note that this value can be set only in the DHCP Options|Scope Properties menu option.
53	DHCP Message Type	Byte	Specifies the DHCP message type where the message type is 1 for DHCPDISCOVER, 2 for DHCPOFFER, 3 for DHCPREQUEST, 4 for DHCPDECLINE, 5 for DHCPACK, 6 for DHCPNAK, and 7 for DHCPRELEASE.

continues

TABLE 9.1. CONTINUED

Number	Name	Data Type	Description
54	Server Identifier	IP Address	Used by DHCP clients to indicate which of several lease offers is being accepted by including this option in a DHCPREQUEST message with the IP address of the accepted DHCP Server.
58	Renewal (T1) Time Value	Long	Specifies the time, in seconds, from the initial IP address assignment to the time when the client must enter the renewal state. Note that this value cannot be specified manually because it is based on the lease time as set for the scope.
59	Rebinding (T2) Time Value	Long	Specifies the time, in seconds, from the initial IP address assignment to the time when the client must enter the rebinding state. Note that this value cannot be specified manually because it is based on the lease time as set for the scope.
61	Client ID	Word	Specifies the DHCP client's unique identifier.

The Microsoft DHCP client and server do not support option overlays. An option overlay is the process of using free space in the DHCP option packet to contain additional DHCP options. So if you are using a third-party DHCP Server instead of the Microsoft DHCP server, you should make sure that your important configuration options are listed first—otherwise, they might be discarded. You also should be sure that these values fit into the Microsoft 312-byte DHCP network packet allocation. The same consideration should be applied if you are using the Microsoft DHCP Server to support your third-party DHCP clients: Fit your most important configuration options first. And although you can use the additional configuration options, as listed in Table 9.2, to support your third-party DHCP clients, these options will not be used by your Microsoft DHCP clients.

TABLE 9.2. THIRD-PARTY DHCP CLIENT CONFIGURATION OPTIONS.

Number	Name	Data Type	Description
0	Pad	Byte	Specifies that the following data fields will be aligned on a word (16-bit) boundary.
2	Time	Long	Specifies the Universal Coordinate Offset Time (UCT) offset time, in seconds.
4	Time Server	IP Address Array	Specifies a list, in order of preference, of time servers for the client.
5	Name Servers	IP Address Array	Specifies a list, in order of preference, of name servers for the client.
7	Log Servers	IP Address Array	Specifies a list, in order of preference, for MIT_LCS User Datagram Protocol (UDP) log servers for the client.
8	Cookie Servers	IP Address Array	Specifies a list, in order of preference, of cookie servers (as specified in RFC 865) for the client.
9	LPR Servers	IP Address Array	Specifies a list, in order of preference, for Line Printer Remote (as specified in RFC 1179) servers for the clients.
10	Impress Servers	IP Address Array	Specifies a list, in order of preference, of Imagen Impress servers for the client.
11	Resource Location Servers	IP Address Array	Specifies a list, in order of preference, of RFC 887 compliant Resource Location Servers for the client.

continues

Table 9.2. continued

Number	Name	Data Type	Description
12	Host Name	String	Specifies the host name (maximum of 63 characters) for the client. Note: The name must start with an alphabetic character, end with an alphanumeric character, and contain only letters, numbers, or hyphens. The name can be fully qualified with the local DNS domain name.
13	Boot File Size	Word	Specifies the default size of the boot image file in 512 octet blocks.
14	Merit Dump File	String	Specifies the ASCII path of a file where the client's core dump may be stored in case of an application or system crash.
16	Swap Server	IP Address	Specifies the IP address of the client's swap server.
17	Root Path	String	Specifies a path (in ASCII) for the client's root disk.
18	Extensions Path	String	Specifies a file that includes information that is interpreted the same as the vendor extension field in the BOOTTP response, except that references to Tag 18 are ignored. Note that the file must be retrievable via TFTP.
19	IP Layer Forwarding	Byte	Specifies that IP packets should be enabled (1) or disabled (0) for the client.
20	Nonlocal Source Routing	Byte	Specifies that datagram packets with nonlocal source route forwarding should be enabled (1) or disabled (0) for the client.

Number	Name	Data Type	Description
21	Policy Filters Mask	IP Address Array	Specifies a list, in order of preference, of IP address and mask pairs that specify destination address and mask pairs, respectively. Used for filtering nonlocal source routes. Any source routed datagram whose next hop address does not match an entry in the list is discarded by the client.
22	Max DG Reassembly Size	Word	Specifies the maximum size datagram that a client can assemble. Note that the minimum size is 576.
23	Default Time to Live	Byte	Specifies the Time to Live (TTL) that the client will use on outgoing datagrams. Values must be between 1 and 255.
24	Path MTU Aging Timeout	Long	Specifies the time-out, in seconds, for aging Path Maximum Transmission Unit values. Note that MTU values are found based on the mechanism defined in RFC 1191.
25	Path MTU Plateau Table	Word Array	Specifies a table of MTU sizes to use when performing Path MTU (as defined in RFC 1191). Note that the table is sorted from minimum value to maximum value, with a minimum value of 68.
26	MTU	Word	Specifies the MTU discovery size. Note that the minimum value is 68.
27	All Subnets are Local	Byte	Specifies whether the client assumes that all subnets in the network will use the same

continues

TABLE 9.2. CONTINUED

Number	Name	Data Type	Description
			MTU value as that defined for the local subnet. This option is enabled (1) or disabled (0), which specifies that some subnets may use smaller MTU values.
28	Broadcast Address	IP Address	Specifies the broadcast IP address to be used on the client's local subnet.
29	Perform Mask Discovery	Byte	A value of 1 specifies that the client should use ICMP (Internet Control Message Protocol) for subnet mask discovery, whereas a value of 0 specifies that the client should not use ICMP for subnet mask discovery.
30	Mask Supplier	Byte	A value of 1 specifies that the client should respond to ICMP subnet mask requests, where-as a value of 0 specifies that a client should not respond to subnet mask requests using ICMP.
31	Perform Router Discovery	Byte	A value of 1 specifies that the client should use the mechanism defined in RFC 1256 for router discovery. A value of 0 indicates that the client should not use the router discovery mechanism.
32	Router	IP Address	Specifies the IP address the client Solicitation will send router solicitation Address requests to.
33	Static Route	IP Address Array	Specifies a list, in order of preference, of IP address pairs

9

Number	Name	Data Type	Description
			the client should install in its routing cache. Note that any multiple routes to the same destination are listed in descending order or in order of priority. The pairs are defined as destination IP address/router IP addresses. The default address of 0.0.0.0 is an illegal address for a static route and should be changed if your non-Microsoft DHCP clients use this setting.
34	Trailer Encapsulation	Byte	A value of 1 specifies that the client should negotiate use of trailers (as defined in RFC 983) when using the ARP protocol. A value of 0 indicates that the client should not use trailers.
35	ARP Cache Timeout	Long	Specifies the time-out, in seconds, for the ARP cache entries.
36	Ethernet Encapsulation	Byte	Specifies that the client should use Ethernet version 2 (as defined in RFC 894) or IEEE 802.3 (as defined in RFC 1042) encapsulation if the network interface is Ethernet. A value of 1 enables RFC 1042, whereas a value of 0 enables RFC 894 encapsulation.
37	Default Time to Live	Byte	Specifies the default TTL the client should use when sending TCP segments. Note that the minimum octet value is 1.

continues

TABLE 9.2. CONTINUED

Number	Name	Data Type	Description
38	Keepalive Interval	Long	Specifies the interval, in seconds, for the client to wait before sending a keepalive message on a TCP connection. Note that a value of 0 indicates that the client should send keepalive messages only if requested by the application.
39	Keepalive Garbage	Byte	Enables (1) or disables (0) sending keepalive messages with an octet of garbage data for legacy application compatibility.
40	NIS Domain Name	String	An ASCII string specifying the name of the Network Information Service (NIS) domain.
41	NIS Servers	IP Address Array	Specifies a list, in order of preference, of IP addresses of NIS servers for the client.
42	NTP Servers	IP Address Array	Specifies a list, in order of preference, of IP addresses of Network Time Protocol (NTP) servers for the client.
43	Vendor Specific Info	Byte Array	Binary information used by clients and servers to pass vendor-specific information. Servers that cannot interpret the information ignore it, whereas clients that do not receive the data attempt to operate without it.
45	NetBIOS Over TCP/IP NBDD	IP Address Array	Specifies a list, in order of preference, of IP addresses for NetBIOS datagram distribution (NBDD) servers for the client.

9

Number	Name	Data Type	Description
48	X Window System Font	IP Address Array	Specifies a list, in order of preference, of IP addresses of X Window font servers for the client.
49	X Window System Display	IP Address Array	Specifies a list, in order of preference, of IP addresses of X Window System Display Manager servers for the client.
64	NIS + Domain Name	String	Specifies a list, in order of preference.
65	NIS + Server	IP Address Array	Specifies a list, in order of preference.
255	End	Byte	Specifies the end of the DHCP packet.

Installing the DHCP Service

You can install the DHCP Server service through the Control Panel Network applet. But before you install the service on your current server, check for the existence of other DHCP servers on the network. These could be other Windows NT Servers or a UNIX server.

To install the DHCP Server service, follow these steps:

Note

In order to install the DHCP Server service, you must be a member of the Administrators group on the computer on which you want to install the service.

1. Launch the Control Panel Network applet to display the Network Settings dialog box.
2. Click the Add Software button to display the Add Network Software dialog box.
3. Select TCP/IP Protocol and Related Components in the Network Software drop-down listbox. Then click the Continue button. The Windows NT TCP/IP Installation Options dialog box appears, as shown in Figure 9.4.

Figure 9.4.
The Windows NT
TCP/IP Installa-
tion Options
dialog box.

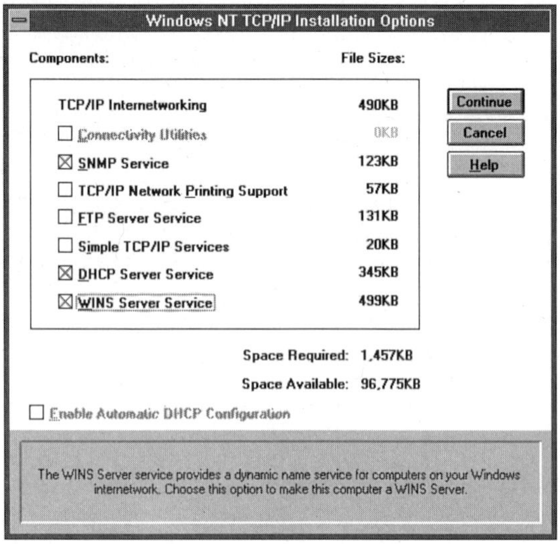

Windows NT TCP/IP Installation Options

Components:	File Sizes:
TCP/IP Internetworking	490KB
☐ Connectivity Utilities	0KB
☒ SNMP Service	123KB
☐ TCP/IP Network Printing Support	57KB
☐ FTP Server Service	131KB
☐ Simple TCP/IP Services	20KB
☒ DHCP Server Service	345KB
☒ WINS Server Service	499KB

Space Required: 1,457KB
Space Available: 96,775KB

☐ Enable Automatic DHCP Configuration

The WINS Server service provides a dynamic name service for computers on your Windows internetwork. Choose this option to make this computer a WINS Server.

4. Enable the DHCP Server Service checkbox. You also may want to install the WINS Server service at this time by enabling the WINS Server Service checkbox, as depicted in Figure 9.4.

Tip

If you want to use SNMP to configure the DHCP Server service remotely, be sure to install the SNMP Service by enabling the SNMP Service checkbox as well.

5. Click the OK button. When prompted, enter the path to the distribution files and click the Continue button to return to the Network Settings dialog box.

6. Click the OK button.

7. Because the DHCP server cannot also be a DHCP client, when prompted, enter the TCP/IP address, subnet mask, default gateway, and WINS Server IP addresses. If you have multiple network adapters installed (a multihomed system), click the Advanced button and configure the additional adapters.

Tip

If you also are going to be interoperating with a UNIX network, at this same time, you should click the DNS button and configure your Windows NT Server DNS client to use your UNIX DNS server for additional name resolution. As part of this process, you also should click the Advanced button and enable the Enable LMHOST Lookup checkbox and import your existing LMHOST file. Do not enable the Enable DNS for Windows Name Resolution checkbox unless you want to use your existing UNIX DNS server as your NetBIOS name re-solver instead of WINS.

8. When prompted, restart your system. After the system restarts, the DHCP Server service should be activated. If not, check your system event log for any error messages.

Managing Your DHCP Server with the DHCP Manager

Your interface to managing the DHCP Service is the DHCP Manager. It is installed in the Network Administration Program Manager group and requires administrative privileges to use. With the DHCP Manager, you can do everything but stop or start the DHCP Service. To stop or start the service, you need to use the Control Panel Service applet and specify the Microsoft DHCP Server as the service to control. Or, you can issue the following commands from a console prompt:

```
net stop dhcpserver
net start dhcpserver
```

The DHCP Manager's primary function is to work with scopes. This section discusses creating, deleting, activating, and deactivating scopes. Next, you will learn how to manage your DHCP clients. This includes managing your client leases and reservations, as well as setting individual DHCP properties for a reserved client that differ from those defined for the scope as a whole. Finally, you will learn about the DHCP database administration required from time to time. This should provide you with a well-rounded education and prepare you for your duties as a network administrator so that you can manage your TCP/IP-based network.

Managing DHCP Scopes

Before you can use the DHCP Server to assign TCP/IP IP addresses and relevant configuration options to your DHCP clients, you must create a DHCP scope. A scope is the heart of your DHCP Server service. It is based on an IP address range, or subnet, if you prefer. It can include only a single subnet, but within that subnet, you can define the IP range to be used as the basis for your DHCP client's IP address assignment, the subnet mask, any IP addresses to exclude from the scope, a lease duration, a name for the scope, and a comment that describes the scope. This section discusses how to create, delete, activate, and deactivate DHCP scopes. Next, it moves on to configuring global, local, or default scope properties.

When you run the DHCP Manager for the first time, it does not have any scopes defined, although it does include a listing in the DHCP Server's window for the local machine. Before you start creating scopes, I suggest that you add the additional DHCP Servers on your network to the DHCP Manager. When you do, your DHCP Manager includes a listing in the window of each DHCP Server on your network (see Figure 9.5). This gives you the capability to manage your other scopes, and you can use these additional scopes as a reference point when creating new scopes.

Figure 9.5.
The Microsoft
DHCP Manager
with multiple
DHCP servers
and scopes.

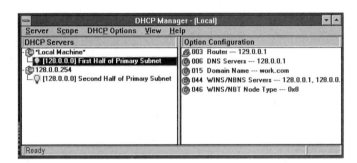

To add additional DHCP Servers to your local DHCP Manager, follow these steps:

1. Choose Add from the Server menu, or press Ctrl+A to display the Add DHCP Server to Server List dialog box.

2. Enter the IP address of the DHCP Server in the DHCP Server field and click the OK button. The IP address appears in the DHCP Server window.

3. Repeat these steps for each DHCP Server you want to add to your local DHCP Manager.

Note

Because the DHCP Server service does not replicate its database and configuration information to other DHCP Servers, you must configure the DHCP Manager on each server in order to manage all the DHCP scopes from any computer with the DHCP Manager installed on it.

Working with DHCP Scopes

Working with DHCP scopes consists of four possible functions:

◆ Activating a scope: Before you can use a newly created scope, you must activate it. Once you have an active scope, your DHCP clients can be assigned an IP address and relevant TCP/IP configuration information from the scope.

◆ Creating a scope: This is the beginning process to automating your DHCP client TCP/IP configuration.

◆ Deactivating a scope: Before you delete a scope, you should deactivate it. Deactivating a scope prevents a client from renewing its current lease and forces it to obtain a lease from another DHCP scope. This is a means of migrating clients to a new scope without manual intervention.

◆ Deleting a scope: After you finish using a DHCP scope, you can delete it.

To create a scope, follow these steps:

1. Select the DHCP Server in the DHCP Server window where you want to create the new scope. If you are creating a new scope on the computer running the DHCP Server service, this entry will be Local Machine; otherwise, it will be an IP address.

2. Choose Create from the Scope menu. The Create Scope dialog box appears, as shown in Figure 9.6.

Figure 9.6.
The Create Scope
dialog box.

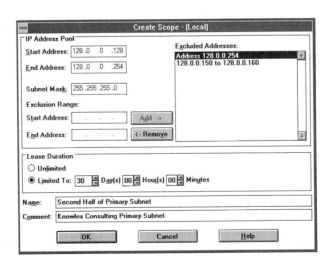

3. In the Start Address field, enter the beginning IP address of your subnet.

4. In the End Address field, enter the last IP address of your subnet.

Tip

> If you are not planning to divide your subnet between two DHCP Servers, enter the complete IP address range of your subnet. However, if you are planning to split your subnet (as I have), enter only half of your IP address range in the Start and End Address fields. This is easier to work with, and prevents complications with the second DHCP Manager's defined scope.

5. In the Subnet Mask field, enter the subnet mask to be assigned to your DHCP clients.

6. If your scope includes statically assigned addresses, such as those assigned to your network adapters in the computer or to the Remote Access Service, enter these addresses in the Exclusion Range group. To exclude a single IP address, enter the IP address in the Start Address field and click the Add button. To enter more than one consecutive IP address to be excluded, enter the beginning IP address in the Start Address field and the last IP address in the End Address field; then click the Add button. This places the IP address range in the Excluded Addresses box.

   To modify or remove an address range, select it in the Excluded Addresses box and click the Remove button. This places the range in the Exclusion Range fields where you can modify it and later add it back to the Excluded Addresses box.

7. In the Lease Duration group, choose the Unlimited or Limited To radio button to specify the lease type. If you choose Limited To, which is the default, specify the length of time for your DHCP clients to keep their assigned IP addresses.

   Choose your lease time based on the frequency at which your computers are upgraded, replaced, or moved between subnets. If you have a high movement of computers, choose a lease of approximately two weeks. If you have an extremely low movement of computers, choose a monthly, tri-monthly, or bi-yearly lease.

Warning

> Do not assign the Unlimited lease type unless you are absolutely sure that no computers will ever be upgraded, replaced, or moved. It is very improbable that you will be in this situation, I can assure you. If you choose an unlimited lease, you will not be able to automatically recover IP addresses that have been assigned to a DHCP client.

8. In the Name field, enter a name for the scope. Your name can be a floor or building location, or a description for the type of subnet. This name, along with the scope address, is listed in the DHCP Server window.

9. In the Comment field, enter a description for the scope.

Tip

To modify the scope properties for an existing scope, just double-click on it. This displays the Scope Properties dialog box, which is identical to the Create Scope dialog box (aside from its name, of course). You can change any of the options described in the earlier steps.

10. Click the OK button. A message box appears, prompting you to activate the scope. However, you should not activate the scope now, unless all your default scope properties are correct, as described in the next section.

11. Repeat these steps for each new scope you want to create.

You should activate a scope only after you have configured it. To activate a scope, choose Scope | Activate.

Before you delete a scope, you should deactivate it. To do so, choose Scope | Deactivate. When the scope lease time expires and you are sure that no DHCP clients are using a lease from the scope, you can delete it.

To delete a scope, follow these steps:

1. Select the DHCP Server in the DHCP Server window containing the scope you want to delete. If you are deleting a scope on the computer running the DHCP Server Service, this entry is Local Machine; otherwise, it is an IP address.

2. The scopes for the server are listed. Select the scope you want to delete.

3. Choose Delete from the Scope menu. A warning message appears, informing you that clients still may have active leases. Click OK to delete the scope.

4. Repeat these actions for each scope you want to delete.

Tip

If you delete a scope with active clients, you can force the client to discontinue using its current lease and obtain one from another DHCP Server by issuing the IPCONFIG /RENEW command at a command prompt. On a Windows 95 computer, you can use the WINIPCFG program. Click the Renew button to release the active lease and obtain a new lease.

CONFIGURING DHCP SCOPE OPTIONS

Scope options are divided into two classes. You can have a global scope setting, which applies to all scopes for the DHCP Server, or a local scope setting, which applies only to the current scope. Local scope properties override globally defined scope properties. This rule gives you the capability to define common properties that apply to all scopes you create, and then to customize the scope properties for each scope you create. Suppose that you define the global router setting to contain the IP addresses for your routers based on subnets. Then, after you create a new scope, you can delete the first entry in this list and then add it back. This places the IP address entry at the end of the list. In effect, it changes the order of router preference so that the router closest to the user is used first. You can repeat this sequence to continue moving the router addresses for each subnet you create without having to type each router address manually.

To modify a scope property, follow these steps:

1. Select the DHCP Server in the DHCP Server window containing the scope you want to modify. If you are modifying a scope on the computer running the DHCP Server Service, this entry is Local Machine; otherwise, it is an IP address.

2. After the connection to the DHCP Server has been established, the scopes for the server are listed. Select the scope you want to modify.

3. Choose Global from the DHCP Options menu to display the dialog box shown in Figure 9.7. Here, you can set global properties for all scopes. Or, you can choose Scope from the DHCP Options menu to set local scope properties.

Figure 9.7.
The expanded
DHCP Options
dialog box.

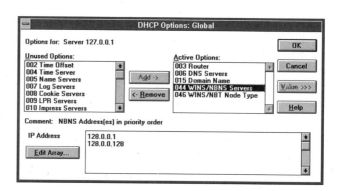

> **Note**
>
> The dialog box displayed by choosing the DHCP Options | Scope menu selection is the same as the dialog box displayed by choosing the Global menu option, aside from the name of the dialog box.

4. In the Unused Options drop-down listbox, select the option that you want to modify, and then click the Add button to move the highlight to the Active Options drop-down listbox.

5. Click the Value button to expand the dialog box and display the edit field where you can click the Edit Array button to modify an array of IP addresses or just edit the field for a single entry type.

6. Repeat steps 3 through 5 for each option to modify. When you finish modifying the options, click the OK button.

Tip

To modify an existing option, select the option in the Active Options listbox, and then click the Value button to expand the dialog box so that you can edit the entry.

CREATING NEW DHCP SCOPE OPTIONS

Not only can you modify the predefined scope properties with the DHCP Manager, but you also can modify the name, unique identifier, and comment of existing configuration options. And if your DHCP clients can use them, you can even create new scope options to be assigned to your DHCP clients. However, the fact that you can modify an existing configuration option or create new ones doesn't mean that you should do so arbitrarily. Only do so if absolutely necessary.

To change an existing configuration option default value, follow these steps:

1. Choose Defaults from the DHCP Options menu to display the DHCP Options dialog box, as depicted in Figure 9.8.

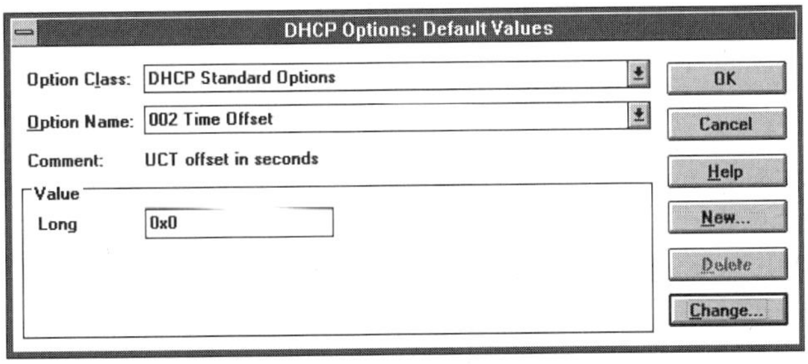

Figure 9.8.
The DHCP
Options: Default
Values dialog
box.

2. In the Option Class drop-down listbox, select the class for the option you want to modify. The default is DHCP Standard Options.

3. In the Option Name drop-down listbox, select the entry for the option class to modify.

4. In the Value group, specify the new value for the option.

To change a configuration option's name, unique identifier, or description, follow these steps:

1. Repeat steps 1 through 3 of the preceding procedure.
2. Click the Change button to display the Change Option Type dialog box.
3. You now can change the name of the option in the Name field, the DHCP unique identifier number in the Identifier field, or the description in the Comment field.

Warning

Changing the name or identifier may prevent a DHCP client from functioning properly. Only an expert who is aware of the consequences should modify any of these settings.

4. After you complete all changes, click the OK button.
5. Repeat these steps for each option you want to change.

To add a new configuration option, follow these steps:

1. Repeat steps 1 through 3 as described in the procedure to change an existing configuration option default value.
2. Click the New button to display the Change Option Type dialog box.
3. In the Name field, enter a name for the new option.
4. In the Data Type field, specify a data type. This can be one of the following:
   - ◆ Binary: An array of bytes
   - ◆ Byte: An 8-bit unsigned integer
   - ◆ Encapsulated: An array of unsigned bytes
   - ◆ IP address: An IP address in the form of ###.###.###.###, where # represents an octal digit (0 – 8)
   - ◆ Long: A 32-bit signed integer
   - ◆ Long integer: A 32-bit unsigned integer
   - ◆ String: An ASCII text string
   - ◆ Word: A 16-bit unsigned integer

   If the Data Type is an array of elements, enable the Array checkbox.
5. In the Identifier field, enter a unique number between 0 and 255.
6. In the Comment field, enter a description for the new option.

Warning

Adding a new configuration option should be performed only by an expert who is aware of the consequences and needs to support non-Microsoft DHCP clients that require the additional options.

7. After your changes are complete, click the OK button.

8. Repeat these steps for each option you want to add.

MANAGING DHCP CLIENTS

Managing your DHCP clients consists of working with client leases and client reservations on the DHCP Server and forcing the client to release or renew its lease on the client workstations. The management options on the server are discussed a little later in this section. Right now, however, you'll look at the options for the command-line program IPCONFIG.EXE.

The syntax for IPCONFIG follows:

```
IPCONFIG [adapter] /all  /release /renew
```

Explanations of the syntax for this command follow:

[adapter]: An optional component that is the specific adapter to list or modify the DHCP configuration. Use IPCONFIG with no parameters to obtain the adapter names.

/all: Lists all the configuration information. This includes the host name, DNS servers, node type, NetBIOS scope ID, whether IP routing is enabled, whether the computer is a WINS Proxy Agent, and whether the computer uses DNS for name resolution (instead of WINS). It also includes per adapter statistics, which include the adapter name and description, the physical address (network adapter Ethernet address), whether the DHCP client is enabled, the IP address, the subnet mask, the default gateway, and the primary and secondary WINS server IP addresses.

/release: Releases the current DHCP lease. If specified for all adapters (or if there is only one adapter), TCP/IP functionality is disabled.

/renew: Renews the lease. If no DHCP Server is available to obtain a valid lease, TCP/IP functionality is disabled.

Tip

Use the /renew option to manually force a client to obtain a new lease from a new DHCP Server or a new DHCP scope.

Note

Windows 95 does not include IPCONFIG; instead, it includes a Windows
GUI application called WINIPCFG.EXE.

If executed with no parameters, the current DHCP configuration is displayed. This
can be useful for determining the installed adapters and IP addresses. The following
output is displayed on my WinBook XP, for example:

```
Windows NT IP Configuration
Ethernet adapter Elnk31:
IP Address. . . . . . . . . : 206.170.127.70
Subnet Mask . . . . . . . . : 255.255.255.240
Default Gateway . . . . . . : 206.170.127.65
Ethernet adapter NDISLoop9:
IP Address. . . . . . . . . : 129.0.0.1
Subnet Mask . . . . . . . . : 255.255.255.0
Default Gateway . . . . . . : 206.170.127.65
```

MANAGING CLIENT LEASES

Managing your DHCP client leases, for the most part, consists of informational
displays. When you select an active scope and choose Active Leases from the Scope
menu, the Active Leases dialog box appears, as shown in Figure 9.9.

Figure 9.9.
The DHCP
Manager Active
Leases dialog box.

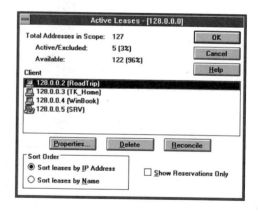

You can perform the following actions in the Active Leases dialog box:

◆ View the active or reserved leases for the scope. By default, all the leases
  are displayed in the dialog box. However, if you enable the Show Reservations Only checkbox, only the reserved leases are displayed.

◆ View the client properties. Select an IP address/computer name in the
  Client list and click the Properties button. The Client Properties dialog box
  appears, as shown in Figure 9.10. This can be a very useful dialog box,
  because it displays the Media Access Control (MAC) adapter address in the

Unique Identifier field, and there are several Windows NT Server applications, including the DHCP Manager (when reserving a lease, for example) that require a MAC address.

Figure 9.10.
The Client
Properties dialog
box.

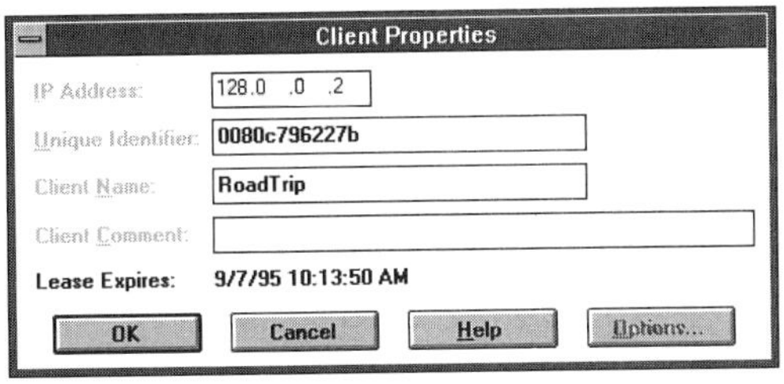

Client Properties	
IP Address:	128.0 .0 .2
Unique Identifier:	0080c796227b
Client Name:	RoadTrip
Client Comment:	
Lease Expires:	9/7/95 10:13:50 AM

[OK] [Cancel] [Help] [Options...]

◆ Update the DHCP database after a restoration from a backup database copy. If, for some reason, your DHCP database has to be restored from a previous backup, (automatically updated by the system or manually updated by you), then you should click the Reconcile button to update the database. This adds lease entries for any leases that are not in the database.

Tip

You can delete a lease by selecting the lease in the Client list and clicking the Delete button. However, this is not an action to be taken lightly, because you could wind up with a duplicate IP address on the network if the original lease is used by another computer. Suppose that you delete an active lease because you want to move the client to a new IP address. As soon as you delete the lease, reserve it (as described in the next section) to prevent the client from reusing the same IP address. Then force the client to establish a new lease by issuing the IPCONFIG /RENEW command on the client workstation. Or, you can use the WINIPCFG command on a Windows 95 client and then click the Renew button to obtain a new lease.

MANAGING CLIENT RESERVATIONS

Client reservations can be more useful than your average lease because you can preassign an IP address for a DHCP client. You also can change the DHCP configuration options for a DHCP client with a reserved lease. This is a pretty powerful option because it gives you the capability to define global and local scope options for the majority of your DHCP clients when you create the scope, and then specify the specific DHCP options for those special DHCP clients that happen to be the exception to the rule.

To create a reservation for a client, follow these steps:

1. Select the DHCP Server in the DHCP Server window containing the scope you want to modify. If you are modifying a scope on the computer running the DHCP Server Service, this entry is Local Machine; otherwise, it is an IP address.

2. Select the scope where you want the client reservation to occur.

3. Choose Add Reservations from the Scope menu to display the Add Reserved Clients dialog box.

4. In the IP Address field, enter an IP address within your current DHCP scope to be assigned to the client.

5. In the Unique Identifier field, enter the MAC address (the network adapter's unique identifier) for the client's network adapter.

6. In the Client Name field, enter the client computer name.

7. In the Client Comment field, enter an optional description for the client computer.

8. Click the Add button.

9. Repeat steps 3 through 6 for each reservation to add to the scope.

Changing the configuration options for a reserved lease requires a little more work. To change a configuration option, follow these steps:

1. Select the DHCP Server in the DHCP Server window containing the scope you want to modify. If you are modifying a scope on the computer running the DHCP Server Service, this entry is Local Machine; otherwise, it is an IP address.

2. Select the scope you want to modify.

3. Choose Active Leases from the Scope menu to display the Active Leases dialog box.

4. Select the reserved lease you want to modify and click the Properties button. If there are too many leases to scroll through, enable the Show Reservations Only checkbox. The Client Properties dialog box appears.

5. Click the Options button to display the DHCP Options dialog box. This dialog box is exactly the same as the other DHCP Options dialog box.

6. In the Unused Options listbox, select the option you want to modify and then click the Add button to move the option to the Active Options listbox. If the option to modify is already in the Active Options listbox, just select it.

7. Click the Value button to expand the dialog box and display the edit field, where you can click the Edit Array button to modify an array of IP addresses, or a field to edit the existing value.

8. Repeat steps 4 through 6 for each option to modify. When you finish modifying the options, click the OK button.

9. Repeat steps 3 through 7 for each reservation you need to modify. When you finish modifying all the reservations, click the OK button.

Managing the DHCP Databases

As your DHCP Server operates day in and day out, the databases may grow or shrink as records are added or deleted. These databases are located in the SystemRoot\System32\DHCP directory and include the following:

- ◆ DHCP.MDB: The DHCP database
- ◆ DHCP.TMP: A temporary file created by the DHCP Server
- ◆ JET*.LOG files: Files that contain transaction records
- ◆ SYSTEM.MDB: Structural information about the DHCP databases

Database growth affects the performance of the DHCP Server. So, as your DHCP.MDB database approaches the 10MB limit, you should compact it.

To compact your database, follow these steps:

1. Stop the DHCP Server Service from the Control Panel Services applet or issue the net stop dhcpserver command from a console prompt.

2. From a console prompt, run the JETPACK.EXE program located in your SystemRoot\System32 directory. The syntax for this program follows:

   JETPACK DatabaseName TemporaryDatabaseName

   DatabaseName is the name of the database to compact, and it can be a fully qualified path name.

   TemporaryDatabaseName is a name to use as a temporary database. It also can be a fully qualified path name.

Caution

Do not compact the SYSTEM.MDB file. If you do, the DHCP Server Service will fail to start. If this occurs, restore your configuration from a previous backup. Or, delete all your files from the SystemRoot\System32\DHCP and SystemRoot\System32\DHCP\backup\Jet directories. Next, expand the SYSTEM.MDB file from your source media and restart the DHCP Server Service. Then reconcile your database by choosing Scope | Active Leases and clicking the Reconcile button.

3. Start the DHCP Server Service from the Control Panel Services applet or issue a net start dhcpserver command from a console prompt.

Tip

Because the potential for failure is possible with the compact utility and data corruption is possible on your SystemRoot partition, you should back up your DHCP databases regularly, and definitely before you compact them. Just stop the DHCP Server Service temporarily and copy the files in the `SystemRoot\System32\DHCP` and `SystemRoot\System32\DHCP\backup\Jet` directories to another directory, or even another computer occasionally.

USING DHCP SERVER REGISTRY KEYS

Like most Windows NT services, the configuration information for the service is contained in the Registry. For the most part, you should use the DHCP Manager to modify your configuration. These listed Registry keys are not configurable from the DHCP Manager, and instead require that you use the Registry Editor (`REGEDT32.EXE`). The Registry Editor can be a dangerous tool to use. Appendix B (which is included on the CD-ROM with this book) includes additional information about using the Registry Editor. If you are administering a remote computer with a configuration problem so severe that the service cannot be started, then you can modify the Registry and restore the database configuration remotely. After these changes are made, you can restart the service using Server Manager.

The Registry keys are stored in the `HKEY_LOCAL_MACHINE\Systems\CurrentControlSet\Services\DHCPServer\Parameters` subkey. If you modify any of these keys (aside from the RestoreFlag), you must restart the computer in order for your changes to be applied.

The keys of interest follow:

◆ APIProtocolSupport: This key's value specifies the transport protocol to be supported by the DHCP Server. The default is 0x1 for RPC over TCP/IP protocols. However, it also can be 0x2 for RPC over named pipe protocols, 0x4 for RPC over LPC (Local Procedure Calls), 0x5 for RPC over TCP/IP and RCP over LPC, or 0x7 for RPC over all three protocols (TCP/IP, named pipes, and LPC).

◆ BackupDatabasePath: Specifies the location for the backup copy of the DHCP database. The default is `%SystemRoot%\System32\DHCP\Backup`. For additional fault tolerance, you can specify another physical drive in the system. Note: You cannot specify a network drive because the DHCP Manager does not support remote drives for backup or recovery.

◆ BackupInterval: Specifies the default backup interval in minutes. The default is 60 (0x3C).

- DatabaseCleanupInterval: Specifies the interval, in minutes, for the time to remove expired client records from the database. The default is 1,440 (0x15180) minutes, or 24 hours.

- DatabaseLoggingFlag: Specifies whether to record the database changes in the JET.LOG file. This file is used to recover the database if a system crash occurs. The default is 1 (enable logging), but if your system is extremely stable, you can set this value to 0 to disable logging and increase overall system performance slightly.

- DatabaseName: Specifies the database filename to be used by the DHCP Server Service. The default is DHCP.MDB.

- DatabasePath: Specifies the location of the DHCP database files. The default is %SystemRoot%\System32\DHCP.

- RestoreFlag: Specifies whether the DHCP Server should restore the DHCP database from its backup copy. Set this value to 1 to force a restoration, or leave it at 0 to continue to use the original database file. Note: If you change this value, you must stop and then restart the service in order for the changes to be applied.

THE WINDOWS INTERNET NAME SERVICE

The Windows Internet Name Service (WINS) can be used as a replacement for a Domain Name Service (DNS) to provide NetBIOS name resolution for computers using the TCP/IP protocol. WINS is based on the protocol specifications defined in RFC 1001/1002 and can interoperate with any other NetBIOS Name Server (NBNS) that also supports these protocols. I have included RFCs 1001 and 1002 on the accompanying CD-ROM as RFC1001.TXT and RFC1002.TXT, in case you would like a fuller understanding of these protocols.

This discussion of WINS begins with some of the design goals of the service, along with some of the concerns when implementing WINS on your network. It then moves on to planning your WINS Server installation, which includes some guidelines for the number of WINS Servers and WINS Proxy Agents to install. Following that, you will look at the actual installation steps required to install the service. Once that is out of the way, you'll move onto managing and configuring the WINS Service with the WINS Manager. And because a major portion of WINS concerns client-related administration, you will see how you can manage your WINS clients with the WINS Manager and learn about some specific quirks for MS-DOS clients using the Microsoft Network Client network software. Finally, you will look at managing your WINS database, using the Performance Monitor to monitor your WINS service, and using some of the Registry keys that control the behavior of the WINS service.

LOOKING AT DESIGN GOALS FOR THE WINS SERVICE

The primary purpose of the WINS Server Service is to make an Administrator's job easier by automating the process of mapping computer names to IP addresses for NetBIOS name resolution in a TCP/IP-based network. It can replace a UNIX DNS service, which uses a static text file (one or more host files) to define the computer-name-to-IP-address mapping. There is more to WINS than just automating the name resolution process, however.

The WINS design also includes the following:

◆ Centralized management: Along with the WINS Server Service, Windows NT Server also includes the WINS Manager. And with the WINS Manager, you can administer other WINS Servers and set up replication partners. You'll learn more about replication partners in later sections of this chapter.

◆ Dynamic address mapping and name resolution: Every time a WINS client starts, or whenever the renewal time expires, the WINS client registers its name with the WINS Server. When the WINS client terminates, such as when the computer shuts down, the name is released. This gives a client computer the capability to change subnets or to change its IP address and still be accessible from other computers and alleviates the manual modifications to host files required by a UNIX DNS service. These three stages (registration, release, and renewal) operate in the following manner:

Registration: A name registration request is sent to the WINS Server to be added to the WINS database. The WINS Server accepts or rejects a client name registration based on its internal database contents. If the database already contains a record for the IP address under a different computer name, the WINS Server challenges the registration. A challenge is a means of querying the current holder of the IP address to see whether it is still using it. If it is, the new client request is rejected. If the current holder of the IP address is not using the IP address, then the new client request is accepted and is added to the database with a timestamp, a unique incremental version number, and other information.

Release: Whenever a computer is shut down properly by the user (meaning that it did not crash or have a power failure), it informs the WINS Server, which marks the name entry in the database as released. If the entry remains marked as released for a specific period of time, the entry is marked as extinct and the version number is incremented. Version numbers are used to mark a record as changed so that changes to WINS partners are propagated to all WINS Servers.

If a record is marked as extinct and a new registration arrives at the WINS Server with the same name but a different IP address, the WINS Server does not challenge the registration. Instead, the new IP address is assigned to the name. This might occur with a DHCP-enabled portable computer (or another DHCP-enabled computer) that is moved to a different subnet, for example.

Renewal: Periodically, when half the renewal time has expired, a WINS client reregisters its name and IP address with a WINS Server. If the renewal time expires completely, the name is released, unless the client reregisters with the WINS Server.

◆ Domain-wide browsing: If you are using WINS Servers, your clients (Windows NT, Windows 95, Windows for Workgroups, LAN Manager 2.x, and MS-DOS computers using the Microsoft Network Client 3.0) can browse for computer resources on a Microsoft network across a router without having to have a domain controller on each side of the router.

◆ Reduction of broadcast traffic: A WINS Server provides the capability to lower the amount of broadcast messages by supplying an IP address when a name query message is received for a computer name from its local database on a WINS server or from its cache on a WINS Proxy Agent. A broadcast occurs on the local subnet only if the name query request fails.

◆ Interoperation with non-WINS clients: WINS can interoperate with non-WINS clients to provide name resolution, but only if you have one or more WINS Proxy Agents installed on the subnet. A WINS Proxy Agent is a computer running the WINS client service, which captures a name query request from a UNIX client, for example, obtains the IP address from the WINS server, and then passes this back to the requesting non-WINS client (the UNIX client, for example).

Tip

Instead of using a WINS Proxy Agent you might want to consider using the Microsoft DNS service. It provides a more transparent method for interoperability with non-WINS-aware clients.

PLANNING YOUR WINS INSTALLATION

For a small Microsoft-based network, all you really need for your WINS installation is to install the DHCP and WINS Services on each domain controller. This provides the means to configure your TCP/IP-based network clients to fully interoperate with any other server or client on the network. This recommendation is based on the fact that a single WINS Server can accommodate about 1,500 name registrations and

760 name query requests per minute. In theory, this means that you can use one WINS Server, with a backup WINS Server for every 10,000 clients. However, I prefer to use a WINS Server per logical grouping to provide additional fault tolerance and load balancing.

Note

These name query requests can be routed to other WINS Servers and WINS Proxy Agents to ensure that a request eventually will be fulfilled. If you enable replication of your WINS databases, however, each WINS Server will have a complete listing of every WINS client name and IP address. Then, when a name query request is received, an IP address will be returned without broadcasting on the network. This mechanism provides the capability to lower the amount of broadcast traffic on the subnet.

This logical grouping should be based on the physical layout of your Windows NT Server domain controllers or servers. A logical group could be based on domain controllers or servers in separate physical buildings or floors. It even could be based on domain controllers on the other side of a WAN link or similar property. For every three to five domain controllers or servers, I like to install the WINS Service. This provides for fault tolerance, in case of required maintenance or a WINS Server failure, and also limits the load on a single WINS Server. At the very least, you should have a minimum of two WINS Servers on your network supplying NetBIOS name resolution to prepare for a failure of the primary WINS Server, just as you should have a primary and backup domain controller to provide logon authentication in case of a primary domain controller failure.

This scenario works very well for Microsoft-based networks that use the Microsoft TCP/IP protocol stacks. But it will fail if you use third-party TCP/IP protocol stacks that do not support WINS on your network clients. This does not mean that you cannot use WINS in this situation, however. Instead, it only implies that you also need to install WINS Proxy Agents or use the Microsoft DNS service. A WINS Proxy Agent should be installed on each subnet, as depicted in Figure 9.11, to provide a linkage between your non-WINS clients and the WINS Servers. Your WINS Servers also should share their database to provide complete coverage of the entire network. This sharing process is provided by WINS replication, which is discussed in detail later in this section.

Note

You also can create static mappings, which will add a permanent computer name to IP address mapping in the WINS database to support your non-WINS clients.

Figure 9.11.
Supporting your
non-WINS clients
in a multiple
subnet network
with WINS
servers.

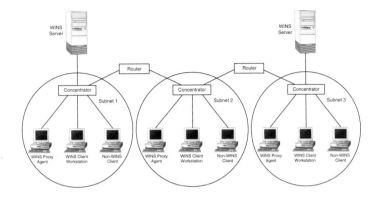

You need to have a WINS Proxy Agent per subnet because broadcast messages are not passed across routers. When a non-WINS client tries to find another computer, it uses a broadcast message to get the IP address of the requested computer. If the computer is on the same subnet, the request succeeds, but if it is on a different subnet, the request fails (unless you have domain controllers on both sides of the routers). This is where the WINS Proxy Agent comes into play, as shown in Figure 9.12.

Figure 9.12.
A WINS Proxy
Agent inter-
operating with
non-WINS
clients.

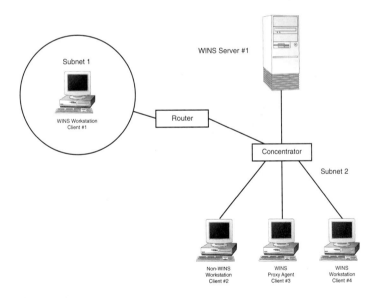

In Figure 9.12, Client #1 is a WINS client, Client #2 is a non-WINS client, Client #3 is a WINS Proxy Agent, and Server #1 is a Windows NT domain controller running the WINS service. When the WINS Client #2 attempts to access WINS Client #1 by broadcasting to obtain the IP address for Client #1, the request fails because Client #1 and Client #2 are on different subnets. The broadcast is intercepted by Client #3, however, which then caches this name and IP address. Client #3 also returns the IP address for Client #1 to Client #2 so that a TCP/IP connection can be established. If another WINS client on a different subnet attempts to access Client #2 by issuing a name query request, the cached IP address for Client #2 that Client #3 has stored is returned to the requesting client.

A WINS Proxy Agent will not store information obtained from a broadcast in the WINS Server's database. You therefore must have a WINS Proxy Agent on each subnet that contains non-WINS clients. In this case, the WINS Proxy Agent can respond to name query requests from WINS clients or WINS Servers, and then broadcast on its local subnet to find the non-WINS client. After the non-WINS client is found, the IP address can be passed to the WINS client or server that issued the name query request.

When a WINS client requires access to another computer, it issues a name query request. This name query request can be routed to WINS Servers, but this occurs only if the primary or secondary WINS Server for the WINS client does not contain a registration for the requested computer. If the routed name query request cannot be resolved by any WINS Server, the WINS client then issues a broadcast message. Both broadcast messages and routed name query messages eat network bandwidth that could be used to pass data. If your WINS Servers have a complete listing of the computer names and IP addresses, however, the primary WINS Server then can respond to the name query request, limiting the number of routed name query requests and broadcast messages.

This leads to the next performance and planning tip, which is that every WINS Server on a network should replicate its database to other WINS Servers on the network so that every WINS Server has a complete listing of every WINS client's name and IP address. This method provides the fastest mechanism for resolving names to IP addresses and limiting broadcast messages and routed name query messages.

WINS Servers provide two mechanisms for replication:

◆ Push partners: A push partner is a WINS Server that sends update notifications to its pull partners. After the pull partner receives this update message, it requests the changes from the push partner. The push partner then sends a replica of its database to the requesting pull partner.

◆ Pull partners: A pull partner is a WINS Server that requests updates from its push partner, and when the push partner responds, it receives the database replica.

As you can see from the description of a push and pull partner, these are part of a circular process. In order to replicate the WINS database one way, one WINS Server must be a push partner and the other must be a pull partner. To completely replicate a WINS database between two or more WINS Servers, each WINS Server must be a push and pull partner of the other. This is a two-way nonlinear chain, as shown in Figure 9.13, which can be used to replicate every WINS database to every other WINS database. You can see in Figure 9.13 that some WINS Servers receive update notifications from more than one WINS Server, which can lead to increased network traffic.

Figure 9.13.
A WINS Server
push and pull
replication in a
nonlinear chain.

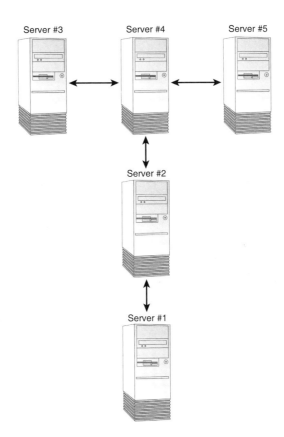

A better method, although a bit slower, is to create a linear chain, as shown in Figure 9.14, where one and only one WINS Server is the push or pull partner of another WINS Server. Only at a WAN link is this rule broken, where the WINS Server on the LAN side is a push and pull partner of a WINS Server on the LAN, and where it is also a push and pull partner of a WINS Server on a WAN link. And this leads to another point: How often should you replicate? My basic methodology is based on the distance between replication points and the speed of the link. For your local area network, 10 to 15 minutes is a good choice because the network throughput is quite high. For local, heavily used WAN links, you should limit your replication period to between 30 and 60 minutes. Lower the rate only if you have a high turnover rate. For longer WAN links, choose a value of between 45 to 90 minutes. And for intercontinental WAN links, choose 6 to 12 hours and schedule it for the nonpeak hours. The idea here is that the more heavily the link is used, the lower the replication frequency (or the higher the number of scheduled minutes between replication attempts).

Figure 9.14.
A WINS server
push and pull
replication in a
linear chain.

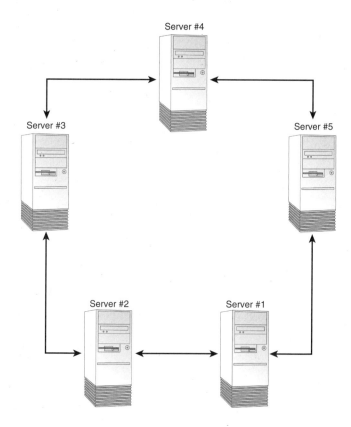

INSTALLING THE WINS SERVICE

You use the Control Panel Network applet to install the WINS Server Service.

Note

In order to install the WINS Server Service, you must be a member of the administrators group on the computer on which you want to install the service.

Follow these steps to install the WINS Service:

1. Launch the Control Panel Network applet to display the Network Settings dialog box.
2. Click the Add Software button to display the Add Network Software dialog box.
3. Select TCP/IP Protocol and Related Components in the Network Software drop-down listbox. Then click the Continue button. The Windows NT TCP/IP Installation Options dialog box appears.
4. Enable the WINS Server Service checkbox.

Note

Normally, you will be installing the DHCP Server as well as WINS, unless you are creating just a WINS Server or WINS Proxy Agent. If you are installing the DHCP Server Service, when prompted, enter the TCP/IP address, subnet mask, default gateway, and WINS Server IP addresses. You can use the local computer IP address as the primary WINS Server address, but you should select another IP address for the secondary WINS server just in case the service fails to start on the local computer. If you have multiple network adapters installed (a multihomed system), make sure that you click the Advanced button to configure the additional adapters.

Tip

If you want to use SNMP to configure the WINS Server Service remotely, be sure to install the SNMP Service by enabling the SNMP Service checkbox as well.

5. If this computer will be only a WINS Server, check the Enable Automatic DHCP Configuration checkbox.
6. Click the OK button. When prompted, enter the path to the distribution files and click the Continue button. The Network Settings dialog box appears.
7. Click the OK button.
8. When prompted, restart your system. After the system restarts, the WINS Server Service should be activated. If not, check your system event log for any error messages.

CONFIGURING THE WINS SERVICE WITH THE WINS MANAGER

The first time you use the WINS Manager, it displays only the WINS Server on the local computer. To add additional WINS Servers to the WINS Manager, choose Server | Add WINS Server and then supply the IP address or computer name in the Add WINS Server dialog box. To delete a WINS Server from your WINS Manager list, select it and then choose Server | Delete WINS Server. After adding your additional WINS Servers to the local WINS Manager, you need to configure the local WINS Server for optimal performance. This includes setting your WINS Server configuration, replication partners, and preferences. Each of these options performs a slightly different task, which you will learn about in this section.

The first recommended option is to choose Server | Configuration, which displays the WINS Server Configuration dialog box (see Figure 9.15).

Figure 9.15.
The expanded
WINS Server
Configuration
dialog box.

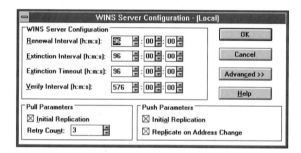

You can set the following options in the WINS Server Configuration dialog box:

◆ Renewal Interval: Specifies how often a WINS client has to register its name with the WINS Server. The default is 4 days.

◆ Extinction Interval: Specifies the time interval between when a record is marked as released and when it is marked as extinct. The default and maximum time is 4 days.

◆ Extinction Timeout: Specifies the time interval between when a record is marked as extinct and when it is scavenged from the database. The default is 4 days and the minimum is 1 day.

Note

The extinction interval and extinction default for a fully configured WINS Server is based on the renewal time and whether the WINS Server has replication partners on the replication time interval.

Tip

You can manually scavenge the database by choosing
Mappings | Initiate Scavenging. This process removes outdated
records from the database.

◆ Verify Interval: Specifies the time interval in which a WINS Server must
verify that old names owned by another WINS Server are still valid. The
default (24 days) is dependent on the extinction interval. The maximum is
24 days.

◆ Pull Parameters: The pull partner replication interval is set in the Preferences dialog box, as described later in this section. If you want the replication to be triggered when the WINS Server Service starts, enable the Initial
Replication checkbox and specify a number in the Retry Count listbox.

◆ Push Parameters: To configure push partner configurations, you can enable
these checkboxes:

Initial Replication: If this setting is enabled, push partners are informed that a change has occurred when the WINS Server Service is
started.

Replicate on Address Change: If this setting is enabled, push partners
are informed whenever an entry in the database changes or when a
new entry is added.

◆ The Advanced button: You can access the following options by clicking the
Advanced button to expand the WINS Server Configuration dialog box:

Logging Enabled: Specifies that the WINS Server service will log
database changes and inform you of basic errors in the system event
log. The default is enabled.

Log Detailed Events: Specifies that detailed events will be written into
the system event log. It should be used only for a limited time, such as
when you are troubleshooting WINS Server problems, because it can
consume considerable resources and impact system performance. The
default is disabled.

Replicate Only with Partners: Allows replication only with push or
pull partners. If this option is disabled, you can replicate data from
any unlisted WINS Server. The default is enabled.

Backup on Termination: Automatically backs up the WINS database
whenever the WINS Server Service is shut down. It does not perform
a backup whenever the system is shut down, however. The default is
enabled.

Migrate On/Off: Enables or disables the treatment of static or
multihomed records as dynamic whenever they conflict with a new

registration or replica (data copied from another WINS Server). This option should be enabled if you are upgrading a non-Windows NT System (such as a LAN Manager server) to a Windows NT Server. The default is disabled.

Starting Version Count: Specifies the highest database version number. Normally, you do not need to change this value; however, if you restore the WINS database from a backup because your primary database is corrupted, you should increment this value to a number higher than any other copy of the WINS Server partners to ensure proper replication.

Note

You can display the current value by choosing View | Database from the menu. If you want to see the version numbers on other WINS Servers, choose the WINS Server before making the menu selection.

Database Backup Path: Specifies the full path to use for the backup copies of the WINS Server database.

My next suggestion is to set your preferences for the WINS Manager and default settings for the WINS Service. You can access these preferences by choosing Options | Preferences to display the dialog box shown in Figure 9.16.

Figure 9.16.
Specifying the
WINS Manager
preferences and
WINS Server
Service defaults.

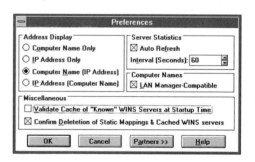

You can take the following actions from this dialog box:

◆ Specify how the WINS Manager displays the names for the WINS Servers it is connected to and, incidentally, the mechanism used for connecting to the service. These options follow:

Computer Name Only: Specifies that the computer name will be displayed and uses named pipes to connect to the WINS Server.

IP Address Only: Specifies that the IP address will be displayed and uses TCP/IP to connect to the WINS Server.

Computer Name (IP Address): Specifies that the computer name will be displayed first and then the IP address, and uses named pipes to connect to the WINS Server.

IP Address (Computer Name): Specifies that the IP address will be displayed first, followed by the computer name; also specifies that TCP/IP will be used to connect to the WINS Server.

◆ Specify the refresh interval for updating the WINS Manager display. If you enable the Auto Refresh checkbox, then you also should specify a value (number of seconds to wait before updating the display) in the Interval field.

Note

The WINS Manager display also is refreshed automatically whenever you initiate an action with the WINS Manager.

◆ Specify the NetBIOS name compatibility. If the LAN Manager Compatible checkbox is enabled (the default setting), then NetBIOS names are limited to 15 bytes to contain the name, whereas you have a limit of 16 bytes for a special code for static mappings. If you use other applications that require a 16-byte NetBIOS name, such as Lotus Notes, this option should be disabled. The special codes follow:

0x0   Specifies that the NetBIOS name is used by the Redirector.

0x1   Specifies that the NetBIOS name is used by the master domain browser.

0x3   Specifies that the NetBIOS name is used by the messenger service.

0x20 Specifies that the NetBIOS name is used by a LAN Manager server.

0x1B Specifies the master browser name that clients and browsers use to contact the master browser.

0x1E Specifies that the NetBIOS name is used for a normal group.

0x1D Specifies that the NetBIOS name is used for client name resolution when an attempt is made to contact the master browser for server lists.

0x1C Specifies that the NetBIOS name is an Internet group name. An Internet group name contains the addresses of the primary and backup domain controllers for the domain. This name is limited to 25 addresses.

◆ Specify the miscellaneous support options:

Validate Cache of "Known" WINS Servers at Startup Time: If this option is enabled, whenever you start the WINS Manager, it attempts to connect to all WINS Servers you have added. If a WINS Server cannot be contacted, you are prompted to remove the WINS Server from the list of connected servers. The default is disabled.

Confirm Deletion of Static Mappings and Cached WINS Servers: This option, if enabled (the default), prompts you with a message box whenever you attempt to remove a static mapping or cached WINS Server. I find the constant message boxes a bit annoying and usually disable this setting. However, before you do so, I suggest that you become a bit more familiar with the WINS Manager.

◆ If you click the Partners button, the dialog box expands and enables you to set defaults for the partner replication. These settings follow:

New Pull Partner Default Configuration: The entries in this group specify the default replication settings for new pull partners that you create for the currently selected WINS Server. These options follow:

Start Time: The time to start your WINS Server database replication. There is no default, although I like to start at 12:00 a.m.

Replication Interval: The interval at which to repeat the WINS Server database replication. There is no default, although I generally choose a 15-minute interval for local area network WINS Servers.

New Push Partner Default Configuration: The entry in this group specifies the number of changes that have to occur in the WINS Server database before a push notification is sent to the push partners that you create for the currently selected WINS Servers.

Update Count: Specifies the number of changes that have to occur before a push notification is sent. There is no default, although I recommend a value of 1,000.

My next suggestion is to set the replication settings for the local WINS Server by choosing Server | Replication Partners. This displays the Replication Partners dialog box shown in Figure 9.17. Click the Add button to add the WINS Servers to be configured as the local push or pull partners. You can choose to replicate to any or all WINS Servers in a nonlinear fashion, or you can choose to pull from one WINS Server and push to another WINS Server in a linear fashion. These techniques were described in more detail earlier, in the section "Planning Your WINS Installation."

Figure 9.17.
Specifying the
WINS Server
replication
partners.

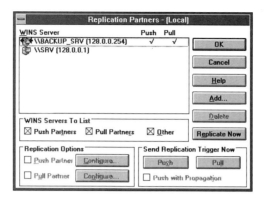

Note

To remove a WINS Server from the WINS Server list, select it and press the Delete key.

After you add your WINS Servers, you can take the following actions:

◆ Specify the WINS Servers to display in the WINS Server list by enabling or disabling the options in the WINS Servers To List section. These options follow:

Push Partners: If enabled (the default), push partners of this WINS Server are displayed.

Pull Partners: If enabled (the default), pull partners of this WINS Server are displayed.

Other: If enabled (the default), any nonpartner of this WINS Server is displayed.

◆ Specify the individual settings for the currently selected WINS Server to be a push, pull, or both partner in the Replication Options section. When you select a WINS Server that already is configured as a push or pull partner, the following Configure buttons are enabled:

Push Partner: Specifies that the selected WINS Server is a push partner. You then can click the Configure button to display the Push properties dialog box, where you can view or set the update count.

Pull Partner: Specifies that the selected WINS Server is a pull partner. You then can click the Configure button to display the Pull properties dialog box, where you can view or set the start time and replication interval.

Tip

If you specified the default values in the Preferences dialog box, these settings are set automatically for new push or pull partners. If you are configuring a push or pull partner across a WAN link, however, you should set higher values, as described in the section "Planning Your WINS Installation."

◆ Initiate a replication trigger immediately instead of waiting for it to occur based on the replication times set in the Configuration dialog box by setting the following values in the Send Replication Trigger Now group:

Push: Initiates a push trigger to send to the selected WINS Server.

Pull: Initiates a pull trigger to send to the selected WINS Server.

Push with Propagation: Modifies the Push message to indicate that changes sent to the selected WINS Server should be propagated to all other pull partners of the selected WINS Servers.

Tip

You can initiate a complete replication to the selected WINS Server by clicking the Replicate Now button.

MANAGING YOUR NON-WINS CLIENTS

Managing your non-WINS clients consists of creating static mappings, which is a permanent computer-name-to-IP-address record, and viewing your current database records. When you create a static mapping, it is also a good idea to create a reservation (as described earlier in the section "Managing Client Reservations") for this IP address to provide a more manageable environment. You can add static mappings by choosing Mappings | Static Mappings, which displays the Static Mappings dialog box, as shown in Figure 9.18. After you click the Add Mappings button, the Add Static Mappings dialog box appears. Here, you can enter a computer name, IP address, and type that will be added to the WINS Server database. Table 9.3 describes the special names the WINS Server uses and how WINS manages these names. You can delete a static mapping by selecting the mapping in the Static Mappings dialog box and then clicking the Delete Mapping button.

Figure 9.18.
The Static
Mappings dialog
box.

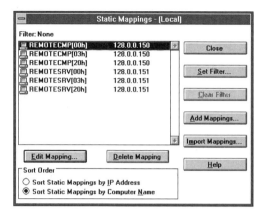

Tip

You can import a series of static mappings by importing a host file
from a DNS server to support your non-WINS computers.

TABLE 9.3. WINS SERVER SPECIAL NAMES.

Type	Description
Unique	A normal name, implying that only one computer name will be associated with the IP address.
Group	Does not have an associated IP address. Instead, when a group name is registered with the WINS Server and a name query request for this name is received, the WINS Server returns the broadcast address (FFFFFFFF) and the requesting client issues a broadcast message to find the requested computer.
Multihomed	A name that has multiple IP addresses associated with it. A multihomed device contains two or more network adapters that can register each individual IP address associated with the computer by sending a special name registration packet. A multihomed group name can contain a maximum of 25 IP addresses.
Internet	A group name that contains domain controller IP addresses. WINS gives preference to this name registration to the closest 25 addresses. After a request is received for the domain, the domain controller address and the additional 24 (maximum) IP addresses are returned to the client.

MANAGING WINS DATABASES

Because your WINS Server also uses the same database format (a modified Access database), it has the same basic issues as the databases for the DHCP Server. As records are added and deleted, the database grows. The WINS databases are located in the SystemRoot\System32\WINS directory and include the following:

◆ WINS.MDB: The WINS database

◆ WINSTMP.MDB: A temporary file created by the DHCP Server

◆ JET.LOG: Contains transaction records

◆ SYSTEM.MDB: Contains structural information about the WINS databases

The database growth affects the performance of the WINS Server. As your WINS.MDB database approaches the 30MB limit, you should compact it. To do so, follow these steps:

1. Stop the WINS Server Service from the Control Panel Services applet, or issue the net stop wins command from a console prompt.

2. From a console prompt, run the JETPACK.EXE program, which is located in your SystemRoot\System32 directory. The syntax for this program follows:

   JETPACK DatabaseName TemoraryDatabaseName

   Here, DatabaseName is the name of the database to compact. It can be a fully qualified path name.

   TemporaryDatabaseName is a name to use as a temporary database. It also can be a fully qualified path name.

Caution

Do not compact the SYSTEM.MDB file. If you do, the WINS Server service will fail to start. If this occurs, restore your configuration from a previous backup.

3. Start the Windows Internet Name Service from the Control Panel Services applet, or issue a net start wins command from a console prompt.

Tip

Before you back up or compact the database, you should choose the Mappings | Initiate Scavenging command to delete old records that are no longer needed.

Tip

Because the potential for failure or just plain data corruption on your SystemRoot partition is possible with the compact utility, you should back up your WINS databases regularly, and definitely before you compact it. You can do this by choosing Mappings | Backup Database. Make sure to perform a full backup by disabling the Perform Incremental Backup option if you plan to use this copy to restore your configuration.

MONITORING THE WINS SERVER SERVICE

Although the WINS Manager displays the same statistics as those used by the Performance Monitor, the WINS Manager can display only the statistics for the currently selected WINS Server. If you use the Performance Monitor, however, you can monitor multiple WINS Servers simultaneously. This can be of enormous benefit when you are comparing the performance of multiple WINS Servers. Table 9.4 lists the available WINS Server performance object counters that you can use to monitor your selected WINS Server.

TABLE 9.4. THE PERFORMANCE MONITOR OBJECT TYPES AND OBJECT COUNTERS FOR THE WINS SERVER.

Object Counter	Description
Failed Queries/sec	Total number of failed queries per second.
Failed Releases/sec	Total number of failed releases per second.
Group Conflicts/sec	The rate at which group registration received by the WINS Server resulted in conflicts with records in the database.
Group Registrations/sec	The rate at which group registrations are received by the WINS Server.
Group Renewals/sec	The rate at which group renewals are received by the WINS Server.
Queries/sec	The rate at which queries are received by the WINS Server.
Releases/sec	The rate at which releases are received by the WINS Server.
Successful Queries/sec	Total number of successful queries per second.
Successful Releases/sec	Total number of successful releases per second.

continues

TABLE 9.4. CONTINUED

Object Counter	Description
Total Number of Conflicts/sec	The sum of the unique and group conflicts per second. This is the total rate at which conflicts were seen by the WINS Server.
Total Number of Registrations/sec	The sum of the unique and group registrations per second. This is the total rate at which registrations are received by the WINS Server.
Total Number of Renewals/sec	The sum of the unique and group renewals per second. This is the total rate at which renewals are received by the WINS Server.
Unique Conflicts/sec	The rate at which unique registrations and renewals received by the WINS Server resulted in conflicts with records in the database.
Unique Registrations/sec	The rate at which unique registrations are received by the WINS Server.
Unique Renewals/sec	The rate at which unique renewals are received by the WINS Server.

Tip

To get a feel for how well your WINS Server is performing, you should monitor the total number of conflicts, registrations, and renewals. You also should monitor the failed queries and releases.

USING WINS SERVER REGISTRY KEYS

The WINS Server Service also stores its configuration information in the Registry, just as the DHCP Server Service does. And, once again, you may need to modify the Registry to modify one or more configuration settings if you cannot set them from the WINS Manager or you are administering an inactive WINS Server. I am issuing this warning again because if improperly used, the Registry Editor can damage your system beyond repair. Refer to Appendix B, "The Registry Editor and Registry Keys," (which is located on the included CD-ROM) for additional information and some tips for backing up your current Registry before using the Registry Editor (REGEDT32.EXE).

The following primary Registry keys are located in the HKEY_LOCAL_MACHINE\System\CurrentControlSet\Services\WINS\Parameters key:

- DbFileNm: Specifies the full path name to the locations of the WINS database file. The default is `%SystemRoot%\System32\WINS\WINS.MDB`.

- DoStaticDataInit: If this item is set to 1, the WINS Server initializes its database with records from one or more files in the DataFiles subkey. This initialization is performed at the time the process is executed and whenever a change to a key in the Parameters or Datafiles subkey occurs. If set to the default (0), this initialization does not occur.

- InitTimePause: If this entry is set to 1, the WINS Service starts in the paused state. It stays in this state until it replicates with its partners (push or pull) or fails in the replication attempt (at least once). If this entry is set to 1, the WINS\Partner\Pull\InitTimeReplication subkey should be set to 1 or removed from the Registry for proper operation. A value of 0 (the default) disables this option. Note that you can set the InitTimeReplication key value by choosing Options | Preference and clicking the Advanced button to expand the dialog box.

- LogFilePath: Specifies the location for the WINS Server log files. The default is `%SystemRoot%\System32\WINS`.

- McastIntvl: Specifies the time interval, in seconds, for the WINS Server to send a multicast and announce itself to other WINS Servers. The minimum and default value is 2400 (40 minutes).

- McastTtl: Specifies the number of times a multicast announcement can cross a particular router. The default is 6, and the range is 1 to 32.

- NoOfWrkThds: Specifies the number of worker threads used by the WINS Server. The default is one per processor on the system, with a range of 1 to 40. Note: You can change this value and place it into effect without restarting the WINS service.

- PriorityClassHigh: If set to 1, this entry enables the WINS service to run in the high priority class. This prevents other applications and services running in lower priorities from preempting the WINS service. The default is 0. Note: If you choose to enable this setting, make sure that you monitor the system with the performance monitor to make sure that the WINS service is not using too much processor time and that other applications and services continue to function properly.

- UseSelfFndPnrs: This option is used to configure the WINS service to automatically find other WINS servers and configure them as push and pull partners. Set this entry to 1 (to enable it) or 0 (to disable it). The default is 0. If the push and pull partners are configured manually with the WINS Manager, the partnership information no longer is maintained automatically when a change occurs.

Note

> If the UseSelfFndPnrs option is enabled, the WINS Service only configures WINS Servers as push and pull partners across routers if the routers support multicasting. Otherwise, only WINS Servers found on the local subnet are configured automatically as partners. If your routers do support multicasting, UseSelfFndPnrs can be a very useful item to set because it relieves you of the burden of configuring your push and pull partners manually.

You can configure the following Registry keys by choosing Server | Configuration and modifying the entries in the WINS Server Configuration dialog box:

◆ BackupDirPath: Specifies the full path name to the location to be used to back up the WINS database.

◆ DoBackupOnTerm: If enabled (1), the WINS database is backed up whenever the WINS Service is terminated. If disabled (0), the database is not backed up when the service is terminated. The default is 1. Note that the backup does not occur if the system is shut down. A backup occurs only when the service is stopped manually.

◆ LogDetailedEvents: If enabled (1), verbose logging of WINS events occurs. The default is disabled (0).

◆ LoggingOn: If enabled (1), WINS messages are placed in the event log. If disabled (0), no events are placed in the event log. The default is 1.

◆ RefreshInterval: Specifies the time, in seconds, for the client to register its name with the WINS Server. The default is 0x54600 (4 days).

◆ RplOnlyWCnfPnrs: Enables (1) or disables (0) the capability to replicate a WINS Server from a WINS Server that is not a partner. The default is 1.

◆ MigrateOn: Enables (1) or disables (0) the treatment of unique and multihomed records as dynamic when a registration conflict is detected. The default is 0.

◆ TombstoneInterval: Specifies the time, in seconds, between when a client record is released and when it is marked as extinct. The default is 0x54600 (4 days).

◆ TombstoneTimeout: Specifies the time, in seconds, between when a client record is marked as extinct and when it is scavenged from the database. The default is 0x54600 (4 days).

◆ VerifyInterval: Specifies the interval in which the WINS Server must verify that old names, which it does not own, are still valid. The default is 0x1FA400 (24 days).

The following Registry keys for partner replication are located in the `HKEY_LOCAL_MACHINE` `\System\CurrentControlSet\Services\WINS\Partners` key:

◆ PersonaNonGrata: Specifies IP addresses for WINS Servers from which you do not want to replicate data. This key may be very useful for Administrators to block replication from WINS Servers that are not under their control.

◆ Pull\<IPAddress>\MemberPrec: Specifies the preference order of addresses in an Internet group. Values can be 0 for low precedence or 1 for high precedence. The default is 0. Note: This entry appears under an IP address (of a WINS Server).

Using the Domain Name System

The primary purpose of a Domain Name System is to supply friendly computer names instead of an IP address to locate a resource. This process is often referred to as NetBIOS name resolution. The Domain Name System utilizes a hierarchical architecture. If a DNS server is unable to resolve an IP address at the local level, it will query other DNS servers at a higher level to resolve the name. If you do not mind maintaining multiple DNS servers and their associated configuration files, you could use DNS in place of DHCP and WINS. I prefer to use all three components together because, in the Microsoft implementation, the three complement each other and provide ease of administration as well as maximum compatibility.

The Design Goals for the Microsoft DNS Service

While you could use other DNS servers on your network, they may not support the Microsoft WINS service. If such is the case, then you may also lose the ability to manage a dynamic network. This is the real difference between the Microsoft DNS implementation and other DNS servers that run under Windows NT. The Microsoft implementation fully supports WINS, which in turn is aware of DHCP. If you use DHCP, WINS, and DNS together then you, too, can achieve the following:

◆ Utilizing DHCP, your clients automatically allocate dynamic IP addresses. This allows you, the Administrator, to provide dynamic IP addresses to your network clients as they move between subnets (a consultant, or temporary employee, perhaps).

◆ Utilizing WINS, your clients automatically register their computer name and IP address, every time they start up their computer. If the computer moves between subnets, this information is automatically updated as well.

◆ Utilizing DNS, your clients can find any non-WINS-aware resources through the static mappings maintained in the configuration files. This also works in reverse. Any non-WINS-aware client that uses DNS to resolve names and has a static mapping to your DNS service, can locate a WINS client as long as the Microsoft DNS server is configured to use a WINS server for additional names resolution.

This combination of DHCP, WINS, and DNS provides additional benefits, too. Dynamic address allocation also means dynamic address recovery. When a new IP address is allocated to a client on another subnet, the old address is released back to the DHCP scope's address pool. This can prevent the confusion caused by duplicate IP addresses on the network. The only thing DHCP and WINS really will not do for you is make it easy to get on the Internet. One of the requirements for registering your domain (often your company name) with the InterNIC is that you maintain two, or more, DNS servers on your network so that clients that want to connect to your server, most likely your WWW page, can find you. Many Internet Service Providers (ISP) don't know how to deal with, or support, DHCP and WINS either, so you may as well get used to using a DNS server if you plan to connect to the Internet. But you don't have to go through all the hassle of modifying your configuration files every time you move or add a client to your network if you also use DHCP and WINS.

There are some additional benefits of using a DNS server because it can provide some additional name resolution capabilities that WINS cannot. A DNS server includes e-mail name resolution by supporting the MX record type, which associates an e-mail address with a host name. And when a DNS server cannot resolve a name locally, it will refer the name query to another DNS server higher up the chain in an effort to resolve the name.

PLANNING YOUR DNS INSTALLATION

There are a few items to consider before you install a Domain Name System server on your network. If you plan to connect to the Internet, the most important of these is security. For this reason, I suggest you consider how this will affect your implementation. The other items are less serious, but equally important.

First, consider who will be in charge of maintaining the configuration files. This person will maintain a master copy of all shared configuration files. Everyone else will use a replicated copy of the master copy. Second, if you will have more than one person modifying any configuration file, make sure they are trained to maintain the files in the same way. Make sure this training includes a standard naming convention for filenames, host names, and verification of IP addresses.

Caution

A duplicate host name or IP address on your network can cause serious problems. Make sure your administrators are aware of this, and that your registration plan includes the capability to register a name and IP address before it is reassigned. An access database could be used to maintain information (host name, IP address, filename, and so on.) about your network and could be queried to verify that the host name and IP address are not in use.

INSTALLING THE DOMAIN NAME SERVER (DNS) SERVICE

The DNS service is based on the UNIX BIND (Berkley Internet Name Domain) service. It provides a means to map computer names to IP addresses, or IP addresses to computer names, much as the WINS service does. The primary difference between WINS and DNS is that DNS uses a static mapping mechanism based on host files. Even if you plan to use WINS, you should install the DNS service because it can provide additional functionality when connecting to the Internet. To install the DNS service, follow these steps:

Note

There have been several versions of the Microsoft Domain Name Server service made available at one time or another. The original version, on the Resource Kit, has been replaced by versions obtainable from service pack upgrades or via the Microsoft WWW site at `http://www.microsoft.com`. This section looks at the latest version. Your version may use slightly different host file formats.

1. Execute `install.bat` (located in the Resource Kit *InstallationRoot*\DNS subdirectory—where *InstallationRoot* is the root directory where you installed the resource kit) from a console window. This will install the appropriate files and configure the service control manager so you can control the service operation.
2. After the files have been copied to your `SystemRoot\System32` directory, launch the Control Panel Services applet.
3. Next, click the Startup button to display the Service dialog where you may configure the Startup Type from Manual to Automatic. This will then start the DNS service when the server starts instead of requiring you to manually start the service each time you power up the server.

4. Then click OK to close the Service dialog. Once this has been accomplished you may click the Close button to exit the Services dialog.

5. At this point, you should modify your host files (located in the `SystemRoot\System32\DNS` or `SystemRoot\System32\drivers\etc` subdirectory, depending on which version you have installed) as described in the following section titled "The DNS Service Configuration Files." Once this has been accomplished, you may restart your system. After the system restarts, the DNS service should be activated. Even if the service is running, you should check the system event log for any error messages produced by the DNS service. Sometimes this is the only indication that you have incorrectly configured a record in one of your host files.

THE DNS SERVICE CONFIGURATION FILES

The configuration files used with the Microsoft DNS server can be replaced by those from a UNIX BIND installation if you are migrating, or interoperating, with a UNIX system, although you may need to modify the files if you are using some outdated BIND commands. These configuration files are divided into four basic types:

◆ BOOT: This file controls the startup behavior of the DNS server. It includes information on the default directory where the configuration files reside, the cache filename, the domain name that the DNS server will service, and the domain name for secondary DNS servers.

◆ CACHE: This file contains information for Internet connectivity.

◆ PLACE.DOM: This file contains information on host names within the domain. It also includes references to reverse lookup filenames and WINS servers.

◆ ARPA-###.REV: These files (there should be one per subnet) include information to resolve an IP address to a hostname.

BOOT

There are not very many commands supported in the boot file, so the syntax for the commands, as summarized in Table 9.3, are fairly easy to remember. A sample BOOT file for a simple network, such as the one in my office, looks like this:

```
;   DNS BOOT FILE
;   CACHE FILE
cache    .        cache
;   PRIMARY DOMAINS
primary  nt-guru.com              nt-guru.dom
primary  127.170.206.in-addr.arpa     arpa-206.rev
primary  0.0.127.in-addr.arpa         arpa-127.rev
```

Table 9.3. Applicable commands for the BOOT file.

Command	Required	Description	Note
;	No	Starts a comment.	Avoid using unnecessary comments because the file is parsed line by line. Each comment added to the file slows down name resolution for any name not in the cache.
directory *PathName*	No	Describes the location of the DNS configuration files where *PathName* is a fully qualified path. The default if not specified is %SystemRoot%\System32\DNS.	If the directory cannot be found, the DNS service will fail to start.
cache *FileName* service	Yes	Describes the location of the cache file that is used to find additional name servers where *FileName* is the name of the file.	If the file cannot be found, the DNS will fail to start.
Primary *DomainName* *FileName*	Yes	Specifies a domain name for which this DNS server is authoritative and a configuration filename that contains information for the domain.	
Secondary *DomainName* *HostList* *FileName*]	No	Specifies a domain name and associated IP address array from which to download zone information.	If a filename is specified, the zone information will be downloaded and used if the domain DNS server, or alternate, cannot be located.

CACHE

The cache file is used for additional name resolution. When your DNS server cannot resolve a name, it queries the additional name servers listed in this file. If you are using this DNS server to resolve names on the Internet, your file should look similar to the following:

```
;    DNS CACHE FILE
;    Initial cache data for root domain servers.
;    YOU SHOULD CHANGE:
;         - Nothing if connected to the Internet.  Edit this file only when
;           update root name server list is released.
;            OR
;         - If NOT connected to the Internet, remove these records and replace
;           with NS and A records for the DNS server authoritative for the
;           root domain at your site.
;    Internet root name server records:
;         last update:   Sep 1, 1995
;         related version of root zone:   1995090100
; formerly NS.INTERNIC.NET
.                        3600000  IN  NS    A.ROOT-SERVERS.NET.
A.ROOT-SERVERS.NET.      3600000      A     198.41.0.4
; formerly NS1.ISI.EDU
.                        3600000      NS    B.ROOT-SERVERS.NET.
B.ROOT-SERVERS.NET.      3600000      A     128.9.0.107
; formerly C.PSI.NET
.                        3600000      NS    C.ROOT-SERVERS.NET.
C.ROOT-SERVERS.NET.      3600000      A     192.33.4.12
; formerly TERP.UMD.EDU
.                        3600000      NS    D.ROOT-SERVERS.NET.
D.ROOT-SERVERS.NET.      3600000      A     128.8.9.90
; formerly NS.NASA.GOV
.                        3600000      NS    E.ROOT-SERVERS.NET.
E.ROOT-SERVERS.NET.      3600000      A     192.203.230.10
; formerly NS.ISC.ORG
.                        3600000      NS    F.ROOT-SERVERS.NET.
F.ROOT-SERVERS.NET.      3600000      A     39.13.229.241
; formerly NS.NIC.DDN.MIL
.                        3600000      NS    G.ROOT-SERVERS.NET.
G.ROOT-SERVERS.NET.      3600000      A     192.112.36.4
; formerly AOS.ARL.ARMY.MIL
.                        3600000      NS    H.ROOT-SERVERS.NET.
H.ROOT-SERVERS.NET.      3600000      A     128.63.2.53
; formerly NIC.NORDU.NET
.                        3600000      NS    I.ROOT-SERVERS.NET.
I.ROOT-SERVERS.NET.      3600000      A     192.36.148.17
; End of File
```

Tip

An updated version of this file can be found at the InterNIC FTP site `ftp.rs.internic.net`. Just log on anonymously, change to the `domain` directory and download the file called `named.root`.

If this DNS server will *not* be used for Internet name resolution, you should replace the name server (NS) and address (A) records with the authoritative DNS server for your domain.

PLACE.DOM

This file is the heart of your DNS server's operation. It contains several record types, as summarized in Table 9.4, which are used to provide name resolution for the domain. Because the example file that is included with the Microsoft DNS service contains information for a non-existent domain, you should rename the file and modify it as appropriate for your domain. The following is a copy of my replacement file, called nt-guru.dom. I use a naming convention of *DomainName*.dom, and I recommend you do so too. This is particularly useful when administering multiple domains.

```
;    nt-guru.dom
;
;    Lookup file for nt-guru.com domain.
;    START OF AUTHORITY
@    IN  SOA     srv.nt-guru.com.  admin.srv.nt-guru.com. (
                            1           ; serial number
                            10800       ; refresh [3h]
                            3600        ; retry   [1h]
                            604800      ; expire  [7d]
                            86400 )     ; minimum [1d]
;    NAME SERVERS
@               IN  NS      srv.nt-guru.com.
srv             IN  A       206.170.127.65
;    WINS Record
@    IN  WINS 206.170.127.65 206.170.127.65
;    LOCAL HOST
localhost       IN  A       127.0.0.1
;    E-MAIL SERVERS
@               IN  MX      10      srv
srv             IN  A       206.170.127.65
;    CNAME RECORDS
ftp             IN  CNAME   srv
www             IN  CNAME   srv
gopher          IN  CNAME   srv
mail            IN  CNAME   srv
```

The first entry in the file must be a start of authoritative (SOA) record. This record should include parameters that describe the source host (where the file was created), an e-mail address for the administrator of the file, a serial number (or version number) of the file, a refresh interval (in seconds) that is used by secondary servers to determine when a revised file should be downloaded, a retry time (in seconds) that is used by secondary servers to know how long to wait before reattempting to download the file in case of error, and an expiration time (in seconds) that is used by secondary servers to determine when to discard a zone if it could not be downloaded. Then your name servers (or DNS servers) for the domain should be listed, followed by their IP addresses. Next, include the local host identifier that is used for loop back testing, the name and address of any mail servers, and finally any host name aliases. A host name alias is used to provide a host (such as my server, SRV) with more than one host name. This is particularly useful when you want your WWW site to be accessible in the commonly used format `WWW.DomainName.COM` (`www.nt-guru.com`, for example) rather than `ServerName.DomainName.COM` (`srv.nt-guru.com`, for example).

> ### Note
>
> When you specify a fully qualified domain name (FQDN) it must be appended with a period. Otherwise the domain name will be appended to the host name for resolution and cause the name query to fail. For example, if I had specified my domain name as `nt-guru.com` in line 7, instead of as `nt-guru.com`, the domain name of `nt-guru.com` would be appended once again (`srv.nt-guru.com.nt-guru.com`) when trying to resolve the host name `srv.nt-guru.com`. Because there is no host by that name, the query would fail.

TABLE 9.4. SUPPORTED DOMAIN NAME RECORDS.

Identifier	Record Type	Description
A	Address	Specifies the IP address of the associated host name.
CNAME	Class Name	Specifies an alias for the associated host name.
MX	Mail	Specifies the e-mail server host names.
NS	Name Server	Specifies the DNS servers in the domain.
SOA	Start of Authority	The first record in any configuration file and is used to specify the host where the file was created, an e-mail contact address, version number, refresh time, expiration time, and retry interval.
WINS	WINS	Specifies the IP addresses of WINS servers that are used for additional name resolution.

ARPA-###.REV

This file is used for reverse lookups of host names within a domain. Instead of resolving a name to an IP address, a reverse lookup resolves an IP address to a host name. For example, for my domain, which only has one subnet (206.170.127.64), the reverse lookup file is as follows:

```
;    arpa-206.rev
;    Reverse lookup file for 127.170.206.in-addr.arpa. domain.
;    START OF AUTHORITY
@    IN  SOA     srv.nt-guru.com.  admin.srv.nt-guru.com. (
                                1          ; serial number
                                10800      ; refresh [3h]
                                3600       ; retry   [1h]
                                604800     ; expire  [7d]
                                86400 )    ; minimum [1d]
;    NAME SERVERS
@       IN  NS      srv.nt-guru.com.
;    NBSTAT Record
@    IN  NBSTAT     nt-guru.com.
;    PTR RECORDS
65      IN  PTR     srv.nt-guru.com.
68      IN  PTR     roadtrip.nt-guru.com.
70      IN  PTR     backup-srv.nt-guru.com.
71      IN  PTR     tk-home.nt-guru.com.
```

Once more, the first record should be an SOA record. The next record lists the name (or DNS) server for the domain, followed by an NBSTAT record, then the individual PTR records for each host in the domain. These records, and their usage, is summarized in Table 9.5. What most people find confusing are the PTR records. Instead of supplying a complete IP address (such as 206.170.127.65) for the host, you only supply the last digit of the IP address (such as 1) followed by the fully qualified host name (host + domain name).

TABLE 9.5. SUPPORTED REVERSE LOOKUP RECORDS.

Identifier	Record Type	Description
NBSTAT	NBSTAT	Specifies the domain name to append to any host name found by an NBSTAT lookup.
NS	Name Server	Specifies the DNS servers in the domain.
PTR	Pointer	Specifies an IP address for a host.
SOA	Start of Authority	This is the first record in any configuration file and is used to specify the host where the file was created, an e-mail contact address, version number, refresh time, expiration time, and retry interval.

SUMMARY

The focus in this chapter was on implementing the DHCP, WINS, and DNS Services on your network. You learned about the design goals for the DHCP and WINS Services, basic planning issues, and the management options available for manipulating your DHCP and WINS clients.

You looked at specific issues for using DHCP and WINS in a mixed Windows NT and UNIX environment. You also learned how to prepare for the possibility of a failure of the services database, how to configure some Registry keys that are otherwise unconfigurable options, and how to implement some basic performance tips.

In the next chapter, you will look at how you can configure your network hardware and software to obtain the best possible performance.

CHAPTER 10

Using the Internet Information Server

The Internet Information Server is Microsoft's answer to providing Internet publishing capabilities for Windows NT Server. You can obtain the Internet Information Server from Microsoft using several methods. It is included on disk 4 of the BackOffice 2.0 CD-ROM set; it could also be included as part of your Windows NT Server installation set if you purchased the Windows NT Server Value Pack; it can be purchased separately from Microsoft; and it is included in the Microsoft Developer Network (MSDN) package. You can also download it from the Internet at http://www.microsoft.com/msdownload. If you are going to pay for the Internet Information Server (IIS) as a separate product, or before you spend the time downloading it from the Internet, you may want to refer to Chapter 2, "Planning Your Network Installation," to understand just what it is you are getting. This chapter focuses on installing the Internet Information Server and learning how to configure the Internet Information Server using the Internet Server Manager.

Note

If you would like a more in-depth Internet Information Server reference, you can pick up another book of mine called *Microsoft Internet Information Server 2 Unleashed* from Sams Publishing. This book includes information on how to use the Internet Database Connector or Microsoft dbWeb to access your ODBC databases interactively, an HTML primer, Windows tools you can use for Web page development, and much, much more.

INSTALLING THE INTERNET INFORMATION SERVER

After all the work that you had to perform in the preceding sections to prepare for your Internet Information installation, you will be happy to know that installing IIS is going to be a piece of cake. To install IIS, just follow these simple steps:

1. If you have the BackOffice 2.0 CD-ROM set, insert disk 4 and execute the setup.exe program located in the INFOSERV directory. Otherwise, execute the install.exe program located on your floppy disk or CD-ROM, or from the copy that you downloaded to your hard disk from the Internet.

2. You will be greeted with the Microsoft Internet Information Server 1.0 Setup dialog. Click OK to continue.

3. Next the dialog shown in Figure 10.1 appears. To specify a different installation directory from the default of c:\INETSRV, click the Change Directory button. This displays the Select Directory dialog where you can specify a different location for your IIS installation.

Figure 10.1.
Installing the
Internet Informa-
tion Server.

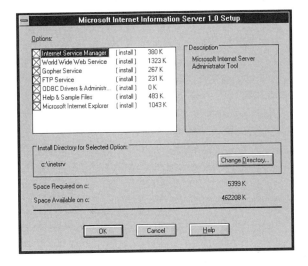

4. If you do not want to install all of the IIS services, administration tools, help files and documentation, ODBC drivers, or the Internet Explorer, you may uncheck specific items in the Options: field. I recommend, however, that you install all of the options for now. When you no longer need them, you can easily execute the IIS setup program to remove specific components. You can also use this application to install components that you may have removed or not installed.

5. Once all of your choices have been selected, click OK to proceed with the installation. If your installation directory does not exist, you will be prompted to create it.

6. Next the Publishing Directories dialog appears. In this dialog, you can choose a directory to contain your data for the WWW, FTP, and Gopher services. For maximum performance, you should seriously consider putting the data for each service on a separate physical drive (or a striped set or striped set with parity), if at all possible. To specify a different drive or directory, click the browse button and choose a new location.

7. When you have specified all of your data locations, click OK to continue the installation. You will be prompted once again to create each directory if it does not already exist. The IIS files will then be copied to your computer, in the locations you specified, the publishing services will be started, and a new group will be created in Program Manager.
8. Next you will be prompted to install the ODBC drivers. The default driver, and only driver, is the SQL Server driver. Select the driver and click OK.

Note

If you will be using a different ODBC driver, you will need to use the ODBC-32 Control Panel applet to install and configure the driver.

9. The Internet Explorer will then be installed, and a program item will be added to the Microsoft Internet Server group. Once this has been completed, a confirmation dialog appears informing you that IIS was successfully installed. Click OK to exit the setup application.

You are now ready to configure the IIS service (as described in the next section, "Using the Internet Service Manager"), to install the data to be published on your server in the service's root directories and to begin to publish data on the Internet.

USING THE INTERNET SERVICE MANAGER

One of the really nice features of Windows NT is that almost every service can be configured by an application specifically designed for it. The Internet Information Server is no different. It includes a tool called the Internet Service Manager (see Figure 10.2). By default, this tool is installed in the Microsoft Internet Service group. Because the focus of this chapter is on managing your Internet Information Server sites using the Internet Service Manager, the following sections will discuss how to control the basic operations of your IIS sites, how to configure the WWW, FTP, and Gopher services, and how to use the ODBC connector to log all of your IIS site activity to a database. While it is possible to use any database that has an ODBC driver, our focus will be on using the ODBC connector to connect to a SQL Server database.

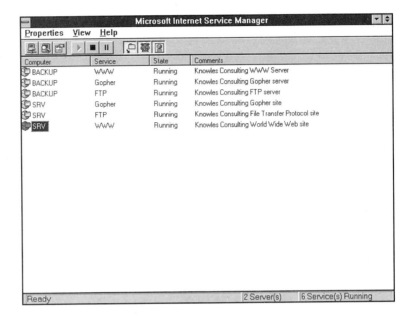

Figure 10.2.
The Internet
Service Manager.

BASIC OPERATIONS OF THE INTERNET SERVICE MANAGER

The Internet Service Manager has a very simplistic set of controls. In fact, there are only three main menu commands and nine toolbar buttons. These are the Properties, View, and Help menu commands. These commands are really all that is needed to manage your IIS services on a local computer, or on a remote computer. Out of these commands, only the Properties and View commands offer real functionality. Even though there are not very many commands, a lot of care went into the design to make managing your IIS sites quite easy.

Our discussion will start with a look at how you can use the Internet Service Manager to control the individual Internet services. Next you will learn how to manage a single, or multiple, Internet Information Server sites. As a continuation of this theme you will also learn how to choose a view to make finding the appropriate Internet services on multiple sites easier as well.

CONTROLLING THE INTERNET SERVICES

One of the requirements of a site manager (that's you) is the ability to control the operating state of the individual Internet services. This can be performed on a local, or a remote server. Before you can control a service, however, it must first be added to the Internet Service Manager. This should be performed automatically the first time you execute the Internet Service Manager as it will browse the network in an attempt to locate all available sites. If this should fail, however, just choose one of the following options from the Properties menu item:

◆ Find All Servers: Scans the entire network looking for IIS sites. Also available by pressing Ctrl-F, or click on the Find Internet Servers button (second from the left) on the toolbar.

◆ Connect to Server: Displays the Connect to Server dialog where you can specify the computer name of the server running the Internet Information Server. This option is also available by pressing Ctrl-O, or clicking the Connect to a Server button (first button on the left) on the toolbar.

Once you have connected to the appropriate servers, the IIS services are displayed in the main window of the Internet Service Manager. To start, stop, pause, or continue an IIS service on a connected server, follow these steps:

1. Select the appropriate service by clicking the server name in the Computer column.

2. From the Properties menu, choose either Start Service, Stop Service, or Pause Service. If you prefer, you can use the Start Service, Stop Service, Pause/Continue Service buttons on the toolbar. These are the third, fourth, and fifth buttons respectively.

Note

When you pause a service, the Properties | Pause Service menu option will have a check mark next to it to indicate that the service is paused. To continue the service, just choose the Pause Service menu option once more or use the toolbar Pause/Continue Service button.

Another way to control the state of the Internet services is to use Server Manager. This shows all the computers in the domain. To control a service, choose Computer | Services from the menu to display the Services on *ComputerName* dialog box. Then scroll down the list until you find the appropriate service (FTP Publishing Service, Gopher Publishing Service, or WWW Publishing Service). Select the service, then click on the Start, Stop, Pause, or Continue buttons.

Note

In order to control the state of a service, you must have administrative privileges on either the local computer or a remote computer.

MANAGING INTERNET INFORMATION SERVER SITES

Once you have more than a couple of IIS sites on your network, managing them becomes more difficult because you have to scroll through the lists of servers and services to check the state of each one. The Internet Service Manager makes this a little easier by including several options that let you rearrange the display to show the information you are most concerned with at the moment. These options are accessible through the View menu command and include:

◆ Sort by Server: Orders the display based on the computer name. This is the default sort order.

◆ Sort by Service: Orders the display based on the type of service. This will change the order to FTP, Gopher, then WWW.

◆ Sort by Comment: Orders the display based on the service description.

◆ Sort by State: Orders the display based on the execution state of the service. This is particularly useful for determining whether you have any services that are not executing. The default sort order is not alphabetical, however. Instead, stopped services appear at the top of the display, running services in the middle, and paused services at the bottom.

USING A VIEW TO MANAGE MULTIPLE SITES

The various view options accessible from the View menu offer another very useful sorting method for managing multiple sites. The default view is the Reports view, but the Servers view and the Services view offer additional benefits. First of all, the state of each service is represented by the color of the stop light—red for stopped, yellow for paused, or green for running—so you can determine it at a glance. Second, you can expand or collapse the display to show just the type of services you want to see. Finally, the right mouse button will activate a pop-up menu to control the state, or properties, of the service, as shown in Figure 10.3.

If you have many IIS sites, you may find that even this view could use a little more room on the display so that you can see the services that interest you. If you want to remove a service from the display you can choose the View | FTP, View | Gopher, View | WWW commands or the seventh, eighth, or ninth buttons on the taskbar. In each case the commands work to toggle the current state. For the menu commands, if a check mark appears next to the command name, the service is visible; otherwise, the service is removed from the display. The buttons work pretty much the same way, except the button will be depressed to represent a checked state, or raised to indicate an unchecked state.

Figure 10.3.
Using the Service
View to manage
your IIS sites.

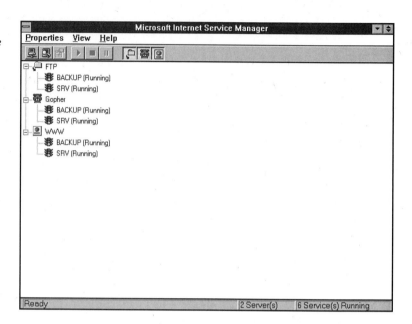

CONFIGURING THE WWW SERVICE

Before you make your WWW site available to the world, you should configure it to suit your individual needs. The default configuration provides some protection from Internet hackers, and if Internet security is your primary concern, then I recommend you take a look at Chapter 11, "Securing Your Network from the Internet," to see what options are available to you. For the rest of this discussion, we'll assume you are just interested in the basics of configuring your WWW Publishing Service.

Configuring the WWW Publishing Service can be broken down basically into four options. You can configure the general properties of the WWW service, specify the WWW directories and create virtual WWW servers, log the activity on your WWW site, and limit access to your WWW site. All of these options are obtained from the WWW Service Properties for *ComputerName* dialog box. To access this dialog box, select the appropriate WWW server then choose Properties | Service Properties from the menu, click the Properties button on the toolbar (third button from the left), or right-click the service when in the Services view or Server view. The dialog box has four tabs, which we will discuss in detail in the following sections.

CONFIGURING THE WWW SERVICE BASIC PROPERTIES

The WWW Service Properties sheet, shown in Figure 10.4, includes these options:

Figure 10.4.
Configuring
the WWW Service
General
Properties.

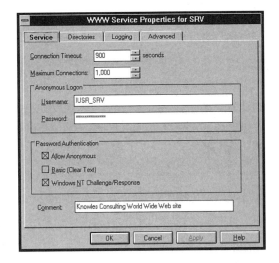

10

◆ Connection Timeout: Specifies the time, in seconds, before an inactive user's connection will be terminated. This is used to ensure that even if the Web server fails to close a connection when a user exits the site, eventually it will be closed. The default is 900 seconds, or 15 minutes.

◆ Maximum Connections: Specifies the maximum number of simultaneous users that can be connected to your Web server. The default is 1,000.

◆ Anonymous Logon: This group box defines the user account and password for users that connect to your site using an anonymous logon. Most Web servers support the anonymous logon. If you want your site to support users that are not members of your domain, which most of us do, then any time a user connects using an anonymous logon their access will be based on the user account and password specified in the following fields:

> Username: Specifies either a local user account or a domain user account. By default this account is called IUSER_*ComputerName* where *ComputerName* is the name of the computer where IIS was installed.

Caution

By default, this group is added to the Guests local group. If your server is a member of the domain, then the account is also a member of the Domain Users global group. You should verify the privileges of the group to ensure that this account cannot be used to access secure network resources. My personal preference is to either move the user account to the Domain Guests global group or create a new group for the account. In either case, minimize the privileges associated with the user account or group. Chapter 11 describes this in more detail.

Password: Specifies the password to be used with the anonymous user account. If you change the password here, you must also change the password using User Manager (for a server) or User Manager for Domains (for a domain controller).

Tip

It is a good idea to change the password for this account once in a while (every 30–45 days is recommended) to enhance the security of your site.

◆ Password Authentication: This group specifies the method to be used by users attempting to connect to your Web server. It has the following options:

Allow Anonymous: When this box is checked, any user may connect to your server using the anonymous logon procedure. When they do, the user account and password specified in the Anonymous Logon group is used to supply their account privileges. If this box is unchecked, anonymous logons are not allowed and a valid user account and password must be supplied to obtain access to your WWW site.

Basic (Clear Text): When checked, this option specifies that the password associated with a user account be transmitted in an unencrypted format.

Warning

Using the Basic password authentication option opens the possibility of a serious security breach. Internet users with access to a sniffer might be able to capture network packets sent to your site. This could provide them with a valid user account and password which they could then use to access network resources.

Windows NT Challenge/Response: When checked, specifies that the password be transmitted in an encrypted format when an anonymous logon is denied. This means that in order to secure your site to domain members only (such as for an intranet WWW site), and support only encrypted passwords, you must also uncheck (disable) the Allow Anonymous and Basic (Clear Text) options.

Note

Currently the only Web browser that supports the Windows NT Challenge/Response authentication mechanism is the Microsoft Internet Explorer version 2.0 or higher.

◆ Comment: Specifies a description to be displayed on the Internet Service Manager while in Report view for the WWW Publishing Service.

Configuring the WWW Service Directories

Configuring the directories for the WWW Publishing Service offers a bit more than you might think at first glance. Not only can you configure a few basic operating characteristics, but you can create virtual directories, and virtual WWW servers. A virtual directory is a directory tree that is not physically attached to the parent WWW directory. By default, the parent WWW directory is `IISRoot`/WWWRoot where `IISRoot` is the directory where you installed the Internet Information Server (such as `F:\MS\InetSrv`). When you create a virtual directory, this directory is viewed by your WWW clients as being a subdirectory of the parent WWW directory. A virtual directory can be physically present on the same server as the WWW Publishing Service, or it can be on a remote computer.

A virtual server is a WWW server which does not exist as a physically separate entity. You could create a WWW server by installing the WWW Publishing Service on a new computer. You could then assign an IP address to the computer's network adapter and register the domain name so that users can find your site using the familiar form of `www.domainname.com`. This would be considered a physically separate entity; it is totally self-contained.

On the other hand, you can create a virtual server that uses the WWW Publishing Service on your current computer. You will still need to assign an IP address to it and register the domain name, but the mechanism varies just a bit. Instead of assigning an IP address to a new network card, you can add it to your current network card. In essence, your WWW Publishing Service would now support two separate WWW sites. Each site would have its own root directory which could be on the local server or on a remote server. Your clients would not know that the Web site was just one of many Web sites running on the same server. Pretty nifty, isn't it?

Configuring the WWW Service Basic Directory Properties

When you select the Directories tab on the WWW Service Properties dialog, the Directories properties sheet appears, as shown in Figure 10.5. This offers two basic configuration options. If you check the Enable Default Document option, then you may specify an HTML document name in the Default Document field. The default document name is `default.htm`, but I prefer to use the default name of `index.htm` as this name provides a more accurate description. What this does for you is specify that this HTML document will be loaded as the default document when a client specifies a URL without a specific document name. For example, a client may specify `http://www.nt-guru.com/Company Information`, and the `index.HTM` document would be loaded automatically. This is better than specifying `http://www.nt-guru.com/index.htm`, as it provides a means for the client to navigate your Web site without having to know the name of each document.

Figure 10.5.
The Directories
properties sheet.

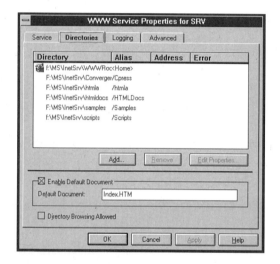

The other basic option is Directory Browsing Allowed. If this option is checked, then a client can browse your entire Web site. The client's ability to browse your site, however, depends on the state of the Enable Default Document option. If this option is checked, and the default document resides in the directory, the default document will be loaded into the client's Web browser. If either the Enable Default Document option is unchecked, or the option is checked but the default document is not resident in the directory, the client will see a list of files in the directory. This list is a hypertext list. If the user clicks a document name, the document will be loaded.

This ability has both a good and a bad side to it. The good side is that clients will not be disappointed and see an error code on their Web browsers. It can also be useful for intranets with a large number of documents, as it provides the ability to load a document without creating a master (or index) document, thereby lessening the administrative burden. The bad side is that it opens up the possibility that an unauthorized client will stop by and browse around and view information that should be off limits. Maybe the client got there by typing an incorrect URL, or perhaps an old employee mentioned the URL—but how the client got there is not as important as the fact he got there at all. So what can you do about limiting this type of problem? Well, you can take one of the following actions:

- Disable the Directory Browsing Allowed option.
- Make sure that every subdirectory of the WWWRoot directory has a default document in it.
- Install IIS to an NTFS partition, then use File Manager or the Windows Explorer to set permissions on subdirectories with sensitive information. The permissions can be configured to limit access to only domain members that require access. By default then, any non-member of this group will be denied access. This is the preferred method if you support directory browsing as you can both control access to the directories and audit the directories to determine who is accessing them, their subdirectories, and the files they contain.

HOW TO CREATE A VIRTUAL DIRECTORY

Creating a virtual directory is not difficult, but you need to decided whether the virtual directory will reside on a local computer or on a remote computer. To create a virtual directory, follow these steps:

1. In the Directories properties sheet, click the Add button. The Directory Properties dialog box appears, as shown in Figure 10.6.

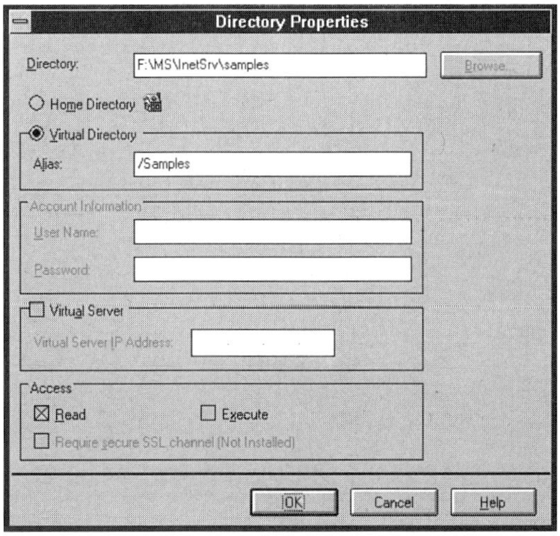

Figure 10.6.
Creating a virtual
directory.

2. To create a virtual directory on the local computer, specify a directory name in the Directory field, or click the Browse button to select a directory.

   If you use the Browse button, the Select Directory dialog box appears. In it you can choose an existing directory from the Directories listbox, or you can enter the name of a new directory to create in the New Directory Name field. Once you have entered the requested information, click OK. Your selected directory will then be displayed in the Directory field of the Directory Properties dialog box.

3. To create a virtual directory on a remote computer, specify a UNC filename (such as \\Backup_Srv\C\WWWRoot) in the Directory field.

4. If the Virtual Directory radio button is not enabled, click it to enable it.

5. Enter a name for the virtual directory, such as Samples, in the Alias field.

6. If the virtual directory will reside on a remote computer, enter a user name in the User Name field and a password for this user account in the Password field. The user name and password will be used to connect to the remote share.

7. In the Access group, specify the type of access your clients will use. By default the Read checkbox is enabled, specifying that the client will have read access to the directory. If this directory will include executable code, such as a CGI script, enable the Execute checkbox as well. If you have an SSL certificate, and have installed it on your Web server, then the Require secure SSL channel option will be available as well. This option can be used to provide a secure method of accessing the directory contents.

8. Click OK to create your virtual directory and return to the Directories Property sheet.

9. Click OK to exit the Directories properties sheet.

HOW TO CREATE A VIRTUAL SERVER

Creating a virtual server is almost identical to creating a virtual directory. In fact a virtual server can use a virtual directory created on the local computer, or a directory on a remote computer. To create a virtual server, follow these steps:

1. In the Directories properties sheet, click the Add button and the Directory Properties dialog box appears, as shown in Figure 10.7.

Figure 10.7.
Creating a virtual
server.

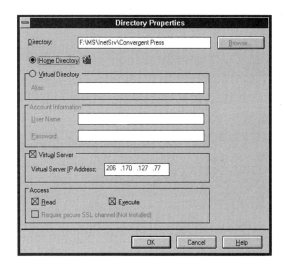

2. To create a virtual directory to be used as the root directory for the
    virtual server on the *local* computer, specify a directory name in the Direc-
    tory field. Or click the Browse button to select a directory.

    If you use the Browse button, the Select Directory dialog box appears. In it
    you can choose an existing directory from the Directories listbox, or you can
    enter the name of a new directory to create in the New Directory Name
    field. Once you have entered the requested information, click OK. Your
    selected directory will then be displayed in the Directory field of the Direc-
    tory Properties dialog box.

3. To create a virtual directory to be used as the root directory for the
    virtual server on a *remote* computer, specify a UNC filename (such as
    `\\Backup_Srv\C\WWWRoot`) in the Directory field.

4. If the Home Directory radio button is not enabled, click it to enable it.

5. If the virtual directory will reside on a remote computer, enter a user name
    in the User Name field and a password for this user account in the Pass-
    word field. This user name and password will be used to connect to the
    remote share.

6. Click on the Virtual Server checkbox to enable it.

7. Enter the IP address to be assigned to the virtual server in the Virtual
    Server IP Address field.

8. In the Access group, specify the type of access your clients will use. By
    default the Read checkbox is enabled, specifying that the client will have
    read access to the directory. If this directory will include executable code,

such as a CGI script, enable the Execute checkbox as well. If you have an SSL certificate, and have installed it on your Web server, then the Require secure SSL channel option will be available as well. This option can be used to provide a secure method of accessing the directory contents.

9. Click OK to create your virtual server and return to the Directories properties sheet.

10. Repeat steps 2 through 9 for each virtual server you want to create.

11. Click OK to exit the Directories properties sheet.

Once you have added all of your virtual servers, you must add the IP addresses and subnet masks to your network adapter. This is accomplished by following these steps:

1. Open the Control Panel Network applet to display the Network Settings dialog box.

2. Select the TCP/IP Protocol, then click the Configure button to display the TCP/IP Configuration dialog box.

3. Click the Advanced button to display the Advanced Microsoft TCP/IP Configuration dialog box.

4. Enter an IP address and subnet mask in the IP Address and Subnet Mask fields. Then click the Add button. This will add the new IP address and subnet mask to the IP Address and Subnet Masks fields.

5. Repeat step 4 for each virtual server.

6. Click OK to exit the Advanced Microsoft TCP/IP Configuration dialog box and return to the Microsoft TCP/IP Configuration dialog.

7. Click OK to return to the Network Settings dialog box.

8. Click on the OK button to close the Network Settings dialog box. The Network Settings Change dialog box is displayed. Click Yes to restart the computer. Once the server reboots, your virtual servers will be available.

Note

Before your virtual servers will be available to the public, you must have registered your domain name. This means that the IP address and subnet mask you assigned must be the same as that assigned to your domain name. Your ISP should provide you with these, as well as configure their DNS servers and set up the necessary routing tables so that clients will be able to find your virtual servers.

LOGGING WWW ACTIVITY

Logging your WWW activity is one way of determining how active your site is. It can also help you find out whether or not someone is accessing data they should not have access to. There are two methods you can use to log your WWW site's activity. You can store the information in a standard text file, or you can store it in an ODBC database. If you use an ODBC database, you must create the database and then set up an ODBC data source name (DSN) using the ODBC Control Panel applet. Creating an ODBC database and setting up the DSN is discussed later in this chapter in the section titled "Logging Site Access with SQL Server." To enable logging follow these steps:

1. Click on the Logging tab in the WWW Service Properties dialog box to display the Logging properties sheet as shown in Figure 10.8.

Figure 10.8.
Configuring the
WWW Service to
Log Activity.

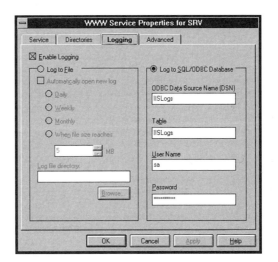

2. Click the Enable Logging radio button.
3. To log your WWW site's activity to a text file click the Log to File radio button. This will enable the following options:

    ◆ Automatically open new log: Specifies that a new log will be created based on one of the following criteria:

    ◆ Daily: Every day.

    ◆ Weekly: Once a week.

    ◆ Monthly: Once a month.

    ◆ When log file size reaches: Whenever the log file exceeds the size specified in the MB field.

    ◆ Log file directory: Specifies the location where the log file will reside.

4. To log your WWW site's activity to an ODBC database, click the Log to SQL/ODBC Database radio button. This will enable the following options:

◆ ODBC Data Source Name (DSN): Specifies the name of the data source to use to access the ODBC database.

◆ Table: Specifies the table within the ODBC database to use for logging.

◆ User Name: Specifies a user name to use to access the table within the ODBC database.

◆ Password: Specifies a password for the associated user account.

5. Click OK to close the WWW Site Properties dialog box and return to the Internet Service Manager.

LIMITING ACCESS TO YOUR WWW SITE

Almost everyone is concerned about the security of their WWW site. And I admit that I, too, fall into this group of concerned Web site administrators. The Internet Service Manager does provide a limited means of securing your Web site against possible intruders, but these features are not too useful if you plan on providing the public with access to your site. If you will be using IIS for an intranet, it is a very useful means of limiting access to sensitive data. To limit potential damage to your system from the public, however, I suggest you look at Chapter 11 to see how you can restrict access to your network. In the meantime, you can limit access to your Web server by following these steps:

1. Click the Advanced tab in the WWW Service Properties dialog box to display the Advanced properties sheet (see Figure 10.9).

Figure 10.9.
Configuring the
Advanced WWW
Publishing
Service
Properties.

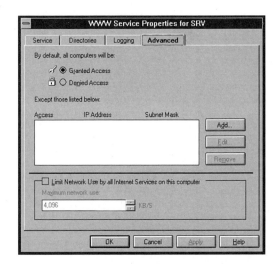

2. To limit access to a specific set of clients, click the Denied Access radio button. Then click the Add button to display the Grant Access On dialog box. To specify a single computer to give access to your Web site, click the Single Computer radio button and enter the IP address of the computer in the IP Address field. To specify multiple computers to give access to your Web site, click the Multiple Computers radio button and specify an IP address and subnet mask in the IP Address and Subnet Mask fields. Then click OK.

3. To grant access to all but a specific set of clients, click the Granted Access radio button. Then click the Add button to display the Denied Access On dialog box. To specify a single computer to deny access to your Web site, click the Single Computer radio button and enter the IP address of the computer in the IP Address field. To specify multiple computers to deny access to your Web site, click the Multiple Computers radio button and specify an IP address and subnet mask in the IP Address and Subnet Mask fields. Then click OK.

4. The IP addresses and subnet masks you specified in step 2 or step 3 will appear in the Except Those Listed Below listbox. Repeat step 2 or step 3 for each additional set of computers you want to deny or grant access to your Web site.

5. To limit the amount of network bandwidth used by your IIS services, click Limit Network Use by all Internet Services on this computer to enable the checkbox. Then specify a value in the Maximum Network Use field.

6. Click OK to close the WWW Site Properties dialog box and return to the Internet Service Manager.

Configuring the FTP Service

Just as you need to configure your WWW Publishing Service before making it available to the public, you need to configure your FTP Publishing Service. This can be divided into five options: You can configure the general properties of the FTP service, specify the messages users will see when they connect to your FTP site, specify the FTP directories, log the activity on your FTP site, and limit access to your FTP site. The logging and limiting access property sheets follow the same basic methodology as the WWW service. So rather than repeat this information I will refer you to the sections titled "Logging WWW Activity" and "Limiting Access to Your WWW Site." All of these options, however, are accessed from the FTP Service Properties for *ComputerName* dialog box. This dialog is accessible by choosing Properties | Service Properties from the menu, clicking the Properties button on the toolbar (third button from the left), or right-clicking the service when in the Services view or Server view.

The FTP Service Properties sheet, as shown in Figure 10.10, includes the following options:

Figure 10.10.
Configuring the
Basic FTP
Publishing
Service
Properties.

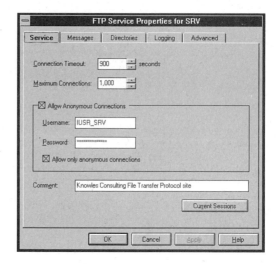

◆ Connection Timeout: Specifies the time, in seconds, before an inactive user's connection will be terminated. This is used to ensure that even if the Web server fails to close a connection when a user exits the site, eventually it will be closed. The default is 900 seconds, or 15 minutes.

◆ Maximum Connections: Specifies the maximum number of simultaneous users that can be connected to your Web server. The default is 1,000.

◆ Allow Anonymous Connections: This checkbox enables you to specify a user account and password for users that connect to your site using an anonymous logon. Most FTP servers support an anonymous logon. If you want your site to support users that are not members of your domain, which most of us do, then any time a user connects using an anonymous logon their access will be based on the user account and password specified in the following fields:

Username: Specifies either a local user account, or a domain user account. By default this account is called IUSER_*ComputerName* where *ComputerName* is the name of the computer where IIS was installed.

Caution

By default, this group is added to the Guests local group. If your server is a member of the domain, the account is also a member of the Domain Users global group. You should verify the privileges of the group to ensure that this account can not be used to access secure network resources. For additional information, Chapter 11 describes this in more detail.

Password: Specifies the password to be used with the user account mentioned above. If you change the password here, you must also change the password using User Manager (for a server) or User Manager for Domains (for a domain controller).

Tip

It is a good idea to change the password for this account once in a while (every 30–45 days is recommended) to enhance the security of your site.

◆ Allow only anonymous connections: When this box is checked, only users that use an anonymous logon may connect to your FTP site.

Warning

Since the FTP protocol does not encrypt passwords, Internet users with access to a sniffer may be able to capture network packets sent to your site. This could provide them with a valid user account and password which they could then use to access network resources. It is therefore best to enable the Allow only anonymous connections.

◆ Comment: Specifies a description to be displayed on the Internet Service Manager while in Report view for the FTP Publishing Service.
◆ Current Sessions: Click this button to display the FTP User Sessions dialog box and see who is active on your FTP site.

CONFIGURING THE FTP SERVICE MESSAGES

When a user connects to your FTP site, you can display a greeting message, an exit message, and an error message if the maximum number of clients are currently connected. Not all FTP clients, however, can display these messages. Nor will all Web browsers. It is still a good idea to specify them for those FTP clients that support them, however. To do so, follow these steps:

1. Click the Messages tab to display the Messages properties sheet, as shown in Figure 10.11.

2. Enter a greeting message, or a warning message (such as "This site is only for authorized users") in the Welcome message field.

Figure 10.11.
Specifying the
FTP Publishing
Service Messages.

3. Enter an exit message, to be displayed when the user disconnects from your FTP site, in the Exit message field.

4. Enter an error message in the Maximum connection message field to inform users that they cannot connect to your FTP site because the maximum number of simultaneous clients have already connected.

5. Click OK to return to the Internet Service Manager.

CONFIGURING THE FTP SERVICE DIRECTORIES

Configuring the directories for the FTP Publishing Service does not offer as much functionality as the WWW Publishing Service does. You cannot create a virtual server, although you can create virtual directories. When you select the Directories tab on the FTP Service Properties dialog box, the Directories properties sheet appears, as shown in Figure 10.12.

Figure 10.12.
The FTP Publish-
ing Service
Directories
properties sheet.

This offers two configuration options. You can specify that a directory listing will follow the UNIX or MS-DOS convention by enabling the UNIX or MS-DOS radio button. Or you can create virtual directories.

Creating a virtual directory is pretty simple. The only decision you need to make is whether the virtual directory will reside on a local computer or on a remote computer. To create a virtual directory, follow these steps:

1. In the Directories properties sheet click the Add button. The Directory Properties dialog box appears, as shown in Figure 10.13.

Figure 10.13.
Creating a virtual
directory.

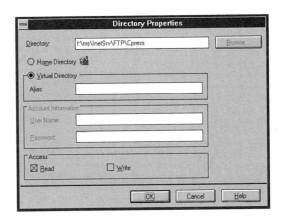

2. To create a virtual directory on the local computer, specify a directory name in the Directory field, or click the Browse button to select a directory.

   If you use the Browse button, the Select Directory dialog box appears. In it you can choose an existing directory from the Directories listbox, or you can enter the name of a new directory to create in the New Directory Name field. Once you have entered the requested information, click OK. Your selected directory will then be displayed in the Directory field of the Directory Properties dialog box.

3. To create a virtual directory on a remote computer, specify a UNC filename (such as `\\Backup_Srv\C\WWWRoot`) in the Directory field.

4. If the Virtual Directory radio button is not enabled, click it to enable it.

Tip

> While you cannot create a virtual server, you can create multiple home directories by enabling the Home Directory radio button. This can provide your FTP site with multiple root directories, although your FTP clients will need to know the directory names in order to access them. They could use `ftp://ftp.nt-guru.com/WinBook` to access the files in the `WinBook` home directory, for example, instead of `ftp://ftp.nt-guru.com` which would put them in the *IISRoot*/FTPRoot directory.

5. Enter a name for the virtual directory, such as Samples, in the Alias field.

6. If the virtual directory will reside on a remote computer, enter a user name in the User Name field and a password for this user account in the Password field. This user name and password will be used to connect to the remote share.

7. In the Access group, specify the type of access your clients will use. By default the Read checkbox is enabled, specifying that the client will have read access to the directory. If this directory will be used to upload files, enable the Write checkbox as well.

8. Click OK to create your virtual directory and return to the Directories properties sheet.

9. Click OK to exit the Directories properties sheet and return to the Internet Service Manager.

CONFIGURING THE GOPHER SERVICE

Just like the WWW and FTP services, before you make your Gopher site available to the world, you should configure it to suit your needs. Configuring the Gopher Publishing Service can be categorized as follows: You can configure the general properties of the Gopher service, specify the Gopher directories, log the activity on your Gopher site, and limit access to your Gopher site. All of these options are accessed through the Gopher Service Properties for *ComputerName* dialog box. This dialog box can be accessed by choosing Properties | Service Properties from the menu, by clicking the Properties button on the toolbar (third button from the left), or by right-clicking the service when in the Services view or Server view. The logging and limiting access property sheets follow the same format as the WWW service. So rather than repeat this information I will refer you to the sections titled "Logging WWW Activity" and "Limiting Access to your WWW Site."

CONFIGURING THE GOPHER SERVICE

The Gopher Service Properties sheet includes the following options, as shown in Figure 10.14:

Figure 10.14. Configuring the basic options of the Gopher Service.

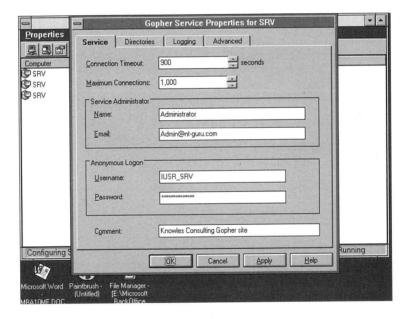

◆ Connection Timeout: Specifies the time, in seconds, before an inactive user's connection will be terminated. This is used to ensure that even if the Gopher server fails to close a connection when a user exits the site, eventually it will be closed. The default is 900 seconds, or 15 minutes.

◆ Maximum Connections: Specifies the maximum number of simultaneous users that can be connected to your Gopher server. The default is 1,000.

◆ Service Administrator: A Gopher client provides additional information to its users. This information includes:

Name: Specifies a contact name or administrator of the Gopher site.

Email: Specifies an e-mail address for the contact name or administrator of the Gopher site.

◆ Anonymous Logon: This group box defines the user account and password for users that connect to your site using an anonymous logon. Most Gopher servers support the anonymous logon. If you want your site to support users that are not members of your domain, which most of us do, then any time a user connects using an anonymous logon their access will be based on the user account and password specified in the following fields:

Username: Specifies either a local user account or a domain user account. By default this account is called IUSER_*ComputerName* where *ComputerName* is the name of the computer where IIS was installed.

Caution

By default, this group is added to the Guests local group. If your server is a member of the domain, then the account is also a member of the Domain Users global group. You should verify the privileges of the group to ensure that this account can not be used to access secure network resources. For additional information, refer to Chapter 11.

Password: Specifies the password to be used with the anonymous user account. If you change the password here, you must also change the password using User Manager (for a server) or User Manager for Domains (for a domain controller).

Tip

It is a good idea to change the password for this account once in a while (every 30–45 days is recommended) to enhance the security of your site.

◆ Password Authentication: This group specifies the method to be used by users attempting to connect to your Gopher server. It has the following options:

◆ Comment: Specifies a description to be displayed on the Internet Service Manager while in Report view for the Gopher Publishing Service.

Configuring the Gopher Service Directories

Out of all the publishing services, the Gopher service has the simplest options for managing directories. All it can do is create virtual directories. When you select the Directories tab on the Gopher Service Properties dialog, the Directories properties sheet appears, as shown in Figure 10.15.

Figure 10.15. The Gopher Publishing Service Directories properties sheet.

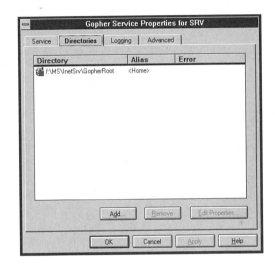

Creating a virtual directory can be accomplished by following these steps:

1. In the Directories properties sheet, click the Add button and the Directory Properties dialog box appears, as shown in Figure 10.16.

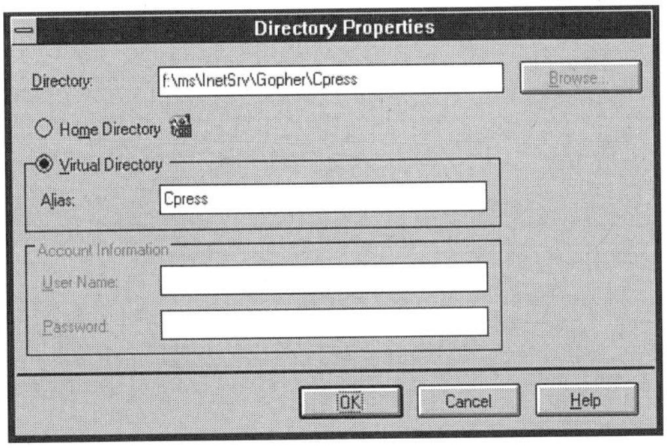

Figure 10.16. Creating a virtual directory.

10

Using the Internet Information Server

2. To create a virtual directory on the local computer, specify a directory name in the Directory field, or click the Browse button to select a directory.

   If you use the Browse button, the Select Directory dialog box appears. In it you can choose an existing directory from the Directories listbox, or you can enter the name of a new directory to create in the New Directory Name field. Once you have entered the requested information, click OK. Your selected directory will be displayed in the Directory field of the Directory Properties dialog box.

3. To create a virtual directory on a remote computer, specify a UNC filename (such as `\\Backup_Srv\C\WWWRoot`) in the Directory field.

4. If the Virtual Directory radio button is not enabled, click it to enable it.

Tip

While you cannot create a virtual server, you can create multiple home directories by enabling the Home Directory radio button. This can provide your Gopher site with multiple root directories, although your Gopher clients will need to know the directory names in order to access them. They could use `gopher://gopher.nt-guru.com/Library` to access the files in the `Library` home directory, for example, instead of `gopher://gopher.nt-guru.com`, which would put them in the `IISRoot/GopherRoot` directory.

5. Enter a name for the virtual directory, such as Library, in the Alias field.

6. If the virtual directory will reside on a remote computer, enter a user name in the User Name field and a password for this user account in the Password field. This user name and password will be used to connect to the remote share.

7. Click OK to create your virtual directory and return to the Directories properties sheet.

8. Click OK to exit the Directories properties sheet and return to the Internet Service Manager.

Logging Site Access with SQL Server

While you can use any ODBC database to log your IIS site's activity, this section will only describe how to use SQL Server, as this is the most commonly used database engine. Configuring an IIS service to log the activity to an ODBC database is described in the section titled "Logging WWW Activity," so I will not repeat that here. What you will learn, though, is how to build the database to contain your logs, how to create a user account to access this database, and how to create an ODBC data source to access the logs from your IIS services.

Building the Database

The IIS services actually write their logging information to one or more tables. These tables, however, must be contained within a database. While you can create the IIS table(s) in any database, I recommend that you create one specifically for the Internet Information Server. This can be accomplished by following these steps:

1. Create two new devices using the SQL Enterprise Manager. This is accomplished by selecting the Database Devices folder, right-clicking it, then selecting New Device from the pop-up menu.
2. Specify a name for the new device (like `IISDatabaseDevice.DAT`) in the Name field.
3. Specify where the device should reside in the Location field.
4. Specify the size of the device in the Size field. If you plan on having a very active Web site and don't plan to dump your database too often, you might want to start with 30MB.
5. Click OK to create the device.
6. Repeat steps 2 through 5 to create the log device, but use a name like `IISLogDevice.DAT` and specify a size of 10MB.
7. Next you need to create the database. To do so, select the Databases folder, right-click it, and choose New Database from the pop-up menu.
8. In the New Database dialog box, specify the database name (such as IISLogs) in the Name field.
9. In the Data device drop-down listbox, choose the device you created in step 2 (IISDatabaseDevice).
10. In the Log device drop-down listbox choose the device you created in step 6 (IISLogDevice).
11. Click the Create Now button to create the database.
12. After the database has been created, you can create the table(s) using the following script:

```
USE DATABASE IISLOGS
GO
CREATE TABLE dbo.IISLog (    ClientHost varchar (255) NOT NULL ,
username varchar (255) NOT NULL , LogTime datetime NOT NULL ,
service varchar (255) NOT NULL , machine varchar (255) NOT NULL ,
serverip varchar (50) NOT NULL , processingtime int NOT NULL ,
bytesrecvd int NOT NULL , bytessent int NOT NULL , servicestatus int NOT NULL,
win32status int NOT NULL , operation varchar (255) NOT NULL ,
target varchar (255) NOT NULL , parameters varchar (255) NOT NULL)
GO
```

Note

The above script will create one table called IISLog. If you want to create individual tables for each service, just change IISLog to WWWLog and run the script. Then change it to FTPLog, or GopherLog, and rerun the script to create the additional tables.

ASSIGNING PERMISSIONS TO ACCESS THE DATABASE

After you have created the devices, the database, and the tables as described in the preceding section, you will need to assign permission to access the database. You can use an existing user account, or you can create a new one. The method you will use depends on the security model of your SQL Server installation. The following will work, though, for a standard or mixed model:

1. Expand the Databases folder using the SQL Enterprise Manager.
2. Select the Groups/Users folder, right-click it, and choose New User from the pop-up menu.
3. Enter a user account in the Name field. This is the name used by SQL Server.
4. Specify a name in the Login field. This is usually the name of an existing SQL Server account (like sa) or a domain account (such as IUSR_SRV).
5. Click the Add button. This will give the user account permission to access the database.
6. Next choose Object | Permissions from the menu. Click the Grant All button, then the Set Button to give full permissions to the objects (like the tables you created) within the database.
7. Click the Close button to exit the dialog box and return to the SQL Executive Manager.

BUILDING THE ODBC DATA SOURCE

The final step is to create the link between your ODBC client (the IIS services) and the ODBC server (SQL Server). This can be accomplished by performing the following steps:

1. Open the Control Panel ODBC applet that will display the Data Sources dialog box.
2. Click the System DSN button to display the System Data Sources dialog box.

3. Click the Add button to display the Add Data Source dialog box.

4. Select the SQL Server entry in the Installed ODBC Drivers listbox. Then click OK.

5. The ODBC SQL Server Setup dialog box appears. Click the Options button to expand the dialog box (see Figure 10.17).

Figure 10.17.
Creating an
ODBC data
source for IIS
logging.

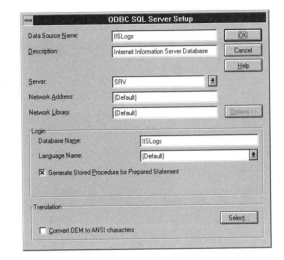

6. In the Data Source Name field, enter a unique name (such as IISLogs).

7. In the Description field, enter a comment to describe the DSN.

8. Specify the SQL Server to connect to in the Server field.

9. In the Database Name field, enter the name of the SQL Server database you created (such as IISLogs).

10. Click OK to return to the System Data Source dialog box.

11. Click Close to return to the Data Source dialog box.

12. Click Close to return to the Control Panel.

And that's all there is to creating an ODBC data source name. If you will be using a different ODBC database, just choose the ODBC driver in step 4 to match your ODBC-compliant database.

SUMMARY

In this chapter you learned what defines the Internet Information Server as a product. You learned how to install the Internet Information Server on your server. You learned how to configure the Internet Information Server using the Internet

Server Manager. You even learned how to create an SQL Server database to keep the logs of your WWW, FTP, and Gopher publishing services. These logs are important, as they can play a part in keeping your network secure from potential intruders. In the next chapter, you will look into this possibility a bit more as you examine some of the potential trouble spots for any network that is connected to the Internet.

- Security and the Internet

- Security and Windows NT Server

- Determining Who Is Using Your System

CHAPTER 11

Securing Your Network from the Internet

Security is a major issue with Internet connectivity. In this chapter you will learn about some of the potential risks and ways to avoid them. You will start with a look at the two basic types of security—downloaded data and access limitations. Next you will look into some of the capabilities provided with Windows NT Server to secure your data and your network. Finally, you'll look at some of the tools you can use to determine who may be using your system, as well as who may be accessing your IIS site.

SECURITY AND THE INTERNET

When you connect to the Internet, an entire world of information is available to you. Much of it is provided by manufacturers to promote or support their products. Sometimes it is provided by an individual who wants to share ideas or provide a useful tool to other members of the online community. And unfortunately, sometimes what you download from the Internet is provided by someone who gets a sick enjoyment out of causing mental anguish or destroying data. You really need to watch what you download, because you never know what it will do until after you try it. Sometimes this is too late!

The flip side of accessing information from Internet sites is that an Internet client might be accessing your site as well. Not only can you access sites all around the world, but users from the entire world may be accessing your site, too. Of course, this ease of access is also one reason why you decided to get on the Internet in the first place. You want people all around the world to view your site. This opens up the possibility, however slight, that an external user might attempt to use your site in unexpected, and dangerous, ways.

Because of the potential damages that can occur, you should seriously consider all the possibilities for harm. This section will look into two of them. First, you will learn about some of the security concerns involved with downloading objects from the Internet. Second, you will learn about some of the issues involved with having external users connect to your site. In both cases, you will learn about strategies that you can implement to minimize the potential damages.

APPLICATION AND DOCUMENT SECURITY ISSUES

Most new Internet users love the Internet because they can find so much information, or applications, that they can download to their computer for free. I will be one of the first to admit that this is an attractive capability. I will also be one of the first to mention that this can be a dangerous opportunity, too. Not everyone who provides files for you to download does it out of the goodness of his heart. Some people only provide a file without cost because they want to see how much damage to your system they can cause. This is not typically the intention of an Internet site administrator, although it could be. Take the following scenario, for example:

An Internet administrator creates a Web page to provide an easy-to-use interface for downloading a nifty shareware or freeware utility. This Web page has a hypertext link to an FTP site. This site could be local (on the same computer as the Web site), or remote (on someone else's FTP site). Now suppose some nasty person replaces the file on the FTP site with a copy that has been infected with a virus. The Web administrator may not even be aware that this has occurred, but he will be aware of it soon—after he reads his e-mail from all the users who downloaded and executed the utility!

If you download a file from a private bulletin board system (like the Microsoft Network, CompuServe, or America Online), you can take some comfort in the fact that before a file is made visible to members it is checked for possible viruses. So the safety factor is increased, but not necessarily eliminated. Public bulletin board systems and the Internet have a higher security risk which you must be prepared to deal with or you shouldn't be using them. In this section you will learn about some of the types of problems that could occur, and what you can do to prepare yourself for such an eventuality.

VIRUSES AND TROJAN HORSES

A virus is an application containing code that is usually destructive to your computer system. A virus can also be embedded in a data object that supports a built-in macro language, like a Word for Windows document, for example. Some viruses are not destructive, but just cause the loss of a service (such as your ability to receive your e-mail) or create user apprehension. A virus is a self-replicating snippet of code. It works, basically, as follows:

1. An infected application is executed on your computer.
2. The infected application either modifies the boot sector on your primary hard disk or infects other applications.

   The boot sector on your hard disk contains 512 bytes of executable code that is called the master boot record (MBR). This boot record is then used to load the rest of the operating system. If the boot sector is replaced by a virus, the original boot sector is copied to a hidden file on your hard disk as part of this process. The first step after loading the infected boot sector is to load the rest of the virus's executable code. Then the virus will load the original boot sector. Because this process happens so quickly, and because the original operating system loads, you may not even be aware that your system has become infected. But any new disk that you load on your system may be infected with the virus. Thereafter, any person who uses one of these disks to boot their system will also infect *their* boot disk.

   If the virus is not designed to replace your boot sector, when it executes it often looks for other executable programs (most commonly *.EXE, or

*.COM files) and infects them with a copy of the virus. Every executable program has a program header that tells the operating system what type of application it is (MS-DOS, 16-bit Windows, 32-bit Windows, OS/2, or POSIX), where the application should be loaded in memory, and where the starting point of the application's executable code begins. A virus might add its executable code to the original application and then change the application's header to point to the virus's startup code. After the virus loads into memory, it loads the application into memory and you continue working as you normally would.

Tip

Windows NT is somewhat protected from most viruses because direct hardware access is not supported by MS-DOS applications except through Windows NT device drivers. So it is less likely that a MS-DOS application will be able to infect the boot sector or other applications if the infected application is executed in a console window under Windows NT. If you boot your system from an infected floppy, however, it is possible that the boot sector could be infected because at this point Windows NT is not running to protect you. In most cases (in fact in all that I have encountered to date), the next time you try to boot Windows NT the system will fail to boot. So if your system fails to boot, you should check it immediately for a boot sector virus. For more information, see the section titled "Recovering an Infected System" later in this chapter.

A macro virus, such as the Prank macro virus found in a Word for Windows document in 1995, usually infects other data objects by hooking into a macro that is executed automatically whenever the document object is loaded into the source program. Thereafter, any new document that is created will be infected as well. Any user who opens one of these infected documents on a non-infected system will infect their system with the virus.

Warning

One of the really nasty problems with a macro virus is that it is not platform-specific. Most viruses are designed to infect a particular operating system platform, like MS-DOS, but a macro virus is designed to infect the source application, such as Word. This means that the same macro virus could infect installations of the application that run under MS-DOS, Windows, Windows NT, Macintosh, OS/2, UNIX, or any other platform where the source application shares the same macro language capabilities.

3. If the virus is a malicious virus, one day the program might activate and wipe away all the data on your hard disk. If the virus is not malicious, you might just loose control of your system while a message is printed on the screen, or some similar action takes place. In most cases with a non-malicious virus, to regain control of your system you will be required to reboot.

A Trojan horse is an application that is designed to be hidden from the user and to capture sensitive information (like a user account and password) that is then passed to another person for nefarious purposes. A Trojan horse is very unlikely to succeed under Windows NT, but it is possible. Windows NT requires that you use a specific mechanism to log on to the system. This is the familiar logon dialog box that is displayed when you press the Ctrl-Alt-Del key sequence. This sequence is used only after the system has loaded.

If an MS-DOS Trojan horse was activated at boot time to display the same logon dialogs, when the user pressed Ctrl-Alt-Del one of two things would occur:

◆ The system would immediately reboot since the Ctrl-Alt-Del key sequence is trapped by the system and is used to perform a warm boot.

◆ If the Ctrl-Alt-Del sequence was trapped by the Trojan horse, the user account and password could be captured by the application. But Windows NT would not be able to load afterwards.

In either case users should be able to notice readily whether a Trojan horse is present on their systems. If either type of activity is noted, users should immediately notify their system administrator. It will then be up to the system administrator to take any corrective action.

ACTIVE CONTENT SECURITY ISSUES

Web browsers that can display active content, such as the Internet Explorer 2.0 or Netscape Navigator, incur additional security risks. These types of Web browsers can create interactive content by utilizing a scripting language, such as a Visual Basic Scripting Edition (VBScript) or JavaScript, which executes on the local computer. Even though most of the language constructs (such as direct I/O) that could cause damage to your system have been removed, the potential is still there for damage to your system or loss of confidential data to occur.

Much of this risk is possible because these scripting languages are still in early stages of their life cycle. In an early release of Java-enabled Web browsers, for example, two potential security risks were identified. In the first case it was possible for an invisible window to remain active on the client. This provided the capability for the invisible application to remain in contact with the host Web server and potentially pass data to the Web server. The Web browser user would not even be aware that this was occurring. In the second case, a Java application was able to access any computer on the network where the application was executing. This was a serious issue because it essentially provided a means for the application to bypass the network firewall.

Java-enabled Web browsers from Netscape have been on the market for a little longer than Web browsers from Microsoft that support VBScript or JavaScript. So some of the potential security leaks have been eliminated. The real problem, however, is that neither of these Web browsers have been available long enough to eliminate all possible problems. It's doubtful that they ever will be able to eliminate all of them. Consider the following capabilities of an active content Web browser:

◆ ActiveX Controls: An ActiveX control is a dynamic link library that executes in the context of the current user. Dynamic link libraries can be used to extend the functionality of an application, and may call other functions in other dynamic link libraries.

◆ Scripting: Both VBScript and JavaScript are interpreted languages that are OLE-enabled. They may load additional ActiveX controls or access additional applications using OLE.

◆ Object Linking and Embedding: OLE can be used to control the behavior of an OLE-aware application.

By creating a package that is downloaded by the user and then executed, it might be possible to create applications that can damage the system. It might even be possible to access shared network resources. This could occur by building a series of dynamic link libraries that would be executed by an ActiveX control, an interactive script, or a stand-alone application (like Word for Windows). It is possible to execute other functions in dynamic link libraries or spawn a downloaded application using an OLE-enabled application (like Word for Windows) that could cause damage to your system.

It is difficult to say with 100 percent certainty whether this could occur, simply because the products are either still in beta or newly released. In either case they have not been completely tested to ensure that no security breach could occur. Nor do I believe this is entirely possible, because the ability to extend the functionality of an application opens up the possibility that someone will do so with the intent to cause harm. One thing I have learned from my years of experience is that if it can be done, someone will find a way to do it.

Recovering an Infected System

Once a computer system becomes infected with a virus, you are in trouble unless you can get rid of it. If your computer system uses the FAT file system, you have more options to remove a virus than if your system uses the NTFS file system. This is simply because there are not very many tools that operate under Windows NT, and currently only a Windows NT application can access the NTFS file system. In this section you will learn a few methods for dealing with viruses that may have infected your system. These options follow:

◆ If Windows NT is active, try the following:

The easiest virus-removal process it to run a virus scanning tool under Windows NT. Many MS-DOS–based or 16-bit Windows-based tools will not work, but the Norton Anti-Virus and McAffee Virus Scan tools are available as native Windows NT applications. These tools will scan each file on your hard disk, and if a virus is detected either remove the virus or delete the infected file if the virus cannot be removed.

◆ If Windows NT is not active and your boot partition is a FAT partition, try the following:

Boot from a clean, write-protected MS-DOS system disk. Execute your virus scanning software. If it succeeds, reboot the computer and run a native Windows NT virus scanning application to check your NTFS partitions for applications that might contain a virus.

◆ If Windows NT is not active, you cannot boot NT, and your boot partition is an NTFS partition, try the following:

The first thing to try in this situation is option 2 described above, because this scenario generally occurs when you boot from an infected floppy disk and a boot sector virus replaces the boot sector on your hard disk.

If option 2 fails to remove the boot sector virus, boot from a clean, write-protected MS-DOS system disk. Then use the MS-DOS command FDISK / MBR, which will replace the master boot record (MBR). In some cases this will remove the infected boot sector, and Windows NT will then be able to boot normally.

If, after using the FDISK /MBR command the boot sector virus was removed but Windows NT will still not boot, you can try the emergency repair process. This is accomplished by booting your system using the original Windows NT installation disk. During the install process you are prompted to set up Windows NT or repair the current installation. Choose the repair option. When prompted, insert your emergency repair disk. Later you will be prompted about what actions to take. Choose to verify the startup files, verify the boot sector, and compare the system files. This will then restore the system configuration.

Note

The only time I have seen the repair process fail to replace the boot sector and system files is when Windows NT no longer recognizes the disk partition. Most times this can be corrected by using the FDISK /MBR option in conjunction with the repair disk process; but if this option fails, your only other option is to wipe the disk (if it is a SCSI drive, you can low-level format it), repartition it, reformat it, and then reinstall Windows NT. Finally, you can restore your last Windows NT configuration using a previous backup.

USING FIREWALLS, PROXY AGENTS, AND OTHER ALTERNATIVES TO LIMIT ACCESS

The first thing that you should consider when planning your Internet Information Server installation is the security of your data. As part of your plan to install IIS, you might want to consider putting it on a network segment that is isolated from your primary network. After all, if the whole world can access your network, there might come a time when someone will decide to try to access more than the information you are making freely available to the public. Preventing an external user from accessing unauthorized areas on your computer (or your entire network), or preventing your internal network clients from accessing external resources (such as Internet resources), is where you will enter the realm of firewalls, proxy agents, and other alternatives.

These topics will be discussed in the following sections, but there is just too much material to make a single chapter an all-inclusive reference. Instead, the discussion will be general and will describe the technologies that are involved in limiting access to your network. There is one sure statement I can make about this entire process of limiting access to your network, and that is: There is no 100 percent guarantee that you can prevent experts from working their way into your system from the Internet. At best, you can be aware of an intrusion; at worst, the intruder could bypass all of your safeguards and do whatever he wants. These are unlikely scenarios, but the longer you are connected to the Internet, the more likely they will become. It is therefore imperative that you do one of two things:

◆ Place the server that provides your Internet connectivity on a stand-alone network. This guarantees that the worst an intruder can do is damage this particular server. He will not be able to worm his way into your internal network since there is no physical connection between them.

◆ If you cannot use a stand-alone server because you are also providing Internet connectivity to your network clients, consider a third-party firewall or proxy agent. At the very least use the capabilities provided within Windows NT Server 4.0 to limit the damage that could occur. (See the section titled "Security and Windows NT Server" later in this chapter.)

Tip

There is one other safeguard you can use that has absolutely nothing to do with limiting access to your computers. It's a pretty simple mechanism but nonetheless is very important. Just make daily, weekly, and monthly backups of your server and your network client computers! At least if you have a backup, you can restore your previous configuration.

USING A FIREWALL TO RESTRICT ACCESS TO YOUR NETWORK

A firewall is an intermediary computer that stands between the Internet and your network. (See Figure 11.1.) A firewall basically performs the same task as the security guard at your office: it checks your credentials at the door and then either lets you into the building or refuses you access. If your company allows visitors to enter the building, the guard may require them to sign in a log book and show proof of identity (such as a driver's license) to verify that they are who they say they are. These two features, restricting access and logging access, are the fundamental functions that a firewall performs for your network.

Figure 11.1.
Using a firewall
to protect your
network.

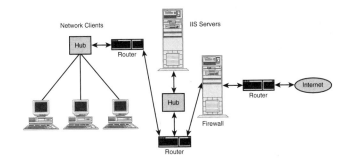

A firewall restricts access to your network by utilizing the information contained within a network packet. For Internet services that utilize the TCP/IP protocol, this information can be divided into five basic components as summarized in Table 11.1. These basic components include the protocol, destination IP address, destination IP port, source IP address, and source IP port. As a comparison, consider the way you make a phone call. You pick up the phone, you dial a 1 for long distance (perhaps you dial 9 first to access an external line), dial the area code, and finally dial a 7-digit phone number. When the other party hears the phone ring, he picks up the receiver and you begin your conversation. You might say something like "Hello, Valda, this is Art." If you want Valda to call you back, you exchange phone numbers. When you have finished your conversation, you hang up.

In this example, your area code could be considered as the source address, you would be considered as the source port, Valda's phone number would be the destination address, and Valda would be the destination port. The method you use to dial the number, initiate, and end the conversation would be considered the protocol. If your destination party's phone company supports caller ID and your destination party has the appropriate hardware, he can determine who is calling before picking up the phone. Some caller ID hardware devices can even record the number of the calling party (you) and the duration of the call.

A firewall functions in a similar manner. By using the destination and source IP addresses and IP port information contained within the packet, the firewall can either accept or reject the packet. It can also accept or reject packets based on the protocol contained within the packet. The firewall can also log this activity, much as a caller ID hardware device does, to determine who may be attempting to access the network.

Some firewalls go beyond the basic packet-filtering mechanism and utilize a network session as their key means to accept or reject a network request. A network session occurs at the user or application level rather than at the IP transport level. Each network session will utilize a different IP port, so each session is guaranteed to have a unique identifier consisting of the five basic components previously described. Session-based firewalls offer increased security and more efficient client-activity recording options, so if you are looking at purchasing a firewall, check to see whether it supports session-based security.

Many people think that a firewall is the only protection that they need for their network. This is not true, however, because a firewall filters information. If you close the filter completely, you are secure. But this also prevents you from utilizing any of the Internet resources. If you open up the filter to provide access to the Internet, you are also creating a window of opportunity for someone to access your system. This follows the same analogy as the services provided by your security guard on the night shift. If he locks the building, he can prevent thefts from occurring. Of course he also prevents any employees from entering the building and performing any work (such as cleaning the offices). By opening the doors of the building, the work can proceed. By making his rounds at night he can help prevent thefts from occurring by his presence, but he cannot prevent all occurrences because he cannot be every place at once. All a security guard can do for you is lessen the chance of a theft occurring. All a firewall can do for you is lessen the risk associated with an Internet connection; it cannot remove all risk entirely.

TABLE 11.1. THE FIVE BASIC COMPONENTS USED BY A FIREWALL IN AN INTERNET ENVIRONMENT.

Component	Description
Protocol	Transmission Control Protocol (TCP) or User Datagram Protocol (UDP).
Destination IP Address	Identifies the location of the computer receiving the data transmission.
Destination IP Port	Identifies the application on the computer that will receive the data transmission.
Source IP Address	Identifies the location of the computer initiating the data transmission.
Source IP Port	Identifies the application on the computer that initiates the data transmission.

USING A PROXY AGENT TO RESTRICT ACCESS TO YOUR NETWORK

A proxy agent is really another type of firewall. Rather than working at the packet level, it operates at the application level. This means that it also uses a network session as its primary means of denying access as a session-based firewall, but it includes one additional feature not provided by session-based firewalls: It can mask the address and IP port of the source computer from the destination computer. This can prevent unauthorized access to your network while still providing access to external users. Let's take a look at how this would work. Assume for the moment that your network includes a server running the Internet Information Server on one computer and a proxy agent as shown in Figure 11.2. The IIS and the proxy agent are both connected to a router which in turn is connected to the Internet. Your network clients' only means of access to the Internet, however, is through the proxy agent. So all network traffic to or from these network clients and the Internet must go through the proxy agent.

11

SECURING YOUR NETWORK

Figure 11.2. Using a proxy agent to protect your network.

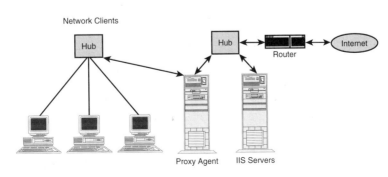

When you create your proxy agent, you also assign an IP port address for the proxy agent to monitor. You may assign one IP port address for all Internet service (such as WWW, FTP, Gopher, and so on), or one port address for each Internet service. Your network clients will then connect to the port on your proxy agent. The proxy agent determines the destination IP address and IP port the client wants to utilize. If the connection is not authorized, the connection will be terminated. If the connection is authorized, the proxy agent will connect to the external source. As data is received from this external source, it is passed to the network client. Any requests from the network client will be passed to the external source, through the proxy agent. In essence, the proxy agent masquerades as the destination computer to the network client, and as the network client to the destination computer.

In order for external users to gain access to your internal network they will have to know the IP address of the client computer, the IP address of the proxy agent, and the IP port the proxy agent is monitoring. They will also have to be on the allowed access list (usually based on the external client's IP address). If any of these items are unknown, the external user cannot connect to the client on the other side of the proxy agent.

USING MULTIPLE NETWORK PROTOCOLS TO PREVENT ACCESS TO YOUR NETWORK

A less expensive, and less secure, method for limiting potential access to your network is to use different network protocols on your internal network and your IIS server. You could use the IPX/SPX protocol on your internal network. You would then use both TCP/IP and IPX/SPX on your IIS server. (See Figure 11.3). This way your network clients would be isolated from external Internet users, but they would still be able to access the shared directories on the IIS server. In this fashion you could provide a limited means of accessing data on an FTP site, for example.

Figure 11.3.
Using multiple
protocols to
protect your
network.

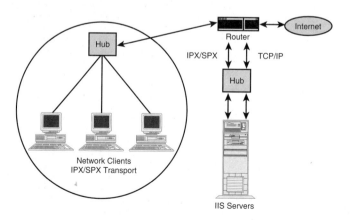

The only drawback to this type of solution is that your network clients would not be able to access the Internet. A solution does exist for multiple-protocol-based networks, however. It is possible to use a gateway (another piece of hardware located between the network clients and the Internet connection) that would convert network requests from your clients using the IPX/SPX protocol to the corresponding TCP/IP protocol. This solution generally also requires specially modified Internet utilities that are based on the IPX/SPX protocol rather than on the standard Internet protocols.

SECURITY AND WINDOWS NT SERVER

By now you should be getting the idea that security is a very important issue with any computer connected to the Internet. With Windows NT Server you have several tools in your arsenal that you can apply to limit access to your network, and thereby limit the risk associated with the Internet. In this section you will look at four of the possibilities. The first item on the agenda is user account policies. Next you will a look at how you can use the NTFS file system. If you will be supporting Remote Access Service clients or connecting to the Internet using a Remote Access Service connection, there are a few configuration options you can apply to make it more difficult for someone to cause damage to your network.

USING USER ACCOUNTS TO LIMIT ACCESS

The starting points in securing your server or your entire network from unauthorized access are the user accounts that you create. These accounts will be created on your server if it is a stand-alone computer, or on your domain controller if you are supplying full Internet connectivity to your clients. These user accounts may be used differently depending on whether you are using the Internet Information Server to supply Internet or intranet services. This may be a bit confusing to some of you, so a more thorough discussion may help to clarify the situation.

When you are using IIS to create an intranet site, your network is usually physically secure. The possibility of someone connecting a packet sniffer to your network and capturing clear text password authentication is not very likely. If you use IIS to provide an Internet presence, however, this may change rapidly as anyone with a packet sniffer can capture network packets transmitted over the Internet. It is also possible that someone will go hunting in an attempt to locate a list of valid user accounts and their associated passwords. It may be that someone is doing this in an attempt to obtain a valid user account and password for your network right now. To prevent these possibilities you need to:

◆ Protect your user accounts and passwords. Do not leave any lists of user accounts and passwords where they can be easily found. Do not throw out any list of user accounts and passwords. Instead, lock any lists up in a secure location (not your desk drawer), and if you dispose of any lists be sure to shred them first.

◆ Make sure your Internet service provider supports an encryption mechanism for any of your clients who will be connecting to your network over the Internet. (See the section titled "Limiting Access Over a Remote Access Service Connection" for additional information.)

◆ Make sure your Internet tools support the Microsoft challenge-response authentication mechanism. If this is not possible (since currently only the Microsoft Internet Explorer 2.0 or higher supports this option), consider obtaining a security certificate and using the Secure Socket Layer (SSL) to provide access to your server for sites with sensitive data.

CONFIGURING THE IIS USER ACCOUNT

If you will be providing Internet access to your IIS site, then you will want to make a few modifications to the user account that is created by the IIS setup program. By default, a user account called IUSR_ServerName, where ServerName is the name of your computer where IIS is installed, is created. This account is added to the Guests local group if you installed IIS on a stand-alone server. If your server is a member of a domain, the account is also a member of the Domain Users global group. My personal preference is to move the user account to the Domain Guests global group. If you have modified the privileges for the Domain Guests global group, and you will have multiple IIS installations, create a new group and assign the IIS user accounts that are created to this new group. Make sure you remove the IIS accounts from all other global groups. If your IIS sites will be on stand-alone servers and you have not modified the Guest account, the default IIS user account privileges should suffice.

Note

In order to use the Guest account on a domain, the account must be enabled. The default for the Guest account is for the account to be disabled. You can change this property by double-clicking the Guest account and clearing the Account Disabled checkbox.

If you create a new global group for the IIS user account, however, make sure that only the Log on locally privilege has been granted to the user account. This can be verified using User Manager, or User Manager for Domains, and choosing Policies | User Rights. This will display the User Rights Policy dialog box. Enable the Show Advanced User Rights checkbox so you can view all rights, not just the basic rights. Then in the Right drop-down listbox, select each right. As you do, the user accounts and groups that have been assigned the selected right will be displayed in the Grant To listbox.

Using NTFS to Protect Your Data

The New Technology File System (NTFS) is another item in your arsenal, which, if properly utilized, can aid you in your goal of preventing unauthorized access to your data. You can think of NTFS as your personal security system. In action it is similar to the numerous code key-door lock systems in use on doors in secure areas. In order to open the door, you must supply a code, use a badge with a preset code, or wait for someone on the other side of the door to escort you in. All access to this secure area is monitored by security cameras and logged by a security guard. If someone attempts to break in, an alarm is sounded, the guards run to the source of the alarm, and the culprit is taken into custody.

With Windows NT Server, an alarm could be created by using the Performance Monitor, in Alert view. By monitoring the Server object counters Errors Logon and Errors Access Permissions, you can be alerted if the frequency of bad logon or data access attempts are occurring in real time. Once informed of the event, if the culprit is a local network client, you certainly can physically confront him face-to-face. If the culprit is a remote user, you can kick him off of the system. The key to being able to determine who is using your system and what they are doing, however, is based on system resource auditing. Auditing directory or file access is only supported on an NTFS partition. For more specific information on how to configure your system and use this auditing information, refer to the section titled "Determining Who Is Using Your System" later in this chapter. I also recommend that you set permissions on all of your directories and files contained on NTFS partitions as this can help eliminate additional security risks. For more information on how to set directory and file permissions, see the following section titled "Setting Permissions on a Directory or File."

During the Internet Information Server setup process, the default root installation directory for your WWW, FTP, and Gopher services is the C:\InetSrv directory. This is not such a good idea, for at least two reasons:

◆ This directory is accessible from the Windows NT hidden administration share C$. While you can delete the sharepoint for the C$ administration share, this could cause numerous problems with remote administration of the server.

◆ Second, if your boot partition has a data error, it's possible to lose not only your Windows NT installation but your Internet service's data as well. It is a much better choice to create a new root directory on another physical drive, such as D:\InetSrv. By creating a new root directory, you can control

11

SECURING YOUR NETWORK

access by deleting the root administration share (D$, for example). You also increase your recoverability options in case your boot partition fails. In the worst case you can reinstall Windows NT Server and have your Web site back up and running in a couple of hours.

Tip

Wherever you install the Internet Information Server files, you should choose an NTFS partition if you have one available. You can then assign permissions to the executable files, as well as to all of the root directories for your content files.

Another capability to consider involves using the fault tolerant capabilities of Windows NT to limit the downtime that could occur in case of a disaster. You can use a stripe set with parity for increased performance and improved fault tolerance, a mirrored set for data redundancy, or both. For maximum fault tolerance, create a mirrored set for your SystemRoot partition to protect you against boot partition errors, and a striped set with parity for the partition used as your IIS root directory. But just because you are using a fault tolerant partition, don't think that you do not need to make system backups.

Plan on daily, weekly, and monthly backups in case all other alternatives fail. This way if you install Windows NT Server as a stand-alone server, you have a way to restore your site. This restoration can occur on the same physical computer that failed (after you replace the failed hardware) or on another computer on your network.

SETTING PERMISSIONS ON A DIRECTORY OR FILE

You can prevent unauthorized access to a network resource by setting permissions on a directory of one or more files. Directory- and file-level permissions are discussed in detail in Chapter 7, "Resource Management Tools," in the section titled "Setting Permissions on Directories and Files." As you will be opening up your server to the Internet, with the possibility that someone will try and bypass your security restrictions, it is a good idea to set permissions on all of your root directories. This permission setting can be propagated to all of your subdirectories as well.

While it may be a problem to reset all of the permissions on your server, because you have a lot of user subdirectories that you will have to reset the permissions on later, it still may be worthwhile to do so. If you cannot afford the time to reset all of the permissions on your disk drives, you should consider using a dedicated server to support the Internet Information Server.

Security and Remote Access Service

The Windows NT Remote Access Service does not provide a high level of security for your network. There are, however, at least two choices you can make that can improve the situation. First, you can configure your dial-out and dial-in connections to use encryption. Second, you can choose to allow all network clients that connect to access just the computer that is providing the Remote Access Service connection, or the entire network. The choice about which encryption setting to use and whether or not to provide full access to your network, will be determined by your requirements.

If you are supporting dial-in connections for remote clients who must access the entire network and for remote clients who do not require full access to the entire network, set up multiple dial-in connections on two or more modems. Each of these remote clients can then access the appropriate modem using a specific phone number that you will provide. This lessens the chance of a security breach. To configure your dial-in connection to enable or disable full access to the network, follow these steps:

1. Open the Network Control Panel applet.
2. Select the Remote Access Service and click the Configure button to display the Remote Access Setup dialog box.
3. Select the appropriate connection and click the Network button. This will display the Network Configuration dialog box.
4. In the Server Settings group, click the Configure button next to the appropriate network protocol under the Allow remote clients running title. This will display the RAS Server Protocol Configuration dialog box, where the protocol is NetBEUI, TCP/IP, or IPX/SPX.
5. In the Allow Remote Protocol clients to access field, where the protocol is NetBEUI, TCP/IP, or IPX/SPX, check the Entire network radio button to grant access to all computers on your network, or the This computer only radio button to limit access to just the server providing the dial-in connection.
6. Click OK to return to the Network Configuration dialog box.
7. If you will be supporting multiple network protocols, repeat steps 4 through 6 for each additional protocol. When you are finished, click OK to return to the Remote Access Setup dialog box.
8. For each additional connection to configure, repeat steps 3 through 7. Then click OK to return to the Network dialog box.
9. Click OK to close the Network dialog box. You will then be prompted by the Network Settings Change dialog box to restart your system. Click Yes to

11

SECURING YOUR NETWORK

restart your system so that the changes will be applied when the system restarts, or No to defer the update until the next time the server is restarted.

To modify your dial-in connections to require password or data encryption for increased security, follow these steps:

1. Open the Network Control Panel applet.
2. Select the Remote Access Service and click the Configure button to display the Remote Access Setup dialog box.
3. Select the appropriate connection and click the Network button. This will display the Network Configuration dialog box.
4. In the Server Settings group, click one of the following options to specify your encryption requirements:

    Allow any encryption including plain text: Specifies that any supported (MS-CHAP, SPAP, PAP) encryption method can be used. A connection will be attempted using the Microsoft password encryption (MS-CHAP) first, and then the standard Internet encryption method (SPAP), followed by a plain text (PAP) authentication.

    Require encrypted authentication: Specifies that a connection will be attempted using the Microsoft password encryption (MS-CHAP) first, and if that fails the standard Internet encryption method (SPAP).

    Require Microsoft encrypted authentication: Specifies that a connection will be attempted using only the Microsoft password encryption (MS-CHAP) method. If this item is selected, you can also enable the Require data encryption checkbox to encrypt your data as well as your password.

5. Click OK to return to the Network Configuration dialog box.
6. If you will be supporting multiple network protocols, repeat steps 4 through 5 for each additional protocol. When you are finished, click OK to return to the Remote Access Setup dialog box.
7. For each additional connection to configure, repeat steps 3 through 6. Then click OK to return to the Network Control Panel.
8. Click OK to close the Network Control Panel. You will be prompted by the Network Settings Change dialog box to restart your system. Click Yes to restart your system so that the changes will be applied when the system restarts, or No to defer the update until the next time the server is restarted.

In order to use the Remote Access Service to connect to the Internet, you will need either a PPP (Point-to-Point Protocol) or SLIP (Serial Line Internet Protocol) account from an Internet Provider. Once you have obtained an account, all that is needed is to create a phone book entry with the Remote Access client. Follow these steps:

1. In the Edit Phone Book Entry dialog, click the Advanced button to expand the dialog. Click the Network button to display the Network Protocol Settings dialog.

2. Disable the NetBEUI and IPX protocols in the PPP entry if you will be using a PPP connection to connect to the Internet service provider. If you have a preassigned IP address or a DNS IP address from your Internet service provider, click the TCP/IP Settings button to enter this information.

3. If you will be using a SLIP connection to connect to your Internet service provider, enable the SLIP radio button, instead of the default PPP radio button, as in step 2.

4. Click the Security button to display the Security Settings dialog box.

5. Choose a security option, which can be one of the following:

   Allow any encryption including plain text: Specifies that any supported (MS-CHAP, SPAP, PAP) encryption method can be used. A connection will be attempted using the Microsoft password encryption (MS-CHAP) first, and then the standard Internet encryption method (SPAP), followed by a plain text (PAP) authentication.

   Use clear text Terminal Login only: Specifies that if you use a terminal setting to log on to your ISP, you may transmit a clear text—no encryption—user name and password.

   Accept only encrypted authentication: Specifies that a connection will be attempted using the Microsoft password encryption (MS-CHAP) first, and if that fails, the standard Internet encryption method (SPAP).

   Accept only Microsoft encrypted authentication: Specifies that a connection will be attempted using only the Microsoft password encryption (MS-CHAP) method. If this item is selected, you can also enable the Require data encryption checkbox to encrypt your data as well as your password.

Note

Many Internet service providers support Microsoft encryption, so you should try this option first. If it fails, then try the Require encrypted authentication. Only if both methods fail should you enable the Allow any encryption including plain text checkbox.

6. Click OK to close the Security Settings dialog box. Then click OK to return to the Edit Phone Book Entry dialog. Finally, click OK again to return to the Remote Access client main window.

After you complete the preceding steps, double-click on your new entry to dial out and connect to your Internet provider.

11

SECURING YOUR NETWORK

DETERMINING WHO IS USING YOUR SYSTEM

Determining who might have accessed your system in the past or who might be accessing your system now is very important to anyone connected to the Internet. Among the best tools you have for determining whether a security breach occurred in the past or whether one is occurring now are the security logs created by Windows NT and the Internet Information Server. Determining who might be accessing your system or attempting to access restricted data files, however, requires that the system first be configured to audit events. Restricting access to your sensitive files or enabling auditing of your files requires that you use File Manager (or Windows Explorer). Viewing your system events requires that you use the Windows NT Event Viewer, but to view your IIS event logs you can use a text editor (like Notepad) if you configured the service to write a text file, or you can use an ODBC front end (like Access) to view logs that were created on an ODBC-compliant database.

CONFIGURING THE SYSTEM TO ENABLE AUDITING

If you want to be able to determine who is using your shared network resources or even who is abusing their privileges on your network, you need to enable the auditing features provided in Windows NT Server. Auditing is divided into several categories, however, and is not enabled in a single application.

To audit a system event related to account usage or modification and the programs running on your server, in User Manager for Domains choose Audit from the Policies menu to display the Audit Policy dialog box. (See Figure 11.4.)

Figure 11.4.
Enabling system
auditing with
User Manager for
Domains.

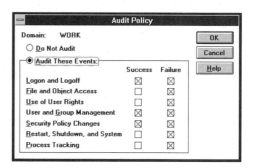

To audit any event, you first need to enable auditing by enabling the Audit These Events radio button in the Audit Policy dialog box (even if you select no options here to audit) and then choosing the application's audit options. To audit the use of files, use File Manager; for printer auditing, use Print Manager. Both of these have an Auditing option on the Security menu that displays a dialog box similar to the Audit Policy dialog box. There, you can specify the events to audit.

When you select an event to be audited, it is entered into the security log, which you can view with the Event Viewer. You can select to audit the successful use of a privilege, failure to obtain access (which indicates a security violation attempt), or both.

You can audit the following events:

◆ Logon and Logoff: Determines who has logged on or off your network. I recommend that you enable both these checkboxes (Success and Failure) to determine who may be using your network.

◆ File and Object Access: Works with other applications that have been used to specify auditing. You can use File Manager to enable auditing of a directory, for example. You can enable the Success or Failure events for the File and Object access in order to record any access to the audited directory.

◆ Use of User Rights: Provides the capability to audit any use of a user right, other than logon and logoff, such as the capability to log on as a service.

◆ User and Group Management: Gives you the capability to track any user account or group management—whether a new user is added, an existing user password is enabled, or new users are added to a group, for example.

If you have constant problems with a particular user account or group being modified and cannot determine who is making these changes, you should enable both Success and Failure for this option. This can help you determine who may be making the changes. I've seen a few problems caused by personnel who have been granted administrative privileges but who are not trained in their use, for example. By using this option, you can determine who needs additional training, or even who should have administrative privileges revoked.

◆ Security Policy Changes: Helps you determine who may be making changes to your system audit policies, user right policies, or trust relationships. Enable this option for both Success and Failure to determine who may be modifying your network policies. This is a good idea particularly if you have several Administrators and find that things have been changing without anyone admitting responsibility.

◆ Restart, Shutdown, and System: Enables you to determine who may be shutting down your servers or performing any event that affects system security or the security log.

◆ Process Tracking: Determines which applications are executing on your system.

Caution

Auditing the Success events for Process Tracking can fill up your security log in a matter of minutes. Only enable this event for Success when absolutely necessary.

AUDITING DIRECTORIES AND FILES

If you want to monitor who is using your network resources or you are concerned about users who constantly attempt to bypass your security restrictions, you can use the auditing features to determine who is doing what with your shared directories or files. Suppose that you have an HTML document as a template on your server that is used by many users on your network. These users should save their copy of the data file under a different name. But suppose that someone inadvertently saves his version of the file and replaces the original. Then, to hide his mistake, he deletes the file. If you have enabled auditing of the file, you will know which user modified or even deleted it. You then can have a serious talk with him about network security. Another possible use of security auditing is to identify an Internet user who may be trying to access restricted data using a stolen user account and password, or maliciously deleting files on your FTP site.

Note

Auditing is available only on NTFS partitions.

You can view this auditing information by using the Event Viewer and examining the security log. This is covered in Chapter 6, "Basic Administrative Tools," in the section "Using the Windows NT Event Viewer." For now, just take a look at what is required to enable auditing of directories and files with File Manager. The first thing to consider is that in order to enable auditing at the system level, you have to use User Manager for Domains and choose Policies I Auditing to turn on the auditing features. This is discussed in Chapter 6 in the section titled "Enable Auditing." After you enable system-wide auditing, you can follow the steps outlined in Chapter 7 in the section titled "Auditing Directories and Files" to audit the directories on your server.

USING THE WINDOWS NT EVENT VIEWER

You use the Event Viewer to display status events that occur on your computer. These events are divided into three categories. Each category is contained in a specific log: The system log includes events related to the operation of the operating system, the application log includes application-specific events, and the security log includes auditing events. Of these three logs, the most important to you is the security log as this can be used to determine if someone is attempting to access restricted data, or if someone is trying to break into your system by guessing passwords for a known user account. The next most important log is the system log as it can show, by service, the anonymous logon requests that have occurred on your system. It can also display other publishing service events.

Note

You should use the Event Viewer to view your logs on a daily basis for your file servers, and at least once a week for a workstation. If you do not review your logs in this time frame, you might be unaware of system errors that could propagate to a system failure, and you will not be aware of possible attempts to violate the security of your network.

Instead of just throwing away the events in your event logs when you fill them up, you should archive them. This gives you the ability to load them at a later date for comparison with current logs to isolate any potential security problems. You also can use these logs with Excel or any database that can import a comma-separated value or ASCII text file. You can use this imported data to spot trends that can indicate a potential network trouble spot or hardware-related failure.

THE INTERNET INFORMATION SERVER LOGS

While you can use the Windows NT Event Viewer to look at the security and system logs, these logs do not contain as much information about who is doing what with your Internet services as the Internet Information Server logs. Your IIS logs contain the following fields:

- Clienthost: Specifies the IP address of the connected client.
- Username: Specifies the name supplied by the user to log on to the specified service.
- Logtime: Specifies when the user started the connection in MM/DD/YY HH:MM:SS time format.
- Service: Specifies the service to which the user connected. This will be MSFTPSVC for the FTP Publishing Service, W3SVC for the WWW Publishing Service, or GopherSvc for the Gopher Publishing Service.
- Machine: Specifies the IIS on which the service is executing.
- ServerIP: Specifies the IP address of the server on which the service is executing.
- Processingtime: Specifies the time the client was connected.
- Bytessent: Specifies the number of bytes sent to the client.
- Bytesreceived: Specifies the number of bytes sent by the client.

◆ Servicestatus: Specifies a service-specific status code.

◆ Win32Status: Specifies a Windows NT 32-bit API-specific status code.

◆ Operation: Specifies the service operation type for the client request.

◆ Target: Specifies the data object name requested by the client.

◆ Parameter: Specifies any additional command parameter.

By saving these logs and reviewing them (at least once a week), you can obtain performance characteristics such as how many users visited your site. You can also use these logs to determine if someone was trying to access data on your site to which they should not have access by looking for user logon failures. If you see several of these from the same IP address, you may want to prevent that IP address from logging on to your site by configuring the advanced options for the service as described in Chapter 6.

SUMMARY

This chapter covered a lot of material, and it only touched on some of the complex security issues. One key concept you should remember is that a security policy needs to be placed into effect to protect you from data you download from the Internet, as well as a policy to limit access to your network. You also learned how to further protect your data by using the NTFS file system in conjunction with the ability to apply permission to directories and files. In the latter part of this chapter, you learned about some of the tools you can use to enable system auditing, set auditing on directories and files, and how you can use the Event Viewer to see if anyone is accessing any files you enabled auditing on. In the next chapter, you will look at how you can configure your network hardware and software to obtain the best possible performance.

- Basic Performance Issues

- Software Configuration

- Hardware Upgrades

CHAPTER 12

Getting the Most from Your Microsoft Network

Optimizing your Windows NT Server to provide the most efficient server performance sometimes can be a daunting task. There are so many options that you can be overwhelmed at times. You always have the option of just throwing money at bigger and better hardware (which always increases some performance aspect), but that's not a very cost-effective solution. It's better to spend some time working with what tools are available first and then to make the determination as to how to best spend your money to increase performance. And that's where this chapter starts— by looking at some of the basic performance options. This chapter includes a discussion of items that can be useful in planning the initial hardware purchase of the platform you will use as your server. It covers the different hardware platforms available for running Windows NT Server, the peripheral I/O buses available on today's computers and when to choose each of them, and the various disk subsystems and how to make the most of them. Finally, you will look at the options that always increase the performance of your server compared to the default system configuration. I call these the no-brainer performance improvements because these solutions use the hardware you already have, but in different configurations.

After you learn about these basic performance modifications, you will take a look at some of the basic software selectable configuration options to optimize your Server service. Then you will see how you can use some of the hardware-based solutions. This chapter discusses options such as implementing hardware RAID (Redundant Array of Inexpensive Disks) solutions, load balancing your network by adding additional network adapters and adjusting the network bindings to increase performance, and adding additional processors.

BASIC PERFORMANCE ISSUES

You can enhance server performance by just choosing a faster processor (or making use of the scalability of Windows NT Server by installing it on an entirely different processor platform); using an ISA-, EISA-, PCI-, or VLB-based peripheral; or using software RAID solutions. In this section, you will examine some of these options to obtain the maximum performance from your server without purchasing additional hardware. You also can use this section as a guide to help make purchasing decisions.

SERVER PLATFORMS

Windows NT Server 3.51 includes the capability to run on several different processor platforms. These platforms include the Intel processor line and several different RISC (Reduced Instruction Set Computer) processors. You currently may use the MIPS, Alpha, or PowerPC RISC processors. There are two major differences between these platforms, aside from the purchase price. First, the Intel processor line is the only processor that can execute OS/2 16-bit character mode applications. It is also the only processor line that can be used in a dual-boot mode to boot MS-DOS. If these are not real concerns, then you can ignore these options and just consider the second difference: pure performance. Depending on the RISC processor line you choose and the clock speed of the processor, one of these platforms may perform better for you than the Intel processors.

It is getting very difficult to make a recommendation for a RISC processor over the Intel processor line because the Intel processor line keeps improving. And when you consider that the primary job of a server is to share resources (generally file and printer resources), then the speed of the processor is not the most relevant issue, although it is a concern because Windows NT is more processor intensive than other network operating systems. Instead, you should be concerned with the I/O bus performance and the peripherals you choose.

I/O BUS CONSIDERATIONS

The next step after determining which processor platform you will use as your server is to determine the I/O bus architecture. As with processor platforms, you have several flavors of I/O buses to choose from, each with specific capabilities. The item to consider here is which bus will perform best for a particular function. Consider how well it will perform for a video adapter, network adapter, and SCSI adapter, for example, because these are the most common performance-oriented peripherals. These are the adapters that must function at their peak. Adapters that are not performance intensive are items such as your sound card, a modem card, a parallel port, a mouse adapter, or even your joystick adapter.

Tip

Many Intel-based computers have an advanced BIOS Setup option to increase the speed at which the I/O expansion bus operates. Increasing this bus speed above the default of 8 MHz can increase performance. Most of today's peripherals are rated for a minimum of 12.5 MHz, although some will operate at higher speeds.

Warning

If you do increase the speed at which your I/O expansion bus operates, make sure that you perform a reliability test before placing the unit in service because not all adapters operate reliably at speeds above 8 MHz. Make sure that when you perform this test, you at least test for full disk controller, network controller, video adapter, and communications port functionality.

12

YOUR MICROSOFT NETWORK

Several I/O expansion bus types are currently in use on today's computers:

◆ ISA (Industry Standard Architecture): The original expansion bus introduced on the IBM (AT) Personal Computer. The original PC (XT) used an 8-bit I/O bus, which the AT computer extended to 16 bits, although the ISA standard includes both the 8- and 16-bit I/O buses. Most of today's peripherals are 16-bit peripherals and offer excellent value. If performance is not an issue, this is the choice to make when purchasing a peripheral. You should use this bus for your 8-bit expansion cards, filling up your 8-bit slots first, and then your 16-bit expansion cards. ISA is a good choice for your sound cards, modem cards, and other peripherals. Try to avoid this expansion bus for your network, SCSI, and video cards unless you have no other option. ISA is a good choice for secondary network and SCSI adapters.

Note

The ISA expansion bus is able to directly access only the first 16MB of system RAM. If you use a bus master controller (such as a SCSI disk controller) and if your system has more than 16MB of RAM, all disk access must be double buffered (the data first has to be copied to a buffer in the first 16MB and then copied above that to the application's data buffer), which therefore decreases overall system performance. Although this is not a significant performance hit on most systems, it is very noticeable on others, depending on the system architecture.

◆ EISA (Enhanced Industry Standard Architecture): An expansion bus that is an extension to the ISA bus. It stretches the I/O bus to a full 32 bits and offers software configuration of peripherals through a configuration disk. An EISA expansion slot also can use ISA adapters because it uses a layered connection mechanism. An ISA adapter only fits halfway down this connection, thus enabling a connection to all the standard ISA expansion pins, whereas an EISA adapter fits all the way down and can reach the additional I/O and bus connectors. The EISA bus is a good choice for network adapters, video adapters, and SCSI adapters. It performs well in most conditions and enables you to install several bus master adapters concurrently.

Note

A bus master adapter has its own processor on it and, in most cases, its own Direct Memory Access (DMA) controller. The idea behind a bus master adapter is that it can use its own processor and DMA controller to pass data to and from the adapter and to and from system memory, thus letting the processor on the motherboard continue to process data requests instead of spending time passing data to and from system memory and to and from the adapter. You can think of it as a poor man's multiprocessor platform.

Tip

Although many people talk about PCI and VLB as the buses to use on the desktop, they tend to forget about performance-oriented servers. These machines can make excellent use of the EISA bus to add additional network adapters, SCSI adapters (there are never enough SCSI channels), and even multiport communications boards (such as those from DigiBoard) to add functionality while maintaining performance. My recommendation for an I/O bus is to find a PCI/EISA bus combination if you can. This offers you the greatest level of performance and compatibility with a long-term growth potential.

- ◆ MCA (Microchannel Architecture): IBM introduced this I/O bus as a replacement for the ISA expansion bus. It was designed for IBM's new PS/2 line of computers. Although it offered increased performance compared to the ISA bus, it was completely incompatible with the ISA bus. This led to increased cost of the adapters and a limited number of available peripherals for the consumer to purchase. This bus is a dead end in my opinion and should be avoided for new purchases.
- ◆ VLB (Video Local Bus): In order to increase performance of video adapters, a method was created to access an adapter by tying it directly to the system memory bus. This increased performance considerably but is limited to three VLB adapters. The current implementation is a 32-bit wide data bus with an extension to 64 bits on the way. This bus is an excellent choice for your primary video adapter and in my limited testing (using the same adapter in VLB and PCI versions), it outperforms the PCI bus. And al-

12

YOUR MICROSOFT NETWORK

though it can be used for multiple purposes, such as a video adapter, disk controller, and network adapter, it is not the best choice for multiple adapters. Use it over an ISA bus for these purposes, but realize that you will not obtain optimum performance for simultaneous access. By this, I mean that in most cases, the performance of a video card as the only VLB adapter is better than if you have both a video card and disk controller installed.

◆ PCI (Peripheral Component Interconnect): This bus was designed to overcome the limitations of the ISA, EISA, MCA, and VLB expansion buses. It's designed to offer true Plug and Play functionality by automatically configuring the adapters (no software configuration program is needed), outperforming all other buses in data-transfer rates, and offering more than three expansion slots. However, it has not lived up to the last goal. Current implementations still limit you to three PCI expansion slots, which is why you generally will see the PCI bus paired with the ISA, EISA, or even the VLB bus. PCI is an excellent choice for multiple adapters, such as your video card, SCSI (or IDE disk controller) adapters, and network adapters. Keep in mind, however, that you probably will have only three PCI expansion slots, which can severely limit your performance options. If PCI is your choice as a primary I/O bus, try to find one that is paired with an EISA expansion bus. This gives you the capability to use the PCI bus for your video and two SCSI adapters, while using the EISA bus for network adapters. And if you need to expand your disk subsystem again, you always can add SCSI adapters to the EISA expansion bus and still maintain adequate performance (as compared to a PCI SCSI adapter).

◆ PCMCIA (Personal Computer Memory Card Industry Association): This bus originally was designed to add memory components to hand-held and portable computers, but it has since become an industry standard I/O bus used to connect SCSI adapters, network adapters, video capture cards, miniature hard disk drives, and just about anything else you can think of to portable computers. It is the first Plug and Play device to live up to its name under MS-DOS and Windows 95. Under Windows NT, you still need to choose an IRQ, I/O port, and possibly a memory address to configure the device driver. And this is because Windows NT does not support the Card and Socket services that provide the Plug and Play functionality. Although this is not a high-performance I/O bus, it still performs relatively well.

Tip

If you need to demonstrate Windows NT Server or even the complete BackOffice product line, consider installing Windows NT Server on a portable computer. With today's hardware, you can find Pentium models (both 75-MHz models, which give excellent runtimes of 2.5 to 3 hours, and 120-MHz models, which offer limited runtimes of 1 to 2.5 hours and excellent performance) with disk drives in the 1GB range. I use my Toshiba T4600c portable and Windows NT for classes and demonstrations. With the addition of supported PCMCIA network and SCSI adapters, it offers true plug and play capabilities in the sense that you can just plug your portable computer into your clients' networks and immediately be fully functional. Not only can you access their resources, but they can access yours as well. It makes an impressive demonstration or training platform, and you can pack it up and hit the road in minutes to catch that flight.

Caution

Avoid an architecture with a mixture of more than two I/O buses, such as ISA, PCI, and VLB, for your server. Although these platforms do offer the capability to use more types of peripherals on a single computer, they do not perform as well. It is better to choose a platform with a dedicated ISA/PCI or ISA/VLB bus and to use the faster bus for your video, disk, and network adapters.

CHOOSING A DISK SUBSYSTEM

The most important single component on your system, aside from the processor, is your disk subsystem. If your server cannot access the data fast enough to handle your client requests, it slows down the entire network as your clients wait to access the data. And poor performance means that you will be notified sooner or later by your superiors and it rarely will be a happy meeting. Four types of disk subsystems are available on the market:

12

◆ **Antique Systems:** If you have one of these in your file server, you are in real trouble. Replace it immediately or suffer the consequences. These antiquated systems are based on the standard disk interface and are all part of the ST-506 family and include MFM (Modified Frequency Modulation), RLL (Run Length Limited), ERLL (Enhanced Run Length Limited), and ESDI (Enhanced Small Device Interface). All these disk subsystems have been replaced by more able (less expensive, too) disk subsystems. Computers using these types of disk subsystems should be converted to WINS Proxy Agents, print servers, communications servers, or other computers that perform less stressful tasks.

◆ **IDE (Integrated Drive Electronics):** This drive interface is an outgrowth of the ST-506 interface and is designed to replace a dedicated (smart) disk controller with a host (dumb) adapter and a smart disk drive. In this particular scheme, the disk controller is really just an interface between the host computer and the smart peripheral. You can add disk drives, tape drives, or even CD-ROM drives to a host adapter. The current limitation includes a maximum of four IDE peripherals in a single system. It accomplishes this by using both the primary and secondary I/O addresses defined for ST-506 hard disk controllers (370-37F and 170-17F) and, in some cases, actually provides separate interrupts for each I/O channel. The good news about IDE disk drives is that they are very inexpensive and can offer acceptable performance for a workstation computer. The bad news is that they are not fast enough for a server. The real bad news is that most IDE disk controllers are PIO (Programmed I/O) devices. This means that the host processor (on your motherboard) must transfer the data to and from the adapter and to and from system memory. This decreases the efficiency of your server and should be avoided if at all possible.

◆ **EIDE (Enhanced Integrated Drive Electronics):** This is an extension to the current IDE standard and is designed to increase the data-transfer rates. It does this by reading multiple sectors of the disk whenever a data-access request is specified. It also increases the maximum size of a disk drive from 512MB to 8GB. But you still are limited to a maximum of four IDE peripherals in a single system.

◆ **SCSI (Small Computer System Interface):** This is my recommendation for a primary disk subsystem, although you can mix and match a SCSI system with any other subsystem mentioned earlier and use it as a secondary disk subsystem. SCSI is another expansion bus—not just a disk I/O bus like IDE. Like IDE drives, however, the electronics for controlling the drive and accessing the data are located on the disk drive. You can add SCSI tape drives, SCSI scanners, SCSI printers, and any other SCSI device to your

SCSI host adapter. The standard SCSI interface offers a single disk channel that can add up to seven SCSI peripherals, whereas enhanced versions offer the capability to add up to 15 SCSI peripherals on two separate channels (seven on one channel and eight on the other channel; the remaining SCSI ID on the first channel is used by the host adapter). Most SCSI adapters are also bus masters, which can increase performance quite a bit. Other factors include the capability to attach and detach the SCSI peripheral from the SCSI bus so that another SCSI peripheral can access the bus while the first is processing a data request, queuing multiple disk commands for later processing, and replacing bad sectors with spare sectors on command.

Note

SCSI currently comes in several flavors: the original SCSI, which you should avoid when purchasing SCSI peripherals; SCSI II, which is the most used; SCSI III, which is on its way to becoming the new standard; and then FAST SCSI and WIDE SCSI. FAST SCSI extends the data-transfer rate from 10MBps to 20MBps, whereas Wide SCSI extends the I/O interface from 8 bits to 16 bits. In some cases, you can even find a combination of FAST and WIDE SCSI, which extends the data-transfer rate to 40MBps. Some manufacturers also use the term ULTRA WIDE SCSI instead of FAST WIDE SCSI, and you may even see an ULTRA WIDE SCSI implementation that provides 60MBps, or higher.

Tip

When adding a CD-ROM to Windows NT, always try to choose a SCSI II CD-ROM drive. These types of CD-ROM drives are the easiest to add to an NT system.

With each type of disk controller you use, there is a limit to the number of disk drives and controllers, and the maximum data-transfer rate you can achieve. Table 12.1 summarizes this information. An ST-506 disk controller can use a primary or secondary I/O address. This means that it is possible to use two disk controllers to double the total number of disk drives you can install in your system for MFM, RLL, ERLL, ESDI, IDE, and EIDE controllers. SCSI controller limitations are based on the number of I/O addresses or BIOS support, which differs among manufacturers; however, you generally can install at least four SCSI adapters in a system.

12

YOUR MICROSOFT NETWORK

TABLE 12.1. DISK SUBSYSTEM CHARACTERISTICS.

Type	Data Transfer Rate (MBps)	Maximum Number of Peripherals per Adapter
MFM	2–4	2
RLL	2–4	2
ERRL	2–4	2
ESDI	20	2
IDE	3.3–8.3	2
EIDE	13.5–16.6	4
SCSI I	5	7
SCSI II	10	7
SCSI III	20	15
FAST SCSI	20	15
WIDE SCSI	20	15
FAST WIDE SCSI	40	15
ULTRA WIDE SCSI	60	30

NO-BRAINER PERFORMANCE GAINS

You can increase the general performance of your Windows NT Server by applying some basic techniques. These techniques involve balancing the load of your disk subsystem to increase the I/O performance. In this particular aspect, you will be concentrating on using SCSI subsystems (because they provide the most benefits), but you can use other disk subsystems (such as IDE or EIDE) as well.

This section takes a look at this in a couple of steps:

- ◆ A single disk subsystem, in which there is only one disk controller with multiple disk drives.
- ◆ A multiple disk subsystem, in which you have at least two disk controllers with one or more disk drives per controller.
- ◆ The ultimate disk subsystem, in which you have multiple disk subsystems with multiple disk drives per disk controller.

SINGLE DISK SUBSYSTEM

This particular installation has limited performance gain options. This doesn't mean that there is nothing you can do; it just means that the options for increasing your server's performance are based on the number of physical disk drives you have installed on your system and how much work you are willing to put into obtaining the maximum benefit. First look at the minimum performance gain option because it is also the easiest.

Assume that you have one disk controller with two disk drives. Each disk drive is 500MB. They can be IDE, EIDE, or SCSI. Each drive has a single primary partition of 500MB. In this particular case, you have installed Windows NT Server to your drive C in the WINNT35 directory (the installation default). This directory is called your SystemRoot. In fact, you have a special environment variable called SystemRoot that equates to the installation directory. In this example, the SystemRoot environment variable is C:\WINNT35. Because this is where all the system files and paging file are located and where all the print jobs are spooled, it is a heavily used disk drive.

To help balance the load, you can do two things. First, install another paging file on the second disk (drive D). This gives Windows NT the capability to use both paging files (the one on drive C and the one on drive D) when it needs to make use of virtual memory. If one disk is in use, the other disk can be used to access its paging file to fulfill the virtual memory request. Second, you can place all your BackOffice and support files on the second disk drive. You can even go so far as to split up your user sharepoints between both drives so that the load is balanced equally. This gives relatively good performance with a minimum of complexity.

Note

Windows NT Server makes heavy use of its paging file, and the most significant performance gain can be realized by placing your primary paging file on a stripe set. The only alternative to paging to disk is to have enough physical memory installed on your system to avoid paging at all. And if you have the funds available, a 256MB Windows NT Server can be an outstanding network server. Adding additional processors can increase its capabilities even more as an application server. An application server is a server designed for the client/server environment (such as SQL Server) and not a file server that shares applications (such as Microsoft Office).

The alternative method requires that you prepartition your hard disk drives into four equal sizes of 250MB each before you install Windows NT Server; partition it as part of the install process (the easiest method); or back up your current NT Server installation and repartition, reformat, reinstall NT, and then restore your backed up version (the toughest method). The idea here is to use two partitions (one on each physical disk) and to create a stripe set of 500MB. Alternatively, you could create four partitions with two partitions of 150MB and two partitions of 350MB to create a 700MB stripe set.

12

Note

I do not recommend less than 150MB (and even that is cutting it close) for the system partition because the available free space dwindles as you install additional software or print jobs are spooled. And, after this partition is filled, you will be required to back up, repartition, reformat, reinstall, and then restore your previous NT installation. This is a lengthy and tedious process, to say the least.

You cannot create the stripe set until after you install Windows NT, of course, so your first task is installing NT to your first primary partition (drive C). After you install NT and create the second primary partition (drive D), you can create the stripe set (drive E) with the Disk Administrator. (See Chapter 6, "Basic Administrative Tools," if you need additional information on how to create partitions and stripe sets.) Now you can follow a similar process, as mentioned earlier, to install your BackOffice software and then create your paging files and user directories. In this case, however, you should create small paging files for your C and D drives (something in the 10- to 30MB range) with your largest paging on your drive E (possibly in the 100- to 250MB range, depending on your server load). Then you can place the user directories on your drive D and place all your other software on drive E (the stripe set). This provides a moderate increase in system performance and increased I/O capacity for your shared network files.

Caution

Because you are using a stripe set without parity, there is no fault tolerance. Your only means of ensuring data integrity is your system backups, so be sure to schedule daily backups. And remember that in order to back up open data files (user files or SQL Server database devices), you must close them first. You can accomplish this by forcing all users off the system (do it gracefully by pausing the service, broadcasting a message to the users informing them of your intentions, and then stopping the Server service) and shutting down SQL Server prior to running your back up. I have included sample batch files to automate this process in Appendix D, "Example Batch Files and Logon Scripts," which is included on the CD-ROM that comes with this book. You can use these files as templates for your system.

MULTIPLE DISK SUBSYSTEM

In this scenario, you will build on your previous performance optimizations by assuming that you have two disk controllers: one EIDE disk controller and single disk drive that shipped with the computer, and an optional SCSI disk controller with at least two (preferably, three to five) SCSI disk drives. In this case, you will install Windows NT Server to the EIDE drive (drive C) and devote this drive completely to Windows NT and the BackOffice system files. The SCSI subsystem will be used to create a stripe set or, if you have enough disk drives (at least three), a stripe set with parity.

Tip

> When creating a stripe set or a stripe set with parity, the more drives you add, the better the performance you will achieve. This is because a stripe set stripes the data among the disk drives in a sequential fashion. If you have three disk drives in a stripe set, for example, in theory, you can read or write three times as much data; in actuality, the performance is not quite that scaleable but is still significant. If you used the same configuration for a stripe set with parity, it only achieves two reads or writes for the same logical drive, because a complete stripe includes two data blocks with one ECC (the parity) block. It is even more important for a stripe set with parity to use more than three drives to obtain equal performance with a regular stripe set.

After you create the stripe set (or stripe set with parity) on drive D, you can install the BackOffice system files. These files should be installed on drive C with all the data files (SQL Server devices, databases, and so on) installed to drive D (the stripe set). All the additional user data files and shared applications also should be installed to drive D to take advantage of the increase in the I/O subsystem. This provides a significant increase in overall system performance and a noticeable improvement in I/O capacity for your shared network files and SQL Server databases.

ULTIMATE DISK SUBSYSTEM

To obtain the ultimate in I/O performance without using a hardware RAID solution, you can use multiple disk controllers with multiple disk drives. In this example, assume that you have three disk controllers: one EIDE disk controller with one disk drive (drive C) and two SCSI disk controllers. One SCSI controller (SCSI 1) will have two disk drives (although more is better), and the other SCSI controller (SCSI 2) will have three or more disk drives. The single EIDE drive once again will become your SystemRoot partition where you will install Windows NT Server and all the BackOffice system files, along with a small system paging file.

12

YOUR MICROSOFT NETWORK

The SCSI 1 disk controller and disk drives will be used to create a stripe set, where you will install the system paging file and, alternatively, the printer spool files as well. In this case, using a stripe set increases system throughput without causing you to worry about data integrity because print jobs can be resubmitted if an error occurs. If an error occurs on this stripe set, then the small paging file you created on the SystemRoot partition is used to keep the system up and running.

All your user data files, shared applications, and SQL Server devices and databases will be installed on the stripe set with parity, which you will create on the SCSI 2 disk controller. This provides an additional level of fault tolerance for your data files and increases I/O performance as well. This gives you the best overall system performance and I/O capacity for your server.

Tip

If you use any of these scenarios with multiple disk controllers in a multiprocessor platform, your performance will increase even more. This is achieved due to the Windows NT symmetric processing model, in which any processor can service interrupts and thereby can achieve an additional level of I/O concurrency over a uniprocessor platform.

In order to really get SQL Server to benefit from the increased I/O capabilities of your stripe set with parity, you need to make a few SQL Server configuration changes. Specifically, you need to increase the max async I/O from its default of 32. The number varies based on the number of disk drives and controllers you have available for the SQL Server installation. For more details, see Chapter 14, "An Introduction to Microsoft SQL Server."

SOFTWARE CONFIGURATION

There are a couple of ways you can tune specific components in Windows NT Server. You can use the provided Control Panel interfaces and you can use the Registry. This section covers a few of the Control Panel interfaces and what they do for you. Appendix B, "The Registry Editor and Registry Keys" (which is included on the CD-ROM), describes the Registry Editor and the major keys of interest. For now, take a look at the Control Panel applets.

The System applet has two provided interfaces for modifying your system and directly impacting your performance. The first is the Virtual Memory button, which displays the Virtual Memory dialog box, as shown in Figure 12.1. In this dialog box, you can create your paging files on a per-drive basis. You also can set the minimum and maximum sizes for your paging files. At a minimum, your paging files should total your physical memory plus 12MB. Your maximum should be about four times your physical memory size for optimum performance, although you can increase this value if necessary (particularly if you do a lot of work with it interactively).

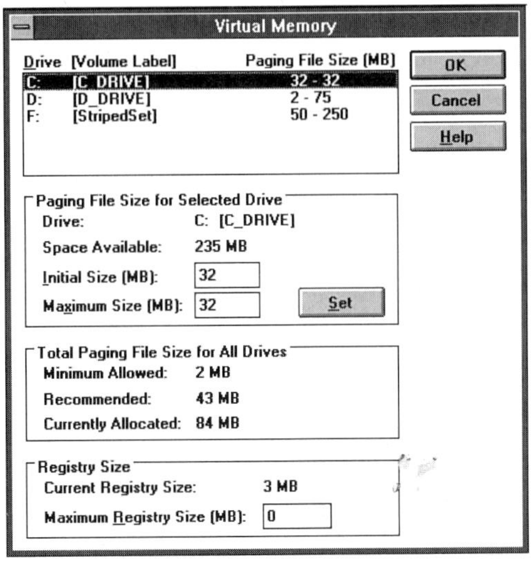

Figure 12.1.
The Virtual
Memory dialog
box.

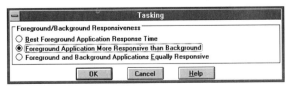

The second option is the Tasking button, which displays the Tasking dialog box, as shown in Figure 12.2. You use this dialog box to set the runtime percentage of all the applications running on your system. The default is to use the Best Foreground Application Response Time option, but this is a poor choice for a server. This setting steals processor cycles from your background processes (such as your Server service) to provide the best performance for the application you are currently using. This choice definitely makes the application you are using perform well, but all other processes suffer. It is an excellent choice for Windows NT Workstation, however, because the goal there is to provide optimum user interaction. I recommend that you use the Foreground Application More Responsive Than Background option if you plan to use this server interactively (to create user accounts, to add computer accounts, or to perform other administrative duties, for example). This choice provides adequate response time and steals fewer processor cycles from the background applications.

Figure 12.2.
The Tasking
dialog box

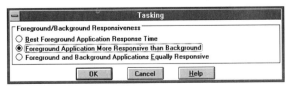

12

YOUR MICROSOFT NETWORK

For optimum performance, you should choose the Foreground and Background Applications Equally Responsive option, which gives every process the same priority and distributes the processor time equally among them. This choice generally makes the server a very poor interactive partner, however, because applications take quite a while to refresh the screen, and any network activity can bring your interactive usage to a crawl. This is not a major problem, however, because you can perform all administrative duties from your desktop if you install the client-based administrative tools mentioned in Chapter 3, "An Introduction to Windows NT Server."

Note

When you install SQL Server, it changes the tasking setting to Foreground and Background Applications Equally Responsive in order to increase SQL Server performance. If you use this computer for interactive administration, be sure to change the tasking setting back to your previous setting.

The other commonly missed performance modification is to change the server service properties in the Control Panel Network applet. The path to displaying this dialog box is fairly simple, but it is hidden from casual modification. To get to it, run the Network applet. Then, in the Installed Network Software listbox, scroll down the list until the Server entry is visible. Then just double-click on it and the dialog box shown in Figure 12.3 appears.

Figure 12.3.
The Server dialog
box.

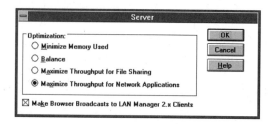

You can choose one of four optimization settings in the Server dialog box:

◆ Minimize Memory Used: This setting is best for servers with 10 or less clients connected to them. If you are in this situation, you have a very small network and, in most cases, you can just use Windows NT Workstation as your server.

◆ Balance: This setting preallocates enough buffers for a maximum of 64 simultaneous network client connections. This is the default setting for networks that only support NetBEUI as their transport protocol.

◆ Maximize Throughput for File Sharing: This setting is best used for any network with more than 64 simultaneous network client connections. Not only does it preallocate buffers, but it also provides the capability to allocate additional buffers on an as-needed basis. It is the best setting to maximize your network client's capability to share network resources such as directories, files, and printers.

◆ Maximize Throughput for Network Applications: This setting also is recommended for large networks with more than 64 simultaneous clients. In this case, there is a trade-off, however. Instead of maximizing performance for resource sharing, the performance optimization is for RPC buffers that will increase the performance of an application server (SQL Server, for example).

Note

When you install SQL Server, it changes the Server settings to Maximize Throughput for Network Applications. If this is not what you want (and in many cases, it will not be), change this back to the previous setting after the installation.

Tip

If you have installed multiple network providers, such as the Gateway Service for NetWare, you also may want to step through the Network Provider Search Order dialog box. You access this dialog box via the Networks button so that you can change the default search order to place the network you use most frequently at the top.

One other option you may want to consider when looking at optimization is using printer pools. This is covered in detail in Chapter 6, "Basic Administrative Tools." A printer pool takes advantage of the capability to use multiple connections to identical printers to form a single logical printer. If one printer in the pool is in use, the next in the chain is used to print the client print jobs. If you have five printers connected to your computer as a single printer pool, for example, your clients can print their jobs five times faster, and they only have to create one printer connection to do so.

HARDWARE UPGRADES

The first rule in maximizing your Windows NT Server performance is to add additional system memory. The next rule to consider is using a hardware RAID

12

YOUR MICROSOFT NETWORK

configuration to increase your I/O capacity. Then think about adding additional network adapters and load balancing your system. If your system is very CPU intensive (it is running SQL Server, Systems Management Server, SNA Server, and Microsoft Mail on the same server, for example), you might want to look at adding processors if your system is capable of being upgraded in this fashion. In this section, you will look at each of these options and learn about some of the benefits each has to offer.

SYSTEM MEMORY UPGRADES

Memory upgrades can be divided into two types: secondary processor cache upgrades and main system memory upgrades. Most people are familiar with upgrading main memory or the memory on the motherboard, but many do not consider upgrading the secondary cache memory at the same time. Perhaps this occurs because they are unfamiliar with the benefits associated with increasing the secondary cache size. So take a moment to look into what a secondary cache can do for you.

You use a secondary (level 2) cache to hold a copy of main system memory that is accessed frequently to pre-read and hold sequential data requests from main memory, or you can use this cache to buffer data writes to main memory. This cache provides increased memory access times because cache memory operates in the 15-to-20 nanosecond range, whereas system memory operates in the 60-to-100 nanosecond range. You use a cache because today's processors operate at speeds that exceed the main memory access time. System memory is based on Dynamic Random Access Memory (DRAM) chips, which require a refresh cycle before they can be accessed again, which doubles or even triples the time between concurrent memory access rates, depending on the system architecture and wait cycles. Secondary cache chips, on the other hand, are based on Static Random Access Memory (SRAM) chips, which do not require a refresh between concurrent data access cycles. My recommendation is to increase the size of your secondary processor cache based on the size of your system memory. Use a minimum of 256KB for a 16MB system, use a 512MB cache for systems up to 64MB, and use at least 1MB of cache for anything larger than 64MB, if possible. Not all systems have upgradable secondary caches.

Many Intel computers offer an advanced BIOS Setup option to configure the secondary cache and main system memory refresh times and wait states. If you can, set your secondary cache to offer write-back (which buffers writes to system memory) functionality because this increases system performance. If data integrity is an issue, set your secondary cache settings to write-through (which pass all data writes directly to main memory) and only cache memory reads requests. If you decrease your refresh times and wait states, you also may increase system performance. But be careful about changing memory refresh rates and wait states, because not all memory chips are created equal and they may not be able to function reliably at faster speeds. One indication that you have gone too far in this regard is if you start to see Nonmaskable Interrupts (NMI), which equate to an F002 blue screen error code under Windows NT.

Upgrading your system memory offers at least three benefits. It cuts down the requests to page memory to disk, thereby increasing overall performance (memory access is in the nanosecond range, whereas disk access is in the millisecond range). The additional memory can be used by the Cache Manager to cache both local and network I/O requests, thereby increasing both local disk and remote disk data access requests. And finally, you can increase the performance of your SQL Server by preallocating a larger amount of system memory for SQL Server's use, creating the tempdb (the temporary database is used to process temporary tables created by SQL Server on your behalf to answer a query or to sort your tables) in RAM, or using both these options.

Windows NT can perform as well as, if not better than, most caching disk controllers with the addition of the same amount of RAM. If you compare a caching controller with 16MB of RAM and Windows NT Server with an additional 16MB of RAM, for example, you will find that the performance is about the same. This is because the caching controller is limited by the expansion bus to transfer the requested data, whereas the Cache Manager uses system memory and therefore accesses cached data based on the memory bus speed. If the caching controller only has 4MB of RAM, even the base installation of Windows NT (with 16MB of RAM and no caching disk controller) performs as well as, if not better than, the same system with a caching disk controller. You also should consider that there are very few caching disk controllers supported by Windows NT. These types of controllers require specific device driver support in order to use the cache on the disk controller. Most device drivers for caching disk controllers turn off the cache when used with Windows NT.

Tip

If you have an EISA-based computer, make sure that the EISA memory setting (based on the EISA Setup utility disk application) correctly identifies the amount of physical memory you have installed on your system. If it does not, Windows NT uses the ISA setting (what it finds based on the BIOS setting), which may limit the amount of memory that Windows NT uses.

12

YOUR MICROSOFT NETWORK

HARDWARE RAID ALTERNATIVES

When you are selecting a disk subsystem, keep in mind that, if you have the budget, nothing performs better than a hardware RAID system. This is because a hardware-based RAID device generally has an internal battery backed up memory buffer (in case a power failure occurs during a disk write), which adds additional fault tolerance over a software-based RAID solution. It also has its own processor so that the overhead involved in calculating the ECC stripe is performed by the disk controller rather than the host processor.

Note

This discussion focuses only on the use of a RAID 5 solution, although there are several RAID levels currently in use with Windows NT Server. This includes RAID 0 (data striping), RAID 1 (disk mirroring), and RAID 5 (striping with parity). RAID levels 2, 3, and 4 generally are used by higher-end mainframes instead of with Windows NT. And each of these levels is just a slightly different variation of a stripe set with parity.

With a hardware RAID system, you also can mirror these RAID drives in software with Windows NT. Or, you can even go so far as to stripe multiple RAID drives, because NT sees these RAID drives as a single logical drive. If you stripe them, there is no need to use a stripe set with parity because this already is being performed on the hardware level. Another advantage of the hardware-based RAID solution is that most of these systems support hot swapping of a failed disk drive. Hot swapping is the capability to change a failed disk drive for a new working drive without powering off the entire computer system. After the drive is replaced, the RAID controller begins to rebuild the missing data blocks based on the available data blocks and ECC blocks in the background. Replacing a software-based RAID solution requires powering off the system to replace the drive. Then, after your system is powered back up, you need to use the Disk Administrator to regenerate the missing data.

Tip

When selecting your disk drives for a RAID solution, either hardware- or software-based, it is better to choose smaller and more disk drives rather than larger and fewer disk drives to build an equivalent logical drive. Suppose that you want about a 5GB logical drive. You could select six 1GB disk drives or three 2GB drives for a maximum logical drive of 4.8GB (RAID drives use one-fifth of the storage for the ECC stripe). Either solution gives the exact same logical drive size, but the unit based on the six 1GB drives generally outperforms the unit based on three 2GB drives.

ADDING ADDITIONAL NETWORK ADAPTERS

Even if you have an optimized disk subsystem, multiple processors, and an abundance of physical RAM, your network server will not perform well if it has a slow network adapter or too many network requests to handle. And when you take the time to consider it, if you only have one network adapter installed on your server, it had better be a 100MB FDDI or Fast Ethernet adapter if you want to get the data out to your network clients as quickly as possible. And you may even want to use more than one adapter for a couple of reasons.

Note

Although I mention 100MB network adapters in this section, you do not need them to obtain increased performance. You can get the same benefits by using the techniques discussed later in this section for 10MB network adapters.

First consider the network transports you will be using. If they are all bound to one network adapter, then that adapter constantly will be changing modes to send out a broadcast name to find an associated resource when a network request is received. Assume that you are looking for a NetWare client using the IPX/SPX transport, for example. In order to find this client, your server probably will send out name requests over the NetBEUI, TCP/IP, and IPX/SPX (assuming that this is the default binding order you have established) transport protocols—and all through the same adapter. After the client is found, all further requests are routed just through the IPX/SPX protocol. But the time it takes to switch modes and send out these name requests and process them is just wasted and decreases the capability of your server to process additional client requests over that same adapter, thereby decreasing overall network throughput.

To increase your network throughput, you can change your default binding order to use the most requested network transport. Assume that you are using one adapter with multiple network transports (NetBEUI, TCP/IP, and IPX/SPX, for example). Also assume that you have an integrated network with Windows NT Server, UNIX, LAN Manager, and Novell servers along with Windows NT, Windows for Workgroups,

12

YOUR MICROSOFT NETWORK

and Novell clients. About 75 percent of these clients use TCP/IP and 15 percent use IPX/SPX, with the remaining 10 percent using NetBEUI as their primary transport. In this case, you can achieve the best client support by changing the binding order for the Server service to TCP/IP, IPX/SPX, and then NetBEUI. By changing the binding order to move the most frequent protocol to the top of the chain, you decrease the overhead involved in servicing the clients that use this protocol, thereby increasing client performance.

Note

The Server service is used by clients that access your server. This service provides the means to share your network resources. The Workstation service is used by your server to access other servers' shared resources (when it is a client rather than a server).

You modify the binding order by following these steps:

1. Open the Control Panel Network applet and access the Network Settings dialog box, as shown in Figure 12.4.

Figure 12.4.
The Network
Settings dialog
box.

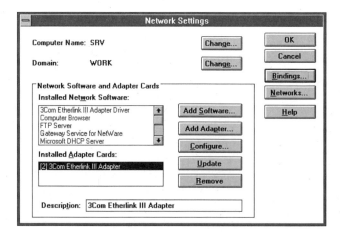

2. Click the Bindings button to access the dialog box shown in Figure 12.5.

3. To change the binding order for the Server service, first select Server from the Show Bindings For drop-down listbox. The Network Bindings dialog box appears, which should look similar to the dialog box shown in Figure 12.6.

Figure 12.5.
The default
Network Bind-
ings dialog box.

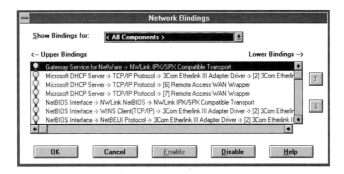

Figure 12.6.
The Server service
bindings dis-
played in the
Network Bind-
ings dialog box.

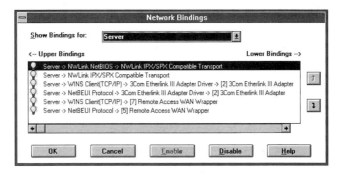

4. Notice that the uppermost binding is NetBIOS; this appears before the IPX/
SPX Compatible Transport because it is Microsoft's default binding order.
Select the WINS Client (TCP/IP) and then click on the up arrow to the right
of the box to move this protocol to the top, as shown in Figure 12.7. This
changes the default binding order to TCP/IP, NetBIOS, IPX/SPX, and then
NetBEUI for your network adapter.

Figure 12.7.
The modified
Server service
bindings.

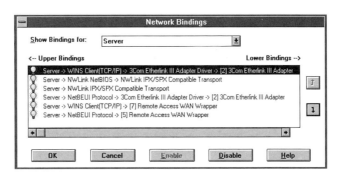

12

YOUR MICROSOFT NETWORK

Note

> If you are not using DHCP and WINS on your Windows NT Server, your binding listing may list TCP/IP instead of WINS Client (TCP/IP).

5. Repeat these steps for the Workstation, NETBIOS Interface, and Remote Access Server service to change their binding orders as well.

As an additional performance option, you can use multiple network adapters, with each adapter bound to a single network transport. You follow a similar procedure as the preceding list, but instead of changing the binding order, you can just disable the bindings for the transports you do not want supported on the particular network adapter. Just follow these steps:

1. Open the Control Panel Network applet and access the Network Settings dialog box. Then click the Bindings button to access the default Network Bindings dialog box.

2. Select the appropriate protocol in the Show Bindings For drop-down listbox. In the example shown in Figure 12.8, the TCP/IP Protocol is selected.

Figure 12.8.
The TCP/IP
Protocol bindings
for the Network
Bindings dialog
box.

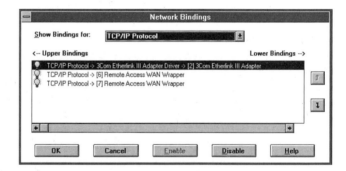

3. Select the transport binding for the appropriate network adapter.

4. Click the Disable button. Figure 12.9 shows the disabled network transport protocol. Instead of a bright yellow lightbulb, the disabled protocol shows a gray (dimmed) lightbulb, indicating that the binding has been disabled.

Note

> In this example, I selected the Etherlink III adapter, and because this is my only physical network adapter, if I disable it, I will be able to share resources only with the TCP/IP protocol for remote access clients. The Remote Access WAN Wrapper is a wrapper around a logical network adapter (the modem, for example).

Figure 12.9.
Disabling the
TCP/IP Protocol
bindings for an
Etherlink III
network adapter.

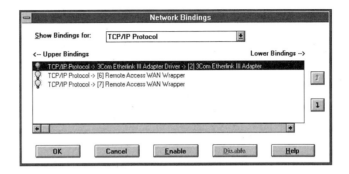

If you want to increase network performance, you may even want to go so far as to use multiple network adapters to split your entire network into discrete components, commonly referred to as segments. This limits the impact these network clients have on each other for accessing resources. The network client request requires access to a resource outside its default segment only if it will impact other network client users. If you use segments on a TCP/IP-based network, however, each network adapter physically installed on your server must have its own IP address, and in order to route network requests from one segment to the other, you must enable IP routing.

This can be accomplished with these basic steps:

1. Open the Network Control Panel applet. The Network Settings dialog box appears.

2. Select the TCP/IP Protocol in the Installed Network Software listbox and click the Add Software button. The TCP/IP Configuration dialog box appears.

3. Click the Advanced button. The Advanced Microsoft TCP/IP Configuration dialog box appears. Then enable the IP Routing checkbox.

4. Work your way back by clicking the OK button as prompted, and then reboot your computer when prompted for the changes to be put into effect.

ADDING PROCESSORS

Windows NT Server is more processor intensive than other network operating systems such as Novell NetWare or UNIX on identical hardware platforms. So, in most cases, adding an additional processor to a uniprocessor platform can make a significant difference in network throughput or an application server's (such as SQL Server) performance. This performance increase is not quite two-fold for a dual-processor system, however. And as you increase the number of processors, this performance ratio decreases. As it stands now, four processors give the greatest

12

multiprocessor benefit on standard Intel (Pentium) platforms. This is because most motherboard manufacturers use the Intel multiprocessor support chipset, which supports only four processors. Supporting more than four processors depends on the proprietary design of the system motherboard.

The problem with multiple processors is that the Windows NT design model requires that all processors have equal access to all system resources. That is what the symmetric multiprocessing model defines. This means that the overhead involved in synchronizing access to hardware resources (such as an I/O port on a SCSI controller) increases as you add additional processors. Even problems with cache management cause grief because each processor generally has its own secondary cache, and as a thread is moved from one processor to another processor, the cache must be flushed in order to ensure the integrity of system memory. All these little problems begin to build, until adding additional processors no longer increases performance, or at best only increases it a small fraction.

Tip

One of the interesting keys I've found in the Registry is the one that specifies how many processors are supported on a particular multiprocessor hardware abstraction layer (HAL). If you look in `HKEY_LOCAL_MACHINE\SYSTEM\CurrentControlSet\Control\SessionManager`, you will find the value RegisteredProcessors. This entry normally has a maximum setting of 4 for Windows NT Server or 2 for Windows NT Workstation. You can increase this value to support additional processors, however, if your HAL can support them and thereby increase performance on some platforms. The performance increase is based on the architecture of the particular platform; some will perform better than others, even if they have the same number of processors.

SUMMARY

In this chapter, you looked at some of the basic performance tuning issues and trade-offs. For the most part, tuning your server consists of the following:

◆ Choosing the right hardware platform and expansion bus to maximize performance of your peripherals

◆ Optimizing your disk subsystem to provide the maximum benefit for virtual memory usage and file sharing

◆ Configuring your application tasking options to optimize the time each process uses before the next process gets its chance and the Server service improves the Server response time.

- Upgrading your hardware by increasing the amount of physical memory or adding a hardware-based RAID solution
- Balancing the load of your network subsystem by adding additional network adapters
- Increasing processing performance by adding additional processors

In the next chapter, you will look at using the Performance Monitor to isolate bottlenecks so that you will know which components need to be modified or upgraded.

12

YOUR MICROSOFT NETWORK

CHAPTER 13

Tuning Your Server

In this chapter, you will learn how to use the Performance Monitor to isolate performance bottlenecks and what you can do about them. You also will use the Performance Monitor in other chapters to help you tune the additional BackOffice components, so gaining a basic understanding of its usage is quite important. If you find that the Performance Monitor is just not your cup of tea for performance tuning, it still can be useful for generating alerts. An alert is a means of notifying you of a problem, such as when a server is short on disk space.

This discussion starts with the basic functions of the Performance Monitor, including creating and configuring charts, logs, reports, and alerts. You then will move on to specific performance-tuning examples. In these examples, you will touch on the topics of finding processor, memory, disk, and network bottlenecks.

Note

> Keep in mind that this subject can be very complex (performance tuning with the Performance Monitor is an art, not an exact science). Entire books are devoted to just this particular program and its usage, so it may take some time for you to really get the hang of using the Performance Monitor and the associated performance counters.

PERFORMANCE TUNING WITH THE PERFORMANCE MONITOR

You use the Performance Monitor to monitor a system in real time. This means that the event objects you monitor are occurring right now, and the value you see for the event object reflects the actual value of the event object with a minimal time lag. You can use the Performance Monitor on the computer you want to monitor, which will affect the performance on that computer slightly. Or, you can use it remotely from another computer, which impacts your network bandwidth more than it does the performance of the computer you are monitoring. The amount of performance degradation varies from unnoticeable to appreciable, depending on the number and frequency of monitored events.

The Performance Monitor defines events as objects. An object is an item such as the system, processor, process, thread, or similar item. Objects are divided further into counters. The system object includes counters for %Total Processor Time (total amount of processor usage on the system), %Total Interrupt Time (total number of interrupts generated on the system), %Total Privileged Time (total amount of processor time spent in the kernel on the system), and so on. And within a counter, you also may have one or more instances. If you have more than one processor on your system and view the processor counter %Processor Time (total amount of the processor used), you will find multiple entries in the Instance field. Instance counts start with 0 and increase by 1 for each additional item. If you have two processors, your Instance field will include 0 for the first processor and 1 for the second processor. You also can have multiple named instances rather than numbers. If you monitor the RAS Port object counter, for example, the Instance field can include COM1, COM2, COM3, and up to as many RAS connections as you have installed.

Note

A complete list of the performance counters you can use with Windows NT Server and other BackOffice components is included in Appendix C, "The Performance Monitor Objects," which is located on the CD-ROM. If you add other third-party components, you may have additional object counters not included in the appendix.

The Performance Monitor supports four types of views; each displays the performance object counters in a different format to provide you with unique capabilities. These views follow:

◆ Chart: This view can display values for performance counters in a line (graph) or bar (histogram) chart. This is the most useful view to use to quickly display performance data over a period of time with a line chart or performance peaks with a histogram chart. This view can become cluttered and difficult to read if you attempt to view more than 10 active performance counters.

◆ Log: This view is used to capture all the performance counters for a particular object to a file. This captured file may be read into the Performance Monitor at a later date for in-depth analysis. You can load in a log file and then chart it, for example.

Tip

When using the Log view, you should remember that you can view only object counters that you have previously captured. You do not have to view all the object counters that you did capture, however. You can select a subset of these counters to view. This is one way to start with the big picture and then narrow it down to a specific incident. So it is always better to capture any performance counters that you think you might need, instead of limiting the capture to a few specific performance counters that you know you will need.

◆ Report: This view is used to display a large series of performance object counter values in real time. It is an instantaneous view of the performance counters, so you can view only the current value. This value changes at the next update interval, which means that the value you are monitoring may be reset to zero before you can evaluate it depending on the update interval frequency.

◆ Alert: This view is used to set conditions based on performance object counters and to alert you when this condition is met. You may want to be informed when your server's paging file grows beyond its current minimum allocation, for example. This way, you can increase the minimum allocation size and increase overall system performance because any time a paging file grows beyond the minimum size, there is a significant amount of overhead involved in expanding the page file. Additionally, any page file expansion may be fragmented, which slows down retrieval of paged data.

THE PERFORMANCE MONITOR TOOLBAR

The Performance Monitor toolbar, as shown in Figure 13.1, provides quick access to the Performance Monitor feature set.

Figure 13.1.
The Performance
Monitor toolbar.

Table 13.1 lists each toolbar button and the function it performs.

TABLE 13.1. THE PERFORMANCE MONITOR TOOLBAR.

Icon	Button Name	Function
	View a Chart	Changes the default view to the Chart view.
	View the Alerts	Changes the default view to the Alert view.
	View Output Log	Changes the default File Status view to the Log view.
	View Report Data	Changes the default view to the Report view.
 +	Add Counter	Displays the Add To Item dialog box, where Item can be Chart, Alert, Log, or Report. Use this as a quick mechanism to add performance object counters.

Icon	Button Name	Function
	Modify Selected Counter	After you select an object counter in the legend and click this button, the Edit Item Entry dialog box appears. Here, you can change the item's color, scale, line width, and line style if viewing a chart or other attributes for alerts, logs, and reports.
	Delete Selected Counter	Deletes the object counter selected in the legend from a chart, alert, log, or report.
	Update Counter Data	Updates the display after you set the update time to Manual Update.
	Place a Commented Bookmark into the Output Log	Inserts a comment into a log file to refresh your memory of the usage of captured object counters.
	Options	Displays the Options dialog box for the selected view.

CREATING CHARTS

Creating a chart consists of selecting the performance objects, configuring the view, and then saving the chart for future use. You can follow these steps to create the chart:

1. Make sure that the default view is for a chart, as shown in Figure 13.2. If a different view is displayed, you can click the View a Chart button on the toolbar, choose Chart from the View menu, or press Ctrl+C.

2. Choose Add to Chart from the Edit menu, click the Add Counter button on the toolbar, or press Ctrl+I. The Add to Chart dialog box appears, as displayed in Figure 13.3. You use this dialog box to select the performance object counters to monitor.

3. In the Object drop-down listbox, choose the event type (performance object) to monitor.

4. In the Counter drop-down listbox, choose the event subtype (object counter) to monitor.

Figure 13.2.
The Performance
Monitor Chart
view.

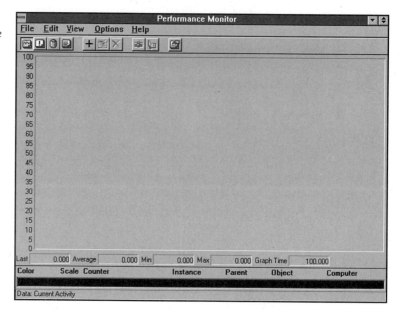

Figure 13.3.
The Add to Chart
dialog box.

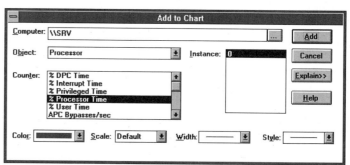

Tip

If you are unsure of the object counter's properties, click the Explain button. This expands the Add to Chart dialog box and displays a short description of the counter.

5. In the Instance box, choose an instance of the object counter, if applicable. An instance is used to differentiate between one or more occurrences of an object counter. Not all object counters will include an instance number.

Tip

> You can select a different source to monitor by specifying the name of a remote computer in the Computer field. Or you can click the button at the end of the Computer field to display the Select Computer dialog box, where you can browse the network for the computer you want to monitor. After you select the computer, repeat steps 3 through 5. This can be particularly useful if you want to monitor multiple servers simultaneously for comparison.

6. In the Color drop-down listbox, select a color to specify a different color for the performance object counter to use for its display.

7. In the Scale drop-down listbox, select a multiplier or divisor to change the default scale for the object counter. This can be very useful when a performance counter peaks at the top of the chart or is too low to be readily visible.

8. In the Width drop-down listbox, change the line thickness displayed in the chart.

9. In the Style drop-down listbox, select a pattern to change the line from a solid line to a series of dashes or dots to differentiate chart lines of the same color.

10. After you make all your choices, click the Add button to add the object counter to the Performance Monitor's display list.

11. Repeat steps 2 through 10 for each object counter to monitor. When you finish, click the Done button to return to the Performance Monitor Chart view.

Tip

> To select a range of object counters, select the first counter in the range. Then, while pressing the Shift key, select the last counter in the range. To select noncontiguous items, select the first counter and then, while pressing the Ctrl key, select the next counter. Repeat this process for each counter. Repeat these steps for the Instance field if you want to monitor multiple object counters for multiple instances. The Performance Monitor automatically selects a color and line width for each item.

To modify the chart configuration, choose Chart | Options to display the Chart Options dialog box, where you can select the following items:

◆ Legend: Displays a map legend at the bottom of the chart that contains each monitored item. This includes the color of the item, item name, instance, parent, object, and computer.

◆ Value Bar: Displayed just above the legend and contains the last value, average value, minimum value, maximum value, and graph time of a selected legend item. The graph time is the time it takes in seconds for a performance counter to completely fill the display area.

◆ Vertical Grid: Subdivides the vertical chart axis. When selected, vertical reference lines are drawn on the displayed window.

◆ Horizontal Grid: Subdivides the horizontal chart axis. When selected, horizontal reference lines are drawn on the displayed window.

◆ Vertical Labels: Enables or disables the vertical scale numbers displayed at the left of the chart window.

◆ Gallery: Selects the chart type. You can display a line chart by selecting the Graph option or a bar chart by selecting the Histogram option.

◆ Vertical Maximum: Specifies a different maximum scale for the vertical axis. The default is 100.

◆ Update Time: Specifies the time when the chart should be updated. You can specify to automatically update the chart by supplying a value (in seconds) for the Periodic Update option or a manual chart update by choosing the Manual Update option. If you select the Manual Update option, the chart is updated only after you choose Options | Update Now, click the Update Counter Now toolbar button, or press Ctrl+U.

After all this work, you should save the chart in case you want to use it again. Choose the File | Save Chart Settings As option to display the familiar File Save As dialog box the first time you save the chart or to just update the file thereafter; here you can specify the filename and directory to store the file. To load a previously saved chart, choose File | Open.

Tip

To save all Performance Monitor views (Chart, Log, Report, and Alert), choose File | Save Workspace. This saves all chart views and the selected performance counter objects, along with the window placement, to a file.

CREATING LOGS

Creating a log consists of selecting the performance objects, configuring the log options, and then starting the log capture. After you capture performance data to a log, you can load this data back into the Performance Monitor for analysis.

Follow these steps to create the log:

1. Make sure that the default view, as shown in Figure 13.4, is for a log. If a different view is displayed, you can click the View Output Log File Status button on the toolbar, choose Log from the View menu, or press Ctrl+L.

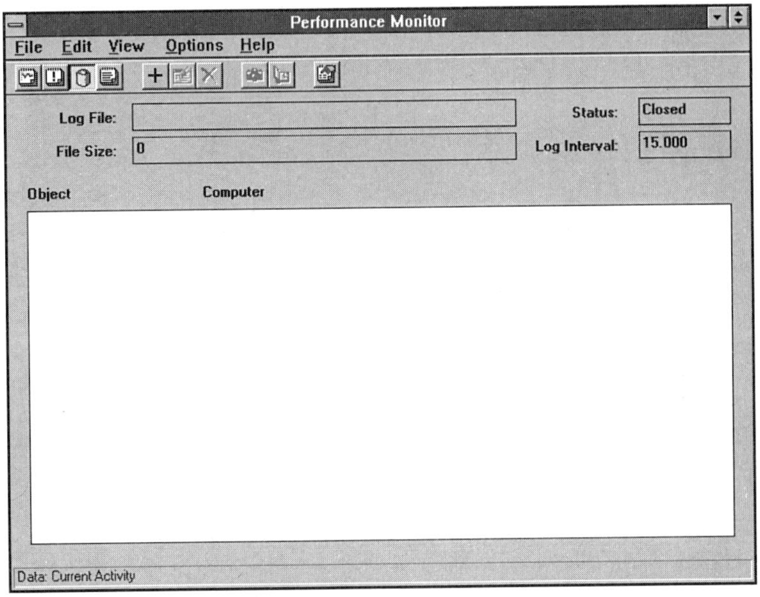

Figure 13.4.
The Performance
Monitor Log view.

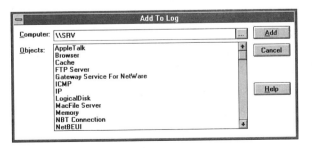

2. Choose Add to Log from the Edit menu, click the Add Counter button on the toolbar, or press Ctrl+I. Any of these commands displays the Add to Log dialog box shown in Figure 13.5.

Figure 13.5.
The Add to Log
dialog box.

3. You use the Add to Log dialog box to select the performance object to monitor. To select an object, highlight the object in the Objects listbox and then click the Add button. To select a range of object counters, select the first counter in the range and, while pressing the Shift key, select the last counter in the range. To select noncontiguous items, select the first counter and, while pressing the Ctrl key, select the next counter.

Tip

If you are unsure of the events to monitor for your first time use, select them all. Only capture these events for a maximum of five minutes, however, because the log file can become quite large.

4. After you make your choices, the Cancel button changes to the Done button. Click this button to return to the Performance Monitor's main window.

5. Now all the performance objects are listed in the Log window. However, you are not ready to capture data yet. First you have to modify the log options to specify a file to place the captured data in, and you need to specify an update interval. These features are accessible from the Log Options dialog box. To display this dialog box, choose Log from the Options menu, press the Options button on the toolbar, or press Ctrl+O.

Note

After you access the Log Options dialog box, you can automatically update the log by specifying a value (in seconds) for the Periodic Update option. To manually update the log, select the Manual Update option. If you select the Manual Update option, the chart is updated only after you choose Update Now from the Options menu, click the Update Counter Data button on the toolbar, or press Ctrl+U.

6. To start your data capture, click the Start Log button in the Log Options dialog box. After this option is enabled, the Status field changes from Closed to Open, and the File Size field displays the size of the data capture file. The longer you capture data, the larger this file will be, so you should not capture data on a drive containing your network client files, because this could prevent a client from being able to save its data files. Of course, this assumes that you are capturing a large amount of data over a significant amount of time.

After you capture all the data you want for analysis, open the Log Options dialog box and click the Stop Log button to close the log file. To actually use this captured data, choose Options | Data From to display the Data From dialog box, where you can load a log file. After you load a log file, you can chart it or use it to generate alerts or reports. You also can change the object to log by redisplaying the Add to Log dialog box and adding additional objects. Before you can append these new objects, however, you must be sure to select the Options | Data From menu option and change the setting from Log File to Current Activity. You then can click the Start button in the Log Options dialog box to append your data to the capture file.

Tip

Don't forget to save your log options by choosing the File | Save Log Setting As menu option.

CREATING REPORTS

The Report view is useful for viewing large amounts of performance object counters simultaneously. The only hitch is that the counter values displayed are always the last known value of the particular counter. You cannot view a series of values over a period of time. Only a Chart view in Line Graph mode can display a series of counter data over a period of time. You will find the Report view most useful for monitoring complex items, such as your entire network.

Network-related counters, for example, include objects such as AppleTalk, Browser, FTP Server, ICMP, IP, Gateway Services for NetWare, MacFile Server, NBT Connections, NetBEUI, NetBEUI Resource, Network Interface, Network Segment, NWLink IPX, NWLink SPX, NWLink NetBIOS, RAS Port, RAS Total, Redirector, Server, Server Work Queues, TCP, UDP, and WINS Server. Now that is an awful lot of object counters to monitor. And if you have installed other network components or third-party products, you may have even more object counters.

To create a report, follow these steps:

1. Make sure that the default view, as shown in Figure 13.6, is for a report. If a different view is displayed, you can click the View Report Data button on the toolbar, choose Report from the View menu, or press Ctrl+R.

2. Choose Add to Report from the Edit menu, click the Add Counter button on the toolbar, or press Ctrl+I. Any of these actions displays the Add to Report dialog box, as shown in Figure 13.7. This dialog box is similar to the Add to Chart dialog box, and is used to select the performance object counters to monitor.

3. In the Object drop-down list, choose the event type (performance object) to monitor.

4. In the Counter drop-down listbox, choose the event subtype (object counter) to monitor.

Figure 13.6.
The Performance
Monitor Report
view.

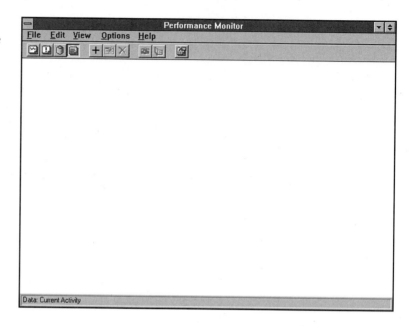

Figure 13.7.
The Add to
Report dialog box.

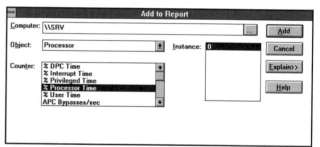

Tip

If you are unsure of the counter's properties, click the Explain button.
This expands the Add to Report dialog box and displays a short
description of the counter.

5. In the Instance box, choose an instance of the object counter, if applicable.

Tip

You can select a different computer to monitor by specifying the name
of a remote computer in the Computer field. After you select the
computer, repeat steps 3 through 5. This field is very useful for
monitoring multiple servers simultaneously to quickly check the load
of a particular server.

6. After you make all your choices, click the Add button to add the object counter to the Performance Monitor's display list.

7. Repeat steps 2 through 6 for each object counter to monitor. When you finish, click the Done button to return to the Performance Monitor Report view.

Tip

Don't forget to save your report configuration by choosing the File | Save Report Settings As menu option. You never know when you might want to use this configuration again.

CREATING ALERTS

Using the Alert view is the best way to be informed automatically of a problem with your server. You can use this view to receive notifications of low disk space, high processor utilization, network errors, or items that concern you. One thing to keep in mind about alerts is that an alert can be sent only if the Performance Monitor is running. If you want to automate specific alerts, then you should obtain the Windows NT Resource Kit or check the Microsoft FTP site (ftp.microsoft.com) for a downloadable copy. This includes the DATALOG.EXE program, which can perform the same alerting and logging features of Performance Monitor but runs as a service. You use the MONITOR.EXE program to install the service and stop and start the alert or logging features.

Note

In order to use MONITOR.EXE, you first must create a Performance Monitor workspace file containing your alert and log settings. If you will be monitoring any activity on a remote computer, be sure to create a user account with sufficient network privileges. When configuring the service startup values, configure the service to use the Logon Account option in the Log on As group.

To create an alert, follow these steps:

1. Make sure that the default view, as shown in Figure 13.8, is for an alert. If a different view is displayed, you can click the View the Alerts button on the toolbar, choose Alerts from the View menu, or press Ctrl+A.

2. Choose Add to Report from the Edit menu, click the Add Counter button on the toolbar, or press Ctrl+I. The Add to Alert dialog box appears, in which you can select the performance object counters to monitor. (See Figure 13.9.)

Figure 13.8.
The Performance
Monitor Alert
view.

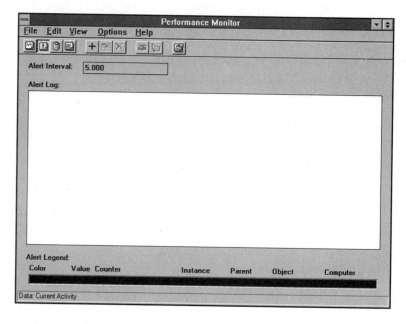

Figure 13.9.
The Add to Alert
dialog box.

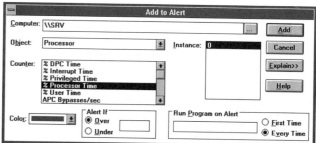

3. In the Object drop-down listbox, choose the event type (performance object) to monitor.

4. In the Counter drop-down listbox, choose the event subtype (object counter) to monitor.

Tip

If you are not sure what the object counter is used for, click the Explain button. This expands the dialog box and displays a short description of the counter.

5. In the Instance box, choose an instance of the object counter, if applicable. An instance differentiates between one or more occurrences of an object counter, and not all object counters include an instance number.

6. In the Color drop-down listbox, specify a different color for the performance object counter to use for its display.

7. In the Alert If group, choose Over or Under and specify a value in the data field for the alert condition. If you want an alert sent when your disk drive has less than 10MB free, for example, you should choose the LogicalDisk object, the Free Megabytes counter, select the Under radio button, and specify the value as 10.

Tip

> To specify the same alert condition for multiple instances (like two or more logical disks), select a range of instances by highlighting the first instance in the range and, while pressing the Shift key, select the last instance in the range. To select a noncontiguous range, select the first instance. Then, while pressing the Ctrl key, select the next instance. Repeat this process for each instance. The Performance Monitor automatically selects a color for each instance.

8. In the Run Program on Alert field, you can specify a command line to be executed every time the alert condition is met (Every Time) or only the first time the alert condition is met (First Time) by enabling the corresponding radio button.

Tip

> The Run Program on Alert option is particularly useful if you have a pager and a command-line program that can be used to dial up your pager and send you a notification message.

9. After you make all your choices, click the Add button to add the object counter to the Performance Monitor's display list.

10. Repeat steps 2 through 9 for each object counter to monitor. When you finish, click the Done button to return to the Performance Monitor Alert view.

To modify the alert configuration, choose Options | Alert, which displays the Alert Options dialog box shown in Figure 13.10.

Figure 13.10.
The Alert Options
dialog box.

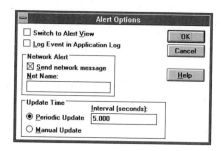

In the Alert Options dialog box, you can select these items:

◆ Switch to Alert View: Automatically switches the Performance Monitor to the Alert view when an alert condition is met.

◆ Log Event in Application Log: Logs the alert condition in the computer's application log.

◆ Send Network Message: Broadcasts a message to the domain users specifying the alert condition. To send a message to a specific user, enter a name in the Net Name field. You can specify a name from a different domain by prefacing the user name with the domain name (DomainName\UserName).

◆ Update Time: Specifies the alert update interval. You can specify an automatic update interval by specifying a value (in seconds) for the Periodic Update option or a manual alert update interval by choosing the Manual Update option. If you select a manual update option, the alert conditions are checked only after you choose Options | Update Now, click the Update Counter Now toolbar button, or press Ctrl+U.

Tip

It is a good idea to save the alert settings by choosing File | Save Alert Settings As and specifying a file in which to save your settings.

Not all performance object counters are useful for specifying alert conditions. The object counters I find most useful, and which you might find useful as well, are summarized in Table 13.2.

Table 13.2. Performance object counters for alerts.

Object	Counter	Instance	Condition	Description
LogicalDisk	% Free Space	Per Drive	Under	Useful for notification in a low free space situation. Specify the minimum percentage of free space per drive in the Alert If value field. Set this value to 10 or higher for useful warnings. Any value less than this may notify you too late for your users' comfort.
LogicalDisk	Free Megabytes	Per Drive	Under	Useful for notification in a low disk space situation. Specify the minimum free space in MB in the Alert If value field. On a large drive (more than 1GB), set this value to 100 or less if you want to run on the ragged edge.
Memory	Pages/sec	5 to 10	Over	Set this to 5 for a notification that the system is paging too often and as an indication that a memory upgrade may improve performance if consistent alerts are sent. Set this value to 10 to be

continues

TABLE 13.2. CONTINUED

Object	Counter	Instance	Condition	Description
				notified that a memory upgrade is required because the system definitely is paging too much.
Network Interface	Current Bandwidth	Per Network Transport Protocol	Over	Set this value to 50000000 (in bits per second) for a notification that your network transport protocol has reached 50 percent capacity.
Network Segment	%Network Utilization	Per Network Adapter	Over	Set this value to 50 for a notification that your network segment has reached 50 percent of its carrying capacity.
Redirector	Network Errors/sec	N/A	Over	If you have any errors, you should spend more time isolating the error, so this value should be sent to 1.
Server	Error System	N/A	Over	Any value greater than 1 indicates a problem with the server. If a problem is detected, you should examine the system log for the cause of the error or spend some time with the Performance Monitor, as

Object	Counter	Instance	Condition	Description
				specified in the "Finding Network Bottlenecks" section, later in this chapter, to help isolate the cause.
Server	Errors Logon	N/A	Over	Notifies you that someone is attempting to hack into your system. A good threshold value is from 3 to 10.
Server	Errors Access Permissions	N/A	Over	Informs you of potential users trying to access files they should not be attempting to access in order to gain access to privileged data. A good threshold value is from 3 to 10.
Server	Pool Nonpaged Failures	N/A	Over	Should be set to 1 because this indicates a lack of nonpageable memory for the server service. An error indicates that the server will be unable to process a client request for lack of resources. This value also may indicate a physical memory shortage.

continues

TABLE 13.2. CONTINUED

Object	Counter	Instance	Condition	Description
Server	Pool Paged Bytes	N/A	Over	Should be set to 1 because this indicates a lack of pageable memory for the server service. An error indicates that the server will be unable to process a client request due to a lack of re sources. This value also indicates a physical memory shortage or that the pagefile setting is too low.
Server Work Queues	Work Item Shortages	Over	Per Network Adapter	Should be set to 0 because any indica- tion represents a problem with the server service. If errors are encoun tered, the MaxWorkItems value should be increased.

PERFORMANCE TUNING

Performance tuning is based on finding your bottleneck (the item causing a performance limitation) and then doing something to correct the situation. The primary goal with performance tuning is to provide adequate system performance. And this basically falls into four categories: the processor, memory, disk subsystem, and network. If these components are performing well, your users generally will not complain to you about system performance. This section looks at each of these areas and provides example Performance Monitor workspaces to illustrate the process of finding bottlenecks in these areas. You will also look into some of the performance objects and counters, to aid you in your Internet Information Server optimization efforts.

Note

You can find sample Performance Monitor charts, alerts, reports, logs, and workspace files in the \MBADMIN\Projects\UPS Monitor Service subdirectory on the CD-ROM included with this book.

One thing to consider about performance bottlenecks is that when you find and solve one bottleneck, it always exposes another bottleneck. Look at an example that helps illustrate this point.

Suppose that you have a server with a 100MHz Pentium processor, 32MB of main memory, a really fast pair of EIDE disk drives, an EIDE disk controller, and a 16-bit network adapter. Your primary concern is providing a fast user response time for shared files and SQL Server access. Where do you think the performance bottleneck would be? The processor? Memory? The disk subsystem? The network adapter? Well, based on my experience, it would turn out to be the disk subsystem. This would be caused by the EIDE controller. This controller would use the standard ATDISK driver provided with Windows NT Server. And this driver can support only one pending I/O request at a time. It's not really the fault of the driver, though. Instead, it is the hardware it supports. Almost all IDE (and EIDE) disk controllers use programmed I/O (or PIO). A PIO controller uses the processor to move data from the disk, through the disk controller, and to system memory. This requires a high percentage of processor time and limits the device to one I/O request at a time.

The solution would be to replace the EIDE disks and controller with SCSI disk drives and a bus master SCSI controller that supports direct memory access (DMA). A bus master controller that supports DMA moves data from the disk to system memory without processor intervention. Although, even here, you need to exercise good judgment. Don't choose an 8-bit or 16-bit SCSI controller if you have a 32-bit expansion bus. Both these require that you copy data from the disk drive to memory below 1MB for an 8-bit controller and below 16MB for a 16-bit controller. This data then must be copied to the application or system buffer above 16MB if you have more than 16MB installed on your system. This coping of data is referred to as double buffering, and it can severely hamper system performance.

Instead, choose a 32-bit SCSI bus master controller. The basic idea is to choose a disk controller with the largest I/O bus that your expansion bus supports for the fastest data-transfer rate. But now that you have increased the performance of your I/O subsystem (and performance does increase compared to the base system), another performance bottleneck may be exposed. This most likely would be the processor. SQL Server can be very processor intensive. Adding an additional Pentium processor and dedicating this processor to SQL Server increases SQL Server performance. And once this has occurred, you'll probably find that replacing your network adapter with a 32-bit network adapter and adding additional memory increases performance even more. And this can go on and on. Literally, forever. Eventually, you have to draw the line based on your budget and your acceptable performance requirements.

FINDING PROCESSOR BOTTLENECKS

Finding processor bottlenecks on your server is not an easy task, but it is possible. The starting point is to use the performance counters that I have included in Processor.pmw on the CD-ROM. This workspace file includes Processor Chart, Alert, and Report View settings. These object counters are listed in Table 13.3, which includes a description of each object counter.

TABLE 13.3. PROCESSOR PERFORMANCE OBJECT COUNTERS.

Object	Counter	Instance	Parent	Description
System	% Total Processor Time	N/A	N/A	Percentage of processor time currently in use on your system. The basic formula for calculation is ((% CPU in Use on CPU 0) + (% CPU in Use on CPU1)... + (% CPU in Use on CPU x)) / Total number of CPUs.
System	System Calls/ sec	N/A	N/A	Number of system service calls executed per second. If this value is lower than the number of interrupts/ sec, then this indicates that a hardware adapter is generating excessive interrupts.
System	Context Switches/ sec	N/A	N/A	Frequency of switches between executing threads. A high value

Object	Counter	Instance	Parent	Description
				indicates that a program's usage of critical sections or semaphores should have a higher priority to achieve a higher through-put and less task switching.
System	Processor Queue Length	N/A	N/A	Number of threads waiting in the processor queue for processor cycles. A consistent value of 2 or higher indicates a processor bottleneck. This value always is 0 unless at least one thread is being monitored.
System	Inter-rupts/sec	Per Processor	N/A	Number of interrupts the system is servicing.
Thread	% Processor Time	Per Processor	Idle	Percentage of processor time the thread is using.

The first step to finding a processor bottleneck is obtaining a baseline chart to gain a familiarity with your system in an idle state. (See Figure 13.11.) Then you should use the same counters to obtain a baseline in a normal working state.

The next step is to use these counters on an active system. Examine the % Total Processor Time statistic. If this value is consistently more than 90 percent, then you have a processor bottleneck. It then is time to examine each process in the system to see which one is using more of the processor than it should. If you have too many processes to view in a chart, then you can use the Report view. To select these processes, choose Edit | Add to Chart and select Process as the object type. Then select the % Processor Time in the Counter column. Next, select each application listed in the Instance column. The process that has the highest peak is generally your performance bottleneck. Take a look at this process in a little more detail and with a sample performance hog.

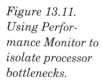

*Figure 13.11.
Using Perfor-
mance Monitor to
isolate processor
bottlenecks.*

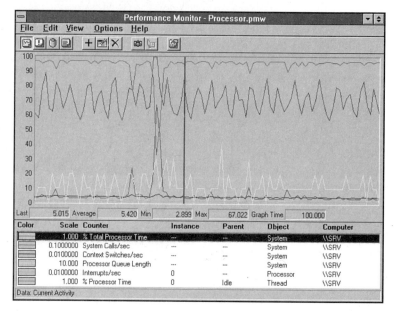

In a multithreaded environment, such as Windows NT Server, a processor shares CPU cycles among multiple threads. Each of these threads can be running or waiting for execution. If you have an application that is waiting for user input or is waiting for a disk I/O request, for example, while it is waiting, it is not scheduled for execution. So other threads that can perform work execute instead. This is based on the application design, however, and in this regard not all applications are created equal. Many applications have been ported from a different application environment and may not make efficient use of the Win32 APIs. If you ported an MS-DOS application to a Win32 console application, for example, you may have left programming constructs that constantly poll for user input, increment a counter, or something similar. The following code shows an example of this process:

```
#include <stdio.h>
#include <stdlib.h>

int main (void)
{
unsigned long uMaxNumber,x;
char chUserInput;
for(x=0;x=4294967295;x++)
{
uMaxNumber=x;
}
```

```
printf("Counter = %d", uMaxNumber);
chUserInput=getchar();

return (0);
}
```

When this application executes, it uses between 80 to 98 percent of the processor, as shown in Figure 13.12. This is the definition of a processor-intensive application. Notice that I have the Process object selected for the BadExample.EXE application (or instance). This is the same object counter you will use (but, of course, you will use different process instances) to determine what percentage of the processor your applications are using and which process is the bottleneck.

Figure 13.12.
An example of
a processor-
intensive appli-
cation displayed
with Performance
Monitor.

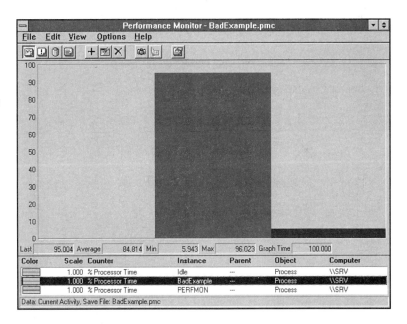

The Visual C++ project file, source code, and executable for this application is included in the \MBADMIN\Projects\Chapter13\Process Hog Example subdirectory on the CD-ROM and is called BadExample.mak, BadExample.C, and BadExample.EXE, respectively. On a uniprocessor system, this little code snippet will use most of your available processor cycles, but on a multiprocessor system, the other processors will remain available to process other application requests. If you have a multiprocessor system, try this application and add the Processor %Total Processor Time for each processor to your chart. One of these processors will show 80 to 98 percent utilization, while the other processors will continue to function normally.

To see how a multithreaded processor-intensive application affects performance on a multiprocessor system, take a look at BadExp3.mak, BadExp3.C, and BadExp3.EXE. This is a multithreaded version of the application. It will spawn three threads and will equally distribute the load among them. This is demonstrated in Figure 13.13. Of course, my system is only a uniprocessor machine, so the load per thread is between 30 and 33 percent. But if you have three or more processors, then three of these processors should show 80 to 90 percent processor utilization. Notice in this example that the Thread object has been selected. This is the object counter you will use to determine which thread of a process is using more of your processor than you would like and is the bottleneck.

Figure 13.13.
A multithreaded
example of a
processor-
intensive appli-
cation displayed
with Performance
Monitor.

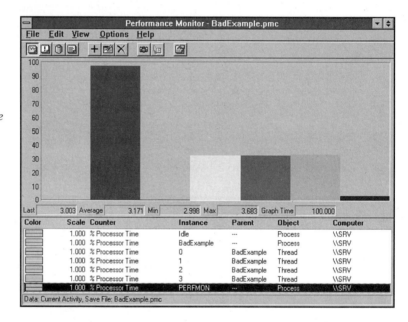

So after you isolate a performance-intensive application, what can you do about it? There are several things you can do, depending on your resources and the application. This breaks down into two categories.

If you have access to the source code, you can do the following:

◆ Use a profiler to modify the application to be less processor intensive. This can include making more efficient use of critical sections or semaphores. If your application spawns multiple threads, for example, you should set the thread priorities to make more efficient use of these control mechanisms so that the threads are not constantly being switched in and out of the processor queue and performing less work than the overhead involved in switching them in and out of the processor queue.

◆ Rewrite the application to spread the load by distributing it among several computers.

◆ Rewrite the application to use thread affinities so that the application uses a specific processor (or processors) in a multiprocessor system. This can achieve higher system performance because the threads will not be constantly switched to different processors. As a thread is switched, it often requires that the processor cache be flushed to maintain data coherency. And that slows down the overall system performance.

If you do not have access to the source code, you can try the following actions:

♦ Inform the manufacturers of the problem and try to get them to fix it by using the earlier suggestions.

♦ Run the application at nonpeak times by using the scheduler service.

♦ Start the application from the command line with the start command at a lower priority. For example, use start `AppName/low`, where `AppName` is the name of the application to execute.

♦ Add additional processors. This provides additional benefits only if you have multiple threads/processes to execute. For the Microsoft BackOffice products, this can provide significant benefits because these applications are designed with multithreading/multiprocessing concepts.

♦ Upgrade the processor. Change from an 80486 to a Pentium, or from an Intel processor to a RISC processor.

♦ Upgrade the processor to a processor with a larger internal cache. The 486/DX4 (75MHz and 100MHz) models, for example, include a 16KB cache over the default 8KB cache of the other 486 models.

♦ Upgrade the secondary system cache. This item is very important when adding additional memory to the system. As you increase system memory, the cache has to map a larger address space into the same size cache. This can increase the cache-miss ratio and degrade performance.

FINDING MEMORY BOTTLENECKS

If you do nothing else to your system, adding additional memory almost always increases system performance. This is because Windows NT Server uses this memory instead of virtual memory and decreases paging. It also is used by the Cache Manager to cache all data accesses. This includes remote (network) or local resource access. The other Microsoft BackOffice components also can benefit from this increased memory. SQL Server, for example, can use some of this memory for its data cache, its procedure cache, and for the temporary database.

And just like finding processor bottlenecks, you have to start with the big picture and then narrow down the search to a specific application to find the memory resource hog. A good starting point is to use the performance counters listed in Table 13.4 to see whether you have a problem. If you find a problem, you can use the process memory-related counters to see which application is the resource hog.

TABLE 13.4. MEMORY PERFORMANCE OBJECT COUNTERS.

Object	Counter	Instance	Description
Memory	Pages/sec	N/A	Number of pages read from or written to disk to resolve memory references to pages that were not in physical memory at the time.
Memory	Available Bytes	N/A	Amount of free virtual memory.
Memory	Committed Bytes	N/A	Amount of memory that has been committed to use by the operating system, as opposed to memory that merely has been reserved for use by the operating system.
Memory	Page Faults/sec	N/A	Number of virtual memory page faults that occurred on the system because the physical page was not in the process' working set or main memory. A page may not need to be read from disk if the page is available on the standby list or is in use by another process that shares the page and has it in its working set.
Memory	Cache Faults/sec	N/A	Number of page faults that occur in the Cache Manager in reference to a memory page that is not in the cache.
Paging File	% Usage	Per Page File	Amount of use of a specific page file.
Paging File	% Usage Peak	Per Page File	Maximum use of a specific page file.

Tip

You can use the Windows NT Diagnostics applet (WINMSD.EXE) located in your Administrative Tools group to get a quick indication of your memory usage. Just click the Memory button to display the Memory dialog box. In the Available Physical Memory field, check the value to see whether it is higher than 1MB for a Windows NT Server computer

or higher than 4MB for a Windows NT workstation. If this value is
less then those mentioned, you have a performance degradation due to
excessive paging. The Memory Load index indicates this in a color bar
chart—green for good, yellow for warning, and red for a system in
trouble.

The first step in isolating the memory bottleneck is to load the Memory.PMW workspace
file into the Performance Monitor. This workspace includes basic counters for the
Chart, Alert, and Report views. Once more, you want to obtain a baseline for an
inactive system and then a baseline for your normally active system. If you have a
memory-intensive process, then your chart will look similar to that shown in Figure
13.14. This particular chart is based on a log file (Memory.LOG), which I captured while
running the MemHog.EXE program. However, the same basic object counter activity will
be displayed in real time for a memory-intensive application as well.

Figure 13.14.
An example of a
system-wide
memory shortage
displayed with
the Performance
Monitor.

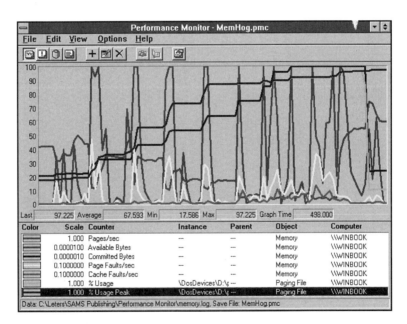

Notice the behavior of these counters. The behavior displayed in Figure 13.14 is an
indication of memory-related problems. Specifically, you should note the following
behavior:

◆ Pages/sec: Notice the high peaks for this counter. This indicates a great
   deal of paging activity, generally because your system does not contain
   enough physical memory to handle the demands placed on it by the application. If you see such activity on your system, you should look closer to see

which application is placing such a load on the system. It may be normal behavior for the application, in which case you should add more physical memory to increase system performance.

◆ Page Faults/sec: Notice here that the peaks follow the peaks for the Pages/sec counter. This also is an indication that your system is paging heavily. A consistent value of more than 5 indicates that your system is paging more than it should. A consistent value of 10 or more is a desperate cry for help. Adding additional physical memory is the only cure. Notice in the example in Figure 13.14 that these counters only peak to a high value and then drop back to a normal level. On an active file or application server, however, the activity should be more linear.

◆ Available Bytes: This counter indicates the amount of virtual address space available to your system. As applications use memory and page to disk, this value decreases. When it drops to less than 10MB, you most likely will see a message warning you that virtual memory is running low and you should close some applications or increase your virtual memory settings. If this counter is consistently low after running an application, this generally indicates a system memory leak.

◆ Committed Bytes: As the Available Bytes counter decreases, the Committed Bytes counter increases. This demonstrates that the process is allocating memory from the virtual address space, but is not necessarily using it. Still, your virtual address space is a limited resource, and you should watch this counter to check for applications that allocate memory but do not use it. This behavior should be noted, and you should discuss this problem with the manufacturer to fix it. Notice in Figure 13.14 that this counter steps up as the paging file activity steps up. This is an indication that the application is making use of the memory it is allocating. High consistent values are an indication that adding additional physical memory will increase system performance. You also should note the counter value when an application ends; if this counter does not return to the original value, then the application has a memory leak or a hidden process that is not terminating properly.

◆ Cache Faults/sec: This counter should be compared with the Page Faults/sec counter to determine whether you really are paging too much in a normal system. If this counter is less than the Page Faults/sec counter, then you definitely are paging too much and you should add additional physical memory.

◆ %Usage: This counter indicates your current paging file activity. If this value is consistently larger than your minimum paging file size, then you should increase your minimum paging file size. A significant amount of system overhead is involved in growing the page file, and any page file growth is not contiguous, which means that more overhead is involved in accessing pages stored in this section of the page file. Notice here that the paging file usage is incremental in steps of 10MB and that when the application terminates, the usage counter drops back to the original (or a little less) value. If your usage counter does not return to the original value after running an application, it has a memory leak or a hidden process that is not terminating.

♦ %Usage Peak: This counter indicates the maximum usage of your page file. If this value consistently reaches 90 percent, then your virtual address space is too small and you should increase the size of your paging file. When it hits above 75 percent, you generally will notice a significant system performance degradation.

You can find the MemHog.EXE program and make file in the \MBADMIN\ Projects\Chapter13\Memory Hog Example subdirectory on the CD-ROM that ships with this book. This program allocates up to 100MB of memory in 1MB allocations. For every 10MB of memory allocated, the program sleeps for 30 seconds. I have the program suspend execution for 30 seconds for every 10MB allocated because, when making heavy use of the paging file, the system uses quite a bit of the processor to grow the pagefile and allocate the memory.

This heavy processor utilization masks the memory-utilization curve of the application. And the purpose of this program is to simulate an application that is making heavy use of your system memory. You will not find many commercial programs that allocate 100MB in less than 10 seconds. Also, this program uses the memset command to write a series of asterisks to each 1MB memory block so that the memory is actually accessed. If you do not perform this step, then the memory merely is allocated but not used. The Committed Bytes object counter then peaks momentarily as the virtual memory address space is increased, but no paging activity takes place because no memory was physically used.

The example shown in Figure 13.14 illustrates a general system-wide, memory-related problem. But in the real world, you need to find the specific cause of the problem. This too can be achieved with the Performance Monitor. Instead of looking at system-wide object counters, you want to narrow the search to the Process object counters, as shown in Figure 13.15, to find the process that is using your system memory.

Doesn't this look quite similar to the display shown in Figure 13.14? Notice that the same basic peaks occur for Memory Page Faults/sec as for Process Page Faults/sec. If you could directly overlay the Memory Page Faults/sec with the Process Page Faults/sec, you would notice that the Memory counter is a bit higher than the Process counter. This is because the Memory counter is a system-wide counter and includes other paging activity from other processes. Table 13.5 lists the corresponding system to process counters to help you in your analysis.

*Figure 13.15.
Using Perfor-
mance Monitor to
isolate a memory-
intensive applica-
tion.*

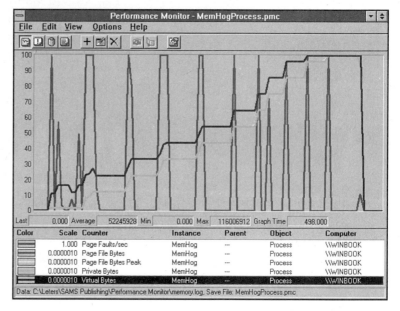

TABLE 13.5. CORRESPONDING SYSTEM TO PROCESS OBJECT COUNTERS.

Object	System Counter	Process Counter
Memory	Page Faults/sec	Page Faults/sec
Memory	Available Bytes	Virtual Bytes
Memory	Committed Bytes	Private Bytes
Paging File	Usage	Page File Bytes
Paging File	Usage Peak	Page File Bytes Peak

Of course, I knew which process was the problem, so my chart only includes the
MemHog application. In order to find a real-world application problem, you should
select all the process instances except for the system processes, unless you are
looking for a system process memory leak. A couple of other Process object counters
that you might find useful in your diagnosis of a memory-intensive application
follow:

◆ Pool Nonpaged Bytes: The nonpaged pool is a system resource area devoted
to system components. Allocations from this area cannot be paged out to
disk. This is a finite resource, and if you run out of nonpaged pool bytes,
some system services may fail.

◆ Pool Paged Bytes: The paged pool is also a system resource area devoted to
system components. Allocations from this area may be paged to disk,
however. It is also a finite resource, and if you run out of paged pool bytes,
a system service may fail.

Note

> Both the Pool Nonpaged Bytes and Pool Paged Bytes counters are very useful in tracking down a process that is incorrectly making system calls and using all the available pool bytes.

◆ Virtual Bytes Peak: This counter is the maximum size of the virtual memory address space used by the process.

◆ Working Set: This counter indicates the size of the application's working set in bytes. The working set includes pages that have been used by the process' threads. When memory is low, pages are trimmed from the working set to provide additional memory for other processes. As the pages are needed, they are pulled from main memory if they have not been removed or read from the paging file.

◆ Working Set Peak: This counter indicates the maximum working set size in bytes.

Tip

> By monitoring the working set for a particular process and comparing that to the working set peak, you can determine whether adding additional memory will increase the performance of the process. The idea here is to add memory until the Working Set and Working Set Peak values are equal, which will provide the maximum benefit to the process. You should consider that this may prove to be an unrealistic goal if your budget is limited.

Finding Disk Bottlenecks

Finding disk bottlenecks is easier than finding processor or memory bottlenecks because these performance degradations are readily apparent. However, before you can search for a disk bottleneck, you must enable the disk Performance Monitor counters. This is achieved by executing the following command:

```
DISKPERF \\ServerName /Y
```

Here, ServerName is the name of the computer on which to enable the Performance Monitor counters.

To disable the counters, use this command:

```
DISKPERF \\ServerName /N
```

There are really only four performance counters to monitor for bottlenecks:

- ◆ **% Disk Time:** This counter is the percentage of elapsed time that the disk is servicing read or write requests. It also includes the time the disk driver is waiting in the disk queue.

- ◆ **Disk Queue Length:** This counter indicates how many pending I/O requests are waiting to be serviced. If this value is greater than 2, it indicates a disk bottleneck. On a multidisk subsystem, such as a stripe set or stripe set with parity, a little calculating is in order to determine whether a disk bottleneck is occurring. The basic formula follows:

    Disk Queue Length–Number of Physical Disk Drives in MultiDisk Configuration

    If this value is greater than 2, a disk bottleneck is indicated. If you have a stripe set with three disk drives and a queue length of 5, for example, then 5–3 = 2. And 2 is an acceptable value.

- ◆ **Avg. Disk Transfer/sec:** This counter is the time in seconds of the average disk transfer. It is not used just for this information, however; it is used in connection with the Memory Pages/sec counter.

- ◆ **Memory Pages/sec:** Use this counter and the Avg. Disk Transfer/sec counter in the following formula to tell you how much of your disk bandwidth is used for paging:

    % Disk Time Used for Paging = (Memory Pages/sec × Avg. Disk Transfer/sec) × 100

When I perform disk diagnostics, I break my Performance Monitor charts into two different settings. I use the % Disk Time, Disk Queue Length, and Avg. Disk Transfer/sec counters, as well as the Memory Pages/sec counter from the LogicalDisk object to determine the performance on a drive letter basis. I then use the same counters from the PhysicalDisk object to determine my hardware disk performance. If you look in the `MBADMIN\Projects\Chapter13\Performance Monitor Example` subdirectory on the CD-ROM, you will find the `LogicalDisk.PMW` and `PhysicalDisk.PMW` Performance Monitor workspace files. These files include basic chart, alert, and report examples for you to use as a starting point.

If you want to see these examples in action, run two copies of the Performance Monitor and load `LogicalDisk.PMW` into one copy and `PhysicalDisk.PMW` into the other. Then run the `DiskHog.EXE` program. This program takes one command-line argument: the drive letter to write its data file to (for example, `DiskHog H:`). If no drive letter is specified, the default is drive C. This program writes up to 1,000 1MB blocks of data to the file (`DumpFile.DAT`), which can total almost 1GB. The purpose of this program is two-fold. First, you can use it to demonstrate disk activity on logical drives (see Figure 13.16) and disk activity on physical drives. (See Figure 13.17.)

Second, you can use it to test your alert conditions for low disk space. When the program finishes writing the data file, it informs you of how much data was written and prompts you to press a key to continue. It then deletes the data file it created.

Figure 13.16.
A disk-intensive
application
displayed with
Performance
Monitor on
logical drives.

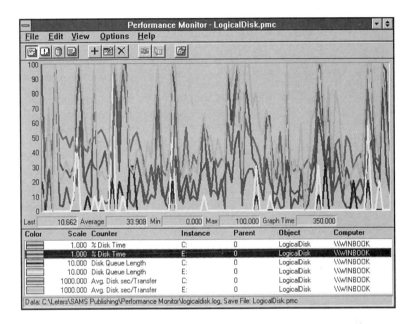

Figure 13.17.
A disk-intensive
application
displayed with
Performance
Monitor on
physical drives.

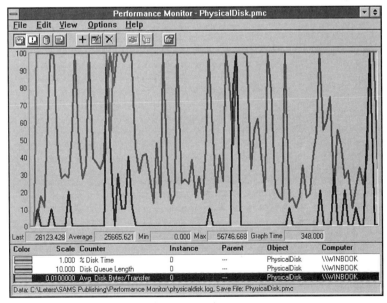

Keep in mind that DiskHog.EXE is a simulation designed to overload your disk I/O subsystem. As such, it cannot be used to demonstrate a normal usage pattern for a file server. It is designed only to give you an idea of what to look for in finding performance bottlenecks with the Performance Monitor.

If you run the DiskHog.EXE program and place the data file on a compressed drive, it most likely will run to completion and write almost 1GB of data, even if you have less than a couple of hundred MB free on the drive. This is because the data block it writes is composed of 1MB of asterisks (*) and is easily compressible. Also, if you interrupt the program, it may not erase its data file. So be sure to look for and delete the DumpFile.DAT data file after a manual interruption.

Tip

When using Performance Monitor to determine disk activities, you may want to change the default capture rate. I break mine down into 5-second, 1-second, 1/10-second, and 1/100-second intervals, depending on the amount of data I want to capture and the server activity.

If you find a bottleneck, you can take several actions that weren't mentioned in the beginning of this section:

◆ Create a mirror set. This can double your read performance if your disk driver can support multiple asynchronous I/O requests. This rules out most IDE and EIDE controllers, which use the default ATDISK driver.

◆ Create a stripe set or stripe set with parity. This can increase both read and write performance if your disk driver can support multiple asynchronous I/O requests. The best choice for this is to use a 32-bit SCSI bus master controller.

◆ If your budget is limited, spend your money on a fast SCSI controller and average disk drives (in terms of seek time) because the SCSI controller has more of an impact on a two-drive system.

◆ If you have sufficient funds, purchase drives with the lowest seek time because the time spent seeking tracks (to find the data) versus the data-transfer time is 10 to 1 or higher. This is more noticeable on subsystems with more than two drives.

◆ Distribute the workload (this is one reason to use the LogicalDisk.PMW example) to place highly accessed data files on different drives. You can place the application files for Microsoft Office on your first physical drive and your SQL Server databases on your second physical drive, for example. Do not place them on different logical drives on the same physical drive because this defeats the purpose of distributing the load.

- If you use a FAT file system, defragment it occasionally. This prevents the multiple seeks required to read or write data to the disk.

- If you have a volume of more than 400MB, you should choose the NTFS file system. NTFS partitions make more efficient use of the disk to provide better performance. A FAT partition can support a maximum of 65,536 clusters, for example. On a large partition, the cluster size may be as large as 64KB. A cluster is the minimum allocation unit, so if you store a 512-byte file, you have wasted 63.5KB. NTFS partitions can have up to 2^{64} clusters to access the partition, so the cluster size can be much smaller and therefore wastes less space.

Note

Executive Software has a disk defragmenter called DiskKeeper, which runs as a Windows NT Service. It can defragment both your NTFS and FAT partitions.

FINDING NETWORK BOTTLENECKS

*Figure 13.18.
Using Perfor-
mance Monitor to
isolate network
bottlenecks.*

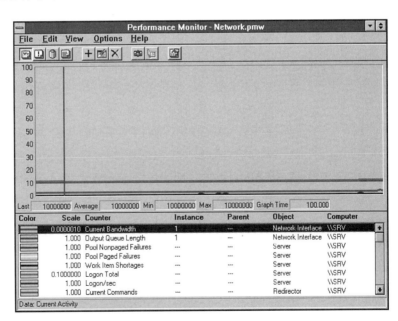

In the preceding chapter, you learned about most of the network performance tuning options provided by the graphical interface tools, such as the Control Panel applets and the hardware alternatives. You may want to look at Appendix B, "The Registry Editor and Registry Keys," (located on the CD that ships with this book); this appendix includes some other mechanisms for configuring the Windows NT Services. Keep in mind that altering any of the Registry keys may prevent a Windows NT Service from automatically tuning itself for maximum performance. Figure 13.18 shows another example Performance Monitor workspace file, `Network.PMW`, which includes a Chart, Alert, and Report view to aid you in your network diagnostics.

The performance object counters included in the Chart and Alert views give you a means to monitor how busy your server is and help you determine basic network utilization. Table 13.6 lists the object counters I consider important for making these determinations.

TABLE 13.6. NETWORK PERFORMANCE COUNTERS.

Object	Counter	Instance	Description
Network Interface	Current Bandwidth	Per Interface	An estimated value of the current network utilization in bits per second.
Network Segment	Network Utilization	Per Adapter	An estimated value of the percentage of the network bandwidth currently in use on the network segment.
Server	Pool Nonpaged Failures	N/A	Number of times allocations from the nonpaged memory pool have failed.
Server	Pool Paged Failures	N/A	Number of times allocations from the paged memory pool have failed.
Server	Work Item Shortages	N/A	Number of times a work item could not be allocated. This counter can indicate that the InitWorkItems and MaxWorkItems parameters for the LanMan Server service need to be increased.
Server	Logons Total	N/A	A total count, since the computer was last rebooted, of all interactive logons, remote logons, service logons, and failed logons.

Object	Counter	Instance	Description
Server	Logons/sec	N/A	The rate at which all interactive logons, remote logons, service logons, and failed logons are occurring.
Server Work Queues	Work Item Shortages	Per Processor	Indicates the number of failed work item allocations. A number greater than 1 is an indication that the MaxWorkItem parameter should be increased.
Server Work Queues	Queue Length	Per Processor	Indicates the number of requests currently waiting in the server queue. A number consistently higher than 4 indicates that a faster processor could improve performance.
Redirector	Current Commands	N/A	Indicates the number of outstanding network requests waiting to be serviced. If this number is greater than the number of network adapters installed on the computer, a network bottleneck is present. Adding an additional network adapter may increase performance.
Redirector	Network Errors/sec	N/A	Indicates that serious network errors have occurred. These errors generally are logged in the system event log, so you should look there for further information. If an error occurs, you should take immediate notice and attempt to resolve the situation.

Note

> The Network Interface Current Bandwidth counter is available only if you install the Network Monitor Agent. You can use it to determine whether your network is overloaded. A value of 50000000.0000 is the 50-percent mark that indicates you should consider segmenting your network. Some network Administrators prefer to plan for additional growth and split the network segment at the 30-to-40-percent mark. The Network Segment Network Utilization counter applies only if you have the TCP/IP protocol installed. This counter is in fractional percentages, and at an indication of 50 percent or higher, the network segment should be split as well.

FINDING INTERNET INFORMATION SERVER BOTTLENECKS

Depending on the size and activity of your Internet Information Server installation, you may run into a few performance-related problems. But before you try to configure the IIS services for better performance, you should try using the Performance Monitor to look at processor, memory, disk, or network bottlenecks, as described in the preceding sections. Only after you have done your best to solve those problems should you move on to optimizing your IIS services. This is because a WWW, FTP, or Gopher server essentially performs the same tasks as a file server—to share file, print, and processor services with their clients. There are several IIS counters you can use to determine just how heavy a load your IIS server is carrying, as well as counters to scrutinize each service.

You should start your performance tuning with the general IIS counters, described in Table 13.7, to get a basic look at how well your IIS server is performing. To determine how well a specific service is performing, you can use the counters in Table 13.8 for your WWW Publishing Service, Table 13.9 for your FTP Publishing Service, and Table 13.10 for your Gopher Publishing Service. You should pay particular attention to the global cache counters mentioned in Table 13.7, because you may modify the size of this cache by modifying the registry key `HKEY_LOCAL_MACHINE\System\CurrentControlSet\Services\InetInfo\Parameters\MemoryCacheSize`. The default is to allocate 3MB (3072000 bytes), and the legal values range from 0 (which disables caching entirely) to FFFFFFF (or 4GB). If you are encountering large numbers of cache flushes or misses, or if you have a poor hit ratio, increasing this value may improve performance. You should be careful, however, to make sure that you use only physical memory that is not required by the base operating system or SQL Server; otherwise, you may affect these systems and cause poor IIS performance.

Tip

For more information on using the Registry Editor and other IIS specific registry keys, refer to Appendix B, "The Registry Editor and Registry Keys."

TABLE 13.7. SUMMARY OF GLOBAL IIS PERFORMANCE COUNTERS.

Counter	Description
Cache Flushes	Specifies how often a cached memory region expired due to changes in IIS files or the directory tree.
Cache Hits	Specifies how often a reference to a file, a directory tree, or an IIS-specific object was found in the cache.
Cache Hits %	Specifies the hit ratio of all cache requests.
Cache Misses	Specifies how often a reference to a file, a directory tree, or an IIS-specific object was not found in the cache.
Cache Size	Specifies the size of the shared memory cache.
Cache Used	Specifies the total number of bytes in use (file handles, IIS-specific objects, and so on) in the cache.
Cached File Handles	The total number of file handles contained in the cache.
Current Blocked Async I/O Requests	The total number of current asynchronous I/O requests blocked by the bandwidth throttle.

continues

TABLE 13.7. CONTINUED

Counter	Description
Directory Listings	Specifies the total number of directory listings contained in the cache.
Measured Async I/O Bandwidth Usage	Specifies the total amount of asynchronous I/O bandwidth averaged over a minute.
Objects	Specifies the total number of objects (file handle objects, directory listing objects, and so on) contained in the cache.
Total Allowed Async I/O Requests	The total number of asynchronous I/O requests permitted by the bandwidth throttle.
Total Blocked Async I/O Requests	The total number of asynchronous I/O requests blocked by the bandwidth throttle.
Total Rejected Async I/O Requests	The total number of asynchronous I/O requests rejected by the bandwidth throttle.

TABLE 13.8. SUMMARY OF HTTP SERVICE PERFORMANCE COUNTERS.

Counter	Description
Bytes Received/sec	Specifies the rate (in bytes/sec) at which the HTTP server is receiving data.
Bytes Sent/sec	Specifies the rate (in bytes/sec) at which the HTTP server is transmitting data.
Bytes Total/sec	Specifies the total amount of data that is being transmitted, or received, by the HTTP server in bytes/second.

Counter	Description
CGI Requests	Specifies the number of Common Gateway Interface (CGI) requests received by the HTTP server.
Connection Attempts	Specifies the total number of attempts made to connect to the HTTP server.
Connections/sec	Specifies the number of connections to the HTTP server per second.
Current Anonymous Users	Specifies how many anonymous users are currently connected to the HTTP server.
Current CGI Requests	Specifies how many CGI requests are currently being processed by the HTTP server.
Current Connections	Specifies the current number of connections to the HTTP server.
Current ISAPI Extension Requests	Specifies the current number of ISAPI requests being processed by the server.
Current NonAnonymous Users	Specifies the total number of users currently connected to the HTTP server using a domain user account.
File Received	Specifies the total number of files received by the HTTP server.
File Sent	Specifies the total number of files transmitted by the HTTP server.
File Total	Specifies the sum of the total number of files transmitted and received.
Get Requests	Specifies the total number of HTTP requests using the GET method.
Head Requests	Specifies the total number of HTTP requests using the HEAD method.
ISAPI Extension Requests	Specifies the total number of ISAPI requests being processed by the server.
Logon Attempts	Specifies the total number of logon attempts that have been made by the HTTP server.
Maximum Anonymous Users	Specifies the maximum number of simultaneously connected anonymous users.
Maximum CGI Requests	Specifies the maximum number of simultaneous CGI requests processed by the HTTP server.

continues

TABLE 13.8. CONTINUED

Counter	Description
Maximum Connection	Specifies the maximum number of simultaneous connections to the HTTP server.
Maximum ISAPI Extension Requests	Specifies the maximum number of simultaneous ISAPI requests processed by the HTTP server.
Maximum NonAnonymous Users	Specifies the maximum number of simultaneously connected users using a domain user account.
Not Found Errors	Specifies the total number of requests that failed because of a missing document.
Other Requested Methods	Specifies the total number of HTTP requests that do not use the GET, HEAD, or POST methods. This can include PUT, DELETE, LINK, or other methods.
Post Requests	Specifies the total number of HTTP requests using the POST method.
Total Anonymous Users	Specifies the total number of anonymous users that have ever connected to the HTTP server.
Total NonAnonymous Users	Specifies the total number of users that have ever connected to the HTTP server using a domain user account.

TABLE 13.9. SUMMARY OF THE FTP SERVICE PERFORMANCE COUNTERS.

Counter	Description
Bytes Received/sec	Specifies the rate (in bytes/sec) at which the FTP server is receiving data.
Bytes Sent/sec	Specifies the rate (in bytes/sec) at which the FTP server is transmitting data.
Bytes Total/sec	Specifies the total amount of data that is being transmitted or received by the FTP server in bytes per second.
Connection Attempts	Specifies the total number of attempts made to connect to the FTP server.
Current Anonymous Users	Specifies how many anonymous users are currently connected to the FTP server.

Counter	Description
Current Connections	Specifies the current number of connections to the FTP server.
Current NonAnonymous Users	Specifies the total number of users currently connected to the FTP server using a domain user account.
File Received	Specifies the total number of files received by the FTP server.
Files Sent	Specifies the total number of files transmitted by the FTP server.
Files Total	Specifies the sum of the total number of files transmitted and received.
Logon Attempts	Specifies the total number of logon attempts that have been made by the FTP server.
Maximum Anonymous Users	Specifies the maximum number of simultaneous connected anonymous users.
Maximum Connections	Specifies the maximum number of simultaneous connections to the FTP server.
Maximum NonAnonymous Users	Specifies the maximum number of simultaneous connected users using a domain user account.
Total Anonymous Users	Specifies the total number of anonymous users that have ever connected to the FTP server.
Total NonAnonymous Users	Specifies the total number of users that have ever connected to the FTP server using a domain user account.

TABLE 13.10. SUMMARY OF GOPHER SERVICE PERFORMANCE COUNTERS.

Counter	Description
Aborted Connections	Specifies the total number of connections that failed due to errors or over-limit requests made to the Gopher server.
Bytes Received/sec	Specifies the rate (in bytes/sec) at which the Gopher server is receiving data.
Bytes Sent/sec	Specifies the rate (in bytes/sec) at which the Gopher server is transmitting data.

continues

TABLE 13.10. CONTINUED

Counter	Description
Bytes Total/sec	Specifies the total amount of data that is being transmitted or received by the Gopher server in bytes/second.
Connection Attempts	Specifies the total number of attempts made to connect to the Gopher server.
Connections in Error	Specifies the number of errors that occurred while being processed by the Gopher server.
Current Anonymous Users	Specifies how many anonymous users are currently connected to the Gopher server.
Current Connections	Specifies the current number of connections to the Gopher server.
Current NonAnonymous Users	Specifies the total number of users currently connected to the Gopher server using a domain user account.
Directory Listing Sent	Specifies the total number of directory listings transmitted by the Gopher server.
File Sent	Specifies the total number of files transmitted by the Gopher server.
Gopher Plus Requests	Specifies the total number of Gopher Plus requests received by the Gopher server.
Logon Attempts	Specifies the total number of logon attempts that have been made by the Gopher server.
Maximum Anonymous Users	Specifies the maximum number of simultaneous connected anonymous users.
Maximum NonAnonymous Users	Specifies the maximum number of simultaneous connected users using a domain user account.
Maximum Connections	Specifies the maximum number of simultaneous connected users to the Gopher server.
Searches Sent	Specifies the total number of searches performed by the Gopher server.
Total Anonymous Users	Specifies the total number of anonymous users that have ever connected to the Gopher server.
Total NonAnonymous Users	Specifies the total number of users that have ever connected to the Gopher server using a domain user account.

13

SUMMARY

This chapter discussed the basics of using the Performance Monitor to create charts, logs, alerts, and reports. It also included specific performance object counters for you to monitor each of these views as a starting point to finding system bottlenecks or just for monitoring purposes.

You also saw some example Performance Monitor charts, alerts, reports, and workspace files to use on your network server. These files were used with sample programs to illustrate how to find processor, memory, disk, network, and Internet Information Server bottlenecks.

The goal of this chapter was not to explain every detail of the Performance Monitor; instead, the goal was to give you a good understanding of the features and to show you how to use the Performance Monitor in your day-to-day activities.

In future chapters, you will look at the Performance Monitor again, as well as optimizations for other BackOffice components.

In the next chapter, you will take a look at SQL Server and learn some of the terms you will need to understand in order to actually install and use the product. It covers such items as the client/server model, the relational database model, integration with Windows NT, the basic SQL Server components, and the SQL Server management tools.

PART III

SQL Server for
Windows NT

- The Client/Server Model

- The Relational Database Model

- Integration with Windows NT

- SQL Server Components

CHAPTER 14

An Introduction to Microsoft SQL Server

Are you looking to implement a shared database on your network? Do you need a database that offers you, the network administrator, centralized administration? Is the data to be stored in the database critical to your company's well being? Is the performance of your database engine a factor? If the answer to these questions is "Yes," then Microsoft SQL (pronounced see-quell) Server could be just what you need. Although you can use other database products on your network, such as Microsoft Access, Microsoft FoxPro, Borland Paradox, Borland dBASE, or other multiuser-aware databases, none of these can offer the same features provided by Microsoft SQL Server. Perhaps you are wondering just what is so different about these database engines. After all, a database is just a collection of data stored in a file, right? For the most part, that statement is true, but how the data is stored and how it is accessed can be quite different.

The differences between a regular sharable database implementation and a SQL Server implementation are the primary focus of this chapter. The idea here is to introduce you to some of the features provided by Microsoft SQL Server to prepare you for implementing and administering databases for your company. This chapter starts with a look at the basic client/server model and then moves on to a brief discussion of the relational database model. These two concepts are the foundation on which you will build to design and implement the database to be used by your network clients. Next, you will look at the integration of Microsoft Windows NT and Microsoft SQL Server and just what this means to you. You'll also examine the basic SQL Server concepts and the tools provided by Microsoft to aid you in the design, creation, and administration of your SQL Server databases.

THE CLIENT/SERVER MODEL

A client/server database has two discrete components, as shown in Figure 14.1. The first part is the back-end (or server) component, which executes on a computer on your network. This computer could be your file server, but it does not have to be because SQL Server can run on any Windows NT computer on your network. If you are planning to have more than 10 simultaneous connections to your SQL Server, however, you should use Windows NT Server. To provide maximum performance, you should use Windows NT Server executing in server mode, not as a domain controller. The second part is the front-end client (or user interface) component, which executes on your client workstation.

All that passes (via the network libraries) between these two components are commands from the front-end application to the SQL Server database engine and the actual data that has been selected by these commands from the SQL Server database engine to your front-end application. In essence, only SQL Server commands and the data contained in the result set pass over your network interface. Compare this client/server flow with the normal flow for a standard database application using a shared database file on your network, as depicted in Figure 14.2. If you were using a Microsoft Access database stored on your network file server, for example, all the data processing and data display would occur on the client workstation. This workstation would run the Microsoft Access program locally but would access the database's tables stored in the file on the network server—row by row and column by column—to find the requested data. All this data passes over your network interface, eating up valuable network bandwidth.

Figure 14.1.
A client/server
database model.

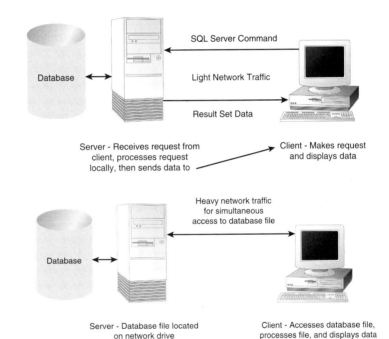

Figure 14.2.
A monolithic
database model.

14

MICROSOFT SQL SERVER

By separating the database engine from the user interface, as provided in the client/ server model, you obtain the following benefits:

◆ Cost effectiveness: Because the actual work of searching through the database for the requested data and sorting the data occurs on the server's processor, you can use a high-end computer to maximize your database engine's performance. The client computer, however, can use a more mainstream configuration because it is used only to query the database server and to display the returned data. So, instead of using Pentium super servers on the desktop with gigabytes of storage, you can use one of these for your database server and a 486/33 (or less, if desired, but not recommended) with a standard sized (200–500MB) local disk drive as your client workstation.

◆ Increased performance: Microsoft SQL Server is a native Windows NT application and, as such, is a multithreaded application. This means that if you have multiple processors on your server, you can process data requests faster.

◆ Scalability: Microsoft SQL Server is available for the Intel, Alpha, and MIPS processors (and with the SQL Server 6.5 and PowerPC processor as well), which gives you the capability to increase performance by changing hardware platforms.

◆ Efficient use of network bandwidth: Instead of having multiple client workstations access a shared database file to read and write to it simultaneously and using a high percentage of your network bandwidth, you can use SQL Server to process the data requests locally on the server and only transmit the requested data over the network, making more efficient use of your limited network bandwidth. This actually makes it feasible to use a RAS connection to query your SQL Server database—by a sales representative at a client office, for example.

THE RELATIONAL DATABASE MODEL

This section explores some key features of the relational database that you can use to make your administrative duties a little easier. Although a complete discussion of the relational database model is outside the scope of this book, you will learn the key points you need to know here.

The first item to consider is how a relational database differs from a nonrelational database. Well, for starters, a nonrelational database generally stores the format of the database or table as a header record in the file that also contains the data, but a relational database stores this information in system tables. This is what I refer to as the first rule of a relational database. As you work with SQL Server, you will become familiar with many of these system tables. Table 14.1 lists system tables included in each database and those system tables included only in the master database. In Chapter 17, "Managing Your Database Server," you will directly interact with some of these tables as you begin your management duties.

Table 14.1. The SQL Server 6.5 system tables.

Table Name	Located in Every Database	Located in Master Database Only	Contains
sysalternates	X	X	User account aliases. These aliases are mapped to a login account in sysusers.
sysarticles **	X	X	Names and information relevant for published articles.
syscolumns	X	X	Names and data characteristics for every column in a table or view.
syscomments	X	X	SQL definition (or creation statement) for every default, procedure, rule, table, trigger, or view.
sysconstraints **	X	X	Information for each primary and foreign key, check, default, and unique constraint.
sysdepends	X	X	Relationships between dependent entities, such as a view to a table, a procedure that references a table or view, or a trigger that references a table.
sysindexes	X	X	Information for each table without an index, as well as information for each clustered or nonclustered index defined for a table.
syskeys *	X	X	Information for each key (primary, foreign, or common) defined for a table.
syslogs	X	X	Transaction log for the database.

continues

14

Microsoft SQL Server

TABLE 14.1. CONTINUED

Table Name	Located in Every Database	Located in Master Database Only	Contains
sysobjects	X	X	Object (tables, views, procedures, and so on) definitions.
sysprocedures	X	X	Preparsed and optimized trees for views, rules, triggers, and stored procedures.
sysprotects	X	X	Permissions for user access to objects, such as tables, views, or procedures.
syspublications **	X	X	Name, description and other relevant information for each publication.
syssubscriptions **	X	X	Contains information about each subscribed publication.
sysreferences **	X	X	Foreign key constraint information.
syssegments	X	X	Database partitions that can be used to control the growth of a database object and subsegment it at a lower level.
systypes *	X	X	System and user-definable data types.
sysusers *	X	X	User accounts that can access the database.
syslogins		X	User accounts, passwords, and configuration defaults for SQL Server login.
syscharsets **		X	Information about installed character sets and sort orders.

Table Name	Located in Every Database	Located in Master Database Only	Contains
sysconfigures		X	Values for the system configuration to be used the next time SQL Server is started.
syscurconfigs		X	Current system configuration values.
sysdatabases		X	Name, owner, status, and other configuration information for each database.
sysdevices		X	Information about preallocated physical storage (files), which are used for database allocations or backup devices (tape, disk, or floppy).
sysusages		X	Information concerning allocations of physical storage to individual databases.
sysprocesses		X	Information about each user who is logged onto SQL Server.
syslocks		X	Information about current locks on tables. Note: This is a memory-resident table. If the SQL Server fails or is shut down, all locks are released.
syslanguages		X	Information about all the installed language sets, except for the us_language set.
syscharsets		X	Installed character sets or sort orders.

continues

14

Microsoft SQL Server

TABLE 14.1. CONTINUED

Table Name	Located in Every Database	Located in Master Database Only	Contains
sysmessages		X	Server-specific error messages.
sysservers		X	Mappings for each remote SQL Server installation.
sysremotelogins		X	Login identifiers for users logging onto the current SQL Server from a remote SQL Server installation.

* - Applies only to SQL Server 4.2x.

** - Applies only to SQL Server 6.x.

The second basic rule of a relational database is that all operations on a table create new tables (or result sets). These operations are restricted to a specific set of commands defined as Transact SQL. Transact SQL is similar to, but not exactly the same as, the set of commands defined by the ANSI SQL command set. The Transact SQL command set is used, much as any other programming language, to build procedures that you can use to manipulate the data stored in your tables. You will learn more about Transact SQL in later chapters as you explore areas that require command-line maintenance or administration.

Finally, you should know about two very important but often misunderstood concepts provided by a relational database: transactions and transaction logs. A transaction is an atomic operation performed on one or more tables in one or more databases. An atomic action is simply one that succeeds completely or fails completely; there is no middle ground. The transaction log is used to store all the changes that are occurring until the operation succeeds. If the operation does succeed, the changes are applied to the database. If the operation fails (perhaps because an attempt is made to insert a duplicate row, for example), the information stored in the transaction log is used to roll back the database and restore the original data.

INTEGRATION WITH WINDOWS NT

Have you been wondering just how integrated Microsoft SQL Server is with Microsoft Windows NT? Is SQL Server an add-on piece of software that happens to run under Windows NT as it does under OS/2? Or is it so tightly integrated that once installed, it functions as if it were an integral part of the operating system that automatically takes advantage of performance enhancements, such as additional processors, memory, or hard disk drives? What happens to the performance of Windows NT Server when SQL Server is added to the mix? How well does SQL Server perform when your network users employ your Windows NT Server as a file and print server? Well, these are some of the questions I hope to answer for you right here and now.

This discussion starts with a look at the integration issue first, because this also plays a part in the performance issues. To start off, consider that Microsoft has rewritten the basic SQL Server code provided by Sybase to take advantage of the Windows NT architecture. The Microsoft version of SQL Server was designed from the ground up to run as a native multithreaded Windows NT service. The basic design model, as shown in Figure 14.3, differs from the design of Microsoft SQL Server for OS/2 in that the OS/2 design is based on providing multiprocessor support at the process level, instead of the thread level provided by the Windows NT design. This means that the Windows NT version of SQL Server is more tightly integrated than the OS/2 version of SQL Server.

Figure 14.3.
A comparison of the OS/2 SMP design versus the Windows NT SMP design of SQL Server.

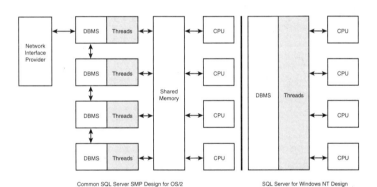

Note

Along with the SQL Server service, Microsoft has supplied a companion service called the SQL Monitor. This service monitors the status of the SQL Service, and if the service terminates abnormally, the SQL Monitor service restarts the SQL Server service. Neither the SQL Server nor the SQL Monitor service is enabled to start automatically; you must configure them to do so. Chapter 16, "Installing SQL Server," covers this topic in more detail in its discussion of the installation and initial configuration.

The Microsoft version of SQL Server uses a series of worker threads to perform the services required by the database engine. There is one thread for each network interface (NetBEUI, IPX/SPX, TCP/IP, or Banyan VINES) that it expects clients to connect to—for example, another thread to process database check points, a pool of threads to handle each connected user, and a pool of miscellaneous threads for other system-related tasks. This method provides for better dynamic load balancing and scalability (the capability to gain additional performance) as additional processors are added to the system.

Note

The capability to add more processors to increase SQL Server 4.21-a performance in order to support additional users has its limits. The most noticeable increase occurs when you add a second processor to a uniprocessor system; this increase tapers off after the fourth processor. Using more than four processors is not very cost-effective. This lack of scalability has been addressed in the later versions of SQL Server (version 6.0 or higher).

Tip

Often, better SQL Server performance for a dual-processor system can be achieved by enabling the multiprocessor support option for SQL Server to use a single processor for SQL Server and the other installed processor for Windows NT. This performance improvement occurs because the threads of execution are not switched among the processors. Normally, as a thread is switched between processors, a context switch occurs and the processor cache must be flushed to make sure that the memory subsystem is consistent. This constant context switching and cache flushing can seriously degrade performance.

Windows NT schedules threads rather than processes for execution. The overall impact on Windows NT Server or SQL Server is not hampered seriously when users connect to Windows NT Server to use the file and print services, or when users connect to SQL Server to access the database services. This differs greatly from the impact on the servers or database performance when compared to SQL Server implementations for OS/2 or NetWare. Just because Microsoft SQL Server uses threads and takes advantage of multiple processors does not mean that it automatically takes advantage of other system enhancements. If you add additional memory to your server, this may improve overall system performance and therefore will impact SQL Server performance slightly due to increased disk caching and less paging to disk. You can achieve better SQL Server performance by changing the SQL Server configuration to use more of this memory directly. The same concerns are evident when adding additional disk drives; achieving maximum performance requires intervention by you. You will learn more about these aspects in Chapter 18, "Optimizing SQL Server."

One of the less-used features provided with Microsoft SQL Server is the integration with the domain user account database. The Microsoft SQL Server includes three security modes you can use to limit access to your installation:

- Standard: Uses the user accounts defined in the SQL Servers syslogins table.

- Integrated: Provides access to the SQL Server databases based on the user accounts contained in the domain user account database.

- Mixed: Uses the user accounts contained in the domain user account first, and if no match is found, it uses the user accounts defined in the syslogins table.

SQL SERVER COMPONENTS

Just as the databases you may be familiar with include multiple components, so does Microsoft SQL Server. These components combine to create the whole object (or database) that your users will access. But your users will not see the whole picture; they will just see the slice you give them access to manipulate. Chapter 17 looks into the following items much more closely. For now, though, I'd just like to give you a little background information about the various components you will be using:

- Devices: A device is a preallocated amount of physical storage on your disk drive. It is a named file that is subdivided into 2KB allocation units. Each of these 2KB units is called a page. Eight pages are grouped into an extent, and 32 extents are grouped into a single allocation. A device is required to contain your databases and transaction logs. When you install SQL Server, the master device (`master.dat`) is created to contain the master database. You are required to create additional devices to contain your databases.

Note

A device also can consist of a backup medium such as a tape backup unit or a floppy disk. The default devices for floppy disks are created during the installation, but you must manually create a tape device.

◆ Segments: A segment resides in a device and is used to subdivide a database or database index to control the growth of a database or index and to potentially increase performance.

◆ Databases: A database resides on a device and must be preallocated. As a database grows beyond this allocation, it must be extended on the same device or on another available device. It contains all the tables, views, rules, triggers, and other database-related components. The minimum size of a database that you can create consists of four allocations, which is where the 2MB minimum database size rule comes into play, as you will see in Chapter 17.

◆ Tables: A table consists of columns of data, as listed in Table 14.2, which, when combined as a unit, is referred to as a row. You can consider a row as a single record of fixed or variable length, depending on your column data type definitions.

◆ Indexes: An index can be clustered or unclustered. A clustered index, of which you can have only one per table, determines the physical sort order of the table. Unclustered indexes are used only to speed access to the data contained within the table. You can have as many as 249 unclustered indexes per table.

◆ Views: A view is a preparsed select statement that can be used to retrieve data from a table, or, it can be used as if it were an actual table itself. It generally is used to restrict access to an entire table and to provide only a subset of the data contained within the table to members not authorized to have complete access to the table's contents.

◆ Triggers: A trigger is used to ensure the referential integrity of your database or to enforce a specific business policy. A trigger can be assigned to insert, update, or delete actions.

◆ Rules: A rule is used to enforce business rules for a column's data. You may create a rule to ensure that a specific column can contain only the values 0 through 9, for example, or to specify that it must follow a specific pattern such as a telephone number pattern of area code, prefix, and suffix—(999) 999-9999, for example.

◆ Defaults: A default is used to insert a specific value into a column when the user does not supply a value.

◆ Stored procedures: A stored procedure is a preparsed and optimized series of Transact SQL statements that have been saved as a named item. A stored procedure can accept command-line arguments and return a value.

◆ Extended stored procedures: An extended stored procedure is a compiled executable in the form of a dynamic link library that is called as if it were a

14

stored procedure. Instead of being interpreted as a stored procedure, however, it is a 32-bit executable program and therefore executes much faster than a stored procedure. You can add extended stored procedures to enhance the capabilities of your SQL Server installation.

Table 14.2. Microsoft SQL Server data types.

Data Type	Size in Bytes	Description
INT	4	A signed 32-bit integer.
SMALLINT	2	A signed 16-bit integer.
TINYINT	1	An unsigned 8-bit integer.
DECIMAL	2 – 17	Specifies an exact numerical value based on the user-supplied precision (number of decimal digits to the left of the decimal point) and scale (the maximum number of digits to the right of the decimal point).
NUMERIC	2 – 17	Same as DECIMAL.
REAL	4	A single-precision floating point value.
FLOAT	4 – 8	A 4-byte (single precision) or 8-byte (double precision value). The actual range of legal values and internal representation is processor dependent, but normally is stored as a double precision (8-byte value).
BIT	1	A value that holds a 0 or 1. Note that only 1 bit of this byte is used; the other 7 bits can be used to contain other bit data types defined for a column.
CHAR	1 – 255	Character data of fixed length determined at the time of allocation.
VARCHAR	1 – 255	Character data of variable length, of which the maximum length is predetermined at the time of allocation.

continues

TABLE 14.2. CONTINUED

Data Type	Size in Bytes	Description
TEXT	0 – 2,147,483,647	Character data of variable length, of which the maximum is predetermined at the time of allocation. Increments are allocated in 2,024-byte units.
IMAGE	0 – 2,147,483,647	Binary data of variable length, of which the maximum is predetermined at the time of allocation. Increments are allocated in 2,024-byte units.
BINARY	1 – 255	Binary data of a fixed length that is determined at the time of allocation.
VARBINARY	1 – 255	Binary data of variable length, of which the maximum length is determined at the time of allocation.
DATETIME	8	Date and time stored as two 4-byte integers with a value and accuracy in milliseconds. The first 4 bytes contain a count of days since 1/1/1990 and can have a legal value from 1/1/1753 to 12/31/9999.
SMALLDATETIME	4	Date and time stored as two 2-byte integers with a value and accuracy in minutes. The first 2 bytes contain a count of days since 1/1/1990 and can have a legal value from 1/1/1990 to 6/6/2079.
MONEY	8	Monetary values stored in two 4-byte values. The first value contains the whole number and the second value contains the fractional amount.
SMALLMONEY	4	Monetary values stored in two 2-byte values. The first value contains the whole number and the second value contains the fractional amount.

Data Type	Size in Bytes	Description
TIMESTAMP	8	An internally (by SQL Server) incremented value.

SQL Server Management Tools

Microsoft has provided two levels of management tools for administrators to use when administering SQL Server. These levels include the standard command-line interface and system stored procedures or graphical user interface (GUI) tools. For the most part, the GUI tools are provided to aid users who are not familiar with SQL Server management, but some of these tools, such as the SQL Security Manager and SQL Transfer Manager, have no command-line interface. This section shows you what GUI tools are available. For more details, see Chapter 17.

You can use these GUI tools with SQL Server 4.2x:

◆ SQL Administrator: This is the heart of your GUI administrative tools because it provides the interface to support the creation of your devices, segments, and databases. It also provides an interface to give you the capability to configure the server, to manage your user and group accounts, and to manage the individual connection to SQL Server.

◆ SQL Object Manager: Just like the SQL Administrator, this application is the heart of managing your individual databases. With this tool, you can create and delete tables, views, stored procedures, rules, defaults, and indexes. You also can use this application to manage the user permissions for objects and to dump the database schema so that you can re-create the database when you want.

◆ SQL Tape Utility: You use this tool to restore a database dump and to verify the datasets that have been dumped to a tape.

◆ SQL Transfer Manager: You use this tool to migrate an existing SQL Server database on a remote SQL Server to your current SQL Server installation.

You can use these GUI tools with SQL Server 6.x:

◆ SQL Enterprise Manager: This tool includes most of the functionality of the SQL Administrator, SQL Object Manager, SQL Tape Utility, and SQL Transfer Manager in a single application. It is also used to manage your database replication.

◆ SQL Server Web Assistant: You can use this tool to create HTML pages from your SQL Server databases for publishing on the Internet or an intranet.

You can use these GUI tools with SQL Server 4.2x or 6.x:

◆ SQL Security Manager: You use this tool to migrate and manage your domain user account mappings in the SQL Server syslogins table.

◆ ISQL/W: This tool is a GUI version of the command-line ISQL utility. You can use it to optimize your queries by displaying a graphical representation of the optimization plan that SQL Server will use and to display the I/O results of the query.

◆ Performance Monitor: When you install SQL Server, it adds additional performance object counters that you can use to tune your server for maximum performance. In Chapter 18, you will look at this tool in much greater detail.

SUMMARY

This chapter discussed some of the basics as an introduction to Microsoft SQL Server to help prepare you for your duties as a network and database administrator. Even if you will not be the database administrator, this chapter should at least have helped you to understand some of the issues and prepared you for some of the problems a database administrator needs to address. Although these issues, for the most part, are separate from a job as a network administrator, some of these issues will occur based on your installation.

This is part of what you will be exploring in the next chapter. You'll learn how to plan for your installation, determine who will be in charge of your SQL Server installation, and how this will impact you. You also will learn how to determine the physical hardware you will need, and how to determine your storage needs by calculating the size of your database.

CHAPTER 15

Planning Your SQL Server Installation

Microsoft SQL Server is fairly integrated with Windows NT Server. You could just install SQL Server on the server of your choice, but you will achieve better results if you spend some time planning your installation. Also, consider how you will use your SQL Server installation. Will you use it just for the Systems Management Server (SMS) database, or will you make it available for other users to use as well? Will you have more than one SQL Server installation on your network? Who will be in charge of these SQL Server installations? Will you, the network administrator, be performing the duties of the database administrator (DBA) as well as your network duties? Or will you have a dedicated DBA to administer the SQL Server installations? If you have a dedicated DBA, will you give him administrative privileges on the network too? Only after you answer these questions should you move onto other areas.

After you determine who will be in charge of the SQL Server installation, you should consider the requirements needed for your SQL Server installation. This includes the type of Windows NT Server installation (domain controller or server) you will use with SQL Server. And just what type of hardware resources will be required? Will you need to add additional memory, hard disk drives, modems, or other hardware to obtain adequate SQL Server performance? While you are considering your hardware requirements, where do you start? What will you do to restore your SQL Server databases if a system failure occurs?

These are a lot of questions to answer, but this chapter should help you answer many of them. Just keep in mind that every network is unique, and depending on your company's business policies, you may need to modify some of the suggestions you will look at in this chapter.

DETERMINING WHO IS IN CHARGE

The decision that you make to determine who will be in charge of your SQL Server will impact more than just your SQL Server installation. It could impact your entire network. And this works the other way as well; a domain administrator could impact the SQL Server installation. And if a network administrator or a database administrator causes problems in the other's fiefdom, you could have a range war as these two sides battle it out trying to assign blame to the other party. This will not help to resolve the problem or get your users up and running again. So you should consider very carefully just who will be in charge right from the beginning and delineate the areas of responsibility that each group will have to maintain.

You should start with the most common installation to understand the difficulties that might arise. Assume that you have installed SQL Server on one of your domain controllers. This is fine if this SQL Server installation will be used only to contain the Systems Management Server's SQL Server databases. But installing SQL

Server on your domain controller is a poor choice if this installation will have to support your other SQL Server clients in addition to SMS—particularly if you also will have a dedicated DBA to administer SQL Server. Now look at this example a bit more closely to understand the reasons behind this decision.

Whoever is in charge of the SQL Server will have to be able to administer the SQL Server. This means that the person will have to be able to create new domain user accounts if you plan on using the integrated security model, or just accounts in SQL Server if you plan on using the standard security model. This same person will have to have sufficient privileges to log onto the domain controller and stop or start the SQL Server service. And this is fine if only SMS will be using the SQL Server installation, because SMS is an administrative tool designed to help a network administrator in his day-to-day duties. But review the following considerations for anyone who is not trained as a network administrator and is unaware of the impact he may have on the server:

◆ At a minimum, the SQL Server administrator's user account must be a member of the Server Operators and Account Operators groups. The Server Operators group gives the DBA the capability to stop or start the SQL Server service so that any configuration changes he makes to SQL Server can be applied immediately. The Account Operators group gives the DBA the capability to create new user accounts on the domain and to manage existing domain accounts to give these users access to the SQL Server.

   Do you really want to give someone who is not trained the capability to manage all the servers in your network in this fashion? Along with the capability to manage the SQL Server service, the Server Operators group also provides the capabilities to manipulate all the services on your server, to manage the shares on your server, and even to shut down the server. The Account Operators group provides the capabilities to manipulate the user account properties and to set non-administrative user rights.

◆ Consider also what will happen to your domain controller's performance as the DBA tunes SQL Server for increased performance. As part of this tuning process, memory allocations must be made to optimize SQL Server's performance. What will happen to your server's performance if too much memory is allocated to SQL Server? Or what will happen if the DBA allocates disk space for SQL Server devices so that he can increase the available storage for databases? How will this impact your users' capabilities to store files in their home directories? And don't forget what will happen in a multiprocessor system if the DBA enables the multiprocessor support option for SQL Server. This definitely increases SQL Server performance, but only at the expense of overall server performance. Are these decisions to be made by untrained personnel, when you will be the one who has to explain why the network performance has suddenly decreased?

If you do not give the DBA the permissions required to manage SQL Server because you are unsure of what damage the DBA may wreak on your network, you must split up the management responsibilities:

◆ User account management: If you are using the integrated security model and decide to add new users or remove existing users from SQL Server, it will be up to the network administrator to use the SQL Security Manager to add and remove the account. After this occurs, the DBA can use the provided SQL Server tools to assign and remove the appropriate access permissions to SQL Server databases.

◆ SQL Server tuning: If the DBA has full System Administrator (sa) privileges on SQL Server but no administrative privileges on the domain controller, then the DBA cannot stop or start the SQL Server service. The DBA still can make configuration changes, however, although the changes are not applied until the server is restarted. So, in effect, the DBA still can affect your network performance by allocating too many resources for SQL Server and not enough for the domain controller.

To prevent the DBA from impacting your domain controller's performance, you must revoke the System Administrator (sa) privileges from his SQL Server account. This prevents the DBA from being able to change the configuration of SQL Server. But you still can provide the DBA with control over a particular set of databases by making the DBA the owner of the appropriate databases. After the DBA is selected as the owner, he can modify the databases as he sees fit and assign permissions to access it.

◆ SQL Server administration: If you do revoke the system administrator privilege from the DBA, the network administrator will have to be available to create new SQL Server devices, add and remove user accounts, tune the SQL Server, make the appropriate database dumps, and perform additional management duties that the DBA no longer is permitted to perform.

If installing SQL Server on a domain controller is not the best choice because of possible problems with the DBA permissions, where should you install SQL Server and how should it be installed? The first option you might want to look into is having more than one SQL Server installation. Choose one for the SMS database, which you can install on a domain controller. For this installation, you can use the integrated security model so that your network administrators can fully use SMS and SQL Server.

Then choose a Windows NT Server operating in server mode to install SQL Server with the mixed or standard security model for use by your other SQL Server clients. For this installation, you can make the DBA a member of the local administrators group, which gives the DBA the capability to completely manage both the server and SQL Server. Any user accounts will be created by the DBA only on SQL Server, which requires the SQL Server clients to maintain both a domain user account and a SQL Server account. No matter what the DBA chooses to do, however, only that server will be affected.

Tip

> The only problem with making the DBA a member of the local administrators group is that once this occurs, the DBA could lock you out. If he removes the Domain Admins global group from the Administrators local group, you lose the capability to administer the server. So you might want to consider making the DBA a member of the Power Users local group instead. This gives the DBA most of the required administrative functions but also requires some additional support from a domain administrator to modify the hardware, partition disk drives, or perform other actions that the DBA is unable to perform.

DETERMINING WHERE TO INSTALL SQL SERVER

In the preceding section, you looked at where to install SQL Server from a control-and-permissions-related point of view. This section focuses on other points of view. You really have four choices when installing SQL Server. You can install it on a primary domain controller, a backup domain controller, a server, or a workstation. Out of these four choices, the first and the last choices should be used only if there is no other choice. The reasons for this are quite simple: A primary domain controller is the originator of your user and group account database and any security policies and, as such, it is used by all your other servers on the network. This includes such tasks as replicating the user database and pass-through authentication for trust relationships, which is more than enough work for a server to perform on a large network. A workstation has a 10-user connection limitation, which means that you can have a maximum of 10 users connected to your SQL Server database, which severely limits the usefulness of this as a SQL Server platform.

This leaves backup domain controllers or servers as choices for SQL Server. And when you consider this, the installation method used most is to use the least heavily used domain controller for your SQL Server installation. The big question here that needs to be addressed is not always a simple one. Is this the right choice? As much as I'd like to answer this with a definitive yes or no, I can't do this. Instead, to make the determination as to whether this is a good choice, consider the following:

◆ The company budget: Just how much money do you have for equipment purchases? Can you afford to purchase another server dedicated to SQL Server? A medium-range server optimized for SQL Server performance can cost upward of $50,000. On the other hand, a low-end server can run between $7,000 and $15,000 and might be within your budget constraints. If you don't have the money for a dedicated server, there really is no other choice but to use what you have available. Good or bad, you'll have to deal with the results. And to make this situation easier to live with, you will look into techniques you can use to optimize the performance of your SQL Server in later chapters.

◆ The available personnel: How many people do you have to support your network activities? Do you have enough people so that you can dedicate one or more persons to support your SQL Server installations? Or will you have to mix the responsibilities of the network administrator and the database administrator and assign them to one or more network administrators?

◆ System performance: SQL Server requires a significant amount of system resources for adequate performance. The domain controller should have at least 32MB of system memory, preferably 64MB or more if possible. At least half of your system's memory, or possibly more, should be allocated to SQL Server. SQL Server also is highly I/O dependent and CPU intensive, which means that SQL Server will impact user logons and any shared resources on the domain controller. Can you accept the decreased performance?

Note

If you have a dual- or quad-processor system fully tricked out with a RAID 5 disk subsystem and more than 128MB of memory, you still can achieve good overall system performance. The performance level depends on how you configure the system and what other services you have running on the domain controller. If you also have Systems Management Server installed on this domain controller, for example, this impacts overall system performance because SMS uses quite a bit of the processor bandwidth and relies heavily on SQL Server. And if you do not change the SQL Server defaults or tune SQL Server, this causes SMS performance to degrade, which in turn causes the domain controller's performance to degrade.

◆ SQL Server usage: If your SQL Server installation will be used to support SMS and your other SQL Server databases, your SQL Server will be performing double duty. This is okay if you are supporting a small set of workstations with SMS, but if you have more than 100 workstations, your other SQL Server clients might complain about poor performance. These complaints will, of course, lead you to an attempt to increase performance by purchasing additional hardware (memory disk drives, for example) and possibly another complete server. If you are going to go this route, you might be better off placing SQL Server on a server dedicated to its use.

◆ Mission-critical data: Will this installation of SQL Server be used to support data required for your company's well being? If so, it should not be used for anything other than SQL Server to minimize potential problems. And in this particular case, you should consider using another server with SQL Server installed, which you can use as a backup in case the first server fails for any reason.

The best choice for SQL Server performance is to use a Windows NT Server operating in server mode. This particular server should not have any other installed software unless absolutely necessary. It is perfectly okay to install SMS worker services on the same server with SQL Server, for example. I do not recommend installing SMS worker services on a SQL Server platform that is to be used to support On-Line Transaction Processing (OLTP) or other business-related data processing, however. Nor should you install any other third-party software on the same server if you use SQL Server for your day-to-day business activities. The two primary goals for using SQL Server for your company's business are reliability and performance, and any other installed software can impact these goals.

Determining Your Hardware Requirements

Just how much system hardware you will really need to support your SQL Server installations depends on what you want to do with SQL Server. The more you expect to get out of SQL Server, the more hardware you will require. But there are limitations to how much hardware you can throw at your SQL Server installation to achieve any real-world performance increases. This installation basically falls into two categories: determining your processor requirements and determining your storage requirements. As part of the determination of your storage requirements, you will need to calculate your table and index sizes.

DETERMINING YOUR PROCESSOR REQUIREMENTS

Windows NT Server and SQL Server execute on the Intel, MIPS, and Alpha processors. I would like to just suggest a platform based on the number of transactions supported on the particular platform, but I have found that this varies too much from system to system. There are so many dependencies that numbers I would suggest here might not be accurate when you compare them to your systems. Based on some early test results and recommendations from colleagues, I can say that the Intel Pentium Pro and DEC Alpha are superb performers.

At a minimum, you should consider only Pentium-based systems when considering the Intel processor line. This is because SQL Server is both processor and I/O-intensive—and the faster the processor, the faster SQL Server performs and the more clients it can accommodate. When making your purchasing decision, you might want to consider purchasing a uniprocessor platform that is expandable to a multiprocessor platform. This gives you the capability to increase your SQL Server performance levels by adding additional processors if necessary.

DETERMINING YOUR STORAGE REQUIREMENTS

The type of storage you purchase for your system greatly impacts your SQL Server performance. It also determines the maximum size of the databases you can support on your SQL Server installation. The first step in determining just how much storage you need is to determine the size of your database (this is discussed in the following section). You will need more storage than the estimated amount you calculate, however, if you want to have a workable SQL Server installation. At the very least, you should consider these points:

◆ Database dumps: Plan on extra space for your database and transaction dumps. Having these available on your hard disk can provide a quick recovery if a failure occurs or your database becomes corrupted.

◆ Bulk copies: You should plan on additional disk space so that you easily can re-create or resize your database based on the data you have copied to your hard disk. A database dump can be used to restore a database, but unlike a bulk copy, it requires the same storage allocations previously defined for the database. This prevents you from changing the size of the database. This bulk copied data also can be imported into other databases, such as a Microsoft Access database. This imported information could be used to support a mobile sales force, for example.

◆ SQL Server schemas: A small amount of disk space should be reserved to contain your database schemas and SQL stored procedures.

◆ Temporary database: Nothing eats up more disk space than your temporary database. This database starts out at a default size of 2MB, and for small databases this actually works. But the minute you start working with real-world databases that require extended joins or numerous sorts, you run out of temporary space rapidly. And this lack of space causes your queries to fail. I have seen instances where the temporary database needed to be between 64MB and 512MB. Remember this basic rule when calculating the size of your temporary database: For each user performing a sort, the minimum space required in the temporary database is approximately three times the size of the table being sorted. If you have a really large number of users and large databases, don't be surprised if you need 1GB or more of temporary space.

◆ Paging file: Depending on your installation, you may need to extend the size of your Windows NT Server paging file. This paging file determines the maximum number of clients that can connect to and use your SQL Server databases. This occurs because SQL Server needs the additional resources, and each connection to SQL Server uses its own thread. Each thread needs additional storage for its internal structures and to process the requested data.

◆ Total disk space: This should be at least three times the estimated database size. Five times the estimated database size is not out of the question. This rule takes into account the additional space needed to create new devices as your database grows beyond your initial estimate. It also includes the additional space needed to rebuild an index. Rebuilding a clustered index, for example, requires enough temporary storage to contain the table plus 1.21 times the size of the original index.

Along with the size of your paging file, you should consider the type of storage you plan to use. You should avoid any device that uses Programmed I/O (PIO) or any disk subsystem that uses the ATDISK.SYS driver, including all EIDE or IDE disk drives. Any disk subsystem that uses the ATDISK.SYS driver can support only one outstanding I/O request at a time, which severely limits your SQL Server performance. The best choice is to use a hardware RAID 5 device based on a SCSI disk controller because this provides the maximum performance. If you cannot afford a hardware RAID solution, consider a software-based solution that also uses a SCSI subsystem. If your budget is sufficient, purchase two identical hardware RAID devices. Create your database devices on one of these RAID drives, and then build a mirror image (using the SQL Mirror command) on the second RAID drive to increase performance even more.

CALCULATING DATABASE SIZE

You should determine the amount of storage required for your database based on the amount of storage required for each table in your database, each clustered index, and each nonclustered index. The formulas for calculating database sizes for tables that use fixed-length columns are the easiest to calculate and give the most accurate results. Database tables that contain variable-length columns must be averaged. The same principle applies to tables that use text or image columns. In this section, you will look at some of the formulas you can use to estimate your database sizes.

Calculating your database size requires that you first calculate the size of your table and then calculate the size of your indexes. Then combine these values.

Note

The values that follow are overhead values used internally by SQL Server, unless noted differently.

To calculate table size, follow these steps:

1. Obtain the number of pages required to hold the data in the table. Determine the size of a single data row. This can be expressed for a data row with fixed-length column (defined as not null) as the following:

```
RowSize = 4 + (Sum of bytes of all fixed length columns)
```

Tip

Refer to Table 14.2 to determine the size in bytes of a column.

For a data row with mixed, fixed, and variable-length data columns; or for a column with a data type defined as null; the formula can be expressed as the following:

```
RowSize = (4 + (Sum of bytes of all fixed length columns) +
_(Sum of bytes of all variable length columns)) +
_((((4 + (Sum of bytes of all fixed length columns) +
_(Sum of bytes of all variable length columns)) / 256) + 1) +
_(Number of variable length columns + 1) + 2)
```

2. Determine the number of data pages required to hold the rows of data. This can be expressed as the following:

```
NbrOfDataPages = (Number of rows in the table) / (2016 / RowSize)
```

Note

The value 2016 is the size of a data page based on the default fill factor size. If you change the fill factor percentage to 100, you should not subtract 2 when calculating the row size. If you change the percentage to a value other than 100, the new data page size can be expressed as (2016 * Percentage / 100). If you use a fill factor of 60 percent, the new data page size is 1210. This value is actually (2016 * 60 / 100) = 1209.6, but you should round up calculations for data pages.

3. Determine the number of data pages required to hold your clustered index. First, determine the size of the clustered index. This varies based on whether the clustered index uses fixed- or variable-length columns. For a fixed-length column, the formula can be expressed as the following:

```
ClusteredIndexSize = 5 + (Sum of bytes of all fixed length columns)
```

For a variable-length column, the formula can be expressed as the following:

```
ClusteredIndexSize = (5 + (Sum of bytes of all fixed length columns) +
_(Sum of bytes of all variable length columns)) +
_((((5 + (Sum of bytes of all fixed length columns) +
_(Sum of bytes of all variable length columns)) / 256) + 1) +
_(Number of variable length columns + 1) + 2)
```

4. Determine the number of data pages required to hold the clustered index. This can be expressed as the following:

```
While
  ((NbrOfIndexPages = (NbrOfDataPages / (2016 / ClusteredIndexSize) - 2 ))
  _> 1)
  (
  SumOfNbrOfClusteredIndexPages = SumOfNbrOfClusteredIndexPages +
  NbrOfIndexPages
  )
```

5. Determine the number of data pages required to hold your nonclustered index. First, determine the size of the leaf index row. This varies based on whether the nonclustered index uses fixed- or variable-length columns. For a fixed-length column, the formula can be expressed as the following:

```
SizeOfLeafRow = 7 + (Sum of bytes of all fixed length columns)
```

For a variable-length column, the formula can be expressed as the following:

```
SizeOfLeafRow = (9 + (Sum of bytes of all fixed length columns) +
_(Sum of bytes of all variable length columns) + 1) +
_((((5 + (Sum of bytes of all fixed length columns) +
_(Sum of bytes of all variable length columns)) / 256) + 1))
```

6. Determine the number of leaf pages in the index, which can be expressed as the following:

```
NbrOfLeafPages = (2016 / SizeOfLeafRow)
```

7. Determine the size of non-leaf rows. This can be expressed as the following:

```
SizeOfNonLeafRows = SizeOfLeafRow - 4
```

8. Determine the number of pages used by the non-leaf data. This can be expressed as the following:

```
While
 ((NbrOfNonLeafPages = (NbrOfLeafPages / (2016 / SizeOfNonLeafRows) - 2 ))>
 _1)
     (
     SumOfNbrOfNonLeafPages = SumOfNbrOfNonLeafPages + NbrOfNonLeafPages
     )
SumOfNbrOfNonclusteredIndexPages = SumOfNbrOfNonLeafPages + NbrOfLeafPages
```

9. Repeat steps 1 through 8 for each nonclustered index for the table.

10. Calculate the total number of data pages used by your table. This can be expressed as the following:

```
TotalNbrOfPages = NbrOfDataPages + SumOfNbrOfClusteredIndexPages +
SumOfNbrOfNonclusteredIndexPages
```

11. Calculate the total size of your table in megabytes. This can be expressed as the following:

```
TableSizeInMB = (TotalNbrOfPages * 2048) / 1048576
```

EXCEPTIONS TO THE RULES

These calculations for variable-length fields use the maximum length, but if you know what the average size is of your variable-length fields, you can use that in the summary calculations. And if you use text or image fields, the size of the column will be a minimum of 16 bytes (for the pointer to the text/image page) plus the number of data pages. A data page for text or image can be calculated as:

```
NbrOfDataPages = LengthOfData (Rounded to nearest 2KB value) / 1800
```

PREPARING FOR DISASTER

Many people think, that because SQL Server is a relational database and uses a transaction log, that their data is safe. Don't be caught in this trap; problems do occur with SQL Server. Some of these are recoverable, but some are not. This can leave you in a very bad position if you get caught with no data backups. You can prepare for a nonrecoverable disaster by using one of the following plans:

◆ Install a tape dump device. (This device is described in more detail in Chapter 16, "Installing SQL Server.") Then dump your database to tape on a weekly basis, and dump your transaction log to the same tape on a daily basis. Use a different tape every week, and make sure that you have enough tapes for a three-month supply. Do not reuse a tape unless it is older than 90 days and archive one tape a month to a permanent storage vault. You use multiple tapes so that you will be able to restore a previous configuration, and to give you a greater chance of restoring your data to a known good configuration. Sometimes an error in the database may go unnoticed for weeks or even months.

◆ Install a disk dump device and dump your database and transaction logs to a local disk drive. Follow the same basic dump times as outlined in the preceding bulleted item. You can back these up to tape with the Windows NT tape backup application.

Note

Although a default installation also will include dump devices for your installed floppy drives, this is not really a viable alternative. Dumping your database to floppy disks is a very slow process and requires an inordinate number of floppy disks.

◆ Periodically dump your database schema to a file with the Object Manager, and then use Object Manager to bulk copy your data to a file. You can use the command-line bulk copy program BCP.EXE if you want. You might be wondering why you should bulk copy your data if you can dump it to tape instead. A database dump requires the same amount of storage as is allocated for the database, but a bulk copy requires only enough storage to contain the data in the tables. If you have created a 500MB database that only has 50MB of data in the tables, for example, a dump to disk or tape still requires 500MB, but a bulk copy requires only 50MB.

Tip

You also can use bulk-copied data to resize your database to a smaller allocation. In fact, prior to SQL Server 6.x, this was the only supported method to shrink a database allocation. Although you could extend a database by allocating additional storage for the database on an unused device, there was no method for releasing a prior database allocation.

◆ Put your database schema on paper. Although the Object Manager database schema rebuilds your entire database, sometimes it is helpful to have a layout of your physical design on paper. This type of layout is easier to visualize than just a series of SQL statements.

◆ Periodically stop the SQL Server service and perform a full backup of the server. If you use this method, you easily can rebuild not only your SQL Server installation, but your complete system configuration. This method is a fail-safe insurance policy in case the entire server fails.

Note

You must stop the SQL Server services in order to close the files containing the SQL Server devices, which incidentally contain your SQL Server databases. If these files are open and in use, they will not be backed up to tape.

Tip

When making a full backup, don't forget to back up the system Registry and verify your files. Without the Registry files, you cannot restore your exact working configuration, although you can restore your data. And a backup that has not been verified is suspect.

SUMMARY

This chapter discussed some of the issues you should consider before installing SQL Server. Specifically, you learned how and why you should make a determination as to who will be in charge of the specific installation. You also looked at where you should install SQL Server.

And as part of this discussion of where to install SQL Server, this chapter also covered how to determine your hardware requirements and gave you some tips on disk storage. You now should be able to calculate your storage requirements based on the estimated size of your tables and indexes.

The final topic in this chapter was a look at disaster planning to prepare you for the worst possible occurrence—the loss of your data. This topic should not be overlooked by anyone who wants to keep his job.

The next chapter steps through the installation and upgrade process. And after SQL Server is installed, you will look at what you should do to your initial installation to configure SQL Server for use.

CHAPTER 16

Installing SQL Server

For the most part, installing SQL Server is quite simple. You should consider a few items before you install SQL Server for the first time, however—items such as the location of the default system device and master database, the types of network clients you want to support, and other incidental information. That is what this chapter is all about: pointing out the information you need to know before you install or upgrade your SQL Server installation.

As this chapter steps through the installation and upgrade process for SQL Server, you will learn about the required settings and configuration information. This chapter also discusses some of the pitfalls you should avoid. The installation and upgrade discussions here are subdivided into SQL Server 4.21a and SQL Server 6.5 sections. These versions differ just enough that separating them will provide you with a better understanding of the subject matter, with less confusion than would be generated by jumping back and forth between the different versions.

After you learn how to install or upgrade SQL Server, you will turn your attention to what you should change in your initial SQL Server configuration. Every network administrator or DBA should be concerned with these items, because forgetting to change these configuration settings could cause unnecessary complications. And finally, this chapter spends a little time discussing some of the troubleshooting topics for a failed installation.

Tip

Before you install SQL Server, you always should read the `readme.txt` file located on the installation disk or from a subdirectory under the `\SQL65` root installation directory (`\I386`, `\MIPS`, `\ALPHA`, `\PPC`), if installing from CD-ROM. This file contains last-minute changes to the software, as well as information concerning the upgrade process.

INSTALLING SQL SERVER FOR THE FIRST TIME

Before you install SQL Server, you should consider a few points. These suggestions are not requirements for installing SQL Server; instead, they are recommendations to aid you in case things go wrong later:

◆ Windows NT Server includes a tape backup utility called `NTBACKUP.EXE`, which is included in the Administrative Tools Program Manager group. Use it! Make a complete system backup, including the Registry, of all drives on your system. If you are unsure of how to use the tape backup utility, refer to Chapter 8, "Additional Administrative Tools."

◆ Back up your system Registry with the Repair Disk Utility. This utility is not installed in any Program Manager group, but may be run from the command line. Just run RDISK.EXE from any command prompt.

INSTALLING SQL SERVER 4.21A

Installing the SQL Server software is generally an easy task. You can use the SQL Server installation program to install SQL Server on a local computer or on a remote computer. There is more to a functional SQL Server installation than just installing a few files, however. Yet you cannot complete your SQL Server installation without first installing the system files, so that is where you will start.

Note

If you will be upgrading your SQL Server installation, stop reading this section for now and read the instructions in the following section, "Upgrading a SQL Server Installation." Then return to this section.

To install SQL Server:

1. Execute setup.exe. The actual directory for this varies based on the platform on which you are installing SQL Server. It is \I386 for an Intel-based processor platform, \ALPHA for a DEC Alpha-based processor platform, or \MIPS for a MIPS R4000-based processor platform. The Welcome dialog box appears.

2. You can click the Help button (or press F1) for additional instructions, click the Exit button (or press F3) to exit the install, or click the Continue button to begin the installation.

3. After you click the Continue button, you are prompted to enter your name and company name. Enter these names and click the Continue button. A confirmation dialog appears. If you made a mistake entering the information, click the Change button. Otherwise, click the Continue button.

   The SQL Server Setup for Windows NT – Options dialog box appears. (See Figure 16.1.) You will become quite familiar with this dialog box during your SQL Server management duties. (Chapter 17 discusses the options it provides in detail.)

   For a first-time install, this dialog box enables only the following options:

   ◆ Install SQL Server and Utilities: This option, which is the default, installs SQL Server as well as all the SQL Server management utilities. These utilities include the SQL Server setup program, the SQL Administrator, the SQL Object Manager, ISQL/W, the SQL Server Security Manager, and the SQL Server Transfer Manager.

◆ Upgrade SQL Server: If you have a previous SQL Server installation that was detected by the Setup process, this option is the default. If the previous SQL Server installation was not detected and you want to upgrade it to SQL Server for Windows NT 4.21a, then you should choose this option instead of the Install SQL Server and Utilities option. You also can use this option to reinstall SQL Server in case you have damaged system files.

◆ Install Utilities Only: Installs only the 32-bit utilities. You can use the Install Utilities Only option to install the appropriate system DLLs and applications on your Windows NT Server or Windows NT Workstation computer so that you can manage your SQL Server installations remotely.

Figure 16.1.
The SQL Server Setup for Windows NT – Options dialog box.

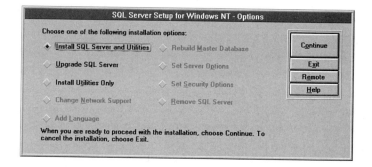

4. For now, assume that you selected the Install SQL Server and Utilities option and clicked the Continue button. The SQL Server Installation Path dialog box appears, where you can specify a disk drive and path for your SQL Server system files. The default for this is c:\SQL. After you specify a drive and system path, click the Continue button.

The disk drive and system path you choose can make a difference in how well SQL Server performs and also can impact your management capabilities. If you install SQL Server on the same drive as your Windows NT Server system files (which is the default setting), then the increased competition for file access may decrease performance. And if you install SQL Server to a FAT partition instead of an NTFS partition, you lose the capability to use built-in compression support. Although compression should not be used for production databases because it does decrease performance, it is very useful for test configurations, data archiving, or any database in which performance is not the primary issue.

Installing SQL Server on a Remote Computer

To install SQL Server on a remote computer, click the Remote button to display the Remote Setup dialog box. In this dialog box, you first must enable the Remote Installation checkbox, and then specify the name of the remote computer (\\BACKUP_SRV, for example). Then you can specify the shared drive to use for the SQL Server installation drive. You also can specify different shares for the Windows NT installation drive (the SystemRoot partition) and the master database installation drive. If you want to choose a different drive for the Windows NT system files and master database, be sure to set the SQL Server installation drive first. Otherwise, when you specify this drive later, it will overwrite the settings for the Windows NT and master database locations that you have chosen.

You also should note that the drive letters you choose in this dialog box are based on the hidden administrative shares (C$, for example, for the default drive C), and that these administrative shares will be mapped to a logical drive letter on the remote server (for example, \\BACKUP_SRV\C$ might be mapped to z: for use as the drive letter that SQL Server will use).

After you complete the Remote Setup dialog box, click OK to return to the SQL Server Setup for Windows NT – Options dialog box, where you can continue the remainder of the installation as outlined in the following steps. The only exception to this is that the mapped drives you specified will be used in the dialog boxes in steps 4 and 5. These mapped drives should not be deleted on the remote computer; if they are, your SQL Server installation will fail to operate.

Tip

16

If you are looking for maximum performance from SQL Server, then you should install it on a hardware RAID subsystem. You can choose a RAID 0 (data striping) for maximum performance but no fault tolerance or a RAID 5 (striping with parity), which increases performance over a standard configuration and provides an additional layer of fault tolerance. If you cannot use a hardware-based solution due to budget constraints, you should use the software alternatives provided by Windows NT Server instead. Data striping can increase the possible I/O bandwidth of your Windows NT Server installation and SQL Server can take advantage of it.

5. You use the next dialog box (MASTER Device Creation) to specify the drive, path, filename, and size of the SQL Server master device. The default drive will be the same as the drive chosen in step 4, and the path will be a subdirectory of the system path specified in step 4—generally, SQL\DATA. The default name is master.dat and the default size is 15MB. Although you can obtain a slight performance increase by installing the master device to a different drive than that used for the Windows NT Server system files and the SQL Server system files, I normally just use the defaults and install the master device on the same drive as the SQL Server system files for convenience.

You should change the default size of the master device from 15MB (the minimum) to at least 25MB. This is because the master device cannot be easily expanded later. Also, as you will see in a later section, "Upgrading a SQL Server Installation," newer versions of SQL Server almost always require additional storage. Just how large your master device should be is open to debate. Your master device is used to contain your initial allocation for the temporary database (2MB), the initial model database (2MB), your master database (8MB), the PUBS sample database (2MB), the system tables, and the default system procedures. You should not need to exceed a 40MB master device unless you have plans to increase the size of your model database beyond a reasonable size, add gobs of complex stored procedures, or add additional databases to the master device (additional databases are best created on separate devices anyway).

6. After you make your choices and click the Continue button, the SQL Server Setup for Windows NT Installation Options dialog box appears, as shown in Figure 16.2.

Figure 16.2.
Modifying the
default SQL
Server configura-
tion.

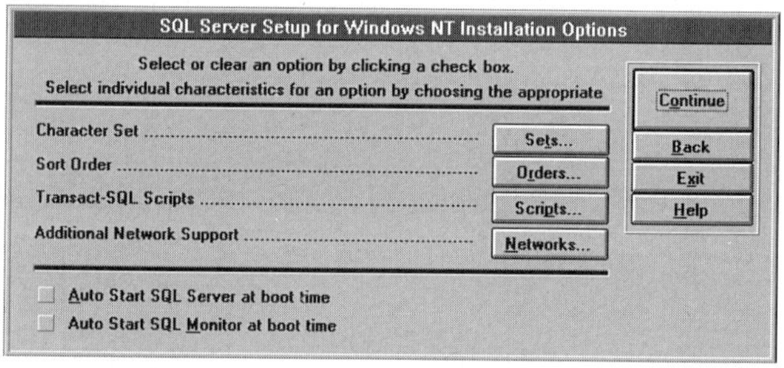

This dialog box is one of the most important configuration dialog boxes and includes the following options:

◆ Character Set: Determines the character sets that SQL Server will support. Click the Sets button to change from the default Multilingual (code page 850) character set. This includes the U.S. English (code page 437), ISO Character set (ISO 8859-1, which is the default character set used by Sybase SQL Server for UNIX or VMS), or a custom character set (which requires an OEM disk). If you plan to store data that uses the MS-DOS graphical characters (ASCII codes 128–255), you should use the U.S. English character set for maximum compatibility.

◆ Sort Order: Specifies how SQL Server sorts data for queries using the GROUP BY, ORDER BY, or DISTINCT clause. The default and fastest sort order is the Binary order, which is based on the ASCII character values 0–255. Click the Orders button to choose a different sort order if you are concerned with strict alphabetical rules and case-sensitivity compliance.

Tip

Although you can use different sort orders included with Windows NT SQL Server to specify how your data will be displayed, changing your sort order can cause a degradation of up to 35 percent of your SQL Server performance. Appendix A of the SQL Server Configuration Guide, "Character Sets and Sort Orders," includes the specifics on the various sort orders and performance-related information.

◆ Transact-SQL Scripts: Click the Scripts button if you do not want to install the sample PUBS database, SQL Scripts used by the Object Manager and SQL Administrator GUI tools, and the built-in Transact SQL Help stored procedure (`sp_helpsql`). You do not need the PUBS database unless you want an example database for your SQL Server clients to use for training purposes. You should keep the SQL Tools and SQL Help stored procedures. Many new SQL Server users find the graphical tools helpful, but these cannot be used without the stored procedures. And the on-line Help facility provided by `sp_helpsql` is useful for anyone accessing SQL Server from an ISQL command prompt.

Tip

If you do install the PUBS database, one of the first things you should do is dump this database to tape or disk so that you can re-create it easily. After all, if it is to be used for training purposes, you will have to restore it to its original configuration for each user or class.

◆ Additional Network Support: Specifies additional Net Libraries that SQL Server uses to listen for client connections. The default is to use named pipe support, which cannot be disabled. This optional support includes the Banyan VINES, NWLINK IPX/SPX, and TCP/IP Net Libraries.

If you specify the Banyan VINES support, you are required to supply a Banyan VINES StreetTalk name; the default is your computer name. In order for your network clients to be able to find your SQL Server installation, however, the StreetTalk name you supply must be entered in your Banyan VINES StreetTalk directory.

If you choose NWLINK IPX/SPX, then you must supply a Novell bindery name. The default for this name is your computer name.

If you choose TCP/IP, then you must supply a TCP/IP port number. The default is 1433, although you should choose a unique port number for your SQL Server installation.

◆ Auto Start SQL Server at Boot Time: By default, this option is disabled. You should enable it if you want SQL Server to start whenever Windows NT Server is started.

◆ Auto Start SQL Monitor at Boot Time: By default, this option is disabled. You should enable it if you want the SQL Monitor service to start whenever Windows NT Server is started. The SQL Monitor service is used to monitor the SQL Server service and restart it in case SQL Server shuts down abnormally.

Tip

You should enable the auto start options for both the SQL Server and SQL Monitor services so that in the event of a system shutdown and restart, the services will start automatically. Otherwise, a network administrator will have to log on and start the services before your clients can access SQL Server. If you are using this SQL Server installation for SMS and SQL Server is not running, this can cause a series of failures throughout the network.

7. After you specify all the installation options, click the Continue button to copy the SQL Server system files.

8. The Setup program scans your disk drives for existing Net Library files and renames them. If you have a problem caused by this update, you can use the prior versions. Before renaming the old versions, be sure that you make a copy of the current files.

9. The next step creates your master device, master database, model database, PUBS database, and stored procedures. Because this can take a while, I suggest that you take a short break.

10. When you return from your break, you should find that the SQL Server for Windows NT group has been created. You now are prompted to reboot your system or return to Windows NT by the Setup program. Before you can start SQL Server, you must restart the computer. Do this now, unless you have to schedule this to occur at a later time due to current network activity.

You probably would like to think at this point that you have completed your SQL Server installation. You still have a little more work to do, however, before you can use SQL Server. Now that you have installed the base software, your next task is setting your SQL Server options, which include setting the auto start settings, mail configuration, tape configuration, SQL Server priority, multiprocessor support, event logging, and Performance Monitor integration. After you complete this process, you need to choose a security model. And finally, there are some additional configuration options that you should apply to your SQL Server installation before making it available for general use.

INSTALLING SQL SERVER 6.5

SQL Server 6.5 includes many enhancements that will change the way you manage your SQL Server installations on your network. These management tools are discussed in the next chapter, but for now you need to focus your attention on installing the product. Instead of describing the installation process in a step-by-step method as in the preceding section, this section looks only at the differences between these installation processes.

Note

If you will be upgrading your current SQL Server installation to SQL Server 6.5, stop reading this section for now and read the instructions in the following section, "Upgrading a SQL Server Installation," before continuing.

The first noticeable difference is that SQL Server 6.5 Setup suggests that you create a user account in User Manager for Domains for use by the SQL Executive, which is a replacement for the SQL Monitor and many of the related SQL Server utilities. You should create and use this user account, even though you also can use the Local System account, just as previous versions of SQL Server did. If you do use the Local System account, however, you will be unable to use the additional functionality provided by the SQL Executive to access domain-wide resources.

To create a user account for the SQL Server Executive, follow these basic steps:

1. Launch User Manager for Domains, which is located in the Administrative Tools group.
2. Choose New User from the User menu to display the New User dialog box.
3. In the Username field, enter a user name, such as SQLAdmin, for the user account that the SQL Executive will use.
4. In the Full Name field, enter a descriptive name, such as System Account.
5. In the Description field, enter a comment for this account, such as SQL Executive Administrator Account.
6. In the Password field, enter a password for the account, and then enter it once more in the Confirm Password field to verify that it was typed correctly.

Note

Do not cut and paste the password from the Password field to the Confirm Password field. Instead, be sure to type it twice. Otherwise, you run the risk of a misspelled password being assigned. And if the password is not what you specified, then you will be unable to use this user account during the Setup process because part of the Setup process is a verification of the user account and password you specified.

7. Disable the User Must Change Password at Next Logon option.
8. Enable the Password Never Expires option.
9. Click the Groups button to display the Group Memberships dialog box. In the Not Member Of field, choose the Administrators group or the Domain Admins group and then click the Add button. This moves the selected group to the Member Of field. If you choose the Domain Admins group (my choice), then you can select this group in the Member Of field and click the Set button to assign the Domain Admins group as the primary group. You then can select the Domain Users group and click the Remove button. This removes the extraneous Domain Users group, leaving only the Domain

Admins group. Then click the OK button. You are returned to the New User dialog box.

10. Click the Add button to add this user account to the domain database.

11. Click the Close button to close the New User dialog box.

12. Choose User Rights from the Policies menu to display the User Rights dialog box.

13. Enable the Show Advanced Right checkbox.

14. Choose Log on as a Service in the Right drop-down listbox.

15. Click the Add button, which displays the Add Users and Groups dialog box, and add the user account you specified for the SQL Server Executive.

16. Click the OK button to close the User Rights dialog box and then exit User Manager for Domains.

After you create the user account, you are ready to install SQL Server 6.5. It follows the exact same procedure as specified earlier in "Installing SQL Server 4.21a," except for the following differences:

♦ When prompted for your name and your company name, you also are prompted for a product identification number. This identification number can be located on the back of the CD-ROM jewel case and is required every time you reinstall, so do not lose this jewel case.

♦ When prompted to supply a master device size, the minimum size is 25MB instead of 15MB.

♦ When prompted to select the network support or Net Libraries to install, you also can choose the AppleTalk, DecNet, Multi-Protocol, or Named Pipes Net Libraries. The AppleTalk and DecNet Net Libraries were optional components included on the Supplemental Services disk, and Named Pipes was a required Net Library and could not be changed for previous versions of SQL Server. The only new Net Library is the Multi-Protocol Library.

Tip

You should install the Multi-Protocol Library if you want to take advantage of the capability to encrypt data and passwords over the network, or if you want to use the integrated security model over other Net Libraries than named pipes. With the Multi-Protocol Net Library, you can use RPC over any of the supported network protocols, including TCP/IP, IPX/SPX, and NetBEUI as your connection mechanism.

◆ When prompted to set your server options, you also can enable the Auto Start License Logging option, which helps you keep track of the license requirements for SQL Server client connections. This can be particularly useful to inform you when you need to purchase additional licenses to allow for system growth. You also can enable the xp_cmdshell–Impersonate Client option, which uses the connected client's user account in place of the SQL Servers account context. This then uses the client account's access rights to access directories, files, or network applications (such as a named pipe application). If the client has insufficient user rights, access to the object is denied.

Upgrading a SQL Server Installation

If you have a previous version of Microsoft SQL Server installed on your system and choose to upgrade it, you should make some preparations just in case of a system failure, installation failure, or SQL Server incompatibility. You can do this by using the following options:

◆ Dump each and every database to tape or disk. This is the quickest method to back up a database and then restore it in a single step. Although it might be the quickest method, it is not always a portable method. Different tape formats, or even different data structures, can make a tape dump unusable. The main reason to create a dump to a tape device is so that you can use the dump to restore your database in case of a catastrophic installation failure. If this occurred, you also would restore your previous operating system, your previous version of SQL Server, and the database from your dump.

Tip

If you will be using a database dump to re-create a database from an OS/2 SQL Server 4.2 to a Windows NT SQL Server 4.2x, then the dump must be a dump to disk, not to tape. Just create a disk dump device, and then for each database, dump it to the disk dump device and rename the disk dump file that is created.

◆ Bulk copy the data contained in each table to disk. This might seem to be a bit extreme because it requires a lot of work from the DBA, but if you bulk copy your data to disk using the character mode format, you can reuse this data file on almost any SQL Server. A bulk copied data file is also the only means you can use to shrink a database.

BATCH FILE TIPS

It is a good idea for a DBA to create a series of batch files to automate the unloading and loading of your databases with the Bulk Copy utility. If you combine these batch files with the ISQL command-line program, you can automate the creation of your SQL Server devices, databases, and tables. These batch files can provide you with the means to manage your databases from the command line.

You could use a series of batch files to unload all your data. For example, drop the databases and devices, stop the SQL Server service, and delete the device files to completely clean the resources used by a database on SQL Server.

Then you can go through the process of re-creating this database by starting the SQL Server service, creating the devices, creating the databases, creating the tables, creating the views and other objects (such as stored procedures, rules, defaults, and so on), uploading the data, creating the indexes and triggers, and assigning user rights. All this can be achieved without intervention from the DBA.

Appendix E, "ISQL Sample Procedures" (located on the accompanying CD-ROM), includes some examples of this basic process to help you create such batch processes.

◆ Create a database schema for each database. If you are using a previous version of Microsoft SQL Server for Windows NT, you can use the SQL Object Manager to create your database schemas. If you do not already have this utility installed, use the Microsoft SQL Server Windows 3.1 Client Utilities disks to install the utilities on a computer that you can use to connect to your SQL Server.

◆ Create a complete system backup, including the system Registry, with the built-in tape backup utility. Make sure when you do this that you first stop the SQL Server service. This enables you to access the SQL Server devices, which usually are open files when the service is running and therefore would not be backed up to tape.

Of course, you do not have to perform all these steps, but if you do, you can be assured that you will be able to restore your data from a previous configuration no matter what. If you were using a compatible version of SQL Server, you can just use the database dumps to re-create the databases and restore the data in one step. But you can't always count on this, which is why I also recommend that you create a database schema and bulk copy your data to disk. If all else fails and you need to have your system up and running in the same day, you can use the system backup to restore your previous configuration.

Tip

Although you cannot upgrade non-Microsoft SQL Servers with Microsoft SQL Server for Windows NT, you can use the SQL Transfer Manager, described in the next chapter, to migrate the databases.

You cannot upgrade a Microsoft SQL Server for Windows NT from one platform to another, such as from an Intel processor platform to a MIPS processor platform. You also cannot use database dumps to restore a database from one platform to another. You can use the SQL Transfer Manager, however, to accomplish the same task.

UPGRADING TO SQL SERVER 4.21A

You can use SQL Server 4.21a to upgrade an OS/2 1.x, OS/2 4.2, or Windows NT 4.x installation. In all cases, you should back up your data as described in "Upgrading a SQL Server Installation" before proceeding, just in case the unthinkable happens. You should keep some additional considerations in mind when upgrading an OS/2 1.x version of SQL Server:

◆ Check to make sure that your master database has at least 2560KB free. If less than this is available, you will be unable to install SQL Server for Windows NT. To determine the amount of free space remaining, you can use the Transact SQL script MSTRFREE.SQL, located on disk #1, or your installation directory on the CD-ROM.

◆ If you have insufficient free space to continue the installation, you can try one of the following options:

◆ Connect to your SQL Server from an ISQL prompt and increase the size of the master database by issuing this command:

```
alter database master on master = 2
```

This adds an additional 2MB from the master device to the master database. If you have insufficient free space on your master device, you may need to create a new device. This new device can be used to increase the size of your master database.

◆ Connect to your SQL Server from an ISQL prompt and dump your transaction log by issuing this command:

```
dump transaction master with truncate_only
```

This may free up enough space to continue the installation.

◆ Connect to your SQL Server from an ISQL prompt and delete tables from the master database, or delete the pubs sample database. You can do this by using the following command:

```
drop table DatabaseName.Owner.TableName
```

In this command, DatabaseName is the name of the database that contains the table, Owner is the name of the user account that created the table, and TableName is the name of an existing table.

Note

Before dropping a table, use the bulk copy program (BCP.EXE) to copy the data to disk so that you can restore it later if necessary. The pubs database can be re-created from the Transact SQL script INSTPUBS.SQL.

◆ If you have marked any databases as read-only, you must remove this attribute by connecting to your SQL Server from an ISQL prompt and issuing this command:

```
sp_dboption DatabaseName, 'read only', false
```

After the upgrade is complete, you can issue the following command to set the database back to read-only mode:

```
dp_option DatabaseName, 'read only', true
```

◆ If any databases are reported as suspect by SQL Server during the start-up process, drop them with DBCC by connecting to your SQL Server from an ISQL command prompt and issuing this command:

```
dbcc dbrepair DatabaseName, dropdb
```

In this command, DatabaseName is the name of the suspect database. These suspect databases are listed in the SQL Server error logs.

When upgrading an existing OS/2 4.2 or Windows NT 4.2x SQL Server, you should execute the MSTRFREE.SQL script as described in the preceding steps to make sure that you have at least 750KB free. If not, try one of the earlier steps to increase your available free space.

Note

If necessary, you can move your Windows NT SQL Server 4.2x databases back to an OS/2 SQL Server 4.2 simply by setting your tempdb to use physical storage rather than RAM by executing this command from an ISQL command prompt:

```
sp_configure "tempdb in ram", 0
```

16

INSTALLING SQL SERVER

> Then, you can execute DNNT42.SQL, which is located in the
> SQL\INSTALL directory. After this is complete, you can physically move
> the database files to an OS/2 SQL Server.

If you are upgrading a Windows NT installation, you also have to make sure that no SQL Server applications are running because this prevents the Setup program from replacing the Net Library files that have been loaded into memory. In some cases, you may have to stop the SQL Service, log off from your Windows NT Server, and then log back on again in order to free these dynamic link libraries so that you can run the Setup program successfully.

Tip

> You also should check your system paths and, in particular, your
> libpath environment variable path manually to make sure that no
> other SQL Server DLLs (such as NTWDBLIB.DLL, for example) are in any
> directory other than the SQL\DLL directory. If these system DLLs are in
> a system path other than SQL\DLL, this can cause a setup failure or
> incorrectly update the system procedures in the master database.

UPGRADING TO SQL SERVER 6.5

Unlike an upgrade from an OS/2 SQL Server 4.2 to a Windows NT SQL Server 4.2x, which you can restore to your previous version, an upgrade to SQL Server 6.5 is a one-way ticket. And for this reason, you should make absolutely sure that you back up all your databases and your system configuration before proceeding with the upgrade. The upgrade cannot be reversed because the system tables are changed, new data types are added, and other system-related components are modified. Another consideration if you are still using an OS/2 SQL Server 1.x version is that an upgrade to SQL Server 6.5 is not directly supported. Instead, in order to perform the upgrade, you first must convert it to a SQL Server 4.2 installation, use the SQL Transfer Manager to migrate the databases, or dump the database schemas and bulk copy the data so that you can re-create it on the new SQL Server installation.

Before you upgrade your current SQL Server to version 6.5, you should run the Check Upgrade utility (CHKUPG.EXE), even though the Setup program runs this utility as part of the upgrade process. You should run it manually, before your upgrade, because it is possible that the Setup program may replace some of the system files before an error is reported to you by the upgrade utility. The syntax for the upgrade utility follows:

```
CHKUPG65.EXE /UUserName /PPassword /SServerName /oOutputFileName
```

Explanations of this syntax follow:

> `/U`: Specifies the user account for the System Administrator (sa) account.
>
> `/P`: Specifies the password for the System Administrator account.
>
> `/S`: Specifies the SQL Server name to connect to. If not specified, the server name of the local computer is assumed.
>
> `/O`: Specifies a fully qualified filename, such as `C:\SQL\ INSTALL\UPGRADE.TXT`. Note: The directories specified already must exist or the reporting process fails.

After the upgrade report is created, use Notepad to view it. Any errors reported will have to be fixed before the upgrade can be performed. The Upgrade utility checks the syscomments table to make sure that the text description in the Text field is valid. The Text field is used to convert or upgrade the data type for an object. If this data is missing (probably because a System Administrator deleted it), the upgrade cannot continue. In order for the upgrade to continue, you must drop and re-create the object. If the object is a table, then you should bulk copy the data out, re-create the table, and then bulk copy the data back.

If the Upgrade utility reports that any databases are marked as read-only, you must remove this attribute by running this command from an ISQL command prompt:

```
sp_dboption DatabaseName, 'read only', false
```

where `DatabaseName` is the name of the read-only database. After the upgrade is complete, you can issue this command from an ISQL command prompt:

```
dp_option DatabaseName, 'read only', true
```

This sets the database back to read-only mode.

COMPLETING YOUR INSTALLATION

Now that the SQL Server service has been installed and is operating normally (if it is not working, then jump to the section "Troubleshooting a Failed Installation"), it is time to choose your additional configuration options and finish your installation. After this is accomplished, you will want to be sure that it continues to work as you expect and set the various system defaults.

Chapter 18, "Optimizing SQL Server," examines other configuration settings and discusses the options available for obtaining maximum performance from your SQL Server installation.

16

FINISHING YOUR SQL SERVER INSTALLATION

Although you could use the SQL Server installation that you just finished installing just as it is, I don't really recommend it. If you use it as is, then you also lose a lot of additional functionality. This section helps you choose among these various configuration options by describing what each option will do for you and how to configure these options.

To set the initial configuration options, follow these steps:

1. Launch the SQL Setup program, which is located in the SQL Server for Windows NT Program Manager group. Then click the Continue button. A confirmation dialog box appears, stating that this installation already has been installed. Again, click the Continue button. The SQL Server for Windows NT – Options dialog box appears.

2. Enable the Set Server Options checkbox and click the Continue button. The SQL Server Setup for Windows NT dialog box appears, as shown in Figure 16.3.

Figure 16.3.
Setting the initial
SQL Server
configuration.

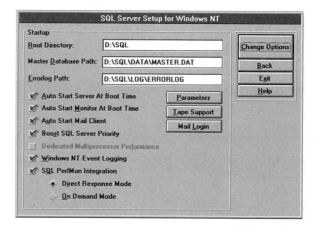

3. The SQL Server Setup for Windows NT dialog box has the following options, which you can modify:

   ◆ Root Directory: Specifies the root directory where SQL Server was installed.

   ◆ Master Database Path: Specifies the complete path and filename to the master device.

   ◆ Errorlog Path: Specifies the complete path and filename to the location of the SQL Server error logs.

Note

You should change these options only if you move SQL Server from its original location. If you do move SQL Server, be sure to click the Parameters button and specify the new locations for the master device and error log.

◆ Auto Start Server At Boot Time: Sets SQL Server to start automatically when the server boots, even if no user is logged onto the system.

◆ Auto Start Monitor At Boot Time: Sets the SQL Monitor service to start automatically whenever the server is restarted.

◆ Auto Start Mail Client: Sets the SQL Server mail client to start automatically whenever the server is started. If you enable this option, it is also a good idea to configure the mail client. This is accomplished by clicking the Mail Login button. Then, in the dialog box that appears, specify the mail account user identification and password to use. You also should enable the Copy SQLMail From Current User Account checkbox to specify the location of the post office and other default configuration information required for a successful mail client.

In order to copy the current mail configuration, the user account you currently are using must already have been configured as a mail client. This requires running Microsoft Mail at least once under the current user to specify the location of the mail server and a mail account. At this same time, you should create the mail account for use by the SQL Server mail client. For more specifics on this, you can refer to Chapter 8, "Additional Administrative Tools," if you are using the built-in mail software provided by Windows NT. Or, if you are using the full-blown Microsoft Mail software (version 3.x), you can refer to Chapter 28, "Optimizing Your Mail Server," for a description of how to manage your post office accounts.

If you are planning on using the built-in mail functionality provided with SQL Server and also are executing the service using the LocalSystem account instead of a specific user account, you also should enable the Allow Service to Interact with Desktop checkbox after accessing the Control Panel Services applet. Just scroll down the list of services, select the SQL Server service, and click the Startup button.

◆ Boost SQL Server Priority: Increases the performance of your SQL Server installation by raising the priority of the SQL Server worker threads. This option also decreases the capability of your server to

16

INSTALLING SQL SERVER

share other network resources, however, so you should enable this option only if the server will be dedicated to SQL Server.

◆ Dedicated Multiprocessor Performance: Increases the performance of SQL Server if you have more than one processor installed on your computer. This degrades the server's capability to service other network users for shared resources, however, so it should be enabled only if the server usage will be dedicated to SQL Server, or you are willing to accept the general performance decrease.

◆ Windows NT Event Logging: Places SQL Server events in the Windows NT application log as well as the SQL Server error log.

◆ SQL PerfMon Integration: Adds additional performance counters to your Windows NT system and enables you to monitor your SQL Server performance.

◆ Direct Response Mode: Gathers statistics from SQL Server and provides the best response, but the statistics gathered will be one refresh interval behind.

◆ On Demand Mode: Gathers statistics from SQL Server and provides the most accurate data, but places a greater load on SQL Server. If you enable this option, be sure to set the refresh interval to a high enough value so that you do not overload SQL Server with requests for statistics.

4. If you have a tape drive installed on your server (and you should), you also should configure the tape time-out interval. Click the Tape Support button in the SQL Server Setup for Windows NT dialog box. This gives you three choices:

◆ Wait Indefinitely: Waits indefinitely for you to insert a tape into the tape backup device in order for a database or transaction log dump to continue. This is the default option.

◆ Try Once and Quit: Attempts to access the tape drive once, and if no tape is available, the dump process is discontinued.

◆ Try for X Minutes: Waits for the number of minutes you specify to access a tape before discontinuing the dump process in case no tape is available.

5. After you complete your changes, click the Change Options button. This updates your configuration and prompts you (via a button) to return to Windows NT.

Tip

If you want your changes to be placed in effect immediately, you first must stop and then restart the SQL Server service.

The next step in this initial configuration process is to choose a SQL Server security mode. Follow these steps:

1. Launch the SQL Setup program as described earlier and click the Continue button until the SQL Server for Windows NT – Options dialog box appears.

2. Enable the Set Security Options checkbox and click the Continue button. The Set Security Options dialog box appears, as shown in Figure 16.4.

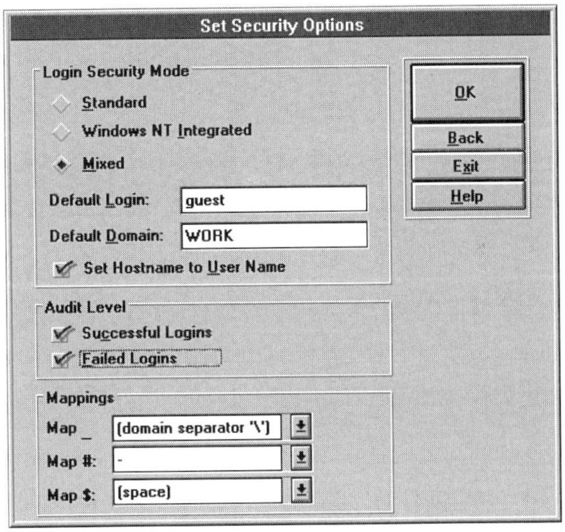

Figure 16.4.
Choosing a
security model
with the Set
Security Options
dialog box.

3. The default security model is the Standard model. However, I prefer to use the Integrated or Mixed security model. Descriptions of these security models follow:

   ◆ Standard: Uses the same security mechanism as all other Sybase SQL Server installations, in which all user account and logon information is maintained internally in SQL Server tables.

   ◆ Windows NT Integrated: Uses the domain user account database for user account authentication over a trusted connection. A trusted connection is available only for clients using a named pipe. Currently, these clients include Microsoft Windows NT, Windows 95, Windows for Workgroups, and LAN Manager. You cannot establish a trusted connection for clients that do not use a named pipe, however, such as those using a TCP/IP socket as their connection mechanism.

16

♦ Mixed: Uses the integrated security model if a trusted connection can be established. Otherwise, the standard security model is used.

When you choose the Windows NT Integrated or Mixed security model, you can set the default user name to be used for a client that is not in the domain database, set the default domain, and enable the Set Hostname to User Name option. This replaces the SQL Server login name that a client uses with the actual network user name for the client, but only if the client connects using a trusted connection.

4. You also can find out just who has been using or attempting to use your SQL Server by enabling the Audit Level options. If you enable the Successful Logins option, a record is inserted into the Windows NT security event log for each user that connects to SQL Server successfully. If you enable the Failed Logins option, you can use the security event log to determine who is having a problem remembering their SQL Server user account and password, or who might be trying to bypass your security and hack his way into your SQL Server databases.

5. The Mappings group is provided to let you change the default mapped characters between those that Windows NT uses and those that SQL Server can accept. SQL Server cannot use a hyphen (-), for example, although Windows NT can, so this character is mapped to an underscore (_). You can change these character mappings if desired, but unless you really have a need, you should leave them as they are.

6. After you finish your changes, click the OK button. You are prompted to supply your System Administrator (sa) password. Enter this (if you have not changed it yet, then there is no password to supply) and click the Continue button. This updates your configuration and then prompts you (via a button) to return to Windows NT.

Note

The changes you have made are not placed into effect until you restart the SQL Server service.

The final step is to install any additional Net Libraries to support your additional network clients. You can use the drivers provided in the Microsoft SQL Server Supplemental Services disk, which provides support for AppleTalk and DecNet clients, or an OEM disk from your manufacturer.

To install additional Net Libraries, follow these steps:

1. Launch the SQL Setup application as described earlier and work your way through the dialog boxes until you reach the SQL Server for Windows NT – Options dialog box.

2. Enable the Change Network Support option and click the Continue button.

3. In the next dialog box, enable the User Provided checkbox and click the Continue button. A dialog box specifying the drive and root directory installation paths appears.

4. You should have to change these paths only if you have more than one SQL Server installation on your server. Then click the Continue button.

5. You are prompted to enter the complete drive, path, and filename of the supplied Net Library file. For the supplied AppleTalk driver, this is

```
A:\ADSP\ProcessorType\SSMSADSN.DLL
```

and for the DecNet driver, this is

```
A:\DECNET\ProcessorType\SSMSDECN.DLL
```

where `ProcessorType` is I386 for an Intel-based processor, MIPS for a MIPS-based processor, or Alpha for a DEC Alpha-based processor platform.

6. If you specified a floppy drive as the source, you are prompted to insert the disk. Do so and click the OK button.

7. You are required to supply a network address. For the AppleTalk Net Library, this can be the name of your server, and for the DecNet Net Library, this can be any unique DecNet object ID. For a numeric ID, preface the number with the # sign (#220, for example). Click OK to exit the dialog box.

8. Your configuration is updated and you are prompted (via a button) to return to Windows NT.

FINISHING YOUR INITIAL SQL SERVER CONFIGURATION

After you finish with your configuration choices, you will want to make sure that these choices remain in effect until you decide otherwise. You also might want to make some system-related configuration changes to set defaults for future database storage allocations, dump devices, and set default data types. These choices and others are discussed in this section in order of importance.

Note

During the discussion in the following steps, I use the command-line tools instead of the graphical tools. This is not because I am a command-line bigot (I actually like the GUI tools); instead, it is because the Microsoft Certification exams focus only on the command-

> line tools. And no matter what Sybase (or derived) SQL Server you
> use, these same command-line procedures can be used to achieve the
> same basic results. The various tools and options are discussed in the
> next chapter, but for now, I'll give you step-by-step examples to help
> walk you through the process.

SECURE YOUR SQL SERVER INSTALLATION

Believe it or not, this step often is overlooked by the average Administrator. But you should consider yourself a step above the average; after all, you purchased this book didn't you? So be sure to change the default System Administrator (sa) password. After you change the password, be sure to reconfigure the SQL Server and SQL Monitor services to use the new password.

To change the default SQL Server sa password, follow these steps:

1. Log onto SQL Server using the ISQL command-line utility. If you are performing this on the local computer where SQL Server is installed, you can issue the following command from a Windows NT command prompt:

   ```
   ISQL /Usa /P
   ```

   If you are going to change the sa password for a remote SQL Server, issue this command:

   ```
   ISQL /Usa /P /SServerName
   ```

   This command uses the following options:

   /U: The account to use for the SQL Server log on.

   /P: The password to be used for the specified account.

   /S: The computer name for the server where SQL Server is installed.

2. Change the password by executing the sp_password stored procedure. The syntax follows:

   ```
   sp_password OldPassword, NewPassword, <AccountID>
   ```

   Explanations of the syntax follow:

   OldPassword: Current password for the account.

   NewPassword: New password to be assigned to the account.

   AccountID: Optional component specifying the account for which you want to change the password.

If you logged onto SQL Server using the default sa account, for example, to change your initial sa account password to `newpassword`, you should use this syntax:

```
sp_password null, newpassword
```

If you logged onto SQL Server with another administrative account, you can use this command:

```
sp_password null, newpassword, sa
```

Note

One day I walked into a client's office to install Windows NT Server and then SQL Server. When I was finished, I used the SQL Administrator to change the System Administrator password for the SQL Server I had just completed and was amazed to find six previous SQL Server installations on their shared network. And not a single one of the DBAs for these SQL Server installations had bothered to change the default password. I was able to connect to all of them using the default sa account and password. This was a very scary situation because all these installations contained data critical to the well-being of the companies involved. If I had any malicious intents, I could have put these companies into potential bankruptcy. Instead, I graciously notified them of their security breaches.

Note

You cannot specify a null parameter by entering a set of quotation marks (`""`) for a string as you might be familiar with using in other applications. Instead, you must enter the keyword null, as in the example for a stored procedure.

3. After entering the preceding command, press Enter. Another numerical prompt appears. Type the word `go` and press Enter. This executes the stored procedure (`sp_password`) that you entered previously. Then you can enter the quit command to be returned to a command prompt.

4. Change the SQL Monitor password by issuing the following command from a Windows NT command prompt:

```
netsql SqlMonitor /NEWPASSWORD=NewPassword
```

Here, `NewPassword` is the password you chose for the sa account earlier.

16

INSTALLING SQL SERVER

A VERY BRIEF OVERVIEW OF ISQL

The Interactive SQL (ISQL) command prompt is a tool you can use to connect to SQL Server and execute any Transact SQL statement. When you use ISQL, a numerical prompt appears for each statement to be executed. After you enter the go keyword to execute your statement(s), a result set or message appears. When you change the sa password using the earlier steps, for example, the input and output (presented in bold text) look like the following:

```
D:\users\default>isql /Usa /P
1> sp_password null, newpassword
2> go
Password changed.
1> quit
```

You also can use ISQL to process a series of Transact SQL statements in a batch file by specifying a filename that contains the Transact SQL statements to execute—for example, ISQL /Usa /P /iISQLFile.SQL. The last two statements in a Transact SQL batch file should be go to execute the batch and quit to exit the SQL command interpreter. Or, you can use the /q switch to execute the query (the same as the go command) or /Q to execute the query and then exit (the same as the go and quit commands). For more information on the ISQL command-line switches, just enter ISQL /? at a command prompt.

CHANGE THE DEFAULT DEVICE

The default device is master.dat after you install SQL Server, but you should change this as soon as possible to prevent the actual creation of user-related databases in this device. This device is a system device, and if you have to re-create it for any reason, any databases you have installed in this device must be restored from a previous backup. If you run out of space in the master device due to these user databases, you must spend time moving them to other devices. This can be a lengthy process, so it is best to avoid this possibility right from the start.

To create a new default device, follow these steps:

1. Log onto the SQL Server, as described earlier.

2. Create a new device by issuing the disk init command. The syntax for this command follows:

```
disk init name = 'LogicalName', physname = 'PhysicalName', vdevno =
➥_UniqueNbr,
size = Nbr2Kbpages, [, vstart = VirtualAddress] [, cntrltype = ControllerNbr]
➥_[, contiguous]
```

Explanations of this syntax follow:

LogicalName: A unique name that will be used in future database or log allocation statements.

PhysicalName: A unique, fully qualified path name to contain the physical storage.

Vdevno: A unique number to represent the device internally by SQL Server.

Size: Number of 2KB (2048 byte) pages to be allocated. The minimum is 512 for a 1MB device.

VirtualAddress: Specifies the virtual offset or the starting address in 2KB blocks.

ControllerNbr: Specifies the disk controller.

Contiguous: Specifies that the disk allocation should be made in a single allocation with no fragmentation.

Note

The last three settings are optional and generally are not used. These should be used only if specified by a Microsoft technical support person after a serious problem has occurred.

To create a 20MB device called MyDefaultDevice in the D:\SQL\DATA directory with a filename of MyDefDvc.DAT and a device number of 3, for example, you would issue this command:

```
disk init name='MyDefaultDevice', physname='D:\SQL\DATA\MyDefDvc.DAT',
➥_vdevno=3, size= 10240
```

3. Execute the disk init command.

4. Disable the master device as the default device with this command:

```
sp_diskdefault master, defaultoff
```

5. Execute the command.

6. Enable the new default device with this command:

```
sp_diskdefault MyDeviceName, defaulton
```

7. Execute the command.

8. Exit the SQL command interpreter by typing quit at a command prompt and pressing Enter.

534 PART III ◆ SQL SERVER FOR WINDOWS NT

REMOVE THE DISKDUMP DUMP DEVICE

The default disk device only performs one action: dumping a database or a transaction log to a nonexistent (or null) device. Although you or another user might think the database has been backed up, in reality, all that occurred is that you lost the capability to restore a previously known good configuration. So to avoid this possibility, use the following command to remove this dump device from the system:

```
sp_dropdevice diskdump
```

Tip

For quick access to the built-in help engine for a SQL command, you can use the `sp_helpsql` command or the SQL Help item in the SQL Server for Windows NT Program Manager group.

SET THE DEFAULTS IN THE MODEL DATABASE

The model database is used as the starting point for each and every database that you create. So if you modify the model database, every database you create in the future will contain those modifications. You can use the `sp_addtype` command to add user-defined data types.

Be careful, though, about adding too many stored procedures or other objects to the model database because each added object consumes additional space. You may be better off creating system-wide stored procedures in the master database rather than the model database and just providing execute permission to these procedures.

SET YOUR TEMPORARY DATABASE SIZE

The default database size of 2MB generally is not large enough to handle real-world queries and sorts. So you should create a new device and then extend the temporary database to use the additional space on that device. This is accomplished with the `disk init` command as described earlier and the `alter database` command. After creating your new device (which you'll call DeviceYouCreated), you can issue this command:

```
alter database tempdb DeviceNameYouCreated = 16
```

This increases the size of `tempdb` from 2MB to 18MB (2MB + 16MB = 18MB). Exactly how large you should make your temporary database is determined by the types of queries you will be using as well as the number of simultaneous connected users, but a 16–32MB temporary database is a good starting point.

Tip

You can extend the size of a database by creating a new device and then using the `alter database` command to use the additional storage. You cannot release this space after it is allocated without rebuilding the master database. So you should increase the size of `tempdb` in small increments.

SET THE NUMBER OF USER CONNECTIONS

The number of simultaneous connections to your SQL Server should be changed from the default of 5 if you expect to get any real work done with SQL Server. What is often not understood about user connections is that each query you make with ISQL/W, or each window you have open in the graphical tools, uses one of these user connections. Other SQL Server related applications—even third-party applications—can use more than one user connection at a time. Before you set your SQL Server user connection to the maximum limit of 32767, you should be aware that each connection requires 37KB of memory. You don't want to set the user connections number any higher than you really need. To change the number of user connections, you can use the `sp_config` procedure. For example, to set a maximum of 100 connections use this command:

```
sp_configure 'user connections', 100
```

My basic rule of thumb to determine the number of user connections to allocate is based on the average number of simultaneous users that will connect to SQL Server. For each regular user, I normally allocate a minimum of five user connections. For each network Administrator or DBA that will use SQL Server, I allocate 10 user connections. Of course, your needs might be a bit more extreme, and you should consider this as well. You still should start with a lower number of user connections than the maximum you expect to use, however, because as a user runs out of connections, he will be informed that no more connections are available and that he should close an open window to free up a connection. If this happens too often, your users will be sure to let you know about it; then you should increase the number of available connections.

TROUBLESHOOTING A FAILED INSTALLATION

It is a rare occurrence for a SQL Server installation to fail, but it can happen. The most common reason for an installation failure is a lack of free space on the destination disk drive, which may be caused by temporary files being stored on the destination drive or a growing page file. If one of these situations occurs, you should choose another drive for your installation or delete files to increase the amount of free space.

The next possibility you should check is the amount of system memory installed on your server. The minimum requirement is 12MB of RAM, although you should have a minimum of 32MB of RAM for adequate system performance.

There could be other reasons, which for the most part will be listed in one of the installation logs. These logs are located in the SQL\INSTALL directory and have an .OUT file extension. You should examine these to see whether you can isolate the cause of the installation failure.

If you cannot determine the cause of the failure, you can run the SQL Setup program in debug mode. The syntax for this follows:

```
setup /t Debug = On
```

You must enter this command exactly as shown. This includes the space on each side of the equal sign.

If you still don't know what caused your installation failure and you still cannot install SQL Server, you might want to take the drastic step of deleting the SQL Server Registry key and trying the installation again. The full path to the Registry key is HKEY_LOCAL_MACHINE\Software\Microsoft\SQLServer. This key contains all the configuration information for the SQL Server service, the SQL Monitor service, SQL Server setup, and the SQL Server applications.

Caution

If you delete this Registry key and are attempting to upgrade an installation or reinstall the SQL Server software, be absolutely sure that you choose the Upgrade SQL Server installation option rather than the default Install SQL Server and Utilities option. Otherwise, you run the risk of losing any information in the previous SQL Server installation.

Another reason for an installation failure can be network related. If a Windows NT Workstation system configuration does not have the networking software installed or a Windows NT Server has a network-related failure, for example, the SQL Server installation fails. In the first case, you can just install the network software from the Network Control Panel applet. In the second case, you should find the cause of the network failure and fix it before restarting the server.

Tip

Before you restart your server, you should install the MS Loopback adapter from the Network Control Panel applet's Add Adapter button. This enables you to log onto the server even if your network adapter has failed.

Still another cause of a failed installation is a hardware or software driver incompatibility with Windows NT Server. This could be a storage device that corrupts data written to the disk, for example. And if this is the case, the problem should be very noticeable because your Windows NT Server should be generating error messages or blue screen system dumps. The only solution to this type of problem is to replace the hardware or software and then continue your installation.

Tip

Windows NT SQL Server includes three supplemental procedures, and although they are not officially supported by Microsoft, they can be quite useful:

`sp_diskblock`: Translates a SQL Server virtual disk page and block number to a SQL Server device, database, and logical page number. This particular procedure can aid you in diagnosing a problem when SQL Server informs you of a read/write error associated with a corrupted object.

`sp_resetstatus`: Removes the suspect flag on a suspect database and possibly provides you with a means to recover your data, depending on the level of database corruption.

`sp_marksuspect`: Sets the suspect flag on a database. These stored procedures can be installed from the INSTSUPL.SQL script file, which is located in the SQL\INSTALL directory.

SUMMARY

In this chapter, you took a look at the basic installation process for SQL Server. Specifically, you looked at how to install SQL Server for Windows NT 4.21a, including upgrading from previous versions of SQL Server for Windows NT as well as SQL Server for OS/2.

You even looked at the installation and upgrade requirements for SQL Server for Windows NT 6.5. And you should be reminded that this version of SQL Server is designed from the ground up as an enterprise-wide system. No longer will you have to manage individual servers from the local workstations and manually replicate user databases, because this new version provides many enhancements to help you automate these types of tasks.

Your final stop was a look at completing your SQL Server configuration after you finish installing the actual software: how to set your additional server options, choose a security model, and how to install additional Net Libraries. And although SQL Server 6.5 improves upon this situation, it does not alleviate all the manual installation.

16

INSTALLING SQL SERVER

And as part of this final configuration, you also looked at some of the configuration changes you should apply to your installation to secure it and prevent unauthorized modifications: changing the default device so that your users and you do not inadvertently create databases on the master device, setting defaults in the model database to help you in future management tasks, and performing other miscellaneous tasks.

In the next chapter, you will look at managing your databases with the management tools provided with SQL Server for Windows NT 4.21a—both from the command line, which will help you pass the Microsoft Certification exams, and from the GUI tools, which will help you in your day-to-day duties. And as part of this process, you will take a look at the SQL Executive, which you use to manage all your SQL Server installations.

- SQL Server 4.21a
  Management Tools

- SQL Server 6.x
  Management Tools

- Shared Management
  Tools

CHAPTER 17

Managing Your Database
Server

An administrator's life is not always an easy one. Whether you are a network administrator or a database administrator, life is tough. There are so many things to keep track of and so many different procedures to follow. And of course, every procedure seems to have different syntax rules to follow. Not only are you supposed to know everything there is to know about the products you manage, but you also are supposed to cope with the stress induced by your administrative tasks as if it didn't exist. However, solving problems with a smile on your face is why you make the big bucks.

This doesn't mean that you can't try to make your job a little easier, though. Although you can use the command-line tools and interfaces to manage your database servers, you will find that the graphical user interface tools can make it a lot easier on you. And that is the primary focus of this chapter: What tools are provided with Microsoft SQL Server and how to use these tools to manage your database servers. Although the focus is on the GUI tools, this chapter also includes relevant information on the command-line tools and SQL Server stored procedures. This information serves three purposes. The first is to provide an alternative to the GUI tools and to give you a way to automate some of your tasks by using batch files. The second is to help you prepare for the Microsoft SQL Server certification exams. The third is to familiarize you with some of the command-line tools you can use to administer your Sybase and compatible SQL Server database servers.

This discussion falls into three categories. The first is specific to SQL Server 4.2x and includes the SQL Administrator and SQL Object Manager. The second is specific to SQL Server 6.x and is dedicated to the SQL Enterprise Manager. The third category discusses tools common to both versions of SQL Server.

SQL SERVER 4.21A MANAGEMENT TOOLS

The two most useful tools provided with SQL Server 4.2x are the SQL Administrator and the SQL Object Manager. You will start your tour of duty with SQL Server by using the SQL Administrator to manage the basic SQL Server functions. With SQL Administrator, you can create, delete, or modify devices, databases, connections, and remote user logins. If you are using the standard SQL Server security model, you will use it to create, delete, or modify local SQL Server groups and user login accounts. If you are using the integrated security model, you can use the SQL Administrator to assign permissions to access databases or to set the default database for the user.

The SQL Object Manager is where the majority of your time working with SQL Server will be spent. This tool is used to manage all the objects within a database. This includes creating, deleting, or modifying tables, indexes, triggers, keys, views, rules, defaults, and stored procedures. You also will use Object Manager to set permissions on these objects, to bulk copy data to and from tables, and to generate database schemas.

USING SQL ADMINISTRATOR

The key to successfully using the SQL Administrator is realizing that it is a multiple document interface (MDI) application and, like most MDI applications, the menu options change based on the active window. So when you are attempting to create a new device, for example, make sure that the Device Management window is the active window. You can open these windows by clicking the appropriate button from the main application window after you connect to a Microsoft SQL Server (see Figure 17.1).

Figure 17.1.
Connecting to a
Microsoft SQL
Server with
the SQL
Administrator.

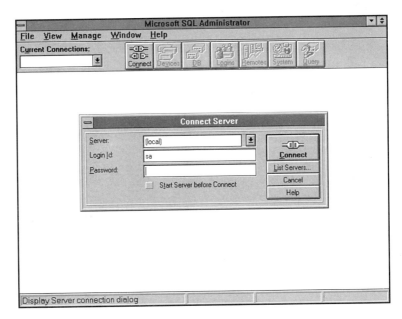

You can choose the following buttons in the main application window (see the top of Figure 17.1):

◆ Connect: Displays the Connect Server dialog box, where you can specify the SQL Server to connect to or a connection to a SQL Server to drop. You can have multiple connections to different servers active at once.

◆ Devices: Displays the Device Management window, which includes the devices, the device type, size, filename, device number, available space, and whether the device is mirrored.

◆ DB: Displays the Database Management window, which specifies the installed databases, size, owner, available free space, and the creation date.

◆ Logins: Displays the System Logins Management window, which shows the user accounts, whether the account has remote server access, the default database for the account, and the default language for the account.

◆ Remotes: Displays the Remote Server Management window, which includes the remote server name, computer name, status, and identification number.

◆ System: Displays the Sys Options/Active Resources window, which shows the process identification number, process status, login identification, host name, whether the process is blocked, the active database, and the command type/status.

◆ Query: Displays a query window, where you can open an existing SQL script and execute it; or write a new SQL script, execute it, or save it. You also can use this window to perform query optimization or to obtain information from a query.

Whenever you launch the SQL Administrator, the Connect Server dialog box appears to prompt you to connect to a specific SQL Server. After you are connected to the server, the buttons along the top of the main application window become active.

To connect to a Microsoft SQL Server, follow these steps:

1. In the Server drop-down list, specify the SQL Server to connect to. If you leave this field blank, you will connect to the SQL Server resident on the local computer. To see a list of active SQL Servers on the network, click the List Servers button. The list of servers you see include the locally configured SQL Servers you established with the SQL Client Configuration utility. If you want to connect to SQL Server using the TCP/IP, IPX/SPX, DecNet, or AppleTalk transport protocols, you must configure a client connection as described in "Using the SQL Client Configuration Utility," later in this chapter.

Tip

The fastest connection to SQL Server is a local connection because this uses local procedure calls (LPCs) instead of remote procedure calls (RPCs). If you specify a connection to a server by name, you will use RPC even if the SQL Server is a local installation.

2. In the Login ID field, specify the user account you want to use.

3. In the Password field, specify the password for the user account and click the Connect button. If a connection can be established, the Current Connections drop-down listbox in the main window of SQL Administrator changes

to display the connection and the buttons become active. At this point, you are ready to use the SQL Administrator.

Note

To disconnect a SQL Server connection, click the Connect button in the main Window. When the Connect Server dialog box appears, choose the connection to drop from the Server drop-down listbox. The Connect button then changes to the Disconnect button. Click it, and the connection is dropped. Or, just close SQL Administrator and all connections are dropped.

MANAGING DEVICES

The starting point to your SQL Server management is creating or deleting devices. A device is the physical storage used to contain your database and all database objects. This type of device is called a database device, but you also can create dump devices. You can dump (SQL technospeak for back up) a database to a hard drive, disk, or tape.

To create a new device, follow these steps:

1. Click the Devices button in the main application window to display the Device Management window.

2. Choose Devices from the Manage menu and choose Create from the submenu that appears. The Create Device dialog box appears.

3. In the Logical Name field, specify a name for the device. This name can contain up to 30 characters and can be a combination of upper- and lower-case characters.

4. Press Tab to move to the Physical Name field. SQL Administrator automatically fills out this field using the default path of SQL\DATA and the first eight characters of the logical name with a .dat extension. If you prefer, you can modify the filename to use a long filename of up to 255 characters to provide a more accurate description of the device.

5. In the Type section, choose one of the following:

    ◆ Database: Specifies that the device will be used to contain SQL Server databases or transaction logs.

Tip

Always create separate devices for your databases and transaction logs for any production database. Otherwise, you will not be able to dump and load just the transaction log. Instead, you will have to dump and load the entire database. Separate devices also can improve performance. The size of the transaction log device should be approximately one-third the allocation size of the database device.

- ◆ Disk Dump: Specifies that the device will be used to back up and restore a database and will use the filename specified in the physical name to contain the dump.
- ◆ Floppy Dump A: Specifies that the device will be used to back up and restore a database. The file will be created on the first floppy drive installed on your system and will use the filename specified in the Physical Name Field to contain the dump.
- ◆ Floppy Dump B: Same as Floppy Dump A, except the dump will be on the second installed floppy drive on your system.
- ◆ Tape Dump: Specifies that a locally connected tape drive will be used to contain the dump. This option is available only if you installed a tape device driver. The default name is

  `\\.\Tape#`

  where `\\.` specifies that the device is on the local server and # is the number of the installed tape device. For a single tape drive, this number is 0.

6. In the Size field, specify the size of the device to be created in megabytes. The default is 2MB.

7. The Device # field is assigned automatically by the SQL Administrator. By default, this number is one more than the first free device number. Device numbers start at 0 and are used by the master device (`master.dat`). You can assign your own device number by specifying a number in the Device # field, but I suggest that you do this only if you have a real need to do so.

Note

The Size and Device # fields are available only if you specified a database as the device type.

8. Click the OK button to create the device.

Note

You also can create a device with the DISK INIT command, as specified in the preceding chapter.

To delete an existing device, just select the device in the Device Management window and choose Manage | Devices | Drop. You receive a warning if any databases currently are using the device. If you drop the device, all databases on the device are dropped as well, so you should dump the databases to disk or tape first, just in case you might want to restore them later.

After a device has been dropped, the physical file is still resident on your system. To delete it, you must stop and restart SQL Server. After SQL Server is restarted, you can delete the file.

Tip

An alternative to SQL Administrator is the sp_dropdevice procedure. The syntax is

sp_dropdevice LogicalName

where LogicalName is the name SQL Server uses to address the device.

To specify the default device on which SQL Server will create new databases, select the device and then choose Manage | Devices | Default. If the device you choose is already the default device, then this status will be toggled off.

Tip

You also can use the sp_diskdefault procedure to toggle the default device status. The syntax is

sp_diskdefault LogicalName, {defaulton¦defaultoff}

To determine which databases are currently on the device, how much space is used by each database, the usage, and the owner, select the device and choose Manage | Devices | Properties or just double-click the device in the Device Management window.

One of the more interesting aspects of device management is what to do in case of a device failure. If the device has a bad page or becomes corrupted, what happens to SQL Server and your databases stored on the device? Well it's really pretty simple. If SQL Server cannot repair the damage and access the device, then your device and all the databases are history. If the device happens to be the master device, then SQL Server will not even start, and you are in a serious world of hurt because the only way to recover is to rebuild the master database or to reinstall SQL Server, and then restore the master database from a previous backup.

To help prevent such an occurrence, SQL Server provides the capability to mirror a device. This means that you will use twice the storage, but if a failure occurs, the mirrored copy is used instead of the original device to keep the system up and running. To mirror a device, select the device and choose Manage | Mirroring | Mirror and then specify a physical device name to copy the device to. If you are not using a stripe set or stripe set with parity, the device should be located on a physically separate disk from the current device to increase your chances of recovery in case of a disk failure.

To unmirror a device, select the device and choose Manage | Mirroring | Unmirror. Select the device type to remove: the database or the mirror. (After you choose one device, the other is used as the replacement physical device storage. You would choose the database to replace the original device with the mirror device, for example.) Then choose the mode: Retain (to keep the physical file) or Remove (to delete the physical file). If you choose to reestablish a mirror after breaking the original mirror relationship, just select the device and choose Manage | Mirroring | Remirror. You can use this option only if you retained the original mirror file, however; otherwise, you have to use the Manage | Mirroring | Mirror command to re-create the mirror file and establish the mirror relationship.

Tip

> At the very least, you should mirror your master device to prevent the possibility of a severe SQL Server error that will prevent you from starting the service.

When choosing to mirror a device, you may specify a write type of serial or nonserial. A serial write means that the original device is written to first, and then the mirror device is written to. A nonserial device means that the writes can occur simultaneously. Windows NT SQL Server supports only serial writes. You should use the nonserial write only for OS/2 4.2 SQL Servers.

You can use the Transact SQL DISK MIRROR command to establish a mirror set, the DISK UNMIRROR command to break a mirror set, and DISK REMIRROR to reestablish a mirror set. The syntax for DISK MIRROR follows:

```
DISK MIRROR NAME = 'LogicalName', MIRROR = 'PhysicalName',
_[WRITES = {SERIAL¦NONSERIAL}]
```

To break a mirror, you can use the DISK UNMIRROR command with this syntax:

```
DISK UNMIRROR NAME = 'LogicalName', [{SIDE = PRIMARY¦SECONDARY}],
_[{MODE = RETAIN¦REMOVE}]
```

Here, the PRIMARY option corresponds to the database and the SECONDARY option corresponds to the mirror. RETAIN keeps the physical file and REMOVE deletes the physical file.

The syntax to remirror a device follows:

```
DISK REMIRROR NAME = 'LogicalName'
```

MANAGING DATABASES

The next step after allocating the physical storage is to store your databases and transaction logs. After you create the database, you probably will want to assign permissions to group or user accounts so that they can access the database, create their tables, and load their data. As the amount of data grows in these databases, you will need to allocate additional storage to accommodate it. This process of adding storage is referred to as altering the database. It actually consists of two steps. First, you need to allocate an additional device if there is not enough space left in the original device to accommodate your database growth. While you are at it, allocate an additional device for the transaction log growth as well. Second, you need to alter the database properties to use this available storage.

To know when to allocate additional storage, you need to be on your toes and check the properties of the database on a daily, weekly, or monthly basis. How often you will need to check your database allocations depends on how active the database is and on how much free space is available. At the very least, you should check once a week; if it is a production database, check it every day. Just remember that it is better for you to take a proactive stance and determine how much of the allocated space is actually in use, instead of waiting for your users to inform you of the problem. You can automate much of this process by using custom Transact SQL scripts with the stored procedures and extended stored procedures.

Tip

> You can select a database in the Database Management window and choose Manage | Database | Properties | Full to obtain the statistics for the selected database.

Now that you have looked at what some of the administrative duties will consist of, take a look at how to accomplish these tasks. The first part of this process is creating your databases. To do so with SQL Administrator, follow these steps:

1. Click the DB button along the top of the main application window to display the Database Management window.

2. Choose Database from the Manage menu, and then choose Create from the submenu that appears. The Create Database dialog box appears, as shown in Figure 17.2.

3. In the Database Name field, enter a name for the database. The name can contain up to 30 characters and is case-sensitive.

4. In the Data Device drop-down list, select a device that will be used to contain the data portion of your database.

5. In the Data Size (MB) field, specify the amount of storage, in megabytes, to use from the associated device. Because data objects include tables, indexes, triggers, and so on, it is better to overestimate your requirements than to underestimate them. The default value is to allocate all the free space in the device, but you can change this if desired.

6. In the Log Device drop-down list, you can specify a device for the transaction log if desired. This is an optional device and is not required but is highly recommended.

7. If you do specify a log device, you then can use the Log Size (MB) field to specify the amount of storage, in megabytes, to allocate for the transaction log. The default is to allocate all the free space but you can change this if you want.

8. Click the OK button and the database is created. You are notified of the number of pages (each of which is 2KB) allocated for the database and transaction log on the specified device.

Figure 17.2.
Creating a SQL
Server database
with the Create
Database dialog
box.

Tip

You can use the Transact SQL statement CREATE DATABASE from an ISQL command line to create a database. The syntax follows:

```
CREATE DATABASE DatabaseName, [ON {DEFAULT¦DeviceName} [= SizeInMB]],
_[LOG ON { DeviceName} [= SizeInMB]]
```

Here, DEFAULT is the default device, DeviceName is the logical name of a SQL Server device, and SizeInMB is the amount of storage to allocate from the device in megabytes. If you want, you can use multiple ON and LOG ON entries for your allocations. To do so, just add a comma after the initial entry and repeat the statements. The following syntax, for example, allocates a database with a total size of 26MB, with 20MB allocated for data and 6MB allocated for the transaction log:

```
CREATE DATABASE SampleDatabase, ON DataDevice = 10, ON NewDataDevice
 = _10, LOG ON LogDevice = 3, LOG ON NewLogDevice = 3
```

You can change the size of a database by following these steps:

1. Select the database in the Database Management window. Then choose Database from the Manage menu and choose Alter Database to display the Alter Database dialog box. This dialog box is essentially the same as the Create Database dialog box, except that you cannot change the name of the database.

2. In the Data Device drop-down listbox, choose a device to increase the amount of free space for storing data.

3. In the Data Size (MB) field, choose the amount of storage to allocate from the device.

4. In the Log Device drop-down listbox, choose a device to increase the amount of free space for storing the transaction log.

5. In the Log Size (MB) field, specify the amount of storage to use.

6. Click the OK button to allocate the additional storage.

Tip

Changing the size of a database and its corresponding transaction log from the command line is a little different than changing the size for just a database. You must first use the ALTER DATABASE Transact SQL procedure to allocate additional storage for the transaction log, using the device you previously allocated or a new device. Then issue the stored procedure sp_logdevice to use the newly allocated space. Finally, use the ALTER DATABASE statement to allocate additional storage for the database. These statements, for example, allocate an additional 10MB for the log and 20MB for the database:

```
ALTER DATABASE SampleDatabase ON DefaultLogDevice = 10
```
followed by
```
sp_logdevice DefaultLogDevice
```
followed by
```
ALTER DATABASE SampleDatabase ON DefaultDataDevice = 20
```
in a single batch.

If it becomes necessary, you can delete a database and free up the allocated storage by selecting the database in the Database Management window and choosing Manage|Database|Drop Database.

Tip

You can use the DROP DATABASE Transact SQL command from an ISQL command prompt to delete a database and recover its allocated storage. The syntax is
```
DROP DATABASE DatabaseName
```

You also can use the Manage|Database|Options menu option to set various properties for a database. After you select this option, the Database Options dialog box appears, which includes a value field where you can change the current setting. These configurable settings follow:

◆ ALL SETTABLE OPTIONS: Sets all the following options to the value you choose. The default setting is False for all options.

◆ dbo use only: When set to True, only a database administrator can access the database.

◆ no chkpt on recovery: When set to True, SQL Server does not add a checkpoint record to the database during the startup recovery process. Instead, the database is updated immediately.

◆ read only: When set to True, the database cannot be modified.

◆ select into bulk/copy: When set to True, the database can accept nonlogged operations. This includes bulk copying data to a table within the database, for example.

Note

If you set the Select into Bulk/Copy option to bulk copy data to a table, you should reset this value to False and dump the database. Until you

> do this, you will not be able to execute the dump transaction statement to dump the log.

- ◆ single user: When set to True, only one user at a time can access the database.
- ◆ trunc. log on chkpt: When set to True, the transaction log automatically is truncated during the checkpoint process. The checkpoint process occurs about once a minute. This option should be set to True only for noncritical databases because this option negates the possibility of dumping the transaction log (which can be used to recover a database).

MANAGING USER ACCOUNTS AND GROUPS

Before a user can actually use a database, he first must be assigned permission to do so by the database administrator. Even if you are using the SQL Security Manager to migrate your domain user accounts, you still have to assign permission to these user accounts to grant permission to access the databases. There is no getting around this administrative chore. You can make it easier on yourself, however, by assigning users to groups and then using these groups to assign permissions to databases. This process becomes even more important if you decide to use the built-in stored procedures to manage your SQL Server installation.

Using SQL Administrator for this purpose is similar to using User Manager for Domains to manage your Windows NT network client user accounts and File Manager to assign permissions to shares based on these accounts. The only difference is that managing these accounts is more difficult than using User Manager for Domains because you do not have a single interface for user and group management. Using the SQL Security Manager is discussed later in this chapter in "Using SQL Security Manager," but for now, take a look at the options for managing your user accounts with SQL Administrator.

You can use the SQL Administrator to create, delete, or modify SQL logins. A login is similar to a domain user account in that it contains an account name and password—although, in SQL terms, this account name is referred to as the login identifier (login ID). Along with this account information, you can specify a language, such as French, which then is used to display SQL Server messages in the appropriate language for the user, a default database, and a user name. Don't confuse this user name with the login identifier, though; the user name is used only for display purposes.

You can use this user name field to give a more informative message to a user. Suppose that you have a specialty database called Marketing that is maintained by a specific person with the login ID of MarketingDbo. This account is being used when another user attempts to access a locked database. The user might be informed that the database is in use by the MarketingDbo if you do not change the default user name for the account. To many users, this might be meaningless, but if you specify a user name like Fred_x4234, the user will know that Fred is at extension 4234 and the user can call Fred to find out when the database will be available.

To create your SQL login accounts, follow these steps:

1. Click the Logins button in the main application window to display the Systems Login Management window.
2. Choose Add Login from the Manage menu to display the System Login Properties dialog box.
3. In the Login ID field, enter a unique name that the user will use to connect to SQL Server.

Note

If you are using the standard or mixed security model to support users who connect to SQL Server using an alternate to named pipes (such as a TCP/IP socket) then this login is the identifier the user will use to connect to SQL Server. This login does not have to be the same as the user's domain user account, but it might be easier on the user if it is.

4. In the Password field, enter a password for this login.
5. Select a language from the Language drop-down listbox if the default language is not used for this account.

Note

You also can select languages that you installed previously. You can install these languages by using the SQL Server Setup program.

6. Choose a default database for the login in the Database drop-down listbox. This database will become the default database for all objects created by the user.

   If you do not choose a default database, the master database is assigned as the default. This is not a good idea because the master database contains system-related information, and if you run out of free space because of user objects, you are in trouble. Instead, you should specifically choose a database for the user. You can choose any previously created database, and if you have not yet created a database for your users, you should do so before you create your user accounts.

Tip

> If you do not want your users to create permanent objects by accident, you can assign the temporary database as their default database. Just specify `tempdb` as the default database. In this case, the user will specifically have to change his database in order to create a permanent object because anything created in `tempdb` has a limited life span.

7. In the User Name field, specify a descriptive name for the user.

Tip

> If you do not specify a user name, the account will not be granted access to use the default database automatically. Instead, you will have to use the process discussed later in this section to grant user access to a database. Or, you should use the `sp_adduser` stored procedure to explicitly grant access for the user account. The syntax for `sp_adduser` follows:
>
> ```
> sp_adduser LoginId [,UserName [,GroupName]]
> ```
>
> If no user name is specified, the login name is used. If no group name is specified, the user is added to the public group for the database.

8. Click the OK button to add the login to SQL Server. If everything is successful, you will receive a few message boxes informing you that the login was added. If everything was not successful, check the error message carefully for the cause of the failure.

   The most common error message is caused by a duplicate identifier. Logins must be unique. If you want to use a login with the same name, use a mixed case. If you have a login of guest for local users of your domain, for example, but you want to allow users of a different domain similar access, use a login of Guest. By doing this, you can assign different languages, default databases, and different user names for these accounts.

Tip

> To create a user login from an ISQL command prompt, use the `sp_addlogin` stored procedure. The syntax follows:
>
> ```
> sp_addlogin LoginId [, Password [,DefaultDB [,DefaultLanguage]]]
> ```
>
> To grant access to the database and specify the user name, use the `sp_adduser` stored procedure.

Tip

> To change the default language, default database, or user name
> properties later, just double-click on the login account. The System
> Login Properties dialog box appears, where you can change these
> properties.

Other basic duties of an administrator are changing passwords for accounts when
a user forgets his password and deleting old accounts. You can accomplish these
tasks by selecting the login account and choosing Manage | Password, which dis-
plays a dialog box where you can specify a new password for the login. You can choose
Manage | Drop Login to delete the user account. Before you delete a user account, it
is a good idea to first check to see what objects the user owns. You can do this by
selecting the user account and choosing Manage | Zoom Login.

At this point, you might be thinking that the user-management process is not all
that bad, and if this were all there was to the job, I'd probably agree with you.
Unfortunately, life is about to take a little twist on you, because you still have to
assign permissions to access specific databases. If you followed the earlier steps for
assigning a default database and specified a user name in the process, you do not
have to grant permission for the user to access (read the default database). But if you
want to allow the user to modify the database or create objects, you still have to
assign permissions. And you have to do this for each database. This is where your
use of groups becomes very handy indeed. Before you can assign permissions to
groups, however, you first must add users to the database, create the group, and
then assign individual users to the group.

To give an individual user login access to a database, follow these steps:

1. Select the database you want to assign user access to in the Database
   Management window. Then choose User from the Manage menu and choose
   Users/Groups from the submenu that appears. The Database Users/Groups
   window appears.

2. Choose Add User/Alias from the Manage menu to display the Database
   User Properties dialog box.

3. In the Login ID drop-down listbox, choose the user login that you want to
   assign access to the database.

4. In the User Name field, assign a unique user name for the user login unless
   you want to use an alias. An alias is a user account that is mapped to an
   existing SQL user login.

Note

If you are using the integrated or mixed security models, and you configure the security settings to Set Host Name to User Name, this value is overridden for any Microsoft client connecting to SQL Server with named pipes.

5. In the Alias drop-down listbox, you can choose a SQL Server login account to use for access to a database, but only if you left the User Name field blank.
6. In the Group drop-down listbox, you can specify that the User Name be added to an existing group by choosing from the list of available groups.
7. Click the OK button and the user will be granted permission to access the database.

Tip

You can give a user logon access to a database by using the `sp_adduser` stored procedure from an ISQL command prompt. The user will be added to the current database, so you should change your default database first with the `USE DatabaseName` SQL statement, where `DatabaseName` is the name of the database to change to. Then you should issue the `sp_adduser` stored procedure command. The syntax for `sp_adduser` follows:

```
sp_adduser, LoginId [,UserName] [,GroupName]
```

Here, `LoginId` is the SQL Server login, `UserName` is the name to be displayed for the specific login account, and `GroupName` is the name of the group to which the login will be added.

Follow these steps to create the group and assign user names to the group:

1. Click the DB button in the main application window to display the Database Management window.
2. Select the database to which you want to add the new group. Then choose Users from the Manage menu and choose Users/Group from the submenu that appears. The Database Users Groups dialog box appears.
3. Choose Add Group from the Manage menu to display the Group Membership dialog box.
4. In the Group Name field, enter a name for the group. This name must be unique within the database.

5. In the Users Not in Group field, choose the individual user accounts to assign to the group and click the Add button. This moves the account to the Users in Group field.

6. Repeat these steps for each user to assign to the group. If you make a mistake, select the user name in the Users in Group field and click the Remove button to move the account back to the Users Not in Group field.

7. Click the OK button to create the group.

Tip

To create a new group from an ISQL command line, use the `sp_addgroup` stored procedure. The syntax is `sp_addgroup GroupName`.

To assign permission to modify a database for a group or user account, follow these steps:

1. In the Database Management window, choose the database to which you want to assign permissions. Then choose Users from the Manage menu and choose Permissions from the submenu to display the Command Permissions dialog box, as shown in Figure 17.3.

2. The first step is to choose the permissions to apply in the Permissions group. You can choose from these options:

   ◆ Create Default: The user/group will be able to create defaults to be applied to columns in a table.

   ◆ Create Procedure: The user/group will be able to create stored procedures in the database.

   ◆ Create Rule: The user/group will be able to create rules to be bound to columns in a table.

   ◆ Create Table: The user/group will be able to create tables within the database.

   ◆ Create Database: The user/group will be able to create a backup copy of the database and log.

   ◆ Create View: The user/group will be able to create views within the database.

   ◆ Dump Database: The user/group will be able to make a backup copy of the database.

   ◆ Dump Transaction: The user/group will be able to make a backup copy of the transaction log or dump the inactive transactions in the log.

◆ All: The user/group will have all the permissions listed in the Permissions group.

◆ None: The user/group will have no permission to create any objects.

3. In the Other Users drop-down listbox, select the user account or group and click the Add button to move the account to the Users With Permissions box.

Figure 17.3.
Granting group
permissions to a
database with the
Command
Permissions
dialog box.

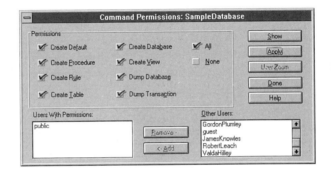

> **Note**
>
> To see who already has these permissions, click the Show button. Any users or groups with the privileges you specified will be listed in the Users With Permissions box.

4. Click the Apply button to assign the permissions.

5. Click the Done button to exit the dialog box.

To revoke a privilege from a group or user, choose the privilege in the Permissions group, and click the Show button to list the users or groups in the Users With Permissions box. Then select the user or group in the Users With Permissions box and click the Remove button. Then click the Apply button to revoke the permissions. To close the dialog box, click the Done button.

Managing SQL Connections

In order for a client to access your SQL Server, a link must be established between the client application and SQL Server. This link (which uses the client and server Net Libraries) is referred to as a connection. Connections are just like any other resource; there is a limit to the number of available connections. Either you'll reach the maximum number of connections you have configured for performance reasons, or you'll reach the maximum number of connections supported by SQL Server.

Once this limit has been reached, no one else can connect to your SQL Server. Because of this limitation, there will come a time when you may need to determine who is using all these connections.

This is where the SQL Administrator can be a handy tool; you can use it to list all the connections to a particular SQL Server installation. You can use this list to determine who is using all your available connections. Once you know who is using these connections, you can inform the user to release some of these connections. You also can use this list to terminate a connection. You may need to terminate a connection for one of three reasons:

◆ Every now and then, a network client may call you to inform you that his application has stopped responding—this may be due to the application experiencing an internal error or due to a long query process. When this occurs, you can terminate your user's SQL Server connection, which generally terminates the user's application or query. This may cause a loss of data in the application that has the connection to SQL Server, but it also restores the user's capability to continue working with other active applications.

◆ When a user has an active connection to SQL Server and terminates the application or reboots his computer without shutting it down properly, the connection may not be terminated properly. SQL Server may keep the connection in a live state while it waits for the application or user to reconnect. If the application or user does not reconnect, the connection may wind up in limbo. In this case, you might want to terminate the connection to free up SQL Server resources and to provide another available connection for your next network client to use.

◆ You have run out of available connections and must terminate other inactive or active connections to enable a higher priority job to execute. Before you take this step, however, you should be sure to inform the user that you are going to terminate his connection so that he has a chance to save his data.

To display the list of connections in SQL Administrator, click the System button from the main application window to display the Sys Options/Active Resources window. This window, as shown in Figure 17.4, lists all the connections by process identification, process status, SQL login identifier, host name, whether the process is in a blocked state, which database is in use, and what state the command is in. This information can be particularly useful in your day-to-day management duties because you can use this information to determine who is using your SQL Server, how many connections are currently in use, which databases are used most frequently, and how many connections actually are performing a real task and not just sleeping (a sleeping task is actually a suspended thread; it does not use any processor time) because the task is idle or blocked.

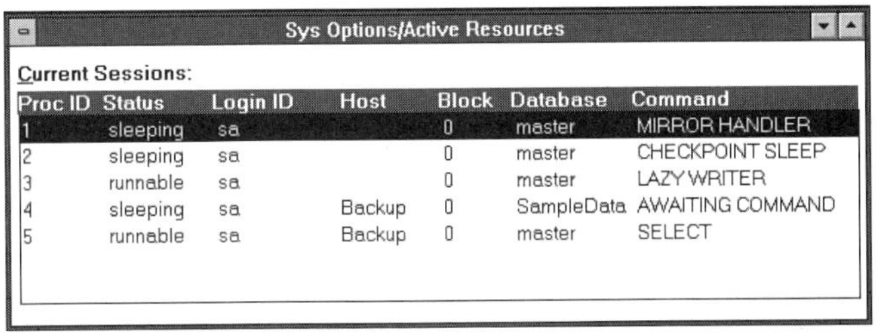

Figure 17.4.
Displaying SQL
Server connec-
tions with the
SQL Admini-
strator.

Proc ID	Status	Login ID	Host	Block	Database	Command
1	sleeping	sa		0	master	MIRROR HANDLER
2	sleeping	sa		0	master	CHECKPOINT SLEEP
3	runnable	sa		0	master	LAZY WRITER
4	sleeping	sa	Backup	0	SampleData	AWAITING COMMAND
5	runnable	sa	Backup	0	master	SELECT

Of all this information, the most important is knowing when a connection is blocked. A blocked connection generally occurs because some other process is inserting or updating data, which creates a temporary lock. This temporary lock could prevent other processes from continuing their execution. If this is caused by a very complex Transact SQL statement that takes a significant amount of system resources to complete, you might want to look at optimization techniques that could speed up the processing task. If, on the other hand, this temporary lock becomes a permanent lock because the Transact SQL statements contain a programmer error and loop forever, your only choices are to wait for a time-out to occur on the client side and discontinue the action when prompted, or to kill the task immediately if the time-out interval is too long a period to wait. You will not find a menu option to kill a task, but you can select the task in the Sys Options/Active Resources window and press the Delete key to kill it. Before doing this, you should be aware that you will not receive a confirmation message before the task is killed; the action occurs immediately.

Tip

You can determine who is using a database and his status, so you can determine if you need to kill the task by using the sp_who stored procedure with the Transact SQL kill statement. If you just execute the sp_who procedure, you will receive the same list as that supplied in the Sys Options/Active Resources window. Or, you can be more selective by including a login identifier or process identifier with the command to list only entries specific to the login identifier or process identifier. Once you have a process identifier, you can kill the connection represented by the process identifier. The syntax for sp_who follows:

```
sp_who [LoginId ¦ 'ProcessId']
```

The syntax for kill follows:

```
KILL ProcessId
```

Managing Remote Servers

There are two types of remote server management. You can choose to connect to a SQL Server installation using SQL Administrator to manage that server as if it were a local server, or you can manage the remote server's login identifiers so that you can make use of stored procedures on the remote server. This section discusses the latter type of remote server management. This option enables you to use a central repository for stored procedures. Or you can use these remote stored procedures to access data that is otherwise inaccessible to a client. This latter possibility occurs because you can map a login identifier from a local server to a remote server with a different login identifier. So, in effect, when a user runs a procedure located on the remote server, he does so with the mapped login identifier rather than his own login identifier. Of course, this process does not occur without the DBA's permission because the default is to provide no access to remote servers.

To configure your local SQL Server to support these remote logins, follow these steps:

◆ Click the Remotes button in the main application window to display the Remote Server Management window.

◆ Choose Add Remote Server from the Manage menu to display the Remote Server dialog box. In this dialog box, you can choose the SQL Server installations to add to your local server's list of current remote servers.

◆ Now you need to configure the remote logins for each remote server. Select the remote server in the Remote Server Management window and then choose Remote Logins from the Manage menu to display the Remote Logins window.

◆ Choose Add Remote Logins from the Manage menu to display the Remote Login Properties dialog box.

  If you leave the default settings, as shown in Figure 17.5, all remote login identifiers will be the same as their local login identifiers. This is the easiest migration method, but also requires intervention on the remote server to assign the appropriate permissions to these accounts on an object basis so that these accounts can use the stored procedures.

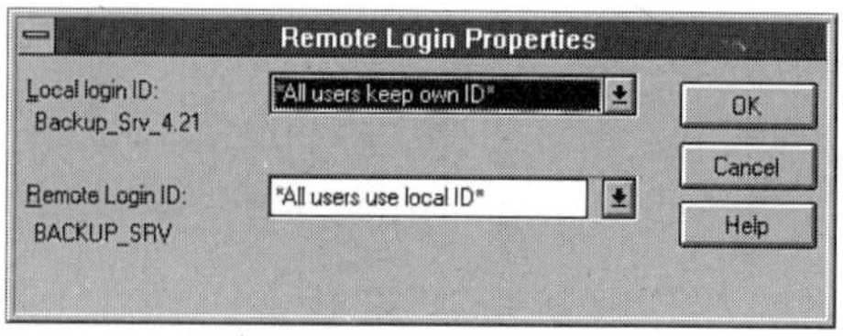

Figure 17.5.
Adding remote
login accounts
with the Remote
Login Properties
dialog box.

This is where the other options come into play. If you choose *All Users Keep Own ID* in the Local Login ID drop-down list, but choose a specific user login in the Remote Login ID drop-down list, you can assign all local users to a specific user login on the remote server. You can even assign a permission level that is higher than the local user login. This enables the user to access data he normally is not allowed to access. This is a controlled access, however, because the stored procedure determines what actions will be undertaken on the user's behalf. The final alternative is to choose a specific user login in the Local Login ID drop-down list and a specific user login in the Remote Login ID drop-down list so that you can perform a one-to-one mapping of user logins. The primary difference between the default setting and this choice is that you can map a local account to a different remote account. Deleting a remote server or remote login follows a similar principle. To delete a remote server, select the server and choose Manage | Drop Remote Server!. To delete a remote user login, just select the user login and choose Manage | Drop Remote Login!.

Tip

To add a remote server, add a remote login, drop a remote server, or drop a remote login from an ISQL command line, you can use the `sp_addserver`, `sp_addremotelogin`, `sp_dropserver`, and `sp_dropremotelogin` stored procedures. The syntax follows:

```
sp_addserver RemoteServerName [, LocalServerName]
sp_addremotelogin RemoteServerName [, LocalLoginName [, RemoteLoginName]]
sp_dropserver RemoteServerName [, DROPLOGINS]
sp_dropremotelogin RemoteServerName [, LocalLoginName [, RemoteLoginName]]
```

You can use the DROPLOGINS option to drop all remote logins corresponding to the local login accounts when the remote server is dropped.

USING SQL OBJECT MANAGER

A SQL Server database really will not do you much good unless you populate it with database objects. These objects consist of any items contained within the database, such as tables, indexes, triggers, views, and so on. At the very least, you must create tables to contain your data. After a table has been created, however, how do you make sure that data entered into it is valid? Do you just give your users a list of rules they must follow when entering, updating, or deleting data within a table and hope for the best? Or will you take charge and assign format specifications for a column, choose default values for a column, and create procedures to ensure that the parent-child data relationship will be maintained properly? Anyone can create a poorly designed database; it requires careful thinking and real work to properly design your database.

Designing your table layout is one of the most important aspects of your database design, and you should consider it carefully. There are two basic trade-offs with table design. You can normalize all your tables to strictly follow the relational database model. Or, you can be space conscious and performance minded, and allow duplicate data and formats in separate tables. I recommend that you normalize your table design when it makes sense to do so, but do not go overboard and waste too much storage or inhibit performance. Consider an example to help clarify this point.

Everybody needs a database of names and addresses at one time or another, and there are several ways in which you could design it. The obvious choice is a free-form table, as shown in Figure 17.6, with three fields to include the name, address, and phone number.

Figure 17.6.
A simple name
and address table
design.

However, a free-form table design is too simplistic for the following reasons:

◆ It is an inefficient design for queries. If you want to search for a particular person by last name, city, or zip code, your query must retrieve the entire field and then break the field into the specific subcomponents.

◆ It does not support an efficient sorting mechanism. The physical sort order is based on the clustered index, and there can be only one clustered index per table. This is discussed in more detail later in this section. Although you can index the Name field, the sort order will be based on the first name, rather than the more common last name. And if you choose the Address field, the sort order will be based on the house number. Once more, this is probably not what you want to accomplish.

◆ It includes only a single address and phone number field. What about business addresses, work numbers, home numbers, cellular numbers, beeper numbers, and fax numbers? If you do not use a clustered index instead of a unique clustered index, you could support duplicate entries for names, addresses, and phone numbers. However, this is not a space-conscious design.

There are probably more reasons why you should not consider a free-form table design, but this points out the more serious flaws. Perhaps you now are considering breaking this design up a bit more and using a single table with a first name, middle initial, last name, home address, home city, home zip code, business address, business city, business zip code, home phone number, work phone number, cellular phone number, and beeper number. This design addresses the issues mentioned earlier and provides for quick data retrieval, but is still not as efficient as you could make it. Not every record will contain multiple addresses or phone numbers, for example, but the design will allocate space for them even if these fields are not used.

So instead of using a single table, you might consider multiple tables, as shown in Figure 17.7, with a parent table that includes links to other child tables. Your design could include a Names table, an Address table, and a Phone Number table. The Names table, which would be your parent table, could include the First Name, Middle Initial, Last Name, Address Link, and Phone Link fields. Each of these link fields could be an integer that supports a maximum of 2 billion entries per address or phone table, which should be more than enough for most users. These links in the parent table would be used as the primary keys, which uniquely identify the record. The same fields in the child table, which are used as the links, are called the foreign keys.

Figure 17.7.
A relational
database model
implementation
of the name,
address, and
phone number
table design.

Names Table (Parent)

| First Name |
| Middle Initial |
| Last Name |
| Home Address Link |
| Work Address Link |
| Home Phone Number Link |
| Work Phone Number Link |
| Cellular Phone Number Link |
| Beeper Phone Number Link |
| Fax Phone Number Link |

Home Address (Child)

| Home Address Link |
| Work Address Link |
| Home Phone Number Link |
| Work Phone Number Link |
| Cellular Phone Number Link |
| Beeper Phone Number Link |
| Fax Phone Number Link |
| Address |
| City |
| Zip Code |

Work Address Table (Child)

| Home Address Link |
| Work Address Link |
| Home Phone Number Link |
| Work Phone Number Link |
| Cellular Phone Number Link |
| Beeper Phone Number Link |
| Fax Phone Number Link |
| Address |
| City |
| Zip Code |

Home Phone Number Table (Child)

| Home Address Link |
| Work Address Link |
| Home Phone Number Link |
| Work Phone Number Link |
| Cellular Phone Number Link |
| Beeper Phone Number Link |
| Fax Phone Number Link |
| Phone Number |

Work Phone Number Table (Child)

| Home Address Link |
| Work Address Link |
| Home Phone Number Link |
| Work Phone Number Link |
| Cellular Phone Number Link |
| Beeper Phone Number Link |
| Fax Phone Number Link |
| Phone Number |

Cellular Phone Number Table (Child)

| Home Address Link |
| Work Address Link |
| Home Phone Number Link |
| Work Phone Number Link |
| Cellular Phone Number Link |
| Beeper Phone Number Link |
| Fax Phone Number Link |
| Phone Number |

Beeper Phone Number Table (Child)

| Home Address Link |
| Work Address Link |
| Home Phone Number Link |
| Work Phone Number Link |
| Cellular Phone Number Link |
| Beeper Phone Number Link |
| Fax Phone Number Link |
| Phone Number |

Fax Phone Number Table (Child)

| Home Address Link |
| Work Address Link |
| Home Phone Number Link |
| Work Phone Number Link |
| Cellular Phone Number Link |
| Beeper Phone Number Link |
| Fax Phone Number Link |
| Phone Number |

The Address table and Phone table, which are child tables, could include the link fields mentioned earlier, plus the Address, City, State, and Zip Code fields, whereas the Phone table could include the link fields mentioned earlier, plus the Phone Number fields. The link fields in the Address and Phone Number tables would be used as the foreign keys. Primary- and foreign-key relationships are the mechanism you will use to create triggers automatically with SQL Object Manager. These keys are used to ensure the referential integrity of your data. Primary and foreign keys follow the relational model and also make it easier to create triggers for the novice, which ensures that data is inserted, updated, or deleted properly.

If you are looking to minimize the space used in your database and do not mind writing your own triggers, then your design, as shown in Figure 17.8, could include a Names table, Home and Work Address tables, and multiple Phone Number tables. The Names table could include the First Name, Middle Initial, Last Name, Home Address Link, Business Address Link, Home Phone Link, Work Phone Link, Cellular Phone Link, Beeper Link, and Fax Link fields. The Address tables could include a link field, Address, City, and Zip Code fields. And the Phone Number tables could include a link field and a Phone Number field. At this point, you may be wondering about all these links. Don't they waste space too if they are not used? The answer to this is yes, the links do waste space, but not as much as empty Address or Phone Number fields.

Figure 17.8.
A non-relational
database imple-
mentation of the
name, address,
and phone
number table
design.

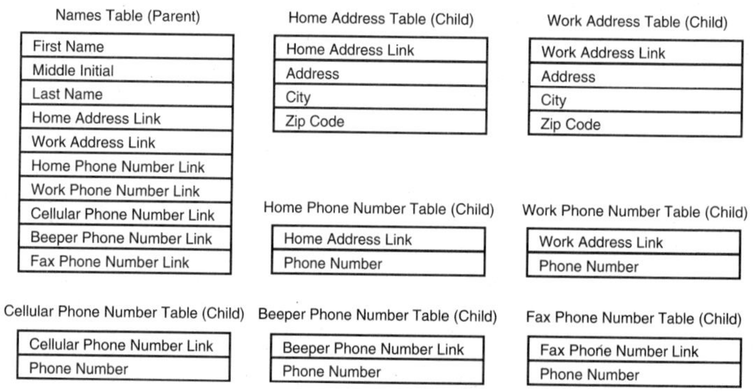

All the links defined in your tables would be used as common keys rather than the primary and foreign keys in your previous design. This cuts down on the space wasted in each table for a complete copy of the primary key, but common keys are used only to inform SQL Server of implicated relationships between tables, and are used to suggest connection points for joins or views. This design does not follow the relational model completely, but it will produce similar results as long as you create the appropriate defaults, rules, triggers, indexes, and stored procedures.

Note

These three database designs are included in the `\MBADMIN\ Projects\Chapter 17` directory located on the CD-ROM that accompanies this book. The first example is in the script file `BadSample.SQL`, the second is in `EasySample.SQL`, and the third is in `FinalSample.SQL`. You will look at parts of these designs as you progress through the rest of this section.

Although the complete theory behind the relational database model is beyond the scope of this book, you will learn about the mechanisms used to create the database objects with which you will be working. This is where SQL Object Manager comes into play; it provides a graphical mechanism for managing your database objects. It does not provide a 100 percent graphical mechanism (in some areas, you still must work with your objects in a character mode), but using it still can make your life as a database administrator a lot easier. The first step after launching the SQL Object Manager (which is located in your SQL Server for Windows NT Program Manager group) is to connect to an SQL Server. Then, in the Current Database drop-down listbox, change the database from the master database (the default) to the database with which you want to work. Unlike the SQL Administrator, you'll find that the buttons are used only as shortcuts to menu options, and that the menus do not change based on the active window, so finding the right command is a little easier.

MANAGING TABLES

Table management consists of several possibilities: you can create a new table, modify the layout of an existing table, modify the data contained within a table, or delete the table. You should make a backup of the table and its data before you make any modifications. These topics are discussed in this section to prepare you for your day-to-day management tasks.

Creating a table is one of the easier tasks you can accomplish with SQL Object Manager, and it is pretty straightforward. Just follow these steps:

1. Select the database to work with in the Current Database drop-down listbox. Then choose Tables from the Manage menu to display the Manage Tables dialog box, as shown in Figure 17.9.

2. In the Column Name field, enter the name for the column. This field must follow the established SQL Server naming convention: It can contain up to 30 characters and is case-sensitive. My preference is to use a mixture of upper- and lowercase, but this is not a requirement. You should establish a fixed set of rules to follow to make your administrative duties easier.

3. Press Tab to move to the Datatype field and choose the type of data that the column will contain.

4. If your data type has an associated size, such as a character (char) data type, then press Tab to move to the Length field and specify the size of the item. The default value is always the maximum size for the associated data type.

5. If you already have created defaults or rules to be bound to columns in your table, press Tab to move to the Default or Rule field and enter the name of your default or rule. If you are unfamiliar with creating defaults or rules, you can jump to the section "Managing Defaults and Rules."

6. Repeat these steps for each column you want to create.

7. After you complete all the columns to add to your table, click the Create button to display the Specify New Table Name dialog box and enter a name for your table. Then click the OK button to create the table.

Before you actually click the Create button to display the Specify New Table Name dialog box, which you will use to create the new table, you also can choose the database segment to place the table on by choosing the appropriate segment from the Segments drop-down listbox. Using separate segments can improve your users' capability to access the tables by spreading the I/O load among several disk drives. This option is of limited usefulness, however, if you are using a stripe set or stripe set with parity as your device storage.

Figure 17.9.
Creating a new
table with SQL
Object Manager.

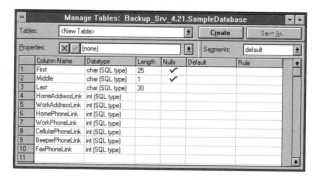

Tip

If you make a mistake with your table layout before you actually create it, you can choose Edit | Delete to delete a column or Edit | Insert to insert a column.

To create a new table from an ISQL command prompt, you can use the CREATE TABLE Transact SQL statement. The syntax follows:

```
CREATE TABLE [[DatabaseName.][OwnerName.]TableName ColumnName,
_ColumnDataType [NOT NULL¦NULL] [,ColumnDataType [NOT NULL¦NULL]...]
_[ON SegmentName]
```

You can specify multiple column names, data types, and whether the value can be null by adding a comma followed by the column name, data type, and null choice.

Modifying the layout of an existing table is possible, but you can add columns only to the end of a table. You cannot change the data type or associated length of an existing column with the SQL Object Manager or a Transact SQL statement. This does not mean that changing a column data type or length is impossible, however. If you need to do so, you can, but this is not a one-step process in most cases.

To add a column to a table, repeat the steps described for creating a table, with one exception. Instead of using the default selection (<New Table>) in the Tables listbox, select the name of the table to add columns to. Your new columns must be added to the end of the table and also must accept NULLS. NULLS must be chosen because current rows will not have any data associated with the new column and therefore will be set to a null value. After you complete all the columns to add, click the Alter button to add the new columns to the table.

Tip

To add columns to an existing table from an ISQL command prompt, use the ALTER TABLE Transact SQL command. The syntax for this command follows:

```
ALTER TABLE [[DatabaseName.][OwnerName.]TableName ADD ColumnName,
_ColumnDataType NULL [,ColumnName, ColumnDataType NULL...]
```

You can specify multiple column names and data types by separating your new column identifiers, data types, and NULL value specifiers with commas.

Modifying a table layout is more complex than creating a table but can be accomplished by using one of these methods:

◆ Make sure that your database supports the Select Into/Bulk Copy option as described in the earlier section, "Managing Databases." Then use the SELECT INTO Transact SQL Statement to create a new table and copy the data from your existing table. After you do this, you can delete the old table and rename the new table. You can use this process to add a column anywhere within a table, to delete a column from a table, or to change column data types.

Tip

Before performing these actions, you should back up your master database, and then you should set the database to single-user mode to prevent any other users from accessing the database while you are making the changes. After you complete your work, reset the Select Into/Bulk Copy option and dump the database to return to a logged database state.

◆ Create a new table and copy your data into it with a `select` statement or the bulk copy transfer as described later in this section. After the new table is populated, you can delete the old table and then rename the new table.

Warning

Before you make any changes to a table, you would be wise to use the Scripts option to generate an SQL script to re-create the table and to bulk copy the existing table's data to a file, just in case things do not work out as you expect.

After you create these new tables, you should reassign your rules and defaults and verify that all your existing triggers, stored procedures, and views still function properly.

You can use two methods with SQL Object Manager to delete a table. First, you can select the table in the Manage Tables dialog box and choose Object | Drop Object. Second, you can select the table from the Database Objects window, which is accessed from the Tools | Manage Object menu option or the Objects button, and then choose Object | Drop Object. The same principle is used to rename a table, except that you use the Object | Rename Object menu choice.

Tip

You can perform these actions from an ISQL command prompt by using the `DROP TABLE` Transact SQL statement or `sp_rename` stored procedure. The syntax follows:

```
DROP TABLE [[Database.]Owner.]TableName [,[[Database.]Owner.]TableName ...]
```

and

```
sp_rename OldTableName, NewTableName
```

COPYING DATA TO AND FROM A TABLE

SQL Object Manager includes a graphical interface to the DB-Library bulk copy functions. These functions enable you to copy data from a table to a file, or from a file to a table. You also can transfer data using views, which is particularly useful because you can use this capability to create flat files for use by external applications. If you want to create mailing lists for customers in a specific state, for example, you can create a view that selects table rows that match the particular state. You then can transfer the data using the view, and the flat file will contain only rows from your tables that match the state, even though you have data in your tables for all 50 states. If you want to create a mailing list for all states but your mailing list must be sorted, then your view can include a GROUP BY clause to sort the data by state.

To bulk copy data from your tables, follow these steps:

1. Choose Transfer Data from the Tools menu or click the Transfer button in the main application window to display the Transfer Data dialog box, as shown in Figure 17.10.

2. Select your transfer option by choosing Export from SQL Server to copy data from a table or view to a file, or Import into SQL Server to copy data from a file to a table. Based on your choice, the arrow will point to the disk graphic on the right for an export or to the server graphic on the left for an import.

3. In the Table Name drop-down listbox, choose your table or view to export from. If you have chosen to import data, this field will be called the Destination Table, and you should select the table to import into.

Figure 17.10.
Transferring data
from a table with
SQL Object
Manager.

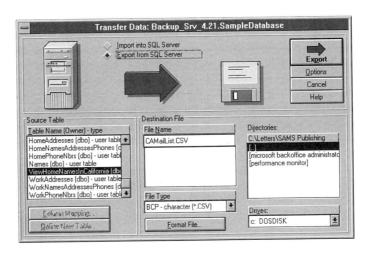

Note

Although you can export data from a view that joins more than one table, you cannot import data from a file using a view that joins more than one table.

4. In the File Name field, specify a filename for the output/input filename. The default is the first eight characters of the table name with a CSV extension, but you can change this if desired. If you are importing data, you can select an existing file from the list.

5. In the File Type drop-down list, choose the type of file to export/import. This can be one of the following:

   ◆ Character *.CSV: This output/input file is an ASCII file with fields separated by commas. Strings are delimited by quotation marks.

   ◆ Character *.TAB: This output/input file is an ASCII file with fields separated by tabs. Strings are delimited by quotation marks.

   ◆ Defined *.DAT: When this choice is selected for an export, the Column Mapping button is enabled. The default output is a fixed-length file based on the size of the column; however, you can change this by clicking the Column Mapping button to display the Data Transfer File Column Specifications dialog box and choosing the columns to export and the length of the output fields. You also can choose to skip a column.

   ◆ Format File *.DAT: This choice uses a bulk copy program (BCP) file format to specify the column mapping, column type, and column length of the data file. Like the Defined *.DAT option, you can choose to create a new table with the Define New Table button on an import.

   ◆ Native *.DAT: This choice copies data in a binary form based on the host processor. Because it needs no conversion, it is the fastest transfer option. Because of its reliance on the host processor, however, it is also not portable to other processor types.

Note

If you choose Import into SQL Server, the Define New Table button is enabled. You can use this option to display the Create New Table dialog box. Here, you can specify the table layout of a new table that will be created to contain the imported data. You also can choose to copy an existing table layout for the new table.

6. If the defaults are not correct, you can choose a different drive and directory in the Directories and Drives fields.

7. If you want to change the default number of rows in a batch or the number of rows to read/write, you can click the Options button to specify these values.

8. Click the OK button to begin your transfer.

When you choose to import data to a table in a logged database, you are asked whether you would like to change the Select Into/Bulk Copy option and drop any indexes on the table. If you choose Yes, the load will occur faster, the Select Into/Bulk Copy option will be set to On, the indexes will be dropped, and the data will be transferred. After this occurs, the Select Into/Bulk Copy option is set to Off and the indexes are rebuilt. After all this, you should verify that the data meets your requirements by executing stored procedures to verify any rules you have defined for the data. Any data that does not meet your requirements should be deleted or modified.

Tip

Before you begin an import, it is a good idea to use the Scripts button in the main application window to generate SQL scripts for your indexes. This enables you to easily regenerate your indexes in case you cancel the transfer or an error occurs and aborts the process. You also should make sure that you have sufficient space to regenerate the index.

MANAGING DEFAULTS AND RULES

SQL Server defaults are used to specify a default value for a table column when a user does not explicitly specify a value for the column during an insert or update. SQL Server rules are used to specify the format of the data contained within a column when a user inserts or updates a column. When you create a default or rule in a database, it can be used only within that database. Just creating a default or rule does not do anything for you until you apply it to a table column, however. This process of applying a default or rule to a column is called binding in SQL Server terminology.

To create a default with SQL Object Manager, choose Manage | Defaults to display the Manage Defaults dialog box, as shown in Figure 17.11. As you can see, this is one of those occasions in which the graphical process breaks down with SQL Object Manager. Defaults can be created only by specifying the SQL Transact SQL statement in the Default Contents drop-down listbox. This same statement can be used from an ISQL command-line prompt.

Figure 17.11.
Creating a
default for a
Phone Number
field with SQL
Object Manager.

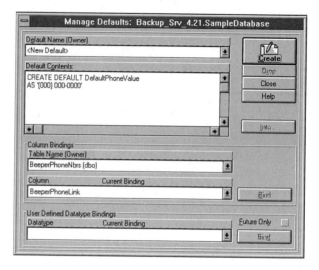

The syntax for creating a default follows:

```
CREATE DEFAULT DefaultName AS DefaultValue
```

Here, `DefaultName` is the SQL object name for the default. `DefaultValue` is the constant value to be inserted into the column when no specific value is specified by the user. This value must follow the rules for data types. If the value to be assigned is a data type, for example, the value should be enclosed in single quotation marks.

After you enter the Transact SQL statement for your default, click the Create button to actually create the default within your database. Then you can bind the default to your table columns by choosing the table in the Table Name field, choosing the table column in the Column field, and clicking the Bind button. Repeat this process for each table column to which you want to bind the default.

You can bind defaults to user-defined data types by selecting the user-defined data type in the User Defined Datatype Bindings drop-down listbox and clicking the Bind button. If you want this default to apply only to future applications of this data type, enable the Future Only checkbox.

Tip

To bind a default to a column from an ISQL command prompt, you can use the `sp_binddefault` stored procedure. The syntax follows:

```
sp_binddefault DefaultName, ObjectName [,FUTUREONLY]
```

Here, `ObjectName` is the name of the table column (such as `'TableName.ColumnName'`) or the user-defined data type.

You can use several methods to delete a default:

- Choose the default in the Default Name field of the Manage Defaults dialog box and then click the Drop button. Or choose Manage | Drop Object!.
- Choose the default in the Database Objects window and then choose Object | Drop Object!.
- From an ISQL command prompt, enter `sp_dropdefault DefaultName`.

Instead of dropping a default, you may just want to unbind it from the column so that you can reuse the default later. To unbind the default, select the column in the Column field. This changes the Bind button to the Unbind button. Click this button and the default will no longer apply to the column. To unbind all the columns from the default, click the Info button to display the Current Bindings dialog box and click the Unbind All button.

Tip

To unbind a default from a column from an ISQL command prompt, use this command:

`sp_unbinddefault DefaultName [,FUTUREONLY]`

To delete a default, use this command:

`DROP DEFAULT [OwnerName.]DefaultName`

To create and manage rules, you follow the same basic process as you use for creating and managing defaults. Even the dialog boxes are the same, aside from the titles. The only difference is the syntax used to create the rule:

`CREATE RULE RuleName AS Expression`

Here, `RuleName` is the SQL object name for the rule. `Expression` is any valid SQL expression statement that can be used in the WHERE clause of a SELECT statement, with the exception that it cannot reference another column in a table or a database object.

Expressions are the heart of the rule statement. You can use any valid SQL expression that contains arithmetic operators (<, >, <=, >=, =, <>, !>, !<) or lists (IN or NOT IN) pattern expressions that use wild cards and the LIKE clause.

The expression statement must include a single parameter that is prefaced by an @. To specify a phone number format that includes the area code, a space, and the phone number, for example, the expression would be

`@VALUE LIKE '([0-9][0-9][0-9]) [0-9][0-9][0-9]-[0-9][0-9][0-9][0-9]'`

This allows only the opening parenthesis and closing parenthesis—characters (and)—and the digits 1 through 9 in the standard phone number format like (123) 456-7890. If an entry does not follow this format, it is rejected during an insert or update.

You can use the following SQL Server wild cards for rule expressions:

%   Any string of zero or more characters.
_   A single character.
[]   Any single character with the specified range. To allow only a digit of 0 – 9, for example, the expression would be [0-9]. To accept only a single character from H – M, the expression would be [H-M].
[^]   Any single character not within the specified range. To accept alphabetic characters but not numbers, the expression would be [A-Za-z^0-9].

Tip

To bind a rule from an ISQL command prompt, use the `sp_bindrule` stored procedure. The syntax follows:

```
sp_bindrule RuleName, ObjectName [,FUTUREONLY]
```

To unbind a rule, use this command:

```
sp_unbindrule RuleName.[,FUTUREONLY]
```

To delete a rule, use this syntax:

```
DROP RULE [OwnerName.]RuleName
```

MANAGING KEYS

When you have a parent table that includes references to child tables, you need to use one or more columns to uniquely identify the relationship between those tables. These columns are referred to as keys. The parent table will contain the primary keys, and the child tables will contain the foreign keys. These primary and foreign keys must be an exact duplicate of each other. If the parent table includes the primary keys First, Middle, and Last, for example, then the child table(s) must contain the foreign keys First, Middle, and Last as well. You also can use additional columns that link to additional tables but are not primary or foreign keys. Instead, these are called common keys and they are used to explicitly inform SQL Server of an implicated relationship in your database design.

At this point, you may be asking yourself just why you should care about these different types of keys. There are two reasons. First, the primary and foreign keys are used to enforce the referential integrity of your database. Referential integrity simply means that the rules you impose on your parent-child tables are maintained properly. It would not be acceptable to delete a parent record but leave the child record, for example. If this occurs, then the child record would be considered an orphan because there is no longer any link to it. The mechanisms you use to impose these rules are called triggers, and they are discussed in the following section. The second reason that keys are important is because they are used by SQL Server to suggest the link between tables for joins. A join is simply the mechanism SQL Server uses to link two or more tables into a single table for you to manipulate.

To create a primary and foreign key, follow these steps:

1. Choose Keys from the Manage menu to display the Manage Keys dialog box, as shown in Figure 17.12.

2. In the Working Table/View drop-down list, choose the table for which you want to create your key. Start with the parent table. Here, you will start with the Names table because this is your parent table.

3. In the Key Type group, choose the type of key to create. You can choose Primary, Foreign, or Common. Because you are working with your parent table, you will start by creating a primary key.

4. In the Columns field under the Working Table/View drop-down list, select the columns to include in the primary key. This will be HomeAddressLink, WorkAddressLink, HomePhoneLink, WorkPhoneLink, CellularPhoneLink, BeeperPhoneLink, and FaxPhoneLink.

5. After you finish adding the fields to be used in the primary key, click the Create button to create the primary key.

6. In the Key Type group, choose the Foreign radio button without changing your Working Table/View entry. This grays out the Working Table/View entries and enables the Related Table/View drop-down listbox.

7. In the Related Table/View drop-down listbox, choose your child table. If this table is a valid table and contains the same keys as the parent table, the keys will be listed in the Columns fields. Click the Create button to create the foreign key. Repeat this step for each table's foreign-key creation.

Figure 17.12.
Managing keys
with SQL Object
Manager.

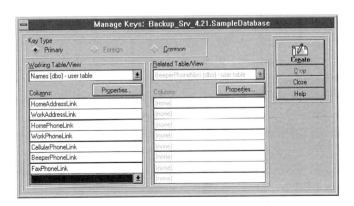

Creating a common key follows a similar process. Just select the Common radio button in the Key Type section, choose your tables and fields, and then click the Create button. Unlike primary and foreign keys, which require the exact same name for the columns, common keys can use any column name. The data types and lengths still must be the same, however.

You can manage keys from an ISQL command prompt by using the `sp_primarykey` to create a primary key, `sp_foreignkey` to create a foreign key, and `sp_commonkey` to create a common key. The syntax follows:

```
sp_primarykey TableName, ColumnName [,ColumnName ..., ColumnName]

sp_foreignkey TableName, PrimaryKeyTableName, ColumnName [,ColumnName ...,
_ColumnName]
sp_commonkey TableName1, TableName2, TableName1ColumnName1,
_TableName2ColumnName1 [,TableName1ColumnName2, TableName2ColumnName2...,
_TableName1ColumnNameX, TableName2ColumnNameX]
```

The syntax to delete a key follows:

```
sp_deletekey, KeyType, TableName, [,DependentTableName]
```

where `KeyType` is primary, foreign, or common and `DependentTableName` is the name of a table with the foreign key when used with the foreign `KeyType`.

Tip

Because keys are used to join tables, you can improve the performance by indexing your keys. These indexes should use a clustered index so that the table is physically sorted based on the key value. Indexes are discussed in detail a little later in this section.

MANAGING TRIGGERS

A trigger is a special type of stored procedure that is executed automatically whenever a row is inserted, updated, or deleted. SQL Server maintains two special tables called inserted and deleted that contain the rows to be inserted, updated, or deleted. Your trigger can use these tables to verify that the table relationships and the table data are valid before a table is modified. If you have a parent-child table relationship and use primary and foreign key definitions properly, then you can use SQL Object Manager to create the appropriate triggers to maintain the parent-child relationship properly. On the other hand, if you only use common keys or want special processing to occur, then you will have to manually write the procedure for the trigger to use.

Note

> The SQL script `EasySample.SQL` uses triggers created by the SQL Object
> Manager, whereas the script `FinalSample.SQL` uses hand-written trig-
> gers to accomplish the same basic process. However, `EasySample.SQL`
> uses primary and foreign keys, whereas `FinalSample.SQL` uses common
> keys in the database design. You can find these samples in the
> `\MBADMIN\Projects\Chapter 17` directory on the CD-ROM. For this discus-
> sion, you will be creating the triggers used in `EasySample.SQL`.

To create a trigger, follow these steps:

1. Choose Triggers from the Manage menu to display the Manage Triggers
   window shown in Figure 17.13.

2. If you will be writing your own trigger, just change the value `<TRIGGER_NAME>`
   to the name of your trigger, change the `DELETE` clause to the type of trigger
   (`INSERT`, `UPDATE`, or `DELETE`), and begin writing your procedure. If you will be
   using SQL Object Manager to create your trigger, which this discussion
   assumes from this point on, then choose the type of trigger to create in the
   Triggers drop-down listbox. The Create Trigger on Table dialog box appears, as shown in Figure 17.14.

*Figure 17.13.
Managing table
triggers with SQL
Object Manager.*

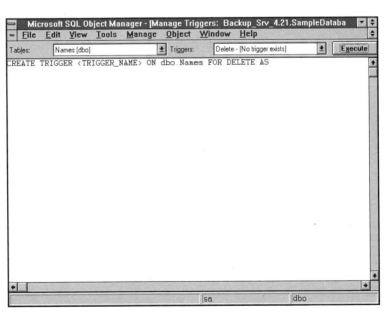

Figure 17.14.
Creating an
insert, update,
and delete
trigger.

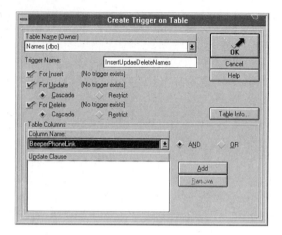

Tip

The syntax for creating a trigger follows:

```
CREATE TRIGGER TriggerName on TableName for {INSERT, UPDATE,
_DELETE} AS SQLStatements
```

Where SQLStatements is the body of your trigger.

You also can use a different format. If you are using the UPDATE clause, this is

```
CREATE TRIGGER TriggerName on TableName for {INSERT,
_UPDATE } AS IF UPDATE (ColumnName..., ColumnName)[AND¦OR (ColumnName...,
_ColumnName)] SQLStatements
```

3. If the default trigger type is not correct, choose the type of trigger to create. You can create a single trigger that can perform all the actions by selecting all three actions. This can be one or more of the following:

   ◆ For Insert: Creates a trigger that will be called wherever data is added to the table.

   ◆ For Update: Creates a trigger that will be called whenever data is modified within the table. If this is a parent table, choose the subtype Cascade; if it is a child table, choose the subtype Restrict.

   ◆ For Delete: Creates a trigger that will be called whenever data is deleted within the table. If this is a parent table, choose the subtype Cascade; if it is a child table, choose the subtype Restrict.

Note

A subtype of Cascade propagates changes from the parent table's primary keys to its foreign keys in child tables. A subtype of Restrict prevents a parent row from being modified if a foreign key in a child row exists.

4. If you want to check the update status of specific keys, you can select them in the Column Name drop-down listbox and choose the AND or OR radio button, although the created trigger automatically includes your primary or foreign key status in the trigger. After you select the key, click Add to add it to the Update Clause box or select the column in the Update Clause box. To remove the key, click the Remove button to remove it from the Update Clause box.

5. In the Trigger Name field, enter a name for the trigger. This name can contain up to 30 characters, must follow the established SQL Server naming convention, and is case-sensitive. I prefer to use the type of trigger (such as Insert, Update, Delete) with the table name appended for a naming convention. What you use is not nearly as important as standardizing a naming convention, however.

6. Click the OK button to create the trigger. This creates the trigger text and returns you to the Manage Triggers window. Click the Execute button to actually create the trigger. Then you can create the next trigger for the table by choosing it from the Triggers drop-down listbox.

Tip

To see additional information about the table you have selected, click the Table Info button.

After you create the trigger, you can use it as is, but if you have used the Restrict option, you will want to change the error message. The default error message for your sample BeeperPhoneNbrs table in the INSERT clause follows, for example:

```
Trigger InsertUpdateDeleteBeeper on table dbo.BeeperPhoneNbrs (HomeAddressLink,
WorkAddressLink, HomePhoneLink, WorkPhoneLink, CellularPhoneLink, BeeperPhoneLink,
FaxPhoneLink): Primary key values not found in table dbo.Names. The transaction is
being rolled back.
```

And that certainly does not give a good description to a user as to why his insert failed. A better choice follows:

```
You must create a row in the Names table prior to creating a
BeeperPhoneNbr row.
```

To modify a trigger, you follow the same basic steps as described earlier, except now that the trigger has been created, when you select the table and then the trigger type, the body of the trigger will be displayed. You then can edit this text to make your modifications. When you are finished, you can click the Execute button to modify the trigger.

You can use several methods to delete a trigger:

◆ Choose the trigger in the Triggers drop-down listbox of the Manage Triggers window. Then click the Drop button or choose Manage | Drop Object!.

◆ Choose the trigger in the Database Objects window and then choose Object | Drop Object!.

◆ From an ISQL command prompt, enter this command:

```
DROP TRIGGER TriggerName
```

MANAGING INDEXES

If you want to decrease your data retrieval access time, you will need to index your tables. Two basic types of indexes exist. The first is a clustered index, which has some special attributes, and the second is a nonclustered index. Why is a clustered index special? First, in a clustered index, the index is physically congruent to the data, and this speeds up the initial access to the data tremendously. Second, access times for set retrieval or stepping through a table row by row is improved because a clustered index specifies the physical sort order of the table. A nonclustered index just includes the index and a pointer to the table row.

Tip

Even though an index speeds up data retrieval, there are penalties associated with its use. First, every index, regardless of type, needs to be updated whenever a table row is inserted, updated, or deleted. And this impacts the performance of your system—both in processor usage and I/O usage. Second, every nonclustered index duplicates the column(s) data and includes a pointer to the table row, which means that you need additional storage. So unless you have unlimited storage capabilities, do not index every field in your table. Only index those fields that you must in order to improve query performance. If you have periodic queries that can be improved by using an index, create the index before you run the query, and then drop the index.

To create an index, follow these steps:

1. Choose Indexes from the Manage menu to display the Manage Indexes dialog box, as shown in Figure 17.15.

2. In the Tables drop-down listbox, select the table on which to create the index.

3. Until you enter a name for the index, you cannot continue, so click the New button to display the Specify New Index Name dialog box. Enter a unique name for the index. Then click the OK button to return to the Manage Indexes dialog box. The name you specified now appears at the top of the column in the Name field.

   The name can contain up to 30 characters, must follow the SQL Server naming convention, and is case-sensitive. I prefer to use a mixture of upper- and lowercase, but you do not need to follow this convention. You should establish a set of standards for your naming convention, however. One of my favorites is to use the type of index, followed by the table name, with an Idx extension—for example, PrimaryKeyForNamesIdx.

4. Choose the type of index to create. This can be one of the following:

   ◆ Clustered: If checked, a clustered index is created. If left unchecked, a nonclustered index is created.

   ◆ Unique: If checked, a unique index is created. This type of index prohibits duplicate indexes (or keys, if you prefer) from being entered into the table. A unique index cannot be created if the table already contains duplicate data.

   ◆ Ignore Duplicate Row: If checked, this property allows an insert or update batch to proceed but does not allow the duplicate row to be inserted or updated in a transaction on a table with a unique clustered index.

Figure 17.15.
Creating indexes
for the Sample
Names table with
SQL Object
Manager.

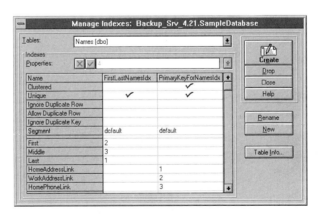

Warning

If the Ignore Duplicate Row property is used during an update (which would cause a duplicate key to be created), the original row and the updated row are deleted from the table. This occurs because an update is really a delete followed by an insert.

◆ Allow Duplicate Row: This property only applies to a nonunique clustered index. If checked, it allows the creation of a clustered index on a table that contains duplicate column data. It also allows the addition of a row to a table that can generate a duplicate key.

◆ Ignore Duplicate Key: This property applies only to a nonunique clustered index. If checked, it disallows the creation of a clustered index on a table that contains duplicate column data. It also disallows the addition of a row to a table that could generate a duplicate key. If a transaction that would create a duplicate row is in progress, only the invalid row is deleted from the insert or update.

◆ Segment: This item specifies the storage location for the index. Using multiple segments is a performance option.

5. Specify the actual columns to index in the lower half of the column by checking them off one by one. Each entry you select is numbered. If you make an error during this process, just click on the field to remove the entry.

6. After you complete your selections, click the Create button to display the Create New Index dialog box. Here you can specify that the data has been presorted (but only if it is in sorted order, please) which speeds up the index-creation process. You also can specify a fill factory by entering a value (a percentage, actually) in the Fill Factor field. Click OK to actually create the index.

Note

The fill factor specifies how much free space will be left in the index for future growth. By default, the fill factor is 0, which leaves room for two new entries. A fill factor of 100 specifies that no free space will be left and should be used only for a table that will not grow. You may want to change the fill factor to increase performance during an insert or update. There is a significant amount of overhead associated with splitting an index to make room for additional entries. The value you specify should be based on the amount of growth you expect will occur on the table. For moderate growth, a fill factor of 75 to 90 generally suffices.

To delete an index, you can list it in the Manage Indexes dialog box and click the Drop button or choose Object | Drop Object. Or, you can select it in the Database Objects window and choose Object | Drop Object.

Tip

You can create an index from an ISQL command line by using the CREATE INDEX Transact SQL statement. The syntax for this follows:

```
CREATE [UNIQUE] [CLUSTERED¦NONCLUSTERED] INDEX IndexName ON
_[DatabaseName[.OwnerName]]TableName (ColumnName...[,ColumnName])
_[WITH {FILLFACTOR=PercentageValue], IGNORE_DUP_KEY, SORTED_DATA
_[,IGNORE_DUP_ROW¦ALLOW_DUP_ROW]}] [ON SegmentName]
```

To delete an index, use this syntax:

```
DROP INDEX TableName.IndexName
```

MANAGING STORED PROCEDURES

A stored procedure is similar to an MS-DOS batch file. It contains multiple Transact SQL statements to automate a process. Instead of being interpreted as a batch file is, a stored procedure is actually compiled and stored as a SQL object. Managing stored procedures is another case in which SQL Object Manager's GUI breaks down. Once more, you have to enter a series of Transact SQL statements to create the stored procedure.

The basic process to create a stored procedure follows:

◆ Choose Stored Procedures from the Manage menu to display the Manage Stored Procedures window.

◆ To create a new stored procedure, select <New Procedure> from the Procedures drop-down listbox.

◆ Specify a name for the procedure in the skeleton Transact SQL statement. Then enter the body of the procedure.

◆ Click the Execute button to create the stored procedure.

The syntax for creating a stored procedure follows:

```
CREATE PROCEDURE ProcedureName [;VersionNumber
_[@Parameter DataType = DefaultValue [OUTPUT]] [WITH RECOMPILE] AS SQLStatements
```

Explanations of the syntax for this command follow:

VersionNumber: A version number for the procedure that differentiates it from other procedures with the same name.

Parameter: A named object of which you can have more than one.

DefaultValue: Specifies the default value for the parameter if none is supplied.

OUTPUT: Specifies that the parameter will return a value.

WITH RECOMPILE: Specifies that each time the procedure is called, it will be reparsed (or rebuilt).

SQLStatements: Series of Transact SQL statements to be executed.

To delete a stored procedure, you can choose it from the list of procedures and choose Manage | Drop Object. Otherwise, you can choose it in the Manage Objects window and choose Manage | Drop Object. To delete a stored procedure from an ISQL command line, you can use this syntax:

```
DROP PROCEDURE [Owner.]ProcedureName
```

MANAGING VIEWS

A view is a means of limiting access to a complete table or joining two or more tables. You can use a view to show only the address and city from the Address table so that your users cannot view or modify the City or State fields, for example. Or, you can create a view to join the Name and Address tables to display a complete name and address table for your users. With SQL Object Manager, you have two choices when creating views: you can write your own view using the skeleton code, or you can use the graphical interface to have SQL Object Manager create it for you.

Assuming that you want SQL Object Manager to create the view, follow these steps:

1. Choose Views from the Manage menu to display the Manage Views window. In the View field, choose <New View> to display the dialog box shown in Figure 17.16.

2. In the Tables drop-down listbox, select your first table. This adds the table columns to the Table Columns drop-down listbox.

3. For each additional table, repeat step 2.

4. After all your columns you want displayed in the view are added to the Table Columns drop-down listbox, select them by choosing them in the order you want them to appear, one at a time, pressing the Ctrl key while you select them. This highlights each field.

5. After all your fields are selected, click the Add To Clause button to add these fields to the SELECT field.

Figure 17.16.
Creating a view
for the sample
Name and
Address tables
with SQL Object
Manager.

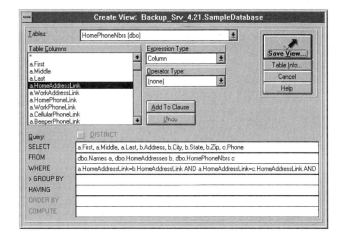

Note

If you want all fields to appear, there is no need to select individual fields. Just leave the asterisk (*) in the SELECT field. On the other hand, if you are choosing individual fields, be sure to remove the asterisk from the SELECT field.

6. Move to the WHERE field and select your operator type. This can be any of the arithmetic, wild-card, or set operators. Then choose your first column in the Table Columns drop-down listbox and click the Add To Clause button. Then choose your column to compare in the Table Columns drop-down listbox and click the Add To Clause button to append this to the current WHERE clause. For each column, remove the comma between the first column and the operator. Repeat this step for each column to compare.

Note

Depending on the type of view you are creating and the clause field you are currently working on, the Expression Type field will contain different entries from which you can choose.

7. Move to the GROUP BY field, which sorts your output based on the column order you specify, and choose your first column in the Table Columns drop-down listbox. Then click the Add To Clause button. Repeat these actions for each column to include in the sort order.

8. If applicable, continue steps 2 through 7 for the HAVING, ORDER BY, and COMPUTE clause.

9. When all your selections are complete, click the Save View button, enter a unique name, and click the OK button to create the view.

You can delete a view by selecting it in the Manage Views window and choosing Objects | Drop Object. Alternatively, you can select it in the Manage Objects window and choose Objects | Drop Object.

Tip

The syntax for creating a view from an ISQL command line follows:

```
CREATE VIEW ViewName AS SQLStatements
```

The syntax for deleting a view follows:

```
DROP VIEW ViewName
```

MANAGING OBJECT PERMISSIONS

Now that you have created all these database objects, you have to assign permissions to these objects to let your clients access them. If you do not assign permissions to these objects, then only the owner or database administrator (the DBA can use the SETUSER command to assume the identity of a user and gain access) can make use of them. Unfortunately, there is no easy way to assign permissions to multiple objects using the tools provided with SQL Server. Each object's permissions must be assigned individually, either from an ISQL command prompt or with SQL Object Manager.

One thing you can do to make your life easier in this regard is to use groups for your permission management. This way, you only assign permissions to objects using groups, and your groups contain the users to whom you want to assign the specific permission. In this way, after permissions are assigned, you can give one or more users access by making them members of the appropriate groups. You can have a group called ReadTables, for example, which only grants SELECT permissions to tables in your database, and another called FullTables, which gives INSERT, DELETE, SELECT, and UPDATE access to your tables. You can create several groups to assign varying levels of permissions to objects.

To assign permissions with SQL Object Manager, follow these steps:

1. Choose Object Permissions from the Object menu. The Object Permissions dialog box appears, as shown in Figure 17.17.

2. In the Name (Owner)–Type drop-down listbox, choose the object for which you want to assign permission.

Figure 17.17.
Managing object
permissions with
SQL Object
Manager.

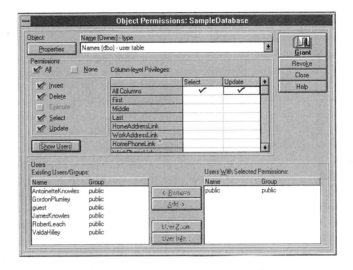

Note

To get more information about a particular object, click the Properties button.

3. In the Permissions section, choose the permission level. This can be one of the following:

   ◆ All: Sets Insert, Delete, Select, and Update permission levels for the object.

   ◆ None: Removes all permission levels.

   ◆ Insert: Allows a user to insert data into a table or view.

   ◆ Delete: Allows a user to delete data in a table or view.

   ◆ Execute: Allows a user to run a stored procedure.

   ◆ Select: Allows a user to read data from a table or view.

   ◆ Update: Allows a user to modify data in a table or view.

4. If you will be setting permissions on a table, you can assign individual permissions on specific columns by selecting them in the Column-Level Privileges drop-down listbox. Select grants read-only access, and Update grants modification access. To assign permissions on all columns, just check the All Columns field in the Select or Update column.

5. To see what users or groups currently have the selected permissions, click the Show Users button. This displays the appropriate names in the Users With Selected Permissions field.

6. To give a user or group the selected permissions, choose the user or group in the Existing Users/Groups field and click the Add button. This moves the appropriate name to the Users With Selected Permissions field.

7. After all users or groups have been moved, click the Grant button to actually assign the selected permissions.

To remove specific privileges from a user or group, choose the appropriate name in the Users With Selected Permissions field and click the Revoke button. For information on specific object permissions, choose the user or group in the Existing Users/Groups field and click the User Info button. To view all object permissions assigned to a user or group, select it in the Existing Users/Groups field and click the User Zoom button.

Tip

You can assign and remove object permissions from an ISQL command prompt if desired. The syntax to assign permissions follows:

```
GRANT (ALL¦PermissionList} ON {TableName[(ColumnList)]
_¦ ViewName[(ColumnList)]
¦ StoredProcedureName ¦ ExtendedStoredProcedureName} TO {PUBLIC ¦
_UserOrGroupNameList}
```

To remove permissions, use this syntax:

```
REVOKE (ALL¦PermissionList} ON {TableName[(ColumnList)] ¦
_ViewName[(ColumnList)] ¦ StoredProcedureName ¦
_ExtendedStoredProcedureName}
_FROM {PUBLIC ¦ UserOrGroupNameList}
```

CREATING DATABASE SCHEMAS

Because it takes many hours to actually create your database, populate it with various objects, create your user logins and groups, and assign permissions for your users' access, I hope you will take the time to back it all up. SQL Object Manager includes a facility to generate Transact SQL scripts that can delete, create, and assign permissions on your database objects. It can even rebuild your user logins and groups. To access the script generator, click the Scripts button or choose Tools I Generate SQL Scripts to display the Generate SQL Scripts dialog box.

In this dialog box, you can choose the defaults, which generate a script including all objects, drops, and dependencies. You also can choose just individual objects, permissions, logins, or groups. After you make your selection, just click the Generate button to create the script and save it to a file. Or, click the Preview button to generate the script and display it in an edit window.

Note

The scripts I have supplied to create the sample names and address databases were created with the transfer script feature discussed earlier.

SQL SERVER 6.X MANAGEMENT TOOLS

If you are as busy as I think you are, you will be very happy to know that Microsoft has been listening to you when you tell them you need a single tool to manage your SQL Server installations. Aside from the tools mentioned in the next section (Shared Management tools), SQL Server 6.x includes the SQL Enterprise Manager. This tool is aptly named because you can use it to manage all your Microsoft SQL Server installations on your network. The SQL Enterprise Manager encompasses the features of SQL Administrator and SQL Object Manager in a single user interface and offers many new enhancements.

The majority of these enhancements can be used only on SQL Server 6.x and include database replication, task scheduling, alert configuration, setting SQL Server configuration options, and viewing server usage. You still can use the SQL Enterprise Manager with your older SQL Server installations, however, to create devices, databases, tables, and other database objects.

What makes the SQL Enterprise Manager so easy to use is its use of the new custom controls introduced in Windows NT 3.51. These controls provide you with an easy-to-traverse tree of objects and the capability to right-click on an object to display a menu of object properties, as shown in Figure 17.18. Those of you who have been using Windows 95 will be quite familiar with the object-property concept, but for those of you who are unfamiliar with using object properties, you will be happy to know that the same options are available from the main menu.

For the most part, managing your database objects—including tables, views, stored procedures, rules, and defaults—uses similar dialog boxes as those used in SQL Administrator or SQL Object Manager. So instead of looking at features already discussed, this section concentrates on the new feature set. Generally, this revolves around SQL Server consolidation, management, and database replication.

MANAGING GROUPS AND SERVERS

When you first execute the SQL Enterprise Manager, it prompts you to register your server. The registration process is merely a means of specifying the server name, the login and password, and the group to which it belongs. By default, the first server is added to the SQL 6.x group. Your next step is to create new groups and add each SQL Server to one of these groups. Groups by themselves do not offer you any special characteristics; their only function is to consolidate servers into manageable units that serve two purposes. First, they help you find the appropriate server. Instead of using the groups SQL 6.x and SQL 4.21, which I have included in my displays, you can use more descriptive names such as Marketing Servers, Accounting Servers, or similar names. Second, groups limit the clutter displayed in the Server Manager window. By grouping servers, you can expand or collapse entire groups, which can limit the confusion when working with many servers on the network.

Figure 17.18.
Managing your
SQL Server
installations with
the Microsoft
SQL Enterprise
Manager.

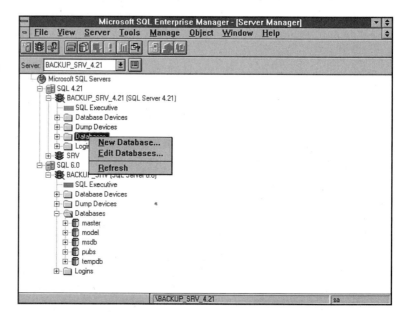

To create a group, follow these steps:

1. Choose Server Groups from the Server menu. Or, right-click on an existing group in the left window of the Server Manager screen and choose New Server Group to display the Manage Server Groups dialog box.

2. In the Name field, enter the name of your group. This name can contain up to 30 characters and is case-sensitive.

3. Just like directories in File Manager, you can create a new root group called a top level group or a subcomponent group called a sublevel group by choosing the Top Level Group or Sub-Group Of radio button.

4. A subgroup is created in the highlighted group, so make sure that you select the appropriate group in which to create your new subgroup by choosing the appropriate group or subgroup first. Then click the Add Group button.

5. If you make a mistake in placing your group, just select the group and click the Remove Group button.

6. If you want to rename the group, select the group, enter a new name in the Name field, and click the Change Group button.

7. After you complete all your group additions, click the Close button to return to the Server Management window.

After you create your groups, it is time to add your SQL Server installations to these groups so that you can start your management duties.

To add servers to groups, follow these steps:

1. Choose Register Server from the Server menu, press Ctrl+R, or right-click on an existing server and choose Register Server to display the Register Server dialog box.

2. To obtain a list of nonhidden SQL Servers on the network, click the List Server button. All the active servers are displayed, and you can select one at a time.

3. If you already know the name of your server or you already have configured a connection with the SQL Client Configuration utility, just add the server name to the Server drop-down listbox.

4. Select the Use Trusted Connection or Use Standard Security radio button in the Logon Information section. If you choose the Use Standard Security option, enter your SQL Server login in the Login ID field, along with the associated login password in the Password field.

Note

The security radio button you choose depends on the security model of your SQL Server installation. If you have chosen to configure your SQL Server for standard security where all logins are maintained within SQL Server tables, then you should choose the Use Standard Security radio button. If you have chosen the mixed or integrated security model, then choosing the Use Trusted Connection radio button is your best choice if you already have a valid account on the domain. Otherwise, you can choose the Use Standard Security radio button and use the System Administrator (sa) account—assuming, of course, that you know the password.

5. Select the group to which you want to add the server in the Server Group field and click the Register button.

Tip

> If you want to add a new group in which to place the server, click the Server Groups button to display the Manage Server dialog box, as described in the preceding section.

6. If you want to delete a server from a group or change the group a server is associated with, select the server from the Server drop-down listbox. Then click the Remove button to delete it, or select the new group and click the Modify button to move the server to the new group.

7. After you complete all your server additions, click the Close button to return to the Server Management window.

Tip

> You can enable the Display Server Status in Server Manager checkbox in the Register Server dialog box to display the state of the server by using the Server Stop Light icon. A red light appears if the SQL Server service is stopped, a yellow light indicates that it is paused, a green light indicates that it is running, and a lightning bolt indicates that it is connected to the server.

LOOKING AT SQL SERVER 6.X ENHANCEMENTS

If you are managing a SQL Server 6.x installation, you also have the option to configure database replication, schedule tasks, configure alerts, configure the server, determine the current activity on the server, and view the SQL Server error log. You should realize that only replication is a completely new feature—most of the other features are possible now with your current Windows NT SQL Server installation. They just require using different tools and, in some cases, a bit more work.

If you want to schedule tasks or batch jobs, for example, you can access the scheduler server for the remote computer using the AT command. To configure alerts, use the SQL Performance Monitor. To determine the current activity, use SQL Administrator and click the System button. To view the error log, use SQL Administrator and choose the Manage | Error Log menu option. The capability to consolidate all these tasks is the new feature here, which is made possible by the SQL Executive service. If you want to be able to manage all your SQL Servers and fully use all the task-management options, you should consider upgrading all your servers to version 6.x.

Using Server Replication

Server replication does not include the capability to keep two or more databases synchronized; instead, it provides a means of distributing a database to two or more servers to distribute the load. If you have an inventory database, for example, that is accessed by many users, both locally and remote, and you are experiencing performance-related problems, then you can use the replication feature to make a read-only copy of the database on additional servers. These read-only copies can be accessed by other users to increase performance of their queries. Of course, updating the database requires that changes be made on the master copy of the database.

Note

> In order to use the replication feature, the Windows NT Server computer must have a minimum of 32MB, and the master database server must be configured with a minimum of 16MB allocated to SQL Server.

The basic idea behind replication is that you have SQL Server installations containing the data to be replicated. These servers are known as publication servers. Servers that receive replicated data are called subscription servers. For optimal performance, you can dedicate a server to distribute the replicated data. This server is called the distribution server. Data that is replicated from a table is called an article.

Note

> Your publication server also can be a distribution server if you prefer. It even can be a subscriber to a different publication/distribution server. This can enable you to split a table into multiple components, which can be distributed in a round-robin fashion to additional servers. In effect, you can create a large distributed database that resides on several servers; only the owned table component should be updated and the rest will be replicated.

In order to use the replication features, you have to configure the server first. Select the server and then choose Server | Replication Configuration | Install Publishing to display the Install Replication Publishing dialog box. Then, if your server will be both the publishing server and the distribution server, select the Local – Install New Local Distribution Database radio button. Then specify the database name, the database and log device names, and the size for the devices. If you will be using a separate SQL Server as the distribution server, select Remote | Use Existing Remote Distribution Server and specify the name of the server in the drop-down listbox. Then click the OK button.

Next, choose Manage | Replication Configuration | Publishing and choose the articles to publish. Then, on your server that will be receiving the replicated data, choose Server | Replication Configuration | Subscriptions and configure the servers from which you will accept replicated data, along with the associated databases. After you have performed the initial configuration, you can then choose Manage | Replication | Publications to create new publications to replicate or Manage | Replication | Subscriptions to create new subscriptions.

Tip

Because of this methodology, you might want to view a graphical representation of your publication, distribution, and subscription servers. You can do this by choosing Manage | Replication Configuration | Topology.

SCHEDULING TASKS

Automating jobs with the Task Scheduler is pretty easy because the graphical interface is very intuitive. To configure your tasks, select the SQL Executive icon below the SQL Server, and then choose Tools | Task Scheduling, press Ctrl+S, or right-click and choose Edit Tasks to display the Task Scheduling dialog box, as shown in Figure 17.19.

Figure 17.19.
Scheduling tasks
with the SQL
Enterprise
Manager.

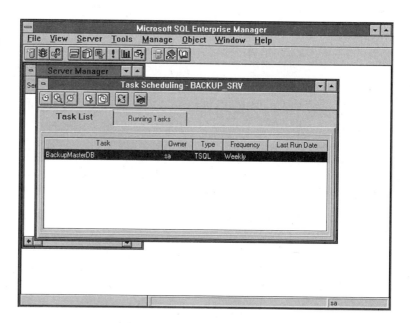

17

You can use the buttons at the top of the dialog box for these functions:

New Task	Creates a new task
Edit Task	Edits the selected task
Delete Task	Deletes the selected task
Run Task	Runs the selected task
Task History	Displays a history of the task
Refresh	Refreshes the display
Task Engine Options	Specifies the history log options.

To create a task, follow these steps:

1. Click the New Task button to display the New Task dialog box.

2. In the Name field, specify a unique name for the task.

3. In the Type drop-down list, choose the type of task you will enter in the Command field. This can be one of the following:

    ◆ CmdExec: A command line executable application

    ◆ Distribution: A replication distribution command

    ◆ LogReader: A replication log reader command

    ◆ Sync: A replication synchronization command

    ◆ TSQL: A Transact SQL command

4. In the Database drop-down listbox, choose the database on which to execute the command.

5. In the Command field, enter the command (batch file, executable name, or Transact SQL statement, for example).

6. If you want to keep track of these commands or be notified in case of an error, click the Options button. This enables you to configure the NT Event Log options, and if you choose an entry in the Email Operator drop-down listbox, then you also have the option to configure an e-mail address, pager address, and work-day schedule for notification.

7. In the Schedule group, choose the scheduling option. This can be one of the following:

    ◆ On Demand: The command will only be executed when manually selected.

    ◆ One-Time: The command will execute once and then be removed from the task list.

    ◆ Reoccurring: The command will execute more than once. Click the Change button to specify the start and stop characteristics.

    ◆ Auto Start: The task will be execute whenever SQL Server starts up. This property applies only to distribution and log reader commands.

8. Click the Add button to add the task to your task list. Repeat these steps for each additional task to add.

CONFIGURING ALERTS

If your database is critical to the success of your company, then you will want to make use of the capability provided in SQL Server 6.x to be notified whenever a problem occurs. To use the alert capability, select your server and then choose Server | Alerts to display the Manage Alerts dialog box. This dialog box is similar in function to the Manage Tasks dialog box, and even interoperates with it. After you click the New Alert button, you can specify the name for the alert, a SQL Server severity code, a database, and the task to run when the alert condition is met. The task can contain an e-mail address and a pager address to notify you as soon as the error occurs.

USING THE SQL SERVER WEB ASSISTANT

The Web Assistant is available only with SQL Server 6.5. The Web Assistant is not designed to interact with the user, unlike the options provided by the Internet Database Connector (IDC) or Microsoft dbWeb. Instead, it is designed to publish a database on-line. It does this by creating static Web pages; but perhaps *static* is the wrong word. Most people consider a static page to be a Web page that does not change its contents. However, with the Web Assistant these Web pages can be automatically refreshed when a new record is inserted into the database, or when a specific time interval is reached. This means the Web page contents could change. In essence, once more you have the ability to create a dynamic Web page. If you combine the IDC with the Web Administrator, you can build a fully interactive on-line order system, for example.

To create an interactive on-line order system would require an event-driven processing methodology where you respond to actions that occur rather than a hierarchical methodology where you control the data flow in a step-by-step process. Let me show you how this could work. First, let's lay a few ground rules:

◆ You have an ODBC database containing your product inventory. This database contains the quantity, price, and a description of each item.

◆ You want to publish an on-line catalog using this information.

◆ You want to accept client orders from the on-line catalog.

To bring these basic ideas together and build an interactive order-entry database, you'd have to create the following constructs:

◆ On-line catalog: You could use the Web Administrator to build this Web page using a query designed to select all items from your product inventory database whenever the item quantity is greater than one. Anytime the database changes, you could have the Web Administrator rebuild the page. The Web page could include a hypertext link to a Web page with the order form.

◆ Order form: The Order form will use the Internet Database Connector to insert an order record into the Order database.

◆ Order database: This database would contain information about the client and product ordered. It might contain fields for order number, date, name, address, payment, product, and so on. For optimum results, this would be a client/server database (such as SQL Server) rather than an application database (such as Access) so that you could benefit from the ability to execute code automatically (like triggers or scheduled procedures). In this fashion, whenever an order record is entered into the database your code could automatically decrement the quantity for the item contained in your product inventory database. This same code could automatically notify a sales or shipping representative. This same code could update other databases used by applications within your company to automate the shipping and billing process.

◆ The basic work flow to obtain an order would follow these steps:

1. The client connects to your Web site.

2. The client selects your catalog to browse through it.

Tip

> You could create a custom query form using the IDC to search for specific items in your catalog. The description field could be used as a searchable text field, for example, so the client could specify the type of items of interest. The returned result set, based on his query, could be displayed on another custom IDC HTML page. The user could then follow the same order process once he selects the item to order.

3. The client selects an item, and clicks a link to order the item.

4. An order form appears. The user fills out the relevant data fields and submits the form. This submission inserts a record into the Order database.

5. The Order database insert trigger is activated. This could send an e-mail message requesting manual intervention to continue the order and shipping process. Or the trigger could cause a cascade of events to occur where one or more databases are updated (like the quantity field for the item in the product inventory database), applications are executed, and finally the product is shipped to the user.

6. When the product inventory database is updated (to reflect that there is one less item) the Web administrator could update the on-line catalog page so the next user will see an accurate count for the item. If the customer purchases the last item and then attempts to reorder the item based on his cached on-line version of the catalog, your IDC order form would report an error since the query executed by the IDC would return real-time results (the query would return no records because the quantity field in the product inventory database would be zero).

To use the Web Assistant to build your Web pages:

1. Launch the SQL Server Web Assistant, located in the SQL Server 6.5 program group, to display the SQL Server Web Assistant – Login dialog box (see Figure 17.20).

Figure 17.20.
Specifying the
SQL Server
parameters for
the Web Assis-
tant.

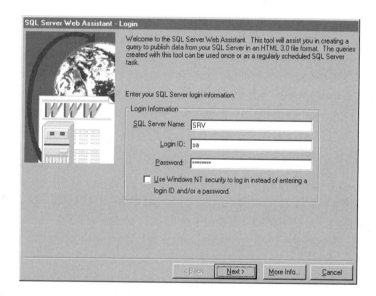

2. Enter the name of your SQL Server installation in the SQL Server Name field.

3. Enter a user name in the Login ID field.

4. Enter a password for the user name in the Password field.

Note

If you are using the mixed, or integrated, security models, you can enable the Use Windows NT Security to Log In Instead Of Entering A Login ID and/Or Password check box. This way, your current credentials will be used.

5. Click the Next button to display the dialog shown in Figure 17.21.

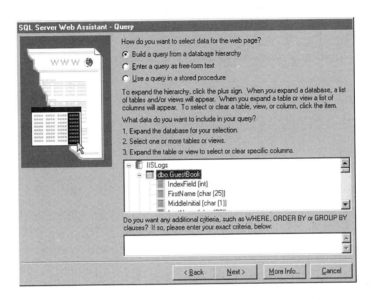

Figure 17.21. Specifying the SQL Server database for the Web Assistant.

6. In the How Do You Want To Select Data For The Web Page? group, specify one of the following:

Build A Query From The Database Hierarchy: This option specifies that the database table you select will be posted on the Web in its entirety, unless you specify additional restrictions in the query window at the bottom of the dialog.

Enter A Query As Free-Form Text: When selected, the dialog box will change to let you choose a database and enter a free-form query. This free-form query will be used to return a result set. This result set will be displayed on the Web page created by the Web Assistant.

Use A Query In A Stored Procedure: When selected, the dialog box will change to allow you to choose a database, choose a stored procedure in the database, and enter any command-line arguments for the stored procedure.

Tip

You can publish multiple tables just by selecting the listbox. If you want to publish only part of a table, you can expand the table item and select the specific fields to publish.

7. When you have made your selection, click the Next button. For this discussion, I will assume you have chosen the Build A Query From The Database Hierarchy option and selected a single table.

8. The SQL Server Web Assistant – Scheduling dialog will appear. Choose one of the following from the Scheduling Options drop-down listbox:

Now: This option specifies that the Web page will be created immediately.

Later: This option specifies that the Web page will be created once at a user-specified date and time.

When Data Changes: This option specifies that the Web page will be re-created automatically whenever the database changes.

On Certain Days of the Week: This option specifies that the Web page will be re-created on specific days at specific times.

On a Regular Basis: This option specifies that the Web page will be re-created at scheduled time intervals.

Tip

For high traffic sites, the On Certain Days of the Week or On a Regular Basis options could be particularly useful. While the data would not be updated in real-time, it could be updated frequently enough to promote a sense of continuity (that is, new products constantly being added to the database) to the client. This could benefit you by lowering the system resource demands on your server during peak activity periods. This lowering of resource requirements means your server could support more simultaneous user connections.

9. Click the Next button, and the SQL Server Web Assistant – File Options dialog box appears (see Figure 17.22).

10. Specify a path and filename for the Web page in the Type The File Name Of The Web Page field.

11. Choose the A Template File Called radio button and enter the name of the HTML template file to be used to format your output. Or, choose The Following Information radio button and specify the Web page title in the What Is The Title Of The Web Page? field, then enter a subtitle in the What Is The Title For The Query Results? field.

12. If you want to add an HTML hypertext link, enable the Yes, Add One URL And Reference Text radio button and supply a single URL and description. Or, enable the Yes, Add A List Of URLs And Reference Text From A Table radio button and specify the table name containing this information.

Figure 17.22.
Specifying the
Web Assistant
Web page
parameters.

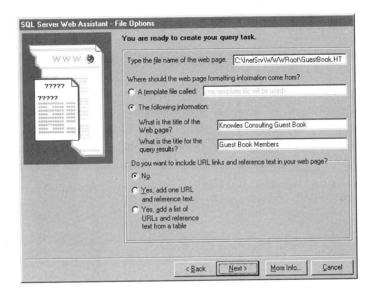

13. Click the Next button to display the SQL Server Web Assistant – Formatting dialog box, shown in Figure 17.23.

Figure 17.23.
Specifying the
Web Assistant
Web page
formatting
parameters.

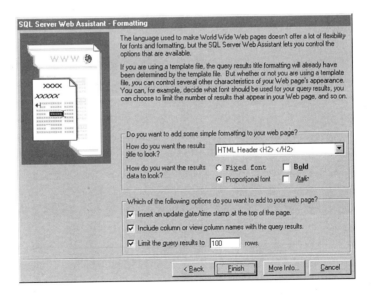

14. Specify the size of the HTML header to be used for the result columns in the How Do You Want The Results Title To Look? field.

15. Specify how the result rows will be displayed by enabling the Fixed Font radio button to use a fixed-width font, or the Proportional Font radio button to use a proportional-width font.

16. To make the results rows more visible, enable the Bold check box. To emphasize the result rows, enable the Italic check box.

17. To insert a time/date timestamp at the beginning of the page, enable the Insert An Update Date/Time Stamp At The Top Of The Page check box.

18. To include column name headers on the output, enable the Include Column Or View Column Names With The Results check box.

19. To limit the number of rows on a single Web page, enable the Limit The Query Results To check box and enter a value in the rows field.

20. Click the Finish button to build your Web page.

SHARED MANAGEMENT TOOLS

Both SQL Server 4.21a and SQL Server 6.x have several applications in common. These include the SQL Service Manager, SQL Security Manager, SQL Transfer Manager, SQL Client Configuration utility, and the command-line utilities. You can use these applications for the following tasks:

◆ SQL Service Manager: Controls the SQL Server services

◆ SQL Security Manager: Migrates your domain user accounts and groups to SQL Server

◆ SQL Transfer Manager: Migrates a database from one SQL Server platform to another SQL Server platform in its entirety

◆ SQL Client Configuration utility: Configures your client workstation to access your SQL Server installation using various client Net Libraries

◆ Command-line tools: Includes an ISQL command-line access tool and the Bulk Copy program to dump and load data in a table

USING SQL SERVICE MANAGER

You use the SQL Service Manager to start, stop, or pause the SQL Monitor. Or, you use SQL Server Service if you are using SQL Server 4.21a, and you use the SQL Executive or SQL Server Service if you are using SQL Server 6.x. Using these tools is far easier and quicker than using the Control Panel Services applet because SQL Service Manager only controls two services instead of all services on the computer. It also uses a traffic light icon to indicate the status of the services.

To use the SQL Service Manager, follow these steps:

1. In the Server drop-down listbox, choose the computer to manage, or enter a remote computer name in the form of \\ComputerName.
2. In the Services drop-down listbox, choose the service to manage.
3. Double-click the green light to start or continue the service, double-click the yellow light to pause the service, or double-click the red light to stop the service.

Using SQL Security Manager

The SQL Security Manager can be used only on SQL Server configurations that are configured to use the integrated or mixed security models. If your server still is using the standard model, you should refer to the preceding chapter on installation to reconfigure your server. Using the SQL Security Manager is an easy task due to its simple graphical interface. The first step in the process is to connect to the appropriate SQL Server.

After you have connected to your server, select the type of accounts to migrate; this can be user level or System Administrator (sa) level. You can choose these options from the View menu, or you can just click the User (looks like a person) or SA (looks like a person next to a computer) button. Then choose Security | Grant New to display the Grant User Privilege dialog box. From there, it is a simple matter of selecting the user or group accounts, enabling the Add Login IDs for Group Members checkbox (if a group is selected), the Add Users to Database checkbox (if you want to grant permission to access a specific database and save you some time with SQL Administrator), and clicking the Grant button. When you finish migrating your accounts, click the Done button.

After you migrate all your accounts, you can manipulate individual accounts in a group by double-clicking on them. This displays the Account Detail dialog box (also accessible by choosing Security | Account Detail), where you can drop the login (revoke the user's permission to access SQL Server) and grant or revoke permissions to individual databases.

Using SQL Transfer Manager

You can use the SQL Transfer Manager to transfer entire databases, portions of a database, or logins from one database to another. The databases can reside on different SQL Servers, but they do not have to. This provides you with two benefits. First, you can migrate a database from one SQL Server platform to another. Second, you can replicate a database. The first step in using the application is to specify the source and destination SQL Servers in the Connect dialog box. After you have connected to the respective servers, the SQL Transfer Manager dialog box appears, as shown in Figure 17.24.

Figure 17.24.
Copying a
database with the
SQL Transfer
Manager.

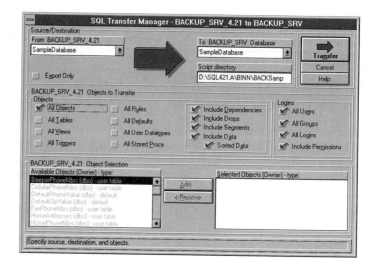

Using SQL Transfer Manager is similar to using the SQL Object Manager's Object Permissions dialog box because you can choose the objects and logins to be migrated. The primary difference is that instead of just generating a script, you are copying the data in the tables as well. To transfer a database, just select the source and destination databases in the From and To fields, respectively. Then choose the objects to migrate, along with the logins and permissions, and click the Transfer button. Once the data starts being transferred, take a break; depending on the size of the database, it will take a while to migrate the database.

Note

Due to the amount of data being transferred across the network, it is a good idea to arrange your database migrations or replications on off-peak hours to minimize the disruption.

USING THE SQL CLIENT CONFIGURATION UTILITY

You can use the SQL Client Configuration utility to configure your client-side connections to SQL Server using various Net Libraries. I mention this here because it is important for you to understand that you do not have to physically use the client computer to verify the proper installation of these Net Libraries to test the service-side Net Library configuration. Instead, you can configure the Windows NT Server client-side connections with the SQL Client Configuration utility to use different names for different client Net Libraries. Then you can connect to SQL Server using any of these named connections with any of the SQL Server tools. If you can connect, the server-side Net Libraries are configured properly. Any client-connection problems you encounter then are network related or are related to the client configuration on the client workstation. The installation and configuration of the server-side libraries is covered in depth in Chapter 16. The SQL Server client-side Net Library installation, configuration, usage, and troubleshooting techniques are covered in Chapter 34, "Windows NT Clients."

Using Command-Line Utilities

The ISQL command-line program provides you with a character-mode interface to SQL Server. With this tool, you can execute Transact SQL statements or create batch jobs. You can use the Bulk Copy program to dump or load data into a table. When you combine the functionality offered by the ISQL and Bulk Copy programs, you can automate the creation of mailing lists or other basic maintenance tasks. Take, for example, a batch file with the following lines:

```
ISQL /Usa /P /SBACKUP_SRV_4.21 /dSampleDatabase /Q "sp_dboption 'select into/
➡bulkcopy', true"
ISQL /Usa /P /SBACKUP_SRV_4.21 /dSampleDatabase /Q "SELECT * INTO TempTable FROM
ViewHomeNamesInCalifornia"
BCP SampleDatabase.dbo.TempTable OUT FlatFile.CSV /Usa /P /SBACKUP_SRV_4.21 /c /t,
➡_/r\n
ISQL /Usa /P /SBACKUP_SRV_4.21 /dSampleDatabase /Q DROP TABLE dbo.TempTable"
ISQL /Usa /P /SBACKUP_SRV_4.21 /dSampleDatabase /Q "sp_dboption 'select into/
➡_bulkcopy', false"
```

This code logs onto the SQL Server BACKUP_SRV_4.21; creates the TempTable table, which contains all the names and addresses for customers who live in California (as based on the view ViewHomeNamesInCalifornia, which joins the Names, HomeAddress, and HomePhoneNbrs tables and limits the selection to the state of California); dumps these rows to the file FlatFile.CSV; and then deletes the temporary table. The file that is created can be imported into any database program that supports the comma-separated values format. This includes almost all Windows database programs, spreadsheets, and word processing programs.

Note

The first statement in the batch file is only there to configure the database to a nonlogged state in order to allow the SELECT INTO operation to proceed. After the temporary table is created, the last statement resets the database back to a logged state. If you want to avoid this temporary toggling of the logged state, you can create a permanent table with the appropriate table layout, use an INSERT statement

> instead of a SELECT INTO statement, and just delete the table's contents before you execute the select statement (in case someone else has played with it) and after the bulk copy (to remove the data that is no longer required).

You can use similar batch files to dump your databases or transaction logs to tape. You might even use a batch process to load data that you have downloaded from a mainframe computer or a CD-ROM containing phone numbers. The bottom line is that you can automate any job that you manually step through now, as long as the application you use accepts command-line arguments to control the application. If you have a Windows program that can create batch scripts, such as Microsoft Test, then you can even automate jobs that use Windows applications.

The syntax for the ISQL command-line program follows:

```
ISQL /ULoginID /PPassword /SServerName /dDatabase
```

Explanations for the syntax follow:

LoginID: The SQL Server login identifier to use.

Password: The password for the SQL Server login identifier.

ServerName: The name of the SQL Server to use.

Database: The initial database to use.

Descriptions of additional ISQL switches follow:

/?: Displays a summary of the command-line switches.

/a: Specifies a different network packet size.

/c: Specifies a replacement for the ISQL command terminator (GO).

/e: Echoes your input to the screen.

/h: Specifies the number of rows to print before a new header is generated; the header specifies column names, followed by a line of dashes to distinguish the printed columns.

/H: Specifies a name other than the default workstation name to be used for identification purposes.

/iInputFilename: Where InputFilename is the name of your Transact SQL script file.

/L: Lists nonhidden SQL Servers.

/m: Specifies the error severity level to use for error message output; messages lower than the supplied level are not displayed.

/n: Removes the numbers on the ISQL command prompts.

/oOutputFilename: Where OutputFilename is the name of the output file to contain the ISQL-generated output.

/p: Prints performance statistics for your SQL statements.

/qCmdLineQuery: Where CmdLineQuery is a SQL statement enclosed in quotation marks to be executed.

/QCmdLineQuery: Where CmdLineQuery is a SQL statement enclosed in quotation marks to be executed; after it executes, ISQL terminates.

/rMsg: Where Msg is 0 to redirect only error messages to the standard error device (stderr) or 1 to redirect all messages.

/s: Specifies the character to use to separate columns of data (default is a space).

/t: Specifies the time in seconds before a command times out; default for a login to SQL Server is 8 seconds.

/w: Specifies the output width.

The syntax for the Bulk Copy program follows:

```
BCP DatabaseName.OwnerName.TableName {IN ¦ OUT} FileName /UUserName /PPassword
_/SServerName
/fFormatFileName /eErrorFileName /FFirstRowNbr /LLastRowNumber /bBatchSize /n /c
_/tFieldTerminator
/rRowTerminator /aPacketSize /vVersionNbr /mMaxErrors
```

The Bulk Copy (BCP) command-line switches follow:

DatabaseName.OwnerName.TableName: The fully qualified name of the table to dump or load.

IN ¦ OUT: Specifies the direction. IN is used to load data into a table from a file, and OUT is used to dump data from a table into a file.

FileName: Name of the file to use.

UserName: SQL Server login identifier to use.

Password: Password for the SQL Server login identifier.

ServerName: Name of the SQL Server to use.

FormatFileName: Name of the BCP format file.

ErrorFileName: Name of the file to contain any SQL Server- or BCP-generated error messages.

FirstRowNbr: Number of the row to start your dump/load from.

LastRowNbr: Number of the row to stop your dump/load from.

BatchSize: Number of rows to process at a time.

/n: Specifies that the SQL Server platform's native data representations format be used.

/c: Specifies that all columns be converted to/from character format.

FieldTerminator: Specifies the value to be used to terminate a column. This can be any ASCII character string up to 30 characters or the following:

\t	Tab character
\n	Newline character
\r	Carriage return character
\0	Null terminator
\\	Backslash character

RowTerminator: Specifies the value to be used to distinguish the end of the row. This can be any of the values described earlier.

PacketSize: Specifies the suggested network packet size to use. The optimal value is 8192 for named pipe clients, and although you can specify a number larger than the default of 512, it may not actually be used. The actual packet size is reported at the end of the bulk copy.

VersionNbr: Returns the version number of the Net Library that is used for the connection to SQL Server.

MaxErrors: Specifies the maximum number of errors that can occur before the bulk copy is terminated. The default is 10 errors.

SUMMARY

This chapter was a fairly complex one, and I hope it has not overwhelmed you. In this chapter, you learned how to manage your SQL Server installation with the SQL Administrator, SQL Object Manager, and SQL Enterprise Manager. You use the SQL Administrator to perform the basic functions, which include device management, database management, group and login management, and other system-management operations. You use the SQL Object Manager to manage your tables, rules, defaults, user-defined data types, views, stored procedures, triggers, and object permissions. To understand object usage, you used components from your sample Name, Address, and Phone Number database to help illustrate the functionality. Of course, you only looked at a few of the individual components. For a fuller understanding, I suggest that you run the sample scripts located on the CD that accompanies this book and review the associated objects with SQL Object Manager. After the discussion of SQL Administrator and SQL Object Manager, this chapter looked at the new features provided in the SQL Enterprise Manager, including basic replication, task management, alerts, and how to use the Web Assistant to create HTML pages from your databases.

This chapter also discussed the shared application, which consists of the SQL Transfer Manager. You can use this to copy a database from one SQL Server installation to another. You explored SQL Security Manager, which you can use to migrate your domain accounts to SQL Server in the integrated or mixed security modes. You also learned about the SQL Client Configuration utility, which you can use to test your server-side Net Library connections. This chapter even discussed how to use the command-line ISQL and BCP (Bulk Copy program) to automate basic recurring tasks. You can use these same tasks with the Windows NT Scheduler service or the SQL Enterprise Manager to help you in your day-to-day management duties.

In the next chapter, you will look at some of the options for tuning your server for optimum performance. This includes a look at using hardware options, configuring various software options, and using the SQL Server Performance Monitor.

- Configuring
  Windows NT Server

- Configuring
  SQL Server

- Using the SQL
  Performance
  Monitor Counters

CHAPTER 18

Optimizing SQL Server

Now that you have SQL Server up and running, you want to maximize its performance and you probably are wondering how to get the most out of it. Do you add to or modify your hardware, such as choosing the fastest disk controller on the market? Do you add additional memory? Maybe even add an additional processor or two? And if you do not add any new hardware, what software configuration choices can you make? Do you make changes to Windows NT Server, or do you modify your SQL Server configuration? There are so many choices available that determining where to start can be very confusing for novice as well as advanced administrators.

These topics and choices are the basis of the discussion in this chapter. After reading this chapter, you should have a much better understanding of where you should start, as well as what you can do to get the most out of your SQL Server installation. This discussion begins with the backbone of your SQL Server installation or Windows NT Server configuration; then it moves on to tell you how to configure SQL Server. Finally, it takes a look at the SQL Server Performance Monitor counters and explains how you can use them to fine-tune your performance.

CONFIGURING WINDOWS NT SERVER

Because SQL Server for Windows NT executes on Windows NT Server, it should be fairly obvious that if Windows NT Server is not optimized for maximum performance, then SQL Server will not be optimized for maximum performance, either. Although this chapter looks at some of the highlights of optimizing performance, it does not discuss it in detail because this is covered in Chapters 12, "Getting the Most from Your Microsoft Network," and 13, "Tuning Your Server." What might not be obvious, however, is the relationship between SQL Server performance and Windows NT Server. When you understand this relationship, optimizing SQL Server becomes much easier simply because you know what trade-offs are involved.

HARDWARE OPTIMIZATIONS

To begin optimizing Windows NT Server, you need to choose a hardware platform. Choose this platform carefully because it determines what options are available to increase performance. You should check the following elements when optimizing Windows NT Server.

PROCESSOR

Make sure that your system has at least a Pentium processor. The faster the processor, the better. But don't stop there; you should try to plan your purchase to include a system that supports at least two processors and preferably four or more.

You do not have to purchase all these processors at once, and the added scalability is well worth the additional expense.

Because many of today's processors are clock doubled, tripled, or even quadrupled, you can achieve a significant performance increase by choosing the right combination of processor speeds based on the memory bus speed. I have an Intel DX4/100, for example, which can be used as a clock-tripled processor when the memory bus is set to 33 MHz, or as a clock-doubled processor when the memory bus is set to 50 MHz. When combined with either a PCI or VLB expansion bus, which also runs at the same speed as the memory bus, you can achieve the best performance by choosing the higher memory bus speed. I gained a 33 percent improvement in video and memory performance by configuring my system to 50 MHz and doubling the processor speed. Many Pentium systems offer similar configuration choices, and you should refer to your system documentation to see whether these possibilities are available to you as well.

MEMORY

There is no doubt about it: You can't go wrong by adding additional memory. Physical memory is the number one optimization option after your processor choice because it decreases the number of page faults, and any extra memory is used to cache I/O access. A page fault occurs anytime Windows NT has to access memory that is not physically present, and therefore must be read from the paging file. Because disk access is in the ms (millisecond) range, whereas memory access is in the ns (nanosecond) range, you can understand that preventing page faults is really a good idea. And this doesn't even include the overhead involved in actually suspending a process, queuing the I/O request, processing the I/O request, and then resuming the thread.

Tip

> A system dedicated to SQL Server should have a minimum of 32MB of RAM. If you want to maximize performance, consider at least 64MB. A system with up to 256MB of RAM is not out of the question, either. This extra RAM can be allocated for direct or indirect use by SQL Server (this is discussed in the next section).

Unlike some operating systems, where you must specify a minimum and maximum size for the disk cache, Windows NT dynamically allocates a cache size based on the system's needs. As more physical memory is required for applications, the cache size shrinks; as less physical memory is required, the cache size increases.

CACHE

This element is tougher to determine, but at a minimum, you should look for a system with at least a 256KB secondary (L2) cache with write-back support. Look for a system that supports the Pentium pipeline burst mode access because this enables you to read/write larger chunks of data in a single cycle. Again, if possible, look for a system that supports a cache that can be expanded to at least 512KB. Some systems support a cache size of 1MB or more. These larger cache sizes are important as you add additional system memory.

Your secondary cache plays a significant role in optimizing the performance of your memory subsystem. If your cache is too small, the data you need will not be in the cache when you need it. You might have heard the term *thrashing* when disk caching performance is described. The same process occurs with your secondary cache. It becomes more of a problem as more threads run on your system because each of these has its own set of localized memory that it needs to access. As each of these threads loads, it accesses memory regions that may differ widely from other threads. This causes the cache to be flushed to load in these new regions of memory. When the thread is suspended (for a task switch, for example), the next thread may require a different region of memory. This causes a previous thread's data to be flushed. All this flushing causes your system to slow down as it writes and reads various memory regions.

Basically, two types of secondary caches exist. You can choose a memory-mapped cache (the most common), which has one location where it can store a specific byte of data based on a series of physical memory addresses, and therefore often is the fastest type of cache. The downside to this type of cache is that it also is more prone to cache thrashing because there is only one location to store more than one physical address, and as your need to access multiple bytes within this address range increases, the cache must read this data directly from the memory bus. The alternative is a set associative cache, which is also the same type of cache used internally within your Intel 80486 and higher processors. This type of cache breaks up the cache memory into two, four, or more banks of memory so that it can store these multiple bytes of data in the required memory range simultaneously. Because the data can be in two, four, or more places, however, it might take longer to locate. For what it's worth, I believe that a set associative cache is the better choice—particularly in a multitasking environment.

EXPANSION BUS

Basically, the faster and wider the bus, the better. This means that PCI is best, followed by VLB, EISA, MCA, ISA, and PCMCIA. When possible, choose a PCI and EISA hybrid rather than PCI and ISA because EISA is a 32-bit bus that still offers 16-bit ISA compatibility.

Note

Whenever possible, avoid the PCI/VLB and ISA hybrid motherboard designs, because these generally have the worst PCI/VLB performance, although they do offer compatibility with your existing peripherals.

PERIPHERALS

This is where it gets a little tougher. Overall, you should start with your fastest bus. If you have a PCI or VLB bus, then use it for your primary disk, network, and video cards. Because PCI currently has a maximum of three expansion slots, which you have just filled, you can understand why EISA makes a good secondary bus choice. Many EISA bus-mastering SCSI and network adapters are widely available and offer good performance.

DISK SUBSYSTEM

While the debate still rages as to which disk type offers the greatest throughput, there is still no doubt that SCSI is the performance king for a server. Why? Simply because a SCSI subsystem can process multiple I/O requests simultaneously, whereas any ST-506 or compatible (ESDI, EIDE, IDE, MFM, or RLL) disk that uses the default ATDISK.SYS driver can handle only one I/O request at a time.

Not only can a SCSI subsystem handle multiple I/O requests, but many SCSI disk controllers are bus masters. This makes it possible for the processor to continue working while the SCSI controller actually moves the data from the disk drive to system memory. In effect, a bus master offloads processing chores from the CPU. Most ST-506 and compatible drives, on the other hand, require the CPU to move the data from disk to memory, which eats up processor bandwidth.

There have been recent market additions to the EIDE disk controller line that do offer bus mastering, hardware disk caching, and command-queuing capabilities that theoretically can provide similar performance as a SCSI disk subsystem. In order to provide these capabilities under Windows NT Server, however, the controller must have a device driver specifically written to support these features. If you use the default ATDISK.SYS driver, then the hardware disk cache generally will be disabled, and only a single I/O request can be processed at a time. This negates the performance options provided by the disk controller.

SOFTWARE OPTIMIZATIONS

The rest of your optimization choices fall into two categories: load balancing and software configuration. Load balancing is a process of spreading a choke point across multiple physical peripherals to lower the load on any one device. If you have a disk drive that contains your mail files and all your applications, for example, I can guarantee that it will be overloaded. Instead, you should put your mail files on one physical drive and your applications on one or more physical drives to even the load. Performance tuning and load balancing Windows NT Server is described in more detail in Chapter 13.

The same principle applies to your network adapters. By adding adapters and binding a single protocol to each adapter, you can spread the load more equally among them to increase network throughput. This also works for processors because Windows NT uses a symmetric processing model. Adding additional processors spreads the processing load and can increase overall performance. Although adding a second processor often almost doubles system performance, the third and fourth processors usually do not triple or quadruple performance because the overhead involved in maintaining concurrency (which includes keeping all the processor caches up to date, handling task switches, and so on) increases with each additional processor added to the system.

SOFTWARE CONFIGURATION CHOICES

Your software configuration choices are much more limited because Windows NT Server is mostly self-tuning. The options I generally modify are described in the following sections.

TASKING

The Control Panel System applet is your interface to specifying how the processes on your server are timesliced. The default in a base Windows NT installation is Best Foreground Application Response Time, which provides the lion's share of the processor to the application running in the foreground. After you install SQL Server, however, the setting changes to Foreground and Background Application Equally Responsive, which gives each process an equal timeslice. This is the best choice to maximize SQL Server's performance, but it makes the system respond sluggishly when used interactively. This is why I prefer to use the Foreground Application More Responsive Than Background option when I use the system interactively (perhaps to administer the system).

Tip

The Windows NT Server CD-ROM includes network administration utilities (User Manager for Domains, Server Manager, User Profile Editor, and so on, contained in the \CLIENTS\ subdirectory), which can be used to remotely administer your network from a remote workstation. If you install the SQL Server utilities on the same remote workstation, you can administer SQL Server for remote administration as well. In this situation, it is best to choose the Foreground and Background Application Equally Responsive setting for maximum performance.

VIRTUAL MEMORY

When your system runs out of physical memory, which surely will happen at one time or another, memory pages to disk or your system grinds to a halt for lack of resources. For this reason, it is best to make sure that you have a sufficient virtual memory allocation. You cannot arbitrarily determine exactly how much virtual memory you need, but you should allocate at least four times the physical memory on your system. If you have 32MB of RAM, for example, allocate a minimum page file of 128MB.

Tip

To determine exactly how large your paging file should be, take a look at the section "Performance Tuning with the Performance Monitor" in Chapter 13. This section explains how to maximize your system based on memory requirements, and the MEMHOG.EXE example shows you just how your system will perform in a low-memory situation.

SERVER CONFIGURATION

You can use the Control Panel Network applet to configure the Server service and to share network resources. You have the following choices:

♦ Minimize Memory Used: Best used when you have 10 or fewer client connections

♦ Balance: Provides support for up to 64 network clients and is the default when the NetBEUI transport is chosen

♦ Maximize Throughput for File Sharing: Allocates additional resources (mainly internal buffers) to maximize the performance for sharing file and print services

♦ Maximize Throughput for Network Applications: The default when you install SQL Server

The Maximize Throughput for Network Applications option allocates additional internal resources and distributes these resources to optimize network-related activity. This is the best choice for large networks and for best SQL Server performance. If you have a small network with fewer than 64 network clients, however, it can be a waste of Windows NT Server resources. Because these resources are limited, you might be able to obtain better overall performance by choosing the Balance option.

NETWORK TRANSPORT

Determining what network transport to use is sometimes just a matter of integration, instead of a performance choice. If you have a Novell Network, for example, you should use IPX/SPX. If you have a UNIX-based network, TCP/IP is the best choice. The fastest transport is still NetBEUI, but it is really only a good choice for small networks. The recommendations are NetBEUI for fewer than 100 clients, IPX/SPX for greater than 100 clients and fewer than 255 clients, and TCP/IP for anything greater than 255 clients. You also might want to use TCP/IP if you have any remote clients.

Tip

Choosing a single network transport can improve performance quite a bit when compared to multiple network transports simply because each additional transport adds additional overhead. When you need to support multiple client platforms, consider TCP/IP as your network transport because you can find TCP/IP stacks for UNIX, Novell, and even Macintosh clients.

CONFIGURING SQL SERVER

After you optimize Windows NT Server to provide the best performance, you can turn your attention to configuring SQL Server. After you make your SQL Server configuration changes, you might need to make changes to your Windows NT Server configuration to fine-tune its performance. The easiest way to modify SQL Server's configuration is with the SQL Enterprise Manager; however, you can use an ISQL command-line prompt, if you prefer. This section looks at the various options and describes both the good and bad sides of these options. In the next section, you will look at using the Performance Monitor to help you determine whether your configuration choices are working as well as expected.

The first requirement is to load the SQL Enterprise Manager. Next, click on a registered server to connect to the SQL Server installation you want to configure. Then, right-click on the server name and choose Configure from the pop-up menu. The Server/Configuration dialog box appears. Choose the Configuration tab; then the available options are displayed on the property sheet. To change the current value, enter a new value Current column for the specific option. Repeat this step for each option to change. After you make all your modifications, click the OK button to return to the SQL Enterprise Manager main window. Table 18.1 lists the options (for SQL Server 6.5) that you can change.

Tip

To set any of these options from an ISQL command prompt, you can use the stored procedure `sp_configure`. The basic syntax follows:

```
sp_configure 'option', 'value'
```

where `option` and `value` are specified in Table 18.1.

18

Optimizing SQL Server

TABLE 18.1. THE SQL SERVER CONFIGURATION OPTIONS.

Option	Minimum Value	Maximum Value	Default Value	Requires Restart to Be Placed in Effect	Description
allow updates	0	1	0	No	Specifies that users with appropriate permissions will be able to modify system tables directly. Use this option with care because it is possible to damage system tables and corrupt a database quite easily.
backup buffer size	1	10	1	No	Specifies the size (in 32-page increments) of the dump and load buffer used to increase the backup performance.
backup threads	0	32	5	Yes	Specifies the number of threads to be reserved for striped operations (such as a dump or load).

continues

Table 18.1. CONTINUED

Option	Minimum Value	Maximum Value	Default Value	Requires Restart to Be Placed in Effect	Description
database size	2	10,000	2	Yes	Specifies the default size, in MB, for newly created databases. This minimum size is based on the model database. If you make a change to the model database, it determines the minimum size of all databases created after the change.
Default language	0	9999	0	Yes	Specifies the default language to use with SQL Server. It is best (and easier) to set this value using the SQL Server Setup utility.
fill factor	0	100	0	Yes	Specifies how full (a percentage from 0 to 100, where 0 specifies the SQL Server default) the data page will be whenever SQL Server creates a new index. You can override this value by using the CREATE INDEX command.

18

Option	Minimum Value	Maximum Value	Default Value	Requires Restart to Be Placed in Effect	Description
language in cache	3	100	3	No	Specifies the maximum number of languages that can be held simultaneously in the system cache.
LE threshold maximum	2	500,000	200	N/A	Specifies the number maximum of page locks that can be held before escalating to a table lock.
LE threshold percent	0	100	0	N/A	Specifies the percentage of page locks that can be held on a table before escalating to a table lock.
locks	5000	2,147,483,647	5000	Yes	Specifies how many locks are available for use by SQL Server. Each lock requires about 32 bytes of memory. If you run out of locks, a process fails or it is suspended until a lock is available. I recommend that you specify a minimum of 50,000 locks. You may need more if you have complex stored procedures

continues

TABLE 18.1. CONTINUED

Option	Minimum Value	Maximum Value	Default Value	Requires Restart to Be Placed in Effect	Description
					or queries, or a large number of users accessing SQL Server.
logwrite sleep	1	500	0	N/A	Specifies the length of time, in milliseconds, before a write to the log that a delay will occur if the buffer is not full.
max async IO	1	50	8	Yes	Specifies the maximum number of asynchronous I/O requests that can be issued by SQL Server. Increase this value if you have a stripe set, a stripe set with parity, or a RAID 5 hardware array. My basic recommendation is to increase this value by half the number of spindles in the system. If you have five disk drives, for example, the entry should be 20 ((5 * 8) / 2 = 20). You can increase this value if you have an exceptionally fast I/O subsystem.

Option	Minimum Value	Maximum Value	Default Value	Requires Restart to Be Placed in Effect	Description
max text repl size	0	2,147,483,647	65,536		Specifies the maximum size, in bytes, of text or image data which may be added to a replicated column in a single insert, update, writetext, or updatetext statement.
max worker threads	10	1024	255	Yes	Specifies the maximum number of threads SQL Server can use to support client connections and perform internal maintenance. Increasing this value if you have more than one processor installed on the system can increase performance.
media retention	0	365	0	Yes	Specifies the length of time you plan to keep each disk used for a database or transaction log.
memory	1000	1,048,576	Based on amount of memory installed	Yes	Specifies the number of 2KB units to physically be used by SQL memory Server. Note: This is the number one item to change for

continues

18

Optimizing SQL Server

TABLE 18.1. CONTINUED

Option	Minimum Value	Maximum Value	Default Value	Requires Restart to Be Placed in Effect	Description
					maximum performance. The basic recommendation is to allocate as much memory as possible for SQL Server's usage. You should leave a minimum of 16MB for Windows NT Server, however. If you have additional services, such as Services for Macintosh, Gateway Services for Novell, DHCP, WINS, and so on, plan on allocating an additional 2MB per service. You can allocate any leftover memory to SQL Server. In a 64MB system, I generally allocate between 32MB and 48MB to SQL Server.
nested triggers	0	1	1	Yes	Specifies whether nested triggers are enabled (1) or disabled (0).
network packet size	512	32,767	4096	No	Specifies the size, in bytes, of the network packet size to use. This value can

Option	Minimum Value	Maximum Value	Default Value	Requires Restart to Be Placed in Effect	Description
					be overridden by the client application.
open databases	5	32,767	20	Yes	Specifies the maximum number of databases that can be opened simultaneously. Each database allocation consumes about 1KB of system memory.
open objects	100	2,147,483,647	500	Yes	Specifies the maximum number of database objects that can be opened simultaneously. Each object allocation consumes about 70 bytes.
procedure cache	1	99	30	Yes	Specifies the amount of memory (a percentage from 0 to 100 percent) to allocate to the procedure cache after the SQL Server allocation demands have been satisfied. If you modify the default settings for memory allocations as recommended, then you also may want to change this value. In a high-memory system

18

Optimizing SQL Server

continues

TABLE 18.1. CONTINUED

Option	Minimum Value	Maximum Value	Default Value	Requires Restart to Be Placed in Effect	Description
					(64MB or more), I generally recommend a value between 30 and 40 percent, depending on the number of users and active stored procedures.
RA worker threads	0	255	3	N/A	Specifies the number of read-ahead worker threads to allocate.
recovery flags	0	1	0	Yes	Specifies what information SQL Server displays during the recovery process. If you have problems, setting this value to 1 enables additional diagnostic messages that may help to isolate the problem.
recovery interval	1	32,767	5	No	Specifies the maximum number of minutes SQL Server can use to recover a database. Increase this value if you have complex or large databases.
remote access	0	1	0	Yes	Specifies that remote SQL Servers can access this

Option	Minimum Value	Maximum Value	Default Value	Requires Restart to Be Placed in Effect	Description
					server (1) or cannot access this server (0).
remote conn timeout	-1	32767	10	N/A	Specifies the maximum number of minutes to wait before closing inactive server-to-server connections.
tempdb	0	2044	0	Yes	Specifies the size (in MB) of RAM to allocate for temporary databases. This is the second most important performance option that you can use because the temporary database is constantly in use for temporary objects (tables, procedures, sorts, and so on). Use this option with care, however, as this directly affects the amount of available RAM that can be used by other system processes. If you have more than 64MB of RAM, it certainly will benefit you to use an additional 16MB to 64MB of RAM for

18

Optimizing SQL Server

continues

TABLE 18.1. CONTINUED

Option	Minimum Value	Maximum Value	Default Value	Requires Restart to Be Placed in Effect	Description
					the temporary database, depending on the type of queries you will be executing.
user connections	5	32,767	10	Yes	Specifies the maximum number of simultaneous user connections that can be established with this server. Each connection consumes about 37KB of system memory. This value should be based on the number of legal license agreements you have purchased, and, for what it's worth, it is better to have a few too many connections than to run out of available connections. At least, you should use the SQL Administrator to check for connections that have been terminated but not removed from SQL Server's connection list and

Option	Minimum Value	Maximum Value	Default Value	Requires Restart to Be Placed in Effect	Description
					manually terminate them to free up available connections.
user options	0	4096	0	N/A	Specifies a bit mask to be used to set various user options which may be overridden on a per user basis using the SET command.

Note

Many of the changes you make will be placed into effect only after you shut down and restart SQL Server.

One of the biggest potential performance gains you can achieve cannot be set using the just-mentioned interface. Instead, you must use the SQL Server Setup utility, as described in Chapter 16, "Installing SQL Server," to enable the Dedicated Multiprocessor Support option. This option basically sets aside a single processor for use by SQL Server. By doing so, it prevents task switches for the threads used by SQL Server from being processed on the additional processors on the system. This can significantly lower the overhead involved in flushing the internal and external caches and can make a dramatic improvement in performance.

USING THE SQL PERFORMANCE MONITOR COUNTERS

SQL Server for Windows NT includes performance counters you can use to monitor the activity of your server for informational purposes and to fine-tune the performance of your SQL Server installation. If you look in the SQL Server for Windows NT Program Manager group, you will find a predefined set of performance counters you can use to check the basic activity of your server. It's not always enough to use just these settings, however, which is why I have included Table 18.2. You can use this table to determine which counters may be of interest to you.

Note

Depending on which version of SQL Server you are using, the counters may be different.

TABLE 18.2. THE SQL SERVER PERFORMANCE MONITOR COUNTERS.

Object	Counter	Description
SQLServer	I/O Log Writes/sec	Specifies the number of log pages written to disk per second. Because almost all database activity is transaction based, which means the changes must be written to the log before they can be applied to the database, this is a good counter to watch to determine whether your disk is a bottleneck for SQL Server performance.
SQLServer	I/O Batch Writes/sec	Specifies the number of asynchronous writes in a single batch (generally as part of the checkpoint process). The higher the value, the better the SQL Server performance. Monitor this value as you make changes to segment and device allocations to see whether your changes are increasing or decreasing performance.
SQLServer	I/O Batch Average Size	Specifies the average number of pages (2KB) written to disk during a batch operation. The higher the value, the better. You use this counter to determine whether your changes to the max async i/o parameter are effective. If you increase the max async i/o value too much, this counter decreases.
SQLServer	I/O Batch Max Size	Specifies the maximum number of pages (2KB) that have been written to disk. The higher the value, the better the overall performance. This counter also can be used to determine whether the max async i/o

Object	Counter	Description
		parameter setting is effective. If this counter lowers after your changes, decrease the value for the max async i/o parameter.
SQLServer	I/O Page Reads/sec	Specifies the number of physical disk reads per second. The lower the number, the better. If this value is too high, you can change the procedure cache percentage to increase the amount of memory allocated to the data cache. A larger data cache lowers the number of physical disk reads.
SQLServer	I/O Single page Writes/sec	Specifies the number of physical disk writes per second. Like the I/O Page Reads/sec counter, a lower number is better. If a high value is encountered, it might be beneficial to increase the size of the data cache.
SQLServer	I/O Outstanding Reads	Specifies the number of pending physical disk reads. You can use this value to determine how well your I/O subsystem is performing. A high value over an extended period of time is an indication that the I/O subsystem is a bottleneck in SQL Server performance.
SQLServer	I/O Outstanding Writes	Specifies the number of pending physical disk writes. Like the I/O Outstanding Reads counter, a high value over an extended period of time is an indication that the I/O subsystem is a bottleneck.
SQLServer	I/O Transactions/sec	Specifies the number of Transact SQL batches per second. A higher value is better.
SQLServer	I/O – Trans. Per Log Record	Specifies the number of transactions that were packed into a single log

continues

18

Optimizing SQL Server

Table 18.2. continued

Object	Counter	Description
		record before being written to disk. A higher value is better.
SQLServer	Cache Hit Ratio	Specifies the percentage of time in which requested data was found in the data cache. The higher the value, the better. If your hit rate routinely drops below 60 percent to 70 percent, increasing the size of the data cache may improve SQL Server performance.
SQLServer	Cache Flushes	Specifies the number of cache buffers that need to be flushed to disk in order to free a buffer for use by the next read. When cache flushes occur, you should increase the size of your data cache or increase the checkpoint frequency to provide additional buffers and increase performance.
SQLServer	Cache – Avg. Free Page Scan	Specifies the average number of buffers that needed to be scanned in order to find a free buffer. When this value increases above 10, increase the size of the data cache or the frequency of the checkpoint process to free additional buffers and increase performance.
SQLServer	Cache – Max Free Page Scan	Specifies the maximum number of buffers that had to be scanned in order to find a free buffer. When this value increases above 10, increase the size of the data cache or the frequency of the checkpoint process to free additional buffers and increase performance.
SQLServer	Cache – Scan Limit Reached	Specifies the number of times the scan limit was reached while searching for free buffers. If this value is consistently high, increase the size of the data cache or the checkpoint

Object	Counter	Description
		frequency to free up additional buffers.
SQLServer	Network Reads/sec	Specifies the number of tabular data stream packets read from the network. A higher value indicates higher network activity.
SQLServer	Network Writes/sec	Specifies the number of tabular data streams written to the network. A higher value is an indication of higher network activity.
SQLServer	Network Command Queue Length	Specifies the number of outstanding client requests waiting to be serviced by the SQL Server worker threads. A higher value is an indication that increasing the number of worker threads may improve performance. If performance does not increase, it may be an indication that the processor is a bottleneck and adding an additional processor may increase overall throughput.
SQLServer	User Connections	Specifies the number of current users connected to SQL Server.
SQLServer-Locks	Total Locks	Specifies the total number of locks currently in use by SQL Server.
SQLServer-Locks	Total Exclusive Locks	Specifies the total number of exclusive (meaning no other process can access the locked area) locks in use by SQL Server.
SQLServer-Locks	Total Shared Locks	Specifies the total number of shared (meaning the lock will not prevent other users from reading the locked data) locks in use by SQL Server.
SQLServer-Locks	Total Blocking Locks	Specifies the number of locks blocking other processes from

continues

TABLE 18.2. CONTINUED

Object	Counter	Description
		continuing. A blocked process is one that requires a lock on the same area.
SQLServer-Locks	Total Demand Locks	Specifies the number of locks blocking other processes that need to obtain a shared lock on the same data area.
SQLServer-Locks	Table Locks – Exclusive	Specifies the number of exclusive locks on tables in use by SQL Server.
SQLServer-Locks	Table Locks – Shared	Specifies the number of shared locks on tables currently in use by SQL Server.
SQLServer-Locks	Table Locks – Total	Specifies the total number of table locks in use by SQL Server.
SQLServer-Locks	Extent Locks – Exclusive	Specifies the number of exclusive extent locks in use on databases (8 pages at a time) that are being allocated or freed.
SQLServer-Locks	Extent Locks – Shared	Specifies the number of shared extent locks in use on databases (8 pages at a time) that are being allocated or freed.
SQLServer-Locks	Extent Locks – Total	Specifies the total number of extent locks in use. An extent lock prevents an exclusive lock from being set.
SQLServer-Locks	Intent Locks – Exclusive	Specifies the total number of exclusive intent locks in use. An intent lock indicates the intention of obtaining the requested type of lock; it does not indicate that the lock has currently been granted. An intent lock prevents an exclusive lock from being granted to another process that needs to lock the same data area.

Object	Counter	Description
SQLServer-Locks	Intent Locks – Shared	Specifies the total number of shared intent locks in use.
SQLServer-Locks	Intent Locks – Total	Specifies the total number of intent locks in use by SQL Server.
SQLServer-Locks	Page Locks – Exclusive	Specifies the number of exclusive locks on pages.
SQLServer-Locks	Page Locks – Shared	Specifies the number of shared locks on pages.
SQLServer-Locks	Page Locks – Update	Specifies the number of update locks on pages.
SQLServer-Locks	Page Locks – Total	Specifies the total number of locks on pages.
SQLServer-User	Memory	Specifies the amount of memory (in 2KB units) allocated to a user connection.
SQLServer-User	CPU Time	Specifies the cumulative amount of time allocated to a user connection.
SQLServer-User	Physical I/O	Specifies the number of disk reads/writes for the currently executing Transact SQL statement.
SQLServer-User	Locks Held	Specifies the number of locks currently held by the user connection.
SQLServer-Log	%Full	Specifies the amount (in a percentage) of the transaction log that is currently in use. Setting an alert for each transaction log on each data base of importance can be a great help, because it can provide you with an early warning.
SQLServer-Log	Size	Specifies the current allocation (in MB) of the transaction log.

18

Optimizing SQL Server

SUMMARY

In this chapter, you saw how you can get the best performance from SQL Server. The first step in the process is optimizing your Windows NT Server platform. This includes choosing the best hardware possible. In this area, you should carefully consider using the fastest possible processor; if possible, plan on a multiprocessor-capable system for later growth. Purchase a minimum of 32MB of RAM; 64MB is the better choice. Choose a system with the largest and fastest expansion bus. PCI should be your first choice, followed by VLB, EISA, MCA, ISA, and PCMCIA. Choose a SCSI disk subsystem and, at the least, use a stripe set (preferably a stripe set with parity) and, if possible, use a hardware RAID 5 configuration.

After your basic Windows NT Server configuration has been optimized, you can begin your optimization of SQL Server. The key item to consider is to allocate as much memory as you possibly can to SQL Server, leaving at least 16MB of RAM for Windows NT Server. If you have the extra RAM, allocate enough memory to contain your temporary (tempdb) database. Finally, use the SQL Performance Monitor to monitor your Windows NT Server and SQL Server activity. Use this tool to fine-tune your performance options.

In the next chapter, you will look at some of the issues involved in recovering the data contained within your SQL Server databases. This includes such topics as how to back up and restore your database with the provided SQL Server utilities, how to automate the backup process, and what you can do to recover your data when you do not have a backup.

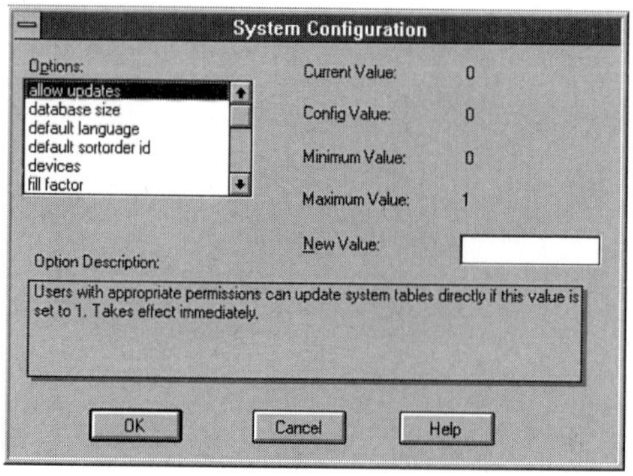

Figure 18.1.
Configuring
SQL Server
performance
with the SQL
Administrator.

CHAPTER 19

Recovering Your Data

Just take a moment to be honest with yourself and admit that perfection is an unattainable dream. No matter how much you strive to attain it, it always seems to slip beyond your grasp. Whether you are dealing with professional or personal goals, nothing is 100-percent reliable. Some events are just beyond your ability to control. This applies as well to the hardware and software you use daily. And as much as I dislike to admit it (but I did say to be honest), even Windows NT Server and SQL Server for Windows NT fall into this category.

You should prepare for the worst possible contingency so that you will not be surprised if and when such an event occurs. When preparing for a hardware failure, you can use a fault-tolerant server that includes redundant power supplies, processors, error-correcting memory, hot-swappable RAID 5 disk drives, and uninterruptible power supplies. All this can minimize the possibility of a data loss due to a hardware failure, but it cannot guarantee it. Consider what would happen if two disk drives in your RAID configuration failed simultaneously, for example. This is an unlikely occurrence, but I have heard of single drive failures that were ignored simply because no one bothered to read the event log and, when the second drive failure did occur, there was a significant data loss. If this happens to you, it could cause you to lose that promotion you were counting on or possibly even your job. So it really does pay to consider beforehand what you can do to minimize such a possibility.

You should apply this philosophy to your software as well. Even Microsoft considers this an important issue and has supplied you with tools to prepare for this eventuality. Not only can you back up and restore your entire database, but you also can make use of the transaction logging capability provided with the SQL model to prepare for incorrect data entry and roll back an entire transaction. Of course, you can roll back a transaction only in a Transact SQL code block that has not been committed to the database with the Transact SQL ROLLBACK TRANSACTION statement. So have you considered what you can do to roll back a transaction that has been committed?

If you have not considered this yet, here are a few guidelines that can help:

- ◆ Make a complete database dump to tape at least once a week and keep these tapes for at least three months. Why wait three months before reusing these tapes? Simply because sometimes an error takes a while to raise its ugly head and be noticed.

- ◆ At the beginning of any Transact SQL block that will modify a database, insert a DUMP TRANSACTION statement. This makes it possible to use the LOAD TRANSACTION statement later and to restore the database to its prior condition, even if the transaction was committed to the database.

◆ When you build your Transact SQL stored procedures or SQL code blocks for interactive use, make use of the transaction capabilities provided with SQL Server. This includes the BEGIN TRANSACTION, COMMIT TRANSACTION, PREPARE TRANSACTION, ROLLBACK TRANSACTION, and SAVE TRANSACTION statements. If you write your code appropriately, then you can roll back changes to the database and recover in a graceful fashion.

◆ Make a complete database dump once a month. This monthly dump should be completely separate from your weekly dump, even if both are made on the same day. This monthly dump should be stored in an outside (of your current physical location) data repository in case of fire, flood, or other act of nature. If nothing else, take the monthly dumps to your home if the company permits it—anything to minimize the chance of a single point of failure.

Having considered the worst, you also should prepare for minor problems that can crop up from time to time. These types of problems include corrupted indexes, corrupted table rows, and corrupted data pages that can cause your database to be marked as suspect. A suspect database is inaccessible and therefore unrepairable in the normal course of events. And a corrupt data page is one of the most perplexing problems because it requires that you first find the object associated with the corrupted page and then fix that particular item. Only then can a suspect database be repaired. If this is not your cup of tea, then you can drop a suspect database with the DBCC utility (Database Consistency Checker) and then restore it from your last database dump. (For more information on the DBCC, see "Using the DBCC Utility," later in this chapter.) This chapter begins with a look at the tools you can use to manage your database dumps and transaction logs. Later in the chapter, you'll learn the process you can use to repair a corrupted database.

BACKING UP AND RESTORING YOUR DATABASE

SQL Server for Windows NT provides two basic mechanisms for backing up your SQL Server databases. You can choose to dump the entire database and in essence make a full backup, or you can dump just the transaction log and make an incremental backup. The big question is how often and what type of backup to make. This question is not easily answered because everyone has different needs. To determine just what you should do, you need to spend a little time discussing what these types of backups can do.

The primary difference between a dump of your database and a dump of the transaction log is that a database dump is a complete copy of the entire database at the time it was taken. This does not necessarily mean that the copy is completely up to date. If a transaction is currently in progress when you make the database dump, then these changes are not reflected in the dump. To ensure that the database dump is a complete copy, make sure that no one else is using the database, or set the database to single-user mode first. Setting the database to single-user mode requires that you set the database attribute and then shut down and restart SQL Server. After you complete your backup, you must reset the single-user mode attribute on the database and restart SQL Server.

Note

Before making a backup of your database with the DUMP DATABASE command, it is a good idea to verify that the database is in a consistent state by running the database consistency checker (DBCC CHECKDB DatabaseName, where DatabaseName is the name of the database to be verified). This utility is discussed in more detail later in this chapter. It is also a good idea to verify that the tape drive and software are working properly by actually using a prior backup and restoring to a temporary database. After all, it is not going to help you much if you make backups but find that the tape drive has an internal problem and all the backups you made are corrupted.

A transaction dump is just a copy of the transactions that occurred in the database. To re-create a database, you first must restore it from your last database dump and then load each transaction dump in the sequence in which you made the original transaction log dumps. The problem with this mechanism is that as each transaction log is loaded, the database goes through a recovery process to apply the changes in the log. This process occurs in real time. This means that if you executed commands that took two days to complete, the transaction log will take two days to recover and restore the database. And if you do not have a copy of every transaction log dump, then you cannot re-create the database in its original configuration.

Tip

The capability to dump your transaction log or restore your database by loading a transaction log is possible only if you have your log on a different device than that used for your database. You therefore should plan on separate devices when you create any database used for production purposes or for any very active (where many changes occur) database.

This is where you need to decide on what type of backup you will use and how frequently you should make the backup. You should choose to back up your databases based on your needs and the time it takes to perform the backup and the restore. If you cannot afford the time it takes to rebuild a database based on your last database dump and the applied sequential transaction logs, then make a database dump nightly and a transaction log dump after each major change to minimize the time it will take to re-create it.

Tip

> You can choose to back up to tape or a file. My recommendation is to always back up to tape because a tape does not overwrite a dump unless specifically requested, whereas a dump to disk overwrites the previous contents. And if you overwrite a transaction dump inadvertently, then you cannot re-create your database because this capability relies on applying a sequential series of transaction logs. If you do decide to dump your database to disk anyway (maybe because you do not have a tape drive) then you should choose a different physical disk than the disk where the SQL Server databases reside for your dumps. This will provide an additional level of fault tolerance so that you can restore your database in the advent that your primary disk fails.

You do have a choice in the tools you use to make your database backups, and you should consider them carefully. First, you can use an ISQL command prompt or query window to execute the DUMP DATABASE or DUMP TRANSACTION command. The syntax for backing up your database follows:

```
DUMP DATABASE DatabaseName TO DumpDevice [WITH [{UNLOAD ¦ NOUNLOAD}]
_[, {INIT ¦ NOINIT}] [, {SKIP ¦ NOSKIP}]
[, {EXPIREDATE = Date} ¦ {RETAINDAYS = Days}] [[,] STATS = Percentage]]
```

Explanations of this syntax follow:

DatabaseName: Name of the database to back up.

DumpDevice: Name of the device where you want to make the backup. This can be a tape, hard drive, or disk device.

UNLOAD: Automatically rewinds the tape and ejects it.

NOUNLOAD: Does not rewind or eject the tape. This option remains in effect until the UNLOAD command is issued. It is useful for making several backups on a single tape or when automating the backup process.

INIT: Makes sure that the dump is the first file on the tape. It overwrites any prior dumps.

NOINIT: Specifies that the backup be appended to the end of the tape.

SKIP: Specifies that the ANSI tape headers will be bypassed.

NOSKIP: Specifies that the ANSI tape will be read. This is the default option.

EXPIREDATE: Specifies a date when the media can be overwritten.

RETAINDAYS: Specifies a number of days, which must elapse, before the media can be overwritten.

STATS: Specifies when statistical information containing the number of pages dumped to the media will be displayed. By default this value is set to 10percent increments.

Note

The SKIP, NOSKIP, EXPIREDATE, and RETAINDAYS options are available only for SQL Server 6.x.

The syntax for making an incremental database backup follows:

```
DUMP TRANSACTION DatabaseName TO DumpDevice [WITH[TRUNCATE_ONLY ¦ NO_LOG ¦
_NO_TRUNCATE][, {UNLOAD ¦ NOUNLOAD}][, {INIT ¦ NOINIT}] [, {SKIP ¦ NOSKIP}]
[, {EXPIREDATE = Date} ¦ {RETAINDAYS = Days}]]
```

Explanations of this syntax follow:

DatabaseName: Name of the database to back up.

DumpDevice: Name of the device where you want to make the backup. This can be a tape, hard drive, or disk device.

TRUNCATE_ONLY: Truncates the inactive portion of the log but does not actually write any data to the dump device. You should use this option only after making a complete backup of the database with the DUMP DATABASE command, and this copy will be your only means of recovering the database in case of a medium failure.

NO_LOG: You should use this option only when you cannot free up enough space using the TRUNCATE_ONLY clause to continue logged operations. It removes all inactive portions of the log and writes a checkpoint record. If you use this option, you should immediately enlarge the size of the log with the ALTER DATABASE command and immediately make a full database backup using the DUMP DATABASE command to ensure your capability to recover the database.

NO_TRUNCATE: Makes a backup copy of the log to the specified dump device but does not remove the inactive portion of the log. This option is useful in recovering an inaccessible database by enabling you to access the transaction log by using a pointer to the log. After you make a copy of the transaction log, you can restore the database from your previous database dump and then apply the transaction logs in sequence to re-create the database.

UNLOAD, NOUNLOAD, INIT, NOINIT, SKIP, NOSKIP, EXPIREDATE, RETAINDAYS: These options have the same functionality as the same options described earlier.

Note

The SKIP, NOSKIP, EXPIREDATE, RETAINDAYS, and STATS options are available only for SQL Server 6.x.

The syntax for restoring a database follows:

```
LOAD TypeOfLoad DatabaseName FROM DumpDevice [WITH [FILE = FileNbr]
_[, {UNLOAD ¦ NOUNLOAD}] [, {SKIP ¦ NOSKIP}] [[,] STATS = Percentage]]
```

Explanations of the syntax follow:

TypeOfLoad: This is DATABASE, which specifies that you want to restore a database from a previous database dump, or TRANSACTION, which specifies that you want to load a transaction log and apply it to the database.

DatabaseName: Name of the database to restore.

DumpDevice: Name of the device that you want to use as the input medium. This can be a tape, hard drive, or disk device.

FileNbr: Number of the file on the tape to load. To retrieve this number, you can use the SQL Tape utility and catalog the tape.

UNLOAD, NOUNLOAD, SKIP, NOSKIP, STATS: These options have the same functionality as the same options described earlier.

Note

The SKIP, NOSKIP, and STATS options are available only for SQL Server 6.x.

Tip

Because the master database does not support a separate device for its transaction log, it can be backed up only with the DUMP DATABASE command. After you perform this chore, however, you should use the DUMP

TRANSACTION WITH TRUNCATE_ONLY command to remove the inactive portion of the log. Failing to remove the inactive portion of the log can prevent you from making system-wide changes if you run out of space in the log for future transactions.

You can schedule these commands to run at specific times by using the Windows NT Scheduler service. I prefer to use the SQL Administrator functions for making my backups, however, because they provide a simple graphical interface. You can even use SQL Administrator to schedule unattended backups.

USING SQL ADMINISTRATOR TO BACK UP OR RESTORE YOUR DATABASE

SQL Administrator certainly can prove useful in managing your tape backups by providing a graphical interface to the DUMP and LOAD commands as well as providing a minimalist tape cataloging procedure. This process is particularly useful for the novice but is handy for the database administrator as well. The only tricky portion of this process is remembering that in order to find the right menu option, the correct window must be active. The SQL Administrator uses the MDI interface, and the menu options change based on the active window.

To back up or restore a database, follow these steps:

1. Choose Databases from the Manage menu, click the DB button in the main application window, or press Ctrl+D to display the Database Management window.
2. Select the database to back up or restore. Then choose Backup/Restore from the Manage menu and choose Backup/Restore from the submenu to display the Backup/Restore Database dialog box, as shown in Figure 19.1.
3. In the Dump Device drop-down list, choose the device to dump or load from. This can be a tape device, hard drive, or disk device. If you choose a disk device, you are prompted to insert and remove disks as required. You should use disks only for the smallest databases, however, because their storage capacity is severely limited.
4. In the Action section, choose the type of dump or load. This can be one of the following:
   ♦ Load Database: Restores a database from a previous full backup.
   ♦ Dump Database: Makes a full backup of the database.
   ♦ Load Tran: Restores a database from a previous incremental backup.

◆ Dump Tran: Makes a copy of a database's transaction log.

◆ Dump Tran/Truncate: Makes an incremental backup of a database and removes the inactive portion of the transaction log.

◆ Dump Tran/No Log: Removes the inactive portion of the transaction log without making a copy of it.

◆ Dump Tran/No Truncate: Makes an incremental backup of a database even if it is inaccessible.

Figure 19.1.
The Backup /
Restore Database
dialog box.

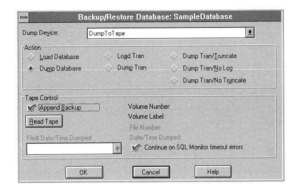

5. If you specified a tape dump device, you also can specify the following tape options in the Tape Control section:

◆ Append Backup: Appends your backup to the current tape. If you leave this option unchecked, the tape is erased during the backup process.

◆ Read Tape: Displays a list of previous backups from which you can select if you are loading a database or transaction. For the selected backup, the tape volume, volume number, file number, date, and time are displayed.

◆ Continue on SQL Monitor Timeout Errors: Continues on time-out errors when accessing a tape. This option normally is checked and should remain this way because most tape operations, such as finding a particular backup entry, exceed the SQL time-out value. If this entry is unchecked and the time-out value is exceeded, the operation is terminated.

6. Click the OK button to make your backup of or to restore your database. If you are restoring a database, after you perform the initial database load, be sure to load each transaction log in order. You can do this by repeating steps 2 through 5 for each transaction log.

USING SQL ENTERPRISE MANAGER TO BACK UP OR RESTORE YOUR DATABASE

Backing up or restoring your database is even easier with the SQL Enterprise Manager because the menu options do not change based on the active window, as they do with the SQL Administrator. You can even specify an expiration time for a backup. This comes in very handy for reusing a dump device that you created on your hard disk. It's also useful for protecting backups on a tape. When the expiration date arrives, the database backup can be overwritten; until then data is appended to the backup.

To back up your database, or to schedule an unattended backup, follow these steps:

1. Choose Database Backup/Restore from the Tools menu and the dialog shown in Figure 19.2 appears.

2. Select the database to back up in the top-most drop-down listbox. Then select one of the following options:

   ◆ Entire Database: Dumps the entire database.

   ◆ Transaction Log: Dumps just the inactive records in the transaction log.

   ◆ Table: If you choose this option, you must also specify a table to back up in the drop-down listbox. This might be a good idea, for example, just before you run that new stored procedure you have been working on that deletes improperly entered records. This way, if the stored procedure does not perform as expected you at least have a backup of the table's data.

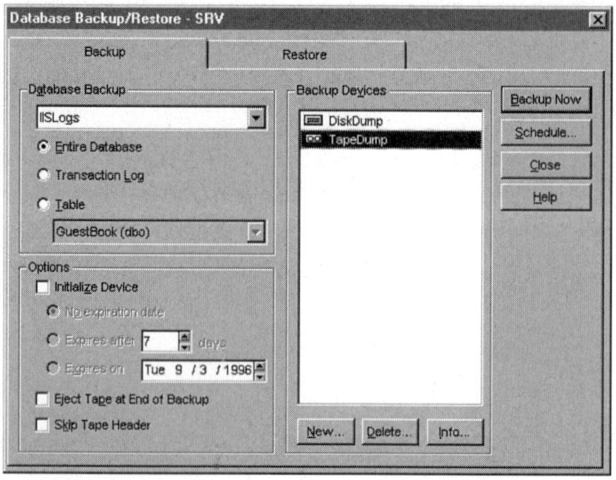

Figure 19.2.
The Database
Backup/Restore
dialog box.

3. Choose the device to dump your database to in the Backup Devices listbox. If you are backing up the database to disk, you can create a new dump device (with associated filename) by clicking the New button. You can also remove a dump device by selecting it and clicking the Delete button, or to obtain information about the device, click the Info button.

4. Then choose your device options in the Options group. These include the following:

   ◆ Initialize Device: Specifies by default that the dump device will be overwritten, or specifies one of the following when checked:

     No expiration date: Specifies that the backup has no expiration time. Any additional data will be appended to the backup.

     Expires after: Specifies that the backup will expire after the number of days set by the user. Once a backup has expired, the space used by the backup may be overwritten.

     Expires on: Specifies that the backup will expire on a date set by the user. To set the date you can enter it manually by selecting Month/Day/Year and entering a replacement value, or by clicking the up/down arrow of the spin box to increase/decrease the value.

   ◆ Eject Tape at End of Backup: When checked, this option specifies that the tape should be ejected from the tape drive when the backup has completed. This is only applicable to tape drives that support a software command to eject the tape (most SCSI tape drives support this feature).

   ◆ Skip Tape Header: When checked, this option specifies that the ANSI tape header be bypassed.

5. Next, click the Backup Now button to perform the backup immediately. Or click the Schedule button to specify a day and time for the backup to occur. If backing up to tape, you may need to specify a volume label. The volume label performs the same basic function as a label on a disk. It identifies the media so you do not accidentally overwrite it.

6. When the backup has completed, or when you have finished entering your scheduled backups, click the Close button to exit the dialog and return to the SQL Enterprise Manager.

AUTOMATING DATABASE BACKUPS

The best reason to use SQL Administrator to manage your database backups and restores is to automate the process of creating these backups. After all, your time is valuable, and you need to save as much time as possible for other tasks. In order to be able to automate this process, the SQL Monitor (or SQL Executive for SQL Server 6.x) service must be running on the local computer. And the best medium to use for this is tape because it can be used to store very large amounts of data and does not overwrite a previous dataset by default.

Automating a backup for SQL Server 6.5 is discussed in the section titled "Using SQL Enterprise Manager to Back Up or Restore Your Database," as the SQL Enterprise Manager integrates this functionality right into the backup process. For an SQL Server 4.2x installation, however, this requires a bit more work. To schedule an automatic backup with the SQL Administrator, follow these steps:

1. Choose Databases from the Manage menu, click the DB button in the main application window, or press Ctrl+D to display the Database Management window.

2. Select the database to back up. Then choose Backup/Restore from the Manage menu and choose Scheduled Backups from the submenu to display the Scheduled Database Backup window.

3. Choose Add Event from the Manage menu to display the Scheduled Backup Event Entry dialog box.

4. In the Database drop-down listbox, choose the database to back up.

5. In the Dump Database To drop-down listbox, choose the dump device for the database. If you want to dump the log as well, choose the dump device for the transaction log in the Dump Log To drop-down listbox.

6. If you are backing up just the transaction log, you can enable the Trunc option to remove the inactive portion of the log after copying the log to tape. To remove the inactive portion of the log and insert a checkpoint record in the database, choose the No Log option.

Tip

When backing up both the database and the transaction log, be sure to enable the Append option beside the Dump Database To drop-down listbox if the tape has previous backups on it. If this is to be a new backup, then only enable the Append option beside the Dump Log To drop-down listbox. This erases the tape when the database backup is performed but appends the log to the tape. If you mistakenly disable both Append options, the log backup overwrites your database backup.

7. In the Frequency drop-down listbox, specify when to make the backup by choosing Daily, Weekly, Bi-Weekly, Monthly-Week1, Monthly-Week2, Monthly-Week3, or Monthly-Week4.

8. Unless you have chosen Daily, you then can specify the day of the week to make the backup on in the Day drop-down listbox.

9. In the Start Time field, specify a time to start the backup and select AM or PM. The best time to schedule a backup is in the off-peak hours; these generally fall between 10:00 p.m. and 4:00 a.m.

Note

If you have enabled the 24-hour time format in the Control Panel International applet, the AM/PM options are disabled.

10. If you have enabled the mail options for SQL Server, then you also can choose an e-mail address to send a message to concerning the status of the backup. You can choose multiple names by separating the names with a semicolon (;). The maximum length is 60 characters.

11. Click the OK button to add the event. Repeat steps 3 through 9 for each event to add.

Note

You can temporarily disable an event from running by choosing the No option in the Enable field. When you want to enable the event, choose the Yes option.

One of the reasons I like the capability to schedule database and transaction log dumps so much is that I also can use it to automate my transaction log management, and I think you'll like this feature too. You can back up your transaction log on even days, for example, and on odd days, you can truncate the log. Why wait to truncate the log rather than truncate it immediately after a scheduled backup? Simply because an error could occur; if it does and you truncate the log, you then will be unable to recover using your transaction logs. This is the primary reason why you should check the e-mail messages or the backup log just to verify that it succeeded.

Table 19.1 lists some options you might find useful as part of this process.

TABLE 19.1. OTHER USEFUL SCHEDULE COMMAND OPTIONS.

Menu Command	Description
Manage | Drop Event	Deletes the selected event from the list of events to execute.
Manage | Start/Stop	Starts or stops the SQL Monitor service on the Backup Engine currently active server.

continues

TABLE 19.1. CONTINUED

Menu Command	Description
Manage I Clear Schedule	Deletes all events from the list of events to execute.
Manage I Clear Log	Clears the history log. The history log contains the status of the scheduled events. Clearing it periodically enables you to determine the status of failed events more readily.
Manage I History	Displays a list of the events you have scheduled, their start/stop times, and a status message.

RECOVERING YOUR DATABASE

If you work with SQL Server long enough, it is going to happen: Sooner or later you will have to recover a corrupted database. In SQL lingo, a corrupted database is called a suspect database. If you are lucky, the problem is not with a table but with an index. An index can just be dropped and re-created. If the problem is with the data contained within a table or with a device or data page, however, you have a much more serious problem. Sometimes you can repair a database and sometimes you can't, depending on the severity of the error. This is why it is essential that you create backups of your database and transaction logs. If all else fails, then at least you have the option of restoring your database.

Tip

> One of the means you have to safeguard your databases from possible problems is to use a SCSI disk subsystem and NTFS partitions. This gives you the capability to use the SCSI disk spare sectoring faculty to replace defective sectors on the disk medium. The NTFS file system also uses a transaction log similar in concept to the SQL Server transaction log, which can help prevent cross-linked clusters. These features can help you avoid a corrupted device or data pages.

The first part of the recovery process is to execute the Database Consistency Checker (DBCC) utility to help you determine the underlying cause of the problem. The DBCC utility also is used to drop a suspect database (a suspect database is otherwise inaccessible), so that you then can re-create it. Sometimes, however, you may find a recurring problem, such as when you run a custom program to load a database, that corrupts data pages. In order to identify the cause, you need to determine where the problem lies. This process requires that you run the DBCC PAGE command, as outlined in Appendix A of the *SQL Server Troubleshooting Guide*, to find the corrupted page and then determine what object is using the page. Once you know the object type, such as an index or table, then you can begin the process to determine why this corruption is occurring. If nothing else, this information may prove useful when you call Microsoft Product Support Services (PSS) for help.

USING THE DBCC UTILITY

The DBCC utility is your primary means of defense in keeping your database free of errors. You can think of this utility as SQL Server's version of the MS-DOS CHKDSK utility, although it includes additional capabilities. Like the MS-DOS CHKDSK utility, which can repair file system errors such as cross-linked clusters, the SQL Server DBCC utility can repair device and data page allocation errors. If these errors are left unrepaired, a device or database can become completely inaccessible.

The DBCC utility statement performs a pretty thorough check of a database or table that includes verification that index and data pages are linked properly, indexes are sorted properly, pointers are consistent, and page data and offsets are reasonable. The syntax for using the DBCC utility to check a database follows:

```
DBCC CHECKDB (DatabaseName)
```

Here, DatabaseName is the name of the database to check or repair allocation errors.

The following code is an excerpt from the DBCC utility when I ran it on my master database, for example:

```
Checking master
Checking 1
The total number of data pages in this table is 11.
Table has 191 data rows.
Checking 2
The total number of data pages in this table is 4.
Table has 52 data rows.
Checking 3
The total number of data pages in this table is 20.
Table has 603 data rows.
   .
   .
   .
Checking 8
The total number of data pages in this table is 1.
```

```
The number of data pages in Sysindexes for this table was 17. It has been corrected
to 1.
The number of rows in Sysindexes for this table was 494. It has been corrected to
15.
*** NOTICE: Notification of log space used/free cannot be reported because the log
segment is not on its own device.
Table has 15 data rows.
.
.
.
Checking 31
The total number of data pages in this table is 1.
The number of rows in Sysindexes for this table was 8. It has been corrected to 7.
Table has 7 data rows.
.
.
.
DBCC execution completed. If DBCC printed error messages, see your System
Administrator.
```

Note

The inability to report the amount of free/used space on the transaction log occurs for any database that does not have the transaction log on a separate device.

To determine what object is associated with the object identification number listed in the DBCC output, you can execute a SELECT statement against the sysobjects table. The following SELECT statement, for example, lists the table objects for numbers 8 and 31, which are really the syslogs and sysusages tables:

```
SELECT * FROM master..sysobjects WHERE id = 8 OR id = 31
name                            id          uid     type userstat sysstat indexdel
schema refdate                      crdate                      expdate
deltrig     instrig     updtrig     seltrig     category    cache
------------------------- ------------- --- -- ---- --- ---- --
- ------------- ------------- ------------- ---
------ ------ ----- ----- ----- ---
syslogs                         8           1       S    0        1       0          0
Jan 1 1900 12:00AM      Jan 1 1900 12:00AM      Jan 1 1900 12:00AM
0       0       0       0       0       0
sysusages                       31          1       S    0        113     0          0
Jan 1 1900 12:00AM      Jan 1 1900 12:00AM      Jan 1 1900 12:00AM
0       0       0       0       0       0
(2 row(s) affected)
```

To check an individual table for allocation errors, use this syntax:

```
DBCC CHECKTABLE (TableName)
```

Here, TableName is the name of a table to check or repair.

You also can check individual subcomponents rather than check all components with the CHECKDB or CHECKTABLE commands. These options follow:

◆ **DBCC CHECKALLOC [(DatabaseName)] ¦ NEWALLOC [(DatabaseName)]**: Checks just the page allocations. The CHECKALLOC statement has been retained for compatibility; however, you should use the NEWALLOC statement because it provides a more detailed listing and does not stop if an error is encountered.

◆ **DBCC TEXTALLOC [({ObjectName ¦ ObjectId} [, FULL ¦ FAST])]**: Performs a check of the text or image fields, where ObjectName is the name of a table, or ObjectId is the object identification number from the sysobjects table. The FULL keyword is the default and, although it is slower, it provides a complete report. The FAST option does not generate a report but still verifies the page-allocation chain.

◆ **DBCC TEXTALL [({DatabaseName ¦ DatabaseId} [, FULL ¦ FAST])]**: Determines what tables in a database have text or image fields and then runs the same process as the TEXTALLOC command on these tables, where DatabaseName is the name of a database or DatabaseId is the object identification number from the sysdatabases table.

◆ **DBCC CHECKCATALOG [(DatabaseName)]**: Verifies the consistency of the system tables, where DatabaseName is the name of a database to verify.

◆ **DBCC DBREPAIR (DatabaseName, DROPDB)**: Drops a suspect database. This is the final option to consider and is probably the most important one. After you drop the database, you then can re-create it and load your backups. You should not use this option unless you have no other choice and just cannot wait to hear from the Microsoft PSS group. Depending on your database design (if you have more than one physical database linked to create a single logical database, for example), it is possible to lose referential integrity.

REPAIRING A SUSPECT DATABASE

Before you actually begin to repair a suspect database, you should take the time to prepare for a worst-case situation. This is not a requirement; it is just insurance. A repair can go wrong, and if you make the situation worse rather than better during your repair attempt, you can restore your original configuration. This preparation entails stopping the SQL Server service and then making a tape backup of the entire SQL Server root directory, all database devices, and the system Registry. If you have the time, you should make two tape backups: one for you to work with, and one to send off to Microsoft PSS if all else fails and you absolutely must recover the data contained within the database.

A corrupted device or data page is the worst type of error you are likely to encounter. Although you can try the procedures outlined in Appendix A of the *SQL Server Troubleshooting Guide* in an attempt to determine and repair the error, my advice is to call Microsoft PSS first. There is a wide variety of possible error conditions, and most of these are outside the scope of this book. If you have an error on a device or data page, it often is best to just drop the database and device, re-create them, and then reload the database from your previous backups.

You need to be aware of a few quirks involved with loading a database dump and applying the transaction log dumps if you want a successful reload. The basic process follows:

1. Try the DROP DATABASE command to delete the database. If this fails, use the DBCC DBREPAIR command as outlined in the preceding section to delete the database.

2. If the error occurred on a device, delete the device with the sp_dropdevice stored procedure.

3. Stop and then restart SQL Server for the changes to be applied.

4. Re-create the device with the DISK INIT command. You could use the DISK REINIT command to reinitialize the device, but if the medium that contains the device has a physical error, this could be a risky option. I prefer to create a new device with the same device number and logical name but a different physical name. This creates a new file to store the new device. You then can delete the physical file used by the old device to recover the storage.

5. Re-create the database. This is the part that must follow a few rules, or the database will not operate properly. You must re-create the database exactly as it was originally created at the time the database was dumped.

    If the original database had an allocation of 15MB for data and a 5MB allocation for the log, for example, and you later extended the database by an additional 10MB for data and 3MB for the log, then this is how you must re-create it. The bottom line is that the physical structure must match exactly, or the load may not operate as expected.

Tip

> Because you must re-create the database exactly as it was originally created at the time the database was dumped, it is best to keep your SQL Server scripts that you use to create and modify the database structure so that you can use them to re-create the database. It is another reason to fully document your database design and changes on paper, because this process can become very complex.

SUMMARY

The primary focus of this chapter was on data recovery. Hopefully, you now are better prepared in case the worst does happen. To prepare for the worst, consider using a SCSI disk subsystem and an NTFS file system to help you minimize the possibility of a corrupt data page, database, table, or index. Make regular backups of your database and transaction logs as a safety mechanism. You never know when you are going to need them. If your database is a production database, consider mirroring the database as described in Chapter 17, "Managing Your Database Server." If you cannot afford the additional storage requirements, at least mirror your master database and make more frequent database dumps.

To minimize the problems associated with the physical layout of a database load, consider using the Bulk Copy utility to dump the data contained in your tables. Then rebuild the database using the required size, but as a single allocation rather than the multiple allocations caused by altering the database. Then rebuild your tables and reload your data.

If all else fails, remember to make a tape backup of your SQL Server root directory, database devices, and system Registry before making any attempt to recover the database. This way, you can at least restore the failed configuration for another attempt at recovering it with the help of Microsoft PSS.

The next chapter begins the discussion of Systems Management Server. It takes a look at why you may need SMS and what SMS can do for you, and also describes some of the basic SMS components.

19

RECOVERING YOUR DATA

PART IV

Systems Management Server

- The Need for Systems
  Management Server

- Defining Systems
  Management Server

CHAPTER 20

An Introduction to Systems Management Server

This chapter is dedicated to providing you with a general understanding of Systems Management Server (SMS). The first thing you will learn is why SMS was developed in the first place. Next, you'll see what SMS really is designed to accomplish for you. Then you'll learn some of the SMS terminology, which is explained in no-nonsense terms, such as the SMS hierarchy (which includes domains and sites, as well as the various components of an SMS site). Finally, you will be introduced to some of the tools you will use to manage your network activities.

This information should help prepare you for actually installing SMS on your network and give you an understanding of what you can do with SMS and the tools you will use to accomplish your goals. Later chapters discuss how to plan your installation, how to actually install SMS, some of the key features of the SMS tools, and how to optimize your SMS installations.

Note

The rest of this discussion on SMS describes SMS 1.1, build 692, with Service Pack 1 installed. You can download the latest Service Pack from The Microsoft Network, Microsoft's FTP site, `ftp.microsoft.com`, or the Microsoft Download Service at (206) 936-6735.

THE NEED FOR SYSTEMS MANAGEMENT SERVER

When computing was introduced to the world, it was limited to a select few with direct access to the computer or mainframe. As time passed and technology progressed, remote terminals were connected to the mainframe to give individuals access to computer resources. These remote terminals were just extensions of the mainframe, however. All the software still was located in a central location, so administration and maintenance tasks were easy to perform for the system administrator. The system administrator maintained complete control on the mainframe. If a user required access to the mainframe (via a user account to log onto the mainframe from a remote terminal), an application, a printer, or any other type of system resource, the user had to request access from the system administrator.

When the personal computer, or PC, was introduced by IBM, these computers originally were used as smart terminals to connect to the mainframe. In this instance, a smart terminal is a program running on the PC to emulate a dumb (or remote) terminal. The "smart" aspect arises from the program's capability to manipulate data locally on the PC and to integrate with local resources, such as a printer connected to the PC. As the computing power of these PCs progressed, the capability to tie them together into local area networks (LANs) became possible.

Now you could have a dedicated server to share resources, with multiple clients to use these resources. With the advent of the LAN, the mainframe methodology declined in stature.

Yet this same abundance of network servers and clients brought the terrible burden of maintaining them. Whereas the mainframe system administrator could perform basic operating system or application upgrades that the user could use immediately, the network administrator was handicapped by the diversity of the PCs connected to the servers. If an upgrade was performed on the server of the network operating service (NOS), in many instances, the network drivers on the client would have to be upgraded as well. This meant long hours for the network administrator to walk around to each client connected to the server and upgrade the various components. It also forced a limited migration because the network administrator could rarely upgrade all the servers and clients in a single weekend.

The maintenance burden for upgrades is just the tip of the iceberg. There are additional—sometimes hidden—expenses required for installing application or operating system software, managing the various assets (personal computers, peripherals, and software), and supporting your network clients in their day-to-day activities. Consider the upgrade to Windows 95. The upgrade takes approximately one hour to install. If your network administrator is paid $35 per hour and you have 1,000 workstations to upgrade, then it will cost $125,000 ($90,000 for the software and $35,000 for the administrator's time) to complete the upgrade. This hidden cost of $35,000 adds almost 30 percent to the cost of the upgrade! If your administrator devotes eight hours a day at a maximum of 40 hours per week, the upgrade will take five weeks to accomplish. And this estimate does not take into account the cost associated with the time it takes to travel from computer to computer and the various hardware upgrades that may be necessary at the client workstation. So what can you do about lowering these hidden costs?

Enter Systems Management Server

Using Systems Management Server is one means you can use to lower these hidden costs associated with supporting your network. The purpose of SMS is to promote the same administration and maintenance principles used in the mainframe environment to LAN and WAN environments. The size of the LAN or WAN is not an issue with SMS. If properly installed and configured, SMS can support multiple domains with 10,000 workstations as easily as it can support a single domain with 100 workstations. You can even scale up your SMS installation to support 20,000, 30,000, or even more workstations if needed. And it doesn't matter whether all the domains are on your LAN or on your WAN. With SMS, you can support them all.

The supported server and workstation platforms vary as well. This is a good thing if you consider the fact that very few networks use a single platform. Many networks include Windows NT Server, Novell NetWare, and LAN Manager servers with MS-DOS, Windows 3.x, Windows 95, Windows NT, and Macintosh workstations. Table 20.1 summarizes the supported server platforms, and Table 20.2 summarizes the client platforms.

TABLE 20.1. SUPPORTED SERVER PLATFORMS.

Server Platform	Comment
Windows NT Server 3.1 or higher	Requires the Services for Macintosh service to support your Macintosh clients and Gateway for NetWare services for your Novell NetWare servers. Note: An NTFS partition is required to support the Services for Macintosh service.
Novell NetWare 3.11	
Novell NetWare 4.x	Requires NetWare 3.x Bindery Emulation mode.
Microsoft LAN Manager 2.1	
IBM LAN Server 3.0/3.1	

TABLE 20.2. SUPPORTED CLIENT PLATFORMS.

Client Platform	Comment
Windows NT Workstation 3.1 or higher	Supports Windows NT Server 3.5 or a higher version operating in server mode.
Windows 3.x	Supports only the Enhanced Redirector mode.
Windows 3.x and Windows for Workgroups 3.x	The full Redirector must be used in order to install and support the SMS client software.
Windows 95	If using a real-mode network Redirector, it must be configured to enhanced mode in order to install and support the SMS client software.
MS-DOS	If using the LAN Manager 2.x Redirector, it must be configured for enhanced mode. If using the Microsoft Network Client, the full Redirector must be used in order to install and support the SMS client software.

Client Platform	Comment
Apple Macintosh	Requires System 7.x or higher.
NetWare 3.11	
NetWare 4.x	Requires NetWare 3.x Bindery Emulation mode.
Microsoft LAN Manager 2.1	
IBM LAN Server 3.0/3.1	

WHAT SYSTEMS MANAGEMENT SERVER CAN DO FOR YOU

The primary focus of a network administrator's job is to support your network clients. In a very small network, it is perfectly feasible to stop by each client computer to install software, to perform diagnostics, or to watch what a user is doing—to see what he might be doing wrong—when a software usage problem occurs. In a large network consisting of multiple domains and possibly thousands of clients (what Microsoft refers to as the enterprise), these same tasks become impossible due to the vast numbers of servers and clients. After all, you can only be in one place at a time, and there is only so much one person can physically accomplish. Right?

Well, not anymore. If you have installed Systems Management Server, you can perform any of the following:

- ◆ Software management: You can distribute, install, and configure software on network servers and clients. When installing software, you can choose to just let the user interact with the installation's Setup program, or you can write a script to automate the installation.

- ◆ Share network applications: With SMS, you can add a new twist to sharing your network-aware applications. Instead of installing and accessing the software on a specific server, your clients can dynamically connect to a server. This gives you the capability to balance your application server load and provides an additional level of fault tolerance.

- ◆ Inventory management: You can remotely inventory all hardware and software on your network servers and clients. The inventory is maintained in an SQL Server database in a central location. You can use predefined queries or write your own queries to pull information from this database concerning the installed software. Or, you can even determine the clients with sufficient hardware to qualify for upgrades of new operating systems, for example.

20

SYSTEMS MANAGEMENT SERVER

◆ Remote administration: You can remotely administer any client computer, subject to client permission, on the network. You can view the display (or capture the display, keyboard, and mouse to take remote control) of MS-DOS, Windows 3.x, or Windows 95 client computers. You even can perform remote diagnostics on MS-DOS, Windows 3.x, Windows 95, and Windows NT computers.

◆ Enterprise-wide alerts: You can create alerts based on a conditional statement for servers and clients. When the condition is met, such as low disk storage, you are notified.

◆ Network protocol diagnostics: You can use the SMS Network Monitor to locally (where you execute the SMS Network Monitor) capture network packets to diagnose numerous network-related problems. You can even remotely (where the Network Monitor Agent software resides) capture network packets to reduce the network bandwidth load on a different network segment.

◆ Customization: Microsoft has published application programming interfaces (APIs) and provided a software development kit (the BackOffice SDK 1.5) so that developers can extend the SMS functionality. You also can use custom front ends to access the SMS database for informational purposes or write custom applications to interact with the SMS database.

WHAT SYSTEMS MANAGEMENT SERVER CAN'T DO FOR YOU

Although Systems Management Server can perform many useful functions, it can't do everything an administrator might need. But then again, I doubt if any single software package can do that. Most of the functionality you will need is provided with SMS, but some features are missing:

◆ Complete automation of the inventory: Automatic inventory of network routers, bridges, or similar devices is currently not possible. Nor is automatic inventory of various computer peripherals, such as tape drives, printers, scanners, or similar equipment. You can create a custom MIF to provide a means for an administrator or user to enter such information in the SMS database, however.

◆ Software licensing: There is no built-in means to support license requirements for network applications. There are third-party solutions, such as Express Meter by Express Systems, to accomplish this task.

◆ Real-time support: Currently, SMS only includes real-time support for remote management. Depending on the size of your network and the available bandwidth, the installation of packages could take hours or days to be distributed. This also means that the inventory from these remote sites could take just as long to be recorded in the central site's database.

◆ Remote control: Currently, the remote control features are limited to MS-DOS, Windows 3.x, and Windows 95. A Windows NT computer can support only remote access, not remote control, to basic diagnostics (the same as that reported by WinMSD), performance statistics (as reported by the Performance Monitor), event log, account database, and Server Manager. Macintosh and OS/2 workstations are even more severely limited.

◆ Installation scripts: Currently, SMS only provides Microsoft Test for automating installation scripts. This tool is not an easy tool to use. There are third-party tools, however, such as WinInstall by On Demand Software, that can make the task much easier.

Defining Systems Management Server

Systems Management Server is a collection of individual components that, when combined, transcend the capabilities of the individual component. This might sound a bit superficial but, nonetheless, it is still true. To understand how you can achieve the dream of administering your network from a single central location, you need to understand the individual components of SMS. This can be broken down into two basic qualifications: the SMS hierarchy and the SMS tools. These are the subjects you will explore in the remainder of this chapter.

The Systems Management Hierarchy

An SMS site is a collection of one or more domains on a LAN or WAN grouped into a logical unit. These domains can be groups of Windows NT Server, LAN Manager, and Novell NetWare servers; and Windows NT Workstation, Windows 3.x, Windows 95, LAN Manager, Macintosh, and MS-DOS clients. (See Figure 20.1.)

SMS sites are based on a hierarchical structure, as shown in Figure 20.2, where components at the lower levels are controlled by components at the higher levels. Lower-level components also report their inventory collections to higher levels, until the highest level has a complete picture of every system. In order for SMS to be truly useful to you, you need to keep this hierarchical structure firmly in mind while you develop a plan to install SMS on your network. If you do not, and you just install it haphazardly, then it will not perform up to your expectations. This should not overly concern you for now because you will learn more about this in the next chapter.

Figure 20.1.
Components of an
SMS site.

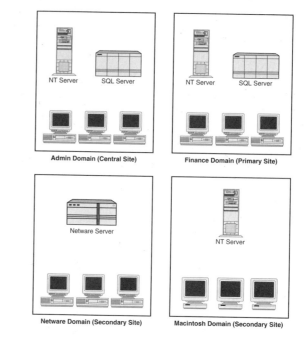

Figure 20.2.
The hierarchical
structure of an
SMS domain.

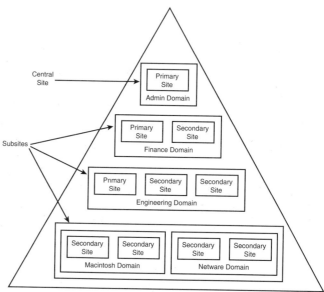

There are three different site types, each of which plays a slightly different role:

◆ Central sites: A central site is the top of the food chain. All other sites can be managed from a central site. A central site must have a copy of

SQL Server available to store the SMS inventory for itself and all its clients or subsites. A subsite can be another primary site or a secondary site. The SMS database is referred to as a site database. The central site is also a primary site, because it includes full administration of all the subsites and contains its own SMS database.

- ◆ Primary sites: A primary site also has a copy of SQL Server available to store the site database for itself and its subsites. A primary site also includes the tools to administer the site as well as any subsites.

- ◆ Secondary sites: A secondary site does not have a site database. It places all the information it collects into the primary site's SMS database. A secondary site does not include any administrative capabilities. It is only a collection point.

After the central site is created, you can add additional subsites. To add a primary site to a central site, you first create the primary site, and then attach it to the central site. To add a primary site to another primary site as a subsite, you first install the primary site, and then attach it to the other primary site. Secondary sites can be installed only from a primary site. This might sound a bit confusing at first, but should become much more defined as you step through the process in the next chapter.

Systems Management Server Components

An SMS site includes many types of components. The majority of these components consists of SMS servers. Each of these SMS servers executes one or more of your network servers (in this case, any server that provides shared resources) to perform a specific set of tasks. These SMS servers can all be on the site server (where SMS was installed) or on various network servers, which includes the Windows NT, Novell NetWare, or LAN Manager platforms. The types of servers follow:

- ◆ Logon server: The central component of a site. It supports configuration, inventory, package installation, and network applications for clients in its domain. Various portions of this server may be relegated to additional servers. A server that provides one or more of these services is called a helper server.

- ◆ Distribution server: A server that stores SMS packages which then are made available to network clients at the site. This type of server generally is used for executable packages such as those supported by the Run Command on Workstation job. A distribution server also can function as an application server.

20

SYSTEMS MANAGEMENT SERVER

Note

Jobs and packages are described in detail later in this chapter in "The SMS Administrator."

◆ Application server: A server that stores and shares an SMS package, which then is made available to network clients at the site. This type of server is used primarily to share network-aware applications and is the result of a Share Package on Server job.

◆ Helper servers: A server running one or more of the site server's additional services. These services follow:

Scheduler: This service monitors the site database (and the SITE.SRV\ SCHEDULE.BOX directory) for jobs. It processes these jobs by compressing the packages, creating send requests, and creating despooler instruction files. The compression of these packages can place a significant load on the server; so, by moving this service to another server, you can gain a significant performance improvement.

Inventory Data Loader: This service monitors the SITE.SRV\DATALOAD.BOX\ DELTAMIF.COL directory for MIFs (used for computer inventories, status, and events) used to update the site database. This is not a high processor cycle service, but if you need to, you can move it to improve performance on an overloaded server. If you do move it, it is best to move it to the same server that contains SQL Server.

Inventory Processor: This service monitors the SITE.SRV\INVENTORY.BOX directory for RAW files (which are used in the computer inventory process and with objects with custom architectures). These RAW files then are processed into MIFs for the Inventory Data Loader. It is not a processor-intensive service, but you can move it if required.

Despooler: This service monitors the SITE.SRV\DESPOOLER.BOX\RECEIVE directory for instruction files and compressed packages created by the Scheduler service. It then uncompresses the files in order to create a package that will be installed on your distribution servers. This process places a heavy load on the processor, and you can gain a significant performance improvement by placing this service on another server.

Aside from your SMS sites, servers, and services, there are a few additional terms you should know. Table 20.3 lists these terms.

Table 20.3. Additional SMS terms.

Term	Description
Outbox	A directory for SMS services to place send request files. A send request file contains instructions for transferring data and instructions to other sites.
Sender	An SMS component contained within the SMS Executive service, which is used to send instructions and data from one SMS site to another SMS site. There are three types of senders. The LAN sender uses a LAN-to-LAN connection. The RAS (a Remote Access Software connection using a modem, ISDN, or X.25 adapter instead of a network adapter) sender uses a RAS-to-RAS connection. And an SNA sender uses an SNA server peer-to-peer connection. Each sender has its own outbox.
Address	Contains the information that defines the server or client connection for a sender. To use a RAS sender at a server to connect to a different site (the client), for example, you must define a RAS entry for the Remote Access client software that contains a user name, user password, description, phone number, network protocol, and communications port. Depending on the address type, there may be additional qualifiers to supply.

The Systems Management Server Tools

You can install SMS on your site server or just install the SMS Administration tools on your Windows NT Workstation in a Program Manager group. Each of these tools serves a particular purpose, as shown in Table 20.4. In Chapter 22, "Managing Your Network with Systems Management Server," you will look more closely at some of these tools.

Table 20.4. The installed systems management server tools.

Icon	Tool	Description
SMS Administrator	SMS Administrator	Your primary means of interacting with Systems Management Server. It is used to manage your site, and is so important that you will get a sneak preview of it in the next section.

continues

TABLE 20.4. CONTINUED

Icon	Tool	Description
SMS Security Manager	SMS Security Manager	Limits user access to the functionality provided with the SMS Administrator. It also is used to set access rights on the SMS database.
SMS Network Monitor	SMS Network Monitor	Performs the same basic function as a dedicated network sniffer. It can be used to capture, filter, and view network packets sent on your network. It also can provide a real-time display of network statistics.
SMS Service Manager	SMS Service Manager	Gives an administrator the capability to manage the individual SMS services on the site. It performs similar functions as the Control Panel Services applet: You can stop, start, pause, or continue a service. You also can use this tool to configure the logging capability of a service.
SMS MIF Form Generator	SMS MIF Form custom Generator	Gives you the capability to create Management Information Forms (MIFs) to collect information not harvested by the SMS inventory service. This can be used to extend the inventory capabilities but does require that the individual recipient of the MIF fill out the form and send it to be collected.
SMS Setup	SMS Setup	Removes (deinstalls) a site or Administration tools from a computer. It also can be used to upgrade a site, shut down a site, reset a site, or edit the SMS and SQL Server logon accounts.

Icon	Tool	Description
SMS Help	SMS Help	A context-sensitive Help file you can use to gain a general overview of SMS, get step-by-step instructions to accomplish specific tasks, access an SMS reference guide, troubleshoot basic tasks, view a glossary of terms, and get instructions on obtaining help from Microsoft PSS.
SMS Release Notes	SMS Release Notes	A context-sensitive Help file containing the same information as the readme file: information on the latest news, problems, and documentation errors.
SMS Frequently Asked Questions	SMS Frequently Asked Questions	Another context-sensitive Help file containing answers to the most commonly asked questions.
SMS Books Online	SMS Books Online	A context-sensitive Help file version of the Administrators Guide. I find this reference to be extremely helpful because it is easier to search than the written documentation.

The SMS Administrator

After you launch the SMS Administrator, you are prompted to select a window type to display. The default is the Sites window. But there are many more window types to choose from, as shown in Figure 20.3, which displays the Sites, Jobs, and Packages windows. What is important to realize about the SMS Administrator is that it is a multiple document interface (MDI) application. As such, the menu commands and toolbar buttons reflect an operation on the active window. Table 20.5 describes each type of window you can open.

Figure 20.3.
The SMS Admin-
istrator.

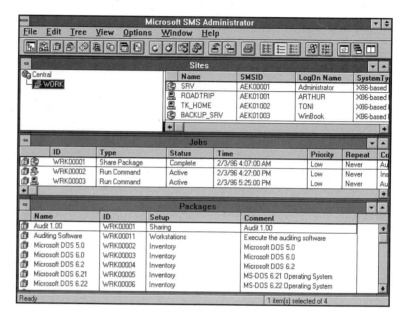

TABLE 20.5. SMS ADMINISTRATOR WINDOWS.

Window	Description
Sites	Functions much as File Manager does when it displays a tree of directories and files. Instead of displaying directories, subdirectories, and files, it displays sites, subsites, and computers.
Jobs	Displays the various jobs you have created. A job can be one of three types. It can be a Run Command on Workstation job, which provides a means to execute a package on the client workstation; a Share Package on Server job, which distributes a package to a server and then shares it on the network; or a Remove Package from Server job, which deletes a Share Package on Server job from the distribution server.
Packages	Displays the various packages you have created. A package is nothing more than an accumulation of software you want to distribute to a server. You can share this package (which can contain a network application) and execute this package on a network client (perhaps to install it or inventory this package) to see whether or not the software has been installed on the network client. By itself, a package is useful only for inventory purposes; in

Window	Description
	order to actually share or execute the package, you also must create a job.
Queries	Maintains the predefined or custom queries you can use to determine which SMS clients meet a specific set of criteria. To upgrade your clients to Windows 95, it would be beneficial to know how many of these clients already meet the minimum hardware requirements. You could use a query to select only computers with an 80386 or higher processor with a minimum of 8MB of RAM and at least 100MB of free disk space, for example.
Alerts	Maintains the various alert conditions you have created. An alert is a query with a conditional statement. It can be applied to any SMS client. When the alert condition is met, such as less than 10 percent free on the local disk drive, then a message can be written into the event log, a program can be executed, and a message can be sent to a computer or user to notify him that the condition has been met.
Machine Groups	Displays the machine groups you have created. You can use a machine group to group computers into a single entity that can be used with jobs to specify where the package should be sent. You might use this to send a package containing a shared network application to all your application servers, for example.
Site Groups	Displays all the site groups you have created. A site group is similar to a machine group, but instead of grouping computers, you group sites into a single entity. This entity can be used with jobs to specify where the package should be sent. You might use this to send an updated application, such as your SMS 1.1 client software, to all your SMS sites.
Program Groups	Displays all the program groups you have created. A program group created here looks and functions just like the program groups you have defined now in Program Manager, with icons and paths to applications. The only difference is that it is dynamically created. The program group is used with a shared network application. You create the package, which contains the application in the Package window, and then you create a Share Package

continues

TABLE 20.5. CONTINUED

Window	Description
	on Server job to actually send it to your distribution servers and share the application. If you do not create a program group for the application, however, your clients have no way to access the application.
Events	Displays SMS events. An event looks and functions similar to events in the Windows NT event log. An alert, for example, might create an informational event that a user has exceeded his disk storage and soon will need a larger disk drive.

SUMMARY

In this chapter, you learned why Systems Management Server was created, some of what it can do for you, and some things it can't do. You also learned a bit about the various components that make up Systems Management Server, as well as some of the terms you need to know. You took a look at the tools that will be created after you complete your SMS installation, and you got a sneak preview at the SMS Administrator.

In the next chapter, you will look at some of the issues involved in planning your SMS installations. Then you will actually walk through the installation process. After you have SMS installed, you will step through some of the configuration issues to get up and running as soon as possible.

- Planning Systems
  Management Server
  Installation

- Installing Systems
  Management Server

CHAPTER 21

Planning and Installing Systems Management Server

Anyone can install Systems Management Server simply by creating the SMS user account, executing the Setup program, and following the installation prompts. On a small network, this is even perfectly reasonable because only a single site is required to manage the entire network. If this is all you do for a medium to large network, however, you most likely will find that although it works, it does not work as well as you expected or do all that you want it to do. This is why planning your installation is so important and should not be performed without careful consideration.

This chapter discusses the concepts and issues involved in planning your SMS installation. After reading this chapter, you will understand how to properly install SMS and obtain the maximum benefit from it. Later in the chapter, you will do a walk-through of the installation process.

PLANNING YOUR SYSTEMS MANAGEMENT SERVER INSTALLATION

As part of the process of building a plan for installing SMS, you need to collect and consider some information. Part of this entails understanding how SMS is organized and how you can make use of this organization. The building block for SMS is the site, so this is where this discussion begins. It then moves on to the process of actually building a plan for your SMS installation. This plan cannot be arbitrarily built for you; instead, you must do this yourself. You can get some help with this process, however, by reading about some of the key issues involved in determining where to install the various components.

The one point I want to make about this entire plan is this: Don't install SMS everywhere all at once. If you do, you may be swamped with support calls you are unprepared to handle. Instead, install SMS on a small test site first. Then you can gradually roll it out to cover the entire network.

BUILDING A PLAN TO INSTALL SMS

There is more to your SMS installation than installing the software. For a successful SMS installation, you should consider the following:

- Where to install the central site
- Where to install the primary and secondary sites
- Your storage requirements
- Your server load
- Your group/user structure

These considerations are discussed in the following sections.

Determining the Location of Your Central Site

Systems Management Server is based on a hierarchical design. You should plan your installation accordingly; you should install your SMS central site to your highest level domain, or at least a domain that is accessible by your domain administrators. This central site, of which there can be only one, is used to manage all your primary and secondary sites. The whole idea behind SMS is that, from one workstation, you can manage your entire network. This really is possible, to a degree, if you plan your installation properly.

The best way to decide which domain to use for your central site is to take a pencil and paper and draw a logical map of your network with all trust relationships. If your network is segmented to provide easy administration, then these are prime candidates for central or primary sites. The highest level domain, or most widely supported, should become the central site. If your network is segmented based on the organization of your company, then the central domain at the top of the company hierarchy should be the central site. Depending on the domain model, you may need to make some revisions to your first choice. Take a look at some examples that further illustrate this point.

Consider a small domain based on the single domain model, as shown in Figure 21.1. There is one server (Admin), which contains all the user and group account information. There are three servers (Finance, Engineering, and Sales).

*Figure 21.1.
Determining the
best location for a
central site for a
single domain
model.*

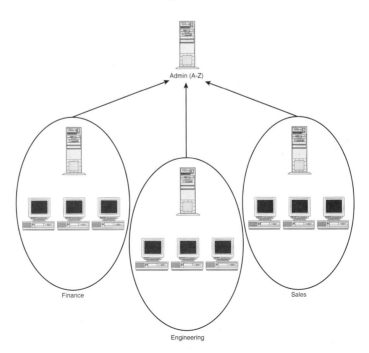

If you look at the arrows, which indicate the direction of authentication, you see that the Admin server is the highest level, and normally would be considered as a prime candidate for the central site. Your primary domain controller is not a good choice, however, because it manages all user account modifications and replication among other duties. So you could use another server, such as Finance, Engineering, or Sales, but each of these is performing services for your network client and, unless you want to impact their performance, they are not good choices either. So what do you do? Well, because you have run out of recommended servers, you should create a new one, call it SMSSrv, and install SQL Server and SMS on it. Normally, I would recommend a different server for SQL Server, and if you have the extra hardware, it is a better solution, but in a small domain, one server for SQL Server and SMS is acceptable. If you have to use your current hardware, then install SQL Server on one server, such as Sales, and SMS on another server, such as Finance. Then move some of the additional SMS Services (as described in Chapter 22, "Managing Your Network with Systems Management Server"), such as the Despooler, to other servers, such as Engineering, to spread the load more evenly.

Now stretch this example a bit further and consider a medium network based on the master domain model (see Figure 21.2).

Figure 21.2.
Determining the
best location for a
central site for a
master or
multiple master
domain model.

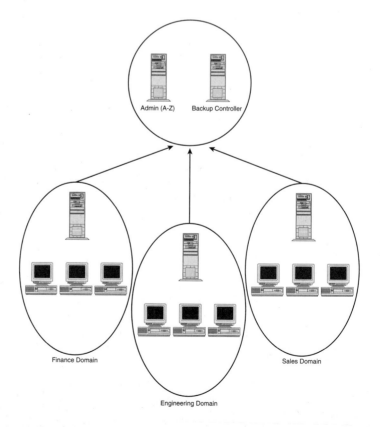

There is one trusted domain (Admin), which contains all the user and group account information. There are three trusting domains (Finance, Engineering, and Sales). If you look at the arrows, which indicate the direction of trust, you see that the Admin domain is the highest level, and that it is a prime candidate for the central site. Once more, though, you do not want to install SMS on the primary domain controller. Instead, pick the least heavily used backup domain controller for SMS. Install Windows NT Server operating in server mode on another computer, and install SQL Server on it. If you do not have enough hardware, you can use two backup domain controllers for SMS and SQL Server and, if necessary, move some of the SMS Services to additional servers.

The final model you should consider is for a medium to large network based on the multiple master domain model (see Figure 21.3).

Figure 21.3.
Determining the
best location for a
central site for a
multiple master
domain model.

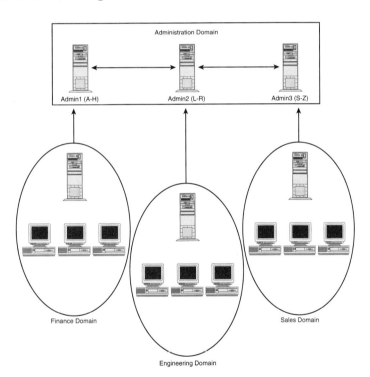

There are three trusted domains (Admin1 through Admin3) that trust each other and contain all the user and group account information. There are three trusting domains (Finance, Engineering, and Sales). The trusted domains can be considered as a single logical domain, which for this example is called the Administration domain. This places it at the same level as the preceding example. The only difference is that there are more servers to work with. The arrows, which indicate the direction of trust, demonstrate that the Administration domain is the highest level and is the best choice for the central site. The big question is, which individual domain (Admin1, Admin2, or Admin3) should house SMS and SQL Server? With many servers to choose from, the best solution is to use the least heavily used backup domain controller for SMS and to install SQL Server on another server.

The only model missing from these examples is the complete trust model; this is because all these domains trust each other equally, so there is no clear indication as to which domain is at the highest level. This model should have SMS installed wherever the most administrators are located to provide support.

DETERMINING PRIMARY AND SECONDARY SITE LOCATIONS

Determining where to install additional primary and secondary sites is not as straightforward as determining where to install your central site. Much of the choice should be based on the site's physical or logical location. You should consider the following points when deciding where to place primary and secondary SMS sites:

- ◆ If you have routers, which most networks include, consider placing an additional site on the far side of the router. The idea here is to limit client access to distribution servers (servers that actually distribute your packages) across routers and to provide more efficient performance as well as to lower network bandwidth requirements.

- ◆ If you will be installing SMS sites on servers located on the other side of a WAN link, you should consider installing SMS as a primary site for increased performance. This also requires SQL Server on this site, but it can improve performance as well as provide local site administration. The reason behind this philosophy is the same as for routers; you want to limit the amount of network traffic sent across the WAN link.

- ◆ For all your sites, consider the amount of traffic you will be sending across your network. Each site will receive one copy of a package. If you have multiple sites, you will send multiple copies of the package—one to each site. It may be better, as far as network bandwidth is concerned, to use one site instead of two or more sites.

- ◆ Consider as well the network protocol behavior you will be using. If you will be using SNA Server to distribute your packages, for example, you should specify SNA BATCH as your transmission mode. If you use SNA INTER (Interactive) mode transmissions, the session will use 100 percent of the network bandwidth until the transmission is completed. Although this is the fastest method of distributing your packages, it does prevent your SNA clients from using the link until the transmission is completed. This problem can be alleviated somewhat by specifying that the SMS link have a lower priority than the SNA client session's priority for the connection.

◆ Finally, consider how you want to manage your network. If you want to provide regional access, then install a primary site at each domain. This gives local administrators access to SMS at the domain level and the capability to manage their own clients. If the domain is large, you can install additional secondary sites. Because each secondary site reports to its primary site and each primary site reports to the central site, the entire network still can be managed from a single location as well by administrators with access to the central site.

DETERMINING YOUR STORAGE REQUIREMENTS

Aside from the basic requirements for SQL Server (memory, disk subsystem, network adapters, and so on), you need to consider just how much physical storage you need for each site to contain the SMS databases. You can get an approximation by using this formula:

```
Primary Site Storage (in MB) = (AvgStoreReqClient ´ NbrOfClients) / NbrBytePerMB
Central Site Storage (in MB) = ((AvgStoreReqClient ´ NbrOfCentralSiteClients) /
_ NbrBytePerMB)+ Primary Site Storage ´ NbrOfPrimarySites
```

Descriptions for the syntax in this formula follow:

> AvgStoreReqClient: 10KB

Note

This estimate is based on small character files used for inventory purposes. If you use large executables for this or collect large files, then your average client requirement must be increased by that amount as well.

NbrOfClients: Number of SMS clients at the primary site, which includes all clients of secondary sites attached to the primary site

NbrBytePerMb: 1048576

NbrOfCentralSiteClients: Number of SMS clients at the central site

NbrOfPrimarySites: Number of primary sites attached to the central site

Suppose that you have 10 primary sites with 500 network clients per site, and one central site with 100 clients attached to it. This gives the following total storage requirement:

Each primary site:

(10240´500) / 1048576 = 4.8828125MB (which I would round up to 5MB)

Primary site total:

5MB´10 = 50MB

Central site:

`(10240´100) / 1048576 =  0.9765625MB` (which I would round up to 1MB)

Central site total:

`50MB + 1MB = 51MB`

For the central site database, you need a minimum of 51MB for the SMS database and at least 5MB for each primary site database. If I will have heavy inventory demands, then I usually double this estimate to 100MB for the central site and 10MB per primary site.

Tip

> For best performance, you should create your SQL Server devices that will be used by the SMS database on a noncompressed NTFS partition.

This takes care of the basic database requirements for SQL Server, but what about the requirements of SMS? This is really where the storage demands soar. A minimum requirement of at least 500MB should be considered for each distribution server (those servers that will distribute your packages), and if you will be submitting large jobs, consider doubling this to 1,000MB. You might be wondering why so much space is needed. The reason is pretty simple: You need space to hold the uncompressed package while it is being compressed, and then you need the same amount of space for the compressed package while it is being uncompressed. If you split these processes (Scheduler and Despooler) to other helper servers, then these servers require half the additional storage (250–500MB) because they will be performing the compression/decompression of the packages.

If you want to calculate a minimum/maximum for how much space you will need, combine all the packages you expect to use. Office 95, for example, requires about 150MB (uncompressed) for my usual install options. Compression usually provides about half the original storage requirements. So this package would require about 75MB of compressed storage with at least 150MB free to decompress the package and distribute it. Now, if you have three or more jobs of this size and you do not stagger your jobs (by forcing everyone to upgrade at the same time, which is not unusual), you need to triple your requirements to 225MB for the compressed packages and 450MB for the decompressed packages for a whopping total of 675MB of free storage.

The bad news with this estimate is that it is not too far out of line. Storage requirements for SMS can be excessive, depending on the types of packages you require. And the worst part about it is that if you have insufficient free space, the decompression fails, which causes the job to fail. So the bottom line is that it is better to overestimate than underestimate your storage requirements.

LOOKING AT SERVER LOAD CONSIDERATIONS

Systems Management Server places a heavy load on your network server, no doubt about it. If you have several servers in your domain, you can spread some of the SMS worker services among them. This can lessen the load produced by SMS on a single server and achieve better performance. If it is at all possible, do not install Systems Management Server and SQL Server on the same server. Instead, spread this load between at least two servers for better overall performance.

Just how you determine your requirements varies based on your expected level of performance. Here are some basic guidelines, based on my experience in the field, to help you determine your server requirements:

◆ An SMS distribution server functions very similar to a file server. Basically, it shares files (or in this case, packages) or shared applications. You can use your experience with your file servers as a rough guide for the requirements of a distribution server.

◆ A Pentium-based server with 64MB of RAM is an acceptable base platform for a primary site. It is capable of supporting the inventory for thousands of clients. If this same server will be used as an application server or distribution server (meaning that you do not split off the services to other helper servers), the total number of clients it can support drops significantly (to between 100 and 300 users).

◆ This same Pentium server platform, if used only as a distribution server, can support between 300 and 600 users with acceptable performance levels. If it also is used to support shared applications, for example, the number of supported clients should be between 100 and 300 users. Although it could support more users, performance will degrade for all users.

◆ A 486/66 or better with at least 32MB of RAM is an acceptable platform for a secondary site. As the number of users climbs, however, more processing power and more memory are required for acceptable performance.

EXAMINING GROUP/USER STRUCTURE CONCERNS

One of the key features of SMS is that you can use it to support fault-tolerant access to shared applications for your network clients. In order to support these network clients in this fashion, you need to create a program group with the SMS Administrator and then assign users or groups to the program group. This can get very messy very quickly if you use users instead of groups. What you should do is assign users to groups, and then assign these groups to the program groups. This is much easier to manage, particularly when you add new users to your domain. The method I usually employ is based on several group levels. The basic steps follow:

1. Create the new user account.
2. Add the user account to each global group that will be used to control access to each application.
3. Assign these global groups to a single local group, based on a higher level.
4. Use the local group to assign permissions to the program group.

In this fashion, you can control access to your shared application quite easily and be as specific about it as you want. If you use the higher levels to designate departments or even divisions, you can assign access rights to huge groups of users all at once. If you have the applications Word, Excel, and Access, for example, you would create four global groups called WordUser, ExcelUser, AccessUser, and OfficeUser. These global groups could be assigned to a local group, such as OfficeGroup. Then when you create your program groups (one for Word, one for Excel, one for Access, and one that includes all three), you can assign the global groups to the individual program groups (for Word, Excel, Access, or all applications) to control access to these individual components. Or, you can use the local group (OfficeGroup) and assign it to the program group that contains all three applications to control access to all the applications. To add a new user and give him access to just Word, all you need to do is to add him to the WordUser group. To give him access to all the applications, just assign him to the OfficeUser group. To provide access to clients on a trusted domain, just add the new global group to the local group OfficeGroup.

INSTALLING SYSTEMS MANAGEMENT SERVER

Installing SMS is a rather easy process because the Setup program walks you through the installation. It does require some preinstallation support before you can successfully install the product, however. After you install it, you must configure it. The basic steps for a successful rollout follow:

◆ Meeting the preinstallation requirements
◆ Installing your central site
◆ Configuring your central site
◆ Installing primary sites
◆ Configuring your primary sites
◆ Installing secondary sites
◆ Configuring secondary sites

After this is out of the way, you will walk through the installation process to create your central site. Then you will learn how to create additional primary and secondary sites. Finally, you will look at how to configure your sites.

EXAMINING SMS PREINSTALLATION REQUIREMENTS

Before installing SMS, you should take care of a few items. These items, if not properly configured, will limit your capability to store or access SQL Server or will prevent you from installing SMS completely. Because you do not want to encounter any of these difficulties, you should take care of these possible problems before continuing the installation. Installing SQL Server is discussed in detail in Chapter 16, "Installing SQL Server," so that information is not repeated here. This chapter does describe the SQL Server configuration modifications that are required, as well as the SMS logon account requirements.

Tip

Another good idea is to read the release notes on the CD-ROM before you actually install SMS. You can find this file (README.TXT) in the root directory.

MODIFYING THE SQL SERVER CONFIGURATION

Depending on the number of SMS clients you will have, some SQL Server configuration values should be modified before continuing the SMS installation. This will prevent inventory collection problems, as well as SMS administration-related access problems. You can modify these configuration settings from the SQL Administrator for SQL Server 4.2x, the SQL Enterprise Manager for SQL Server 6.5, or from any ISQL command prompt.

The primary configuration changes you should make follow:

◆ The first step should be to set your temporary database (tempdb) to a larger value than the minimum of 2MB. Although the default value works for small networks (less than 500 clients), larger networks encounter failed sorts or performance-related problems. It is better to set tempdb to a minimum of 10MB—preferably, 20MB or larger.

◆ Preconfigure the SQL Server user connection limit. The default value requested by the SMS installation program is 25 user connections, although the SMS services only require five user connections. Each additional SMS Administrator needs at least five user connections. If you run out of connections, the SMS Services are unable to perform their tasks and start generating site errors, or you cannot use the SMS Administrator to manage your site. Neither of these results is acceptable, so you should determine the maximum number of connections that will be required. You can calculate this by using the following formula:

```
Maximum User Connections = (NbrOfSites + NbrOfAdministrators) ´ 5
```

You should note that this calculation assumes that all sites and every SMS Administrator are connected simultaneously. This probably will not happen in the real world. And you can take steps to make sure that it doesn't happen by informing each administrator that if he is not using SMS Administrator at the time, he should exit the application and release the user connections.

Tip

Because each user connection requires a license and uses resources on the server, it is best to keep these down to the minimum required to handle your day-to-day activities. One way to determine this value is to use the Performance Monitor to monitor the number of user connections. You also can set alerts to inform you when this value is reaching 75 percent of the user-connection limit you established. You can use the alert to inform you to configure SQL Server for a higher connection limit and eventually reach a stage where you have sufficient, but no more than you need, connections to handle your requirements.

◆ Make sure that you configure SQL Server to use available memory. At a minimum, you should set the memory value to 5000, which allocates 5000 2KB pages, or 10MB of RAM, to SQL Server. If you have a large network, you might need to increase this value.

◆ Set the number of open database objects to 5000 or more. This prevents SQL Server from running out of object handles when accessed by multiple administrators or when performing large queries.

CREATING THE SMS LOGON ACCOUNT

There are fewer rules to follow in order to create the SMS logon account and to successfully install SMS. There are two rules: The user account must be a member of the local administrators account or, preferably, the Domain Admins account (which automatically includes this account in every local administrators account), and the account must be assigned the Log on as Service right.

To create the account, follow these steps:

1. Launch User Manager for Domains.
2. Choose New User from the User menu to display the New User dialog box.
3. In the Username field, enter a name, such as SMSAdmin, for the account.
4. In the Full Name field, enter a value, such as System Account.
5. In the Description field, enter a comment, such as SMS Administrator Account.

6. In the Password and Confirm Password fields, enter a password for the account.

7. Enable the Password Never Expires checkbox, and disable the User Must Change Password at Next Logon checkbox.

8. Click the Groups button and add the Domain Admins account. Remove any other groups. Then click the OK button.

9. Click the OK button to return to the main User Manager for Domains window.

10. Choose User Rights from the Policy menu to display the User Rights Policy dialog box.

11. Enable the Show Advanced User Rights checkbox. Then select the Log on as Service right in the Right drop-down listbox.

12. Click Add to display the Add Users and Groups dialog box. Then select the user account you just created and click the Add button.

13. Click the OK button and the user account should be displayed in the Grant To field. Click the OK button.

INSTALLING THE CENTRAL SITE

You must install SQL Server from the CD-ROM first before you can install System Management Server. You must also have created the SMS user account. If either of these is unavailable, you cannot continue the installation. If these items are available, just follow these steps to install your central site:

1. Execute SETUP.BAT, which is located in the SMS11\SMSSETUP directory on the second CD-ROM of the BackOffice 2.0 set. This runs the appropriate binary for your hardware platform.

Tip

> If the autodetection of your hardware platform fails, you can run the appropriate binary (SETUP.EXE), which is located in \I386 for Intel processors, \MIPS for MIPS processors, and \ALPHA for DEC Alpha processors, subdirectories.

2. After the Welcome screen appears, click the Continue button. A message appears, telling you the build number for the copy of SMS you are about to install. Then a Registration dialog box appears.

3. Enter your name, your company name, and thc registration identification number (located on the back of your CD-ROM jewel case) into the appropriate fields and click the Continue button. A message appears, asking you to confirm your entries in the Registration dialog box.

4. Verify that your entries are correct and click the Continue button to continue the installation, or click the Change button to modify them. The Installation Options dialog box appears, enabling you to finally install the product (see Figure 21.4).

Figure 21.4.
The SMS Installation Options dialog box.

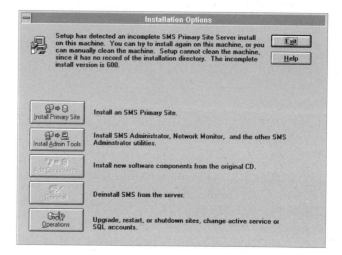

5. Click the Install Primary Site button. You are notified that you must have completed the preinstallation requirements, as described in the preceding section, in order to install SMS.

Tip

You also can use the Installation Options dialog box to install just the SMS Administration tools on any Windows NT computer by clicking the Install Admin Tools button. This is very useful because it enables you to administer all your SMS sites from your desktop, instead of having to walk to the server and run the tools from there.

6. If you have completed the preinstallation requirement, click the Continue button. If not, click the Cancel button, abort the installation, install SQL Server, and create the SMS user account. After you click Continue, the Installation Directory dialog box appears.

7. Enter a drive and directory (the default is c:\sms) on an NTFS partition with at least 100MB of free space. Then click the Continue button. The Setup Install Options dialog box appears, as shown in Figure 21.5.

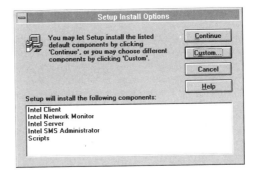

Figure 21.5.
The SMS Setup
Install Options
dialog box.

Note

You must install SMS to an NTFS partition. You cannot install it to a FAT or HPFS partition. If you did not install NT Server to an NTFS partition, or you did not create an NTFS partition, then abort the installation. You can use the CONVERT program to convert a FAT or HPFS partition to NTFS. If you are using a dual boot for MS-DOS or OS/2 and you convert the boot partition, you will no longer be able to boot the prior operating system. Only NT can access an NTFS partition. You can also use the Disk Administrator to create a new partition and format it as NTFS. After you create an NTFS partition, you can restart the installation of SMS.

Caution

The SMS Setup program will not prevent you from installing SMS on a mapped drive, as long as it is an NTFS partition. This option generally fails when the SMS Services attempt to start to verify the installation. It appears that this is not a supported option at this time; it is not really a desirable option either, because having the SMS system files on another server would decrease the overall SMS performance and increase the network traffic.

8. This dialog box automatically includes all the options for your specified hardware platform. If you want to add support for RISC-based or Macintosh client platforms, however, or add the SMS Book Online manuals, click the Custom button and add these components. After you select all your components, click the Continue button. The SQL Database Configuration dialog box appears, as shown in Figure 21.6.

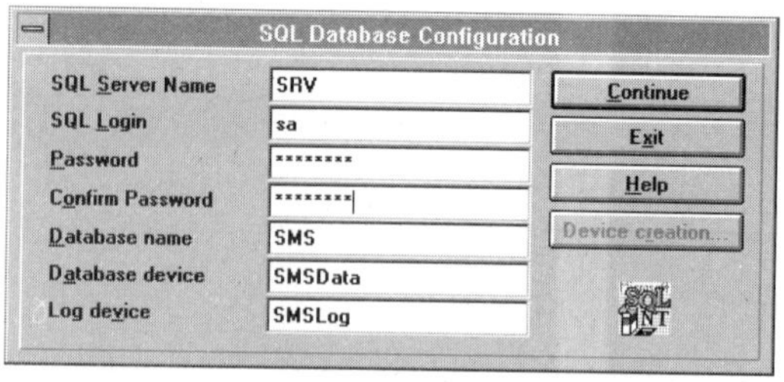

Figure 21.6.
Specifying the
SMS database
options.

Note

If you click the Cancel button in the Setup Install Options dialog box and then click the Install Primary Site button in the Installation Options dialog box to continue the installation, each time you do this you add the basic SMS components to the Setup Install Options dialog box. If you click Cancel and then click Continue, for example, you will see two entries for the Intel Client, Intel Network Monitor, Intel Server, Intel SMS Administrator, and Scripts. You should remove these duplicate entries by clicking the Custom button before continuing the installation.

If you have additional RISC-based Windows NT Server platforms that you will be using for primary or secondary sites, you should install support for these platforms at this time.

9. In the SQL Server Name field, enter the name of your SQL Server, which is usually the computer name where SQL Server is installed.

10. In the SQL Login field, enter a SQL Server administrative account name. The default is sa, however you should create a separate administrative account for use by the SMS services.

11. In the Password and Confirm Password fields, enter the SQL logon password for the account.

Warning

The default for the sa account is a blank (or no password at all). I certainly hope that you have set this to a different value then the default, however, as recommended in Part III. Otherwise, your entire SQL Server installation is open to any user with a tool that can connect to SQL Server (such as most ODBC-compliant applications). If you have not changed this password, do it now and then continue the installation.

12. If you do not like the default names, you already have created devices and the SMS database, or you are using the same SQL Server for more than one site (which is possible, but not recommended) for the SQL Server database, database device name, or log device name, change them in the Database Name, Database Device, and Log device fields. Then click the Continue button. To change the location or the allocations of the database or log device, click the Device Creation button in the SQL Database Configuration dialog box.

13. The heart of your site configuration occurs in the Primary Site Configuration Information dialog box, which appears next (see Figure 21.7).

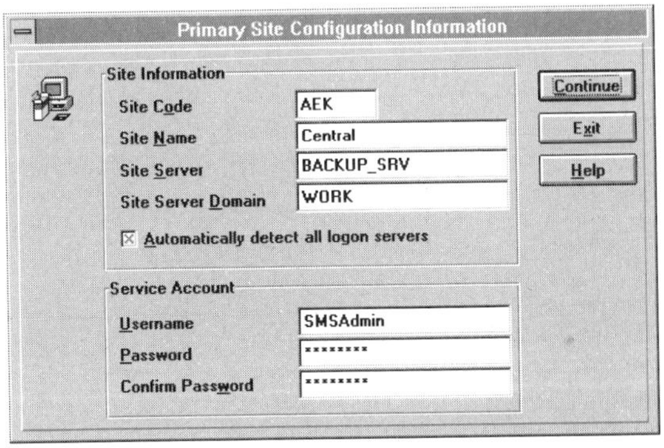

Figure 21.7.
Configuring the
primary site.

Tip

If you are using a non-local SQL Server, meaning that SMS and SQL Server are on different computers (which is the recommended choice), the SMS installation program cannot create the devices or database. Instead, you must do this manually before you can continue the installation. The default size for the database device is 45MB. The default for the log device is 8MB. If you are using an existing device, the installation program prompts you to delete all databases on the device. The installation cannot continue if there are any databases on the device, so it is best if you dedicate devices specifically for SMS. The transaction log must be on a separate device. It cannot be on the same device as the database device. Be sure to create entirely separate devices to contain the database and log when you create the database, and do not use these devices for any other database or log.

You can use the following options in the Primary Site Configuration Information dialog box:

◆ Site Code: Specifies a three-character code. It is not case sensitive, but it must be unique within the SMS domain.

◆ Site Name: Specifies a unique name for the site, which is used within SMS Administrator to identify the site.

◆ Site Server: Specifies the server where the site is located. This should be the same as the computer name.

◆ Site Server Domain: Specifies the name of the domain where the site server resides.

◆ Automatically Detect All Logon Servers: Automatically enumerates all servers used to authenticate your clients and installs the SMS Inventory Agent and Package Command Manager Services.

Note

If you will be performing a limited rollout or want to manually specify the logon servers, clear this checkbox. You later can specify the servers to be used as logon servers with the SMS Administrator.

◆ Username: Specifies the user name that will be used by the SMS Services. This account should have been created as part of the preinstallation requirements.

Note

When specifying the user name for a site on a trusted domain, preface the user name with the domain name. If the account is on the domain WORK and the user name is SMSAdmin, for example, the fully qualified user name is WORK\SMSAdmin.

◆ Password: Specifies the password for the SMS user account.

◆ Confirm Password: Verifies the password for the SMS user account.

Caution

Do not cut and paste the password specified in the Password field into the Confirm Password field because this defeats the purpose of preventing a data-entry error. Instead, enter the password twice as indicated.

Note

> If you will be using Novell NetWare servers in your site for logon
> servers, do not use a password that is the same as the user name.
> Novell NetWare servers have an option to prevent passwords from
> being the same as the user account name.

14. After you complete all entries in the Primary Site Configuration Informa-
    tion dialog box, click the Continue button. At this point, the user account
    and password are verified, and the Setup Progress dialog box appears. This
    dialog box displays the status of the installation. It shows the progress of
    the files being copied, the SQL database initialization, and the service
    installation.

15. Finally, the Network Monitor Service is installed and the Systems Manage-
    ment Server Program Manager group is created. At this point, the installa-
    tion is complete and all services should be running on the site server.

After the installation is complete, you should verify that the following services are
running. You can do this by viewing their status with the Control Panel Services
applet or by issuing the NET START command from a command prompt.

> SMS Hierarchy Manager
>
> SMS Site Configuration Manager
>
> SMS Executive
>
> SMS Inventory Agent for Windows NT
>
> SMS Package Command Manager for Windows NT

If these services are not running, check the application event log for SMS-specific
events, or check the SMSSETUP.LOG file (located in the root directory of your Windows
NT Server installation drive) for possible reasons for the failure.

Tip

> You can use the SMS Setup application to try to restart all the ser-
> vices in case of an error. Click the Operations button in the Installa-
> tion Options dialog box, and then click the Reset Site button in the
> Site Operations dialog box.

INSTALLING A PRIMARY SITE

To create a primary site, you follow the same basic process that you use to create a
central site. After the site is up and running, though, you need to attach it to the
central site (or parent site, if you are creating subsites). A subsite is a child of the

parent. In order for a parent to communicate with its child, the sites must have a sender and address that define the communications linkage. If the sites will be communicating over the LAN or WAN, you can use the default MS_LAN_SENDER, but you still need to create an address. The address defines the site and authentication parameters that will be used. After you define the sender and address, you can attach the site. You create a sender and an address, and attach a site from the SMS Administrator.

To begin the process of installing a primary site, follow these steps:

1. Launch the SMS Administrator (this should be performed at the appropriate site) and open a Sites window.

2. From the Sites window, select the site (the topmost entry) and choose Properties from the File menu or press Alt+Enter to display the Site Properties dialog box. (See Figure 21.8.)

Figure 21.8.
Modifying the
properties of a
primary site.

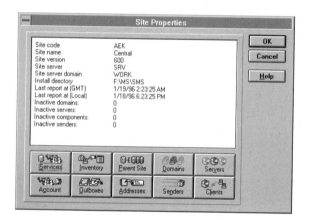

3. Click the appropriate button, as described in the following sections, to create a sender and an address, and to attach the site.

CREATING A SENDER

Create the sender at the parent site first. Then create the sender at the child site. These two senders need to be reciprocals of each other, so, in effect, each site can establish a connection.

To create a sender, follow these steps:

1. Click the Senders button in the Site Properties dialog box to display the Senders dialog box.

2. Click the Proposed Properties radio button.

3. Click the Create button to display the Sender Properties dialog box.

4. In the Type drop-down listbox, choose one of the following:

   ◆ MS_LAN_SENDER: Uses a LAN or WAN connection and is created automatically when the site is created.

   ◆ MS_BATCH_SNA_SENDER: Uses an SNA Server batch session.

   ◆ MS_INTER_SNA_SENDER: Uses an SNA Server interactive (LU 6.2) session.

   ◆ MS_ASYNC_RAS_SENDER: Uses a Remote Access Service (RAS) modem-to-modem connection.

   ◆ MS_ISDN_RAS_SENDER: Uses a Remote Access Service (RAS) ISDN-to-ISDN adapter connection.

   ◆ MS_X.25_RAS_SENDER: Uses a Remote Access Service (RAS) X.25-to-X.25 adapter connection.

5. In the Server field, enter the name of the computer that will provide the connection service. If SMS is installed on the server named SRV, for example, but the RAS server that will be supplying the connection to the remote computer (called BACKUP_SRV) is called RAS_SRV, then the name you should enter is RAS_SRV.

6. Specify the drive letter in the Drive field where the site outbox on the connection server will be created. This will create an SMS root directory, and the outbox will be located in the SITE.SRV\HELPER.SRV\Platform.BIN (where Platform.BIN is X86, ALPHA, or MIPS) and will be shared as SMS_SHRx (where x is the drive letter you specified).

Note

If you are creating an SNA connection, click the Details button in the Sender Properties dialog box and specify the name of the LU 6.2 alias to use.

Note

When creating a RAS connection, you also need to create a RAS phone book entry for the specified type. If you are using the ISDN sender, for example, you must create an ISDN phone book entry. The RAS Server on the remote site also must authorize the local site user account as a valid dial-in client in order for the connection to be established. When you define the address, the user account, and password, these are used for the RAS phone book entry when the connection is established to the remote server.

7. Click the OK button in the Sender Properties dialog box, and then click the OK button in the Senders dialog box to create the new sender.

CREATING AN ADDRESS

Create the address at the parent site first. Then create the address at the child site. Like the sender, these two addresses need to be reciprocals of each other to enable each site to establish a connection.

To create an address, follow these steps:

1. Click the Addresses button in the Site Properties dialog box to display the Addresses dialog box.
2. Click the Proposed Properties button.
3. Click the Create button to display the Address Properties dialog box.
4. In the Destination Site Code field, enter the three-character site code of the remote site.
5. In the Type drop-down listbox, choose one of the following:
   ◆ MS_LAN_SENDER: Uses a LAN or WAN connection and is created automatically when the site is created.
   ◆ MS_BATCH_SNA_SENDER: Uses an SNA Server batch session.
   ◆ MS_INTER_SNA_SENDER: Uses an SNA Server interactive (LU 6.2) session.
   ◆ MS_ASYNC_RAS_SENDER: Uses a Remote Access Service (RAS) modem-to-modem connection.
   ◆ MS_ISDN_RAS_SENDER: Uses a Remote Access Service (RAS) ISDN-to-ISDN adapter connection.
   ◆ MS_X.25_RAS_SENDER: Uses a Remote Access Service (RAS) X.25-to-X.25 adapter connection.
6. Click the Details button. Depending on the type of connection, you are prompted for a remote computer name, user name, password, LU 6.2 alias (for an SNA Server connection), phone book entry (for a Remote Access Server connection), and domain name (which is the SMS site domain name). For a RAS connection, you can specify different user accounts and passwords to establish the connection (RAS Access) and to access the site (Destination Access).
7. Click the OK button in the Address Properties dialog box, and then click the OK button in the Addresses dialog box to create the new address.

ATTACHING A SITE

You can attach a site by following these steps:

1. First create a sender and address at the parent site.
2. Create a sender and address at the child site.
3. From the Sites window, select the site (the topmost entry) and choose Properties from the File menu or press Alt+Enter to display the Site Properties dialog box.
4. Click the Parent Site button to display the Parent Site dialog box.
5. Select the Proposed radio button.
6. Select the Attach to Parent Site radio button.
7. In the Site Code field, enter the three-character site code of the central or primary (parent) site and click the OK button. This attaches this primary site to its parent.

INSTALLING A SECONDARY SITE

You install a secondary site from the SMS Administrator. Before you create the secondary site, however, be sure that you have created a sender and address, as described in the preceding section. Then just follow these steps:

1. From the Sites window, select the site (the topmost entry) and choose New from the File menu or press Ctrl+N to display the New Secondary Site dialog box. (See Figure 21.9.)

Figure 21.9.
Creating a
secondary site.

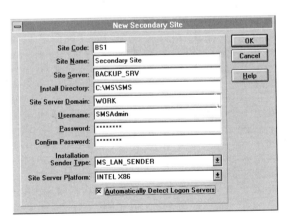

The New Secondary Site dialog box offers the following options:

◆ Site Code: Specifies a three-character code. It is not case sensitive, but it must be unique within the SMS domain.

◆ Site Name: Specifies a unique name for the site, which will be used within SMS Administrator to identify the site.

◆ Site Server: Specifies the server where the site is located. This should be the same as the computer name.

◆ Install Directory: Specifies the location of the SMS root directory.

◆ Site Server Domain: Specifies the name of the domain where the site server resides.

◆ Username: Specifies the user name that will be used by the SMS Services. This account should have been created as part of the preinstallation requirements.

Note

When specifying the user name for a site on a trusted domain, preface the user name with the domain name. If the account is on the domain WORK and user name is SMSAdmin, for example, the fully qualified user name is WORK\SMSAdmin.

◆ Password: Specifies the password for the SMS user account.

◆ Confirm Password: Verifies the password for the SMS user account.

Note

If you will be using Novell NetWare servers in your site for logon servers, do not use a password that is the same as the user name. Novell NetWare servers have an option to prevent passwords from being the same as the user account name.

◆ Installation Sender Type: Specifies the type of sender to use for the connection. This can be one of the following:

MS_LAN_SENDER: Uses a LAN or WAN connection and is created automatically when the site is created.

MS_BATCH_SNA_SENDER: Uses an SNA Server batch session.

MS_INTER_SNA_SENDER: Uses an SNA Server interactive (LU 6.2) session.

MS_ASYNC_RAS_SENDER: Uses a Remote Access Service (RAS) modem-to-modem connection.

MS_ISDN_RAS_SENDER: Uses a Remote Access Service (RAS) ISDN-to-ISDN adapter connection.

MS_X.25_RAS_SENDER: Uses a Remote Access Service (RAS) X.25-to-X.25 adapter connection.

◆ Site Server Platform: Specifies the type of processor at the site.

◆ Automatically Detect Logon Servers: Automatically enumerates all servers used to authenticate your clients and installs the SMS Inventory Agent and Package Command Manager Services.

Note

If you will be performing a limited rollout or want to manually specify the logon servers, clear this checkbox. You later can specify the servers to be used as logon servers with the SMS Administrator.

2. Click the OK button. You are informed that the site-creation process might be a lengthy one, and you are asked if you want to continue. Click the OK button to create the site.

3. Finally, you are informed of the status of the site initiation. If everything is working as expected, it should be a success status. If so, click the OK button and continue your work with the SMS Administrator.

SUMMARY

This was a fairly complex chapter. The complexity is due to the nature of SMS and its requirements. From this chapter, you should remember that planning your installation is very important. Without a good plan, your SMS installation will not work as well as it should. And it may even cause you significant difficulties, rather than provide you with benefits.

When creating primary sites that are not on your local LAN, or if you will use SNA Server as the connection mechanism, be sure to create both a sender and an address on each site to facilitate the site communications. After installing a site, be sure to verify that the SMS Services have started properly.

In the next chapter, you will look into some of the management issues of SMS. You will learn more about managing your shared network applications, remote troubleshooting, and some of the other administrative tools.

- Managing Shared
  Network Applications

- Remote Trouble-
  shooting with the
  SMS Administrator

- Managing Your SMS
  Database Permissions
  with the SMS
  Security Manager

- Using the Microsoft
  Network Monitor

- Managing Your
  SMS Installation with
  SMS Setup

- Using an ODBC
  Application with the
  SMS Database

CHAPTER 22

Managing Your Network with Systems Management Server

There is so much to using Systems Management Server that it cannot be covered in a single chapter. Luckily, the *Systems Management Server Administrators Guide* is a good source of documentation for the product. This documentation includes step-by-step instructions on how to implement packages, jobs, queries, and the like, but it does not always include helpful discussions on why you should use various aspects of the product, how to best use a particular feature, or even how to use it with other applications to provide access to information that is useful to non-administrative personnel. So these are the topics this chapter addresses.

This discussion starts with a look at some of the issues involved in configuring your network to use an SMS application server to manage your shared network applications and, not incidentally, to make your life as an administrator a little easier as well. Then, you will look at one of the more useful administrative features of the SMS Administrator: remote troubleshooting of your MS-DOS, Windows 3.x, and Windows 95 clients. Finally, you will explore some of the other tools, such as the SMS Security Manager, the Network Monitor, and the SMS Setup utility. These tools are used to determine how individual users can use the SMS SQL Server database, capture network packets for troubleshooting purposes, and modify or manage an existing SMS installation.

Although SMS does include many tools, your focus should be on the information contained in the SMS database and how to make use of it. As part of this process of information sharing, the concept needs to be extended to more user-friendly applications, particularly those not designed for the network administrator. To understand this point, you will look at how to configure an ODBC-aware application to access the SMS database.

MANAGING SHARED NETWORK APPLICATIONS

One of the most common reasons for a network is to provide a means of sharing an application with several network clients. This generally requires that the network administrator install the application from a client workstation to a network server using a special version of the application's Setup program or a command-line switch on the Setup program. This uncompresses all the files on the distribution disks and places them in one or more directories on the server. The root installation directory then is shared on the network, and each network client then is required to attach to this shared directory and run the Setup program locally. Then, depending on how the administrator installed the original source material, the user can choose to install a copy of the application on his computer for best performance, install just shared components to provide a slight performance increase, or install just the configuration (INI) files.

Although this process works, it does have a few faults:

◆ Server performance: If only a single server is used to provide a centralized distribution point to make upgrades easier, then the performance of the server is severely affected. After all, there is a definite limit to the number of clients that can connect to a single server to use shared files before all network users are impacted. This can be caused by the server's inability to transmit the data (network bandwidth), the disk subsystem's inability to read the data fast enough to transmit it, or the processor's inabilityto process the data fast enough to interpret the network requests.

◆ Fault tolerance: If the server that contains the user's application files goes down, the user cannot access the applications. In effect, this user will be unable to perform any work with these applications unless he has access to other servers and knows how to connect and configure his workstations if this type of problem occurs.

◆ Upgrade capabilities: If you use multiple servers to spread the load, up-grades become more of a problem because you have to spend time installing the shared application on more than one server. In some cases, you can just copy an installation to another server, but this does not always work. Then, depending on how each user installed the application, he may have to reinstall it all over again.

◆ Roaming users: If a user moves from one network client workstation to another and attempts to access his shared application from this new client workstation, he may encounter problems running the application. If the new workstation's original user installed the software differently, then the application may fail to run. If the user connects to a different server with different sharepoints, the application may fail to run. There are so many ifs in this scenario that I really can't even include them all but, in most cases, the application fails to run.

This is where SMS can help you and, not incidentally, your network clients—by providing multiple servers that can be used to provide a shared network application if properly implemented by the network administrator. The basic requirements to implement this type of scenario with SMS follow:

◆ Create one or more application servers.

◆ Install the application on each of these application servers, and create the program group to provide access to the application.

Note

There is only one real problem with sharing applications in this fashion with SMS 1.1, and it is a humdinger. Only Windows 3.x and Windows NT platforms support dynamic allocation of Program

Manager groups. This means that your Windows 95, OS/2, and Macintosh clients are not supported. This does not mean that you cannot use shared network applications, though; it only means that you must create a manual connection to the shared directory and manually build a program group to the associated applications. These types of clients then will still be able to run the network applications, but they also will be tied to a specific server. Currently SMS 1.2 which does support Windows 95 clients is in beta and should be released in the fourth quarter of 1996.

CREATING AN APPLICATION SERVER

An application server is nothing more than a server with shared applications. This could be your primary or backup domain controller, but these servers are not the best choice to use for sharing your applications because they have more than enough work to do authenticating users or providing additional services. The better choice is to use Windows NT Server operating in server mode as your application server platform. This particular configuration is tuned to provide maximum performance as a file and print server. Just installing NT Server in this way is not always enough, however. The server must have sufficient resources (processor, RAM, disk storage, network bandwidth, and so on) to accommodate all your network clients.

With SMS, however, you can use multiple application servers. When a client then requests access to the application server, the request is dynamically routed to an application server. This provides three benefits:

◆ The load on the server is balanced between multiple servers. The client is connected to a server based on a random connection that performs basic load leveling.

◆ If a server fails or is taken offline for maintenance, the user is connected to another application server when he launches the application.

◆ Application installations and upgrades can be automated. This process includes upgrading the application servers as well as the network clients.

The SMS Administrators Guide often refers to an application server as a distribution server (a server that distributes packages), but this does not always need to be the case. You can use other servers to provide this function. For the purposes of this chapter, you can consider a distribution and an application server as one and the same. When you do use multiple servers to distribute applications, you have to group them into a single logical unit. This logical unit is called a machine group.

To create the group and assign the servers to the group, follow these steps:

1. Open the Machine Groups window by clicking the Open Window: Machine Groups button from the toolbar on the SMS Administrator. Figure 22.1 shows the SMS Administrator toolbar.

2. Choose New from the File menu to display the Machine Group Properties dialog box.

3. In the Name field, enter a name for the new group, such as Application Servers.

4. In the Comment field, enter a description for the new group.

5. Open the Sites window if it is not already open by clicking the Open Window: Sites button.

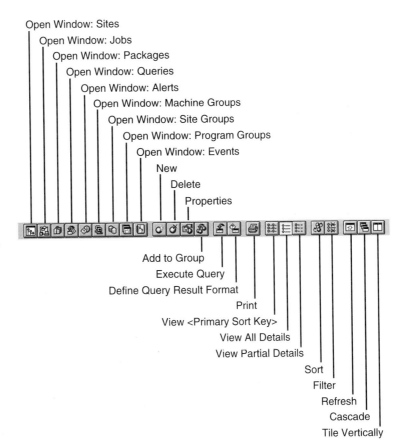

Open Window: Sites
Open Window: Jobs
Open Window: Packages
Open Window: Queries
Open Window: Alerts
Open Window: Machine Groups
Open Window: Site Groups
Open Window: Program Groups
Open Window: Events
New
Delete
Properties

Figure 22.1.
The SMS Admin-
istrator toolbar.

Add to Group
Execute Query
Define Query Result Format
Print
View <Primary Sort Key>
View All Details
View Partial Details
Sort
Filter
Refresh
Cascade
Tile Vertically

6. Expand the site with the servers you want to add to the machine group.

7. In the right window, select the computers to add to the group and choose Add to Group from the File menu, or click the Add to Group toolbar button. You can choose a consecutive range of computers by selecting the first computer name and then, while pressing the Shift key, selecting the last computer name. To choose a nonconsecutive range of computers, select the first computer name and then, while pressing the Control key, select each additional computer name.

8. Repeat steps 6 and 7 for each additional site's computers to add to the group.

Note

If your application server also will be supporting Novell NetWare or Apple Macintosh clients, your application server should have the File and Print Services for NetWare (or you can use a real NetWare server) or the Services for Macintosh installed. Without these services, the network clients cannot access the application server.

INSTALLING THE APPLICATION ON THE SERVER

The next stage in creating an application server is to install the software on the server and make it available to your network clients. Unfortunately, this is not always as easy as it sounds. There are basically three ways to accomplish this task:

◆ You can do this the old way, by just running the application's Setup program to install the software on the server and then sharing the root directory. Although this is easy, it is not as useful because most installations like this are tied to the particular server on which you installed the application. So if you want to install it on more than one server, you have to repeat the installation on each server. Then each client must connect to the server and run the client side of the installation. Now each client is tied to a specific server to access the application. This type of behavior is not really what you are looking to provide for your clients.

◆ You can install the software on a server to create an image you can copy to other servers. This is possible but not very probable in some cases. Some applications—generally those not designed as a network shared application—can be installed to a network share and then copied to multiple servers, and each network client then can use the application without problem as long as each user has a unique home directory for his temp files.

Although this type of application is not tied to a specific server as long as the application can find its source files, it also is not designed for multiple users. Some of these types of applications use configuration files or create temp files in the root directory. If this occurs with the application you want to share, the only recourse is to allow only one user to access the application at a time. This can be accomplished by setting the share limit to one, but a solution such as this is not really very useful.

◆ You can use SMS to install the application on each distribution server. This type of installation is the most useful because it automatically installs the application, creates the shares, copies any required configuration files, and builds an access point that can be dynamically selected by the network client. This option is the best choice but is certainly not the easiest, and it is also the subject of the rest of this discussion.

The basic process for using SMS to install a sharable network application consists of several steps. First, you have to create a package. A package is nothing more than all the source files needed to install the application. For the purposes of this chapter, this is generally the original source media or a copy of the source media's installation directory copied to a disk on the server. Next, you must create a Share Package on Server job to install the package on the application servers. Finally, you must create a program group. If you want to be able to inventory these packages, or even other applications, on a client's hard disk drive you can specify parameters for the package.

Tip

> The SMS 1.1 source media includes several predefined package definition files (PDFs) that describe the contents of the package, as well as scripts for installing applications contained within the package. This should be your first step when installing your shared network applications; if you do not have a predefined PDF or script, you must create one yourself.

To create the package, follow these steps:

1. Open the Packages window by clicking the Open Window: Packages button in the toolbar in the SMS Administrator.

2. Choose New from the File menu to display the Package Properties dialog box.

22

MANAGING YOUR NETWORK

Tip

> If you have a package definition file (PDF) for the application, click the Import button in the Package Properties dialog box. This imports most of the required information to install and inventory the application.

3. In the Name field, enter a name for the package.
4. In the Comment field, enter a description to explain the contents of the package.
5. Click the Sharing button to display the Setup Package for Sharing dialog box.
6. Enter a UNC directory name where the package will be installed in the Source Directory field.

Note

> When this package is installed using the Share Package on Server job, the same root directory name is used as that specified in the UNC filename. The computer name is replaced by the name of the local computer on which the package is installed, however.

7. Enter the name (eight characters maximum) that the install directory will be shared as in the Share Name field.

Note

> Use the Access button to specify the type (Read/Write) permissions for domain users or domain guests who will access the share.

8. Click the New button to display the Program Properties dialog box.
9. In the Description field, specify a comment for the application.
10. In the Command Line field, specify the command line to execute the application.
11. In the Registry Name field, specify a Registry key name to be used by the application.
12. In the Configuration Command Line field, specify the installation program or script name to install and configure the application.
13. Enable the Display Icon in Program Group checkbox if the application should include a shortcut to run the application. Then click the Change Icon button to modify the default application icon, if desired.

14. Enable the Run Local Copy if Present checkbox to enable the user to execute a local copy of the application. If this checkbox is disabled, then the network version of the application always is executed. If it is enabled, the computer is scanned to determine whether a local copy of the application exists. If found, this copy of the application is executed to improve performance.

15. Enable the Run Minimized checkbox to start the application in a minimized state if desired.

16. Choose an entry in the Drive Mode section to determine how the application accesses the installation directory. This can be one of the following options:

   ◆ Runs with UNC Name: This entry should be selected only for applications that are UNC aware. In this mode, no drive letter is assigned, and all access to the installation directory uses the UNC convention (\\ServerName\ShareName).

   ◆ Requires Drive Letter: This entry assigns a drive letter to the shared directory and prompts the user for a specific drive letter assignment if the default is unacceptable.

   ◆ Requires Specific Drive Letter: This entry assigns a specific drive letter (as selected in the Drive Letter listbox) to the share.

17. Choose the platforms the application will execute under in the Supported Platforms field.

18. Click the OK button to complete this item. Then repeat steps 8 through 18 for each additional item.

19. Click the Close button to close the Setup Package for Sharing dialog box, and click the OK button to complete the package setup.

Note

If you will be creating a package to install an application, you also should click the Workstation button and define the methods to start the installation process. If you also want to be able to inventory the package contents, click the Inventory button.

To create the Share Package on Server job, follow these steps:

1. Open the Jobs window by clicking the Open Window: Jobs button on the toolbar in the SMS Administrator.

2. Choose New from the File menu to display the Jobs Properties dialog box.

3. In the Comment field, enter a description that defines the purpose of the job.

4. In the Job Type drop-down listbox, choose Share Package on Server.

5. Click the Details button to display the Job Details dialog box.

6. From the Package drop-down listbox, choose the package (which you created in the preceding set of steps).

7. Enable the Limit to Sites checkbox to specify the site to which to install the package. Otherwise, the package is installed on all sites. If this option is enabled, you also can choose the site or site group where the package should be installed in the Job Target field. If you enable the Include Subsites checkbox, all subsites below the selected site are included as well.

8. Select the Only If Not Previously Sent or Even If Previously Sent radio button in the Send Phase field to determine whether the package should be sent to the sites that have never received this package before or to all sites.

9. In the Distribute Phase section, make sure that the Put on Specified Distribution Servers checkbox is enabled. Then select the machine group name that defines your application servers in the listbox.

10. Click the OK button to create the job.

Tip

If you want to delay the time at which this job is executed, click the Schedule button and specify a time and date to run the job. To check the status of all jobs, click the Status button.

To create the program group, follow these steps:

1. Open the Program Groups window by clicking the Open Window: Program Groups button in the toolbar in the SMS Administrator.

2. Choose New from the File menu to display the Program Group Properties dialog box.

3. In the Name field, enter a name for the Program Manager group.

4. In the Comment field, enter a description to define the group.

5. Click the Packages button to display the Program Group Packages dialog box.

6. In the Available Packages field, you see an entry for each sharable package you have defined. Select the name of the package and then click the Add button to move the package to the Member Packages field.

7. In the Program Items field, select the program items to include in the group. Then click the OK button.

8. Click the User Groups button to display the User Groups dialog box.

9. Select the user groups to be assigned permission to use the program group in the Don't Share with These Groups listbox and click the Add button to move the groups to the Share with These Groups listbox. Then click the OK button.

Note

By creating more than one group, selecting different program items, and assigning different user group permissions, you can limit access to sensitive applications.

10. Click the OK button to create the program group.

Inventorying Applications

One of the nicer features of SMS is the capability to collect data about your SMS clients. By default, SMS will only inventory the hardware of the client computer. However, you can create a package to inventory a specific software application that is installed on the client's computer. This information will then be placed in the SMS database, which you can query at will later. In this section you will learn how to create the inventory package and how to create a query to determine which SMS clients contain the inventoried package.

To create the inventory package, follow these steps:

1. Open the Packages window by clicking the Open Window: Packages button in the toolbar in the SMS Administrator.
2. Choose New from the File menu to display the Package Properties dialog box.
3. In the Name field, enter a name for the package. The name might be something like WinZIP if you want to inventory the WinZIP application by Nico Mak Computing, Inc.
4. In the Comment field, enter a description to explain the contents or purpose of the package—perhaps something like "Windows ZIP archive tool."
5. Click the Inventory button to display the Setup Package for Inventory dialog box.
6. Enable the Inventory this package checkbox.
7. Click the Add AND button to display the File Properties dialog box.
8. Enter the name of the application in the File Name field.
9. In the Properties field, choose a file property in the Properties Available listbox. These properties can be one of the following:

   BYTE: Used to identify a file based on finding a specific byte of data at a specific offset (location) within the file.

CHECKSUM: Used to identify a file based on a checksum of a series of bytes starting at a specific offset within the file. A checksum is basically a series of bytes added together one byte at a time with the result also being stored in a single byte. Since a single byte can hold only the values from 0–255, as a byte of data is appended to the previous total the result field overflows to the next value above 0 but less than 255.

CRC: Used to identify a file based on a cyclic redundancy check (CRC) of a series of bytes starting at a specific offset within the file. A CRC is similar to a checksum in that it sums a series of bytes. The difference, however, is that a CRC can compare the order of the byte sequence which is summed. As such it is a more reliable method of identifying a file than a checksum.

DATE: Used to identify a file based on the date contained within the time-date stamp of the file.

LONG: Used to identify a file based on finding a specific series of 4 bytes (32 bits) of data at a specific offset (location) within the file.

SIZE: Used to identify a file based on the file size.

STRING: Used to identify a file based on finding a specific string of data at a specific offset (location) within the file.

TIME: Used to identify a file based on the time contained within the time-date stamp of the file.

WORD: Used to identify a file based on finding a specific word (16-bits) of data at a specific offset (location) within the file.

10. Click the Add button. A dialog will appear where you may enter the information for the specified property (such as a date for the DATE property). Then the property to test will be moved to the Property to test field.

11. Repeat steps 9 and 10 for each additional property. You may want to use multiple properties to distinguish between software versions, for example, by selecting different file sizes or time-date stamps. If you actually want to copy the file and place it in your SMS database, enable the Collect this file checkbox.

12. Click the OK button to close the dialog box and return to the Setup Package for Inventory dialog. Then click OK to close the Package Properties dialog box and return to the SMS Administrator.

Once you have created the inventory package, you need to create a query to search your SMS database for SMS clients that have the software application installed on their computer. To create the query follow these basic steps:

1. Open the Queries window by clicking the Open Window: Queries button in the toolbar in the SMS Administrator.

2. Choose New from the File menu to display the Query Properties dialog box.

3. In the Query Name field, enter a name for the query. The name might be something like Installed Software.

4. In the Comment field, enter a description to explain the contents, or purpose, of the query—perhaps something like "Finds computers with a user specified software package" if you want to find an application based on a user supplied application name.

5. Click the Add AND button to display the Query Expression Properties dialog box. This dialog box has three fields from which you may select a property that identifies the type of query to perform (in our example this would be the Software Name from the Software group), the type of operator (which in our example would be is) from the Operator drop-down listbox, and an entry from the Value drop-down listbox (in our example this would be <Prompt(Software - Software Name:)> to allow the value to be entered when the query is executed).

Note

There are actually several different groups, software classes, attributes, operators, and values which you can use to build predefined queries. It may be helpful to look at some of the predefined queries to get a feel for the information retrievable from the SMS database before writing your own queries.

6. Click OK to add your expression and return to the Query Properties dialog box. If you have an additional phrase to add to your query, choose the Add AND or Add OR button to extend the query expression.

7. Once you have finished building your query, click OK to close the Query Property dialog box and return to the SMS Administrator.

To execute your query and find out who has the installed software on their computers just select the query (such as Installed Software, which you created above) and choose Execute Query from the File menu. You will then be prompted for the name of the package to find within the inventory database. Once you enter the name, click OK and the result window will appear with any matching SMS clients.

Note

Remember to enter the name of the package (such as WinZip) to find in the query rather than an application name (such as winzip.exe) or the query will fail to find any matching clients.

REMOTE TROUBLESHOOTING WITH THE SMS ADMINISTRATOR

One of the most useful tools included with the SMS Administrator gives you the capability to connect to a client workstation; to run MS-DOS, Windows 3.x, or Windows 95 applications; or to just view a session with a user or take complete control of the computer. This capability is very powerful because it can be used with any client on the network. If you have installed the Remote Access Service on your server and on your network client, you can even use this tool to help your users who are on the road. It will be much slower, but it is still worth the performance penalty if you can help the user.

You should keep the following considerations in mind when using this tool:

◆ First, the client must grant you permission to use it. This is accomplished by using the Help Desk utility on the client to configure the Remote Control Agent. You can use an SMS job and a script to preconfigure all your network clients to automatically support this option, however, if desired.

◆ Second, you can support only Windows or Windows 95 clients who have an 80386 or higher processor. If the client does not have an 80386, you must use the DOS client TSRs, and the usefulness is severely impaired.

◆ Whenever possible, you should use a higher resolution than the client you want to view remotely. This is so that you can view the entire client screen without scrolling.

◆ Finally, your choice of network transport protocols has an impact on the amount of generated datagrams sent over the network. If you are using NetBEUI, you should avoid using the File Transfer, Remote Chat, and Ping Test options.

To configure a client to support remote control, follow these steps:

1. Launch the Help Desk Options utility to display the Help Desk Options dialog box, as shown in Figure 22.2.

   This dialog box displays several checkboxes. Each checkbox performs a different function:

   ◆ Allow Remote Control: Enables/disables the capability to take control of the client computer.

   ◆ Allow Remote Reboot: Enables/disables the capability to reboot the client computer.

   ◆ Allow Chat: Enables/disables the capability to chat with the client computer user. When this option is enabled, a chat window appears on both the client and the SMS Administrator to provide two-way communications.

◆ Allow Remote File Transfer: Enables/disables the capability to send or receive files on the client computer.

◆ Allow Remote Execute: Enables/disables the capability to execute commands (including applications) on the client computer.

◆ Allow DOS Diagnostics: Enables/disables the capability to view the client computer's MS-DOS configuration. This includes items such as the CMOS, ROM information, device drivers, interrupt vectors, and memory configuration.

◆ Allow Windows Diagnostics: Enables/disables the capability to view the client computer's Windows configuration. This includes items such as the Windows memory, Windows module list, Windows task list, Windows classes list, global memory heap, and GDI heap.

◆ Allow Ping Test: Enables/disables the capability to ping the client computer to test for connectivity and network transmission speed.

◆ Visible Signal When Viewed: Visibly signals the user whenever the Remote Control Agent is activated.

◆ Audible Signal When Viewed: Audibly signals the user whenever the Remote Control Agent is activated.

◆ Permission Required: Requires that the computer user actively participate in the remote-control process. If this feature is enabled, then the user is notified of the attempt to take control, and then must grant permission before the remote-control session can be established.

2. To make these settings permanent, click the Save As Default button. To make the settings apply to the current session, click the Save As Current button.

3. Click the Exit button to close the dialog box.

After a user is configured to provide access to the remote troubleshooting tools, you can access the client computer from the SMS Administrator by performing these steps:

1. Open a Sites window and expand the site until the site with the associated client is visible in the left window.

2. Select the site to display all the SMS clients within the site in the right window. Double-click the entry for the remote computer to display the Personal Computer Properties window, as shown in Figure 22.3. This window has several icons in the Properties column that display information about the subject when selected. Table 22.1 describes these icons.

22

MANAGING YOUR NETWORK

Figure 22.2.
Configuring a
client for remote
control.

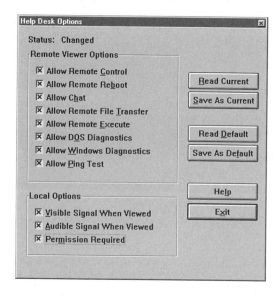

Figure 22.3.
The Personal
Computer
Properties
window.

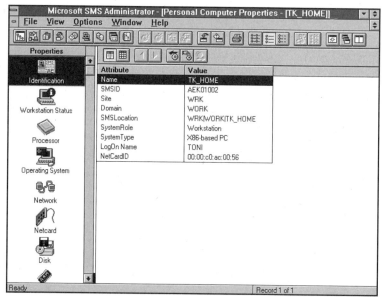

TABLE 22.1. PROPERTIES ICONS AND DESCRIPTIONS.

Icon	Description
Identification	Describes various SMS client attributes.
Workstation Status	Describes various workstation attributes related to the computer's SMS components.

Icon	Description
Processor	Describes the installed central processing units (CPUs).
Operating System	Describes the workstation's operating systems, version numbers, and other relevant information.
Network	Describes the client's network operating system shell, transport protocols, and other relevant information.
Netcard	Describes the client's network adapter and associated resources.
Disk	Describes the client's physical and logical disk characteristics.
PC Memory	Describes the client's physical, virtual, conventional, and extended memory characteristics.
Serial Port	Describes the client's serial port configurations.
Parallel Port	Describes the client's parallel port configurations.
Video	Describes the client's current video mode, video type, manufacturer, BIOS date, and other relevant information.
Mouse	Describes characteristics about the mouse operation.
PC BIOS	Describes the client's computer BIOS, manufacturer, and release date.
IRQ Table	Describes the client computer's interrupt table.
Packages	Describes the packages that have been detected on the client workstation. Note: This option is available only for Windows 3.x and Windows NT computers.
Services	Describes all the services installed on the computer. Note: This option is available only for Windows NT computers.
Environment	Lists all the client's workstation's environment variables.
Help Desk	Enables you to remote control a host, transfer files, reboot the workstation, or chat online.
Diagnostics	Provides information about the host's CMOS configuration, installed device drivers, ROM information, software interrupt table, DOS memory, Ping test, Windows memory, Windows active modules, active Windows tasks, active window classes, the Windows Global Heap, and the Windows GDI Heap.

continues

TABLE 22.1. CONTINUED

Icon	Description
Network Monitor	Enables you to find and start the Network Monitor Agent service on the remote computer.
User Information	Describes the user information entered in the MIF form when the SMS client utilities first were installed.

To remotely control a client computer, as shown in Figure 22.4, select the Help Desk icon and then wait for the connection to be established. After a connection is established, just click the Remote Control button. A window appears that echoes the user's screen. You then can take control of the computer or just view the actions of the local user.

Figure 22.4.
Taking control of
a remote com-
puter.

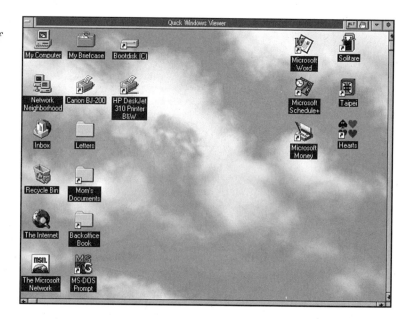

MANAGING YOUR SMS DATABASE PERMISSIONS WITH THE SMS SECURITY MANAGER

You can use the SMS Security Manager with the SQL Security Manager to manage access to your SMS database. You first must use the SQL Security Manager, if operating in mixed or integrated mode, to assign users or groups to SQL Server and the SMS database. If you are using standard mode, you need to assign users or groups with the SQL Administrator, SQL Object Manager, or command-line interfaces. After a user is assigned permission to access the SMS database, you can use the SMS Security Manager to limit access to the data contained in the database. (See Figure 22.5.)

Figure 22.5.
Using the SMS
Security Manager
to limit access to
the SMS data-
base.

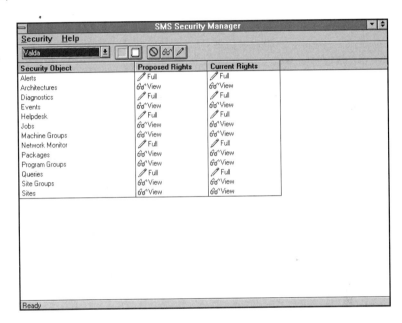

There are five predefined user classifications you can use to restrict access to the tasks a user can perform with the SMS Administrator and to the SMS database objects as well. These classifications are based on the type of job each user is to perform. These classifications follow:

- ◆ Asset Manager: A user responsible for monitoring SMS activity, or who requires the capability to view the types of hardware and software on client workstations.
- ◆ Job Manager: A user responsible for monitoring job activity or creating new jobs.
- ◆ Network Monitor: A user who requires the capability to execute the Network Monitor to view or capture packets on the network.
- ◆ Software Manager: A user responsible for application maintenance.
- ◆ Technical Support: A user responsible for providing technical support to users.

Each user classification specifies a set of access rights to control how a user may interact with the SMS Administrator, as summarized in Table 22.2.

TABLE 22.2. ACCESS RIGHTS.

Table	Asset Manager	Job Manager	Network Monitor	Software Manager	Technical Support
Alerts	No Access	No Access	No Access	No Access	Full
Architectures	View	View	View	No Access	View
Diagnostics	No Access	No Access	No Access	No Access	Full
Events	View	View	No Access	No Access	View
Help Desk	No Access	No Access	No Access	No Access	Full
Jobs	No Access	Full	No Access	No Access	No Access
Machine Groups	No Access	View	No Access	No Access	No Access
Network Monitor	No Access	No Access	Full	No Access	Full
Packages	View	View	View	Full	No Access
Program Groups	No Access	No Access	No Access	Full	No Access
Queries	Full	Full	No Access	No Access	Full
Sites	View	View	View	No Access	View
Site Groups	No Access	View	No Access	No Access	View

You also can provide custom access to the various SMS data by granting an individual right to a user instead of using the predefined rights of a user template. Regardless of the method, the basic steps to assign rights to a user follow:

1. Select the user account in the listbox.

2. The user's current properties are displayed in the Current Rights column. To change a user's rights, select the appropriate item in the Security Object column and then choose No Access, View, or Full from the Security menu. Alternatively, you can use the buttons on the toolbar. These are the third, fourth, and fifth buttons, respectively.

Tip

> To use a predefined set of user rights, choose Security | User Template or click the User Template button (the second from the left).

3. After making the proposed changes to the security objects, choose Save User from the Security menu. Or, click the Save Current Rights button (the first one from the left) to update the user rights.

USING THE MICROSOFT NETWORK MONITOR

There are many reasons for using the Network Monitor, but most of these are quite technical in nature. (See Figure 22.6.) If you are already familiar with using a packet sniffer, then you know what the Network Monitor can do for you. You might want a little explanation, though. The Network Monitor is used to display network statistics and to capture, view, or retransmit captured network packets. For the most part, a network administrator uses this tool only on the behalf of someone else. If you are encountering a problem with a client on a subnet being authenticated, for example, you might want to capture the network packets sent from the client workstation and forward them to Microsoft PSS to help you determine the cause.

Figure 22.6. Using the Network Monitor to monitor network activity.

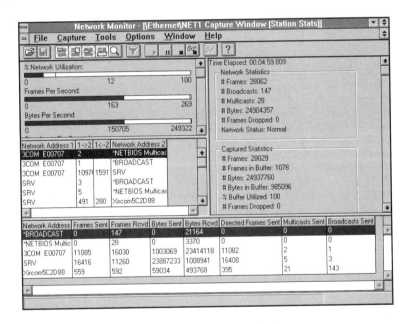

Even though this tool is not designed for the novice, it still can be very useful. If you have the time, you can even teach yourself some of the basics by capturing data and reviewing it at your leisure. If you decide to go this route, the first thing I suggest that you do is capture data from working configurations and save it for comparison when you do encounter a problem. I'll give you an example of when this might come in handy. Suppose that you have captured packets sent from or to a workstation and all your servers during a client authentication sequence. Later, you upgrade your client or server to a new version of the operating system and encounter a problem when you log on (the authentication sequence). If you capture a new series of packets in similar circumstances and compare this with your prior packet capture, you might notice a difference in the data flow.

This actually happened to me one day. The network was a token ring network using NetBEUI as the transport protocol with a bridge that supported both source and transparent routing. The cause of the authentication failure, which could be seen by examining the packets, was that the new WFW 3.11 client would send both a source and a transparent routed packet to the Windows NT Server to establish a session. By itself, this was not really a problem; however, when the Windows NT Server realized that it did not have to send source routed packets (because the bridge routed transparent packets) and switched in midstream to transparent packets, the WFW 3.11 client terminated the session and failed to be authenticated. There were three possible solutions:

◆ Use a different network protocol other than NetBEUI. This was deemed unacceptable; because it worked with LAN Manager, it should have worked with Windows NT Server.

◆ Reconfigure the bridge to support either source routed or transparent routed packets, but not both simultaneously. This also was deemed unacceptable because it required modifying the hardware configuration on every router.

◆ Modify Windows NT Server to always use source routing. This was the preferred solution, and I did modify the Registry to reconfigure the server. But it didn't work. What finally did work was upgrading Windows NT with a service pack so that it used whatever type of packet with which it originally established the session.

So what is the moral of this story? Well, it basically can be said in the old Boy Scout motto, "Be Prepared." If you take the time to become familiar with your network and the basic activity on it, you can use the Network Monitor to aid you in problem solving; even if you are not familiar with it now, you will be if you use it for a while. Most of the steps in using the Network Monitor are covered in the SMS Administrators Guide, so instead of walking you through a step-by step-process, I will just point out a few tips for you:

◆ You can use the Network Monitor to obtain a real-time view of your network activity. This includes the percentage of the network bandwidth on the active segment and frames, bytes, and broadcasts per second that make up this activity. All you have to do to obtain this information is launch the Network Monitor and choose Capture | Start or press F10. This is a good way to gain a bit of familiarity with your network. The only thing to consider is that a capture can use a lot of disk space, so you do not want to operate in this mode for too long.

◆ Capture as much data as you can on the first pass when troubleshooting. This includes both network protocols and specific addresses. After you capture the data, you can use a filter to remove unwanted data. It is better to have more data than you need, however, than not enough. If you do not have all the required data to determine the cause, you must repeat the capture. Only after you have narrowed down the cause of the problem should you limit your captures for best effect.

◆ If you install the Network Monitor Agent on one or more of your Windows NT and Windows 95 computers on each network segment, you can use any of these to capture packets remotely. Instead of capturing the data on the computer you run the Network Monitor on, the data is captured on the remote computer. By using this agent on different segments, you can determine how much of your network bandwidth is in use on each of these segments. You also can use this to capture data on the other side of a WAN connection. This provides quick data captures, and only a small portion of the WAN bandwidth is used when you view the captured data.

Note

To install the Network Monitor Agent on a Windows NT computer, open the Network Control Panel applet. Select Add Software and choose the Network Monitor Agent.

To install the Network Monitor Agent on a Windows 95 computer, open the Network applet, click Add, select Services, click the Have Disk button, and then specify the ADMIN\NETTOOLS\NETMON directory on your Windows 95 CD-ROM as the installation directory.

MANAGING YOUR SMS INSTALLATION WITH SMS SETUP

You can use the SMS Setup application to perform several different functions on an existing SMS site. Some of these were viewed during the installation process, but others aren't available until after the installation. When you execute the Setup program and work your way to the Installation Options dialog box, you have three options:

◆ Add Components: Adds more components to a site, such as additional SMS servers or clients for alternate RISC platforms.

◆ Deinstall: Removes a working or orphaned site. An orphaned site is a secondary site that was not removed using the SMS Administrator when a primary site was removed. If this option is selected, all the SMS components at a site are removed from the server.

◆ Operations: Performs various operations on a site and is really the reason why you should examine the SMS Setup application. After you choose this

22

MANAGING YOUR NETWORK

option, the Site Operations dialog box appears. This dialog box includes the following options:

Upgrade Site: Upgrades a current site from one version of SMS to another. It upgrades all the components (services and files) on the current site, all logon servers, and all secondary sites. Your SMS clients are upgraded automatically to the new software the next time they log on or when they run their current client software.

Reset Site: Causes the current site to enter a watchdog cycle. This consists of stopping all the SMS services on the site; removing, reinstalling, and restarting the SMS Configuration Manager; and forcing two new site configuration files to be written to disk. These configuration files then are evaluated, and the best one is selected. At this point, the new configuration file is used and all the SMS services are restarted.

Shutdown Site: Stops all SMS services running on the current site as well as any logon servers.

Service Account: Changes the SMS user account or password used by the SMS services. It is better to use this option instead of the Control Panel Services applet to modify the user account properties.

SMS Database: Changes the SMS user account that will be used by the SMS services to access the SQL Server SMS database. It also can be used to change the name of the SQL Server and associated database. Normally, this option is used only when you move a SQL Server database using a backup/restore or the SQL Transfer Manager. This option does not actually create or modify an account on the SQL Server. Instead, it just modifies the SMS Services to use this modified information. So you also need to create a user account on the proposed SQL Server installation to match your proposed account properties, if you have not already done so.

Even though it is possible to change some of these options manually, such as using the Control Panel Services applet to specify a different SMS user account, you might run into difficulties if you do so. It is much better to use SMS Setup to handle these types of tasks. If you do get into trouble by manually changing any of these settings, you might need to modify one or more of the SMS configuration settings in the Registry. The root Registry key can be found in HKEY_LOCAL_MACHINE\SOFTWARE\Microsoft\SMS.

USING AN ODBC APPLICATION WITH THE SMS DATABASE

One of the benefits of using SQL Server rather than a proprietary file format to contain the SMS database is that you can use other applications to access or manage the data contained within the tables of the database. Instead of just requiring everyone to use the SMS Administrator, you can create a custom tool. The easiest way to accomplish this task is to use Open Database Connectivity (ODBC) with an ODBC application. This discussion uses Access 7.0, but it could be any ODBC-compliant tool.

To use an ODBC application to access your SMS database, perform the following steps:

◆ Create an ODBC data source that defines the connection to the database.

◆ Grant the user account permission to access the SMS database.

◆ Develop the ODBC application.

CREATING THE ODBC DATA SOURCE

You can create a new data source from the ODBC Control Panel applet. After you launch the applet, the dialog box shown in Figure 22.7 appears.

Figure 22.7.
The ODBC Data
Sources dialog
box.

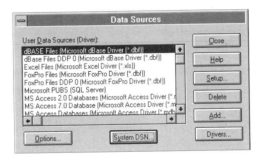

You use the Options button to provide a trace facility so that you can trace the ODBC calls made on your system for troubleshooting. In the ODBC Options dialog box that appears, you can enable or disable the trace facility and specify a file to contain this trace information.

Note

For additional information on how to install the ODBC utilities and set up a data source, refer to Chapters 31 through 33, which describe the steps in more detail for 16-bit and 32-bit client platforms.

You can use the System DSN button to install and configure data sources that can be used by all users of the system. The System Data Source dialog box appears, which looks similar to the ODBC Data Sources dialog box. Adding a system data source follows the same actions as described in the following procedure. The only difference is that data sources configured from this dialog box can be accessed by all users of the computer in the ODBC Data Sources dialog box, whereas the procedure that follows creates data sources for just the current user.

To create the ODBC data source to access your SMS database, follow these steps:

1. Click the Add button in the Data Sources dialog box. The Add Data Source dialog box appears.

2. Select the SQL Server entry and click the OK button. This displays the ODBC SQL Server Setup dialog box.

3. Click the Options button to expand the dialog box, as shown in Figure 22.8.

4. In the Data Source Name field, enter a name, such as SMS Database, which will be displayed in your ODBC-compliant application's Open Data Source dialog box.

5. In the Description field, enter a comment for the data source.

6. In the Server drop-down listbox, enter the name for your SQL Server installation that contains the SMS database. This varies from installation to installation.

7. In the Network Address field, specify the name of the SQL Server address to use. For SQL Server for Windows NT, this is a named pipe and is usually `\\ServerName\pipe\sql\query`, where `ServerName` is the computer name of your server. If you specified a different name for the pipe during the installation, specify that name in the Network Address field.

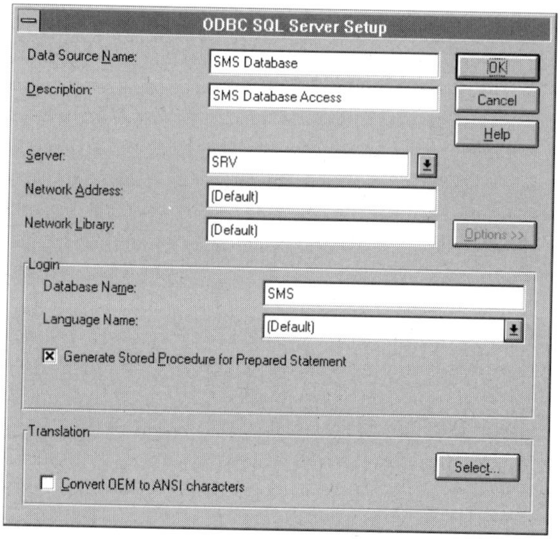

Figure 22.8.
The expanded
ODBC SQL
Server Setup
dialog box.

Note

If you specify (Default), as in Figure 22.8, the default driver library is used for your specified server.

8. In the Network Library field, specify the DB-LIB library dynamic library to be used for your connection. If you specify (Default), the network library specified in the SQL Client Configuration utility for your server name is used.

9. In the Database Name field, specify the SQL Server database name for your SMS database to use; the default for the SMS installation is SMS. This name is case-sensitive, so be sure to specify the correct name and case.

10. If you have installed the optional languages on the SQL Server (version 4.2 or later), you can specify an alternate language driver to use in the Language Name drop-down listbox.

11. The Generate Stored Procedure for Prepared Statement checkbox is a performance option to create stored procedures (precompiled procedures) on the SQL Server that are used by the ODBC drivers. Leave this checkbox enabled unless you are supporting multiple versions of ODBC and are having problems.

12. The Convert OEM to ANSI Characters option normally is disabled and is used to provide a code page translator between your client application and the SQL Server database. If you have a nonstandard code page, you can specify an alternative by clicking the Select button.

13. Click the OK button to add the new data source. You now are ready to access your SMS database from any ODBC-compliant application.

LIMITING ACCESS TO THE DATABASE

Before you develop your ODBC application, you should consider who will be using it. If these users are unsophisticated users, then you should limit access to all tables to prevent users from modifying the data. There are two ways to accomplish this task.

◆ You can use the SQL Security Manager, SQL Administrator, or ISQL command line to grant access to the SMS database and then use the SQL Object Manager to assign permissions for these users or groups of users.

◆ After a user is granted access to the SMS database, you can use the SMS Security Manager, as described earlier, to assign various access rights.

The key item to consider is preventing updates to these tables for all users who are unfamiliar with the structure of these tables. If you properly design your application, though, it is possible to manually update these tables. It is much easier and a great deal safer, however, to develop data-entry screens to just view the data. You also will want to develop your own stored procedures to minimize the risk of corrupting the data. You might even want to go so far as to create an entirely new database containing all the elements your ODBC application will use to access the SMS database. In this fashion, you can prevent direct access to the SMS database and avoid the possibility that it will be inadvertently corrupted.

Developing the Application

After you properly prepare the access to the SMS database, you can develop your application. The basic process to create an Access 7.0 database to access the SMS database follows:

◆ Create a repository to contain the objects. This is nothing more than a file or local database—sms.MDB, for example.

◆ Select the ODBC data source. From the Table tab, choose New | Link and select the ODBC Databases () entry in the Files of Type field. Then select the SMS database data source. The reason to choose a link (which just attaches the tables) instead of importing (which copies the tables and associated data) is that you are only using the Access database as a more user-friendly front end to the SQL Server database. You don't want to actually copy the SMS database to your local computer.

◆ Link to the tables contained within the data source. After you select the data source, you are prompted to select the tables to attach.

◆ Develop your data entry or, in this case, view forms. This is one of the more critical stages because it requires a knowledge of the structure of the SMS tables. In this stage, you are linking multiple tables and creating your view of the data. You do not need to include all the fields of the table—just those you need to view. If you plan to update the tables, you need to include all the fields.

◆ Develop your queries. This process is useful for developing predefined queries that can execute directly on the server for increased performance. But if sufficient permission is granted to the user, these queries also can create ad hoc queries for situations that you did not anticipate.

◆ Develop your reports. By predefining reports, the user can gather summary data in an easy-to-use fashion. These reports then can be exported or imported and used with other applications.

SUMMARY

This chapter's basic focus was on how to use SMS to manage your network applications, how to perform basic troubleshooting, and how to use ODBC to develop custom front ends to access the SMS database. You should remember that application servers are more versatile than the normal file server for sharing network applications. The only hitch is that Windows 95, OS/2, and Macintosh clients cannot dynamically connect to an application server or create a program group with SMS 1.1.

The remote troubleshooting tools are one of your most powerful tools for aiding a user. After all, you are not a gifted psychic and cannot read minds. But this tool can enable you to connect to a remote client over the network or RAS to see exactly what the user sees in order to diagnose a problem.

The Network Monitor is useful for basic network diagnostics in the hands of the novice, and is an extremely useful tool in the hands of an expert. When used with the Network Monitor Agent, you can perform remote packet captures and actually replace dedicated packet sniffers that cost $5,000 or more.

Finally, you can use ODBC and any ODBC-compliant application to connect to your SMS database and provide a more friendly front end. You can even use ODBC to access your database and include useful summary data in your monthly reports.

In the next chapter, you will learn about performance tips you can use to obtain the best possible performance from your SMS installation. You also will look at some of the Performance Monitor object counters you can use to obtain real-time statistics of your installation that can be useful in determining how well your site server is holding up under the strain.

22

MANAGING YOUR NETWORK

- Optimizing Windows NT Server

- Optimizing SQL Server

- Tuning Systems Management Server for Maximum Performance

CHAPTER 23

Optimizing Systems Management Server

Optimizing Systems Management Server (SMS) is a more complex task than optimizing other BackOffice components due to the complex nature of SMS. Most BackOffice components use a few applications that normally run as services to provide their functionality. SMS uses at least 15 services, however. This can place a serious burden on the host processor and memory subsystem (particularly in a multiprocessor system), even though the services execute in a staggered fashion to limit the amount of processor time they use. And like most other BackOffice components, SMS uses Windows NT Server as the base from which it sprouts to provide services to you (the network administrator). But unlike these other BackOffice components, it also relies on SQL Server for Windows NT as a storage medium. If Windows NT Server or SQL Server for Windows NT is not properly configured for optimum performance, SMS will not perform as well as it could.

This is why you'll look at some of the important issues relating to tuning both Windows NT Server and SQL Server for Windows NT before you turn your attention to tuning Systems Management Server. Many of the ideas will seem familiar to you, and they should if you have read the previous chapters already. This chapter only touches on these concepts, however. For an in-depth discussion of issues relating to tuning Windows NT Server, see Chapter 13, "Tuning Your Server." For issues relating to tuning SQL Server for Windows NT, see Chapter 18, "Optimizing SQL Server."

Only after the discussion of tuning the base components will you move on to tuning SMS for maximum performance. The key section describes how you can separate the various components to build a more efficient product. Even though this takes additional hardware, it is a worthwhile effort. Not everyone has the additional resources, however, so this chapter presents alternatives as well. This chapter also tells you how to use the Performance Monitor to perform a long-term analysis of SMS performance.

OPTIMIZING WINDOWS NT SERVER

You probably already know all the topics that will be discussed in this chapter and can spout them in your sleep. As they say, "Practice makes perfect," so it will not hurt to go over them one more time. Besides, you might learn something that you missed in the earlier chapters, and I really do want you to be able to build the best possible network server that you can.

The starting point to building an efficient server is choosing the best possible hardware before you install Windows NT Server. After you have done this, you can work on configuring the software for best performance. If you already have made your choice, or if someone has made it for you, you might want to skip the hardware discussion and move right on to configuring the software. I do recommend that you at least glance at the hardware options for possible future upgrade choices, though.

CHOOSING YOUR HARDWARE

When considering a platform for your server, always keep in mind two concepts. First, the fastest hardware will serve you best. Second, what is fastest today when you purchase it will not be the fastest tomorrow. Technology moves so fast in the computer world that it is almost impossible to keep up. Replacing complete systems is costly in terms of finances as well as time, and your time is a valuable commodity. For these reasons and many more, consider a hardware platform only with these specific attributes:

◆ Upgradable processor: Some systems are designed specifically for a single processor running at a specific processor speed. Although less expensive to purchase, they are a poor choice. This is because today's processors come in several speeds, with faster ones announced every couple of months. Replacing a processor is much cheaper than replacing an entire system later. So look for systems with motherboards that can support systems from 75MHz up to 200MHz (or higher).

Note

You should be concerned with low-end processor speed because you will need to support future clock-doubling, clock-tripling, and clock-quadrupling processors. These processors can be used only if your motherboard supports an appropriate processor bus speed. The greater your flexibility in this area, the greater your chance of being able to use an unannounced processor when it finally does become available.

◆ Upgradable to multiprocessor: Although a faster processor improves performance, sometimes you can achieve better results by adding an additional processor or two rather than increasing processor speed. So consider systems that are upgradable to a multiprocessor model, particularly because adding an additional processor of a later model CPU (like a Pentium 120) usually is cheaper than upgrading to the fastest model processor (like a Pentium 133/150) that is supported.

◆ Upgradable memory: Nothing—and I do mean nothing—is more important for overall performance than having sufficient physical memory in your system. Depending on the type of memory SIMMs (30 – 72 pin) you should consider only systems with sixteen (30) or four to eight (72) slots. Although you can use systems with fewer banks, it may cause you problems later.

Most 30-pin banks can support only 16MB SIMMs, which means that each
bank of four slots can support up to 64MB. However, some 72-pin SIMMs
can support 32MB or 64MB per slot, which can provide a maximum of
128MB to 256MB (512MB if it supports 64MB SIMMs). No matter what
memory type you use, try to consider only systems that support a minimum
of 128MB, and preferably systems that support 256MB or more.

Tip

> Many newer systems support Enhanced Data Out (EDO) SIMMs,
> which are faster than standard SIMMs and offer the capability to read
> larger blocks of data without a refresh cycle.

◆ Upgradable cache: Most of today's systems include a 256KB cache, and
some include a 512KB cache. But you should see whether your cache is
upgradable to 1MB or more for best performance.

◆ Wide I/O expansion bus: Your new server should have a PCI bus rather
than a VLB bus for maximum performance. Most PCI- and VLB-based
systems support only three of these expansion slots as their primary
expansion buses, however. The remainder of the secondary expansion buses
are usually ISA expansion slots. Although ISA is fine for some adapters, it
severely limits your performance options. Instead, consider EISA for your
secondary expansion bus. EISA is a true 32-bit, bus-mastering expansion
bus and provides a wide selection of secondary network, disk, and communications adapters.

◆ Fast and upgradable disk subsystem: Your disk subsystem is critical to
providing outstanding performance on a system designed to support SMS.
If you have a choice, choose a SCSI-based system—preferably, a fast wide
SCSI-based system, because it is easily expandable and provides asynchronous I/O, command queuing, and a detachable I/O bus. If you can't use
SCSI, then try an EIDE-based system. Some EIDE controllers can provide
similar benefits. If all else fails, add additional disk drives. Multiple drives
still can provide additional performance over a single drive by dividing the
various component (NT Server system files, paging files, SMS files, and
SQL Server files) locations among these drives.

◆ Network adapters: Choose the fastest possible network adapter. These are
generally PCI, VLB, or EISA. Look for a bus-mastering adapter with a
memory-mapped I/O buffer for best performance. Consider using more than
one network adapter to segment your network based on network protocols
to increase efficiency.

◆ Network topology: When possible, use fiber-optic or fast Ethernet as your network backbone. If network traffic increases to above 50 percent of your available network bandwidth, consider splitting the network segment.

Tip

For even better performance you could use a network switch instead of standard hub. The hub could be connected to the server using a 100Mbps connection while providing a 10Mbps connection for your network clients.

CONFIGURING THE SOFTWARE

Because Windows NT Server is fairly good at self tuning, there is not much you can do in this area. That doesn't mean that there is nothing you can do to increase performance, however. You can use the following suggestions to increase performance:

◆ Configure the Server service (via the Network Control Panel applet) to maximize throughput for network applications. This configuration favors using system memory for processes rather than the system cache. It allocates additional nonpageable buffers, which are used to increase your server's capability to authenticate users, to increase network response time, and to be used by SMS internally to increase performance.

◆ Configure the system (via the System Control Panel applet) to make the foreground and background applications equally responsive. This ensures that all processes receive equal amounts of processor time and provides a better overall base for SMS.

◆ Finally, do not install additional services not required by the installation. Although you may need the Gateway Services for NetWare or Services for Macintosh to support your NetWare and Macintosh clients, for example, don't install the DHCP, WINS, FTP, or other services. Although these services provide additional functionality, they also require additional resources.

OPTIMIZING SQL SERVER

Getting the most out of SQL Server for SMS is a little different than optimizing general SQL Server performance—but not by much. You still should start by optimizing your basic Windows NT Server platform, as described in the preceding section. After you cover those areas, you should consider the following:

◆ Add additional memory: SQL Server is not a memory hog and operates in a minimum configuration (16MB of total RAM), but it certainly will not perform up to your expectations. You will achieve better performance in a system with 32MB, 64MB, or even more. You will not achieve the performance you expect unless you also configure SQL Server to use it properly, and this is where the next step comes in.

◆ Configure SQL Server: You can configure several options to improve performance. You can set these by using the SQL Administrator or the ISQL command sp_configure for a SQL Server 4.21 installation. Or you can use the SQL Enterprise Manager if you are using SQL 6.x.

Note

For the specific range of values and how to set these values, refer to "Configuring SQL Server" in Chapter 18.

The options you should set, in order of preference, follow:

Memory: Specifies the amount of memory, in 2KB units, to be used by SQL Server. The basic idea is to allocate as much physical memory as possible for SQL Server's use. You should leave a minimum of 16MB of physical RAM for Windows NT Server, however, plus 2MB for each additional service. If you have Services for Macintosh running, for example, you should leave 18MB for the base system. Be sure not to allocate more RAM to SQL Server than you have physically installed. Otherwise, you will use virtual memory, which will wind up decreasing overall performance.

Note

If you will be installing SMS on the same server, be sure to leave at least 4MB free for the Systems Management Server components.

tempdb in ram: Specifies that the temporary database is stored in RAM instead of a physical disk. The temporary database is constantly in use for temporary objects (tables, procedures, sorts, and so on).

Warning

Use the tempdb in RAM option with care, because when you do set it to RAM and increase the size beyond the default of 2MB, it may be difficult to reset it to use a disk storage device. This occurs because when you switch from a database stored on a physical device to RAM and then extend the database, it does not physically extend the allocation of the database on the device. So if you do plan to swap to RAM and then possibly back again, do this only if you first extend tempdb on a physical device first. Then never increase the size of tempdb, unless you first reset tempdb in RAM to Off (0), restart SQL Server for the changes to be applied, increase the size of tempdb, and then reset tempdb in RAM to On (1).

max async IO: Specifies the maximum number of asynchronous I/O requests that can be issued by SQL Server. If you have a stripe set, a stripe set with parity, or a RAID 5 hardware array, increase this value.

max worker threads: Specifies the maximum number of threads SQL Server can use to support client connections and perform internal maintenance. Increase this value if you have more than one processor installed on the system.

pre-read packets: Specifies the maximum number of network packets to read ahead. Increasing this value may increase performance, but this varies from system to system.

◆ Use a multiprocessor system: SQL Server is a processor-intensive application. It benefits from a multiprocessor-based system. If you do install SQL Server on an SMP platform, be sure to enable the SMP support in the SQL Setup application. This maximizes the potential performance increase by configuring SQL Server to use only a specific processor.

◆ Use a stripe set or stripe set with parity: SQL Server is very I/O intensive, as well as processor intensive. It can benefit from a fast disk subsystem by spreading the load among that subsystem to multiple drives. If your budget can accommodate it, use a hardware-based RAID 5 disk subsystem.

◆ Separate your SQL Server and SMS databases: If you do not have a stripe set, stripe set with parity, or RAID 5 drive array, at the very least, separate your SQL Server devices from your SMS devices. Because your databases use these devices to physically store their data, you can spread the load by placing these devices on physically separate drives and increase performance.

TUNING SYSTEMS MANAGEMENT SERVER FOR MAXIMUM PERFORMANCE

There are several methods of installing Systems Management Server. Each of these equations has its own plus and minus sides to provide a stable and efficient platform.

You can install all the various components on a single server or split them up between two or more servers. Each of these options implies certain trade-offs you should consider while attempting to obtain the greatest performance. Although I can tell you about these various trade-offs, only you can determine the best method to implement for your network.

In this section, you'll look at the various methods you can use to separate the various SMS components to build a better solution. It is not a requirement that you separate these components, however, and, in some cases, it is not desirable or even possible for you to separate the components. So this section takes a look at several possibilities and points out both the good and the bad sides of each possible solution.

Your final stop will be a look at the performance counters you can use with the Performance Monitor to help you determine how well your solution is working. Even though SMS does not have any of its own performance counters, there are still counters you can use to provide you with useful information.

DIVIDING AND CONQUERING

Although I recommend separating the primary components of SMS (SQL Server for Windows NT, Systems Management Server, and the various SMS services), this is not always the best solution. It really depends on the hardware configuration you are using and how well it can withstand the load imposed on it by the various components. If you have a superserver (a multiprocessing server with four or more processors, a hardware RAID 5 array, and 128MB to 256MB of RAM), a single server might be able to perform every task you put to it with outstanding performance. If you are using your standard uniprocessor servers, however, you might want to consider breaking up the components to provide a better overall solution. The uniprocessor model is the scenario you will be considering for the rest of this discussion.

Sometimes you cannot divide the components due to a lack of physical resources or because you have insufficient network bandwidth to support this type of configuration. This is why you will first look at providing the best possible configuration on a single server. Next, you will look at how you can use multiple servers to provide a single logical system. This configuration normally outperforms a single system, but it does so only if the individual components are configured properly and if these individual systems have sufficient resources. Your final stop in this area will be a look at dividing the various SMS services among several servers in an effort to spread the load even further. Although this particular method may not always outperform separate servers, it usually provides a more uniform response.

USING A SINGLE SYSTEM

When you install SMS, it must be on a primary domain controller or a backup domain controller. If it is possible, do not install it on a primary domain controller. A primary controller has enough work to do replicating the account database, maintaining trust relationships, and authenticating users, so if you do install SQL Server and SMS on it, you may impact your entire network in a negative fashion. If you overload your primary domain controller, the user administration you perform may not be replicated quickly enough, which may cause user-authentication problems across your entire network. Or performance may degrade so much that your network clients may scream for a pound or two of your flesh. Instead, use a backup domain controller that you can dedicate completely to SQL Server and SMS. If this particular server still has enough processor time to authenticate users, consider it a bonus.

The next part of your optimization struggle should be to follow the ideas presented in optimizing your server and then your SQL Server configurations. Only when these are operating as well as possible should you consider further optimizations. The primary areas you should be concerned with follow:

◆ Adding more memory: I know you are tired of hearing this one, but it is still true that the most significant optimization technique you can use is to make sure that your system pages as infrequently as possible. A single server should have at least 64MB of RAM, and if it is possible, shoot for 128MB of RAM. If you allocate 32MB to 48MB of RAM to SQL Server, and at least 16MB of RAM for the temporary database, then your system will perform well and SMS queries will be quite fast to nearly instantaneous, depending on the size of your network.

Note

A minimum configuration for a primary site that includes SQL Server is 28MB of RAM. For a secondary site without SQL Server, you can get by with as little as 20MB of RAM. However, this is for a bare-bones server or one that does not include DHCP, WINS, Service for Macintosh, Gateway Services for NetWare, or other add-ons. If you will be adding any of these additional components, plan on adding at least another 2MB of RAM for each component.

◆ Increasing your paging file size: Even with sufficient physical RAM, you will find that your system peaks and then must page to disk. Even though NT Server automatically grows the paging file to a size large enough to handle the load, it is better to preallocate your paging file because a lot of overhead is involved in expanding the paging file.

Tip

The best place for your paging file is on a stripe set because it increases read/write performance by spreading the number of asynchronous I/O among the disks that create the stripe. Choose at least three to five drives to create the stripe set. These stripes do not have to be large—each can be from 50MB to 100MB, depending on the number of physical drives and the total load of the server. I prefer to create a drive in the 250MB-to-500MB size, which is usually more than adequate. You may need to create a drive in the 500MB-to-1000MB range if you have insufficient physical RAM or place higher loads on your server, however.

Note

You should not use a stripe set with parity because a paging file is not mission-critical data, so using a stripe set with parity just adds overhead as it creates the parity block.

◆ Adding additional processors: A uniprocessor system does not perform as well as a multiprocessor system when all the SMS components are installed on a single system. To obtain the best possible performance, plan on a dual or quad processor system and then dedicate at least one processor to SQL Server by enabling the Multiprocessor Support option.

◆ Adding additional network adapters: If you will be supporting several protocols for your network clients, use one network adapter per protocol (NetBEUI, IPX/SPX, TCP/IP, AppleTalk, and so on) for best performance.

USING MULTIPLE SYSTEMS

Using multiple systems builds on the previous optimization techniques for Windows NT Server, SQL Server for Windows NT, and the preceding section. The only difference is that you will dedicate two servers for SMS. One of these must be a backup controller, and this is where SMS should be installed. The other should be a backup domain controller or, preferably, a Windows NT Server operating in server mode where you will install SQL Server. Both these servers should be on a fast (100Mb) backbone to facilitate user authentication and data transfers.

Note

You want to use Windows NT Server operating in server mode because it has the least amount of overhead and because it does not participate in user authentication or account replication. It therefore can provide superior performance as a base platform for SQL Server.

For a backup domain controller with SMS, you should consider the following:

◆ It should be dedicated to Systems Management Server. It should not provide any other shared resources. Although you can use it to provide additional services, this may degrade performance based on the size of your network.

◆ You should have a single Pentium or better processor. The faster the processor, the better your ability to provide additional services other than SMS to your network clients.

◆ You should have a minimum of 32MB of RAM. This limits the amount of paging that will occur and provides a good base for SMS.

For a server with SQL Server, consider the following items:

◆ Dedicate it to SQL Server. This server should provide no other shared resources other than SQL Server. For best performance, this installation should not provide any other databases to any other network clients.

Note

If your SQL Server installation is a multiprocessor system with sufficient resources, you can provide additional databases for your network clients. This probably will not degrade SMS performance too much. If your database is used heavily or it uses queries that place a high load on SQL Server, however, it probably will degrade SMS performance. This is a trade-off you must consider based on your individual needs.

◆ Use a multiprocessor system. Use at least a dual-processor system and enable the dedicated processor support in SQL Server to provide the fastest response time.

◆ Allocate a minimum of 64MB of RAM. The more you plan to use SQL Server for additional services, the more memory you need to achieve the same level of performance. This memory should be configured in three ways: first, to be used specifically by SQL Server (32MB is a good starting point); second, to be used for the SQL Server temporary (tempdb) database (8MB or more); third, to be used by the system cache to cache file and network I/O (the remainder after Windows NT Server allocates its needs).

23

OPTIMIZING SYSTEMS MANAGEMENT SERVER

Tip

If you plan to use this installation for more than SMS, consider a system with at least 128MB of RAM. If you will have large databases with many users, consider using 256MB of RAM. The biggest gains come from allocating sufficient memory for SQL Server (64MB or more) and making the temporary database as large as will fit into the remaining amount of RAM. The size of your temporary database and the allocations between SQL Server and this temporary database are dependent on the type of use you plan to make of it. For large sorts or intermediate queries, you want to allocate RAM to the temporary database. For large procedures or large numbers of users, you want to allocate additional RAM to SQL Server. The performance counters you will look at a little later can help you make this determination.

SPREADING THE LOAD

One of the more interesting aspects of SMS is that it is a collection of services. And not all these services must be executed on the server where SMS is installed. You therefore can spread the load imposed by SMS among several servers. If you choose servers that have sufficient free processor cycles and sufficient storage space, you can improve overall performance. This does not magically improve the situation, however, because it is a trade-off between processor cycles (server performance) and network bandwidth. As long as your servers are all on a 100Mb network backbone, you should not see much degradation at all. But if you have servers on a 10Mb segment or a WAN link, this can eat up a lot of your available bandwidth and can cause a noticeable client-performance problem.

To move a service, follow these steps:

1. Open the Sites window, select the site, and choose File | Properties to display the Site Properties dialog box. Then click the Services button to display the Services dialog box shown in Figure 23.1.

Figure 23.1.
Moving a service
to another server.

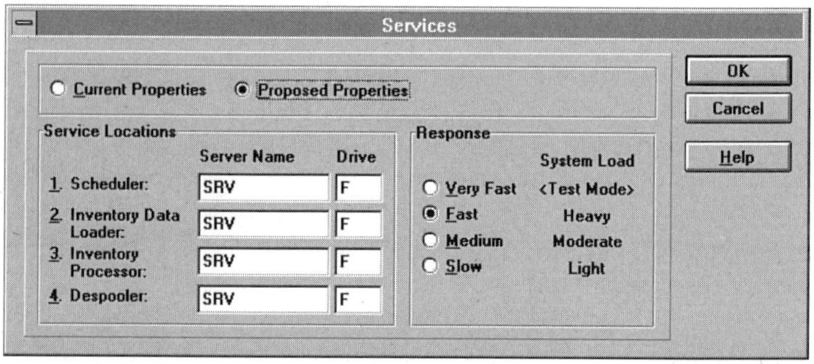

2. Select the Proposed Properties radio button, which then enables the Service Locations fields so that you can modify the location of the following services:

- ◆ Scheduler: This service monitors the site database (and the `SITE.SRV\SCHEDULE.BOX` directory) for jobs. It processes these jobs by compressing the packages, creating send requests, and creating despooler instruction files. The compression of these packages can place a significant load on the server, so by moving this service to another server, you can gain a significant performance improvement.

Tip

If you installed SQL Server on a separate platform and it has sufficient processor cycles and disk storage, you can get the best performance (because the site database is a SQL Server database) by installing the Scheduler service on the same server.

Note

Job compression requires a significant amount of disk storage. So wherever you install the Scheduler service, make sure that there is sufficient free space to accommodate your needs.

- ◆ Inventory Data Loader: This service monitors the `SITE.SRV\ DATALOAD.BOX\DELTAMIF.COL` directory for MIFs (used for computer inventories, status, and events) used to update the site database. This is not a high processor cycle service, but if you need to, you can move it to improve performance on an overloaded server. If you do move it, you should move it to the same server that contains SQL Server.

- ◆ Inventory Processor: This service monitors the `SITE.SRV\INVENTORY.BOX` directory for RAW files (which are used in the computer inventory process and objects with custom architectures). These RAW files then are processed into MIFs for the Inventory Data Loader. It is not a processor-intensive service, but it can be moved if required.

- ◆ Despooler: This service monitors the `SITE.SRV\DESPOOLER.BOX\RECEIVE` directory for instruction files and compressed packages created by the Scheduler service. It then uncompresses the files in order to create a package that will be installed on your distribution servers. This process places a heavy load on the processor, and you can gain a significant performance improvement by placing this service on another server.

Note

> Package decompression requires a significant amount of disk storage.
> So make sure that there is sufficient free space to accommodate
> your needs.

3. In the Server Name field, enter the name of the server where the service will be relocated.

4. In the Drive field, enter the drive letter of the remote server where the service will be installed.

5. Repeat steps 3 and 4 for each service you want to relocate, and then click the OK button.

You can further decrease the load on your server by specifying a different value in the Response group. This value is used to determine the polling rate (the rate at which the services check for status conditions and updates) of the standard services (Site Hierarchy Manager, SMS Alerter, SMS Scheduler, and Applications Manager), as well as the Site Configuration Manager, Maintenance Manager, and Despooler services. Table 23.1 summarizes the polling interval (in minutes) based on the Response setting.

TABLE 23.1. RESPONSE RATES TO POLLING INTERVALS.

Response	Standard Service	Site Configuration Manager	Maintenance Manager	Despooler
Very Fast	1	12	24	24
Fast	5	60	120	120
Medium	15	60	120	120
Slow	30	360	720	720

USING PERFORMANCE MONITOR TO TUNE SYSTEMS MANAGEMENT SERVER

The Performance Monitor is discussed in detail elsewhere in this book, so instead of repeating myself here and boring you to tears, I'll refer you to the other chapters for specifics on how to use the Performance Monitor. The counters of interest to you to help maximize your SMS performance follow:

◆ System | % Total Processor Time: Percentage of processor time currently in use on your system. If this value constantly is above 80 percent, you should consider getting a faster processor, adding an additional processor, or spreading the load.

◆ System | Processor Queue Length: The number of threads waiting in the processor queue for processor cycles. A consistent value of 2 or higher indicates a processor bottleneck that may be alleviated by adding additional processors or by spreading the load. This value always is 0 unless at least one thread is being monitored.

◆ Memory | Pages/sec: The number of pages read from or written to disk to resolve memory references to pages that were not in physical memory at the time. A high value indicates that additional physical memory will improve performance by decreasing the amount of paging that occurs. It also may indicate that you are paging because you have not allocated your memory as efficiently as you could. You may have allocated too much memory to SQL Server or to the temporary database (tempdb), for example.

◆ Memory | Page Faults/sec: The number of virtual memory page faults that occurred on the system because the physical page was not in the process's working set or main memory. A page may not need to be read from disk if the page is available on the standby list or is in use by another process that shares the page and has it in its working set.

◆ Memory | Cache Faults/sec: The number of page faults that occur in the Cache Manager in reference to a memory page that is not in the cache. A high value here indicates that adding additional memory will improve I/O response time.

◆ Paging File | % Usage Peak | Per Page File: The maximum use of a specific page file. A constant high value (between 50 and 75 percent) is an indication that you should increase the size of your paging file, create another paging file on another drive, or add additional physical RAM.

◆ Network Interface | Current Bandwidth | Per Interface: An estimated value of the current network utilization in bits per second.

◆ Network Segment | Network Utilization | Per Adapter: An estimated value of the percentage of the network bandwidth currently in use on the network segment.

◆ Redirector | Current Commands: The number of outstanding network requests waiting to be serviced. If this number is greater than the number of network adapters installed in the computer, a network bottleneck is present. Adding an additional network adapter may increase performance.

◆ PhysicalDisk | Disk Queue Length | DiskInstance: Indicates how many pending I/O requests are waiting to be serviced. If this value is greater than 2, it indicates a disk bottleneck. On a multidisk subsystem, such as a stripe

23

OPTIMIZING SYSTEMS MANAGEMENT SERVER

set or stripe set with parity, a little calculating is in order to determine whether a disk bottleneck is occurring. The basic formula follows:

```
Disk Queue Length - Number of Physical Disk Drives in MultiDisk Configuration
```

If this value is greater than 2, a disk bottleneck is indicated. If you have a stripe set with three disk drives and a queue length of five, for example, then 5 - 3 = 2. And 2 is an acceptable value.

◆ SQLServer | I/O Log Writes/sec: Specifies the number of log pages written to disk per second. Note that because almost all database activity is transaction based, which means that the changes must be written to the log before they can be applied to the database, this is a good counter to watch to determine whether your disk is a bottleneck for SQL Server performance.

◆ SQLServer | I/O Batch Writes/sec: Specifies the number of asynchronous writes in a single batch (generally as part of the checkpoint process). The higher the value, the better the SQL Server performance. Monitor this value as you make changes to segment and device allocations to see whether your changes are increasing or decreasing performance.

◆ SQLServer | I/O Batch Average Size: Specifies the average number of pages (2KB) written to disk during a batch operation. The higher the value, the better. You can use this counter to determine whether your changes to the max async i/o parameter are effective. If you increase the max async i/o value too much, this counter will decrease, which indicates that you set the max async i/o value too high.

◆ SQLServer | I/O Batch Max Size: Specifies the maximum number of pages (2KB) that have been written to disk. The higher the value, the better the overall performance. This counter also can be used to determine whether the max async i/o parameter setting is effective. If this counter lowers after your changes, decrease the value for the max async i/o parameter.

◆ SQLServer | Cache Hit Ratio: Specifies the percentage of time that requested data was found in the data cache. The higher the value, the better. If your hit rate routinely drops below 60 – 70 percent, then increasing the size of the data cache may improve SQL Server performance.

◆ SQLServer | Network Command Queue Length: Specifies the number of outstanding client requests waiting to be serviced by the SQL Server worker threads. A higher value is an indication that increasing the number of worker threads may improve performance. If performance does not increase, it may be an indication that the processor is a bottleneck, and adding an additional processor may increase overall throughput.

◆ SQLServer-Log | Log Space Used (%) | SMS: Specifies the amount (in a percentage) of the transaction log for the SMS database currently in use.

Note

These counters are not the only counters you should use to determine how well your system is performing or where a bottleneck may be. These are just some of the available counters that can give you a quick indication of your overall performance. For an in-depth look at determining the performance of your systems, you should refer to Chapter 13 for the basics and Chapter 18 for an all-inclusive list of counters for SQL Server.

Summary

In this chapter, you considered various aspects to obtain the best possible performance Systems Management Server. You should remember the following key concepts:

Tune for server performance first. Because Windows NT Server is the foundation on which you will install SQL Server and Systems Management Server, you should make sure that it is properly configured and as optimized as possible before installing additional components.

Tune for SQL Server performance second. SQL Server performance really can be defined by two components: processor speed and how much memory you will devote to SQL Server and its temporary database.

Tune for SMS performance last. Use separate dedicated computers for SMS and SQL Server. If you can, split off the additional service to other computers to spread the compression/decompression services and lessen the load on the site server.

The next chapter introduces you to Microsoft Mail. This discussion explores some of the types of e-mail systems that are widely available and looks closely at how Microsoft Mail actually works.

PART V

Microsoft Mail and Microsoft Exchange Server

- What Is Electronic Mail?

- Introduction to Microsoft Exchange Server

CHAPTER 24

Introduction to Microsoft Mail and Exchange Server

This chapter covers the basics of electronic mail (e-mail) by introducing you to some basic concepts and nomenclature. It compares and contrasts different ways in which electronic mail is exchanged to give you a broader view of how various e-mail systems work. During this discussion you will learn how a basic e-mail system sends messages from one user to another user and the difference between how messages are processed by Microsoft Mail and Exchange Server.

The purpose of this chapter is to give you an understanding of several facets of Microsoft Mail and its replacement, Exchange Server. While this chapter could just discuss Exchange Server, that would be a disservice to you, as Exchange Server is not for everyone. If you have a small set of users to support, and you do not need to route messages between postoffices, you might want to consider using the Workgroup Postoffice that is included in the base Windows NT Server package. Creating and managing a Workgroup Postoffice is discussed in Chapter 8, "Additional Administrative Tools." This chapter focuses more on using Microsoft Mail and Exchange Server. It will help you make an informed decision when purchasing and planning your e-mail implementation. It will point out the benefits of using a particular e-mail system that will help you to optimize performance at your particular installation.

WHAT IS ELECTRONIC MAIL?

If you are a new administrator, you may not be familiar with the basic e-mail system concept. The basic idea is the capability to use a software program on your computer to provide a way for people to exchange messages. These messages are generically referred to as electronic mail or e-mail. You may already have used an e-mail system such as that provided by CompuServe, America Online, The Microsoft Network, or other on-line service. In the following section you will examine how some of these various e-mail systems connect to each other to point out the differences between an on-line service (such as CompuServe) and a local area network e-mail service. Once you have looked at the basic methodology of connecting an e-mail system, you will learn how an e-mail system actually sends messages from one system to another.

GENERAL METHODS OF CONNECTION

Fundamentally, an e-mail system requires some sort of link between the various computers. This link can be by local area network (LAN), by wide area network (WAN), or by remote access into a network via modem or other means. Most e-mail systems provide the capability to transfer e-mail over more than one of these media. In fact, this becomes a central issue when marketing the product. An e-mail system that simply allows you to exchange e-mail over a LAN may be fine, but maybe a user needs more. It could be at a competitive disadvantage when compared to a system that lets you exchange e-mail over both a LAN and a WAN, for example. Of course, with our mobile society, adding support for remote users becomes another valuable feature of e-mail software. You will have to decide which features best fit the requirements of your organization.

EXAMPLE E-MAIL SYSTEMS

Some e-mail systems are simply software that runs on top of your existing network topology. Microsoft Mail, Microsoft Exchange Server, and Lotus cc:Mail are examples of these. They can run on networks that use TCP/IP, NetBIOS, IPX, or whatever transport is supported by your network operating system. Figure 24.1 demonstrates how Microsoft Mail is implemented on a Windows NT network. In the case of Microsoft Exchange Server, it is tightly integrated with Microsoft Windows NT Server, so whatever type of network you set up based on Windows NT Server, Microsoft Exchange Server will fit seamlessly on top of it.

Figure 24.1.
Microsoft Mail
on a typical
Microsoft
Windows NT
network.

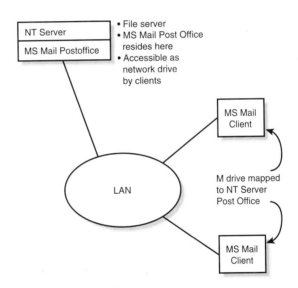

Note

Although classified with Microsoft Mail and Lotus cc:Mail here, Microsoft Exchange Server is vastly different from and superior to those products both in architecture and in implementation. Some of the differences are covered later in this chapter.

BANYAN VINES MAIL

Another type of e-mail system is one that is integrated as part of a network operating system. (See Figure 24.2.) Banyan VINES is one example of a network operating

24

system that provides an e-mail system. With Banyan VINES, when installing the server software on a machine, one of the options is to install a mail service. In this way, the capability to communicate via e-mail is integrated in the networking software. It doesn't matter if you have one server or 100—the VINES messaging system takes care of routing your e-mail properly.

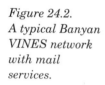

Figure 24.2.
A typical Banyan
VINES network
with mail
services.

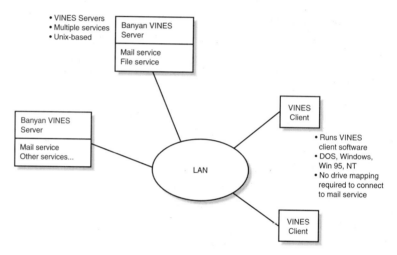

Windows NT is like this to a very limited degree with its built-in Workgroup Postoffice (WGPO). However, WGPO is rudimentary in its feature set because it is basically a subset of Microsoft Mail. Additionally, WGPO does not have any provision for routing mail to other WGPO postoffices. This means you are limited to a single postoffice on your network if you want everyone to be able to share e-mail. This also means that you cannot send e-mail (such as Internet e-mail) outside of your network.

COMPUSERVE MAIL

Other e-mail systems are networks that you connect to remotely. CompuServe, America Online, and The Microsoft Network, are such systems. (See Figure 24.3.) Typically, you use your modem to dial into a local node, and that gets you onto the network. From there, you can do a number of things—one of which is sending and receiving e-mail.

Because CompuServe is really text-based, client software is available to make the environment easier to use. The client software for Microsoft Windows users is called WinCIM. While connected to CompuServe, WinCIM becomes your work environment, part of which is the e-mail interface. You use this software as your link to the CompuServe network for sending and receiving e-mail, in addition to interacting with the service.

Figure 24.3.
CompuServe
mail.

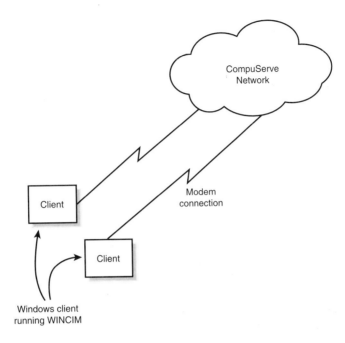

Technically speaking, at its core the CompuServe mail system is probably not too different from the systems discussed earlier. This is a case in which its implementation makes it look much different, however, because it is most often used remotely rather than in a LAN-type environment.

MICROSOFT MAIL

Microsoft Mail is the enhanced version of the Workgroup Postoffice. Or to put this another way, a Workgroup Postoffice is a subset of Microsoft Mail. It uses a set of shared directories to exchange e-mail, store the global address list, and other relevant information. The actual message processing, however, is performed by the client mail application. You will look at these features in more detail in the following sections. For now, I would like to point out a couple of benefits of using Microsoft Mail.

First, since Microsoft Mail is based on a set of shared directories, it requires fewer processor and memory resources than Exchange Server. This relates directly to the second reason to use Microsoft Mail. For a small number of users, or if you are on a tight budget, Microsoft Mail might be a better solution, as you can use Microsoft Mail on older and slower computers. As long as a computer can share a directory, it can be used to store your postoffice files. You can even put your shared directory on a Novell server, a UNIX server, a Windows for Workgroups server, a Windows 95 server, or any other server that your Microsoft Mail clients can access.

24

MICROSOFT MAIL AND EXCHANGE SERVER

SHARED DIRECTORIES

You might be wondering exactly how Microsoft Mail stores and manages all the information in a postoffice. It is accomplished through a shared file system. In other words, the postoffice files must reside on a file server on your network. Figure 24.4 shows a typical single postoffice configuration.

Figure 24.4.
A single Microsoft
Mail postoffice
configuration.

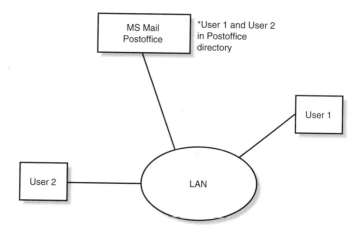

Although this method certainly shows the product's age, it is still a fairly effective way of accomplishing the task of exchanging e-mail. Unfortunately, an undesirable side effect is the complexities that lie in the actual implementation of a mail server that uses a shared directory structure. Every mail client, for example, needs direct access to the subdirectories, which means that an uninformed Microsoft Mail user might run amok and delete data contained in these subdirectories. This is not good! It also means that the computer that is sharing these directories might be a choke point—if too many clients access the directories simultaneously, the hard disk may be unable to keep up with the demand of supplying the data to these clients.

Note

The successor to Microsoft Mail, Microsoft Exchange Server, implements true client-server capabilities in a mail package. This brings more modern e-mail capabilities to the user. See the following section, "What Is MS Exchange Server?" for more details about this type of implementation.

A Microsoft Mail postoffice is composed of a postoffice directory, located on a file server, which is accessible by the user's mail client software. Within the postoffice directory are 19 subdirectories, which are listed in Table 24.1.

Table 24.1. The directory structure of a workgroup postoffice.

Subdirectory	Description
ATT	Contains attachment files for e-mail messages. You will see a number of directories under this—AT0, AT1, and so on. These are strictly for file distribution, so the directory limit for the number of files (imposed by DOS) is not reached.
CAL	Contains Schedule+ calendar files.
FOLDERS	Contains local and public folders for each user in the LOC and PUB subdirectories, respectively.
GLB	Contains the global system files for Microsoft Mail. This is a very crucial directory for a postoffice because it describes the postoffice and what it can do. It contains the postoffice name, serial number, user login and account information, modem connection information, directory synchronization records, and so on.
GRP	Contains local group files and their pointers to mailbags.
HLP	Contains DOS-based Help files for the administrative programs.
INF	Contains per-user information files.
INI	Contains system initialization files used for special Microsoft Mail settings (configuration for EXTERNAL, for example).
KEY	Corresponding file to the MBG (mailbag) file, a KEY file contains counts of unread and new mail along with a record of deleted mail items. It points to which of the 4,096 entries in the MBG files have something in them.
LOG	Contains Microsoft Mail logs for anything that performs logging (EXTERNAL and directory synchronization, for example).
MAI	Contains the actual mail message contents. You will see a number of directories under this—MA0, MA1, and so on. These are strictly for file distribution, so the directory limit for the number of files (imposed by DOS) is not reached.
MBG	Contains the user mailbag files. All the mail headers (up to 4,096) for each user's messages are stored in a MBG file in this directory.
MEM	Pointers to mailbags. These are group related—these files work with the files in GRP.

continues

TABLE 24.1. CONTINUED

Subdirectory	Description
MMF	Contains MMF files. In the Windows and OS/2 Presentation Manager clients, each MMF file contains all the user's messages, inbox, personal folders, and so on. This file is kept by default on the user's local machine, or it can be stored in this directory in the postoffice.
NME	Contains pointer files for the name alias address lists.
P1	Contains envelope information for mail to be routed off the postoffice. EXTERNAL uses this.
TPL	Contains template files.
USR	Contains per-user personal groups for when you define you own private groups.
XTN	Contains external postoffice routing and configuration information.

THE MAIL CLIENT DOES THE WORK

Bear in mind that the Microsoft Mail postoffice is a temporary message store. It holds a message until a user's mail client software retrieves it. Then the message gets stored locally in the user's MMF file (if using the Microsoft Mail client for Windows) and deleted from the postoffice. It is important to understand that the postoffice is a passive entity. In other words, the Microsoft Mail client is doing the real work of routing mail. The postoffice is just a file repository for the mail client to use while shuffling files around.

The exception to this is in a multiple postoffice scenario. The EXTERNAL program, running on a separate machine or in a separate process in a multitasking operating system, has the job of routing mail between servers. In a single postoffice scenario, all the work is done by the mail client.

STORE-AND-FORWARD

Store-and-forward is a term that is fundamental to understanding how e-mail systems, in general, work. It is also fundamental in understanding how Microsoft Mail and Exchange Server work, because both systems are store-and-forward mail systems.

The idea is this: Sent mail is stored in a location until it is determined when and if it should be forwarded to another storage location on the way to its destination. If it doesn't need to be forwarded anymore, the e-mail stays where it is until someone comes to get it. It's a pretty simple concept. In fact, you deal with it every day with your own U.S. postal system.

I'll use the U.S. postal system as an analogy as you look at two examples of mail routing to get the idea. First, you'll see a simple example of mail routing. In the second example, you'll see a more complex example. Both scenarios can be used to demonstrate how e-mail is routed in Microsoft Mail.

POST OFFICE EXAMPLE 1

Suppose that Shelly wants to send Velma a birthday card. Velma lives in the same town as Shelly. After Shelly seals the birthday greeting in the envelope, she writes Velma's address on the outside. Then Shelly drops the mail into her mailbox, where it will be picked up and taken to the local post office. After the mail gets to the post office, a routing decision has to be made. Based on the address, the postal system knows this piece of mail does not need to go any farther than this post office. Why? Because Velma, the recipient, receives her mail from this post office. So the local post office knows that this piece of mail does not get forwarded any further; it simply gets delivered to Velma's mailbox, where it is stored until she picks it up. This scenario is illustrated in Figure 24.5.

Figure 24.5.
A simple mail-
routing dia-
gram—a single
post office.

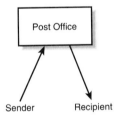

There are a few fundamental concepts I'd like to point out here:

◆ Both Shelly and Velma have a mailbox through which they send and receive mail. This is exactly the way it is with Microsoft Mail; each person must have an e-mail box in order to send and receive e-mail.

◆ Mail is routed through a postal system—in this example, a post office. Again, this is very much like Microsoft Mail. In fact, the Microsoft Mail's repository for e-mail is called a postoffice.

◆ Each post office from this example knows who its own recipients are. So does Microsoft Mail. This is very important, because it implies some knowledge about how to route the mail. It is key in this simple example, but it becomes crucial in example 2 when routing to more than one post office is required.

POST OFFICE EXAMPLE 2

The next scenario, as illustrated in Figure 24.6, is a bit more complex. Now suppose that Shelly wants to send Gary a birthday card. Gary lives in Florida, and Shelly lives in Texas. After Shelly seals the envelope, she writes Gary's Florida address on the outside. As before, she drops the mail into her mailbox, where it will be picked up and taken to the local post office. After the mail gets to the post office, a routing decision has to be made. Based on the address, the postal system knows this piece of mail has to go somewhere else besides this local post office. Why? Because Gary, the recipient, does not receive his mail at this post office. So the local post office knows that mail of this kind has to be forwarded to the regional post office for further routing.

Figure 24.6.
A more complex
mail-routing
diagram—
multiple post
offices.

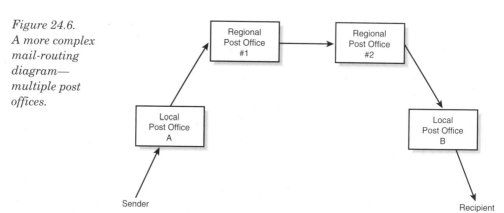

After the mail gets to the regional post office, another routing decision is made. This time, the postal system knows that Gary does not live in this region, so it doesn't forward to any other local post office in the region. In fact, he lives in a completely different state. So the decision is made to put the mail on a truck bound for the Florida regional post office.

After the mail is received by the Florida regional post office, its postal system knows that Gary receives his mail at one of the local post offices in this region. The mail then is forwarded to the local post office in Gary's town, and it is stored there until it is delivered to his personal mailbox. Then, when he opens the mail, he reads the special greeting inside from Texas.

Here are some things I'd like to point out from this example:

◆ This is a classic example of mail being "stored" and "forwarded." It is stored in one post office, and then forwarded to the next post office in the routing sequence until it reaches its destination.

The postoffice in Microsoft Mail works in precisely this fashion.

◆ There has to be some sort of routing system in order to facilitate efficient delivery of mail. Otherwise, in this example, mail going from Texas to Florida might needlessly get routed to California, then to Montana, through Kentucky, and finally to Florida—probably late for Gary's birthday. Not good.

◆ In fact, Microsoft Mail has a routing mechanism—a program called External—that forwards mail between postoffices. As an administrator, you define which postoffices are linked, either directly or indirectly, to a particular postoffice. Combined with the address, Microsoft Mail knows how to route mail from a person based out of one postoffice to another person based out of a different postoffice.

◆ The first post office that gets the mail figures the best route to take. From the start, it knows the route to Gary's local post office based on the address. Combining that information with the post offices it can transport to, it delivers the mail in the most expedient way.

The same applies in Microsoft Mail. The address you use when sending e-mail tells where in the postoffice the mail needs to go. In the case of routing through more than one postoffice, Microsoft Mail has something called EXTERNAL (also called a Message Transfer Agent or MTA) that handles routing mail between other Microsoft Mail postoffices in the system. More on this later.

◆ When there are multiple post offices involved, administration gets more complex. A single post office is the simplest case, and administration is straightforward. As you add more post offices, however, the administrative overhead increases. That is because, among other things, each post office has to know about the other post offices in the system.

◆ In Microsoft Mail, the entity that contains all this information is the Global Address List (GAL). This list contains all the addresses accessible to users at a postoffice. With multiple postoffices, the information in the GAL must be kept in sync among all the postoffices by using directory synchronization or by running the Rebuild utility. The GAL can accommodate more than 500,000 user names.

INTRODUCTION TO MICROSOFT EXCHANGE SERVER

This section discusses a bit about MS Exchange Server, its components, and its architecture. It goes over some differences between MS Mail and MS Exchange Server and points out some of the strong points of MS Exchange Server and its advantages over MS Mail.

One point of clarification before you continue: The term MS Exchange Server can be a bit confusing because it can have three meanings, depending on the context. First, it can refer to the entire product. Second, it can refer to just the server component of the product (not the client component). Third, it can refer to a physical server machine—for example, my mailbox resides on an MS Exchange Server unit called *gurney*. I'll try to make which meaning I am using clear by the context.

WHAT IS MS EXCHANGE SERVER?

Simply put, Microsoft Exchange Server is the replacement for Microsoft Mail. It is software that provides a way for people to exchange messages via computer. More precisely, it is a MAPI-based messaging server that provides e-mail, groupware, information sharing, and group scheduling functions over a network. Figure 24.7 shows a diagram of all the MS Exchange Server components and how they relate to each other.

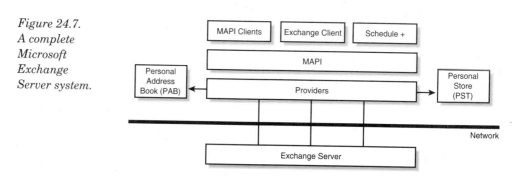

Figure 24.7.
A complete
Microsoft
Exchange
Server system.

One huge difference between MS Mail and MS Exchange Server is that MS Exchange Server is truly a client/server product. Unlike the MS Mail client, the MS Exchange Server client makes a request of the server, and the server carries out the request. As covered earlier in this chapter, with MS Mail the client itself does most of the work and the server is simply a passive message repository. So, although both products send messages back and forth, they accomplish it in vastly different ways.

On the other hand, one big similarity between the two is that they are both store-and-forward mail systems. That is, they are mail storage facilities that forward e-mail to the next storage facility until the e-mail gets to its destination. However, as you will see in this section, the implementation is vastly different.

Each MS Exchange Server has three main divisions, which are (in order from the top down):

◆ Organization

◆ Site

◆ Servers container

An organization can contain many sites. A site can contain many servers in its Servers container. A user's mailbox resides on an individual server within a site. Note that there are other objects in the organization besides the site and the Servers container.

The entire MS Exchange Server system consists of client software, which runs on the user's local computer, and server software, which runs on the computer used as the MS Exchange Server. The MS Exchange Server component runs on the MS Windows NT Server 3.51 operating system, so it can benefit from the features of the operating system. The MS Exchange client component can run on the following operating systems:

◆ Windows NT 3.51, 32-bit client

◆ Windows 95, 32-bit client

◆ Windows for Workgroups 3.11, 16-bit client

◆ Windows 3.1, 16-bit client

◆ MS-DOS 6.x client

In the next two sections, you'll look a bit more closely at the server and client components of MS Exchange Server.

MS Exchange Server—The Server Component

The Server component is by far the most complex part of the entire system. Although the client software is certainly comprehensive in its own right, the server is made up of many processes and threads that comprise four core components:

◆ Directory Service

◆ Information Store

◆ Message Transfer Agent

◆ System Attendant

These four components are discussed later in this chapter.

In addition, there are several other components that may exist in any MS Exchange Server system:

◆ The administrator program: A graphical user interface that handles centralized administration of all MS Exchange Server objects.

◆ MS Mail connector: Provides connectivity to MS Mail systems, including MS Mail for PC Networks and MS Mail for AppleTalk Networks.

24

MICROSOFT MAIL AND EXCHANGE SERVER

◆ MS Schedule+ Free/Busy connector: Provides the capability for the MS Exchange Server to exchange MS Schedule+ free/busy information with MS Mail systems.

◆ Internet Mail connector: Provides connectivity with Internet mail users.

◆ Directory Synchronization: Handles the task of keeping the directories up to date between various MS Exchange Servers.

◆ Key Management: Manages security for digitally signing messages.

◆ Third-party gateways: Provides delivery of messages from MS Exchange Server to disparate mail systems, such as PROFS and SNADS.

SERVER CORE COMPONENTS

Now take a couple minutes to look at the server's core components. Understanding how these interrelate builds the foundation for understanding server installation, migration, and performance issues. Figure 24.8 shows a diagram of the server components.

Figure 24.8. Server core components of Microsoft Exchange Server.

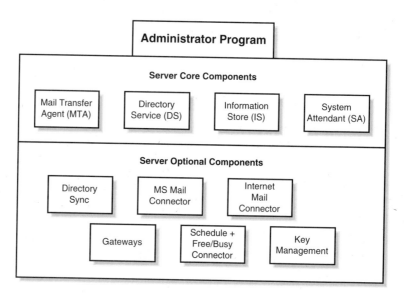

INFORMATION STORE

The Information Store (IS) is comprised of two databases that contain all the users' public and private folders. The store also enforces security on these. In other words, this component is where all your messages and e-mail are stored.

The private store contains your inbox, outbox, wastebasket, and sent messages folders. It resides in a database file called PRIV.MDB. The public store contains folders publicly accessible. It resides in a database file called PUB.MDB. In traditional groupware fashion, these databases can be replicated to other MS Exchange Servers in your installation.

If you are familiar with MS Access, you might be thinking PUB and PRIV are MS Access databases. They are not. In fact, they are designed around a true database design complete with rollback capability, relational features, and a transaction log. In this way, they are similar to industrial-strength databases like SQL Server.

Note

The relational features of the Exchange Server database engine are not available at the user level; they are used only by the underlying database engine. This becomes important for installation and performance considerations.

Directory Service

The Directory Service (DS) is a database that stores information about all the users, lists, public folders, and servers in your installation. This information is replicated automatically to all servers in a site, and it can be configured to replicate automatically to servers in other sites.

The users interact with this component regularly. When addressing an e-mail, for example, the global list of users to choose from is provided by the Directory Service. It also validates that users in the Destination fields are known by the system. This is how the server knows whether it should be able to route a particular e-mail.

Message Transfer Agent

The Message Transfer Agent (MTA) is the component responsible for forwarding messages to other servers. The messages can go to other gateways, other information stores, X.400 MTAs in foreign systems, or other MS Exchange Server MTAs.

This component takes over the function of EXTERNAL, which you learned about in MS Mail. Its job fits in very well with the earlier examples about mail routing in the postal service.

System Attendant

The System Attendant is aptly named because it is sort of a "catch-all" component that takes care of various administrative and maintenance tasks in the server that don't really fit in the scope of the IS, DS, or MTA components. Some tasks it is responsible for include assisting in running monitoring tools, monitoring the condition of connections between servers, and keeping logs for message tracking.

MS EXCHANGE SERVER—THE CLIENT COMPONENT

OK, you spent a good deal of time on the server, so now it's time to take a look at the client. Before you do, however, you should realize that it is in no way nearly as complex as the server, so this section will be a bit less involved. There are three main components to the MS Exchange Server client: the Viewer, Schedule+, and Forms Designer.

THE VIEWER

The Viewer is the main interface the user has with the server, and it is a consistent interface across the supported platforms. The Viewer shows a tree hierarchy that groups many kinds of information into one place. In fact, it might be a bit overwhelming at first, but as you use it, the purpose for everything becomes clear. It is a powerful interface.

The main items contained here are the private mailbox folders (Inbox, Outbox, Sent Items, and Wastebasket) and the public folders, all grouped under the heading of the organization in which you are running. Of course, you can add more private and public folders easily via the Viewer as you need them.

Other items, like folder shortcuts and personal folders, can be viewed here. Personal folders are kind of like the MMF file in MS Mail; they are a store of messages on your local system.

Client software usually is installed on a user's local machine, although it technically could be installed on a file server on the network. The MS Exchange Administrator program can be run on a Windows NT client machine.

MICROSOFT SCHEDULE+

Schedule+ (pronounced *schedule plus*) is a component of the client that is integrated with Microsoft Exchange Server. You also will find its predecessor, Schedule+ 1.0, integrated with Windows for Workgroups, Windows 95, and Windows NT. It provides a calendar, group scheduling, a Contact Manager, and other resources that help a user manage time and tasks.

The calendar works great for keeping track of dates and times for meetings and other important events. There is even an alarm to alert you when it's time to go somewhere. Schedule+ is quite useful for scheduling group meetings and viewing associates' free and busy times. This is useful when you are trying to efficiently set up meeting times and reserve conference rooms. The Contact Manager is a storage place for all the information in that stack of business cards you keep meaning to organize.

Tip

> One of the really nice benefits of Schedule+ is its capability to transfer information (appointments, tasks, contact information, and so on) to the Timex Datalink watch. Since I bought my watch, I haven't missed an important meeting yet.

MICROSOFT EXCHANGE FORMS DESIGNER

The Forms Designer enables the user to design custom forms for use with MS Exchange Server. Such a form can be used for posting and viewing specific customized information, such as customer case-tracking or order forms.

The Forms Designer is not a programming tool; it is a visual design tool that enables the designer to define how aspects of a form will look and behave. However, underneath it is based on MS Visual Basic 4.0, so an understanding of Visual Basic is helpful in order to take advantage of advanced features.

SUMMARY

This chapter discussed the basic concepts involved in an e-mail system. Most of it focused on Microsoft Mail and Microsoft Exchange Server, which makes sense because these products are the heart of your future e-mail system. You should remember that Microsoft Mail is a file-based store-and-forward e-mail system that utilizes a complex directory tree. Microsoft Mail stores files locally on a network drive and then forwards them to their destinations. It is also the Microsoft Mail client software that really performs the work in an MS Mail system.

Microsoft Exchange Server, on the other hand, is a client-server-based e-mail system. Instead of using a complex directory structure to segregate the work load, it uses several server-side applications. Most of the work is performed by the server rather than by the client software.

The next chapter takes this discussion a little further and looks at the planning and installation issues related to your Microsoft Mail and Exchange Server installation.

24

MICROSOFT MAIL AND EXCHANGE SERVER

- Planning Your Microsoft Mail Installation

- Planning Your Microsoft Exchange Installation

- Microsoft Exchange Security Issues

CHAPTER 25

Planning Your Postoffice Installation

There are many important things you should consider when putting together a MS Mail postoffice or MS Exchange Server: planning, migration, administration, performance, and security. One of the most important things is getting the installation right. If you don't do it properly—and this applies to most computer programs—you'll likely have problems down the road. Fortunately, the installation programs for both MS Mail and MS Exchange Server are very good at helping you get it right. You have to know some things about what you're setting up, but if you're armed with a bit of information, you'll get the installation right. And that will make things easier later on.

This chapter will give you a feel for what's coming your way with the installation process of both MS Mail and MS Exchange Server systems. If you have been through this process already, it might be familiar ground. You still can get some good preparatory ideas for the setup process before actually starting the installation, however. Not only can these ideas help you now, they can benefit you in the future. You will also look into some of the security issues involved with using Exchange Server as an SMTP server. Many of these ideas also apply to MS Mail if you install an optional gateway.

One of the key items to consider is whether you should use MS Mail or MS Exchange Server. MS Mail is a good solution if you must reuse older, and correspondingly slower, hardware. Otherwise, you should consider moving right to Exchange Server, as it provides a more robust and efficient mail platform. Exchange Server also offers easier administration of your postoffice, but to provide good performance you will need a higher-end server with at least a Pentium processor, 64MB of RAM, and multiple disk drives.

PLANNING YOUR MICROSOFT MAIL INSTALLATION

This section tells you a bit about the installation of MS Mail. There is always a temptation to jump right in and do the work. With software systems as potentially complex as MS Mail and MS Exchange Server, however, it is a good idea to do some planning before you get started. This section gives you an idea of things you should think about. The list is by no means comprehensive, but reading through these items should prompt you to think about those topics relevant to your installation:

- ◆ Know what your users expect.
- ◆ Understand as much as possible about the software.
- ◆ Draw it on paper first.
- ◆ Select your hardware appropriately.
- ◆ Choose a file server.

◆ Determine your storage requirements.

◆ Be aware of the issues when migrating from a Workgroup postoffice.

◆ Be prepared for issues involving gateways and disparate mail systems.

◆ Decide on a plan for backup.

KNOW WHAT YOUR USERS EXPECT

I think everyone understands the importance of delivering to people what they want and expect. It is no different when preparing to install an e-mail system for your users. In fact, it might be even more crucial to deliver on expectations, because people will be using the tool you are setting up to get their jobs done. That makes it a pretty important tool.

How fast do users want the computer to respond when they are reading new mail? One second? Two seconds? Five seconds? What is tolerable? Usually, I try to follow the two-second rule. If you keep the response time at less than two seconds, you will hardly ever go wrong. Of course, one second or less is ideal, but when you balance that against the potentially large number of users you must support, it becomes a game of trade-offs.

What type of information do users want to exchange with their e-mail systems? Just text? Text and attachments? How large will the attachments be? What about graphical information or voice and video clips? All these have an impact—sometimes a very significant impact—on the way you configure your system.

Do the users need to exchange information with people using other types of e-mail systems? If they will always be using the homogeneous environment of MS Mail, that makes your job simpler. Chances are that sometime they will need to exchange information over the Internet, or with PROFS or with an X.400 system. This is where gateways come into the picture.

All this having been said, the final part to knowing your users' expectations is knowing whether MS Mail can actually meet the expectations of the users. That is when it is crucial that you understand what the software can deliver before committing to giving your users what they are asking for. Believe me, they would much rather you tell them up front that they will not be able to do something instead of three months later when you can't get it to work because of a limitation of the software.

UNDERSTAND AS MUCH AS POSSIBLE ABOUT THE SOFTWARE

This idea can be generalized into a cliché: Look before you leap. There are plenty of areas in life where this is applicable, and preparing to install an e-mail system is certainly no exception.

After you have an idea of what your users expect of the e-mail system, you should do some research on MS Mail to ensure that it can deliver what you need. MS Mail is a good product with powerful features. There are just some things it cannot do, however, and some things that it cannot do well.

Delivering video clips in e-mail is a good example. Although MS Mail certainly can handle the task of transporting an AVI file, for example, it is not one of the things it does well. First, the file might be very large. Because MS Mail is based on a shared file system, the entire file would have to be moved across the network to the postoffice and stored there. If it has to go to another postoffice, there is another trip across the network for a huge file. Then, upon retrieval, the user must bring the file across the network and into the mailbox, which is stored on the local machine. Assuming that there is enough local storage for the file, it then can be played back. This scenario demonstrates a very inefficient method of handling video clips. It serves to illustrate the point that, although it might work to some degree, this is one of the tasks that just isn't well-suited for MS Mail.

DRAW IT ON PAPER FIRST

I cannot emphasize this point enough, especially in large organizations that probably use multiple MS Mail servers. Envisioning the connections between a few MS Mail servers is not too difficult, but as the number increases, it becomes very tough to keep track of how all the pieces fit together.

Take a big piece of paper, stick it to the wall, and make a diagram of your proposed MS Mail network configuration. It will make it much easier to visualize how things fit together. It also will make it easier to spot potential problems, and it will tend to illustrate when you've designed something that doesn't make sense.

MS Mail can be configured to work in many different network configurations. You can configure very simple installations, or you can configure complex ones. You can run a single postoffice or many postoffices, either on the same network or on different networks. Several scenarios are covered in detail in Chapter 3 of the *MS Mail Administrator's Guide*, "Network Scenarios and Applicable Programs." This section looks at a few of these scenarios.

Figure 25.1 depicts the simplest MS Mail installation: one postoffice on a network. This is similar to the WGPO installation, but the similarity ends here because

WGPO cannot support moving messages between multiple postoffices. To have a Workgroup postoffice talk to another postoffice, you have to upgrade to MS Mail and use the EXTERNAL routing program (EXTERNAL.EXE) to route the mail from one postoffice to another. Figure 25.2 shows a typical configuration of multiple postoffices with users on each.

Figure 25.1.
A single MS Mail
postoffice on a
network.

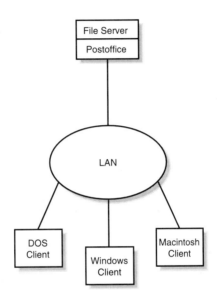

As you can see in Figure 25.1, the configuration is very simple. This is quite adequate for a small installation that doesn't have much volume of mail exchanged. When traffic loads require adding a second postoffice, however, Figure 25.2 illustrates the setup.

Figure 25.2 depicts a dedicated machine running the EXTERNAL program (also called the Mail Transfer Agent or MTA). This is one way to do it if you are only using the DOS version of the MTA. With the advent of Windows NT and OS/2, another approach is to run EXTERNAL on the same Windows NT Server that houses one of your postoffices. This arrangement is shown in Figure 25.3.

The benefit of doing this is obvious: You do not have to deploy a separate machine for each copy of EXTERNAL that you have running. In fact, a multitasking MTA in MS Mail 3.5 is available for Windows NT. This version provides greater throughput and mail-handling capabilities than the DOS-based version of the MTA. For clarity, other figures will show the EXTERNAL machine as separate, but understand that it can be configured as shown in Figure 25.3 if you want.

*Figure 25.2.
Multiple MS Mail
postoffice on a
network with
multiple users on
each postoffice.*

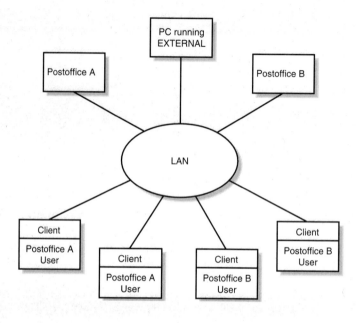

*Figure 25.3.
Multiple MS Mail
postoffices on a
network with the
EXTERNAL program
running on a
Windows NT
postoffice.*

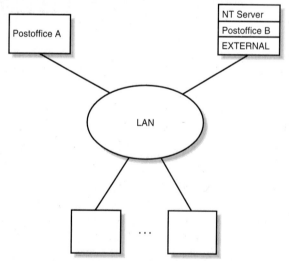

One final example you'll look at is the connection of postoffices deployed on separate networks. This provides the capability to exchange mail between users of MS Mail postoffices that cannot be on the same network. (See Figure 25.4.)

Figure 25.4.
Multiple MS Mail
postoffices on
separate networks
connected via
modems.

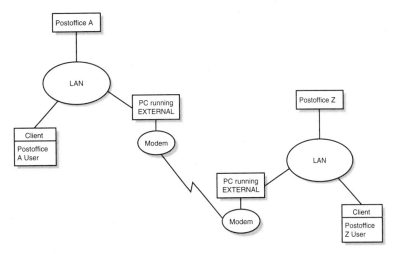

With this approach, you can have postoffices at different remote sites in your company, for example, and tie them together with a modem or other remote link. Again, as shown in Figure 25.3, the EXTERNAL program could be run on a Windows NT Server. You could then install a modem on the NT Server machine to provide the remote connection.

There are other variations of these scenarios, but they are mainly just different combinations of the same general idea. There is the possibility of having a remote user rather than a network-connected user, for example. Then you can have multiple remote users who connect to the same network but use different postoffices. Then there's the notion of a gateway that, like the EXTERNAL program, provides mail communication outside the postoffice. Unlike the EXTERNAL program, however, a gateway links MS Mail with a different type of mail system, such as X.400 or AT&T Mail.

SELECT YOUR HARDWARE APPROPRIATELY

This can be a difficult task to complete accurately. Sometimes it seems as though there is almost no chance that the platform you build or purchase will live up to your expectations. So what you end up with might be a bit different than what you thought you would end up with. This doesn't have to be the case if you follow a few simple rules:

First, stick with mainstream hardware. I am a firm believer that, although price is certainly important, it is difficult to place a price on your reputation. Select first-tier hardware that is a known performer in the market, and stay away from trying to "force fit" a machine into a role for which it was not intended.

If you need a good MS Mail server, you know a few requirements for that system already. First, it must be reliable because it is likely going to be up 24 hours a day, seven days a week. It must be able to take that kind of beating for a long period without breaking. It should have the features you need. Remember, MS Mail is a shared file architecture, so the server you pick needs to have features and performance characteristics that would make it a good file server. It should be fast, and hopefully, it will have advanced features that set it apart from using just a "plain old desktop" for the job.

Tip

> One of the key features in providing a robust mail server is maintaining the shared files. This means that the file system must be kept free of errors. If you are using a lower-end system, such as a Windows for Workgroups or Windows 95 system, you should periodically scan the disk for defects, compress the mail folders periodically, and defragment the disk regularly for optimum performance. You should also back up your shared files regularly. To perform any of these tasks requires that you take your mail system off-line. Therefore, your plan should include a schedule to perform these tasks (at least once a week).

Second, size the hardware according to today's needs with tomorrow's needs in mind. This concept is tied to meeting your users' expectations in two ways. It enables you to deliver the usability your users want in the system. When your users get to a point that necessitates an upgrade or expansion, it should be relatively quick and painless for you to do it. That also keeps your users (and you) happy.

If you know that your users exchange a huge amount of mail with large attachments, for example, purchase a system with a large hard drive to begin with. A server with a hardware array controller provides a good solution because it allows for extensibility of the disk volume while providing excellent performance using RAID drive sets and onboard caching.

Tip

> While a SCSI-based hardware array controller is the optimum disk storage solution, not everyone can afford one. In this case, a good alternative is to use the software-based alternative provided by Windows NT Server. You can use a stripe set with parity for additional fault tolerance or just a stripe set for increased performance.

Third, read the documentation for recommendations on things like how much disk space per user is required, what the maximum number of mail messages per mailbox is, and so on. If you will have a few hundred users, you should consider breaking them up into multiple postoffices rather than running on one single, huge server. There is a break-even point, but exactly where that is depends on your users' usage patterns, their performance expectations, and what type of hardware you have installed or plan to install. So there is no way I can advise you to always roll out a second postoffice after n users on a single postoffice.

I can tell you from experience, however, that a single MS Mail postoffice can realistically support about 200 to 300 consistent users and maintain a respectable performance. This is as long as you have a fast processor, such as a Pentium/66, and a fast disk subsystem, such as the array controller mentioned earlier—all running on a server-class machine with 32MB to 64MB of RAM. If you are reusing older hardware, the number of users you can support decreases sharply. An 80386 with 16MB of RAM might be able to support between 50 and 100 users, and an 80486 with 16MB to 32MB might be able to support between 75 and 150 users. Keep in mind that you are basically building a file server for MS Mail, so the faster the disk subsystem, the better. Also, more RAM dedicated to disk caching will help. You will learn more about tuning and performance in Chapter 28.

Fourth, learn how the product works by using it and studying it. This is a trial-and-error, iterative process. Fortunately, because MS Mail is a shared file architecture, you already know a couple of things about its performance characteristics. First, it tends to be disk-intensive rather than CPU-intensive when users are pounding on it. Along with that, it will be somewhat network-intensive because entire files must be transported across the network. When many users are logged into the postoffice receiving, moving, composing, and sending mail simultaneously, the stress on the server can be quite heavy.

CHOOSE A FILE SERVER

As I've indicated before, an MS Mail postoffice is nothing more than a shared set of files on a file server. These shared files have to be accessible by everyone on the network who will participate in exchanging e-mail. The actual selection of a file server, along with relevant performance topics, is covered in Chapter 28, "Optimizing Your Mail Server." There are some definite items to consider when selecting a good postoffice machine, but for now, it will suffice to just say that you need a network file server. Of course, you already might have file servers set up on your network, so you won't have to go through the process of selecting a new server. Great. In that case, just figure out a file server that provides the appropriate access for the folks you want to use e-mail.

The MS Mail postoffice must be installed on a LAN Manager-compatible network—such as Windows NT, LAN Manager, or Windows for Workgroups—or on a Novell network. To set up the postoffice over the network on a shared resource, you need to have the following access rights:

> Windows NT/LAN Manager: Read, Write, Create, Delete, Attrib
>
> Novell: All except Supervisor, File Scan, and Access Control

DETERMINE YOUR STORAGE REQUIREMENTS

Another issue that no doubt will arise is the amount of space you need on the postoffice file server. This depends on two things: the number of users you want to host, and what type of usage needs you expect the users to have. It's impossible to say exactly how much space each user will require. For light users, a good amount would be 10MB or less, and double that for heavier users. Because you can only realistically host about 200 users on a (very fast) file server, that would translate to 2GB to 4GB (200 × 10MB to 200 × 20MB) of disk space at the most.

You also need to set aside another approximately 10MB on the server for the administrative files and client files so they can be accessed across the network. While I have seen postoffices that used more than 10MB per user, these postoffices encountered many problems. Often the entire mail system would fail. If you need to support large postoffices, you should use Exchange Server instead.

BE AWARE OF THE ISSUES WHEN MIGRATING FROM A WORKGROUP POSTOFFICE

Keep in mind that a Workgroup postoffice (WGPO) is simply an MS Mail postoffice that has no capability to exchange mail with any other external postoffice. Given that fact, the task of migrating from WGPO to MS Mail is pretty straightforward. It basically turns into the same task as restoring MS Mail users to any MS Mail postoffice. The MS Mail documentation discusses this in depth, so I won't go through it here.

The preceding paragraph assumes that you are migrating from WGPO into a *new* MS Mail postoffice. The biggest difficulty, however, arises if you are trying to migrate WGPO users into an existing MS Mail postoffice—one that already has users in it. To accomplish that, you must export the existing WGPO users' folders and then import them into the newly created MS Mail mailboxes in a similar fashion. It can be time consuming, but it ensures a smooth migration.

Warning

You cannot simply use the XCOPY command to place the WGPO directories over the top of the MS Mail directories. That would be disastrous because existing users of the MS Mail postoffice would likely be destroyed in the process.

BE PREPARED FOR ISSUES INVOLVED IN USING GATEWAYS AND DISPARATE MAIL SYSTEMS

This is one subject that is easy to overlook, especially if you are concentrating on getting the basic postoffice working correctly. If your users expect to be able to exchange mail with other non-MS Mail users, however, considerations for external mail gateways must be in your plan.

In the box, MS Mail has a gateway to AT&T Mail. It also has the EXTERNAL program, which enables it to exchange mail with other MS Mail postoffices. This version of EXTERNAL is DOS-based—it is a single-tasking version. You can run multiple instances of the program on a multitasking operating system like Windows NT or OS/2, though. This is useful if you need to increase the number of postoffice links. If you want a multitasking version of EXTERNAL to run on Windows NT or OS/2, a separate product called the Microsoft Mail Multitasking MTA is available that provides this functionality.

In addition, there are several third parties who make gateways for MS Mail. You can use these products to allow MS Mail to exchange messages with a variety of other e-mail systems, such as Lotus cc:Mail, Banyan VINES, and the Internet.

Note

MS Exchange Server includes a Microsoft Mail connector with the product. This gives you a way to route mail between users of MS Exchange Server and MS Mail if you will run both in your organization.

DECIDE ON A PLAN FOR BACKUP

One thing that often gets overlooked is how the system will be backed up, archived, and restored in the event of a disaster. I'm not just talking about your building falling down or something. I'm talking about things that happen every day, like disk crashes, server failures, or just plain old user errors. Any of these things, and some things you won't plan for, require you to restore your system from a backup. And there's nothing worse than not having a backup when you need it.

Obviously, it is best to plan for this before the installation occurs. If you install 4GB of disk space, for example, that old 50MB tape backup unit probably isn't the best choice of hardware for efficient backup. You also need to consider how the system will be used so that you can plan the backup schedule patterns. Another thing to consider is the actual process for backup: Will you do complete backups every day, every other day, or every week?

Chapter 27, "Managing Your Postoffice," addresses this subject in more detail. I just wanted to bring it up now so that you will start thinking about it if you haven't installed yet.

PLANNING YOUR MICROSOFT EXCHANGE INSTALLATION

This section takes a moment to examine some of the issues you might run into when installing MS Exchange Server. Fortunately, the topics discussed later in this chapter in the section "Installing Microsoft Mail" also apply to MS Exchange Server. However, there are a few additional items to consider:

◆ Choose a server.

◆ Determine your storage requirements.

◆ Choose a disk subsystem for your Exchange Server installation.

◆ Understand how MS Exchange Server works.

◆ Understand how your users will install the MS Exchange client software.

◆ Understand the issues when migrating from MS Mail or from a Workgroup postoffice.

◆ Understand the issues involved in using gateways and disparate mail systems.

◆ Connect Multiple Exchange Server sites using the Internet as a backbone.

CHOOSE A SERVER

The server piece of Exchange is the key component. Unlike the MS Mail "server," the Exchange server is not a passive entity. It is a multiprocess, multithreaded set of NT services that are constantly active moving mail, servicing client requests, and so on. This has many implications, including performance and proper selection of a server machine, as discussed in Chapter 28.

Because the server is a very active part of the picture and not merely a file server for its clients, the installation process is a bit more involved. Fortunately, the Exchange installation process is very helpful in guiding you through a successful installation. It is basically composed of two parts: the main Setup program, which copies files and actually installs Exchange Server, and the Exchange Performance Optimizer, which analyzes your system and helps to make the right choices about configuring Exchange.

Unlike MS Mail's Setup program, you typically run Setup on the same machine that is the destination for the Exchange server installation. Setup runs under Windows NT, which is the type of machine Exchange Server must run on.

Basically, during the installation of an Exchange server, you need to prepare a few things. Among these are the destination directory, an administrative account that Setup uses to install the services, and the server components you want to install (MS Mail Connector, Internet Mail Connector, and so on). You also should know whether this is the first server in the Exchange organization or site. If it is the first, think of a name to use for the Exchange organization and site. The Exchange server name will be the same as the NT Server name.

By default, the Setup program is set to install both the Exchange server and the Administration program on the destination machine. You do not have to install the Administration program on the same machine, though. You can install it on any other Windows NT machine on the network that you will use for administrating the server. Chapter 28 gives more details on administration.

You also should keep in mind additional considerations for an Exchange server. I'm just going to list these here and not go into them in detail as not every item will apply to all installations. Some of these topics are addressed further in Chapter 27 on administration and Chapter 28 on performance. Keep these considerations in mind as you plan your installation:

◆ Choose a consistent naming convention for the organization, site, and servers.

◆ Determine whether you will have multiple Exchange sites or a single site.

◆ Plan on creating mailboxes for the clients if you are not migrating from a previous postoffice.

◆ Determine what network protocol(s) will be used.

◆ Plan your server data backup strategies.

◆ Consider your performance options carefully—perhaps you will need a hardware upgrade before installing MS Exchange Server, for example.

◆ Plan your migration from an MS Mail or Workgroup postoffice carefully.

◆ Determine the types of clients you will be supporting—Windows 95, for example.

◆ Plan your connections to external gateways—X.400, SMTP, and so on.

◆ Create a plan to support mobile/remote client access.

◆ Determine whether MS Schedule+ should be used.

DETERMINE YOUR STORAGE REQUIREMENTS

An installation of the Exchange server requires anywhere from about 70MB to 120MB of disk space, depending on the options you choose in Setup. A bare-bones server with no connectors and no Administrator program takes about 70MB.

Another issue is the amount of disk space that the clients require on the server. That question is difficult to answer directly; it depends on what type of activity and usage loads the server will bear. It's not as easy as just planning 10MB per mailbox because Exchange users can do much more than just send e-mail.

You can place limits on a user's disk space usage, however. You can configure each user's mailbox with a 20MB maximum. That way, if you know you will support 100 users, there must be a maximum of 2GB of storage available for the private database store. The actual theoretical maximum will be more than that because you must allow space for the directory store, the Exchange programs, the NT pagefile, the NT programs, and any other items stored on the machine hosting the Exchange server. However, it should give you a place to start.

With the initial release of MS Exchange Server, the private and public stores can each have a maximum size of 16GB. That sounds like a lot, and it is. However, in a large enterprise environment, if you try hosting 1,000 users on a single server or if the users store and exchange huge files like video clips, 16GB suddenly doesn't seem so big. Consider that 300 users, each consuming 50MB of the database store, require 15GB.

Fortunately, to help alleviate this and to make the server more efficient, Microsoft has designed Exchange with single-instance storage. That means there is not a separate instance of duplicate items in the store. If a 5MB video clip is sent to 10 different users, for example, it will not require 50MB of space in the database store—it will only need 5MB. A single instance of the object is stored, and all 10 users have a pointer to it. The last person to delete it actually causes the item to be removed from the database store.

CHOOSE A DISK SUBSYSTEM FOR YOUR EXCHANGE SERVER INSTALLATION

At its core, MS Exchange Server is run by a fully relational database engine. That means it has a database store and transaction logs. If you are familiar with databases such as SQL Server 6, you know the transaction log should be placed on a separate drive from the main database. You certainly can place them together if you have only a single disk drive, but one of the steps in optimizing performance is separating the two. This topic is covered in more detail in Chapter 28.

If you can, you should plan to have at least two separate disk drives in the server that will have MS Exchange Server installed. An even better choice is to use two or more hardware drive arrays or stripe sets for optimum performance.

UNDERSTAND HOW MS EXCHANGE SERVER WORKS

As mentioned earlier, at its core, MS Exchange Server is a database rather than a shared file system. The performance characteristics of the Exchange Server system therefore are quite different from those of the MS Mail postoffice system. With this in mind, you need to think about what your users will be doing with Exchange.

Will they be exchanging only text, for example? Is there a requirement for other forms of data storage? If so, plan the disk space accordingly. A fresh installation of Exchange Server takes approximately 50MB to 100MB of disk space, depending on how many optional components you install. With Exchange Server 1.0, the public and private stores are limited to 16GB each.

One other thing to consider is the increased hardware requirements for MS Exchange when compared to those of MS Mail. A good entry-level MS Exchange Server would be a Pentium/133 with 64MB RAM and a single, fairly large disk drive—1GB to 2GB, for example. From there, you can add memory, add a second hard drive, or upgrade the processor.

Tip

The computer you plan to use for Exchange Server should not execute any other BackOffice components, such as SQL Server, if you want to provide the best possible platform for Exchange Server.

UNDERSTAND HOW YOUR USERS WILL INSTALL THE MS EXCHANGE CLIENT SOFTWARE

Your users can conveniently install the Exchange client software over the network. You should consider how this is to be accomplished. You can place the client install files on the Exchange Server machine and then share the directories for network installs. You don't have to place the MS Exchange client files on the MS Exchange Server itself; however, they can be installed from any file server on the network. You also can pass around the CD if you have a fairly small organization and you don't happen to have an extra file server. This probably isn't a good idea for large organizations.

For a larger organization, SMS is a better method for distributing the Exchange client files. You can create a package with SMS that contains all the Exchange client installation files. Your SMS clients may then install the Exchange client software using the Package Command Manager.

UNDERSTAND THE ISSUES WHEN MIGRATING FROM MS MAIL OR FROM A WORKGROUP POSTOFFICE

An entire portion of the MS Exchange Server manual is dedicated to explaining the process of migrating from MS Mail to MS Exchange Server. You should have an understanding of how MS Exchange Server works before attempting a migration. I highly recommend reading the MS Exchange Server documentation on migration before proceeding.

Fortunately, some migration wizards are included with MS Exchange Server that will work with your existing system and with the Administrator program in MS Exchange to help you with the migration process. If you get the MS Exchange Developer's Kit, you also can create your own custom migration tools if you need to.

Migration wizards help you to perform the following tasks:

◆ Create Windows NT accounts for users.

◆ Create MS Exchange mailboxes from MS Mail mailboxes.

◆ Import mailbox data from MS Mail.

◆ Migrate directory data and custom recipient data from MS Mail.

◆ Migrate Schedule+ data from MS Mail.

Note

Migrating from a WGPO to MS Exchange Server is like migrating from MS Mail to MS Exchange Server. WGPO is just a simplified version of MS Mail, so many of the principles for migrating from MS Mail are applicable.

MS Exchange Server has several features that make migration from MS Mail possible—or at least easier. Keep these in mind when planning the migration:

♦ MS Exchange users can exchange mail with MS Mail users through the MS Mail connector gateway.

♦ The MS Exchange client software can be used with Microsoft Mail postoffices. Just install the MS Mail PC Provider in your profile on the MS Exchange client.

♦ INI files, such as MSMAIL.INI and SHARED.INI, continue to function with MS Exchange clients, as do custom forms and commands.

♦ Third-party add-ons for MS Mail clients that use Simple MAPI and CMC also work with MS Exchange clients.

♦ The migration tools help you move messages in mailboxes, MMF files, personal address book entries, and private folders.

♦ Group folders, shared folders, and Schedule+ calendar information can be migrated with the migration tools.

♦ MS Exchange Servers can perform the task of directory synchronization servers, and they can act as directory synchronization requesters.

UNDERSTAND THE ISSUES INVOLVED IN USING GATEWAYS AND DISPARATE MAIL SYSTEMS

There are gateways included in the box with the enterprise edition of MS Exchange Server, including an MS Mail postoffice connector, an X.400 gateway, and an SMTP gateway. There also will likely be more gateways developed by third parties that you can add onto MS Exchange Server.

If your users will only be using MS Exchange Server, no problem. That is the simplest scenario because you won't have to worry about foreign mail systems. However, if your users want to send and receive mail over the Internet, for example, you must plan for this in your installation.

Migrating to MS Exchange Server also provides advantages when using gateways. Using the X.400 connector in the MS Exchange MTA, for example, provides some advantages over MS Mail:

♦ There is no longer a need for a dedicated computer performing the gateway operations.

◆ You get the benefit of redundant dynamic routing if one MTA is down or is very busy.

◆ You can monitor the performance of the MTA to see how much work it is doing.

◆ You get the benefit of a multithreaded MTA. Along with this, the performance is much improved over the MS Mail X.400 gateway.

◆ It conforms to 1988 standards.

◆ TCP/IP is supported.

CONNECT MULTIPLE EXCHANGE SERVER SITES USING THE INTERNET AS A BACKBONE

If your network has multiple sites in external locations (such as a WAN), you are probably using proprietary means to connect your mail servers so that you can exchange e-mail with all of your network users. This proprietary connection might be a router, a slow modem, or a similar product. As an alternative to proprietary (and costly) connection schemes, you can use your connection to the Internet to connect your external sites. There is a catch here, however, because you get nothing for free. To create an SMTP mail system and connect two Exchange Server sites, you need multiple mail connectors. You can use one of three combinations: one X.400 and one Internet Mail Connector, the Microsoft Exchange Connector (which provides the Site Connector and Dynamic RAS Connector) and the Internet Mail Connector, or two of the same type of connector (such as the Internet Mail Connector).

Note

If you have the Enterprise edition of Exchange Server, or have purchased the Microsoft Exchange Connector, you can use the Site Connector (choose File | New Other | Site Connector) to connect multiple Exchange Server sites. This is a better choice than purchasing multiple Internet Mail Connectors. It is also a more efficient mechanism because it uses Windows NT Remote Procedure Calls over any supported transport protocol that supports NetBIOS or Windows sockets (TCP/IP, IPX/SPX, NetBEUI, and others) to connect the sites. The Site Connector is also required if you want to replicate directories with Exchange Server.

The basic idea is that you will use one Internet Mail Connector to send your SMTP mail to all external e-mail clients (those outside of your organization) and the other connector, whichever one it is, to connect your sites together. You would then set your external sites to forward their SMTP mail to the Exchange Server that provides the outbound SMTP mail service. All outgoing SMTP mail from the external site would be forwarded to this site for final transmission over the Internet. All incoming SMTP mail would be received on this site and then forwarded to all the external sites (using the X.400 Connector, the Site Connector, or the Internet Mail Connector).

MICROSOFT EXCHANGE SECURITY ISSUES

The number-one service most users demand is e-mail. E-mail has revolutionized communications in the industry. This capability, however, also includes inherent risks when you decide to provide Internet e-mail capabilities. You must be prepared to deal with the risks to minimize the potential problems that could occur. In this section you will examine some of these problems and the solutions you can apply to your Microsoft Exchange Server and Microsoft Exchange clients.

PROTECTING YOUR SERVER

Microsoft Exchange Server uses the Windows NT Remote Procedure Call (RPC) mechanism as the communication link between the server and client. It uses the Microsoft Challenge/Response security methodology built into the Windows NT RPC to authenticate client/server and server/server connections. Using this methodology, it is possible not only to encrypt the password associated with a user account, but to encrypt the entire communication stream as well. This means that it is possible to provide a secure means for a user to access his mailbox over the Internet, as well as replicate data between Exchange sites. (For more information on site replication and the Internet, refer to Chapter 27.) But there is more to protecting your server than just using a secure communications link. The following sections address these issues.

PREVENTING A DENIAL OF SERVICE

Have you considered what could occur if one of your network clients annoys someone on the Internet? Suppose this problem occurred on an Internet news group. Your client may have just a nasty message reply (commonly called a *flame*) posted on the news group. If that's all that happens, consider yourself fortunate. Why fortunate? Because it is also possible that this annoyed Internet user may be so upset, or just malicious enough, to decide to send a flood of e-mail to this network client of yours. There could be a series of small messages, a series of large messages, or possibly a series of huge messages that contain megabytes of junk embedded in them. Your server will have to deal with them all.

Because each message requires processing time and server storage, a flood of e-mail could cause what is commonly called a *denial of service*. In essence, this means your server could be overloaded, which would prevent all of your e-mail clients (not just the one user) from sending or receiving e-mail. To prevent such an occurrence from happening, you can perform one of the following actions:

◆ Warn your network clients about posting inflammatory messages on the Internet. Instigate a policy for users to inform you of high message traffic from any Internet user.

◆ Configure the Internet Mail Connector Message size parameter in the General tab of the Internet Connector Properties dialog box to limit the size of incoming and outgoing mail. This will prevent large messages from being received by your network client from an irate Internet user.

◆ Configure the Internet Mail Connector to reject messages sent from the irate Internet user. You do this from the Connections tab of the Internet Mail Connector Properties dialog box. Just enable the Accept or Reject by Hosts option; then click the Security Hosts button. You can then specify the IP addresses of the host computers from which to reject messages.

RESTRICTING ACCESS TO THE INTERNET

Another problem that could occur with network clients who send or receive e-mail over the Internet is that they could send mail containing sensitive information to someone outside of the organization. This could occur, for example, when an e-mail message is received from an external user. Your very friendly network client, thinking that only someone who works for the company would ask for such information and have access to his e-mail account, sends the requested information back as a reply to the original message. He might not even have been aware that the originating e-mail message arrived from an external source. After all, how many network users do you know who check the properties for each e-mail address they receive?

The enhanced version of the Microsoft Exchange Client included with Microsoft Exchange Server attempts to avoid this possibility by displaying a *friendly name* (the actual name of the sender) along with the e-mail address at the top of each message. A message received from the Internet might appear as Arthur Knowles [webmaster@nt-guru.com]. The e-mail address within the brackets [] of the e-mail address is a sure sign that this message originated outside of the organization. Messages that are sent within the organization include only the friendly name, such as Arthur E. Knowles, which you define as the display name for the client mailbox.

To prevent such an occurrence in your organization, you can limit the clients who are authorized to send e-mail over the Internet. You do this using the Delivery Restrictions tab on the Internet Connector Properties dialog box. You can specify individual clients to accept e-mail intended for the Internet in the Accept message from listbox or reject specific individuals in the Reject messages from listbox.

PREVENTING AUTO-REPLIES TO THE INTERNET

One of the really nifty features of the enhanced Microsoft Exchange client is the capability to automatically send a reply to a received message. This is commonly used when a network client will be out of the office for a few days (such as when he is on vacation). It is an appropriate mechanism to inform colleagues at work that you will be unavailable until a specific date, and you might even go so far as to include private data (such as where you can be reached in an emergency). It is not necessarily a good idea, however, to send these types of replies to e-mail received from the Internet.

After all, do you want someone whom you might not know personally to receive private information? Do you want him to know that you will not be at your home for this length of time? Carelessly passing around information like this can lead to trouble. But again, it is easily solved using the Internet Connector Properties dialog box. Just select the Internet Mail tab. Under Message Content Information, choose Interoperability and check the Disable Automatic Replies to the Internet option. This is discussed in more detail in Chapter 27.

PROTECTING YOUR E-MAIL MESSAGES FROM TAMPERING OR THEFT

Because anyone with a network packet sniffer can intercept packets sent over the Internet, you might want to ensure that e-mail messages you send cannot be read by just anyone. There are two encryption features you can use with Microsoft Exchange Server to ensure that your e-mail is secure from prying eyes. First, you can encrypt the data contained within a message; second, you can sign a message digitally to verify the authenticity of the sender (to prevent someone else from sending messages in your name, for example).

Performing this task is a twofold process. First you must install the Microsoft Exchange Key Manager components on your Exchange Server. This is covered in Chapter 27 as well, so I will not step through all the details here. Second, you must configure your Microsoft Exchange clients using the Security tab of the Options dialog box (accessed by choosing Tools | Options from the menu). If you do not install the Key Manager, you cannot create the private and public keys for your network clients. Without these keys, the encryption options of the Security tab are disabled.

Note

Currently, only the enhanced Microsoft Exchange client can support data encryption and digital signatures. If your clients will be sending e-mail to users who do not use the enhanced Microsoft Exchange client, they should not encrypt or digitally sign e-mail to that particular user. If they do, the recipient will not be able to read the message.

PROTECTING YOUR CLIENTS FROM VIRUSES

In the early days of computing, viruses were transmitted primarily through the sharing of floppy disks. Although this still should be a concern for you, the primary vector for virus transmission has changed. Now, viruses are transmitted more easily by downloading files from an Internet WWW or FTP site. They also can be sent directly to you via e-mail as an embedded object. To prevent the spread of viruses in your organization, you should make sure to instigate a policy to protect your users. At the very least, you should follow these guidelines:

◆ At system startup, execute a virus-scanning utility such as those provided by Norton Anti-Virus or McAffee's Virus Scan.

◆ Do not directly activate embedded objects in a mail message that arrive from an external source (such as the Internet). Instead, save the attachment. Then run a virus scanner to verify the contents of the object. Only then should the object be opened.

◆ If a virus is found within an e-mail message, immediately notify the rest of your e-mail clients who may be recipients of a broadcast message containing the object. If you want to be friendly about the situation, notify the sender of the e-mail message that a virus was found within the object (he might not have been aware that his system was infected when he attached the object to the message). If you want to take a stronger stance about the situation, configure the Internet Mail Connector (via the Accept or Reject by Host group options in the Connections property sheet) to reject all e-mail messages from the sender of the infected e-mail message. You can reject all new messages from the sender until he proves, to your satisfaction, that he did not knowingly send you an infected message.

SUMMARY

This chapter discussed some of the issues involved in planning your postoffice installation with either MS Mail or MS Exchange Server. With each product, there are several things to think about: client support, migration from Workgroup Postoffice (WGPO), co-existence with MS Mail postoffices, disk space requirements, the type of machine on which to install, client support, remote usage, and so on. If you plan to connect your mail system to the Internet, there are also some security issues. While you did not look at all of these issues, you did look into the major issues using Exchange Server as a reference. In the next chapter you will actually step through the installation process for both MS Mail and MS Exchange Server.

CHAPTER 26

Installing Microsoft Mail
and Exchange Server

Installing Microsoft Mail or Exchange Server is not a difficult task, but it does require some perseverance as the installation process may be a bit lengthier than expected. The installation of the mail server is also only the beginning of the process to create a fully functional postoffice. This chapter is divided into two sections. The first covers Microsoft Mail and the second covers Microsoft Exchange Server. Both sections cover the basic installation process in a step-by-step fashion that walks you through the actual installation so that there will be no surprises when you create your postoffice.

Following the installation of the postoffice components will be a discussion of the installation process for the mail clients and a brief discussion on using Remote Access to connect to your postoffice. You will also learn about the Microsoft Exchange Migration Wizard which can help you migrate your existing postoffice to Microsoft Exchange Server.

INSTALLING MICROSOFT MAIL

In this section, you will step through the actual MS Mail installation process so there will not be any surprises waiting for you when you actually begin your installation. Once that is out of the way, you will explore some of the client installations so that your MS Mail clients can connect to your postoffice, and exchange mail with each other. Before you can install the MS Mail postoffice, you must have already connected to the shared directory where you want to install your postoffice. This is really only an issue if you are installing the postoffice over the network. The MS Mail installation which follows is performed locally on a Windows NT Server computer.

The basic MS Mail installation process follows these steps:

1. Insert Disk 1 of your Microsoft Mail setup disks and execute SETUP.EXE, and the MS Mail Welcome screen will appear as shown in Figure 26.1.

Figure 26.1.
The MS Mail
Welcome screen.

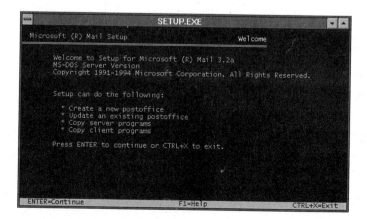

2. Press the Enter key to continue the installation, and the Function Select screen shown in Figure 26.2 will be displayed.

Figure 26.2.
Choosing your
MS Mail
installation type.

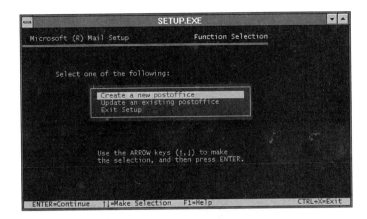

3. The pop-up dialog box includes the options to create a new postoffice, update an existing postoffice, or exit the installation. Choose the Create a new postoffice entry and press the Enter key. The screen shown in Figure 26.3 will be displayed.

Note

If you are upgrading an existing Workgroup Postoffice to an MS Mail Postoffice, choose the Upgrade an existing postoffice option.

Figure 26.3.
Specifying your
postoffice loca-
tion.

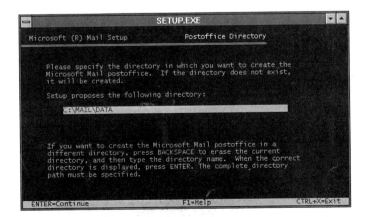

4. The default directory for your MS Mail postoffice is `C:\MAILDATA`. I prefer, however, to create a single directory to contain all of the mail files, so I use

a parent directory of C:\MAIL and the subdirectory DATA (as shown in Figure 26.3) for my postoffice. Once you have specified the location for your postoffice, press the Enter key.

5. The Postoffice Name screen shown in Figure 26.4 appears. Enter the name for your postoffice, such as CONSULTING, then press the Enter key. This name can be up to 10 characters in length and is usually the name of a group within your organization.

Figure 26.4.
Specifying your
postoffice name.

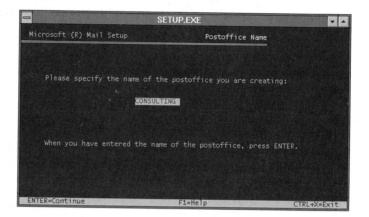

6. Next you will be greeted with a similar screen to define your network name. Enter this name, such as WORK, and press the Enter key. This name can be up to 10 characters in length and is usually the name of your organization. I often use the Windows NT domain name for my network name; you may also want to follow this practice.

7. The Network Type screen then will be displayed as shown in Figure 26.5. For an installation on a Novell server, choose Novell. For an SMB or compatible network such as Windows NT, IBM LAN Server, DEC Pathworks, Windows for Workgroups, Windows 95 or other MSNet/SMB-compatible network, choose Microsoft LAN Manager—compatible. Then press the Enter key.

8. The Server Programs screen, shown in Figure 26.6, appears. Choose each option one at a time and press the Enter key. Start with the Administration and Utilities option and end with the Modem script files option. When all of the options are marked with an asterisk, as shown in Figure 26.6, select the DONE option and press the Enter key.

9. The Server Directory screen will be displayed. This screen looks similar to the Postoffice Location screen shown in Figure 26.3. The only real difference is the default name for the file locations, which is C:\MAILEXE.

Figure 26.5.
Specifying your
network type.

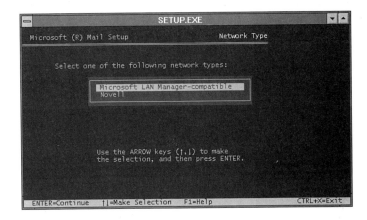

Figure 26.6.
Specifying the
Server Programs
to install.

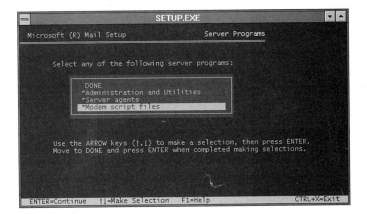

Once more, I prefer to use a single parent directory for my postoffice files, so I use the directory name of C:\MAIL\EXE. When you have entered the appropriate directory name press the Enter key.

10. The Client Programs screen will then be displayed. This screen functions similarly to the Server Programs screen shown in Figure 26.6, except this time you are selecting the types of network clients to support. For Windows 3.x and OS/2 1.x clients, select the Windows and Presentation Manager entry and press the Enter key. To support MS-DOS clients, choose the MS-DOS entry and press the Enter key. When you have made your choices, choose the DONE entry and press the Enter key.

Note

To support your Macintosh clients, you will need to install the Macintosh client from the Apple Macintosh Workstation Version diskette on a Macintosh-accessible volume. This will require that you have also installed the Services for Macintosh on your Windows NT Server installation.

11. The Client Directory screen will then be displayed. This screen is also similar to the Postoffice Location and Server Directory screens. The default directory is C:\MAILEXE, but I prefer to use the C:\MAIL\CLIENTS directory. This enables me to share the subdirectory on the network so that users can install the appropriate mail client without being able to access the MS Mail administration programs. Once you have specified your installation directory, press the Enter key.

12. The Confirm Choices screen, shown in Figure 26.7, then will be displayed. This screen will display the choices you have made in the previous steps. If any information is incorrect, you may scroll down to the appropriate entry and press the Enter key. This will take you back to a previous step so you can make any necessary modifications. Once all of your configuration choices are complete, choose the NO CHANGE option and press the Enter key.

Figure 26.7.
Specifying the
Server Programs
to install.

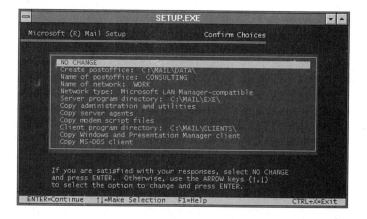

13. The Creating screen appears, which will create the directories you specified, and the file copy process then will begin. Insert each MS Mail diskette as prompted. When all of the files have been copied to your system, the Installation Complete screen will be displayed. Press the Enter key to exit the setup program.

Note

If you will also be using the built-in FAX capabilities, insert the Microsoft FAX setup diskette and run the setup program to install the

FAX support files. If your modem is not listed in the default set, you can install additional support files using the Supplementary Modem Scripts installation diskette.

14. Your final step is to share your postoffice (either `c:\MAILDATA` if you choose the default or `c:\MAIL\DATA` if you followed my example) and the mail applications (located in the `c:\MAILEXE` if you used the default directory or `c:\MAIL\CLIENTS` if you followed my example). The postoffice share must be created with a minimum of Change permissions as each mail user requires full access to all of the mail subdirectories, but the application directory can be shared with Read permissions to prevent inadvertent deletion of the application files.

Note

Creating shares is covered in Chapter 7, "Resource Management Tools," if you need additional information to help you create your shares and assign permissions.

UPGRADING A WORKGROUP POSTOFFICE TO MS MAIL

Presumably, you will be migrating from a WGPO into a new MS Mail postoffice; you will convert a WGPO to an MS Mail postoffice. If this is the case, the simplest thing to do is to run the postoffice upgrade for Microsoft Windows for Workgroups. MS Mail 3.5 on the MS BackOffice CD provides a special Setup program that takes care of upgrading your WGPO to an MS Mail postoffice. It is not the same as the regular MS Mail Setup program, although it looks similar. This makes short work of the upgrade.

At some point, however, you may have to migrate WGPO users into an existing MS Mail postoffice—one that already has active users in it. In this case, you cannot just upgrade the WGPO into a new MS Mail postoffice. Fortunately, it involves simply moving users from the WGPO to the MS Mail postoffice.

By far the easiest way to accomplish the move is with the Move User utility. It is a Windows program, and the process is as simple as dragging and dropping the mailbox from one postoffice into another, deleting the old mailbox, and ensuring that the user's MMF file is accessible at the new location.

Another way to move users is with the Export User and Import User features of the Move User utility. This accomplishes the same thing as moving a user from one postoffice to another, but in two steps. First, you must export the user from the WGPO to an MMU file. Then you must import the user to the new postoffice. This is the way to move users if the source and destination postoffices are not connected to the same network.

Keep in mind that a Workgroup postoffice (WGPO) is simply an MS Mail postoffice that has no capability to exchange mail with any other external postoffice. It is, in essence, a stripped-down version of MS Mail 3.x. Given that, the task of migration from WGPO to MS Mail is pretty straightforward. It turns into the same process as moving MS Mail users between any existing MS Mail postoffices. The MS Mail documentation discusses this in detail.

You cannot simply use the XCOPY command to place the WGPO directories over the top of the MS Mail directories. That would be disastrous because existing users of the MS Mail postoffice would likely be destroyed in the process, or it would otherwise mess everything up.

After the migration, Windows clients should update the ServerPath entry in their MSMAIL.INI file to reflect the location of the new postoffice after being moved to the new postoffice.

Finally, instruct any user being moved to a new postoffice to use Forward rather than Reply when responding to a message received before the move from the old postoffice. This is because after moving to a new postoffice, a reply to a sender might not go to the correct place. A forward ensures that the e-mail goes where you expect.

When you move a user to another postoffice, the following information is copied:

◆ Basic user information, consisting of the mailbox name, user name, and password. The user is added to the destination postoffice and retains all access and folder privileges.

◆ The user's e-mails, which reside on the server. This includes the read/unread state of each e-mail and the contents, including attachments.

◆ The user's private folders, if they are stored on the server.

◆ The user's message file (MMF) and calendar file, if they are stored on the server.

The following information is not transferred during the move process:

◆ Group or shared folders owned by the user.

◆ The user's personal address list (PAL).

◆ Template data.

Note that any personal address books (PAB files) that include this user will be incorrect after the user is copied to the new postoffice. Personal address books are not automatically updated, so this will have to be handled manually.

INSTALLING THE MS-DOS CLIENT

The MS-DOS client for MS Mail, called MAIL.EXE, is a very rudimentary program. It has been around for a while, and it is a holdover from the "old days" of DOS programs. Compared to the Windows version, its functionality is limited and its interface is inelegant. However, it does what it's supposed to do—exchange e-mail.

After the installation of the postoffice, MAIL.EXE will be in the MAILDATA directory (assuming that you accepted the default). Just connect to the file share with MAIL.EXE and run it from a DOS prompt. After you enter your mailbox and password, you'll be in mail. You will also need to connect to the network resource that contains the MS Mail postoffice as drive M:. You can copy MAIL.EXE locally and run it from there.

Note

It doesn't matter whether you use the MS-DOS client sometimes and the Windows client at other times; you still will be able to use your mailbox just the same. The programs access the user's mail information in a common way through MAPI.

To make things easier for your network clients, you may want to automate the drive mapping in their logon script. To make things easier for both you (the administrator) and your network clients, you may want to use SMS to create a package for the MS Mail client. That way you can have your clients run the MS Mail client directly from the shared package. For improved performance you could create an SMS package and a run job or workstation job to install the MS Mail client locally.

See the section "Workstation Software for MS-DOS" in the MS Mail user's guide for more details on the MS-DOS client.

INSTALLING THE WINDOWS FOR WORKGROUPS CLIENT

The Windows client for MS Mail, called MSMAIL.EXE, is a Windows version of the mail program. It runs under Windows 3.1, Windows 95, and Windows NT. Windows 95 and Windows NT include their own improved mail programs; Windows 95 has the Exchange client and Windows NT has MS MAIL32. The Windows version has a much better interface and more functionality than the MS-DOS version of the mail client.

As with the MS-DOS client, the Windows mail client should be found in the MAILDATA directory along with the setup program (SETUP.EXE). Before you run the setup program you should connect to the network resource that contains the postoffice and map this share as drive M: on your local computer. Then run the setup program and install MS MAIL to your local machine. This is preferred to running it from the network share for improved performance. Once more, you can make things easier in this department by automating the mapping of the postoffice to drive M: in their logon script. You can also use SMS to create a package and job for the MS Mail client. That way you can automate the installation of MS Mail and easily perform upgrades in the future.

See the section titled "Windows and Presentation Manager Version" in the MS Mail user's guide for more details.

INSTALLING THE MACINTOSH CLIENT

The Macintosh client for MS Mail is a Macintosh version of the mail program. This program can be run from the network server (if you have installed the Services for Macintosh) or from the user's local machine. It still provides the same basic functionality as the mail clients for DOS and Windows, but for Macintosh users on AppleTalk networks.

Its requirements are minimal. You must have a Macintosh Plus or better with a hard disk, at least 1MB of RAM, and be running System 6.0.3 or higher and Finder or MultiFinder. See the section titled "Workstation Software for the Macintosh" in the MS Mail user's guide for more details.

USING REMOTE CLIENT ACCESS

MS Mail supports clients who use the postoffice remotely—that is, when they are not attached to the network. Remote client users access the postoffice in one of two ways.

The client can use a modem on his remote computer to dial into the postoffice using Microsoft Mail Remote. Actually, the connection is made to the machine running the EXTERNAL program, but all the remote client sees is a connection to the postoffice. The MS Mail Remote program runs under DOS and Windows.

Alternatively, the client can use Remote Access Services (RAS) to attach to the network and then connect to the postoffice and work just as though he were locally attached to the network. This has a few advantages. First, there does not have to be a machine on the network running External, so there is no additional administrative overhead with configuration. Second, RAS is included with and is supported by Windows for Workgroups, Windows 95 (in Windows 95 it's called Microsoft Dial-Up Networking), and Windows NT, so the software already is available on these systems out of the box. There just needs to be a RAS server somewhere on the network where the postoffice resides so that RAS clients can connect to it. Third, when connected with RAS, the remote client has access to network resources other than just the postoffice.

INSTALLING MICROSOFT EXCHANGE SERVER

Preparing for the installation of MS Exchange Server requires some different considerations than its predecessor, MS Mail. Exchange is considerably more powerful and more complex. The good news is that the installation program has been designed to make the process as painless as possible. This section covers some things to think about when installing Exchange, both client and server. When you finish, you should have a better idea of what's ahead when embarking on this task. You'll explore the following topics:

◆ Installing Exchange server components.

◆ Installing the clients.

◆ Migrating an existing postoffice.

◆ Using Remote Client Access.

INSTALLING THE EXCHANGE SERVER COMPONENTS

The installation of the Exchange Server core components is a two-step process. This is because you must first install Service Pack 4 for Windows NT Server before you can install Exchange Server. This adds a step to the install process and also complicates your life a bit more, since any time you add additional Windows NT system components (such as a new service) you must then reinstall the service pack. Failure to reinstall the service pack after installing additional components can lead to unpredictable results. So it's best not to forget!

To install the Windows NT Service Pack, follow these steps:

1. Insert Disc 1 of your BackOffice CD-ROM set into your CD-ROM drive.

2. Change to the WINNT351.QFE subdirectory. Execute the UPDATE.EXE application in the appropriate subdirectory for your processor type. This will be I386 for an Intel processor, ALPHA for a DEC Alpha processor, MIPS for a MIPS processor, or PPC for a PowerPC processor.

3. The replacement files will be copied to your system then you will be prompted to restart your system. Restart the system, and then you may start the Exchange Server installation.

To install Exchange Server, follow these steps:

1. Insert Disc 3 of the BackOffice CD-ROM set into the CD-ROM drive.

2. Change to the EXCHANGE\SERVER\SETUP subdirectory. Execute the SETUP.EXE application in the appropriate subdirectory for your processor platform. This will be I386 for an Intel processor, ALPHA for a DEC Alpha processor, or MIPS for a MIPS processor.

Note

If you cannot find the setup application (SETUP.EXE) using File Manager, this is because the program has the hidden file attribute set for the file. To view hidden files, choose By File Type from the View menu and enable the Show Hidden/System Files checkbox. Then click OK.

3. The Microsoft Exchange Server Setup dialog will be displayed. This dialog informs you that setup cannot proceed if any shared files are in use. Although this is not typically the case, you can just rename files that are in use and continue the setup process. At this point, just click OK, and the dialog box shown in Figure 26.8 appears.

4. This dialog box has four buttons that provide the following options:

   ◆ Typical: Installs a standard installation.

   ◆ Complete/Custom: Choosing this option will allow you to specify which components to install. A complete installation requires about 135MB.

   ◆ Minimum: Installs a minimum installation to conserve disk storage. No sample applications or online documentation will be installed.

   ◆ Change Directory: Choosing this option will display the Change Directory dialog so that you can choose an alternate installation directory. The default is C:\EXCHSRVR for the core system files.

Figure 26.8.
Choosing an
Exchange Server
installation
scenario.

Note

For this example installation, the assumed choice is Complete/Custom.

5. The dialog box shown in Figure 26.9 will then be displayed. This dialog box
   will offer you the following basic options:
   ◆ Microsoft Exchange Server: If this option is checked (the default),
     the Microsoft Exchange Server core files will be installed on the local
     computer. By default, this option installs all of the Exchange Server
     connectors as well.
   ◆ Microsoft Exchange Administrator: If this option is checked (the
     default), the Microsoft Exchange Administrator and additional tools
     will be installed on your local hard disk. If you will not be administer-
     ing Exchange Server locally on the server with the Exchange Server
     installation, then you may uncheck this option.

Tip

You can install just the Microsoft Exchange Administrator program on
another computer to perform remote administration. Just execute the
setup program on the computer you want to use for remote administration and leave only the Microsoft Exchange Administrator option

checked. To specify a different installation directory select the
Microsoft Exchange Administrator option and click the Change
Directory button. The default directory is C:\EXCHSRVR\BIN.

◆ Books Online: If this option is checked (the default), a copy of the
online documentation will be installed on your local hard disk. If space
is at a premium, you may uncheck this option and insert the CD-ROM
whenever you need to use the online documentation.

Figure 26.9.
Specifying the
Exchange Server
basic installation
options.

6. To specify which connectors to install, select the Microsoft Exchange Server
option and click the Change Option button.

7. The dialog shown in Figure 26.10 will be displayed. This will allow you to
choose from the following options:

◆ MS Mail Connector: This connector is used to provide interoperability
with a MS Mail postoffice.

◆ SMTP/Internet Mail Connector: This connector is used to provide the
ability to interoperate with an existing SMTP (Simple Mail Transfer
Protocol) mail system. It can also be used to create a standalone
SMTP mail server so that your network clients can send or receive
e-mail over the Internet.

Figure 26.10.
Specifying the
Exchange Server
connectors to
install.

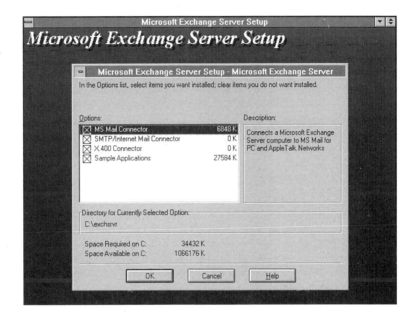

- ◆ X.400 Connector: This connector provides the capability to interoperate with X.400-compatible mail systems.

- ◆ Sample Applications: Installs sample applications to demonstrate Exchange Server's capabilities. It includes a help desk, vacation or sick leave forms, survey forms and a nifty chess application.

8. Once you have made your selections, click OK to return to the Exchange Server Setup—Complete/Custom dialog. Then click OK again to proceed with the installation.

9. The dialog shown in Figure 26.11 will appear. This dialog box is used to specify the license mode for Exchange Server. You have two options. You can use the Per Server license mode and specify the number of licenses you have purchased or the Per Seat license mode. The Per Server mode is useful when you have more clients than licenses. As long as you do not have more simultaneous connections to your Exchange Server than you have licenses, you will not violate your license agreement. The Per Seat mode requires one client license per computer, regardless of whether the client is currently connected to Exchange Server or not.

10. Once you have chosen your licensing mode and specified the number of client licenses if required, click OK.

11. A license dialog, such as that shown in Figure 26.12, will be displayed. You must check the I Agree checkbox to continue the installation. Then click OK.

*Figure 26.11.
Choosing a
licensing mode
for Exchange
Server.*

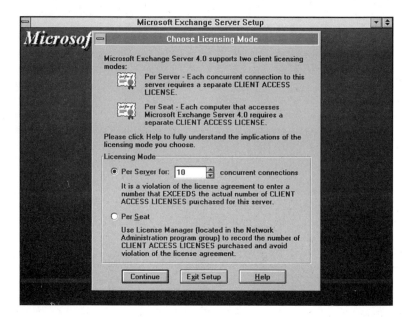

*Figure 26.12.
Confirming your
license agreement
for Exchange
Server.*

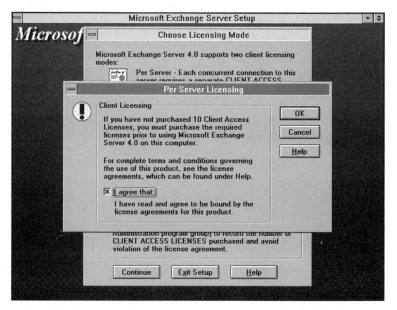

12. The dialog shown in Figure 26.13 will be displayed. This dialog is used to
allow you to join an existing Exchange Server site or to create a new site.
The default is to create a new site. If you will be joining an existing site
instead, choose Join an existing site and specify the name of the computer
in the Existing Server field that contains the site you wish to join. For a

new site, you must specify the name of your organization in the Organization Name field and the name of your site in the Site Name field. The default organization name is your company name (which you should have specified when you installed Windows NT Server) and your domain name will be used for the site name. If these names are not satisfactory, you may change them. If you change them, be sure that you use a consistent naming convention for all of your Exchange Server installations.

Figure 26.13.
Specifying your
Exchange Server
organization and
site information.

13. Once you have specified your site requirements, click OK. A confirmation message box will be displayed. Click Yes to proceed with the installation.

14. The Site Services Account dialog box will be displayed. Here you must specify a user account and password to be used by the Exchange Server services. To specify a different user account, click the Browse button to display the Add User or Group dialog and select a different user account.

Note

By default the account you are currently logged on as will be used for the Exchange Server account. I do not recommend that you use this account. Instead you should create a new account using User Manager for Domains, which is discussed in Chapter 6, "Basic Administrative Tools." The account should have the User Cannot Change Password and Password Never Expires checkboxes enabled.

15. Once you have specified your user account and password, click OK. A message box appears, informing you that the account has been granted the Log on as a Service and Restore Files and Directories user rights. Click OK to proceed.

16. At this point the installation files will be copied to your hard disk drive, the Exchange Server services will be added to the Service Control Manager, the registry will be updated, the Exchange Server directory will be initialized, the Exchange Server program group will be created, and the connectors will be installed.

17. Finally you will be greeted with a dialog box to run the Microsoft Performance Optimizer or exit the setup program. To run the performance optimizer (recommended), click the Run Optimizer button. To exit the setup program, click the Exit Setup button.

Note

The Microsoft Exchange Performance Optimizer is covered in more detail in Chapter 28, "Optimizing Your Mail Server."

At this point you may think that you are finished with your Exchange Server installation. While you have finished actually installing the product, you still have some additional work to do to create a working postoffice. If you have an existing mail system, for example, then you will need to migrate these users to Exchange Server. If you are creating an entirely new postoffice, you will need to create new mailboxes. If you have installed any of the optional connectors, these connectors need to be configured. Finally, you will need to configure the basic Exchange Server properties. All of these options, aside from the migration process, are discussed in the next chapter, "Managing Your Postoffice."

MIGRATING AN EXISTING POSTOFFICE

Migrating an existing postoffice with Exchange Server is pretty easy if you have a Workgroup postoffice, a Microsoft Mail postoffice, or a cc:Mail postoffice, because the Microsoft Exchange Migration Wizard can be used to automate the entire migration process. The basic processes for migrating these postoffices are quite similar. To see just how easy the migration process is, you can use the following steps to migrate a Workgroup or Microsoft Mail postoffice:

Note

If you have an IBM PROFS/OfficeVision, Digital ALL-IN-1, Verimation Memo, or Microsoft Mail for AppleTalk Networks-based mail system, you will find additional tools in the EXCHANGE\SERVER\ MIGRATE directory on Disc 3 of your BackOffice 2.0 CD-ROM set.

1. Execute the Microsoft Exchange Migration Wizard, which is located in the Microsoft Exchange program group. The dialog shown in Figure 26.14 will appear.

2. This dialog offers you the following choices:

Figure 26.14. Starting the migration process.

- ◆ Import Migration Files: Imports a migration file from a migration source extractor or from the migration file created using the Microsoft Exchange Administrator.
- ◆ Migrate from MS Mail for PC Networks: Imports a Workgroup postoffice or MS Mail postoffice.
- ◆ Migrate from Lotus cc:Mail: Imports a cc:Mail postoffice.

3. Once you have specified your choice (in our case, Migrate from MS Mail for PC Networks), click Next.

4. An informational dialog box will be displayed. Click Next.

5. The dialog shown in Figure 26.15 appears. You must enter the location of your postoffice and the administrator account and password.

6. Click Next, and the dialog box shown in Figure 26.16 will be displayed.

7. This dialog box offers you a choice of a single-step process and a two-step process. The single-step process is preferred because of its simplicity, but if you need to modify some of the user properties, you may choose the two-step process. The two-step process will extract the user list from your postoffice.

Figure 26.15.
Specifying your
postoffice location
and account
information.

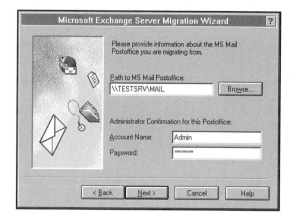

Figure 26.16.
Specifying the
migration type.

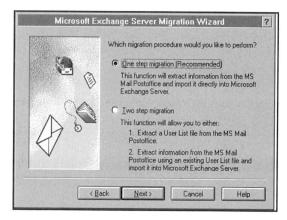

You may edit this list, perhaps to modify the display names for the users, then the Migration Wizard will use it to extract the information from your postoffice and import it into Exchange Server.

8. Once you have made your choice (for this example, the single-step process is assumed to have been chosen) click Next, and the dialog box shown in Figure 26.17 appears.

9. This dialog provides you the ability to choose the information to migrate from your postoffice. You may import information to migrate the user account information to create a mailbox or import their messages, shared folders, address books, and Schedule+ information. (You can even specify a date range for messages to import.) Once you have made your selection, click Next.

Figure 26.17.
Specifying the
information to
migrate from
your postoffice.

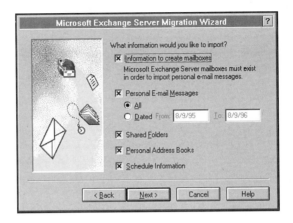

26

10. The next dialog box to appear shows a list of users for the postoffice. This is to provide you the opportunity to limit the users to import to Exchange Server. To select all users, click the Select All button. When you have made your selections, click Next.

11. Now you will be prompted for the name of the Exchange Server computer to which you will migrate the mail accounts and associated information. Once you have entered the name, click Next.

12. If you chose to migrate shared folders, the dialog box shown in Figure 26.18 will appear. This offers you the following choices:

    ◆ No access: This is the default choice and specifies that no users will be granted access to the shared folders.

    ◆ Author access: read, create, edit items: Specifies that all users will be able to read messages, create new messages, and edit messages that they created in the shared folders.

    ◆ Publishing Editor access: includes create folders: Specifies that all users will be granted the ability to read messages, create messages, edit messages, delete messages, and create or delete subfolders within the shared folders.

Tip

You may change the associated permissions with the Microsoft Exchange Administrator after the migration process if you make an incorrect choice during the migration process.

13. Once you have made your choice, click Next and specify a container (the default is Recipients) to hold the user accounts. Then click Next and the dialog box shown in Figure 26.19 appears.

Figure 26.18.
Specifying
permissions for
shared folders.

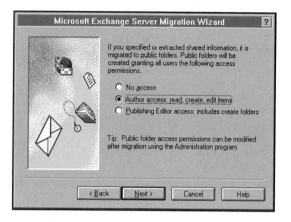

Figure 26.19.
Creating accounts
and passwords.

14. This dialog box offers the following choices:

    ◆ Create accounts and generate random passwords: Specifies that the mail account alias will be used for the Windows NT user account name and the password will be randomly generated. A list of user accounts and passwords will be stored in the file ACCOUNT.PASSWORD.

    ◆ Create accounts and use alias as a password: Specifies that the mail account alias name will be used both for the Windows NT user account name and as the password.

    ◆ Don't create Windows NT accounts: Specifies that no user accounts will be created.

15. By default, these user accounts will be created in the current domain. If you have established any trust relationships with other domains, you may choose another domain from the Choose a Windows NT Domain for accounts drop-down listbox. Once you have made your selection, click Next.

16. At this point the migration process actually begins. When the process has completed (it may take a significant amount of time, depending on the number of users and associated information to migrate), click Finish to exit the Exchange Migration Wizard.

17. A message box will then be displayed instructing you to check the Windows NT event log for further information. This can be particularly useful if any errors were encountered during the migration process.

INSTALLING THE CLIENTS

There is robust client support in MS Exchange. Windows NT, Windows 95, Windows for Workgroups 3.11, Windows 3.1, and MS-DOS clients are all included with the package. The English version of the Exchange clients can be found in the EXCHANGE\CLIENTS\ENG subdirectory of Disc 4 of your BackOffice 2.0 CD-ROM set.

The clients usually are installed over the network by connecting to a file server that contains the client files. However, if you have SMS installed, you can use the predefined package definition files (PDF) located in the EXCHANGE\CLIENTS\SMS\ENG subdirectory to automate the installation process. The Setup program for each operating system provides a common installation routine. Before starting the installation, you should know whether you want to run Schedule+ and whether you already have a mailbox on the Exchange server.

If you are running Windows 3.1 or Windows for Workgroups, you will get a 16-bit version of the Exchange client software. Windows 95 and Windows NT users get the 32-bit version of the Exchange client software. As you may know, Windows 95 already includes an Exchange client. This is really a "lite" version of the Exchange client that ships with the MS Exchange Server package. If you are going to have Windows 95 clients using an Exchange server, you should upgrade them to the full version of the Windows 95 Exchange client. If you run the Windows 95 Exchange client Setup program, it upgrades the Windows 95 Exchange "lite" client to the full version.

Note

In the initial version of MS Exchange Server, there was no Macintosh or PowerPC client support. However, this recently become available, and you may download them from the Microsoft ftp site at ftp:
`//ftp.microsoft.com/bussys/exchange/exchange-public/fixes/`.

26

MICROSOFT MAIL AND EXCHANGE SERVER

USING REMOTE CLIENT ACCESS

The remote Exchange client is supported by dialing into the network that contains the Exchange Server computer. You can accomplish this with Remote Access Services (called Dial-Up Networking in Windows 95) or with a third-party product that provides PPP connectivity. MS-DOS and Windows clients can use ShivaRemote, for example, which is included with Exchange to connect to the network and connect to the Exchange server. Windows 95 clients can use Dial-Up Networking. Windows for Workgroups and Windows NT clients can use RAS.

After the client is remotely connected to the network, things basically function as though the client were locally attached to the network. This is a much better solution than having to use a proprietary remote program, as is the case with MS Mail. The capability to connect to the network (rather than to a server) with a remote access program makes things function more seamlessly. This makes life easier for both the administrator and the user.

SUMMARY

In this chapter you learned how to install both Microsoft Mail and Microsoft Exchange Server. You also learned a bit about the installation of the various mail clients, as well as how to use the Exchange Migration Wizard to migrate your existing Microsoft Mail postoffice to Exchange Server. In the next chapter, you will look into some of the issues involved in managing your MS Mail postoffice. You will learn how to connect multiple postoffices, move users from one postoffice to another, prepare a backup plan, and perform other basic administrative duties.

CHAPTER 27

Managing Your Postoffice

There is obviously a lot to the topic of administration. People have written entire volumes on the subject. In this chapter you will learn some of the basic administration topics of Microsoft Mail and Exchange Server. The purpose of this chapter is not to cover all the details about administration contained in the product documentation or in other books. Instead, the intent is to give you an overview of the administration of your Microsoft Mail postoffice, hopefully providing some insights you might not get from the manuals. Otherwise, this chapter easily could get very big, and you'd probably get really bored reading it all anyway. Then your boss would wonder why you fell asleep while reading such a great book.

You'll also learn some of the more critical details about Microsoft Exchange Server. In this chapter you will learn how to configure Exchange Server, create mailboxes, configure the Exchange Server connectors, and back up your Exchange Server postoffice. This will provide you with a fairly well rounded education of Exchange Server administration. For more detailed information you might want to take a look at *Microsoft Exchange Server System Administrator's Survival Guide,* also by Sams Publishing.

If the information in this chapter saves you some trouble now or in the future, it will be well worth the time you spent reading it. So put on your administrator hat and jump right in!

Note

Admittedly, this chapter tends to be Windows NT-centric; most of the ideas and concepts are brought up with NT Server in mind. In fact, it must be that way when discussing Exchange Server because Exchange runs only on NT Server. Some ideas will apply to any file server or network operating system, but, because this is a BackOffice book, it makes sense to focus on NT Server.

ADMINISTERING YOUR MICROSOFT MAIL POSTOFFICE

The main focus of this section is on Microsoft Mail postoffice administration, and that's what this section addresses. Several facets of this topic are covered:

◆ Administrative tools and utilities

◆ Connecting multiple postoffices

◆ User management and security

◆ Postoffice backup strategy

EXAMINING ADMINISTRATIVE TOOLS AND UTILITIES

Several programs provide the capabilities you need to administer your Microsoft Mail postoffice. Most are DOS, character-based applications. One is a Windows application: Move User. These form the foundation tools for administering your Microsoft Mail postoffice.

THE ADMINISTRATIVE MODULE

The most important administrative tool is the Microsoft Mail Administrative Module: ADMIN.EXE. Figure 27.1 shows Admin's main screen.

*Figure 27.1.
The Microsoft
Mail 3.5 Admin-
istrative Module.*

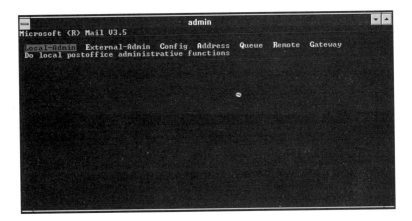

As you can see, the program is a DOS, character-based program. A Windows version of Admin does not exist.

Note

> You will see the terms user and mailbox used interchangeably in this section. They are, for the purposes of Microsoft Mail, synonymous; a user is defined by his mailbox. Do not confuse this with a Windows NT user account or any other network user account; they are not the same.

The functions are split into seven main menus, each of which has submenus that enable you to access various postoffice administrative functions:

◆ Local-Admin: This is where the common administrative functions are carried out—tasks pertaining to the local postoffice. Mailboxes (users) and distribution lists can be created, modified, and deleted. Folder and mailbox compression, default global user options, and printing are accessed here, along with the capability to reset user passwords.

◆ External-Admin: If you have more than one postoffice, you will use this menu a lot. You can define, modify, and delete the list of external postoffices here. You can export a list of your postoffice's users and groups to external postoffices, perform maintenance on the postoffice address list, and display statistics on external postoffices. This menu is also where you configure parameters for external postoffices you connect to directly via modem or X.25.

◆ Config: If your postoffice must communicate with external postoffices, this menu enables you to specify hardware and software parameters. Things like directory synchronization, global address list usage, hop count, and modem parameters are accessed through this menu, too. The local postoffice password can be set here as well.

◆ Address: If you have external postoffices, this menu enables you to add addresses of those external users to your postoffice address list. Maintaining this list is an important administrator responsibility because your users rely on it to get the proper addresses, both for local and external users.

◆ Queue: This menu enables you to manage your postoffice's outbox and its contents. You can return mail to the sender, or you can delete mail from the outbox. This menu is only applicable for mail that is being sent to an external postoffice.

◆ Remote: You use this menu to access administrative tasks for remote users at your postoffice. This is only applicable if you have installed the Modem Mail postoffice module. You set the baud rate and phone number for the postoffice, give remote mail privileges, and perform other remote user administrative tasks.

◆ Gateway: If you have any gateways attached, you will use this menu. Otherwise, it does nothing. This accesses the administrative tasks for external gateways at the postoffice.

As you use Admin, you will quickly become familiar with its menu structure. You also will likely find that it is the administrative tool you spend the most time using.

ADMINISTRATOR UTILITIES

The postoffice administrator uses other tools as well. These main administrative utilities are Re-sort, Folders Compression, Rebuild, Import, LAN Manager Extract, Novell Extract, and Move User. You can find detailed descriptions for each utility in the *Microsoft Mail Administrator's Guide*, Appendix A, "Administrator Utilities."

These utilities are described briefly here:

- Re-sort: RESORT.EXE is an MS-DOS application used by administrators. This utility re-sorts the postoffice address list according to the collating sequence compatible with your postoffice. It is useful for international installations. The mail system should be inactive when Re-sort is run. The simplest way to make sure the postoffice is inactive is to pause the server service, which will prevent new connections to your postoffice. Then you can use Server Manager to send e-mail to any users who are currently connected to the postoffice, asking them to disconnect from the postoffice share. Any unresponsive users can be forcibly disconnected from the postoffice with Server Manager as well, but you want to be careful about forcibly disconnecting a user as this could cause a loss of data.

- Folders Compression: FOLDCOMP.EXE is an MS-DOS application used by administrators and MS-DOS clients. Its purpose is to recover disk space from folders that have space in them left over after deleting mail. FOLDCOMP is used most commonly by MS-DOS clients who want to recover disk space taken up by folders located on their local hard drive.

- Rebuild: REBUILD.EXE is an MS-DOS application used by administrators to rebuild the global address list (GAL). The GAL contains all the addresses accessible by your postoffice users. It contains combined entries from all address lists, including gateway lists. A GAL is optional, and, if you don't use one, you won't need the Rebuild utility. Also, if you use directory synchronization, it rebuilds the GAL.

- Import: IMPORT.EXE is an MS-DOS application used by administrators. It is used to import local postoffice user information, to import external postoffice and gateway user information during directory synchronization, and to import user names extracted with LMEXT and NOVEXT.

- LAN Manager Extract, Novell Extract: LMEXT.EXE and NOVEXT.EXE are MS-DOS applications used by administrators with the Import utility. LMEXT and NOVEXT extract the user names from the network user accounts and create a text file containing the user names and full names. The text file, in turn, is imported by IMPORT to create mailboxes and their respective aliases in the postoffice.

- Move User: MOVEUSER.EXE is a Windows application used by administrators to move users from one postoffice to another. It also can be used to delete users from a postoffice, to export mailboxes to MMU files, or to import mailboxes from MMU files. You must have a login to an Admin mailbox on each postoffice you want to use. Figure 27.2 shows MOVEUSER in action.

27

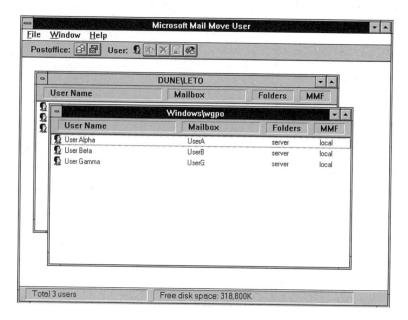

Figure 27.2.
The Microsoft
Mail Move User
utility connected
to two postoffices.

CONNECTING MULTIPLE POSTOFFICES

Most likely, if your installation is of any size, you will have to use more than one Microsoft Mail postoffice. When that happens, there are additional administrative concerns that come up that you didn't have to worry about with a single postoffice. The next three sections cover the EXTERNAL program, global directory synchronization, and the Dynamic Drive Administrator program.

The fundamental idea is this: You have two postoffices, and the users based out of each postoffice need to exchange e-mail with each other. How does Microsoft Mail do it? As you will note in Figure 27.3, there is a computer on the network running EXTERNAL that takes care of routing mail from a user's postoffice to another postoffice (referred to as an external postoffice).

To set things up for exchanging e-mail between postoffices, you have to make some preparations that basically consist of the following:

- ◆ Setting up the postoffices to use EXTERNAL.
- ◆ Ensuring that the directory is synchronized across postoffices.

After you understand this concept for the simplest case of two postoffices, you can expand it to the number of postoffices on your network.

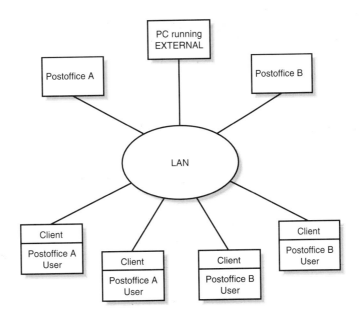

Figure 27.3.
Multiple
Microsoft Mail
postoffices on a
network with
EXTERNAL.

POSTOFFICES AND THE EXTERNAL PROGRAM

The first thing to think about is how to enable postoffices to move mail from one postoffice to another. To do that, you need to use the EXTERNAL program, simply referred to as EXTERNAL. In the preceding chapter, I outlined a few scenarios for configuring multiple postoffices. The most basic scenario is shown in Figure 27.3.

Setting up the postoffices for EXTERNAL is not difficult. The idea is to tell each postoffice about all the other postoffices with which it can exchange e-mail. You can do this by using the External-Admin | Create menu of Admin. You also have to give each user privileges to send e-mail to external postoffices through Admin's Local-Admin menu.

A couple other aspects of configuring a postoffice to use EXTERNAL follow:

◆ Instructing EXTERNAL how e-mail will be routed: directly or indirectly.

◆ Instructing EXTERNAL how e-mail will be transported: MS-DOS drive (over the LAN), modem, or X.25.

The MS-DOS drive transport method is the method for postoffices connected on a LAN, so this transport is used for this example. Depending on the number of postoffices and the network layout, the routing method can be direct or indirect.

Indirect routing is useful if you have many postoffices—too many to connect them all directly. A direct connection requires that an actual connection, such as a network drive, be mapped to the other postoffices. Indirect routing is used when routing mail to a postoffice through a third postoffice. A good example of indirect

27

MANAGING YOUR POSTOFFICE

routing is using a central hub postoffice to handle routing e-mail from several postoffices. For the example of the simplest scenario—two postoffices with users sending e-mail to each other—the direct routing method works best.

OK, after you've told the postoffices about each other, then you can start EXTERNAL. Because you've configured the connection to the external postoffice to be direct-routed over an MS-DOS drive, EXTERNAL must have access to a network drive mapped to the postoffice. In this example, you have two postoffices for EXTERNAL to manage, so you can map them to drives M and N. After you start EXTERNAL and it is running, it looks something like Figure 27.4.

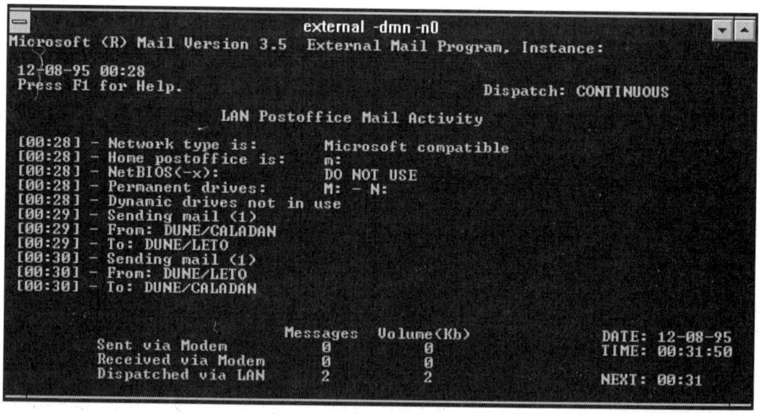

Figure 27.4.
The EXTERNAL
program's
console.

```
                                    external -dmn -n0
Microsoft (R) Mail Version 3.5   External Mail Program, Instance:

12-08-95 00:28
Press F1 for Help.                                    Dispatch: CONTINUOUS

                          LAN Postoffice Mail Activity

[00:28] - Network type is:        Microsoft compatible
[00:28] - Home postoffice is:     m:
[00:28] - NetBIOS(-x):            DO NOT USE
[00:28] - Permanent drives:       M: - N:
[00:28] - Dynamic drives not in use
[00:29] - Sending mail (1)
[00:29] - From: DUNE/CALADAN
[00:29] - To: DUNE/LETO
[00:30] - Sending mail (1)
[00:30] - From: DUNE/LETO
[00:30] - To: DUNE/CALADAN


                         Messages  Volume(Kb)            DATE: 12-08-95
      Sent via Modem         0         0                 TIME: 00:31:50
      Received via Modem     0         0
      Dispatched via LAN     2         2                 NEXT: 00:31
```

EXTERNAL's purpose is to wait until e-mail is ready to be delivered between the postoffices it is watching over. As you can see, mail has been exchanged between two postoffices by EXTERNAL. Pretty cool, huh? Well, this is actually the easy part, because, to enable a user to send e-mail to another user on an external postoffice, there must be a directory entry for that external user. "How does that happen?" you ask. Time to talk about directory synchronization.

GLOBAL DIRECTORY SYNCHRONIZATION

Arguably the most important thing about maintaining a set of postoffices is keeping the directories in sync. Global directory synchronization and EXTERNAL work together to keep the global address list (GAL) up to date on all the postoffices.

Suppose that you want to send e-mail to JohnJ, who resides on postoffice Leto. Your mailbox resides on postoffice Caladan. How can you send JohnJ e-mail? Your postoffice address list doesn't even know JohnJ exists, so you cannot address him. Somehow, your postoffice has to know about postoffice Leto, as well as JohnJ's existence there. That's where the global directory, or GAL, comes into play.

The GAL is kept up-to-date with all the directory entries for all users through the process of global directory synchronization. You specify a postoffice as the directory server, and the other postoffices are directory requestors. Directory synchronization can be done manually using the Rebuild utility, or it can be managed to occur automatically using the Dispatch program.

Now look at DISPATCH.EXE for a minute. The dispatch program is an MS-DOS console-type application similar in appearance to EXTERNAL. Figure 27.5 shows DISPATCH in action. DISPATCH polls the postoffices in the list—there are two in Figure 27.5; Leto attached to M and Caladan attached to N—and checks for any scheduled directory update events on each postoffice.

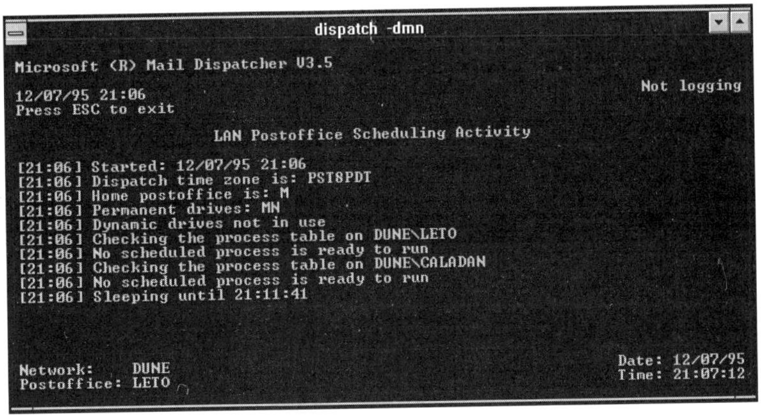

Figure 27.5.
The Dispatch
program's
console.

```
                          dispatch -dmn
Microsoft (R) Mail Dispatcher V3.5
12/07/95 21:06                                        Not logging
Press ESC to exit
                    LAN Postoffice Scheduling Activity

[21:06] Started: 12/07/95 21:06
[21:06] Dispatch time zone is: PST8PDT
[21:06] Home postoffice is: M
[21:06] Permanent drives: MN
[21:06] Dynamic drives not in use
[21:06] Checking the process table on DUNE\LETO
[21:06] No scheduled process is ready to run
[21:06] Checking the process table on DUNE\CALADAN
[21:06] No scheduled process is ready to run
[21:06] Sleeping until 21:11:41



Network:    DUNE                                    Date: 12/07/95
Postoffice: LETO                                    Time: 21:07:12
```

If DISPATCH finds nothing ready to run in the schedules of the postoffices, it merely sleeps until the next polling time. Tough life, eh? This polling interval can be specified by you, so you can make it work harder if you want. But if DISPATCH finds something ready to run in a postoffice's schedule, it kicks off the Microsoft Mail Directory Synchronization Requestor (the MDSR), which runs the directory synchronization utilities. The utilities are called agents, and include the following:

◆ REQMAIN: Processes directory update requests and responses from requestor postoffices.

◆ SRVMAIN: Initiates processing of address updates on the directory server.

◆ IMPORT: Merges the directory updates from the directory sync stream into the local postoffice address lists.

◆ REBUILD: Rebuilds the global address list (GAL).

To synchronize the GAL for all the postoffices, updates go from the requestor postoffices to the directory server postoffice, and then from the directory server

27

postoffice back out to the requestor postoffices. The basic process to manually synchronize the GAL follows (the MDSR follows this same principle):

1. Run REQMAIN in transmit mode for each requestor postoffice and for the directory server postoffice, causing them to queue their directory synchronization mail to be sent to the directory server.

2. Use EXTERNAL to send the queued directory sync mail to the directory server.

3. Run SRVMAIN in receive mode on the directory server, causing it to receive the directory updates sent from the requestors.

4. Run SRVMAIN in transmit mode on the directory server, causing it to queue directory updates to be sent to the requestor postoffices.

5. Use EXTERNAL to send the queued directory sync mail to the requestor postoffices.

6. Run REQMAIN in receive mode for each requestor postoffice and for the directory server postoffice, causing them to receive the directory updates sent from the directory server.

7. Run IMPORT for each postoffice, including the directory server, causing each postoffice's address list to be updated with the new directory entries.

8. Run REBUILD for each postoffice, including the directory server, causing the GAL to be rebuilt on each postoffice.

After this series of programs runs, the directory synchronization process is complete.

There is one important implied aspect of directory synchronization: The EXTERNAL program must be running and accessible by the postoffices being synchronized. "Why?" you ask. Directory updates are shipped back and forth between the directory server and the requestors via mail messages. Guess what program is responsible for doing all that shipping. You got it—EXTERNAL. Hopefully, you can start to see how all these seemingly disparate components interrelate.

Note

You also can include any installed external gateways in directory synchronization.

These topics are covered in detail in the *Microsoft Mail Administrator's Guide*, in the chapters "Global Directory Synchronization," "Setting Up the External Mail Program," and "External Postoffice Administrative Tasks."

DYNAMIC DRIVE ADMINISTRATOR

Dynamic Drive Administrator is another tool you can use if you must administer multiple Microsoft Mail postoffices. This program provides a workaround if you require more postoffices to be connected than can simultaneously connect to a single postoffice (remember that a postoffice resides on a file server).

For purposes of an Microsoft Mail postoffice, Windows NT can assign all unused letters of the alphabet to network drives, but if there are 30 external postoffices that need to connect to your postoffice, there's a problem. You cannot map all of them as a network drive and leave them mapped. This is where Dynamic Drive Administrator comes in. It connects to a network resource when EXTERNAL requires the connection, and it releases the resource when EXTERNAL is done. In this way, many more connections can be made than would otherwise be possible.

You might even want to use dynamic drive assignment even if you don't have more postoffices than your connection limit. Because the network resource is connected only when it is needed and released when it isn't, this can save on network traffic and server resources. It also can help postoffice performance because the file server won't always have to manage all those open network connections. This subject is covered in detail in the *Microsoft Mail Administrator's Guide* chapter, "The Dynamic Drive Administrator Program."

IMPLEMENTING ADVANCED SECURITY

Security is a big deal, right? Well, think about this. In order for a user to work with Microsoft Mail, the user has to be given complete access rights to the postoffice data files directory—usually MAILDATA. The user gets the server and share name, and access rights include the right to delete files, because, during the course of using Microsoft Mail, the Microsoft Mail client has to do all kinds of operations on disk files in the postoffice. As you know, usually this is asking for trouble. Even if you can implicitly trust all the users, accidents do happen. And if anything happens to this directory tree, the postoffice is in big trouble. That means your life just got harder.

Fortunately, you can implement advanced security in Microsoft Mail. The idea is this: The user doesn't have to know what network share he is connected to for the postoffice data files. When the mail client is run, the location of the Microsoft Mail data files is read out of an encrypted file called MAIL.DAT. This allows the Microsoft Mail client to automatically connect to the postoffice for the duration of the mail session. Afterward, the client is disconnected.

Tip

> If the postoffice is on a server which can be browsed by your postoffice clients, with a little sleuthing your postoffice clients could find the shared directory and directly connect to the postoffice. Since you do not want this to occur in the first place or you would not be using the advanced security features, you should hide the server containing your postoffice. This really only removes the server from the browse list of resources on your network; it doesn't prevent anyone from accessing a shared resource if they know the name of the server and the shared resource. To hide your server, you need to create a new entry called Hidden under the `CurrentControlSet\Services\LanmanServer\Parameters` key. Then set the Hidden entry's value to 1. For more details on creating keys and values, you can take a look at Appendix B, "The Registry Editor and Registry Keys."

Now you're probably thinking you can pull some tricks out of your hat and keep these users from hosing the directory. Probably so. Windows NT has many features to manage security at quite a detailed level, for example. But in case you cannot find a solution, advanced security is an option to consider.

PLANNING A POSTOFFICE BACKUP STRATEGY

One serious concern for an Administrator is to have the postoffice data files backed up properly. Nothing can ruin your day faster than to need a backup, only to find that you don't have one around—especially if the boss is asking. Ouch. Therefore, it is prudent to spend some time figuring out how you're going to prevent that situation from happening. So someday when a disk drive suddenly crashes, or when someone accidentally deletes everyone's mail, you will have some recourse to fix things.

It's not too hard, really. All it requires is some forethought and a bit of planning. Then you, too, can be a hero when your boss needs that critical backup data. First, I'll tell you about some data-loss prevention ideas, and then I'll cover two ways to back up your Microsoft Mail postoffice.

PREVENTING DATA LOSS

Before you get into the meat of the topic of backup, it's a good idea to review some ways to take a proactive stance on data loss. In other words, you can make your life easier with techniques to prevent data loss from happening. In reality, you can't actually prevent data loss with 100-percent certainty, but you certainly can minimize the occurrences of data loss. Here are some ideas:

◆ Use mirrored disk drives. Probably the single most effective thing you can do to prevent data loss is to mirror your disk drives. Functionally, it doesn't really matter if you use NT Server's drive-mirroring feature or if you use a third party's disk controller to mirror your drives. The net result is the same: disk fault tolerance with decent performance. There are some performance implications with software versus hardware mirroring, but the bottom line is data protection.

In a mirrored configuration, if—no, when—you have a drive failure, you will have a mirror of the failed drive that contains all the same data. Assuming that the mirror doesn't fail, too (stranger things have happened), in all likelihood your postoffice will not even go down until you take it down to replace the failed drive. And you won't even have to take the system down if you use hot-pluggable disk drives.

◆ Look for redundant systems. This notion of redundancy pays off in other areas, not just with disk drives. Modern server hardware is more and more often equipped with redundancy features, such as redundant power supplies, mirrored disk controllers, and mirrored disk drives.

If a power supply fails, for example, another one immediately kicks in before the system can go down. Some vendors even have external disk drive systems which, in the case of a main computer failure, automatically allow another connected standby computer to come up and use the drives. The new system looks and acts just like the now-failed system to users on the network.

◆ Employ other disk fault tolerance. OK, so your boss didn't want to spring double the money for mirrored drives. I can understand that. Fortunately, there are other solutions. One of the most cost-effective is RAID level 5, also called a stripe set with parity in NT Server. This allows you to deploy n drives in a striped fashion, and you get fault tolerance with the storage space of $n - 1$ drives.

If you deploy four 1GB drives in a RAID 5 configuration, for example, you get 3GB of disk space. If any one drive fails, you simply replace it and the system rebuilds it from the information stored on the other drives.

You must have a minimum of three drives for RAID 5. Also note that RAID 5 does not perform as fast as mirroring, but that's the trade-off for the extra disk space and fault tolerance.

◆ Install an uninterruptible power supply (UPS). This is the simplest idea of them all. If your system loses its supply of electricity, no amount of fault-tolerant features will keep things running. A UPS keeps electricity flowing to the system while the power is out, and, if it needs to, the system can shut itself down gracefully.

27

MANAGING YOUR POSTOFFICE

◆ Use NTFS. Speaking of losing power to the system, funny things can happen to a file system when files are open and the system goes down unexpectedly. With NT Server, you can run your postoffice on the NTFS file system. NTFS has transaction logs built into it that ensure the integrity of the file system if the operating system goes down ungracefully. If that happens, when NTFS reinitializes, it checks the file system integrity. If it needs to, it simply replays the transactions up until the point of failure, putting things back exactly as they should be.

◆ Purchase quality server hardware. How many times have you heard this? Many, I'm sure, but I can't stress this enough. How many people have lost perfectly good hair because they have pulled it all out over poor hardware? Save yourself some time and energy (and hair) by purchasing quality server hardware, especially if you are in a large corporate environment.

◆ Perform regular backups. You knew I was going to say this, didn't you? If you perform regular backups, you will help the cause simply because you have a copy of the data stored somewhere else. And if you have a copy of it, that means it can't be completely lost. Although this doesn't actually prevent data loss, it does help minimize it.

ESTABLISHING A BACKUP ROUTINE

An important element of a successful backup plan is to establish a regular routine of backing up. You never know when catastrophe will strike, so you must be ready at all times.

I recommend backing up once a week at the absolute minimum. Once a day is even better, especially for the postoffice that is the directory server. There is a point of diminishing returns when you start backing up too often to get real benefit, but only you can really determine what that point is.

You can do a full backup each time, for example, copying all the data files to the backup destination. If the postoffice is very large and a full backup takes a while, there are other methods, especially if you are using tape. See the section "Backing Up the Postoffice to Tape," later in this chapter, for more details about this.

BACKING UP THE POSTOFFICE TO A FILE SERVER

One way to back up your postoffice is simply by copying the postoffice data files to another file server on the network. You could even copy the files to another directory on the same machine that houses your postoffice. Regardless, the idea is just to copy and save the data directory somewhere else.

If you will remember, the data directory is the one with the 19 subdirectories. It is where all the critical postoffice data is stored. If you lose the postoffice or if this directory gets corrupted, you have to restore the backup of this directory tree and its contents intact.

You should take the postoffice offline during the backup operation. Here are the general steps to follow:

◆ Ensure that there is no one using the postoffice. Under NT Server, you can see this by opening the Control Panel and running the Server applet. Then click the Users, Shares, or In Use button to see who is actively using the postoffice share. As an alternative, you can use Server Manager, which adds a little bit more functionality, such as the capability to send connected users a message that you are going to disconnect them from the postoffice.

◆ Stop sharing the postoffice on the network. This keeps users from using the postoffice while the backup is in progress. This is the preferred method to use if you must also allow users to connect to other shared resources on the same server. Otherwise you can just pause the Server service—to prevent new users from connecting to the server—and disconnect any currently connected users on the postoffice. But be sure to send these users a message first to provide them with a few minutes to save their data and disconnect from the postoffice first, if this is at all possible.

◆ Copy the data directory to the backup destination, another file server or a different directory on the disk drive.

◆ Resume sharing the postoffice on the network, or continue the Server service if you previously paused the Server service. The postoffice now is ready for users to resume using it.

Technically speaking, you can perform the backup without taking the postoffice off the network if you're absolutely sure that no one will be using it. A problem arises, however, when a user tries to send mail during the backup process. If some files change after they are backed up but other corresponding files change before they are backed up, the postoffice backup is left in an indeterminate state. As a result, the backed up postoffice will have problems if you restore it and try to use it.

There is an added benefit of doing backups to another file server on the network. If your postoffice machine died a horrible death and could not be brought back up, you could just share the backed up postoffice from the backup file server. Users could remap their network drive to it and they would be back up and running.

One other note: If the postoffice data files directories are lost or corrupted, anything that was placed in the postoffice since the last backup is gone. That is another reason why you should consider the preventive measures outlined earlier.

BACKING UP THE POSTOFFICE TO TAPE

A second way to back up your postoffice is by backing up the postoffice data files to tape. This is the same principle as outlined earlier, copying the postoffice data files to another file server on the network. This time, however, the destination is a tape drive, rather than a file server.

First, some tape backup terminology. These definitions are taken from the Windows NT Server Backup software included with NT Server:

◆ Normal: Copies the data to tape and sets the archive bit.

◆ Copy: Copies the data but does not change the archive bit.

◆ Differential: Copies only data files that have been modified but does not set the archive bit.

◆ Incremental: Copies the data that has been modified and sets the archive bit.

◆ Daily: Copies data files that have been modified on that day but does not set the archive bit.

One scenario is to perform a Normal backup every night. This minimizes restore time because all you have to do is restore the last full backup. Another scenario, if you have a large postoffice to back up, is to perform a Normal backup once a week. Then, every other night, perform an Incremental backup. This minimizes backup time and postoffice down time each night. Restore time is increased, however. You must restore starting with the last full backup, and then restore each Incremental backup in sequence until you are through the last Incremental backup. The most commonly used methods are Normal and Incremental, but you can combine any of the methods to customize backups to your specific needs.

As with the first backup procedure outlined earlier, you should take the postoffice offline for the backup operation. Again, here are the general steps to follow:

◆ Ensure that there is no one using the postoffice. Under NT Server, you can see this by opening the Control Panel and running the Server applet, or use Server Manager. Then click the Users, Shares, or In Use button to see who is actively using the postoffice share.

◆ Stop sharing the postoffice on the network or pause the Server service and disconnect any connected users. This keeps users from using the postoffice while the backup is in progress.

◆ Perform the copy of the data directory to the backup destination, either to another file server or to a different directory on the disk drive.

◆ Resume sharing the postoffice on the network or continue the Server service. The postoffice now is ready for users to resume using it.

As noted before, you can perform the backup without taking the postoffice off the network if you're absolutely sure that no one will be using it. A problem arises, however, when a user tries to send mail during the backup process. If some files change after they are backed up but other corresponding files change before they are backed up, the postoffice backup is left in an indeterminate state.

This is even more likely to happen with tape backup than with copying files to another file server because backing up to tape is slower, so the window during which the postoffice can be damaged is longer. Once again, if the postoffice data files' directories are lost or corrupted, anything put in the postoffice since the last backup is gone. That is another reason why you want to consider the preventive measures outlined earlier.

ADMINISTERING YOUR MICROSOFT EXCHANGE SERVER POSTOFFICE

There is a lot to say about Exchange Server administration, and there will be even more as time goes on. To get an idea, just look at the size of the administration manual. As you start looking at the administration of an Exchange Server postoffice, however, you will need to think about several new ideas, as well as remember some established ones.

In this section you will learn how to configure the basic Exchange Server elements to get you started. Then you will learn how to create your user mailboxes, using the Exchange Server extensions to User Manager for Domains. Finally, you will look at the Exchange Server extensions to the Windows NT Backup utility so you can backup or restore your Exchange Server installation.

CONFIGURING EXCHANGE SERVER

Configuring Exchange Server to do just what you want can sometimes be a bit more difficult than expected. This is not because Exchange Server is difficult to administer. Rather, it is because there are so many different items to configure and the documentation and built-in help files just do not tell you exactly where to configure a specific item. This is where I come into the picture, to help you find these items so that your Exchange Server installation will do what you want it to do.

The starting point for all of these configuration issues will be to point out a few of the surprises waiting for you. Once this is out of the way, you will look into configuring the various Exchange Server connectors. A connector is used in one of two ways: to connect two or more mail systems to exchange e-mail with each other, or to provide a means for Exchange Server to interoperate with existing e-mail standards. This section will focus on the issues involved in configuring Exchange

Server to interoperate with existing e-mail systems, such as the Internet standard SMTP (Simple Mail Transfer Protocol). The best way to configure Exchange Server to connect two sites is to use the Exchange Server Site Connector, because this method provides complete directory replication. However, you can also use the Connected Sites tab in a connector to join two or more sites to just exchange e-mail, if desired.

CONFIGURATION SURPRISES

The Microsoft Exchange Administrator uses a Windows 95 Explorer-type view to provide an interface to access the various Exchange Server components. This functions quite similarly to the basic directory and file methodology with which you are already familiar (assuming you have used the Windows 95 Explorer or the Windows NT File Manager). The only problem with this interface is that you expect to be able to select an item in the left window pane and have the configurable components be displayed in the right window pane (much as you'd select a directory in the left window pane and see the files in the right window pane). Unfortunately, it does always work this way, which is why you may sometimes be confused when attempting to find an item to configure. This is why I call these options configuration surprises, since they do not follow the standard methodology.

There are three items of note which every administrator needs to be able to find in order to properly configure their postoffice, and which do not follow the standard method. In this section you will learn where these options are, and how to configure them.

GENERATING THE OFFLINE ADDRESS BOOK

Almost every network includes clients that use portable computers. These portable computer users need to be able to address their e-mail messages while not physically connected to the network. In order to do so, these users must be able to store a local copy of the Exchange Server address book on their computer. In order for a network client to download a copy of the address book, the network client can just choose Tools | Syncronize | Download Address Book. This is the easy part. Unfortunately, your Exchange clients are likely to encounter a misleading error message or two while attempting to download the address book. This is because, before your clients can download the address book, you (the administrator) must create the offline copy of the address book for your clients to download first. This process can be completed by following these steps:

1. Launch the Microsoft Exchange Administrator, located in your Microsoft Exchange program group.

2. Expand the site folder (for my server, this is WORK, for example) so that the Add-Ins, Addressing, Connections, Directory Replication, Monitors, and Servers folders are displayed. (See Figure 27.6.)

Figure 27.6.
Preparing to
configure
Exchange Server's
basic properties.

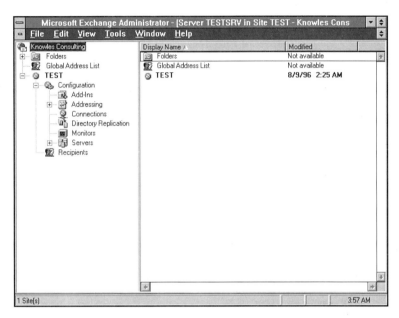

3. Select the Configuration folder, and the configurable items will be listed in the window on the right side. (See Figure 27.7.)

Figure 27.7.
The configurable
components in the
WORK site.

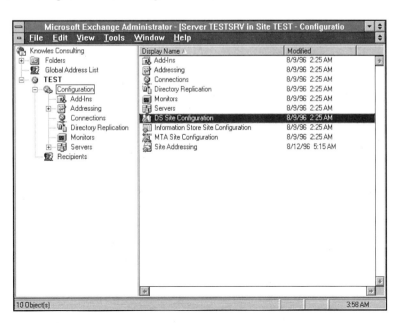

4. Select the DS Site Configuration item and choose Properties from the File menu.

5. The DS Site Configuration Properties dialog will appear.

6. Select the Offline Address Book tab. Then click on the Generate Offline Address Book Now button. A window will appear informing you that the offline address book is being created. Then a message box will appear, informing you that the offline address book was successfully generated. Just click the OK button to close the message box.

7. Then click the OK button to exit the DS Site Configuration Properties dialog box and return to the Microsoft Exchange Administrator.

Tip

Once you have generated your initial copy of the offline address book, you should click on the Offline Address Book Schedule tab and specify the days and times to regenerate the offline address book. This will make sure the offline address book is kept up-to-date. You should then inform your network clients (possible via an e-mail message) that, before they disconnect from the network and hit the road, they should download the latest copy of the offline address book.

CONFIGURING THE EXCHANGE SERVER NAME SPACE

The Exchange Server name space is really the naming convention used by Exchange Server to specify your organization. However, the default names provided by Exchange Server may not really be how you want your e-mail clients to be addressed. The default SMTP name for my network was *UserName*@SRV.KnowlesConsulting.COM. Since I have my own domain name, I preferred to use *UserName*@nt-guru.com. Microsoft has provided a means to change the default names. Unfortunately it, too, is buried in another dialog which many users will overlook. Luckily, I know where this dialog is and plan to share it with you. So, to change your default naming convention, follow these steps:

1. Launch the Microsoft Exchange Administrator, located in your Microsoft Exchange program group.

2. Expand the site folder (for my server, this is WORK, for example) so that the Add-Ins, Addressing, Connections, Directory Replication, Monitors, and Servers folders are displayed. (See Figure 27.6.)

3. Select the Site Addressing item and choose Properties from the File menu.

4. The Site Addressing Properties dialog will appear.

5. Choose the Site Addressing tab. Then select the appropriate name space (such as SMTP) and click on the Edit button. This will display an edit dialog box where you may change the default name to be used for the address space.

6. When you have completed your changes, click the OK button to exit the edit dialog. Then click the OK button to exit the Site Addressing Properties dialog box and return to the Microsoft Exchange Administrator.

Configuring the Exchange Server Message Transfer Agent

The Message Transfer Agent (MTA) is used to transfer your messages from one e-mail system to another, or, to put it another way, the MTA is used to send your e-mail. For most networks the default configuration should be acceptable. However, if you are using a less reliable connection, such as a slow remote access connection over a standard phone line, you may need to change the defaults to better suit your configuration and increase reliability. Alternatively, if you have a reliable high speed connection, you may want to change the defaults to increase performance. You can change these settings by following these steps:

1. Launch the Microsoft Exchange Administrator, located in your Microsoft Exchange program group.

2. Expand the site folder (for my server, this is WORK, for example) so that the Add-Ins, Addressing, Connections, Directory Replication, Monitors, and Servers folders are displayed. (See Figure 27.6.)

3. Select the MTA Site Configuration item and choose Properties from the File menu.

4. The MTA Site Configuration Properties dialog will appear.

5. Click on the Message Defaults tab, shown in Figure 27.8.

6. This property sheet has the following options:

   ◆ RTS values: The RTS (Request to Send) group is used to specify your error control options for sending your e-mail. It has three options, which includes the following:

   Checkpoint size (K): Specifies the amount of data to be sent before a checkpoint record is inserted. A checkpoint record is used to determine where the retransmission of your e-mail will start if an error occurs during the transmission phase. Smaller checkpoint values should be used for less reliable connections, while larger values should be used for more reliable connections. The default checkpoint size is 30.

   Recovery timeout (sec): Specifies the time, in seconds, for the MTA to wait after an error occurs to delete the last checkpoint and retransmit the data. The default is 60 seconds.

27

Figure 27.8.
Configuring the
MTA message
defaults.

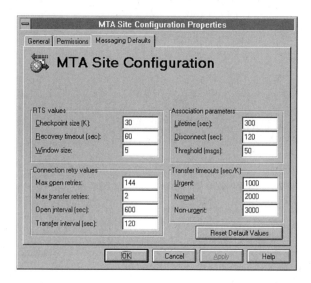

Window size: Specifies the number of checkpoints that can be unacknowledged before the data transmission is suspended. Larger window sizes can be used to increase performance, but should not be used on unreliable connections. The default is 5.

◆ Connection retry values: This group controls connection related parameters and includes the following options:

Max open retries: Specifies the maximum number of times to try to open a connection before a non-delivery report (NDR) is sent to the mail administrator. The default is 144.

Max transfer retries: Specifies the maximum number of attempts to send a message over an open connection.

◆ Association parameters: Specifies the association parameters. An association is a pathway to another system over an open connection. You may have multiple associations per connection. The options you may change include the following:

Lifetime (sec): Specifies the amount of time, in seconds, to keep an association to a remote system open. The default is 300 (or 5 minutes).

Disconnect (sec): Specifies the time, in seconds, to wait for a response to a disconnect message before closing the association. The default is 120 (or 2 minutes).

Threshold (msgs): Specifies the maximum number of messages to allow in a queue before opening another association to transfer the messages. The default is 50.

◆ Transfer timeouts (sec/K): Specifies the timeout parameters for various message types. When the timeout expires, an NDR will be sent to the mail administrator. These timeout options include the following:

Urgent: Specifies the number of Kb/second to wait before an error is assumed to occur when sending urgent e-mail. The default is 1000.

Normal: Specifies the number of Kb/second to wait before an error is assumed to occur when sending normal e-mail. The default is 2000.

Nonurgent: Specifies the number of Kb/second to wait before an error is assumed to occur when sending non-urgent e-mail. The default is 3000.

8. After you have made your changes, click on the OK button to close the MTA Site Configuration Properties dialog and return to the Microsoft Exchange Administrator.

CONFIGURING THE INTERNET MAIL CONNECTOR

Configuring the Internet Mail Connector can be very easy or very complex, depending on how you plan to make use of it. I know this does not sound very encouraging, but it is true. It's true because of the multitude of property sheets you have available to configure the service. So before you collapse from frustration (or information overload), just configure the following basic properties for the Internet Mail Connector:

◆ Specify the Administrator's mailbox. This mailbox is used by the Internet Mail Connector to send all error messages that occur.

◆ Specify MIME (Multipurpose Internet Mail Extensions) or UUENCODE (a conversion scheme to convert 8-bit binary data to a 7-bit format) message encoding for outbound mail messages.

◆ Specify an SMTP address space. The SMTP address space is used to specify the SMTP host from which to accept or reject mail. If the address space is set to *@* (which is the recommended setting to get you started), then all SMTP mail will be accepted by Exchange Server. To accept mail from specific hosts and reject mail from all other hosts, you can specify the individual IP address of the hosts you want to accept mail from.

◆ Specify a relay host or internal DNS server for message delivery. The relay host is usually an external host where all of your mail is sent or received from. It is used for two reasons. First, it can be used internally as a single access point (such as when you have multiple Exchange Server installations but only one has a connection to the Internet) to which to forward all of your outbound mail. Second, it can be used to provide an additional level of fault tolerance (for example, when your e-mail server is down, the relay host will continue to receive e-mail from external clients). A DNS server is used to determine the IP address of the destination hosts and supply basic NetBIOS name resolution (such as when you need to convert the e-mail address of webmaster@nt-guru.com to the destination address of webmaster@206.170.126.65).

Note

Using a relay host based on an Internet mail server (such as those commonly used by Internet Service Providers) requires additional support considerations, generally adds additional complexities to the receipt of your e-mail, and is therefore not recommended unless you need the additional fault tolerance. If you choose to use a relay host, be sure to discuss your requirements with your ISP to determine the methodology for sending stored mail to your Exchange Server installation.

Note

If you will not be using a DNS server, you can map the IP addresses using the HOSTS file or WINS, or by specifying the outbound servers in the Connections property sheet.

To configure the Internet Mail Connector to use these basic properties, follow these steps:

1. Launch the Microsoft Exchange Administrator, located in your Microsoft Exchange program group.
2. Expand the site folder (for my server, this is WORK, for example) so that the Add-Ins, Addressing, Connections, Directory Replication, Monitors, and Servers folders are displayed. (See Figure 27.6.)
3. Select the Connections folder, and the installed connectors will be listed in the window on the right side. (See Figure 27.9.)
4. Select the Internet Mail Connector. Then choose Properties from the File menu, or just press the Enter key, to display the Internet Mail Connector Properties dialog box, as shown in Figure 27.10.

Figure 27.9.
The installed
connectors in the
WORK site.

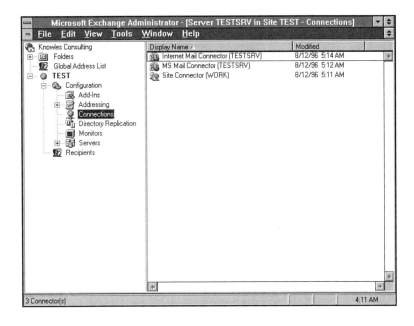

Figure 27.10.
Configuring the
Internet Mail
Connector's basic
properties.

5. Click on the Change button. This displays the Administrators Mailbox dialog box, where you may select an e-mail account to use for all administrative messages. After you select an account, click the OK button to return to the Internet Mail properties sheet.

Note

Some of the other interesting options, which not everyone will need to use, include the Address Type and Message Content Information group fields and the Enable message tracking checkbox. This checkbox is used to create a log file of the routes (or paths) of your e-mail messages to the destination host. The Message Content Information group includes two subgroups called Mime Attachments and Character Set Translation. The Mime Attachments subgroup is used to specify your outbound mail encoding scheme for embedded objects. This encoding scheme can be either MIME, the newer standard with richer content varieties, or UUENCODE, the older but more compatible scheme. When a message is sent, the character set may need to be translated, based on the encoding scheme. This choice is configured in the Character Set Translation subgroup. If you would like to specify this information on a per-domain name basis, you can do so by clicking the E-Mail Domain button.

Tip

When connected to the Internet, some additional features of Exchange become more of a potential problem than a potential benefit. Having your internal e-mail clients send out-of-office (such as when you are on vacation) or automatically generated replies (such as when you need to time-stamp a message) is a nice feature. Sending possibly confidential information (an address to reach you while you are vacation, perhaps) over the Internet, however, can be a possible security hazard. To prevent this from occurring, click on the Interoperability button to display the Operability dialog box. Then check the Disable Out Of Office Responses to the Internet and Disable Automatic Replies to the Internet checkboxes.

6. Click on the Notifications button to display the Notifications dialog box, shown in Figure 27.11. My personal preference is to be notified of all non-delivery events (when a message could not be sent or received), which is accomplished by enabling the Always send notifications when non-delivery reports are generated radio button. You may, however, choose to limit the messages you will receive by enabling the Send notifications for these non-delivery reports radio button. Then you may choose from the following events:

E-Mail address could not be found: Specifies that a message be sent to the mail administrator when either the sending or receiving party could not be located.

Multiple matches for an E-Mail address occurred: Specifies that a message be sent to the mail administrator when there are multiple definitions for an e-mail address in either the sending or receiving party. The most common cause of this message is defining the same SMTP address for multiple Exchange Server recipients.

Message conversion failed: Specifies that a message be sent to the mail administrator whenever an unknown mail format is received. This can often be corrected for future messages by updating the MIME mapping in the MIME Types tab.

Destination host could not be found: Specifies that a message be sent to the mail administrator whenever the destination mail server could not be located. This can be caused for one of three reasons. First, the destination mail server could be down or otherwise unavailable. Secondly, the domain name server for the destination server could be down or otherwise unavailable. Third, there may be no definition in the HOSTS file, located in the SystemRoot\System32\drivers\etc subdirectory.

Protocol error occurred: Specifies that a message be sent to the mail administrator whenever a transport protocol error occurs.

Message timeout exceeded: Specifies that a message be sent to the mail administrator when a message could not be sent to the destination host. This type of failure is called a *timeout error* (these timeout choices can be specified in the Connections property sheet).

7. Click on the Address Space tab to display the Address Space property sheet, as shown in Figure 27.12.

8. Click on the New Internet button to display the SMTP Properties dialog box. Enter a value of *@* in the E-mail domain field. Leave the Cost field as 1. Then click the OK button.

9. Click the Connections tab to display the Connections property sheet, as shown in Figure 27.13.

10. In the Message Delivery field, choose the Use domain name server (DNS) radio button to use your DNS server for NetBIOS name resolution. Or choose the Forward all messages to host radio button and specify the name of the mail server to relay all of your outbound mail to, such as ServerName if another Exchange Server is used internally or ServerName@DomainName.com if using an external (Internet mail server) mail server.

Figure 27.11.
Configuring the
Internet Mail
Connector
message notifica-
tion properties.

Figure 27.12.
Specifying the
SMTP address
space.

Figure 27.13.
Using the
Connections
Properties sheet
to specify the
SMTP address
space.

Tip

I prefer to use the Microsoft DNS service rather than a relay host. Although this does add an additional level of complexity, I consider it a worthwhile effort because it keeps you in control. If you use a relay host, it is up to the administrator of that host to make sure that the DNS service on that site is properly configured. It's easier to use a relay host, but certainly not as satisfying.

11. Click on the OK button to close the Internet Mail Connector Properties dialog box.

At this point you might think you are finished, but you're not. There are still two steps you need to accomplish before you can use the Internet Mail Connector. You need to add your DNS records to your DNS server and configure the Internet Mail Connector's service startup values. To configure your DNS service, follow these steps:

1. Open the file that defines your domain. Mine is `nt-guru.dom`, and the default file supplied with the Microsoft DNS service is `place.dom`, but yours will probably have another name. If you are unsure of the file to use, look in the boot file for a primary entry with the domain name and associated filename (such as `primary nt-guru.com nt-guru.dom`). For additional information, refer to Chapter 9, "Using DHCP, WINS, and DNS."

2. If you left the comments in the file, look for the E-Mail Servers entry. If you did not leave the original comments, you can add the records anywhere in the file. Just make sure not to duplicate the records (in case someone else has already added them). The entries you need to add include an address record (A) and a mail record (MX) and will look like the following:

```
@                IN  MX    10      srv

srv              IN  A        206.170.127.65
```

Be sure to change the value of srv to the name of your computer hosting Exchange Server and the IP address (206.170.127.65) to the IP address assigned to your server. Otherwise you will not be able to send or receive e-mail from the Internet and I will wind up with a lot of non-delivery messages in my administrator's mailbox.

3. Repeat steps 1 and 2 for each DNS server you have hosting a separate Exchange Server installation. If you will only be using one DNS server, repeat step 2 for each Exchange server installation.

4. Save and close your file.

5. Stop and then restart your Microsoft DNS service using the Control Panel Services applet. Or enter NET STOP DNS, then NET START DNS, at a command console prompt.

To configure your Internet Mail Connector's service startup values, follow these steps:

1. Open the Control panel, then launch the Services applet.

2. Scroll down the list until you see the Microsoft Exchange Internet Connector entry in the Service listbox. Select the entry and click the Startup button to display the Service dialog box.

3. Choose the Automatic radio button in the Startup Type field.

4. Click the OK button to close the Service dialog box.

5. If you want to get started right away with the Internet Mail Connector, click the Start button to start the service. Then click the Close button to close the Service dialog box.

CONFIGURING THE MICROSOFT MAIL CONNECTOR

Configuring the Microsoft Mail Connector is much easier to configure than the Internet Mail Connector. You do need to know a few things about your Microsoft Mail postoffice, however, before you can configure the Microsoft Mail Connector. This includes the following information:

◆ Specify the Administrator's mailbox. This mailbox is used by the Microsoft Mail Connector to send all error messages that occur.

♦ Specify the UNC pathname to your Microsoft Mail postoffice. This will be used to connect to the postoffice and extract the network and postoffice names.

To configure the Microsoft Mail Connector to use these basic properties, follow these steps:

1. Launch the Microsoft Exchange Administrator, located in your Microsoft Exchange program group.

2. Expand the site folder (for my server, this is WORK, for example) so that the Add-Ins, Addressing, Connections, Directory Replication, Monitors, and Servers folders are displayed. (See Figure 27.6.)

3. Select the Connections folder, and the installed connectors will be listed in the window on the right side. (See Figure 27.7.)

4. Select the MS Mail Connector. Then choose Properties from the File menu, or just press the Enter key, to display the MS Mail Connector Properties dialog box, as shown in Figure 27.14.

Figure 27.14.
Configuring the
MS Mail
Connector's basic
Properties.

27

5. Click on the Change button. This displays the Administrator's Mailbox dialog box, where you may select an e-mail account to use for all administrative messages. After you select an account, click the OK button to return to the MS Mail properties sheet.

6. Click the Connections tab to display the Connections property sheet, as shown in Figure 27.15.

Figure 27.15.
Preparing to add
a new connection
to your MS Mail
Connector.

7. Next, click on the Create button to display the Create Connection dialog
   box. Then click on the Change button to display the Postoffice Path dialog
   box, as shown in Figure 27.16.

Figure 27.16.
Specifying the
postoffice path.

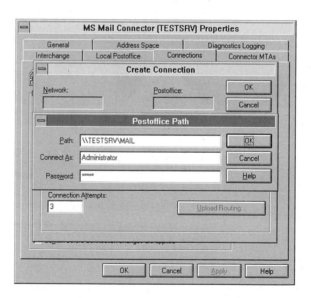

8. Enter a UNC pathname (such as \\TESTSRV\MAIL) to your Microsoft Mail
   postoffice in the Path field. If the postoffice is on a remote server, enter a
   user name in the Connect As field and a password for the user account in
   the Password field. Then click on the OK button.

9. Now the Create Connection dialog box should appear, similar to that shown in Figure 27.17, with the network and postoffice names filled in by the MS Mail Connector. The Apply Changes Now message box will then be displayed, informing you that your changes will be applied immediately. Just click on the OK button to close the message box.

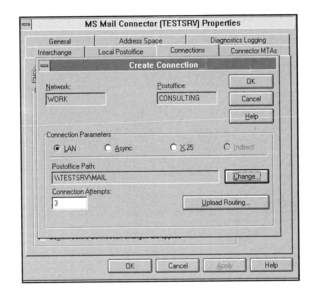

Figure 27.17.
The completed
Create Connec-
tion dialog box.

10. At this point the Connections property sheet will show your Microsoft Mail postoffice connection, below your Exchange Server network/postoffice name.

11. If you have additional Microsoft Mail postoffices to connect to, repeat steps 7 through 10. When you have finished adding all of your Microsoft Mail postoffices, click on the OK button to close the MS Mail Connector Properties dialog box.

At this point you might think you are finished, but you're not. Just as with the Internet Mail Connector, you need to configure your MS Mail Connector's service properties to start up automatically. This can be accomplished by following these steps:

1. Open the Control Panel; then launch the Services applet.

2. Scroll down the list until you see the MS Mail Connector Interchange entry in the Service listbox. Select the entry and click the Startup button to display the Service dialog box.

3. Choose the Automatic radio button in the Startup Type field.

4. Click the OK button to close the Service dialog box.

5. If you want to get started right away with the Internet Mail Connector, click the Start button to start the service. Then click the Close button to close the Service dialog box.

Configuring the Site Connector

If you want to connect two or more Exchange sites together to replicate directory information to share a common user account list then the best way to do this is to use the Microsoft Exchange Site connector. This connector is included with the Enterprise edition of Microsoft Exchange, but may be purchased separately as well. To join two or more sites, follow these steps:

1. Launch the Microsoft Exchange Administrator, located in your Microsoft Exchange program group.

2. Choose New Other | Site Connector from the File menu.

3. The New Site Connector dialog box will appear, where you can enter the name of the computer running Exchange Server (such as SRV) that you want to connect to. Once you have entered the name, click on the OK button.

4. The Site Connector Properties dialog box, shown in Figure 27.18, will be displayed.

Figure 27.18.
The Site Connec-
tor Properties
dialog box.

5. If you do not have a trust relationship established with the remote site, then most likely your local site's service account (the user account that Exchange Server runs under) will lack permission to access the remote site's services as well. In this case, click on the Override tab, shown in Figure 27.19.

Figure 27.19.
Specifying the
service account to
use in the foreign
domain.

6. Enter the remote Exchange Server service's account name in the Windows NT username field.

7. Enter the remote Exchange Server service's account password in the Password and Confirm password fields.

8. Enter the name of the remote Exchange Server's domain in the Windows NT domain name field.

9. Click the OK button. You may be prompted to create a site connector in the foreign domain. If so, accept this option. At this point you have created a connection between two Exchange Server sites. For each site to connect, repeat steps 2 though 9.

CREATING USER MAILBOXES

There are two ways to create a mailbox. You can create the mailbox using User Manager for Domains (see Chapter 6, "Basic Administrative Tools," for more details) or you can use Microsoft Exchange Administrator. In this section you will learn how to use the latter tool to create your mailboxes. It's not very difficult, though there is a lot more data entry to perform than I like. Since most of these entries are optional, however, you can choose which fields to fill out. To create a client mailbox, follow these steps:

1. Launch the Microsoft Exchange Administrator, located in your Microsoft Exchange program group.

2. Expand the site folder (for my server, this is WORK, for example) so that the Recipients folder is displayed. (See Figure 27.6.)

27

3. Select the Recipients folder and choose New Mailbox from the File menu, or use the shortcut key sequence Ctrl-M and a dialog box similar to the one shown in Figure 27.20 will appear.

Figure 27.20.
A properties
dialog box.

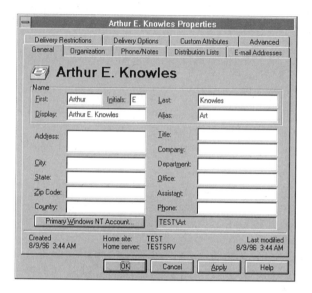

4. Enter the user's first name, middle initial, and last name in the First, Initial, and Last fields respectively. This will automatically create the display name (the name to be displayed in the address book) and alias (the user mailbox name) for you automatically. If you do not care for these names, you may manually change them in the Display and Alias fields.

5. Click on the Primary Windows NT Account button.

6. The Primary Windows NT Account dialog box will appear. Choose the Create a new Windows NT account option to create a new domain user account, or choose the Select an existing Windows NT account (the default) to select an existing domain user account.

7. If you chose the Select an existing Windows NT account option, the Add User or Group dialog box will appear, where you can select the existing user account. Once you have made your selection, click the OK button.

8. If you chose the Create a new Windows NT account option, the Create Windows NT Account dialog box will appear, where you can enter the domain name where you want the account to be created in the NT domain field and a user name in the Account name field. By default, the account name will be the same as the Exchange Server alias name. Once you have made your entries, click the OK button. The user account will be created with the user account password set to the same name as the account name.

Note

The only properties to be set for a user account created by the Microsoft Exchange Administrator will be the username, full name, and password. The new account will also be a member of Domain Users. However, this leaves a lot of additional work for you to perform afterward. You will need to set the user's description, logon script name, profile path, home directory, and any additional account restrictions.

9. At this point you can click on the OK button to return to the Microsoft Exchange Administrator, as the above information is all that is required. However, I prefer to set the information in the following tabs as an account minimum as well:

General: Address, City, State, Zip Code, Country, Title, Company, Department, Office, Assistant, and Phone.

Phone/Notes: Business, home, fax, cellular, and pager phone numbers.

Tip

You can use the Delivery Restrictions tab to specify mail accounts the user can send to or receive from. The Delivery Options tab can be used to specify send on behalf of permissions (to let other users send mail on behalf of this user account), as well as to specify an alternate recipient. The Advanced tab can be used to limit the size of e-mail messages sent by the user or received by the user (to prevent outrageous usage of network bandwidth, for example). The Distribution Lists tab can be used to specify which distribution lists the user can use, and the Organization tab to specify the user's manager or where reports should be directed for the user account.

BACKING UP YOUR POSTOFFICE

There are three methods you can use to backup your Exchange Server postoffice using the Windows NT tape backup applet (NTBACKUP.EXE). First, you can stop all of the Exchange Server services and backup all of the Exchange Server directories (which may be on more than one disk drive). Second, you can use the Windows NT tape backup applet interactively to back up your Exchange Server Directory and Information Store. Or, you can use a batch file to automate the backup process. Using the tape backup applet is discussed in detail in Chapter 8, "Additional Administration Tools," and you've already learned some of the basic backup scenarios in the preceding section on Microsoft Mail, so I will not dwell on the actual mechanics of using the tape backup applet. I do, however, want to point out a few differences between backing up a Microsoft Mail postoffice and an Exchange Server postoffice.

If you plan to stop all of the Exchange Server services, as described in the first option, and back up the actual data directories, then your backup strategy follows the same basic principles as a backup for Microsoft Mail. On the other hand, if you plan to back up your postoffice dynamically (while Exchange Server is active), using the tape backup utility, then you need to consider the integrity of your postoffice. This follows the same basic principles as backing up an active Microsoft Mail postoffice as previously discussed.

The only method you can apply to ensure the integrity of your backups is to make sure that no users are sending or receiving mail on your Exchange Server site. This can be performed by pausing the Server service—to prevent new users from connecting to Exchange Server—and forcibly disconnecting users who may already be using Exchange Server. You might think that this type of action could only be performed interactively and that you may have to be in the office at 2:00 a.m. to perform your backup. However, this is not really required. If you use User Manager for Domains to set your account policies to forcibly disconnect users (choose Policies|Account from the menu) from the server and specify the times (use the Hours button in the User Properties dialog box) a user can be logged on to the server, then you should be able to set aside a time frame for you to make your backups safely.

SUMMARY

This chapter covered the essential topics of postoffice administration. Although the chapter's purpose was not to cover every aspect of administration, it attempted to cover the main items you might encounter when administering a Microsoft Mail or Exchange Server postoffice. The orientation of this chapter was deliberately toward Windows NT Server, although some of the information is generic enough to apply to any type of file server.

Topics addressed included using Microsoft Mail and Exchange Server administrative tools and utilities, connecting multiple postoffices, implementing security, and examining postoffice backup strategies. You also learned about some tips for minimizing and preventing data loss.

In the next chapter, you will look into optimizing your Microsoft Mail and Exchange Server installations. You will explore such subjects as the performance of your postoffice as perceived by the user and by the administrator, which often can be two different views. You also will look into possible hardware configuration tips or upgrade possibilities, which include your network, disk drive, and processor subsystems.

- Defining Performance

- Optimizing
  Performance of
  MS Mail and
  MS Exchange Server

CHAPTER 28

Optimizing Your Mail Server

Optimizing your mail server can be an involved process. In fact, optimizing just about anything on the computer can be an involved process. Ask anyone who has seriously tried to maximize the performance of a complex system.

The entire concept of performance is an interesting one. On the surface, it seems simple: make the system go as fast as it can. So just put in a faster CPU. What could be simpler, right?

Unfortunately, once you dive into it, things get a bit more complicated. Subtleties and interrelationships in the hardware and software become more apparent. Just upgrading a single component may help some, but you may have simply amplified the weakness in another component. It turns out performance optimization is both a science and an art. There are some hard-and-fast rules to follow, and there are definitely some tricks to it that come with practice and experience.

This chapter addresses some of the issues involved in performance optimization and how they specifically apply to MS Mail and MS Exchange Server. You also will take a good look at a valuable performance tool that comes with Windows NT called Performance Monitor. After you finish this chapter, you will have a better sense of how to optimize your MS Mail Postoffice or your MS Exchange Server. Plus, if you are running Windows NT, you will gain some insight into how to effectively use Performance Monitor. So grab something to drink, kick back, and let's talk performance.

DEFINING PERFORMANCE

There is a saying that goes something like this: "Perception is reality." With regard to performance measurement, there is a lot of truth in that statement. There are two main realms of perception you have to deal with: the user's and the system administrator's. Well, maybe three if you include your boss, but we'll include him with the users.

This breaks down into two main viewpoints: client response time (user perception) and system resource utilization (system administrator perception). The user can be experiencing great performance from his point of view, but the system administrator may be pulling hair.

USER VERSUS SYSTEM ADMINISTRATOR PERCEPTION

Suppose that 1,000 users decide to send mail at one time. After they click the Send button, they don't perceive any slowdown in the system unless they try to read more mail or something. The recipients don't know when the mail was sent, so they have no perception of the delay unless it spans several hours perhaps.

Meanwhile, back at the server room, the system administrator is fretting a bit because the system just got a huge influx of traffic and it is choking on all the mail messages it has to process. If this keeps up, users may start noticing the problem. That would be bad, especially because we categorized the boss with the users.

There are several things a savvy system administrator can do here. The first thing is to know the system and the environment. Is this an unusual amount of traffic for your user community? Does this happen often? Has it been observed happening more often? These questions assume that the system administrator has been watching the system and knows something about the history of the environment. Being armed with information of this kind goes a long way toward making intelligent decisions about improving performance.

Most performance problems get visibility because users start screaming about sluggish response time or about e-mail getting lost or delayed. If you plan for optimal performance correctly, that should not happen very often. There certainly will be times when things get crazy and users will complain about performance. But if you, the system administrator, know your system, you will be able to handle this. Forewarned is forearmed.

So you have this notion of user perception, which translates into client response time, and of system administrator perception, which translates into system/server resource utilization. Which one is more important? I'm sure you guessed it—the one the boss is in. The real question is this: Which one do you have more control over?

In the case of MS Mail, the client is really doing most of the work because it has to move files around on the postoffice. A very key point, however, is that a very busy postoffice makes the client perform poorly. That is no fault of the client program; it is just being slowed down by an overworked postoffice. So it's pretty safe to deduce that, with MS Mail, if you have a fast postoffice, you will have fast clients. That means the client response time is better, which improves the user perception of performance. What the administrator sees is a reduced load at the server.

In contrast to MS Mail, in MS Exchange, the server side is doing most of the work thanks to its client/server architecture. Granted, the client has to do some work, but mostly it is the server in the spotlight. Because of this, Exchange can make the client look like it is responding quickly when really the work has just been handed off to the server. With that in mind, you'll have to spend a bit more time examining the server side of performance. These two systems are very different in their performance. Your approach to optimizing them will have to be different as well.

"So how do I tell what is going on in the system?" I'm glad you asked that. First, you must have some tools. Then you need some knowledge of how to use them. After you know what to fix, your system should perform better than ever. Still got that drink?

PERFORMANCE TOOLS

Several performance tools are available for monitoring the performance of various operating systems. The simplest of these is your trusty stopwatch, which can be used for very simplistic data gathering. Crude but useful, the stopwatch can help you measure and understand performance changes on a system. You can go to your user's machine, for example, start a task and your stopwatch at the same time, and then stop the stopwatch when the task is complete. After making some tweaks to the server, you can repeat the exercise and hope things get faster.

There are more elegant ways, though. Better and better performance tools are becoming available as operating systems get more complex and more full-featured. One I have used is a tool for OS/2 from C.O.L. Systems called OSRM2-Lite v3.0. This tool enables you to capture data for the many performance counters in the OS/2 kernel. Then you can report on them using REXX. It is a very powerful and useful tool for those who must try to optimize systems running on OS/2. There are other performance tools, too numerous to mention, for Novell NetWare and UNIX as well.

A similar tool for Windows NT is called the Performance Monitor. It too uses counters in the system kernel, but also can access counters for device drivers as well as application-level software. For the sake of simplicity, this discussion focuses on optimizing your Microsoft Mail Postoffice and Microsoft Exchange. For specifics on using the Performance Monitor, refer to Chapter 13, "Tuning Your Server."

OPTIMIZING PERFORMANCE OF MS MAIL AND MS EXCHANGE SERVER

All right, you've spent some time looking at the perceived performance of your applications and the actual performance of your server. Now it's time to get down to business. Take a few minutes to look specifically at performance issues surrounding an MS Mail Postoffice and an MS Exchange Server system. You'll look at some issues specific to both environments and examine some ideas on how to apply NT Performance Monitor to understand them.

Note

> I'm writing the MS Mail section assuming that you are running on Windows NT Server, but the ideas may apply to other operating system platforms. MS Exchange Server only runs on Windows NT Server, so naturally, everything in that section is oriented toward Windows NT.

OPTIMIZING FOR MS MAIL

Your burning question throughout this chapter has been how to get your MS Mail Postoffice to run faster. First of all, let me clarify something. I may sometimes interchange the terms MS Mail Postoffice, MS Mail Server, and MS Mail. They are really the same in this context, although technically there is not a "server" task running on the MS Mail Postoffice. See Chapter 24, "An Introduction to Microsoft Mail and Exchange Server," for an overview of MS Mail to get more details.

There is one overriding thing to always keep in mind when tuning performance on an MS Mail Postoffice server: It is a shared file environment. Assuming that there is nothing else running on your server, tuning the postoffice is much the same as tuning a file server. Because file servers have been with us for a while, there is abundant information on tuning them.

In the next few sections, you'll visit some issues specific to MS Mail. They are divided into three main sections: Network, Disk, and Processor. All the suggestions pertain to the server on which the postoffice is installed. Some suggestions can be applied to the client machine as well. Then you'll learn about using Performance Monitor with MS Mail.

NETWORK PERFORMANCE

The MS Mail Postoffice tends to be network-intensive, so you probably will want to examine performance of the network subsystem of your server. The interaction of the postoffice with the mail client software is "chatty" on the network. Every time someone requests a mail message or an attachment, the entire thing has to be shipped over the network. There are a few things you can do:

◆ Upgrade your NIC (Network Interface Controller). Your server may be using an old 8-bit ISA card. Upgrade that to a 16-bit NIC. Or better yet, if you have an EISA machine, get an EISA NIC. If you have a VESA or PCI local bus, that is even better. Both the EISA and PCI cards give you the benefit of the 32-bit bus and high data-transfer rates. Use a bus master NIC if you can because this helps alleviate stress on the system processor; some older NICs rely on the system processor to help them get their work done. This is bad in a heavily loaded system because it can multiply your problem; not only is the NIC a bottleneck, but it also places unneeded stress on the system processor.

Tip

When possible, use a memory-mapped NIC. This type of network card maps an internal buffer on the NIC to the system address space. Both the NIC and the operating system can access this buffer directly. This type of adapter generally is faster than an I/O mapped device because memory-to-memory data transfers are faster than I/O-to-memory and memory-to-I/O transfers.

◆ Add another network adapter to your server. If you have a lower performing NIC that is heavily loaded, this tends to spread the load between multiple NICs. So if you've got an extra one lying around not doing anything, put it to work. The same guidelines apply as in the earlier paragraph about using a high-performance NIC. However, if you get a high-quality, high-bandwidth NIC to begin with, you may actually run out of network bandwidth before you run out of NIC bandwidth.

◆ Segment the network. Adding NICs to your system can help, but if your network is clogged, it only gets you so far. The theoretical limit of Ethernet bandwidth is 10Mbps, for example. You can expect to get about 70 to 80 percent of that before so many collisions occur that they impede data transfer. When you're at that limit, adding NICs to the same segment of the network does no good. You are forced to offload some of the traffic onto another network segment. To do this, you still add another NIC to the server, but you connect the NICs to separate network segments. That way, traffic is split between the two segments, and the network load is distributed between the NICs. Now this doesn't guarantee that the loads on the two networks will be equal (that depends on the user load), but it does alleviate the problem of a clogged network. In this scenario, your server becomes a bridge or router.

Note

Most Administrators segment their network when the average bandwidth capacity reaches 50 percent. This allows for peaks in the 70- to 80-percent range, without hindering overall network performance.

◆ Change network protocols. Some network protocols tend to generate lots of network traffic. NetBEUI is very fast, for example, but it generates lots of broadcasts on the network. This is fine when you have a relatively small number of users on the network, but when the number of users grows to hundreds, you might start to see problems. Switching to something like TCP/IP can help. It is much more efficient than NetBEUI, and its performance has improved vastly over the years. In fact, the TCP/IP stack in Windows NT is quite fast. Plus, unlike NetBEUI, it is routable. So if you have a segmented network with dedicated routers, TCP/IP is the way to go.

Tip

If your network is small enough, you can add several NICs to your server and use Windows NT's internal routing of IP addresses to build a multisegment network without external routers. It is not as efficient as dedicated routers, but it is less expensive.

THE DISK DRIVE SUBSYSTEM

This is the most likely area for performance bottlenecks with MS Mail, so you should look here first. The disk is heavily used because of the file-sharing nature of the MS Mail Postoffice. There are many types of disk configurations out there, and I will try to address the main ones that will help you maximize your disk performance. The costs vary greatly between technologies discussed here, so you have to weigh that in your decision.

◆ Upgrade your disk drive. Maybe you have a server with a single hard drive. Chances are that it has been around for a while. Consider upgrading that to a newer drive. Most new drives are both faster and of higher capacity, so this is definitely a win-win option. The only problem is that your disk controller might not be compatible with the newer, faster drives. Read on.

◆ Upgrade your disk controller. If you have an old ESDI drive system, for example, you might not be able to find newer, faster drives than you already have. Most of the new drives are EIDE, Fast ATA-2, or Fast SCSI-2. If you don't have one of these controllers, you'll need to get one. There's a definite benefit in upgrading to these controllers, not only because of the faster drives, but also because of the increased bandwidth. (The extra drive space is nice, too.)

Again, if you have an EISA or PCI (or VESA) local bus system, consider an EISA or PCI disk controller. These controllers are extremely fast, and if you are replacing a controller that is two or three years old, you'll probably notice a significant improvement.

Tip

If you are going to replace your entire disk subsystem (controller and disk drives), stick with a SCSI-based system. These types of systems support bus mastering (where the adapter has its own processor to offload work from the CPU), multiple asynchronous I/O (which any other type of disk subsystem that uses the standard ATDISK.SYS device driver—such as IDE, EIDE, MFM, RLL, and ESDI—cannot support), command queuing, and a detachable bus (so that you can

> continue to pull data from one drive while the other drive is seeking requested data).

One relatively new type of controller is the Fast Wide SCSI-2 controller. If you get an EISA or PCI version, you get the extremely fast performance combined with increased bandwidth: Fast Wide SCSI-2 is 20MBps; Fast SCSI-2 is 10MBps. An even better solution is one of the newer SCSI controllers, such as the Adaptec 3940, which is sometimes referred to as an ULTRA WIDE SCSI controller. These types of controllers include more than one SCSI channel on the SCSI controller. So if you place one, or more, disk drives on each SCSI channel and stripe the disks you can combine the 20MBps data transfer rate of the individual SCSI channels. This can provide a data transfer rate of 40MBps. Some SCSI controllers include up to three separate channels, which means you can achieve a 60MBps data transfer rate.

◆ Install additional drives and set them up as NT stripe sets. Stripe sets, also referred to as software striping, are a feature built into Windows NT Server. It requires multiple physical drives, and you can configure the disks three different ways: as a stripe set, as a stripe set with parity, or as disk mirrors. Disk mirroring is slightly different from stripe sets because it is not actually doing any striping, but I'll group it with stripe sets for this discussion.

When you set up a stripe set, also known as RAID 0, you are distributing the data across multiple disk drives. In this way, the data can be accessed much faster than on a single drive. A stripe set has no fault tolerance—if one drive in the set fails, you lose all data in the stripe set. Of the three configurations, this one provides the best performance. You must have at least two drives to set up a stripe set.

A stripe set with parity, also known as RAID 4 or RAID 5, functions in much the same way as a stripe set except that parity information has to be written to the stripe set along with the data. As an added benefit, it provides fault tolerance. If any drive in the set fails, the data can be reconstructed from the remaining drives in the set after the faulty drive is replaced. If two drives fail at the same time, however, all data in the set is lost. As a trade-off, performance will not be as good as with a plain stripe set because the system processor has to calculate the parity information on-the-fly. The benefit is fault tolerance, however. You must have at least three drives to set up a stripe set with parity.

A disk mirror, also known as RAID 1, is just what the name implies—one disk that is a mirror of another disk. This arrangement is fault tolerant because if one disk fails, the system can use the mirror. When the faulty disk is replaced, the drive is rebuilt from its mirror. Performance typically is better than a stripe set with parity. In fact, performance of a drive mirror should theoretically be the same as with a single disk. You must have two drives in order to set up a mirror. Windows NT Server supports mirroring a maximum of two drives.

◆ Use a hardware drive array controller. This provides all the same benefits from striping as described earlier. It also gives you the additional performance advantage of having this implemented in hardware. This way, you won't even have to bother with NT's software striping support. And the system processor won't incur the overhead of managing the array. Just configure the controller itself for striping and let it do the work. To NT, a stripe set on an array controller looks just like a single logical volume.

An array controller should have its own onboard processor to handle the stripe sets. The processor and operating system do not incur the overhead of managing the stripe set; the array controller takes care of it. Also, the controller should be available in an EISA or PCI version for optimal performance.

An array controller should allow mirroring of more than two drives. With this approach, you get the performance benefits of striping combined with the fault-tolerance benefits of mirroring. You can install six drives in your system, for example—three mirrored with three. Both sets of three would be striped for performance and mirrored for fault tolerance. Although it requires more drives to achieve the same disk space as RAID 0 or RAID 5, it is the best performing fault-tolerant scheme.

Finally, an array controller should have some onboard cache. This is faster than using NT's system cache because the controller uses its cache transparent to NT.

◆ Tell NT to favor the system cache over other system processes. This is one of those parameters you can change to alter the behavior of Windows NT.

From the Control Panel, start the Network applet. In the Installed Network Software listbox, click the Server entry, and then click the Configure button. A dialog box appears, giving you some radio button options. You should click Maximize Throughput for File Sharing. This helps NT make decisions when choosing what to page to disk. With this setting, when NT needs memory, it leans toward preserving the system cache and pages other processes first.

◆ Add more RAM for the NT system cache. As mentioned earlier, Windows NT tunes itself. If it sees a large demand for the disk, it tries to accommodate the request. Now everyone knows the benefits of a large disk cache in a file server. If you give NT extra RAM, rest assured it will put it to good use. Another benefit of adding RAM is that NT pages to disk less often. If your postoffice is heavily used, it will be disk-intensive, and the last thing you want in this case is for NT to page to disk.

Note

I must mention here that there is a point of diminishing returns with adding memory. You can't just keep throwing memory at the system and expect it to continue improving. Somewhere along the line, you will move the bottleneck from memory to somewhere else in the system. Depending on the server load, this point varies for different systems, so there's no way I can give you a set amount and say it will always be the best. If your system has minimal RAM, however (16MB or 24MB), it is safe to advise increasing into the 32MB-to-64MB range.

SYSTEM PROCESSOR PERFORMANCE

In a file-sharing environment, and with file servers in general, the processor is not usually the first component to become a performance bottleneck. So unless you have a really underpowered server or a disk controller that is a pig with the system CPU, this might not be a problem. Check it out with the Performance Monitor to see how things look. If usage is consistently high (above 80 percent), here are some things to consider:

◆ Install the fastest single processor available. If you have a decent-sized level 2 cache (also called processor cache)—512KB, for example, you will get good performance. Some server products provide their CPUs on processor boards complete with L2 cache. Get one with as large an L2 cache as possible—some even go up to 2MB.

Don't worry about installing multiple processors. In a file server, there is generally not much benefit from multiple processors, unless you have the server running other tasks besides handling the MS Mail Postoffice. In that case, you might well benefit from a second processor.

Adding a third or fourth processor is probably not the best investment, however. Of course, if you have money to burn and you want to try squeezing the last drop of performance out of your system, go ahead and buy them. And while you're at it, buy a few hundred more copies of this book. OK, OK, just kidding about the processors.

◆ Free processor bandwidth by using bus-master disk controllers and NICs. This was really already covered in the previous sections. Using bus-master NICs and hardware array controllers, for example, offloads stress from the system processor. That helps you get more mileage out of the CPU because it doesn't have to be bothered with the mundane tasks of managing network and disk I/O.

USING PERFORMANCE MONITOR IN MS MAIL

As you probably have already noticed, there are many, many counters accessible to the Performance Monitor. To help you wade through them, here are a few good ones that will get you started. These counters should prove useful when monitoring usage of your MS Mail Postoffice. They will vary some with your exact implementation— you may not use NetBEUI, so NetBEUI-specific counters won't mean anything to you, for example.

Note

> Don't forget to use `diskperf -y` to activate the disk counters before trying to use the Logical Disk (and Physical Disk) object. After you finish your performance tuning, use `diskperf -n` to disable the disk counters for optimum performance.

Regardless, the general principle is the same, and you can use these counters to begin some exploration on your own:

◆ Cache:Data Map Hits %: Percentage of successful references to the in-memory system data cache. A high hit ratio is preferred because this means the requested data was in the system cache. This means the operating system was able to retrieve the data without having to perform a physical read from the disk drive. Considering that that disk access is in the millisecond range and memory access is in the nanosecond range, you can understand the advantage of a high hit ratio. If you have a low hit ratio, adding additional physical RAM will increase the cache size and usually increase the hit ratio.

◆ Logical Disk:% Disk Time: Percentage of time the disk is busy servicing I/O requests.

◆ Logical Disk:Avg. Disk sec/Transfer: Average amount of seconds it takes the disk to satisfy a disk transfer (read or write).

◆ Logical Disk:Disk Bytes/sec: Rate at which data is transferred to or from the disk during I/O operations.

◆ Memory:Available Bytes: Amount of free memory in the system available for use.

◆ Memory:Cache Bytes: Size of the system cache. Note that the system cache is to cache file access on the local disk drives and remote mapped network drives. Adding additional RAM will usually increase the size of the system cache.

◆ Memory:Pages/sec: Indicates overall paging activity—the rate at which pages are written to or read from the disk. A high value here is an indication that adding additional RAM will improve overall system performance.

◆ NetBEUI:Bytes Total/sec: Amount of NetBEUI data sent to and received from the network.

◆ NetBEUI Resource:Times Exhausted: Number of times the NetBEUI buffers were exhausted.

◆ Paging File:% Usage: Shows what percentage of the pagefile is in use. A high value (above 50%) is an indication that you need to enlarge your pagefile to prevent out-of-virtual-memory errors.

◆ Processor:% Processor Time: Amount of time the processor is busy doing work. This is both User and Privileged (kernel) time combined. A consistent value above 80% is an indication that upgrading your processor could improve overall system performance.

◆ Server Bytes Total/sec: Rate at which the server is sending and receiving data to and from the network.

◆ System:Processor Queue Length (also must monitor one thread from the Thread object for this counter to be nonzero): Number of threads waiting in the processor queue. Numbers above 2, per processor, can indicate processor congestion.

OPTIMIZING FOR MS EXCHANGE SERVER

One of the design goals of MS Exchange Server was to perform well on small and large installations alike. It was designed both to exploit minimal hardware and to scale well with powerful hardware. This enables the product to be a viable solution in environments ranging from small offices to large enterprise installations. Get the idea? I think I'd better move on before you start thinking I'm a marketing type.

When optimizing an Exchange server, there are two main things to remember. One, MS Exchange Server is a client/server system, not a shared file system like MS Mail; Exchange's architecture is vastly different. Two, keep in mind the design goal I outlined earlier. Because of these two items, tuning an Exchange server differs from tuning an MS Mail Postoffice. Although you may find some common optimization topics between them, the products are really nothing alike.

In the next few sections, you will explore some issues specific to MS Exchange Server. Like the "Optimizing for MS Mail" section, these issues are divided into three main sections: Network, Disk, and Processor. Then you'll learn about using the Microsoft Exchange Optimizer (also called PerfWiz) and the Performance Monitor with Exchange.

NETWORK PERFORMANCE

Fortunately, MS Exchange Server does not tend to be network-intensive—at least compared to MS Mail. This is due in large part to the client/server architecture and the hard work of folks on Microsoft's performance team who worked long and hard to optimize and refine the product. As you increase the number of Exchange users, or as you start outgrowing your hardware, however, here are a few ideas to consider when optimizing the network subsystem:

- Upgrade your NIC (Network Interface Controller). Your server may be using an old 8-bit ISA card. Upgrade that to a 16-bit NIC. Or, better yet, if you have an EISA machine, get an EISA NIC. If you have a VESA or PCI local bus, that is even better. Both the EISA and PCI cards give you the benefit of the 32-bit bus and high data-transfer rates.

  Use a bus-master NIC if you can to help alleviate stress on the system processor. Some older NICs rely on the system processor to help them get their work done. This is bad in a heavily loaded system because it can multiply your problem; not only is the processor being stressed by Exchange Server itself, but the processor also is being stressed unnecessarily by the NIC.

Tip

> When possible, use a NIC that supports memory-mapped I/O. This type of network card maps an internal buffer on the NIC to the system address space. Both the NIC and the operating system can access this buffer directly. This type of adapter generally is faster than an I/O-mapped device because memory-to-memory data transfers are faster than I/O-to-memory and memory-to-I/O transfers.

- Add another network adapter to your server. If you have a lower performing NIC that is heavily loaded, this tends to spread the load between multiple NICs. So if you've got an extra one lying around not doing anything, put it to work. The same guidelines apply as in the earlier paragraph about using a high-performance NIC. If you get a high-quality, high-bandwidth NIC to begin with, however, other components in the system probably will become the bottleneck before the NIC does.

- Segment the network. Adding NICs to your system might help, but if your network is clogged, it will only get you so far. The theoretical limit of Ethernet bandwidth is 10Mbps, for example. You can expect to get about 70 to 80 percent of that before so many collisions occur that they impede data transfer. When you're at that limit, adding NICs to the same segment of the network does no good. You are forced to offload some of the traffic onto another network segment. To do this, you still add another NIC to the server, but you connect the NICs to separate network segments. That way, traffic is split between the two segments, and the network load is distributed between the NICs. This doesn't guarantee that the loads on the two networks will be equal (that depends on the user load), but it does alleviate the problem of a clogged network. In this scenario, your server becomes a bridge or router.

◆ Change network protocols. Some network protocols tend to generate lots of network traffic. NetBEUI is very fast, for example, but it generates lots of broadcasts on the network. This is fine when you have a relatively small number of users on the network, but when the number of users grows to hundreds, you might start to see problems. Switching to something like TCP/IP can help. It is much more efficient than NetBEUI for larger networks, and its performance has improved vastly over the years. In fact, the TCP/IP stack in Windows NT is quite fast. Plus, unlike NetBEUI, it is routable. So if you have a segmented network with dedicated routers, TCP/IP is the way to go.

THE DISK DRIVE SUBSYSTEM

Depending on your user load and disk configuration, the disk drive subsystem is a potential area for Exchange Server performance problems. The disk on the server is actually dealing with two types of disk I/O: random and sequential.

There are many types of disk configurations out there, and I will try to address the main ones that will help you maximize your disk performance. The costs vary greatly between technologies discussed here, so you have to weigh that in your decision. As you scale to very large installations, however, the cost of the more powerful solutions may pale in comparison with the cost of poor performance. Fortunately, NT and Exchange exploit the high-powered solutions:

◆ Install a second disk drive and split the database logs from the database store. Probably the most effective performance enhancement you can make to a single disk server is to add a second disk drive. This enables you to place the database logs on one drive and the database stores on the other drive.

You want to do this because I/O to the logs is virtually all sequential writes. I/O to the store is virtually all random reads and writes. If you have both the logs and the store on the same drive, you cannot get the best disk performance because the disk heads always are moving all over the drive, performing a mix of sequential and random I/O. It is much more efficient if you dedicate a drive to the logs, which allows the sequential log writes to occur uninterrupted. Plus, with two drives, log writes can happen in parallel with store I/O. With a single drive, log and store I/O cannot be parallel.

Note

If you are using an ST-506–compatible controller (IDE, EIDE, ESDI, MFM, or RLL) and are using the default ATDISK.SYS driver, then reads/writes are not performed in parallel. Instead, they occur sequentially. You still achieve some benefits from using multiple drives, but not as much as if you used a SCSI-based subsystem that supports bus mastering, command queuing, asynchronous I/O, and a detachable I/O bus.

◆ Upgrade your disk drive(s). Maybe you had a server with a single hard drive and you just added a second one. Now things are better, but maybe those drives have been around for awhile. Consider upgrading to newer drives. Most new drives are both faster and of higher capacity, so this is definitely a win-win option. The only problem is that your disk controller might not be compatible with the newer, faster drives. Read on.

◆ Upgrade your disk controller. If you have an old ESDI drive system, for example, you might not be able to find newer, faster drives than you already have. Most of the new drives are EIDE, Fast ATA-2, or Fast SCSI-2. If you don't have one of those controllers, you'll need to get one. There's a definite benefit in upgrading to these controllers, not only because of the faster drives, but also because of the increased bandwidth. (The extra drive space is nice, too.)

Again, if you have an EISA or PCI (or VESA) local bus system, consider an EISA or PCI disk controller. These controllers are extremely fast and, if you are replacing a controller that is two or three years old, you'll probably notice a significant improvement.

One relatively new type of controller is the Fast Wide SCSI-2 controller. If you get an EISA or PCI version, you get the extremely fast performance combined with increased bandwidth: Fast Wide SCSI-2 is 20MBps; Fast SCSI-2 is 10MBps. An even better solution is one of the newer SCSI controllers, such as the Adaptec 3940, which is sometimes referred to as an ULTRA WIDE SCSI controller. These types of controllers include more than one SCSI channel on the SCSI controller. So if you place one, or more, disk drives on each SCSI channel and stripe the disks you can combine the 20MBps data transfer rate of the individual SCSI channels. This can provide a data transfer rate of 40MBps. Some SCSI controllers include up to three separate channels, which means you can achieve a 60MBps data transfer rate.

◆ Install additional drives and set them up as NT stripe sets. Stripe sets, also referred to as software striping, is a feature built into Windows NT Server. It requires multiple physical drives, and you can configure the disks in three different ways: as a stripe set, as a stripe set with parity, or as disk mirrors. Disk mirroring is slightly different from stripe sets because it is not actually doing any striping, but it is grouped with stripe sets for this discussion.

When you set up a stripe set, also known as RAID 0, you are distributing the data across multiple disk drives. In this way, the data can be accessed much faster than on a single drive. A stripe set has no fault tolerance; if one drive in the set fails, you lose all data in the stripe set. Of the three configurations, this one provides the best performance. You must have at least two drives in order to set up a stripe set.

A stripe set with parity, also known as RAID 4 or RAID 5, functions in much the same way as a stripe set except that parity information has to be written to the stripe set along with the data. As an added benefit, it provides fault tolerance. If any drive in the set fails, the data can be reconstructed from the remaining drives in the set after the faulty drive is replaced. If two drives fail at the same time, however, all data in the set is lost. As a trade-off, performance is not as good as with a plain stripe set because the system processor has to calculate the parity information on-the-fly. The benefit is fault tolerance, however. You must have at least three drives in order to set up a stripe set with parity.

A disk mirror, also known as RAID 1, is just what the name implies—one disk that is a mirror of another disk. This arrangement is fault tolerant because if one disk fails, the system can use the mirror. When the faulty disk is replaced, the drive is rebuilt from its mirror. Performance typically is better than a stripe set with parity. In fact, performance of a drive mirror should theoretically be the same as with a single disk. You must have two drives in order to set up a mirror. Windows NT Server supports mirroring a maximum of two drives.

◆ Use a hardware drive array controller. This provides all the same benefits from striping as described earlier. There is the additional performance advantage of having this implemented in hardware, however. This way, you won't even have to bother with NT's software striping support. And the system processor won't incur the overhead of managing the array. Just configure the controller itself for striping and let it do the work. To NT, a stripe set on an array controller will just look like a single logical volume.

An array controller should have its own onboard processor to handle the stripe sets. The processor and operating system do not incur the overhead of managing the stripe set; the array controller takes care of it. Also, the controller should be available in an EISA or PCI version for optimal performance.

An array controller should allow mirroring of more than two drives. With this approach, you get the performance benefits of striping combined with the fault-tolerance benefits of mirroring. You can install six drives in your system, for example—three mirrored with three. Both sets of three are striped for performance and mirrored for fault tolerance. Although it requires more drives to achieve the same disk space as RAID 0 or RAID 5, it is the best-performing fault-tolerant scheme.

Finally, an array controller should have some onboard cache. This is faster than using NT's system cache because the controller uses its cache transparent to NT.

Although you're using an array, you still should set up two separate logical volumes so that you can split the logs and the store, as described earlier. The effect of doing this is that you get the benefit of array performance on both log and store I/O. And one more thing: You should always set up your logs on a fault-tolerant drive if possible.

◆ Tell NT to favor system processes over system cache. This is exactly opposite to the way you should set it for MS Mail. The Exchange Setup process is supposed to set this during installation, but check it anyway.

From the Control Panel, start the Network applet. In the Installed Network Software listbox, click the Server entry, and then click the Configure button. A dialog box appears, giving you some radio button options. You should click Maximize Throughput for Network Applications. This helps NT make decisions when choosing what to page to disk. With this setting, when NT needs memory, it leans toward leaving the system processes in memory and pages the disk cache. This is fine, because Exchange does not use the system disk cache anyway. It has its own buffers that it uses to cache accesses to the databases.

◆ Add more RAM. For one thing, adding memory allows an increase in the number of database buffers in Exchange. The database buffers function as a disk cache to the Exchange databases, and because Exchange doesn't use the system disk cache, it is very important not to starve the database buffers.

A tool comes with MS Exchange Server called Exchange Performance Optimizer. Its whole purpose in life is to analyze your system and set various Exchange parameters to an appropriate value. It does a very good

28

job at allocating memory to the parts of Exchange that need it, so adding more memory gives Performance Optimizer something to work with.

> ## Note
>
> I must mention here that there is a point of diminishing returns with adding memory. You can't just keep throwing memory at the system and expect it to continue improving. Somewhere along the line, you just move the bottleneck from memory to somewhere else in the system. Depending on the server load, this point varies for different systems, so there's no way I can give you a set amount and say it will always be the best. If your system has minimal RAM, however (32MB, for example), and you want to support a few hundred users, it is safe to advise increasing into the 64MB-to-96MB range.

SYSTEM PROCESSOR PERFORMANCE

The processor is arguably the most important subsystem in an Exchange Server system. Given a reasonably fast disk subsystem, the processor is the most likely candidate to become the next bottleneck. If you have many users on a server (hundreds, for example), Exchange Server puts quite a strain on your system processor. When optimizing your server for Exchange, you might want to follow some of these suggestions:

◆ Install the fastest processor available. If you have a large level 2 cache (also called a processor cache)—512KB, for example, you will get good performance. Some server products provide their CPUs on processor boards complete with L2 cache. Get one with as large an L2 cache as possible— some even go up to 2MB. With Exchange, you will notice a big difference in performance with a system that has a 2MB L2 cache when compared with one with a 512KB L2 cache.

◆ Add a second processor. In a heavily loaded system, Exchange Server benefits significantly from a second processor. This reduces the load on each processor and it increases the overall speed of the system. It also can have the effect of increasing disk throughput because disk I/O can be requested more quickly as execution speed increases.

Unlike MS Mail and typical file server environments, Exchange Server and Windows NT are designed to be scaleable with multiple processors.

In Exchange, this is due in large part to the multiprocess, multithread nature of the server software. This is another good reason to select a server class system for Exchange Server instead of trying to deploy it on a desktop. You can add processors to multiprocessor server machines when you need to.

◆ Add a third and fourth processor. The same general ideas apply here as in the preceding bullet. One caveat, though. As you add third and fourth processors, the system does not benefit as much as from the second processor. Also, the benefit is not so much speed as it is capacity. In other words, speed increases somewhat with the third and fourth processors, but the amount of load your server can sustain increases more.

◆ Free processor bandwidth by using bus-master disk controllers and NICs. This really was already covered in the previous sections. Using bus-master NICs and hardware array controllers, for example, offloads stress from the system processor. That helps you get more mileage out of the CPU because it doesn't have to be bothered with mundane tasks such as managing network and disk I/O.

USING THE MICROSOFT PERFORMANCE OPTIMIZER

When you install Exchange Server, the SETUP program gives you the option of starting the Exchange Performance Optimizer (also known as PerfWiz). This occurs at the end of the installation process once all of the core files have been copied to your hard disk and the services have been started successfully. It is a good idea to start it, because the default Exchange Server configuration is probably not optimized for your system configuration. PerfWiz can also help eliminate a lot of the guesswork in optimizing the Exchange configuration and Exchange Server parameters.

PerfWiz basically takes you through a step-by-step process, asking you pertinent questions along the way in an attempt to optimize Exchange Server for your specific system. For example, it asks how many users you expect to host and adjusts parameters accordingly. It checks system memory and adjusts database buffers and other parameters to appropriate values. PerfWiz will also analyze your disk subsystem and suggest the best placement for various Exchange Server components. Anytime you modify the system configuration—such as when you add additional RAM, install a new disk drive, or install additional services (like the Internet Information Server or the Services for Macintosh)—you should rerun PerfWiz to reconfigure Exchange Server for optimum performance.

If you want to see what PerfWiz is doing, you can run it with the verbose (-v) option:

```
perfwiz -v
```

This will show all the values for parameters as they are set by PerfWiz. This is great for getting an idea of exactly the types of parameters Exchange uses. Be careful about manually changing values, though, because it can have unpredictable effects on your server's performance. The Microsoft Exchange team has done a very good job of refining this tool so it will give the right answers, and a lot of testing has gone into the decisions it makes. It's not always perfect, but it does what it is supposed to do: assist you in optimally configuring Exchange Server. If you decide to manually configure any of the Exchange Server parameters, the next section can be helpful in determining just how well your changes are working.

Using Performance Monitor in MS Exchange Server

As with MS Mail, you can use many of the same counters to help monitor Exchange Server performance. In this section, you will find two sections of counters: the Exchange-specific counters, which are installed when Exchange Server is installed, and the generic counters, which are installed as a part of Windows NT.

Hopefully this list of counters—although only a few of the many available—will get you started exploring the Performance Monitor counters for yourself. There is a wealth of information to be gathered.

Note

Don't forget to use `diskperf -y` to activate the disk counters before trying to use the Logical Disk (and Physical Disk) object.

Exchange-specific objects installed by Exchange Server follow:

◆ MSExchangeDB: Counters for the Exchange database engine
◆ MSExchangeDS: Counters for the Exchange Directory Service
◆ MSExchangeIS: General counters for the Exchange Information Store
◆ MSExchangeIS Private: Counters for the Exchange Private Store
◆ MSExchangeIS Public: Counters for the Exchange Public Store
◆ MSExchangeMTA: Counters for the Exchange Mail Transfer Agent
◆ MSExchangeMTA Connections: Counters for connections to the MTA

There are dozens of counters included in these seven objects. Following are some useful ones to get you going:

◆ MSExchangeDB:% Buffer Available (Instance=Information Store): The percentage of the database buffer cache available for use. This counter and the following one help monitor the effectiveness of your database buffer cache.
◆ MSExchangeDB:% Buffer Cache Hit (Instance=Information Store): The percentage of requests for store data satisfied from the database buffer cache.

- MSExchangeIS:User Count: Number of users connected to the store.
- MSExchangeIS Private:Messages Submitted/min: The rate at which messages are being submitted by clients. If this is consistently higher than Messages Delivered/min, it could indicate that the server can't keep up with the delivery load.
- MSExchangeIS Private:Messages Delivered/min: The rate at which messages are delivered to all recipients. If this is consistently lower than Messages Submitted/min, it could indicate that the server can't keep up with the delivery load.
- MSExchangeIS Private:Send Queue Size: Number of messages in the send queue. Another counter that can indicate when the server is overloaded.
- MSExchangeIS Public:Messages Submitted/min: The rate at which messages are being submitted by clients. If this is consistently higher than Messages Delivered/min, it could indicate that the server can't keep up with the delivery load.
- MSExchangeIS Public:Messages Delivered/min: The rate at which messages are delivered to all recipients. If this is consistently lower than Messages Submitted/min, it could indicate that the server can't keep up with the delivery load.
- MSExchangeIS Public:Send Queue Size: Number of messages in the send queue. Another counter that can indicate when the server is overloaded.

Generic counters that you might find helpful follow:

- Cache:Data Map Hits %: Percentage of successful references to the in-memory system data cache.

Note

A high hit ratio is preferred because this means the requested data was in the system cache. This means the operating system was able to retrieve the data without having to perform a physical read from the disk drive. Considering that disk access is in the millisecond range and memory access is in the nanosecond range, you can understand the advantage of a high hit ratio. If you have a low hit ratio, adding additional physical RAM will increase the cache size and usually increase the hit ratio.

- Logical Disk:% Disk Time: Percentage of time the disk is busy servicing I/O requests.
- Logical Disk:Avg. Disk sec/Transfer: Average amount of seconds it takes the disk to satisfy a disk transfer (read or write).

28

◆ Logical Disk:Disk Bytes/sec: Rate at which data is transferred to or from the disk during I/O operations.

◆ Memory:Available Bytes: Amount of free memory in the system available for use.

◆ Memory:Cache Bytes: Size of the system cache. Note that the system cache is used to cache file access on the local disk drives and remote-mapped network drives. Adding additional RAM will usually increase the size of the system cache.

◆ Memory:Pages/sec: Indicates overall paging activity—the rate at which pages are written to or read from the disk. A consistently high value is an indication that adding additional RAM may improve overall system performance.

◆ NetBEUI:Bytes Total/sec: Amount of NetBEUI data sent to and received from the network.

◆ NetBEUI Resource:Times Exhausted: Number of times the NetBEUI buffers were exhausted.

◆ Paging File:% Usage: Shows what percentage of the pagefile is in use. Can indicate whether you need to enlarge your pagefile. A high value (above 50%) is an indication that you need to enlarge your pagefile to prevent out-of-virtual-memory errors.

◆ Processor:% Processor Time: Amount of time the processor is busy doing work. This is both User and Privileged (kernel) time combined.

◆ Server Bytes Total/sec: Rate at which the server is sending and receiving data to and from the network.

◆ System:Processor Queue Length (must also monitor one thread from the Thread object for this counter to be nonzero): Number of threads waiting in the processor queue. Numbers above 2, per processor, can indicate processor congestion.

SUMMARY

This chapter focused primarily on the techniques to optimize your Microsoft Mail and your Microsoft Exchange Server. For the most part, this discussion centered around hardware, with a brief discussion of Performance Monitor counters you can use to fine tune your system. For specifics on using the Performance Monitor, I suggest that you look at Chapter 13; it includes additional tips with example software to help you determine whether your system is processor, memory, I/O, or network bound.

Both Microsoft Mail and Exchange Server share some basic performance optimizations. You will find that the best performance benefit usually can be obtained by adding additional RAM, considering your disk subsystem, considering your network adapter, and possibly segmenting your network to increase available network bandwidth. When configuring an MS Mail installation for best performance, you should configure your system to use RAM for system caching over system processes. But for MS Exchange Server, configure your system to use RAM for system processes over system caching. You also might want to add additional processors because Exchange Server is a multithreaded client/server application. As such, it can benefit from additional processors.

The next chapter introduces you to SNA Server. You will learn about the SNA Server Architectural model and SNA Server's capabilities.

- An Introduction to
  SNA Server

- Planning Your SNA
  Server Installation

- Installing SNA Server

- Managing Your
  SNA Server Gateway

- Optimizing
  SNA Server

PART VI

SNA Server

- The SNA Server
  Architectural Model

- SNA Server
  Capabilities

CHAPTER 29

An Introduction to SNA Server

If you have an IBM mainframe, IBM AS/400, or System Network Architecture (SNA) compatible product, you have a reason to use SNA Server for Windows NT. It is not a requirement that you use SNA Server for your connectivity solution; you can always use dumb terminals or dedicated 3270/5250 hardware emulation with a dedicated connection to your mainframe instead. These are either of limited usefulness or are quite expensive solutions, however, when you have many users to connect to your mainframe.

This is the primary reason why SNA Server exists: to provide a more useful, easier-to-use, and less expensive connectivity solution. Perhaps you are wondering about the justification behind this statement or, in other words, "Where's the beef?" Maybe the following will help to explain this reasoning:

◆ The first item to consider is usability. A dumb terminal provides access to your mainframe, but that is all. In this scenario, any sharing of data requires software-based solutions on your mainframe and mainframe processor time. And as any mainframe guru will tell you, this is both a very expensive proposition, as well as a cumbersome solution.

On the other hand, if you can use your networked personal computer as your mainframe connectivity solution, you can use your computer for other solutions as well. This includes word processing, spreadsheets, database, e-mail, development, and even entertainment. What makes this solution so capable is that you can use your software connectivity solution to connect to your mainframe, download and upload data, and use any networked resource, such as shared disk drives or printers.

One of the best reasons I find to use this type of connectivity solution is for your mainframe development efforts. You can download a subset of your mainframe data, for example, and then use a COBOL, FORTRAN, C, C++, or other type of compiler to develop and debug your applications. After your application is fully developed, you can upload your source code and recompile it. Then you can use this application on your mainframe. If you do this over the course of a year, it's quite possible that the money you save in processor time (particularly because every mainframe shop I've been involved with will charge back the associated cost based on the processor time used) can pay for your equipment.

You can even downsize your mainframe-based solutions in their entirety in some cases because Windows NT supports many of the same architectural features. These features include a 2GB-per-process address space, 32-bit wide numerical abstracts, large datasets, and high-speed I/O options. Depending on your processor choice and platform, you might even be able to surpass your mainframe computing capacity. What you probably will not be able to surpass is your mainframe's raw I/O speed or dataset capacity.

Tip

It is not always the best solution to downsize a mainframe-based solution to your network; however, it is always good to have the option. Even if you do not downsize the application, you still can downsize enough of it to aid you in your development efforts. With the various relational database servers and compilers available to you today, you can build a solution that your developers will thank you for every day—particularly on those days that the mainframe is over-loaded and running as slow as a dog. And you might even be able to save the company enough money to get them to give you that raise you've been waiting for.

◆ Second, consider the expense required for dedicated hardware-based solutions. Not only do you have to consider the price of the dumb terminal or personal computer with a 3270/5250 hardware adapter, but you also must factor in the cost of the mainframe ports, the cabling, and, in some cases, the additional storage and peripherals. And don't forget the main-frame expertise required to maintain and administer these solutions.

All of this costs big bucks, and if you already have a network with numerous clients plugged in, the network clients can be granted access to the mainframe simply by adding some additional software. Adding a new user is simply a matter of building him a network-capable computer and pulling the cable from the closet to his computer. This administrative chore is well within the scope of most network administrators, whereas a dumb terminal connection requires extensive experience with the mainframe hardware and administrative software.

◆ Next, you may want to reflect on SNA Server's capability to tie into your existing network architecture to provide access to your mainframes from a non-local network client (a WAN, for example) or a client using the remote access software. In either case, the user usually will be able to obtain greater throughput between your mainframe and the client computer than if he dialed up the mainframe directly. You can even use SNA Server with an X.25 connection to provide local low-speed (9600bps) access numbers when your network clients have to travel internationally.

◆ Finally, consider the custom solutions you can build with SNA Server. If you look closely in the DOCS\SDK, DOCS\WINSNA, and SDK directories on the CD-ROM, you'll find documentation and development files you can use to build custom applications to solve your unique problems.

There are at least two other reasons why you might want to use SNA Server. The first is to provide a communications pathway between your mainframe databases and your network databases so that you can keep the various databases in sync. I've found it useful to build data-entry systems at the network level, for example, and then to upload this data to the mainframe databases. The second reason is to support the remote installation of Systems Management Server over a WAN link. The SMS Setup program can use SNA Server to provide a reliable means of installing the software, including SQL Server, if needed.

All these capabilities and more are possible with SNA Server. The rest of this chapter looks at SNA Server in a different light. You'll learn what SNA Server is and how it fits into IBM's architectural model as well as your network model. You'll also take a look at the basic capabilities and learn some of the various acronyms to aid you in your decisions on how to implement SNA Server.

THE SNA SERVER ARCHITECTURAL MODEL

In order to understand how SNA Server's architectural model fits into the IBM networking model, you need to look into what System Network Architecture (SNA) really means. In the beginning, mainframes used proprietary hardware and proprietary protocols to tie these pieces of hardware together, which is still true in some cases today. Then, in the early '70s, IBM developed the System Network Architecture as a means of providing a standard message format and communications interface to integrate its hardware. And because this interface was developed and controlled by IBM, it is a well-documented interface. Because this interface was well-documented, it also was easily understood, which made it possible for third-party manufacturers to provide hardware and software solutions to integrate into IBM mainframe systems. SNA Server is one of these third-party products.

When you look closely at the architectural design of a working IBM mainframe (such as an IBM S/370 or S/390) that uses the SNA architecture, you will see a hierarchical chain of physical devices. (See Figure 29.1.) At the top of the chain is the IBM Central Processing Unit (CPU), which in SNA terms is referred to as a Physical Unit Type 5 (PU5). At this level, the responsibility includes the operating system, system-level applications, and user-level applications. The next level is usually an IBM front-end processor (FEP), which in SNA nomenclature is called a Physical Unit Type 4 (PU4). The FEP is responsible for managing the communications between the CPU and the devices, applications, and users on the network. Just below the FEP is the cluster controller, or, in SNA terminology, the Physical Unit 2 (PU2).

The cluster controller is not as intelligent as the FEP, but it is responsible for controlling the attached devices, such as dumb terminals and printers. These physical devices are not directly accessed by the SNA network software. Instead, each device is accessed through a logical address, rather than the actual physical address of the device, and is treated as a logical unit (LU). An LU2 is a dumb terminal (3278, 3279, or 3178), which is a monochrome, color, or graphics terminal. An LU1 or LU3 is an IBM 3287 or compatible printer.

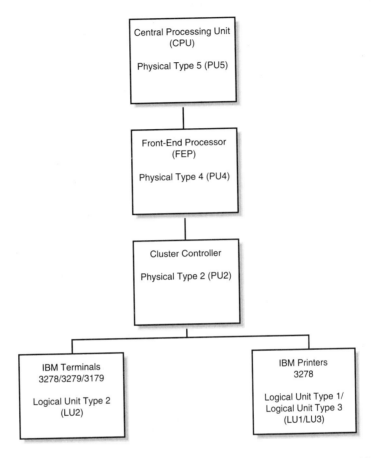

Figure 29.1.
The hierarchical
design of an IBM
mainframe.

This is where SNA Server fits into the picture—as another cluster controller with logical devices attached. (See Figure 29.2.) This figure shows that instead of a physical cluster controller with physically attached dumb terminals or printers, SNA Server replaces the cluster controller with the client applications emulating the various logical units (terminals and printers).

It would be nice to stop right here and say that's all there is to the SNA architectural model but, unfortunately, there is another model to be considered. This model has evolved from the hierarchical model and is IBM's stated direction in future networking concepts. This model is called an advanced peer-to-peer networking (APPN) model and is often found in environments that use IBM AS/400 series computers. For comparison, you can consider the hierarchical SNA model to be similar to a network model that uses a server and network clients. The SNA peer-to-peer model then would be similar to a peer-to-peer network, such as a workgroup of Windows NT, Windows 95, or Windows for Workgroups computers.

*Figure 29.2.
Fitting SNA
Server into the
hierarchical IBM
mainframe SNA
architectural
design.*

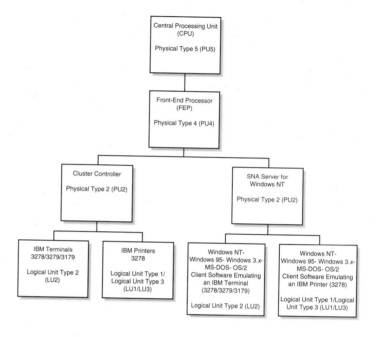

In an APPN model, the topmost item in the food chain is a network node or physical unit type 2.1 (PU2.1), as shown in Figure 29.3. Below that are additional PU2.1 entry nodes, each of which may have additional logical units attached to it. These logical units are of type LU6.2, which includes terminals, printers, or applications. These logical units communicate via the LU6.2 interface. This is a group of protocols called Advanced Program to Program Communications (APPC).

*Figure 29.3.
An advanced
peer-to-peer
networking
model.*

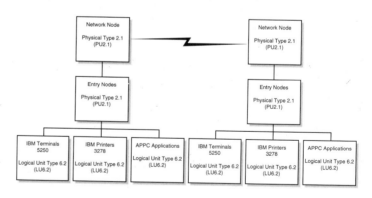

In the APPN model, SNA Server replaces a PU2.1 entry node rather than a cluster controller in the hierarchical model. (See Figure 29.4.) And rather than using LU1, LU2, or LU3 devices, the APPN model uses the LU6.2 protocols (APPC) to communicate between applications and devices. This model is much more flexible and useful than the hierarchical model, simply because applications and devices can communicate directly with other applications and devices.

29

SNA SERVER INTRODUCTION

Figure 29.4.
Fitting SNA
Server into the
advanced peer-to-
peer networking
model.

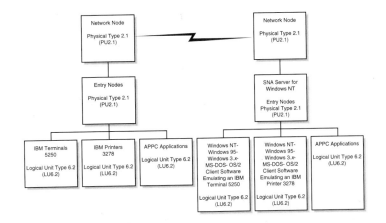

One additional item I would like to point out is that SNA Server communicates with the SNA network via a data link. A data link is a combination of hardware and software—similar to a network card and network protocol (such as TCP/IP). In this case, the hardware is the physical connection to the SNA network, with SNA Server providing the software components. An SNA network provides more data links than currently are supported by SNA Server, however. Future enhancements to SNA Server might support these additional data links but, for now, the supported data links follow:

◆ DFT: A locally attached distributed function terminal.

◆ DLC: The Data Link Control protocol over Ethernet or token ring based networks.

◆ SDLC: The Synchronous Data Link Control protocol over a leased or dial-up telephone line.

◆ X.25: A private or public packet-switched network.

SNA Server Capabilities

Every corporation has unique needs that must be addressed in order for the company to survive, and hopefully flourish. SNA Server can provide a solution to connecting your network clients to your IBM mainframes, but you must carefully consider your needs to determine if and how SNA Server will work in your situation.

Some of the features SNA Server can provide follow:

◆ Support for Windows NT, Windows 95, Windows 3.x, MS-DOS, and other operating system network clients. Before you consider SNA Server a complete solution to your client-connectivity needs, you should be aware that although SNA Server includes 3270/5230 clients software, these are limited to a one-user administrative license. These tools are provided for diagnostic usage only. So you will need to look at third-party (such as Attachmate, Intergraph, WRQ, and so on) connectivity solutions in order for your network clients to access your mainframe via SNA Server.

Note

You can find a listing of supported third-party 3270/5250 software emulations on the SNA Server CD-ROM in the \COLLATRL directory in the ISVCATAL.DOC file.

◆ Support for 2,000 simultaneously connected clients with a maximum of 10,000 sessions per SNA Server installation.

Note

Just because a single server can support 2,000 user connections and 10,000 sessions does not mean that you will achieve adequate performance at the maximum limits. The performance levels you achieve are based on the server load (it may be providing additional services), processor speed, available RAM, network adapters, network bandwidth (including the bandwidth provided by your mainframe connection), and mainframe capacity. The application you use on the client side may also affect your performance and should be considered as well.

◆ Support for the Intel, MIPS, PowerPC, and Alpha processor line. This enables you to scale up your server if more raw processing power is required.

◆ Support for native mode TCP/IP network client connections. This support is particularly important when looking at supporting mainframe connectivity via third-party applications (such as those from Intergraph and WRQ), alternate operating systems (such as UNIX or Macintosh), and wide area network clients.

◆ Support for Macintosh clients using the AppleTalk network protocols. Although there is no built-in client for a Macintosh computer, you can use clients from Attachmate or DCA.

◆ Support for various manufacturers' SNA adapters (such as those from Attachmate, Barr Systems, Microgate, and so on). The device drivers for these adapters are bundled with SNA Server and can be installed during the SNA Server setup.

◆ Support for Channel-attached and TwinAx connections to your mainframe from manufacturers such as McData or Andrew Corporation.

> *Note*
>
> Although SNA Server provides support, it does not provide the device drivers. These drivers must be supplied by a third-party manufacturer. You can find supported products in the `ISVCATAL.DOC` file in the `\COLLATRL` directory on the CD-ROM.

◆ Support for TN3270 servers. This support simply means that you can use third-party products that provide the TN3270 server functionality to interface to SNA Server. You can use a TN3270 server to provide connectivity solutions (perhaps from a UNIX workstation).

> *Note*
>
> You can find a listing of supported third-party TN3270 servers on the SNA Server CD-ROM in the `\COLLATRL` directory in the `ISVCATAL.DOC` file.

Along with all these features, it also might help to know that SNA Server provides the capability for your client software to download and upload data using the IND$FILE protocol and to print data to a local printer or to a mainframe printer.

SUMMARY

This chapter looked at some of the reasons why you might want to use SNA Server on your network. To aid you in your understanding of how SNA Server works and what it can do for you, it also looked into the architectural model and SNA Server's capabilities.

The next chapter looks at the various SNA Server concepts you should know when planning your SNA Server installations.

CHAPTER 30

Planning Your SNA Server Installation

Before you insert your SNA Server CD-ROM and begin installing SNA Server, you had better be prepared to supply a variety of configuration information. Configuration information is not all you need to know, however, and, in fact, is the easy part of the SNA Server installation. This chapter's primary focus is to prepare you for your installation of SNA Server—both on your server and on your various clients.

This chapter explores the following tasks:

◆ Choosing a model: SNA Server for Windows NT groups collections of SNA Servers into a single unit that interoperates within a Windows NT Server domain. This might be confusing at first glance. Yet, by the time you finish looking into this subject in depth, there should be no misunderstanding, and you will be prepared to choose a model and implement your SNA Server installation to best fit your needs.

◆ Choosing your hardware: Determining exactly what hardware you need can be a daunting task. And it requires some interaction with your mainframe administrators, and your network administrators (if you are not performing these duties) as well, to choose the best hardware to suit your needs. This discussion will help you prepare for your meetings with these administrators and help you plan the SNA Server rollout.

◆ Choosing your software: I bet you thought you had this one covered when you chose SNA Server to meet your connectivity needs. SNA Server only provides the connection between Windows NT Server and your SNA-compatible mainframe, however. You still need to determine what client software to use.

CHOOSING AN SNA SERVER MODEL

Planning your SNA Server installation is one of the most critical choices you can make. It is not a requirement; you can just go right ahead and install SNA Server in any way you choose. At least you can do this at first, but later, when you want to add additional servers to improve the increasing demand for mainframe connectivity, you might encounter administrative or performance-related problems. This is one reason why you should think first and act later. You also need to interface with your mainframe administrators (this is discussed in the following section) and network administrators before you can provide this service to your network clients. This is another reason for you to plan your installation rather than just installing it haphazardly.

To begin, there are basically three models from which you can choose. Each offers unique capabilities, but none of them is perfect for every situation. The first, as shown in Figure 30.1, is the centralized model.

Figure 30.1.
Implementing
SNA Server in a
centralized
model.

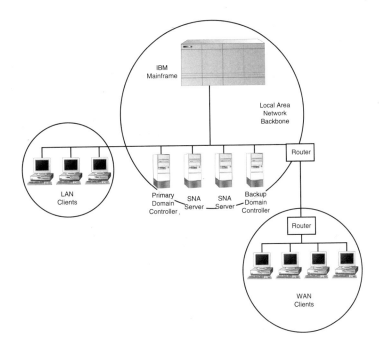

The centralized model provides the following benefits:

◆ Centralized administration: Because all the SNA Servers are located in one physical location, it is easy to administrate. All your administration—either locally on the mainframe or on the Windows NT Servers—is simplified. This limits the requirement to have SNA-savvy administrators located at remote locations and provides the best all-around model for companies that have a centralized MIS shop.

This also places less of a burden on your administrators and increases response time for client requests. How? Just by being physically present in the area most likely to cause a problem. If there is a problem with the mainframe, it can be resolved by working with the MIS personnel. If the problem relates to SNA Server, the people are once more readily at hand. If the problem is a bit tougher, such as those that relate to the connection between SNA Server and your mainframe, you will need members from both groups together simultaneously to provide a fast response time. Phone calls between these groups rarely provide the level of response that you can achieve by putting both groups face to face.

◆ Single network protocol: In this model, you can choose to use a single network protocol—generally, TCP/IP—throughout your entire network. There is no need to concern yourself with routing problems, such as whether your routers can handle the DLC network protocol and can ease connectivity-related issues.

Note

Because only one network protocol is being used, this provides the simplest method of supporting your remote clients—those on the other side of a WAN segment or those who dial into a Remote Access Server.

♦ Easy access to resources: Because all your servers hopefully are connected via a high-speed, fiber-optic backbone, these servers can communicate quite effectively among themselves for authentication purposes. And because all your LAN clients are connected to this same network, they too can easily and efficiently access any resources they need based on your domain model. Even your WAN clients have easy, although not as efficient, access to resources.

Tip

If you place all your servers on a high-speed backbone, you also can increase the load these servers can carry. Specifically, if you also have a high-speed connection to your mainframe, adding additional network adapters to your servers can increase the capacity of these servers to service client requests. You even can add additional SNA adapters to increase the link capacity between your mainframes and SNA Server.

The next model you can choose from is just the opposite of the centralized model. This model is the noncentralized model, as shown in Figure 30.2. Instead of placing all your SNA Servers in a single location, this model splits up access to the mainframe among several groups. Each group directly communicates with the mainframe through an SDLC link. This model's primary benefit is that it offers fast response time to local domain resources. File and print sharing are as efficient as the communications link between the servers and your network clients. You can even support fast response time for application servers, such as SQL Server. Managing the network can be a little easier for your network administrator too because each group is treated as a unique unit—it can be, but it doesn't have to be.

Tip

The primary downside to this model is its slow mainframe connection. Most SDLC connections are quite a bit slower than your direct cable connections to your mainframe. You could use one or more SDLC adapters with a T1 connection to increase the throughput, but this is also a very expensive alternative. I do not recommend this model unless it is the only way to provide connectivity between your mainframe and your network clients.

Figure 30.2. Implementing SNA Server in a noncentralized model.

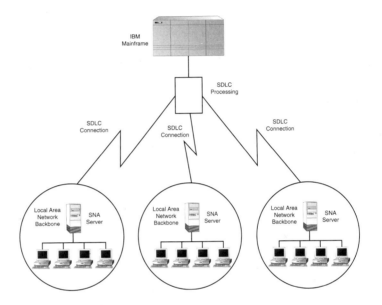

In the noncentralized model, each group will most likely be a single domain. This provides your administrator with an autonomous ability to manage the domain as he sees fit. This can be both good and bad because the local administrator can provide services to his clients without complicating the life of administrators in the other domains. In a real-world situation, however, there is always someone who needs access to external (other domain) resources. This means that a WAN linkage is required as well as dual accounts or a trust relationship between domains. Each domain's local administrator also must be SNA-savvy to be able to manage his SNA Server installation. This duplication of effort can be quite costly, both in personnel and in wasted man hours.

You, therefore, might want to consider grouping these individual physical domains into a single, larger logical domain. This method lowers the personnel and man-hour requirements and provides for a centralized administrative capability. You can even place a backup domain controller in each physically separate group to increase authentication requests and provide a better local response time instead of establishing multiple trust relationships. Of course, this really depends on the size of your network and WAN bandwidth; the larger the network becomes, the more WAN bandwidth is required for replicating the user database between primary and backup controllers. A trust relationship between multiple domains is better because your network increases in size as it lowers the WAN bandwidth requirement while still providing centralized administration and good local response time. A domain based on trust relationships also is easily expanded to include additional domain controllers, resource servers, and application servers.

As you can see, the choices you can make can really drive you crazy with all the "what ifs" that are possible. For this reason, I will take pity on you and give you a few guidelines. Only consider the backup domain controller option for small (fewer than 50) remote groups that require little administration or interaction from your network administrators. In this group, look for someone with the potential to handle day-to-day administrative issues, such as new user accounts and authentication-related issues. If you have more than 50 users or very demanding users, go with multiple domains and trust relationships. This group probably will continue to grow and require additional resources, and the multiple domains with trust relationships provide an easier path for your network administrators to do their jobs, and also provide the means to expand the local resources as required by adding additional servers.

The final model uses the best of both the centralized and noncentralized models and is the model I generally recommend. This model is what I call the mixed model. This model starts with a centralized connection to the mainframe but also provides for the capability to connect external groups directly to the mainframe. At this point, I bet you are thinking, "Now why would I want to do that, when I could just connect these external groups to my domain with a WAN connection?" or something similar. Many companies use external agencies (some refer to this as outsourcing) to provide services and if you consider the following questions, you'll have your answer. How well do you trust these external agencies? Do you want to provide them with direct access to your network, or would you prefer that they only provide their data-entry services and interact with the mainframe directly?

Limiting access to just the mainframe limits potential damage to your network. With the mixed model, you can consider your mainframe as the choke point—similar to an Internet firewall. The external agency still can provide the services you want, but the potential to take down your mainframe and your network simultaneously, or to corrupt data on both systems, is less likely to occur. This model also provides the best performance and long-term growth options. Those members connected to your LAN have a fast connection to your LAN resources and your mainframe. Those connected to your WAN have a slower connection but still can access both your LAN resources and the mainframe. And administration is still centralized. Those users connecting to just your mainframe can access only the mainframe, however. Administering these users falls into the MIS group's dominion, which also means less work for your LAN administrators.

Tip

> One important item to consider when implementing SNA Server when using a WAN to provide a route between SNA Server and your network clients is whether your routers will bridge DLC packets or encapsulate the DLC packet in a routable protocol (like TCP/IP). If they will not, you should choose the centralized model or a variant, in which SNA Server can communicate with your network clients by using a supported routable protocol.

CHOOSING YOUR SNA SERVER OPERATING MODE

When you install SNA Server, you must choose the mode of operation for the installation. It can be a primary configuration server, a backup configuration server, or a member server. This follows a similar model for a Windows NT Server installation, in which each installation can be a primary domain controller, backup domain controller, or server. Much like a PDC manages the other computers (backup domain controllers, servers, and network clients), the account database, trust relationships, and shared resources, a primary configuration SNA Server installation manages the other SNA Server installations (backup configuration servers and member servers), 3270/5250 users, link services, logical units (LUs), and other relevant configuration information.

Tip

> Your SNA Server configuration information is stored in the file COM.CFG, which is located in the SNARoot\System\Config directory. This Config directory is shared on each SNA Server installation so that a copy of this file can be loaded in case of a primary configuration server failure. Because this shared file is critical to SNA Server's function, however, you should install all your SNA Servers to an NTFS partition where you can set directory and file permissions to protect it from inadvertent or malicious changes.

The same principle holds true for backup configuration servers and backup domain controllers. These servers obtain a copy of the configuration file from the primary configuration server, similar to the replicated account database from primary to backup domain controller, so that servers and connections can be managed. Just like a BDC cannot manage account information when the PDC is down, a backup configuration server cannot be used to modify the configuration of the current SNA Server installation when the primary configuration server is down.

A member server provides the same level of interaction as a server because neither contains a copy of the configuration file or account database. All authentications are referred to the units higher up in the hierarchy.

When you plan your installation, you should follow the same rules as when you planned your Windows NT Server installation. You should have a minimum of two servers: one primary configuration server and one backup configuration server. Preferably, you will have one or more backup configuration servers, just in case of failure, and one or more member servers to handle the increased loads on a large network.

CHOOSING YOUR HARDWARE

After choosing how you will fit SNA Server into your current network configuration, you need to consider what physical hardware is required to support your goals. By this, I mean just how much hardware and what type are required to support your network clients. After all, there is a limit to the number of clients and sessions each client can have open on a single SNA Server installation. The actual number varies depending on your hardware platform and its configuration. And even if your server can support all these clients simultaneously, your connection to your mainframe might not. Your connection to your mainframe might be the limiting factor in how many connections you can support at once, simply because, as the available bandwidth is used, your network clients will become very irate at the lengthy mainframe response time. At some point, the system becomes unusable. And this is really the goal I have in mind at this point, because the purpose is to support your users' needs.

The first step in solving this particular problem is to choose a minimum hardware platform. This minimum platform is limited strictly to providing a stable and functional SNA Server platform. If you want this computer to provide additional services other than SNA Server, you should increase the minimum requirements or be willing to suffer the associated performance degradation. The realistic minimum requirement for an SNA Server platform follows:

◆ Windows NT Advanced Server 3.1. For best performance, plan on using Windows NT Server 3.51; it has been enhanced to provide better server performance than Windows NT Advanced Server 3.1.

◆ An Intel 80486 processor operating at 66 MHz or higher. The preferred platform should consist of a multiprocessing Pentium platform with two or more processors. Why more processors? Because the BackOffice components can make use of these processors to increase performance. If you have such a platform, then your system can provide more resources to your network clients without hindering SNA Server performance.

Tip

> Remember that the faster the processors, the better. Windows NT Server requires more computational capability than most other network operating systems. The additional services—such as SNA Server, SQL Server, and Systems Management Server—also require more computational capability than their implementations on other operating systems. A part of this stems from their clientserver architecture and interdependence of the base operating system, which provides increased scalability when compared to alternative operating systems.

Note

> The various RISC platforms also offer acceptable and, in some cases, quite excellent performance for SNA Server platforms. The available device drivers and link services drivers are not as widely available, however. If you choose to use a RISC platform, make absolutely sure that the device drivers you need are available in a retail—not beta— product before you purchase your RISC platform and peripherals.

◆ A minimum of 20MB of RAM. Your preferred minimum should be at least 32MB of RAM. If you expect to use this server for additional services, plan on a minimum of 64MB of RAM to achieve good performance levels. No other single item increases or degrades performance as much as the amount of system RAM you have in your server. Keep this in the front of your mind when determining your server requirements.

Tip

> When making your purchase decision for your server, you also might want to consider a larger level two (L2) cache. Generally, a larger cache can improve system performance by between 10 and 30 percent. If the cache is too small (256KB or less), it does not offer much help when your system exceeds 16MB of system RAM.

◆ A minimum of 11MB of free space on your disk drive. This is for the core files; adding the SNA Server client-connectivity files for administrative troubleshooting requires additional space. A realistic view is to reserve at least 100MB for SNA Server–related files, which includes third-party products.

◆ A supported network adapter. Although any adapter will do, you should choose the fastest possible adapter. If you are not using a 100MB network backbone, consider using more than one adapter to help balance the load. And if you are using more than one network transport, consider using more than one network adapter. You can achieve the best all-around response by using one network adapter per network transport and binding one transport protocol to one specific adapter.

Note

There is actually more to using multiple adapters with multiple network transports for load balancing and increased efficiency. In general, however, this almost always increases performance. The only way to find out for sure beforehand is to use the Performance Monitor to determine whether the current network adapter is a bottleneck. Chapter 13, "Tuning Your Server," includes a more in-depth discussion of load balancing using multiple adapters.

◆ A supported SNA adapter. This is a critical choice and should not be made alone. Consult your mainframe administrators beforehand. Discuss the possible connection possibilities. Consider both the available connections (what is possible with your current mainframe configuration) as well as possible connections based on a future product purchase. It will do you little good to purchase the fastest available product if you cannot connect to your mainframe with it because your mainframe has no open connections or does not support it. Your budget also should consider mainframe hardware purchases to support your connection requirements. This is really where your mainframe administrators can help you in determining just what is possible, now and in the future. Don't skimp on this step or you might find yourself in a serious bind. Table 30.1 includes information about currently supported SNA adapters.

Tip

Just as you can increase your ability to service network requests by adding additional network adapters, you can increase your available bandwidth to your mainframe (assuming that it can handle the additional data traffic) by adding additional SNA adapters. This is particularly useful if your current budget does not include the money to purchase additional mainframe hardware to support your faster SNA adapter hardware. Instead, you can use two or more slower SNA adapters on slower connection pathways. Although it's not the perfect solution, it is a workaround until you can fit the appropriate hardware into your budget.

Note

Interacting with your mainframe administrators, network administrators, PC support technicians, and any other groups involved, can be a time-consuming business. You should factor in the additional time and pad it by 50 percent for the inevitable delays required in your planning to provide a realistic SNA Server delivery date.

◆ To support your network clients, you can use the NetBEUI, IPX/SPX, or TCP/IP network protocol. You can use any one, or all, of these protocols to provide a connection between your server and network clients. To support your Banyan VINES clients, you must use the Banyan Enterprise Client 5.52 or higher for Windows NT. To support your Macintosh clients, you must install the Services for Macintosh.

Note

The Services for Macintosh require an additional 2MB, preferably 4MB or more, of RAM for adequate performance. This also is true for the Gateway Services for NetWare. In fact, for each additional service you add to your Windows NT Server, plan to add a minimum of 1MB of additional RAM. Some applications, like SQL Server or Systems Management Server, require substantially more RAM.

TABLE 30.1. SUPPORTED SNA ADAPTERS.

Manufacturer	Product	Supported Platforms	Description
Andrew Corporation	TwinAx driver	N/A	TwinAx Adapter
Atlantis	Shiva for Windows NT	Intel	SDLC and X2.5 support
Attachmate	Advanced 3270 Adapter	Intel	DFT Adapter (COAX)
Attachmate	SDLC Adapter	Intel	SDLC/X2.5 Adapter

continues

TABLE 30.1. CONTINUED

Manufacturer	Product	Supported Platforms	Description
Attachmate	Advanced Function SDLC Adapter	Intel	SDLC Adapter
Barr Systems	T1-Sync	Intel, MIPS, and Alpha	N/A
Barr Systems	Barr/Channel	N/A	IBM Channel Interface
DCA	IRMA Adapter	Intel	DFT Adapter
DCA	ISCA Adapter	Intel	SDLC/X2.5 Adapter
EICON	WAN Services for Windows NT	Intel and Alpha	SDLC/X2.5 with EiconCard Adapter
IBM	3278/9 Emulation Adapter	Intel	DFT ISA Adapter
IBM	3278/9 Advanced Emulation Adapter	Intel	DFT ISA Adapter
IBM	3270 Connection Model A	Intel	DFT MCA Adapter
IBM	3270 Connection Model B	Intel	DFT MCA Adapter
IBM	MPCA Adapter	Intel, MIPS, and Alpha	SDLC/X2.5 ISA Adapter
IBM	SDLC Adapter	Intel, MIPS, and Alpha	SDLC/X2.5 ISA Adapter
IBM	Multiprotocol Adapter/A	Intel	SDLC/X2.5 MCA Adapter
MicroGate Corporation	MG96 and MG144	Intel, MIPS, and Alpha	SDLC/X2.5 Adapter
MicroGate Corporation	Digital Services Adapter	MIPS and Alpha	SDLC/X2.5 Adapter

Manufacturer	Product	Supported Platforms	Description
MicroGate Corporation	Unified Serial Adapter	Intel, MIPS, and Alpha	SDLC/X2.5 Adapter
Open Connect Systems	Channel Interface Driver	N/A	IBM Channel Interface
Passport Communications	SDLC Adapter	Intel	SDLC/X2.5 Adapter
Synaptel	Syngate Open Services for Windows NT	N/A	ISDN, SDLC, and X2.5 Adapters

Choosing Your Software

Because SNA Server for Windows NT includes only 3270/5250 emulation software for administrative testing, you need to purchase third-party clients to meet your connectivity needs. With these packages, you can choose software to best suit your needs. Table 30.2 includes some additional information on products that are available or will be available soon.

TABLE 30.2. SNA SERVER CONNECTIVITY PRODUCTS.

Manufacturer	Product	Emulation	Supported Clients
Andrew Corporation	Elite for Windows NT	5250	Windows NT
Andrew Corporation	Elite for Windows	5250	Windows 3.x
Andrew Corporation	Transcend	File Transfer Only	Windows 3.x
Attachmate	Extra! for Windows NT	3270	Windows NT
Attachmate	Extra! for Windows	3270	Windows 3.x
Attachmate	Extra! Extended for DOS	3270	MS-DOS
Attachmate	Rally! for AS/400	5250	Windows 3.x
Attachmate	Extra! for Mac	3270	Macintosh

continues

TABLE 30.2. CONTINUED

Manufacturer	Product	Emulation	Supported Clients
DCA	IRMA Workstation for Windows NT	3270	Windows NT
DCA	IRMA Workstation for Windows	3270	Windows 3.x
DCA	IRMA Workstation for DOS	3270	MS-DOS
DCA	IRMA Workstation for Windows OS/2	3270	OS/2
DCA	IRMA Workstation for Windows MAC	3270	Macintosh
DCA	IRMA/400 for Windows	5250	Windows 3.x
Eicon	Access for Windows NT 3270	3270	Windows NT
Eicon	Access for Windows NT 5250	5250	Windows NT
Eicon	Access for Windows	3270	Windows 3.x
Eicon	Access for OS/2 3270	3270	OS/2
Eicon	Access for Windows 5250	5250	Windows 3.x
IBM	PC/3270 for Windows	3270	Windows 3.x
IBM	PC/5250 for Windows	5250	Windows 3.x
Open Connect System	TN3270 Gateway for Windows NT	3270	Windows NT
Wall Data	Rumba for the Mainframe	3270	Windows NT
Wall Data	Rumba for the AS/400	5250	Windows NT

SUMMARY

This chapter spent some time discussing the requirements for installing SNA Server on your network. The goal here was to understand what is required of you, the network administrator, in order to implement the connection between your mainframe and your clients. Before you actually install SNA Server, you should choose the right SNA Server model to suit your needs. Don't accept the basic model if it does not really fit your requirements. Instead, massage it a bit until you feel comfortable with the implementation.

Make sure that your hardware supports your SNA Server domain model and implementation. Remember that not all routers will bridge DLC packets but will almost always route TCP/IP packets. Make sure that your planning includes the inevitable delays that will crop up as you interface with your mainframe, network, or PC support administrators. Make sure that they understand your needs before you install SNA Server.

Discuss your hardware choices with your mainframe administrators before you make your purchases. It does not help you to choose faster SNA adapter alternatives if your current mainframe cannot support them.

The next chapter actually walks you through the installation and upgrade process so that there will be no surprises when you perform your installation.

- Installing the
  Hardware

- Installing the
  Software

- Upgrading
  SNA Server 2.0

CHAPTER 31

Installing SNA Server

This chapter walks you through the process of installing SNA Server 2.1 for Windows NT in an effort to prepare you for your actual installation. It starts with the installation of the SNA adapter and discusses some of the troublesome spots that may arise. Hopefully, by preparing for these situations beforehand, you can minimize any potential problems. The next step is the actual SNA Server installation walk-through. Finally, you'll look into the upgrade process, why you might want to upgrade from a previous release of SNA Server, and what preparations you should make before your upgrade.

INSTALLING THE HARDWARE

For the most part, installing new hardware on your server is an easy task. In fact, it is so easy that many problems can occur later because you did not consider them before you opened up the computer case and installed the hardware. You want to avoid this situation by looking at some of the possible problems first. To make this easier, this discussion is divided into three areas. In the first case, you'll look at some of the architectural problems. In the second case, you'll consider problems based on Distributed Function Terminal (DFT) adapters. A DFT adapter is similar to a network adapter in that the adapter is directly connected to the system expansion bus and it usually has a wire-based connection—generally, a coax or twisted-pair cable—to a server (or in your case, an IBM mainframe computer). The third case focuses on Synchronous Data Link Control (SDLC) and X.25/QLLC (Qualified Logical Link Control) adapters. An SDLC or X.25/QLLC adapter can be an internal or external adapter and can be compared to an internal or external modem because many of the same functions and types of problems apply.

CONSIDERING THE ARCHITECTURE

As a network administrator, you already may be used to dealing with resource conflicts related to your client network adapters. If so, you will not find too much here that is new to you, but it still may be worthwhile reading to learn something about the architecture you work with and to consider some techniques you can apply in the future. The most common problem is a resource conflict: an input/output (I/O) port address, hardware interrupt (IRQ), Direct Memory Access (DMA) channel, or memory address conflict. You can help avoid this potential problem by your choice of a hardware platform, your studious efforts at documenting your computer's architectural configuration, your knowledge of the basic IBM PC/XT/AT architecture, and your use of diagnostic-related software tools.

Your hardware platform can aid you, but cannot completely eliminate potential resource conflicts. Nor should you put your faith in a hardware platform's capability to do so. I'm sure you have heard at one time or another that the MicroChannel

Architecture (MCA) promoted by IBM, the Extended Industry Standard Architecture (EISA), or the Peripheral Component Interconnect (PCI) can eliminate all resource conflicts by using a software-based configuration (MCA/EISA) or hardware-based configuration (PCI) to register an adapter's resource requirements. This is a misconception, however, and you should not be fooled into thinking that all your problems are solved by using an MCA-, EISA-, or PCI-based computer. To date, I have not found any of these platforms to be perfect in this area, and, in some cases, I have found these platforms to cause more trouble than a standard ISA-based computer in eliminating a resource-related conflict.

The reason for this is really quite simple. MCA and EISA configuration methodologies are based on a software-based program and configuration files. The configuration files list various resources required by the adapter. The software configuration program is used to assign these resources to the adapter or, in effect, to configure the adapter to use these resources. The flaw in this methodology is that the configuration file does not list every resource requirement. It generally includes all the interrupts, DMA channels, and base memory addresses, but rarely includes every I/O port address. And to be honest, I've never encountered a configuration file that listed every I/O port address required by the adapter. My understanding of this problem is based on discussions I've had with hardware engineers, and the bottom line is that these resource configuration files have inherent limitations to the definition statements and total file size, which means that not every resource can be placed in the configuration files.

The same problem generally occurs in the adapter's written documentation. The primary interrupt, DMA channel, memory addresses, and I/O port addresses are included, but many I/O port addresses are not. To date, I have only seen one set of documentation that includes all the possible I/O port addresses required, and this is for my Media Vision ProAudio Spectrum 16. That listing covers a couple of pages, and sometimes I have my doubts that every I/O port address is included.

The PCI architecture uses similar techniques, but instead of using a software-based configuration mechanism, which requires your intervention to configure the adapters, it uses a hardware-based configuration methodology. For the most part, this configuration process is automatic. The computer's BIOS is responsible for configuring PCI and ISA Plug and Play (PnP)–compatible hardware. The resources required are stored in each adapter, and the BIOS uses this information to configure the adapter. Some computers' BIOSs only support automatic configuration, whereas others enable you to override their resource determination and manually configure the adapter. Just like the MCA and EISA configuration methods, there are inherent flaws in the architecture that prevent 100-percent perfection in the automatic configuration of peripherals.

31

INSTALLING SNA SERVER

SOMETIMES IT JUST WON'T WORK

As an example of an I/O port resource conflict, I'd like to share a problem that plagued me for many days. I have an EISA/VLB-based computer. I had already installed an Adaptec 1742/a SCSI adapter. This particular adapter is an EISA adapter, and it was quite easy to configure the adapter with the EISA utility. Later, I wanted increased video performance, so I purchased an ATI Graphics Vantage EISA-based video card. This video card is a superset of the IBM 8514/a video card. What I found is that there was no combination of resource assignments that would work in this computer, even though the EISA utility reported no resource conflicts.

Part of the problem stems from the 8514/a architecture, which uses a slew of I/O port addresses all across the I/O address space. Just little chunks here and there. Some of these I/O addresses were not listed in the configuration file or documented elsewhere. And the rest of the problem stems from the fact that each slot in an EISA computer has a specially reserved base I/O address.

This base address is used by the adapter and cannot be used by any other adapter. Unfortunately, my ATI card conflicted with my SCSI card base I/O address. One way around this type of problem is to choose different slots for the EISA adapters. And although this worked for some of my contemporaries with similar EISA platforms and the same adapters, it wouldn't work for me. The only possible solution was to configure the 1752/a to emulate a 1542, which stripped it of many features and performance. Rather than choose this alternative, I sold the ATI card and purchased a Diamond Viper VLB video card. Sometimes this is all you can do with a resource problem: Find another adapter that does not cause the problem in the first place.

Note

One of the potential trouble spots in an EISA- or PCI-based computer is the mixture of ISA peripherals. Only a PnP ISA adapter can report its resource requirements and only then to a PnP-compatible computer. It is up to you to configure non-Plug and Play ISA adapters or software configurable ISA adapters and create the appropriate ISA configuration file and/or documentation to minimize potential resource conflicts.

I hope you will not mistake my intent here. Even though PCI, MCA, or EISA architectures are not perfect in their configuration attempts, they still are better than no attempt to reach the autoconfiguration goal. One day, you may see this actually possible, but I think it will be a long time in coming. And just so you know, even the Macintosh platform has similar problems. Nothing is perfect, and you have to be aware of this in order to do your job. Particularly because nobody cares about your problems—only that you succeed in producing a working platform so your network clients can do their jobs. If you can accept the thought that no platform is perfect, then you are well on your way to solving the potential conflicts that can arise.

So if the hardware, the configuration files, and the written documentation do not include every I/O port address or resource, how are you supposed to eliminate related resource conflicts? The truth of the matter is that you cannot eliminate them—you can only try to avoid them. The first step in avoiding a resource conflict is to recognize that the problem might exist in the first place. After you accept that, you can use the following techniques to try to avoid these problems:

◆ Don't rely on your software- or hardware-based configuration tools to eliminate the possibility of a resource conflict. Use these tools to configure your peripherals, but be aware that they might not work. You might need to change expansion slots for an adapter to change the base I/O port address to move the I/O port resource conflict. Or, you might have to choose another adapter to eliminate the problem.

◆ Do be aware of your adapter's requirements before you install it. Of course, you can't be aware of all the resource requirements, but you can be aware of the major requirements. You will look at some of these potential trouble spots for DFT, SDLC, and X.25/QLLC adapters in the following sections.

◆ Do be aware that although an EISA-, MCA-, or PCI-based adapter can share an interrupt, it can share an interrupt only with another EISA-, MCA-, or PCI-based adapter in the system. Attempting to share an interrupt with an ISA-based adapter will cause an interrupt conflict.

◆ Do keep up-to-date documentation. This documentation should include a listing of the resource requirements for each adapter, as well as potential configurations.

◆ Do use the proprietary, MS-DOS, and Windows NT tools to help you in your documentation attempts. The EISA and MCA software-based configuration tools generally provide the capability to print a resource map. Many adapters also include a configuration and diagnostic tool you can use for this purpose as well. There are many MS-DOS–based tools that you can use to find potential I/O resources in use. And finally, consider using the Windows NT Microsoft Diagnostics (MSD) application in the Administrative Tools group.

This application can list some of the resources in use by your adapters and system motherboard.

Note

If you do decide to use an MS-DOS–based tool, be sure to create an MS-DOS boot disk and only use these tools after booting MS-DOS. Windows NT emulates MS-DOS and prevents direct access to the hardware, which in turn may skew your ability to map resources that are in use.

◆ Do use the Windows NT event log to find potential resource conflicts. If a driver fails to start because of the resource conflict, it usually is listed in the system event log. This also can tell you where the resource conflict is, which enables you to eliminate it. You also can use the Microsoft Diagnostics utility (WINMSD.EXE) to tell you what each functioning adapter is using in the way of resources. This can help you isolate a malfunctioning adapter—one in which the driver did not load due to a resource conflict.

INSTALLING A DFT ADAPTER

Because most DFT adapters are based on the IBM DFT adapters for compatibility, this usually limits you to using the low-end interrupts. These include interrupts 2, 3, 4, 5, and sometimes 7. And this can be a major problem because these interrupts generally are used by other peripherals, as listed in Table 31.1. If the resource is in use already, the only way to free it is to remove or disable the offending peripheral. In some cases, you can share the interrupt, but only if both peripherals support interrupt sharing and are based on the same architecture (MCA, EISA, or PCI).

TABLE 31.1. A LOW-END INTERRUPT USAGE SUMMARY.

Interrupt	Common Usage
2	Cascade interrupt for secondary interrupt controller. Often used by many token ring network adapters. Note: This interrupt still may be used, but in some cases will cause a nonmaskable interrupt (NMI) or parity error.
3	Generally reserved for COM2 or COM4.
4	Generally reserved for COM1 or COM3.
5	Generally reserved for LPT2. Often used by sound cards and 8-bit SCSI adapters.
6	Used by floppy controller.

Interrupt	Common Usage
7	Generally reserved for LPT1. Often used by sound cards and 8-bit SCSI adapters.

Note

All the interrupts shown in Table 31.1 are often used by token ring and some Ethernet network adapters that also only support low-end interrupts. In the case of IRQs 3 through 7, the offending peripheral (COM port, LPT port, sound, or SCSI card) usually is eliminated or disabled to free the resource for use.

Caution

The cascade interrupt (2) really ties IRQ 2 and IRQ 9 into a single interrupt; if IRQ 9 is in use, then IRQ 2 will not be available.

By looking at Table 31.1, you can see that only interrupt 2 is usually available, and most DFT adapters will use this interrupt. This is a potential problem for the Alpha- and MIPS-based platforms because they do not support an adapter that uses this interrupt. Nor is it available if you use a token ring adapter on this interrupt, except with adapters (and platforms) that support interrupt sharing. Considering that the major problem is caused by problems relating to port management, you might want to try the following on any system that is to function as an SNA Server:

◆ First, disable or physically remove any communications or parallel ports from the system.

◆ Second, if the ports cannot be disabled or removed, then disable the serial.sys and parallel.sys device drivers in the Control Panel Devices applet.

Note

If you disable the serial.sys or parallel.sys drivers, Windows NT will not allocate an interrupt for use by these devices. In most cases, this prevents an interrupt conflict, even though the physical device has not been disabled. The basic idea here is that the new device driver (such as a token ring device driver) allocates the interrupt for its usage even though there are two physical devices that could generate the interrupt.

31

INSTALLING SNA SERVER

◆ Finally, consider using a multiport communications board that supports high-end (IRQ 9 through 15) interrupts. These types of boards come in two basic flavors. A nonintelligent (such as those from JDR Microelectronics) board that uses multiple 16450/16550 UARTS, with each UART being assigned a user-specified I/O port and IRQ, and intelligent boards that have a built-in processor to manage from four to 256 UARTS on a single interrupt. The best of these intelligent multiport boards, in my opinion, are made by Digiboard, both because of their functionality and their lifetime support options (meaning that they do supply drivers for almost every operating system out there, and that they supply drivers for newer operating systems).

Other potential problems often overlooked are the memory address and DMA channel requirements of the adapter. Many DFT adapters require a memory window in the 640KB-to-1,024KB range, which commonly is referred to as the upper memory area (UMA). So, to eliminate this type of problem, consider the following:

◆ Do make sure that the required memory range is not used by any other adapter. This includes a partial overlap, as well as a complete overlap. Suppose that you have two adapters, each of which requires a 32KB memory range. The first one is configured for D000–D7FF and the second for D400–DAFF. In this case, the second adapter overlaps the first adapter's address space in the D400–D7FF region. If, for some reason, this overlap does not cause a fatal error at boot time, then when the adapters are used, both of them will try to write to and read from the same address space and cause a loss of data, device driver errors, or generic system errors.

Tip

Common causes for failures in the memory window are caused by using more than one adapter that requires a memory address space. These can consist of DFT adapters, network adapters, disk drive controllers that require their own BIOS address space, and video adapters that use portions of the UMA address space.

◆ Do pay attention to your BIOS configuration settings. Most BIOSs support ROM shadowing, which is used to copy a ROM to RAM, and then map the RAM address space to the ROM address space in order to increase performance. This works well for the boot-strap sequence and for MS-DOS, but does not offer any advantage to Windows NT. And if you mistakenly shadow a memory region required by a network adapter RAM buffer, you probably will encounter a fatal error (generally, a blue-screen text error message).

Note

This is one area in which using an MCA- or PCI-based computer can cause problems. An MCA computer or PCI computer that is Plug and Play enabled generally uses a 128KB BIOS ranging from E000–FFFF. Couple this with the standard video RAM and ROM areas (A000–C7FF), and you are left to work only with the C800–DFFF range. And if you use another disk controller, such as a SCSI disk controller, as your boot device, then you also will lose the C800–CFFF range as well. This only leaves you with a 64KB (D000–DFFF) memory range for your adapters, which makes it quite easy to unintentionally create a memory address overlap condition.

The same principle holds true for DMA channels because they cannot be shared with any other device. This error often is less noticeable, however, and sometimes can be troublesome to track down. Some indications of a DMA conflict follow:

- Scrambled hard disk drive data: Many SCSI adapters and some EIDE adapters use a technique called bus mastering to increase performance. Bus mastering uses a DMA channel to move data to the hard disk from system memory and vice versa without the intervention of the host processor. This means that your computer's (the host) processor can continue to perform other tasks while data is being read from or written to the disk drive. If this DMA channel also is used by any other adapter, however, a conflict occurs because the DMA controller is actually programmed with a specific memory range to read or write. After the DMA controller has been programmed, the data transfer command is executed and the data is moved. But if, during this process, the DMA controller is reprogrammed with a different address by another adapter, data corruption occurs.

- Corrupt network packets: The same principle mentioned with the scrambled hard disk drive data can occur on your network adapters. If your network adapters, including your DFT adapters, encounter data corruption, it may well be caused by a DMA conflict.

- Repeating sounds: Many sound cards use two DMA channels: one in the low range (1–3) and one in the high range (5–7). If your system events (sounds) repeat indefinitely, this is an indication of an interrupt or a DMA channel conflict. If this occurs at the same time you experience data corruption on your hard disk or network adapters, then you have identified the problem.

- Printing problems: Many of the newer parallel ports are Enhanced Communication Port (ECP)–compatible, and this type of port uses a DMA channel in the low range (usually DMA 3) to increase data throughput. If you

31

encounter gibberish when you print to a local printer, a DMA conflict may be the cause. If this problem occurs at the same time as your data corruption on your hard disk or network adapter, you have found the problem.

Note

DMA channel 0 often is used for the system memory refresh but on some systems this channel is available for use. DMA channel 4 is the cascade channel and is system reserved.

INSTALLING AN SDLC OR X.25/QLLC ADAPTER

Installing an SDLC or X.25/QLLC adapter is generally as easy as installing an internal or external modem. These devices use the same basic principles in that they require a communications (COM) port, operate at speeds of up to 57600bps, and connect to another SDLC or X.25/QLLC adapter with a phone line. As such, they also experience many of the same problems as a modem-to-modem connection. These problems can be broken down into a resource conflict or a link-related problem.

Generally speaking, the most likely resource conflict is an I/O port address or interrupt conflict because the ISA standard predefines I/O port addresses and interrupts for COM ports. And because most SDLC and X.25/QLLC adapters use one of the standard I/O port addresses and interrupts, you must be sure to use an I/O address and interrupt that is not already in use, or you must disable the conflicting communications port.

Most SDLC adapters operate at up to 57600bps, but not all UARTS can handle this speed without dropping the occasional byte of data. In theory, a 16450 UART can handle DTE speeds of up to 38400, a 16550 UART that has a 16-byte FIFO buffer can handle speeds of up to 57600, and proprietary UARTS that also use buffering techniques can handle speeds of up to 115,200. These dropped bytes can cause link failures if they occur too often to reestablish the data flow.

Additionally, UARTS generate a lot of interrupts. For a 16450, there is one interrupt for each byte of data transferred, whereas a buffered UART only generates an interrupt when the buffer is almost filled. And if your processor is too busy to handle the interrupts and transfer the data from the UART to system memory (or vice versa), then, once more, a link-related problem can occur. Your best bet in avoiding this type of problem is to use a proprietary UART. Choose an internal adapter that has, at a minimum, a 1KB FIFO buffer, or use external devices that you can connect to an intelligent multiport board (such as those manufactured by Digiboard) that includes its own processor and from 256KB to 512KB of buffer memory.

Note

Another type of link-related problem can occur because the adapter itself cannot handle the communications load. The IBM SDLC, IBM MCPA, and Microgate adapters, for example, do not include a coprocessor and therefore cannot handle a transmission speed greater than 9600bps for an X.25 connection. SNA Server requires a full duplex connection for an X.25 link, and these adapters often will experience link failures at speeds above 9600bps.

INSTALLING THE SOFTWARE

Installing SNA Server is relatively straightforward. You merely execute `setup.bat` (located in the root directory of the CD-ROM), which determines your hardware platform for you and executes the installation program. However, if it were really just a matter of running a setup program to install the software, this section really would not need to discuss it. There are many choices you need to make during this installation process, and some of them may be more than a little confusing. This section focuses on eliminating this confusion by walking you through the installation process. The discussion is divided into two sections. The first section discusses the basic installation process, but only glosses over the installation of the link services. The reason for this is that the configuration of the link services is actually the most critical part of the installation process and can vary quite a bit based on the type of link service, so this option is covered in a separate section to more fully explore the various choices you have available.

Tip

Before you install SNA Server, it is a good idea to read the accompanying `readme.txt` file for any last-minute changes or updates to SNA Server.

INSTALLING THE SNA SERVER SERVICE

Although it is not often that a failure occurs during your installation process, it is possible, so I recommend a full backup of your system, including the Registry, before you install SNA Server. You also should plan on a forced reboot if you have to install additional network services and want SNA Server to become active as soon as possible, so you should plan on this temporary outage by notifying any users beforehand. The basic installation process follows:

31

INSTALLING SNA SERVER

1. Execute the setup.bat program in the root directory of the CD-ROM. This launches the correct executable image (setup.exe) for you. This will be \I386 for the Intel and compatible processor line, \MIPS for the MIPS processors, or \ALPHA for the Alpha AXP processors. A confirmation dialog box appears.

Note

I have explained where the individual binaries for the Setup program are located strictly for users of Intel-compatible processors. Although Windows NT is aware of many of these Intel-compatible processors, more are being produced every day. It may be that your processor is incorrectly identified, in which case you need to execute the appropriate binary manually.

2. If you are ready for your installation (which I hope you are already), click the Continue button. If you need a little refresher, choose the Help button. If you click Continue, the Software Licensing dialog box appears.

3. Enter your name, your company name, and your product identification number. You can find the product identification number on the back of your CD-ROM jewel case or on your license agreement. After you enter this information, click the Continue button to display the confirmation dialog box. If your information is correct, click the OK button; otherwise, click the Back button to reenter the information. After you click Continue, the Installation Path dialog box appears.

Tip

SNA Server does not require much in the way of storage space. Only 11MB is required. Your choice of a file system is very important, however. If you can, choose NTFS because you then can use the security features to restrict access to the SNA Server system files, as well as the shared configuration file.

4. Enter the path for where you want to install SNA Server. The default is C:\SNA. After you complete your choice, click the Continue button. The Select Client/Server Protocols dialog box appears.

Tip

Even though it is a minor pain to fill out all these licensing dialog boxes at the time of installation, it really is worth your time to do so. The software Licensing dialog box embeds this information in the

Registry, and you can call it back up anytime by choosing the Help|About menu option in SNA Server Admin. You might not think you need it now, but if you need to call Microsoft PSS, they will require this information before they will help you with your problems.

5. Choose which network transport protocols to support. For each transport you have installed, you will see a preselected transport. If you do not want to support a particular transport, just click on it to disable the checkbox. The transport choices follow:

   ◆ Microsoft Networking (Named Pipes): Uses the NetBEUI transport for compatibility with existing Microsoft networks.

   ◆ Novell NetWare (IPX/SPX): Provides compatibility with Novell network clients.

   ◆ Banyan VINES: Supports your Banyan VINES network clients.

   ◆ TCP/IP: Supports any client that uses TCP/IP (such as UNIX or remote clients on the other side of a WAN link).

   ◆ AppleTalk: Supports your Macintosh network clients.

After you make your selections, click the Continue button.

Note

If your choice is grayed out, you need to exit the installation program, install the appropriate services (such as Services for Macintosh or Gateway Services for NetWare), restart the server, and then restart the SNA Server installation process. Alternatively, you can continue the installation process, add your additional network services, restart your computer, and then use the Maintenance Setup program (SNA Server Setup, located in your Microsoft SNA Server Program Manager group) to install or remove the client/server protocols.

The Change SNA Server Role dialog box appears next. This is also a critical choice, and you should not take it lightly. You have three options:

   ◆ Primary Configuration Server: There can be only one primary configuration server in your domain. This server maintains the primary configuration file used by all SNA Server installations in the domain. Any modifications to your SNA Server configurations are made on this copy of the configuration file. If, for some reason, this server is unavailable, then no modifications may be made. This server will have a higher load than other SNA Servers and should be a fast machine on a high-speed network backbone, if you have that option.

◆ Backup Configuration Server: You can have more than one backup configuration server. Its purpose is to keep SNA Server up and running in the domain in case the primary configuration server fails. Each backup configuration server maintains a copy of the SNA Server configuration file for this purpose.

◆ Member Server: You also can have more than one member server. This type of SNA Server has no configuration file at all. It relies on the primary or backup configuration server to supply the configuration data. If no primary or backup configuration server is available, your member servers are unusable even if they are up and running.

After you make your choice, click the Continue button.

Tip

It is really a good idea to have more than one, and preferably at least two, backup configuration servers available on your network just in case the primary configuration server fails or must be taken offline for service. This limits the possible down time for your network clients.

6. After you make your choice for your server configuration, you are given the chance to review your choices in the Review Settings dialog box. If you click the Review button, you are returned to step 4 to get the chance to modify your choices. After you make your choice, choose the Continue button to start copying files to your installation directory, create the SNA Server services, update the Registry, and create your Program Manager group.

7. The next choice is your chance to choose a link service from the Link Service Installation dialog box. The basic process consists of selecting the link service, clicking the Install button to install and configure the link service, and then clicking the Continue button to proceed with the installation. Because of the variety of selections for this item, it is discussed in more detail in the next section. You might want to skip ahead at this point to find the relevant type (DFT, SDLC, or X.25/QLLC) for your SNA Server installation and then come back to this section.

8. The Network Settings dialog box appears next while the network bindings are updated. If you have not already installed the DLC protocol, you are prompted to do so and to insert your installation medium as well.

9. Finally, you are informed that you must use the SNA Server Admin program to configure the link service before it can be used. Click the OK button.

10. You are prompted to exit the installation program by clicking the Exit button, or to configure your link service by clicking the Admin button.

After the SNA Server Services are installed, you still have a bit of work to do before your clients can actually connect to your IBM mainframe. At a minimum, you have to configure the link service, the logical unit pools, and your group and user accounts. These configuration options are performed with SNA Server Admin, and are discussed in detail in the next chapter.

INSTALLING THE LINK SERVICES

You have three basic choices when installing a link service with SNA Server's built-in drivers. You can choose to install a DFT, SDLC, or X.25/QLLC link service. You optionally can install a link service for an OEM product, such as a TwinAx or IBM channel interface, if you have the appropriate hardware and a driver diskette from your manufacturer. This discussion uses the DCA DFT, SDLC, and X.25/QLCC link services as examples. There are two methods to display the Link Service Installation dialog box. You can follow the steps in the preceding section, and when you get to step 7, the dialog box is displayed. Or, you can execute the SNA Server Setup applet located in the Microsoft SNA Server Program Manager group after installing the software.

The basic steps for installing the link services follow:

1. Execute the SNA Server Setup program. This is the same executable (setup.exe) you executed from the CD-ROM, but in this case, it is used for maintenance rather than installation. It is located in the root installation directory (c:\SNA, by default).

2. You see a brief message that Setup is examining your configuration, and then the same welcome message you viewed previously is displayed. Just click the Continue button to display the Setup Options dialog box, as shown in Figure 31.1.

Figure 31.1.
Using the Setup
Options dialog
box for SNA
Server mainte-
nance.

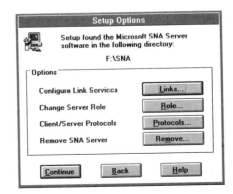

31

The Setup Options dialog box offers the following options:

◆ Configure Link Services: Clicking the Links button displays the Link Service Installation dialog box so that you can install a built-in or OEM link service.

Note

The next three items assume that you have selected the Configure Link Services option and that the Link Service Installation dialog box is active.

◆ Change Server Role: Enables you to change the role of an SNA Server configuration.

◆ Client/Server Protocols: Enables you to add or remove network transport protocols that SNA Server will support to allow your network clients to connect to your mainframe.

◆ Remove SNA Server: Removes all the SNA Server files, Registry entries, and link services from your system. It is the only supported method of removing SNA Server, and you should choose this option rather than manually removing the SNA directory.

3. After you make your choices and click the Continue button, you are returned to the Setup Options dialog box. At this point, click the Continue button to update your network bindings.

4. Finally, a message box will appear and you are informed that you must use the SNA Server Admin program to configure the link service before it can be used. Click the OK button.

5. Exit the installation program by clicking the Exit button, or configure your link service by clicking the Admin button.

Tip

Although the DLC 802.2 Link Service is not used with a specific adapter as are the other link services, it is still a very useful link service that you may want to install. This link service is used by SNA Server to communicate with host, peer, or downstream computers with a token ring or Ethernet network adapter.

INSTALLING A DFT LINK SERVICE

Installing a DFT Link Service varies a bit, but the basic process follows:

1. Select the Link Service to install in the Link Service Installation dialog box and click the Install button. For this example, choose the DCA DFT link service.

Note

If you are installing an OEM link service, then click the Other button. This displays the Link Service Import dialog box, which prompts you for your OEM installation disk and then displays a dialog box to configure the service.

The DCA DFT Link Service Configuration dialog box appears, as shown in Figure 31.2.

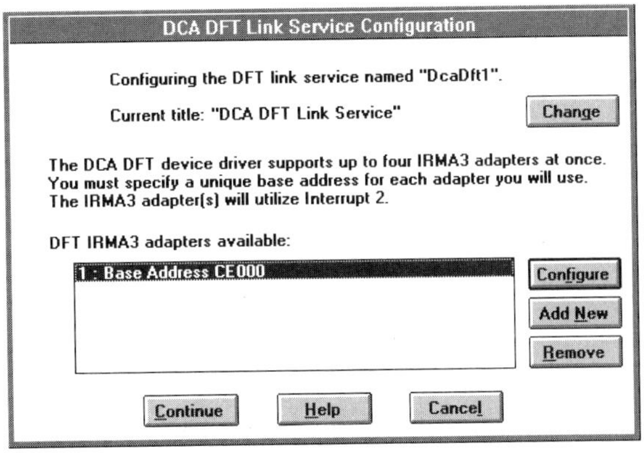

Figure 31.2.
Configuring the
DCA DFT link
service.

The DCA DFT Link Service Configuration dialog box includes the following options:

◆ Change: Changes the title of the displayed link service. It is only useful if you plan to install more than one link service of the same type. Its purpose is to provide you with a unique name for mainte-nance and performance tuning.

◆ Configure: Enables you to choose another memory address for your adapter. If you have installed an adapter at a different address than the default, choose this option to specify the correct memory window.

◆ Add New: Installs additional link services of the same type. For each addition, you need to specify a unique title and memory address.

Note

> Although this dialog box specifies that you can install up to four adapters, with each adapter using IRQ 2, keep in mind that IRQ sharing is only supported on certain platforms (EISA, PCI, and MCA) or for adapters specifically designed to share resources. You also should note that because the MIPS and Alpha AXP platforms do not support using IRQ 2, you cannot install the DCA DFT adapter on these platforms.

   ◆ Remove: Removes the selected entry in the DFT IRMA3 adapter's available field.

2. After you make your choices, click the Continue button. The Link Service Configuration dialog box is redisplayed. The buttons have changed a bit, however. It includes an Add New button instead of an Install button or Other button, which you can use to install additional link services. It also contains a Configure button to enable you to change the configuration parameters for the link service and a Remove button to enable you to remove a link service that is no longer required.

3. Repeat these steps using the Add New button for each additional link service you want to install.

INSTALLING AN SDLC LINK SERVICE

Installing an SDLC link service requires more grunt work than a DFT adapter, but the basic principle still applies. The primary difference is that you now are interfacing with a modem-to-modem adapter rather than a network-to-network adapter interface. Use the following steps to guide you through the installation process:

1. Select the link service to install in the Link Service Installation dialog box and click the Install button. For this example, choose the DCA SDLC link service.

Note

> If you are installing an OEM link service, click the Other button. This displays the Link Service Import dialog box, which prompts you for your OEM installation disk and then displays a dialog box to configure the service.

The DCA SDLC Link Service Setup dialog box appears, as shown in Figure 31.3.

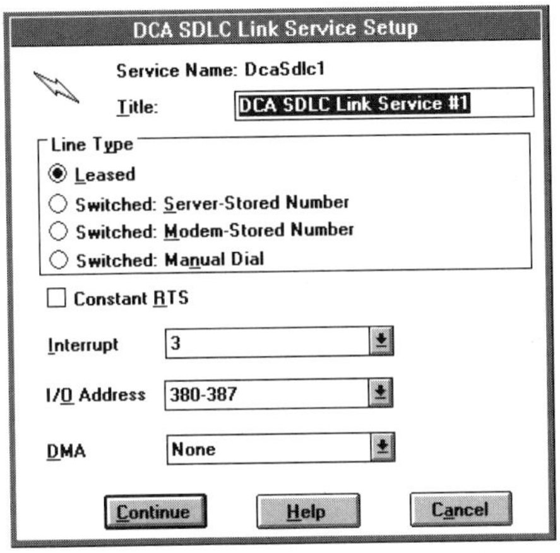

Figure 31.3.
Configuring the
DCA SDLC link
service.

The DCA SDLC Link Service Setup dialog box includes the following options:

◆ Title: You can modify the entry in this field to change the title of the displayed link service if desired. This, of course, is really only necessary if you plan to install more than one link service of the same type.

◆ Line Type: This section specifies the type of phone-line connection you can use. Choices included here follow:

Leased: Choose this option if your phone connection is a dedicated telecommunications line or, in the network jargon, a leased line.

Note

Some dialog boxes use the term *dedicated* rather than *leased*.

Switched: Server-Stored Number: Choose this option if your SDLC adapter has a built-in communications port and can accept a phone number from SNA Server.

Note

In order to use the Switched: Server-Stored Number selection, your SDLC adapter must be configured so that it accepts an ASCII dial command (8 data bits, no parity bit, single stop bit). It must not dial the number when the DTR signal is raised. It must set CTS and DSR to on when it is ready to accept commands. It must set DSR to off after accepting a command. It must then set DSR to on when the connection is made. Then it must change to synchronous mode after the dial-up has finished, and finally change back to dial-up command mode if DTR is raised.

Switched: Modem-Stored Number: Choose this option if your SDLC adapter cannot accept a phone number from SNA Server, or if you want to use the SDLC adapter's capability to store a number to dial directly.

Note

In order to use the Switched: Modem-Stored Number option, your SDLC adapter must dial the number when the Data Terminal Ready (DTR) line is raised.

Switched: Manual Dial: Choose this option only if your SDLC adapter does not support either of the previous choices, or if you want to manually dial the number. SNA Server prompts you to dial the number when required.

◆ Constant RTS: Choosing this option increases performance by enabling the Ready To Send (RTS) signal. When this option is specified, the adapter is in a constant state to send data. If this option is disabled (the default), before the adapter can send data, the Ready To Send (RTS) line must be raised, and the remote adapter must raise the Clear To Send (CTS) signal.

Caution

Do not enable the Constant RTS option for a multidrop connection. This type of connection allows multiple SDLC adapters to use the same physical wire and would cause communication problems if enabled.

Note

If you configure your adapter or SNA Server with the SNA Server Admin utility for full duplex transmission, the Constant RTS option must be enabled. Full Duplex mode is the preferred choice because it allows data to be sent and received simultaneously. Half Duplex mode requires that the data flow be alternated between the two endpoints, effectively halving the possible data throughput.

- ◆ Interrupt: Enables you to change the default interrupt choice for the adapter.
- ◆ I/O Address: Enables you to specify a different I/O port address for the adapter.
- ◆ DMA: Enables you to change the default DMA channel allocation for the adapter.

Note

There are basically only three reasons why you might want to change the interrupt, I/O address, or DMA channel. First, you have installed the adapter with a nonstandard resource. Second, you have installed more than one adapter. Third, you are trying to avoid a resource conflict.

OTHER LINK SERVICE OPTIONS

Depending on your SDLC adapter choice, you may see additional selections, including the following:

Data Rate: Specifies the transmission speed (or baud rate) to be used by SNA Server when it sends a modem command to the adapter.

Baud Rate: This choice is the same as a modem DTE rate configuration choice. Basically, this setting is the rate at which the data flows to and from the communications port from and to the adapter.

DatMode: Specifies whether the adapter communicates in Half or Full Duplex mode.

Com Port: Specifies the communications port number that Windows NT uses.

Incoming String: Specifies a modem string to send to the device when an incoming call is detected.

Outgoing String: Specifies a modem string to send to the device when an outgoing call is detected.

2. After you make your choices, click the Continue button. The Link Service Configuration dialog box is redisplayed. The buttons will have changed a bit, however. You will see an Add New button instead of an Install button or Other button, which you can use to install additional link services. A

31

INSTALLING SNA SERVER

Configure button is included to enable you to change the configuration parameters for the link service, and a Remove button enables you to remove a link service that is no longer required.

3. Repeat these steps using the Add New button for each additional link service you want to install.

INSTALLING AN X.25/QLCC LINK SERVICE

Installing an X.25/QLLC service is the most complex type of service you will install, because it requires the most decisions from you. However, you can use the following steps to guide you through the configuration process:

1. Select the link service to install in the Link Service Installation dialog box and click the Install button. For this example, choose the DCA X.25/QLLC link service.

Note

If you are installing an OEM link service, click the Other button. This displays the Link Service Import dialog box, which prompts you for your OEM installation disk and then displays a dialog box to configure the service.

The DCA X.25 Link Service Setup dialog box appears, as shown in Figure 31.4. It includes the following options:

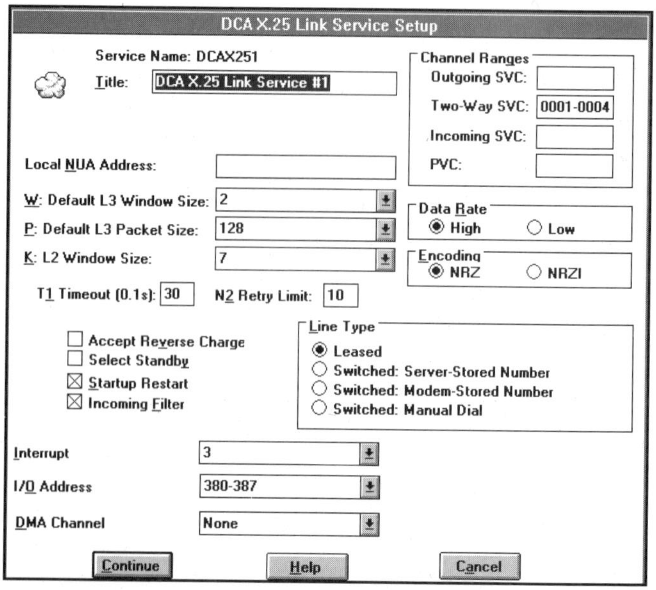

Figure 31.4.
Configuring the
DCA X.25 link
service.

◆ Title: You can modify the entry in this field to change the title of the displayed link service. Of course, this is really only required if you plan to install more than one link service of the same type.

◆ Local NUA Address: This is your local X.25 address. It can contain from 12 to 15 decimal digits with no embedded spaces. The first 12 digits are your actual address, and the final three are used for routing between stations with the same local address. This number should be obtained from your service provider.

◆ W: Default L3 Window Size: Specifies the maximum number of packets that can be sent or received before an acknowledgment is required. The W: Default L3 Window Size setting is valid only for switched virtual circuits (SVC). The default value is 2, with a range from 1 to 7.

◆ P: Default L3 Packet Size: Specifies the maximum size, in bytes, of a data packet sent to or received from a remote computer through an SVC. The default is 128, and ranges from 64 to 512 in 64-count increments.

◆ K: L2 Window Size: Specifies the maximum number of frames that can be sent or received before an acknowledgment is required. The default is 7, with a range from 1 to 7.

◆ T1 Timeout (0.1s): Specifies the time, in .1-second intervals, that the local computer should wait for a response from the remote computer before trying again. The default is 30, with a range of 1 to 100.

Note

The T1 Timeout value should be at least twice the minimum time it takes for a frame to be sent from a local to a remote system.

◆ N2 Retry Limit: Specifies the maximum number of retry attempts. The default is 10, with a range from 1 to 100.

◆ Accept Reverse Charge: Specifies that SNA Server should accept or not accept (the default) incoming calls with a reverse charge facility in the call packet. The default is disabled.

◆ Select Standby: Specifies that you want your secondary line, a backup connection, set to the On position. The default is disabled.

◆ Startup Restart: Specifies that a modem restart should be performed each time the link is activated. The default is enabled.

◆ Incoming Filter: Specifies that incoming packets to nonlocal addresses be filtered out of the data stream. The default is enabled.

31

INSTALLING SNA SERVER

Note

You should know about a couple of rules when assigning channel numbers:

◆ The total number of channels used must be from 1 to 16.

◆ Channel numbers must be unique and not overlap.

◆ Your PVC values should be less than your SVC values.

◆ To accept an incoming call, you must have a channel assigned to receive it in either the Incoming SVC or Two-Way SVC field.

◆ Channel numbers do not need to be consecutive and should be assigned in ascending order of PVCs, incoming SVCs, two-way SVCs, and outgoing SVCs.

◆ Channel Ranges: In this section, you specify the number of switched virtual circuits (SVC) or permanent virtual circuit (PVC) channels that will be used. You can specify the following options:

Outgoing SVC: Specifies the range of switched virtual circuit channels used for outgoing calls. There is no default, with a format of x-y, where x and y can be in the range of 0001–4096.

Two-Way SVC: Specifies the range of switched virtual circuit channels used for incoming and outgoing calls. The default is 0001-0004, with a format of x-y, where x and y can be in the range of 0001–4096.

Incoming SVC: Specifies the range of SVC channels used for incoming calls. There is no default, with a format of x-y, where x and y can be in the range of 0001–4096.

PVC: Specifies the range of PVC channels used by the computer on the X.25 network. There is no default, with a format of x-y, where x and y can be in the range of 0001–4096.

◆ Data Rate: Specifies the communications rate between your communications port and the modem. The default is high.

◆ Encoding: Specifies the encoding scheme used by the local and remote modems. Both these modems must use the same encoding scheme. The default is NRZ (nonreturn to zero), with values of NRZ or NRZI (nonreturn to zero inverted).

◆ Line Type: This section specifies the type of phone-line connection you can use. Choices you may see here follow:

Leased: Choose this option if your phone connection is a dedicated telecommunications line, or in the network jargon, a leased line.

Switched: Server-Stored Number: Choose this option if your SDLC adapter has a built-in communications port and can accept a phone number from SNA Server.

Switched: Modem-Stored Number: Choose this option if your SDLC adapter cannot accept a phone number from SNA Server, or if you want to use the SDLC adapter's capability to store a number to dial directly.

Switched: Manual Dial: Choose this option only if your SDLC adapter does not support either of the previous choices, or if you want to manually dial the number. SNA Server prompts you to dial the number when required.

◆ Interrupt: Enables you to change the default interrupt choice for the adapter.

◆ I/O Address: Enables you to specify a different I/O port address for the adapter.

◆ DMA Channel: Enables you to change the default DMA channel allocation for the adapter.

Note

There are only three basic reasons why you might want to change the interrupt, I/O address, or DMA channel. First, you have installed the adapter with a nonstandard interrupt, I/O port address, or DMA channel. Second, you have installed more than one adapter. Third, you are trying to avoid a resource conflict.

Note

Depending on your X.25/QLLC adapter choice, you may see additional selections, which include the following:

Baud Rate: This choice is the same as a modem DTE rate configuration choice. Basically, this setting is the rate at which the data flows to and from the communications port from and to the adapter.

Com Port: Specifies the communications port number that Windows NT uses.

Incoming String: Specifies a modem string to send to the device when an incoming call is detected.

Outgoing String: Specifies a modem string to send to the device when an outgoing call is detected.

2. After you make your choices, click the Continue button. The Link Service Configuration dialog box appears. The buttons will have changed a bit, however. They will include an Add New button instead of an Install button or Other button, which you can use to install additional link services. You also will see a Configure button, which enables you to change the configuration parameters for the link service, and a Remove button to remove a link service that is no longer required.

3. Repeat these steps using the Add New button for each additional link service you want to install.

UPGRADING SNA SERVER 2.0

Before you actually begin your upgrade process, there are a few things you should be aware of that you might not have considered—or maybe they were too obvious to be thought about—but that might cause you problems. The first item is the realization that although you can mix and match SNA Server 2.11 with SNA Server 2.0 in the same domain, you should do this only as a temporary solution. You should upgrade all your 2.0 installations as soon as you can. Why? Consider these reasons:

◆ In order to support your 2.0 SNA Servers and your new 2.11 SNA Servers, you first must upgrade your current primary configuration server to version 2.11.

◆ Then your new primary configuration server must enable broadcast support for SNA Server 2.0. This option increases the network traffic by submitting a broadcast once a minute, whether or not it is needed. So this option decreases performance of SNA Server 2.11 and increases network traffic.

Note

To enable the preceding selection, choose the Options | Server Broadcast menu option in the SNA Server Admin program. Then make sure the SNA Server 2.0 Servers in Same Domain option in the Server Broadcast dialog box is enabled.

◆ You will only be able to manage your SNA Servers from 2.11 versions of SNA Server, or from SNA Server 2.11 client workstations, because this is the only version that supports the SNA Server Admin program. This could make administering your SNA Server domain a bit more difficult.

◆ Each SNA Server 2.0 installation must be updated. This process only requires replacing the SNACFG.DLL, but it still requires that each service be temporarily shut down so that you can replace this DLL and restart the service.

◆ Finally, SNA Server 2.11 specific functions may not work or may work erratically with SNA Server 2.0. With 2.11, for example, you have the capability to prevent users from running the SNACFG command-line program; however, this will not function correctly on SNA Server 2.0 servers or clients.

This means that your installation plan may require a bit more planning if you want it to be a smooth transition. Normally, the upgrade process from SNA Server 2.0 to SNA Server 2.11 is a painless process that requires little effort to accomplish. Because of this, many administrators choose to just follow the standard upgrade process. I recommend that you be a little more circumspect about it and prepare for the worst possibility. Granted, it probably will not happen to you, but if it does, at least you will be able to deal with the situation.

This modified installation process follows:

1. Prepare for the upgrade process by backing up your entire system. Not just the system directory and data files, but all drives and directories. To do this, you may need to stop additional services, such as SQL Server, WINS, and DHCP. Make sure that you have enabled the option to back up your system Registry as well.

Note

> The preceding option protects you in case of a system-wide failure or the loss of any data on your system. This is a rare occurrence, and if you make the backup, you can be pretty sure you will not need it. But if you don't make the backup, you can almost always be sure you will need it. This is just one of those corollaries to Murphy's Law, "If something can go wrong, it will," that I like to prepare for.

2. Insert a floppy disk into your drive A. Then run the Repair Disk Utility (RDISK.EXE) to update your repair information on your system directory, and then create a new repair disk as well.

Note

> The Repair Disk Utility is one of the preparation tools I always use just in case of a problem. The reason for this update is to protect you in case of a software installation failure or removal. Most products read and write their configuration information directly to the system Registry. If a fault occurs, however, sometimes the Registry is left in an inconsistent state. This could cause you to be unable to remove the rest of the software or to complete your new installation. Just think of

31

INSTALLING SNA SERVER

this as additional insurance that is faster to recover from than a complete system restoration. To use this repair disk, you need to have your original three boot floppy disks that you used to install Windows NT Server but, instead of reinstalling, you should just run through the repair process.

3. Back up your current SNA Server configuration file by choosing Backup from the File menu in the SNA Server Admin. Select a directory that differs from your current SNA Server directory tree (generally, C:\SNA), because this entire directory tree is removed later in the upgrade process.

4. Stop the SNA Server service. You can do this from the Control Panel Services applet, or by choosing Stop Service from the Services menu in the SNA Server Admin program.

Note

If you have any third-party services that rely on the SNA Server service, such as a TN3270 service, stop these services first.

5. Close the SNA Server Admin application.

6. Use the SNA Server Setup program, which should be in your Microsoft SNA Server Program Manager Group, to remove the 2.0 version SNA Server software.

7. Insert your SNA Server 2.11 CD-ROM and execute SNA Server Admin.

8. Choose Restore from the File menu. When prompted for your configuration file, select the same file you chose in step 3. This loads the 2.0 configuration you backed up on the new 2.1 SNA Server installation.

And that is about all there is to the upgrade process. But before you are finished, you also must enable the SNA Server broadcast option, as described earlier, to support your current SNA Server 2.0 installations. Because this option degrades performance, however, as soon as you have upgraded all your 2.0 versions to 2.11, you should disable the broadcast option.

SUMMARY

This chapter looked at some of the basic issues you might encounter when installing your SNA adapters. Specifically, you looked at why the automatic configuration options available cannot solve all your problems. From this discussion, you should remember that an I/O port address is the most difficult resource conflict to detect and sometimes can be solved only by disabling conflicting hardware, changing the hardware expansion slot the adapter is installed into, or replacing a conflicting piece of hardware. An interrupt conflict is the most likely cause of a resource conflict, particularly for token ring, DFT, and SDLC adapters. And corrupted data is an indication of a DMA channel or memory address conflict.

If you cannot disable or remove a conflicting piece of hardware, disabling serial.sys or parallel.sys may prove beneficial in eliminating an interrupt or I/O conflict. You also may find that link failures may be caused by UARTS that generate more interrupts than the processor can support or by an adapter without a coprocessor that cannot handle full duplex transmissions above 9600bps.

This chapter also looked at installing the SNA Server core files and the link services. In fact, you looked at installing and configuring the three types of link services provided with SNA Server: DFT, SDLC, and X.25/QLLC link services. Finally, you learned how to upgrade SNA Server 2.0 to 2.1.

The next chapter looks into the topics relevant to managing your SNA Server domain. These include items such as configuring the link services, creating logical unit (LU) pools, and other basic management duties.

31

- Using SNA Server
  Administrator

- Using the SNA Trace
  Utility

CHAPTER 32

Managing Your SNA Server Gateway

Managing your SNA Server gateway consists of three basic precepts: configuring and maintaining your network, configuring SNA Server, and troubleshooting. The first part deals with specifying your network transport protocols, configuring your routers to pass the appropriate network packets, and maintaining the rest of your physical network. These are readily understood functions of a network administrator, however, and are not the focus of this chapter. Instead, this chapter is concerned primarily with configuring SNA Server with the SNA Server Administrator and performing basic troubleshooting with the SNA Trace utility.

Note

The actual name for the tool is really SNA Server Admin, which can be found in your Microsoft SNA Server Program Manager group. Rather than call it this, however, I prefer to call it the SNA Server Administrator because this more fully describes its function. For the rest of the chapter, this is how I refer to it.

USING SNA SERVER ADMINISTRATOR

The SNA Server Administrator is your primary interface to managing your SNA Server domains. The majority of this chapter focuses on how to use the SNA Server Administrator to perform the following tasks:

◆ Configuring the link services. Because the first thing you must do after installing SNA Server is configure a link service so that SNA Server can provide a connection to your SNA-compatible mainframe, it makes sense to start the discussion here as well.

◆ Managing users and groups. After you configure the link service, you need to specify who can use your SNA Server connection. This is where group and user management comes into play.

◆ Managing logical unit pools. An LU pool is a means of grouping several LUs into a single entity or pool that you can manage. If you are looking for additional means to improve response time, balance the load on SNA Server, and provide additional fault tolerance, then this section can help you achieve your goals.

◆ Managing SNA services, security, and SNA Administrator access. Managing the SNA Server services usually is limited to starting and stopping the various services involved. This chapter discusses these services, along with the means to automate the startup sequence, but the more important aspect is learning how to restrict access to the SNA Server Administration features. After all, you do not want to allow just anybody to play with your SNA Server installation.

CONFIGURING A LINK SERVICE

The first time you open the SNA Server Administrator, it displays the Servers and Connections window, which lists only the servers, because you haven't created any connections yet. (See Figure 32.1.) A connection is the basic building block you use to define a linkage between your SNA-compatible mainframe and your SNA Server clients. This process is what the SNA Server Setup program describes as a link service and is what is discussed here. It is not really a difficult process if you have some help from your technical support personnel. If you do not have this help and do not know what addresses, node identification strings, or other salient reference numbers have been assigned for your use, then you can pretty much forget about a working SNA Server configuration. This means that you will need help from your mainframe MIS department and service provider for an X.25/QLLC connection in order to supply the required information.

Figure 32.1.
Administering
your SNA Server
domain with the
SNA Server
Administrator.

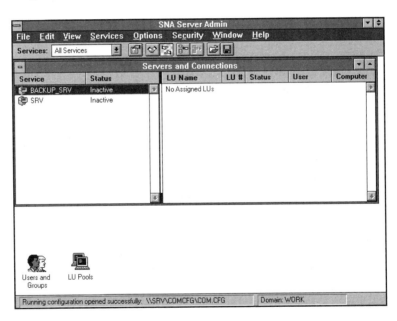

The idea of this discussion is to walk you through the actual process of creating a connection and assigning logical units so that you will understand what information you need to successfully complete your SNA Server configuration. This chapter begins with assigning the properties to your SNA Server that will be used for APPC or AS/400 connections. Then, you'll step through the process of creating connections. Finally, you'll learn how to assign logical units to a connection. Because this discussion includes all the various types of connections and logical units, you might want to skip the parts that do not concern you at this time.

32

ASSIGNING SERVER PROPERTIES

If your SNA Server installation will be supporting incoming calls, advanced peer-to-peer communications (APPC) (which also includes 5250 terminal emulation), or an AS/400 connection, then you must configure the server properties to identify your installation. This is accomplished by selecting the server in the Servers and Connections window and then choosing Services | Properties from the menu. The Server Properties dialog box appears, in which you can assign a comment, network name, and control point name. (See Figure 32.2.)

Figure 32.2.
Assigning server
properties to
uniquely identify
your SNA Server
installation.

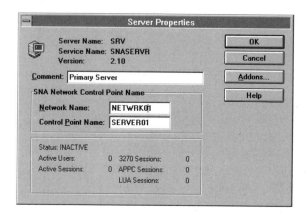

Tip

Alternatively, you can select the server and press Alt+Enter or just double-click on a server to display the Server Properties dialog box.

The comment can contain up to 25 characters, and is used to aid you in identifying your installation when you have more than one SNA Server in your domain. The network name and control point name are the identifiers, which uniquely identify your SNA Server installation on the network. These names are required only for systems using Format 3 XIDs, and define one point of the connection mechanism between SNA Server (the local node) and your SNA-compatible mainframe (the remote node). The remote node names are defined as you create your connections. These values should be supplied by your MIS department, and they vary, depending on how your server is connected to your mainframe.

For an AS/400, the values in the Server Properties dialog box follow:

◆ Network Name: This name will be the RMTNETID value on the AS/400.

◆ Control Point Name: This name will be the RMTCPNAME in the host controller description.

For a VTAM or NCP connection, you will use these values:

◆ Network Name: This name will be the NETID value in the VTAM Start command for the local SSCP. The SSCP is the VTAM connection where SNA Server is attached.

◆ Control Point Name: This name will be the CPNAME in the Physical Unit (PU) definition for the VTAM or Network Control Point (NCP).

Note

The network name and control point name can contain from one to eight alphanumeric characters. They can include the special characters $, #, and @. The first character must be alphabetic. All lowercase characters are converted to uppercase characters. You cannot use just one name; if you supply one of these names, you must supply both names.

Tip

Click the Addons button to display the SNA Server Additions dialog box. By default, this dialog box only includes the SNA Server Trace options, which you can select to configure the Trace utility. If you have added any third-party software, however, you might be able to configure it here as well.

CREATING A CONNECTION

A connection can be considered the means SNA Server uses to communicate with your SNA-compatible mainframe. It is not used directly by your SNA Server clients. Instead, your SNA Server clients use a logical unit (terminal) that has been assigned to a specific connection. Your clients do not need to know what type of connection they are using, but as the SNA Administrator, you do.

SNA Server supports six types of connections:

◆ A Data Link Control (DLC) 802.2 connection: This is a network-adapter-to-network-adapter connection that uses the DLC transport protocol. It can be used on Ethernet or token ring-based networks.

◆ A Distributed Function Terminal (DFT) connection: This type of connection is used to connect SNA Server to a 3270 control unit on your host SNA-compatible mainframe over a coaxial cable connection.

◆ A Synchronous Data Link Control (SDLC) connection: This is a modem-adapter-to-modem-adapter connection that uses the DLC transport protocol. It is a direct (SDLC-to-SDLC), low-speed connection that uses leased or switched phone lines to connect the two adapters.

◆ An X.25/QLLC connection: This is a packet-switching-network-adapter-to-packet-switching-network-adapter connection that uses the Qualified Logical Link Control protocol. It is most commonly used to provide low-speed interstate or international connections through a host packet-switched network. Its primary usefulness stems from local access numbers to a packet-based connection point, which then can be used to connect to your mainframe.

◆ A Channel connection: This type of connection is used to directly connect to a channel attachment on your SNA-compatible mainframe.

◆ A TwinAx connection: This type of connection is used to directly connect to your AS/400 mainframe over a TwinAx connection.

SNA Server has some limitations that you should be aware of that may determine how many SNA Server installations you require and how many adapters per server you need to meet your requirements. Table 32.1 summarizes these limitations.

TABLE 32.1. SNA SERVER CONNECTION AND SESSION LIMITATIONS.

Software/ Hardware	Total Connections	Total Sessions	Note
SNA Server	250	10,000	This includes a maximum of 2,000 clients. A single downstream connection is equivalent to a single client when determining the total number of clients per SNA Server installation.
802.2	250	254	
DFT	1	5	Although you can use up to four DFT adapters in a single system, they must all be controlled by a single link service. This can provide you with up to 4 connections with 20 sessions.
SDLC	1	254	
X.25/QLLC	250	254	If your adapter does not include a coprocessor, you cannot support a duplex transmission with a DTE speed higher than 9600bps.

Software/ Hardware	Total Connections	Total Sessions	Note
Channel	250	254	
TwinAx	1	20	

Note

The total number of sessions applies to 3270, LUA, and dependent APPC LU-LU sessions. For independent APPC LU sessions, the maximum is 10,000 sessions. You cannot use multiple 802.2, X.25/ QLLC, or channel adapters to increase the number of supported connections.

To create a new connection, follow these steps:

1. Select the server where you want the connection to be created in the Servers and Connections window. Then choose New Connection from the Services menu or use the shortcut key F2. The Insert Connection dialog box appears.

2. Select the connection to create. This can be 802.2, SDLC, DFT, X.25, Channel, or TwinAx. Then click the OK button.

3. In the Connection Properties dialog box, enter the relevant information for your connection type, as described in the following sections.

4. Click the OK button to accept the connection definition or press Cancel to abort.

Note

The following sections assume that you have already made your choice in the Connection Details dialog box and that the Connection Properties dialog box for your connection type is active.

CREATING A DLC 802.2 CONNECTION

Creating a DLC 802.2 connection consists of three parts: defining the connection, assigning the basic settings for the connection, and assigning the advanced settings for the connection. To define the connection, follow these steps:

1. When the Connection Properties dialog box appears, enter a name for the connection in the Connection Name field. (See Figure 32.3.) The connection

name can be from one to eight alphanumeric characters. The name can
include the special characters $, #, and @. All lowercase characters are
converted to uppercase characters. The name must be unique and cannot be
the reserved name SNASERVR.

Figure 32.3.
Assigning
connection
properties for an
802.2 connection.

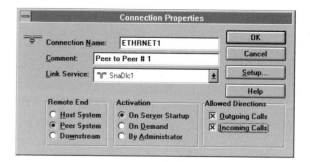

2. In the Comment field, enter a description for the connection. The description can be a maximum of 25 characters.

3. In the Link Service field, choose the service the connection will use to
   communicate with an SNA adapter.

Note

If no entry is available, you need to use the SNA Server Setup program to install a link service. This is discussed in Chapter 31.

4. In the Remote End section, choose the type of remote system for the connection to use. This can be one of the following:

   ◆ Host System: This type of remote system is usually a mainframe that
   controls all interactions between the mainframe and any clients that
   connect to it. This type should be used for dependent APPC, 3270, and
   LUA logical units.

   ◆ Peer System: This type of remote system usually is used for mainframes, minicomputers, and clients that communicate with each other
   as equal partners (independent APPC). The most common reason to
   use this type is for an AS/400 connection or when setting up a
   peer-to-peer connection to be used with Systems Management Server.

   ◆ Downstream: This type of remote system is used by clients, such as
   the IBM Communications Manager/2, that do not support the SNA
   Server client/server interface, but that can still access host connections provided by SNA Server.

Note

When using a Downstream type, be sure to configure the Max BTU setting, as described later in this section, to a value supported by the downstream client.

5. Choose an entry in the Activation section to specify when to make the connection available. This can be one of the following:

   ◆ On Server Startup: Specifies that the connection will be activated (made available to clients) when SNA Server starts.

   ◆ On Demand: Specifies that the connection will be activated on an as-required basis and deactivated when no longer required.

   ◆ By Administrator: Specifies that an administrator must manually activate or deactivate a connection. This option only applies to outgoing connections. If a connection has been configured to accept incoming calls, the connection begins to listen to calls as soon as SNA Server starts.

6. Next, choose the type of connection support to implement in the Allowed Directions section. This can be Incoming Calls, Outgoing Calls, or both. The default is Outgoing Calls.

7. You now have defined the connection, but you are not finished yet. At this point, you must click the Setup button to configure the basic properties for the connection. This displays the 802.2 Setup dialog box, as shown in Figure 32.4.

*Figure 32.4.
Configuring the
basic properties
for an 802.2
connection.*

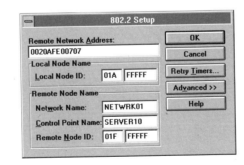

You can configure the following fields in the 802.2 Setup dialog box:

   ◆ Remote Network Address: This 12-digit hexadecimal address specifies the network address of the remote (the system to which you will connect) host, peer, or downstream system. This is one of those times when you need to contact your MIS department in order to find out the correct address. To aid you in this effort, here are a few tips that might help you in identifying your requirements:

For a connection to a 3174, you can use the `configuration response 900` value in the customization program.

For a connection to a 3720, 3725, or 3745 front-end processor (FEP), you can use the MACADDR= value in the NCP configuration.

For a connection to an IBM 3970 mainframe, you can use the MACADDR= value in the VTAM PORT definition.

For a connection to another SNA Server installation, use the network adapter address. This can be determined by executing the `NET CONFIG SERVER` command from a command prompt and using the 12-digit value in the Server Is Active On entry.

Tip

If the server on which SNA Server is installed uses DHCP, then another way to find the network address is to use the DHCP Manager. Just select the primary server and then choose Scope | Active Leases. Then, in the Active Leases dialog box, select the server in the Client field and click the Properties button. The network address will be listed in the Unique Identifier field.

◆ Local Node ID: This is an eight-digit hexadecimal that uniquely defines the local system to the remote system. The first three digits are commonly referred to as the block number, and the final five digits are referred to as the node number. Here are a couple of rules for their usage:

The first three digits cannot be 000 or FFF because these are reserved values.

In order for a remote or downstream connection to use this connection, you must inform the local administrator of your local node identifier.

In order to use a host connection, you must use the IDBLK value for the block number and the IDNUM value for the node number in the VTAM PU definition.

The same local node identifier must be used for all connections on your SNA Server installation.

◆ Network Name: If connecting to a host system that uses a remote network name, this entry should be the NETID value in the VTAM `Start` command for the local SSCP (the VTAM connection where SNA Server is attached). If connecting to an AS/400, this value will be the Network Name of the AS/400 (the RMTNETID value on the AS/400).

♦ Control Point Name: If connecting to a host system using a remote control point name, this value will be the SSCPNAME value in the VTAM Start command of the remote SSCP. For an AS/400, enter the name of the AS/400.

♦ Remote Node ID: This entry is a unique identifier of the remote node. It must be supplied by your MIS department for a host connection or by the local Administrator for a downstream connection. The first three digits cannot be 000 or FFF because these are reserved values.

Note

The network name and control point name can be from one to eight alphanumeric characters. They can include the special characters $, #, and @. The first character must be alphabetic. All lowercase characters are converted to uppercase characters. You cannot use just one name; if you supply one of these names, you must supply both these names.

8. To specify how often to retry a connection operation, click the Retry Timers button. This displays a dialog box in which you can specify the following choices:

♦ Maximum Number of Attempts: Specifies how many times SNA Server will attempt to make a connection. When the maximum value is reached, an entry is made into the event log, and no further attempts are made to connect. The range is from 1 to no limit, and the default is no limit.

♦ Delay After Failed Attempts: Specifies how long to wait, in seconds, between connection attempts. The range is from 5 to 255, with a default of 10.

9. If required, you can configure additional characteristics for the connection by clicking the Advanced button. This expands the dialog box to offer you the following fields:

♦ XID Type: Specifies the type of identifying information SNA Server will send. A Format 0 XID only sends the node ID and should be used only for systems that do not support a Format 3 XID. A Format 3 XID sends up to 100 bytes of identifying information, including the local node ID and control point name.

Note

If you will be using independent APPC LUs on the connection, you must specify a Format 3 XID.

32

MANAGING YOUR SNA SERVER GATEWAY

◆ Remote SAP Address: Specifies the remote system access point (SAP) address. This is a two-digit hexadecimal value in multiples of 4. The default value of 04 should suffice for most installations. If you will be using a 3174 controller for your connection, however, this value should be the same as the `configuration response 900` of the controller's customization program. Or, if you will be using an IBM 9370 host, use the value in the SAPADDR= value specified in the VTAM PU definition.

◆ Retry Limit: Determines how many times the local system will resend a frame when no response from the remote system is received. The range is from 0 to 255, with a default of 10.

◆ Max BTU Length: Defines the size of the basic transmission unit (BTU), also referred to as an I-frame, that can be sent in a single Data Link Control (DLC) frame. The range is from 265 to 16393, and the default is determined by your adapter.

Note

The maximum BTU length should be less than the MAXDATA= value in the VTAM PU definition for a host connection. For a 4Mb token ring adapter, the value should be equal to or less than 4195; for a 16Mb token ring adapter, the value should be equal to or less than 16393; and for an Ethernet adapter, the value should be equal to or less than 1493.

◆ XID Retries: Specifies how often the local system should resend an identifier (XID) message when no response is received from the remote system. The range is from 0 to 30, with a default of 3.

◆ Response (t1) Timeout: Specifies the time that the local system will wait for a response from a remote system before retransmitting. The value specified should be greater than the total time it takes for the data to be relayed between the local system, the remote system, and the network.

Tip

If you choose the default value for Response Timeout, the system maintains two separate time-out values: one for a remote system on the local network and the other for a remote system on a remote network. If you do not use the default value, the value you choose is used both for local and remote networks. The default for a local network is 400 milliseconds and 2 seconds for a remote network.

◆ Receive ACK (t2) Timeout: Specifies the maximum time a local system can delay before sending an acknowledgment to the remote system. The value specified should be less than the response time-out so that the system takes less time to acknowledge a received transmission than it requires to seek a response to a transmission.

Tip

If you choose the default value for Receive ACK Timeout, the system maintains two separate time-out values: one for a remote system on the local network and the other for a remote system on a remote network. If you do not use the default value, the value you choose is used both for local and remote networks. The default for a local network is 80 milliseconds, and the default for a remote network is 800 milliseconds.

◆ Inactivity (ti) Timeout: Specifies the maximum time a link can be inactive before SNA Server assumes that the link is malfunctioning and deactivates it.

Tip

If you choose the default value for Inactivity Timeout, the system maintains two separate time-out values: one for a remote system on the local network and one for a remote system on a remote network. If you do not use the default value, the value you choose is used both for local and remote networks. The default for a local network is 5 seconds, and the default for a remote network is 25 seconds.

◆ Receive ACK Threshold: Determines the maximum number of frames that can be received before the local system must send a response. The value ranges from 1 to 127, with a default of 2.

◆ Unacknowledged Send Limit: This entry, often referred to as the window send size, specifies the maximum number of frames the local system can send without receiving an acknowledgment from the remote system. The range is from 1 to 127, with a default of 8.

Tip

Receive ACK Threshold should be less than Unacknowledged Send Limit so that the local system acknowledges received transmissions more frequently than it requires responses from the remote system to send transmissions.

Tip

If you increase Unacknowledged Send Limit and Receive ACK Threshold, you may achieve greater throughput. You should attempt this only on connections with low error conditions, however, or you may actually decrease throughput.

10. Click the OK button to accept your connection definition.

CREATING A DFT CONNECTION

Creating a DFT connection is much easier than creating some other types of connections. All it requires is the basic definition, which can be accomplished by following these steps:

1. When the Connection Properties dialog box is displayed, enter a name for the connection in the Connection Name field. The connection name can be from one to eight alphanumeric characters. The name can include the special characters $, #, and @. All lowercase characters are converted to uppercase characters. The name must be unique, and cannot be the reserved name SNASERVR.

2. In the Comment field, enter a description for the connection. The description can be a maximum of 25 characters.

3. In the Link Service drop-down list, choose the service the connection will use to communicate with an SNA adapter.

Note

Even though you can use up to four DFT adapters, you must use only one link service for all of them. If no entry is available, you need to use the SNA Server Setup program to install a link service. This is discussed in Chapter 31.

4. Specify when to make the connection available by choosing an entry in the Activation section. This can be one of the following:

   ◆ On Server Startup: Specifies that the connection will be activated (made available to clients) when SNA Server starts.

   ◆ On Demand: Specifies that the connection will be activated on an as-required basis and then deactivated when no longer required.

   ◆ By Administrator: Specifies that an administrator must manually activate or deactivate a connection. This option applies only to outgoing connections. If a connection has been configured to accept incoming calls, then the connection begins to listen to calls as soon as SNA Server starts.

Note

The Remote End section is preset to Host System, and the Allowed Directions section is preset to Outgoing Calls.

5. Click the OK button to accept your connection definition.

CREATING AN SDLC CONNECTION

Creating an SDLC connection also consists of three parts: the first defines the connection, the second assigns the basic settings, and the third assigns the advanced settings for the connection. To create your SDLC connection, follow these steps:

1. When the Connection Properties dialog box is displayed, enter a name for the connection in the Connection Name field. The connection name can be from one to eight alphanumeric characters. The name can include the special characters $, #, and @. All lowercase characters are converted to uppercase characters. The name must be unique and cannot be the reserved name SNASERVR.

2. In the Comment field, enter a description for the connection. The description can be a maximum of 25 characters.

3. In the Link Service drop-down listbox, choose the service the connection will use to communicate with an SNA adapter.

Note

If no entry is available, you need to use the SNA Server Setup program to install a link service. This is discussed in Chapter 31.

4. In the Remote End section, choose the type of remote system the connection will use. This can be one of the following:

   ◆ Host System: This type of remote system is usually a mainframe that controls all interactions between the mainframe and any clients that connect to it. This type should be used for dependent APPC, 3270, and LUA logical units.

   ◆ Peer System: This type of remote system is usually used for mainframes, minicomputers, and clients that communicate with each other as equal partners (independent APPC). The most common reason to use this type is for an AS/400 connection or for a peer-to-peer connection for Systems Management Server.

◆ Downstream: This type of remote system is used by clients, such as the IBM Communications Manager/2, that do not support the SNA Server client/server interface, but that can still access host connections provided by SNA Server.

Note

When using a Downstream system type, be sure to configure the Max BTU setting, as described later in this section, to a value supported by the downstream client.

5. Specify when to make the connection available by choosing an entry in the Activation group. This can be one of the following:

   ◆ On Server Startup: Specifies that the connection will be activated (made available to clients) when SNA Server starts. This is a good choice for connections that use a leased line.

   ◆ On Demand: Specifies that the connection will be activated on an as-required basis and then deactivated when no longer required. This is a good choice for connections that use switched lines.

   ◆ By Administrator: Specifies that an administrator must manually activate or deactivate a connection. This option applies only to outgoing connections. If a connection has been configured to accept incoming calls, the connection begins to listen to calls as soon as SNA Server starts.

6. Next, choose the type of connection support to implement in the Allowed Directions group. This can be Incoming Calls, Outgoing Calls, or both. The default is Outgoing Calls.

Note

When using multiple SDLC connections for incoming calls, all these connections must use the same encoding (NRZ or NRZI) setting. A DFT connection can be configured only for outgoing calls.

7. At this point, you have defined the connection; however, before you can use the connection, you must click the Setup button to configure the basic properties for the connection. This displays the SDLC Setup dialog box, and if you choose the Advanced button (as you have here) the dialog box expands, as shown in Figure 32.5.

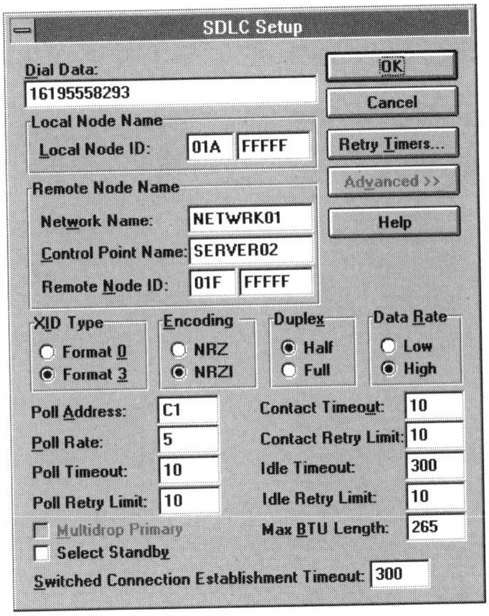

Figure 32.5.
Configuring the
basic and
advanced
properties for an
SDLC connection.

You can configure the following fields in this expanded SDLC Setup dialog box:

◆ Dial Data: Specifies a phone number, from 1 to 40 digits, that will be used for SDLC adapters on a switched phone line.

Note

If the SDLC adapter has a built-in communications port, the number is a phone number that is sent directly to the adapter. If the adapter is configured for a manually dialed number, the number entered here is specified in the pop-up message box that appears whenever the adapter is used for an outgoing call.

◆ Local Node ID: This is an eight-digit hexadecimal that uniquely defines the local system to the remote system. The first three digits are commonly referred to as the block number, and the final five digits are referred to as the node number. Here are a couple of rules for their usage:

The first three digits cannot be 000 or FFF because these are reserved values.

In order for a remote or downstream connection to use this connection, you must inform the local administrator of your local node identifier.

In order to use a host connection, you must use the IDBLK value for the block number and the IDNUM value for the node number in the VTAM PU definition.

The same local node identifier must be used for all connections on your SNA Server installation.

◆ Network Name: If connecting to a host system that uses a remote network name, this entry should be the NETID value in the VTAM Start command for the local SSCP (the VTAM connection where SNA Server is attached). If connecting to an AS/400, this value is the Network Name of the AS/400 (the RMTNETID value on the AS/400).

◆ Control Point Name: If connecting to a host system using a remote control point name, this value is the SSCPNAME value in the VTAM Start command of the remote SSCP. For an AS/400, enter the name of the AS/400.

◆ Remote Node ID: This entry is a unique identifier of the remote node. It must be supplied by your MIS department for a host connection or by the local administrator for a downstream connection. The first three digits cannot be 000 or FFF because these are reserved values.

Note

The network name and control point name can be from one to eight alphanumeric characters. They can include the special characters $, #, and @. The first character must be alphabetic. All lowercase characters are converted to uppercase characters. You cannot use just one name; if you supply one of these names, you must supply both these names.

◆ XID Type: Specifies the type of identifying information that SNA Server will send. A Format 0 XID only sends the node ID and should be used only for systems that do not support a Format 3 XID. A Format 3 XID sends up to 100 bytes of identifying information, including the local node ID and the control point name.

Note

If you will be using independent APPC LUs on the connection, you must specify a Format 3 XID.

◆ Encoding: Specifies the encoding scheme the modem will use. This can be NRZ (Nonreturn to Zero) or NRZI (Nonreturn to Zero Inverted). The default is NRZI.

Note

Both modems (the local and remote modems) must use the same encoding schemes. For connection to a host system, the encoding scheme is specified in the LINE/GROUP definition in VTAM. This value should be specified by your MIS Administrator.

◆ Duplex: This entry is based on your modem configuration. It will be Half or Full, depending on the feature set of your modem. You should refer to your SDLC adapter documentation to determine whether it supports half or full duplex.

Note

If Full is specified, then your SDLC configuration must have the Constant RTS option set. For specifics on this setting, refer to Chapter 31 for details on configuring the SDLC link service.

Tip

If your adapter lacks a coprocessor and you want to use a transmission speed higher than 9600bps, choose Half.

◆ Data Rate: This entry specifies the rate at which SNA Server can communicate with the SDLC adapter. You should refer to your adapter documentation to determine whether it supports a high data rate for optimum performance. If you have communications problems, then choose the low setting.

Note

The Data Rate option can be considered as the DTE rate when compared to a modem. And just like a modem, the maximum DTE rate is determined based on your UART. Even though the UART can handle higher data rates (19200bps for an 8250, 38400bps for a 16450, and 57600bps–115200bps for a 16550), if you specify a rate that is too high for your processor to handle, you will encounter data errors (dropouts), which will require retransmissions.

◆ Poll Address: This two-digit hexadecimal address should be supplied by your MIS Administrator for a host connection. It will be the ADDR= value of the VTAM definition. For a peer connection, this value can be anything but the reserved values 00 and FF because these peers will negotiate an acceptable value.

◆ Poll Rate: For peer or downstream services, this value determines the pool rate. The default is 5, with a range of 1 to 50.

◆ Poll Timeout: For a peer or downstream connection, this value specifies the time, in tenths of a second, for the local system to pause before polling again. The range is from 1 to 300, with a default of 10.

Caution

If you set the Poll Timeout value too low, it may cause link failures.

◆ Poll Retry Limit: For a peer or downstream connection, this entry determines how many times the local system will poll the remote system when no response is received. The range is from 1 to 255, with a default of 10.

◆ Contact Timeout: Specifies the time, in tenths of a second, that the local system will pause between connection attempts. The range is from 5 to 300, with a default of 10.

Note

The Contact Timeout value is not used for incoming calls.

◆ Contact Retry Limit: Specifies how many times the local system should attempt to make a connection to the remote system. The default is 10, with a range of 1 to 10.

Note

The Contact Retry Limit value is not used for incoming calls.

◆ Idle Timeout: For a host or peer connection, this entry specifies the time, in tenths of a second, that the local system will wait for a response from the remote system before resending the data. The range is from 1 to 300, with a default of 10.

Note

If the Idle Timeout value is too small, you may experience link failures.

- ◆ Idle Retry Limit: For a host or peer connection, this value determines the number of times the local system will attempt to send data to a remote system if no response is received. The range is from 1 to 255, with a default of 10.
- ◆ Max BTU Length: Defines the size of the basic transmission unit (BTU), also referred to as an I-frame, that can be sent in a single Data Link Control (DLC) frame. The range is from 265 to 16393, and the default is 265 for an SDLC connection.

Note

The maximum BTU length should be less than the MAXDATA= value in the VTAM PU definition for a host connection. For a downstream service, this value should be equal to or less than the maximum value supported by the downstream service. For specific values, you should refer to your documentation or just use the default value.

- ◆ Multidrop Primary: If you are using a leased SDLC line to a downstream connection and the local system is the primary station for a multidrop connection, this option should be enabled.
- ◆ Select Standby: If your modem supports a standby line (refer to your documentation if you are unsure) and it is enabled, this option should be enabled as well. The default is disabled.
- ◆ Switched Connection Establishment Timeout: If you are using a switched SDLC line, this value defines the maximum time, in seconds, to wait for a connection to be established. The range is from 10 to 500, with a default of 300.

8. To specify how often to retry a connection operation, click the Retry Timers button. This displays a dialog box where you can specify the following choices:
   - ◆ Maximum Number of Attempts: Specifies how many times SNA Server will attempt to make a connection. When the maximum value is reached, an entry is made into the event log, and no further attempts are made to connect. The range is from 1 to no limit, and the default is no limit.
   - ◆ Delay After Failed Attempts: Specifies how long to wait, in seconds, between connection attempts. The range is from 5 to 255, with a default of 10.

9. Click the OK button to accept your connection definition.

CREATING AN X.25/QLLC CONNECTION

Creating an X.25/QLLC connection is similar to creating an SDLC connection because it also consists of three parts: defining the connection, assigning the basic settings, and assigning the advanced settings for the connection. To create an X.25/QLLC connection, follow these steps:

1. When the Connection Properties dialog box is displayed, enter a name for the connection in the Connection Name field. The connection name can be from one to eight alphanumeric characters. The name can include the special characters $, #, and @. All lowercase characters are converted to uppercase characters. The name must be unique and cannot be the reserved name SNASERVR.

2. In the Comment field, enter a description for the connection. The description can be a maximum of 25 characters.

3. In the Link Service drop-down listbox, choose the service the connection will use to communicate with an SNA adapter.

Note

If no entry is available, you need to use the SNA Server Setup program to install a link service. This is discussed in Chapter 31.

4. Choose the type of remote system the connection will use in the Remote End group. This can be one of the following:

   ◆ Host System: This type of remote system is usually a mainframe that controls all interactions between the mainframe and any clients that connect to it. This type should be used for dependent APPC, 3270, and LUA logical units.

   ◆ Peer System: This type of remote system is usually used for mainframes, minicomputers, and clients that communicate with each other as equal partners (independent APPC). The most common reason to use this type is for an AS/400 connection or for a peer-to-peer connection for Systems Management Server.

   ◆ Downstream: This type of remote system is used by clients, such as the IBM Communications Manager/2, that do not support the SNA Server client/server interface, but that can still access host connections provided by SNA Server.

Note

When using a downstream system type, be sure to configure the Max BTU setting, as described later in this section, to a value supported by the downstream client.

5. Specify when to make the connection available by choosing an entry in the Activation group. This can be one of the following:

   ◆ On Server Startup: Specifies that the connection will be activated (made available to clients) when SNA Server starts. This is a good choice for connections that use a leased line.

   ◆ On Demand: Specifies that the connection will be activated on an as-required basis and then deactivated when no longer required. This is a good choice for connections that use switched lines.

   ◆ By Administrator: Specifies that an administrator must manually activate or deactivate a connection. This option only applies to outgoing connections. If a connection has been configured to accept incoming calls, then the connection begins to listen to calls as soon as SNA Server starts.

6. Choose the type of connection support to implement in the Allowed Directions group. This can be Incoming Calls, Outgoing Calls, or both. The default is Outgoing Calls.

7. Select the type of virtual circuit that will be used in the Virtual Circuit Type field. This can be one of the following:

   ◆ Switched (SVC): This type of virtual circuit is the default, and is called and cleared dynamically rather than being constantly active. A destination address is supplied when the circuit is called.

   ◆ Permanent (PVC): This type of virtual circuit is constantly active with a preset destination address.

8. At this point, you have defined the connection; however, before you can use the connection, you must click the Setup button to configure the basic properties for the connection. This displays the X.25 Setup dialog box, and if you click the Advanced button, the dialog box expands.

   You can configure the following fields in the expanded X.25 Setup dialog box:

   ◆ Remote X.25 Address: This entry consists of from 12 to 15 hexadecimal digits (the final three digits are used for routing between installations with the same first 12-digit address) and should be specified by the Administrator of the remote system. If you are connecting to a host using VTAM, the DIALNO= parameter in the VTAM PORT definition should be used.

◆ Local Node ID: This is an eight-digit hexadecimal that uniquely defines the local system to the remote system. The first three digits commonly are referred to as the block number, and the final five digits are referred to as the node number. Here are a couple of rules for their usage:

The first three digits cannot be 000 or FFF because these are reserved values.

In order for a remote or downstream connection to use this connection, you must inform the local administrator of your local node identifier.

In order to use a host connection, you must use the IDBLK value for the block number and the IDNUM value for the node number in the VTAM PU definition.

The same local node identifier must be used for all connections on your SNA Server installation.

◆ Network Name: If connecting to a host system that uses a remote network name, this entry should be the NETID value in the VTAM Start command for the local SSCP (the VTAM connection where SNA Server is attached). If connecting to an AS/400, this value is the network name of the AS/400 (the RMTNETID value on the AS/400).

◆ Control Point Name: If you are connecting to a host system using a remote control point name, this value is the SSCPNAME value in the VTAM Start command of the remote SSCP. For an AS/400, enter the name of the AS/400.

◆ Remote Node ID: This entry is a unique identifier of the remote node. It must be supplied by your MIS department for a host connection or by the local administrator for a downstream connection. The first three digits cannot be 000 or FFF because these are reserved values.

Note

The network name and control point name can be from one to eight alphanumeric characters. They can include the special characters $, #, and @. The first character must be alphabetic. All lowercase characters are converted to uppercase characters. You cannot use just one name; if you supply one of these names, you must supply both these names.

◆ XID Type: Specifies the type of identifying information that SNA
Server will send. A Format 0 XID only sends the Node ID and should
be used only for systems that do not support a Format 3 XID. A
Format 3 XID sends up to 100 bytes of identifying information, including the local node ID and control point name.

Note

If you will be using independent APPC LUs on the connection, you
must specify a Format 3 XID.

◆ Max BTU Length: Defines the size of the basic transmission unit
(BTU), also referred to as an I-frame, that can be sent in a single Data
Link Control (DLC) frame. The range is from 265 to 16393, and the
default is 1033 for an X.25/QLLC connection.

Note

The maximum BTU length should be less than the MAXDATA= value
in the VTAM PU definition for a host connection. For a downstream
service, this value should be equal to or less than the maximum value
supported by the downstream service. For specific values, you should
refer to your documentation or just use the default value.

◆ PVC Alias: Specifies the PVC channel. The range is from 1 to the
configured number of channels. The default is 1.
◆ Packet Size: For a PVC, this entry specifies the maximum number of
data bytes to be sent in a frame. The range is 64 to 1024 in 64-unit
increments with a default of 128. This entry should be specified by
your network service provider.
◆ Window Size: For a PVC, this entry specifies the maximum number of
frames that can be sent without receiving a response from the remote
system. This entry should be obtained from the administrator of the
remote system.
◆ Facility Data: For an SVC, this entry specifies the codes for any
facility data required by your network service provider or administrator of the remote system. The data can be a maximum of 126 hexadecimal characters (63 hexadecimal bytes) in length.

32

Note

Facility data is a coded string that is used primarily to request non-standard functions from your X.25 network.

◆ User Data: For an SVC, this entry specifies the codes for any user data required by your network service provider. It can be a maximum of 32 characters and must be an even number of characters.

Note

User data is a coded string used primarily to specify the protocol to be used. For SNA, this value must be C3, which specifies the QLLC protocol.

9. To specify how often to retry a connection operation, click the Retry Timers button. This displays a dialog box where you can specify the following choices:

   ◆ Maximum Number of Attempts: Specifies how many times SNA Server will attempt to make a connection. When the maximum value is reached, an entry is made into the event log, and no further attempts are made to connect. The range is from 1 to no limit, and the default is no limit.

   ◆ Delay After Failed Attempts: Specifies how long to wait, in seconds, between connection attempts. The range is from 5 to 255, with a default of 10.

10. Click the OK button to accept your connection definition.

CREATING A CHANNEL CONNECTION

Creating a channel connection also consists of three parts, but there is less information to supply. The first part follows the standard to define the connection, the second assigns the basic settings, and the third assigns the advanced settings for the connection.

To define the connection, follow these steps:

1. When the Connection Properties dialog box is displayed, enter a name for the connection in the Connection Name field. The connection name can be from one to eight alphanumeric characters. The name can include the special characters $, #, and @. All lowercase characters are converted to uppercase characters. The name must be unique and cannot be the reserved name SNASERVR.

2. In the Comment field, enter a description for the connection. The description can be a maximum of 25 characters.

3. In the Link Service drop-down listbox, choose the service the connection will use to communicate with an SNA adapter.

Note

> If no entry is available, you need to use the SNA Server Setup program to install a link service. This is discussed in Chapter 31.

4. Specify when to make the connection available by choosing an entry in the Activation group. This can be one of the following:

◆ On Server Startup: Specifies that the connection will be activated (made available to clients) when SNA Server starts. This is the preferred setting for a channel attachment.

◆ On Demand: Specifies that the connection will be activated on an as-required basis and then deactivated when no longer required.

◆ By Administrator: Specifies that an administrator must manually activate or deactivate a connection. This option only applies to outgoing connections. If a connection has been configured to accept incoming calls, then the connection begins to listen to calls as soon as SNA Server starts.

Note

> The remote system will be preset to Host System and the Allowed Directions group will be preset to Outgoing Calls.

5. At this point, you have defined the connection; however, before you can use the connection, you must click the Setup button to configure the basic properties for the connection. This displays the Channel Attached Setup dialog box, and if you click the Advanced button (as you have here) the dialog box expands, as shown in Figure 32.6.

Figure 32.6. Configuring the basic and advanced properties for a channel connection.

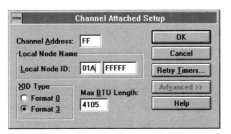

32

MANAGING YOUR SNA SERVER GATEWAY

You can configure the following fields in this dialog box:

- ◆ Channel Address: This hexadecimal entry uniquely identifies the channel. The range is from 00 to FF, with a default of FF.

- ◆ Local Node ID: This is an eight-digit hexadecimal that uniquely defines the local system to the remote system. The first three digits commonly are referred to as the block number, and the final five digits are referred to as the node number. Here are a couple of rules for their usage:

    The first three digits cannot be 000 or FFF because these are reserved values.

    In order for a remote or downstream connection to use this connection, you must inform the local administrator of your local node identifier.

    In order to use a host connection, you must use the IDBLK value for the block number and the IDNUM value for the node number in the VTAM PU definition.

    The same local node identifier must be used for all connections on your SNA Server installation.

- ◆ XID Type: Specifies the type of identifying information SNA Server will send. Format 0 XID only sends the node ID and should be used only for systems that do not support a Format 3 XID. Format 3 XID sends up to 100 bytes of identifying information, including the local node ID and control point name.

Note

If you will be using independent APPC LUs on the connection, you must specify Format 3 XID.

- ◆ Max BTU Length: Defines the size of the basic transmission unit (BTU), also referred to as an I-frame, that can be sent in a single Data Link Control (DLC) frame. The range is from 265 to 16393, and the default is 4105 for a channel connection.

Note

The maximum BTU length should be less than the MAXDATA= value in the VTAM PU definition for a host connection. For a downstream service, this value should be equal to or less than the maximum value supported by the downstream service. For specific values, you should refer to your documentation or just use the default value.

6. To specify how often to retry a connection operation, click the Retry Timers button to display a dialog box where you can specify the following choices:

   ◆ Maximum Number of Attempts: Specifies how many times SNA Server will attempt to make a connection. When the maximum value is reached, an entry is made into the event log and no further attempts are made to connect. The range is from 1 to no limit, and the default is no limit.

   ◆ Delay After Failed Attempts: Specifies how long to wait, in seconds, between connection attempts. The range is from 5 to 255, with a default of 10.

7. Click the OK button to accept your connection definition.

CREATING A TWINAX CONNECTION

Creating a TwinAx connection is just like creating a DFT connection in that it only requires the basic definition. You can accomplish this by following these steps:

1. When the Connection Properties dialog box is displayed, enter a name for the connection in the Connection Name field. The connection name can be from one to eight alphanumeric characters. The name can include the special characters $, #, and @. All lowercase characters are converted to uppercase characters. The name must be unique and cannot be the reserved name SNASERVR.

2. In the Comment field, enter a description for the connection. The description can be a maximum of 25 characters.

3. In the Link Service drop-down listbox, choose the service the connection will use to communicate with an SNA adapter.

Note

If no entry is available, you need to use the SNA Server Setup program to install a link service. This is discussed in Chapter 31.

4. Specify when to make the connection available by choosing an entry in the Activation group. This can be one of the following:

   ◆ On Server Startup: Specifies that the connection will be activated (made available to clients) when SNA Server starts. This is the preferred choice for a TwinAx connection.

   ◆ On Demand: Specifies that the connection will be activated on an as-required basis and then deactivated when no longer required.

   ◆ By Administrator: Specifies that an administrator must manually activate or deactivate a connection. This option only applies to

32

outgoing connections. If a connection has been configured to accept incoming calls, the connection begins to listen to calls as soon as SNA Server starts.

Note

The remote system is preset to Peer System, and the Allowed Directions group is preset to Outgoing Calls.

5. Click the OK button to accept your connection definition.

ASSIGNING A LOGICAL UNIT (LU) TO A CONNECTION

Before your clients can actually connect to your SNA-compatible mainframe, you must assign the logical units (LUs) to a connection. This is performed by selecting the connection in the Servers and Connections window and then choosing Services|Assign LU. The Insert LU dialog box appears, where you can select from one of the following:

- ◆ 3270: Supports users of 3270 emulation software to access an SNA-compatible mainframe. You can define the LU to support a 3270 terminal or a compatible printer.

- ◆ APPC (Remote): Supports advanced program-to-program communications (transaction program (TP) to transaction program (TP) communications), which use the LU 6.2 protocol. It is most frequently used to support SNA-to-SNA communications or 5250 terminal emulation.

- ◆ LUA: Supports Logical Unit Application (LUA) client-to-host communications.

- ◆ Downstream: Supports applications that do not support the SNA Server client server interface, but that still can access host services provided by SNA Server.

After you select the appropriate LU type and click the OK button, a New LU Properties dialog box is displayed, where you can define the LU. Each LU has a slightly different dialog box, which is described in the following sections.

CREATING A 3270 LOGICAL UNIT (LU)

To create a 3270 LU, fill out the following fields in the New 3270 LU Properties dialog box:

- ◆ For a DFT connection, enter the number for the DFT adapter that will be used in the Port Number field. This value can range from 1 to 4.

- For a DFT connection, enter the logical terminal number, as specified in the 3174 FEP, in the LT Number field. This value can range from 1 to 5 and most likely will require help from your MIS Administrator to determine.

- For a DLC 802.2, SDLC, or X.25/QLLC connection, enter a number in the LU Number field to identify the LU. This number should be assigned by the MIS Administrator. It should match the LOCADDR= parameter in the VTAM or NCP Gen on the host system. This value can range from 1 to 254.

- Specify a unique name for the logical unit in the LU Name field. The name can be from one to eight alphanumeric characters. The name can include the special characters $, #, and @. All lowercase characters are converted to uppercase characters.

- Specify a description for the LU in the Comment field. This entry can be a maximum of 25 characters.

- Choose the type of LU in the LU Type field. This will be 3270 for a 3270 terminal emulation, or printer for printer emulation.

- If this LU is a 3270 terminal emulation, choose the default display mode in the Display Model field. If you want to allow your users to choose a different display model, enable the Model Can Be Overridden checkbox.

- Click the OK button.

Tip

> If you have several 3270 LUs to create, you can use a shortcut. Along with selecting the 3270 entry in the Insert LU dialog box, enable the Range of LUs checkbox. Then, in the Add LU Range dialog box, enter a name in the Base LU Name field (such as TERM), the starting number in the First LU Number field (01, for example), and the total number of LUs to create in the Number of LUs field (10, for example).

Tip

> Then click the OK button. This displays the 3270 LU Range Properties dialog box where you should specify a description for the LUs in the Comment field, choose an LU type, and—if the LU type is a 3270 terminal emulation—choose a display mode as well. After you click the OK button, several LUs are created on the selected connection (in this example, these are TERM01 through TERM09).

32

MANAGING YOUR SNA SERVER GATEWAY

CREATING AN ADVANCED PROGRAM-TO-PROGRAM (APPC) LOGICAL UNIT (LU)

There are two types of APPC LUs you can create: an independent APPC LU, which can communicate directly with a peer system and support multiple parallel sessions, or a dependent APPC LU, which requires the support of a host configuration in order to communicate with a transaction program. When creating an APPC LU, keep in mind that you have to create a local and a remote APPC in order to create a link between two transaction programs. The local APPC is created on a server, and the remote APPC is created on a connection.

You should follow a couple of rules for a successful configuration.

For an independent APPC LU, follow these rules:

◆ If your local system will be communicating with a host system transaction program, the host system must use VTAM version 3, release 2, or higher. The host also must use NCP version 5, release 3, or higher. The LOCADDR= parameter should be set to 0 in the VTAM, NCP, and CIS parameters on the host system.

◆ You must use Format 3 XIDs.

For a dependent APPC LU, follow these rules:

◆ The connection should be configured with a remote end of host, rather than a peer.

◆ If using a version of VTAM earlier than version 3, this is the only type of APPC LU you can use to communicate with transaction programs on the host system.

◆ The host system should have the LOCADDR= parameter set to 1 or greater in the NCP Gen.

To create a local APPC LU, fill out the following fields in the New APPC LU Properties dialog box:

◆ First, determine whether you will create a dependent or independent LU in the LU 6.2 type field.

Note

If you will be using a remote APPC LU on a DFT connection, you must configure the local APPC LU for a dependent connection.

◆ Enter a name in the LU Alias field that will be used by local transaction program (TP) applications. The name can be from one to eight characters and can include the special characters %, $, #, and @. The name must be unique on the connection and cannot match an LU on the server.

◆ Enter the name in the Network Name field. The name can be from one to eight alphanumeric characters. They can include the special characters $, #, and @. The first character must be alphabetic. All lowercase characters are converted to uppercase characters.

Note

This name should be obtained from the administrator of the host or peer APPC LU. For a host connection, the name should be the NETID value in the VTAM start command for the VTAM system. If the server will communicate with several hosts over several connections, use the subarea name.

Note

For an independent APPC LU, the network name is required. For a dependent APPC LU, the network name is not required, but is recommended because it is used only by local applications.

◆ Enter a name in the LU Name field to identify the LU. The name can be from one to eight alphanumeric characters. They can include the special characters $, #, and @. The first character must be alphabetic. All lowercase characters are converted to uppercase characters.

◆ Enter a number in the LU Number field if this APPC LU will be a dependent APPC LU. This number should be obtained from your host system Administrator and is usually the LOCADDR= value in the LU definition in VTAM or NCP. The range is from 1 to 254.

◆ Enter a description for the APPC LU in the Comment field.

◆ To enable automatic partnering of APPC LU, set the Enable Automatic Partnering checkbox. This creates LU-LU pairs for all APPC LUs that have the automatic partnering option enabled.

Note

To specify partners manually, click the Partners button and add the specific partners to create your LU-LU pairs.

◆ If you want to specify a default LU for use by transaction programs that do not specify a local LU, enable the Member of Default Outgoing Local APPC LU Pool checkbox.

- To specify a default remote APPC LU to be used by transaction programs that specify a local LU SNA Server does not recognize, select it from the Implicit Incoming Remote LU listbox.
- To specify the number of seconds SNA Server waits for an invokable transaction program to respond to a start request, enter a value in the Timeout for Starting Invokable TPs field. This value can range from 1 to 3600, with a default of 60.
- Click the OK button.

To create a remote APPC LU, fill out the following fields in the New APPC LU Properties dialog box:

- Enter a name in the LU Alias field that will be used by local transaction program (TP) applications. The name can be from one to eight characters and can include the special characters %, $, #, and @. The name must be unique on the connection and cannot match an LU on the server.
- Enter the name of the server in the Network Name field. The name can be from one to eight alphanumeric characters. They can include the special characters $, #, and @. The first character must be alphabetic. All lowercase characters are converted to uppercase characters.
- Enter a name in the LU Name field that identifies the APPC LU. The name can be from one to eight characters and can include the special characters %, $, #, and @. The name must be unique on the connection and cannot match an LU on the server, although it can match the LU Alias name.
- If the APPC LU will be used for a dependent APPC LU, enter a name in the Uninterpreted LU Name field for the remote LU. Generally, this name is the name of the remote LU on the host system, as defined in the SSCP (such as TSO). The name can include the special characters ., #, @, and $.
- Enter a description for the APPC LU in the Comment field.
- If the APPC LU will be used for an independent APPC LU, enable the Supports Parallel Sessions checkbox. If the APPC LU will be used for a dependent APPC LU, clear the checkbox.
- To enable automatic partnering of APPC LU, set the Enable Automatic Partnering checkbox. This will create LU-LU pairs for all APPC LUs that have the automatic partnering option enabled.

Note

To specify partners manually, click the Partners button and add the specific partners to create your LU-LU pairs.

◆ Choose a mode from the Implicit Incoming Mode listbox to preselect a default mode for sessions from remote APPC LUs that specify a mode not understood by SNA Server. This can be one of the following:

#BATCH: A batch session.

#BATCHSC: A batch session that uses minimal security.

BLANK: A session that uses a default mode name specified as eight blank characters in EBCDIC format in BIND.

#INTER: An interactive session.

#INTERSC: An interactive session with minimal security.

QPCSUPP: A session with an AS/400 minicomputer.

◆ To modify the security for the APPC LU, click the Security button. Then you can specify one of the following:

No Session Level Security: The default, which requires no security key.

Security Key in Hex: A maximum of 16 hexadecimal characters.

Security Key in Characters: A maximum of eight characters. The key can include the special characters ., #, @, and $.

Note

If you specify a security key, the session will not be activated unless both APPC LUs have keys that match.

◆ Click the OK button.

CREATING A LOGICAL UNIT APPLICATION (LUA)

To create an LUA LU, fill out the following fields in the New LUA Properties dialog box:

◆ Enter a number in the LU Number field if this APPC LU will be a dependent APPC LU. This number should be obtained from your host system Administrator and is usually the LOCADDR= value in the LU definition in VTAM or NCP. The range is from 1 to 254.

◆ Enter a name in the LU Name field to identify the LU. The name can be from one to eight alphanumeric characters. They can include the special characters $, #, and @. The first character must be alphabetic. All lowercase characters are converted to uppercase characters.

◆ Enter a description for the LU in the Comment field.

◆ Enable the High Priority LU checkbox to give this LU higher precedence over lower priority LUs.

◆ Click the OK button.

CREATING A DOWNSTREAM LOGICAL UNIT (LU)

To create a downstream LU, fill out the following fields in the New Downstream LU Properties dialog box:

◆ Enter a number in the LU Number field if this APPC LU will be a dependent APPC LU. This number should be obtained from your host system Administrator and is usually the LOCADDR= value in the LU definition in VTAM or NCP. The range is from 1 to 254.

◆ Enter a name in the LU Name field to identify the LU. The name can be from one to eight alphanumeric characters. They can include the special characters $, #, and @. The first character must be alphabetic. All lowercase characters will be converted to uppercase characters.

◆ Enter a description for the LU in the Comment field.

◆ Click the OK button.

MANAGING YOUR USERS

Before your users can actually use a connection or logical unit, they must be granted permission to do so. This can be accomplished at the group level or at the user level. As with most other issues relating to security, this is much easier to perform at the group level. The basic series of steps follows:

◆ Use User Manager for Domains to create a new group. In actuality, you will want to create several groups. You might want to segment these groups by department boundaries or specific hardware (such as terminals and printers). As usual, you can create both local and global groups to make your management tasks easier.

◆ Use User Manager for Domains to create new user accounts as required.

◆ Use User Manager for Domains to assign your users to the appropriate groups.

Note

You can find specifics on how to use User Manager for Domains to manage users and groups in Chapter 6, "Basic Administrative Tools," in the section "Using User Manager for Domains."

◆ Finally, use SNA Server Administrator to assign users or groups to logical units.

This last step is the focus of this discussion, and you will be happy to know that it follows the same basic principles as assigning permissions to any other object (such as a directory or file).

The basic steps follow:

1. Open the Users and Groups window.

2. Choose New User from the Users menu to display the Add Users and Groups dialog box.

3. If the default domain, which is where the current SNA Server installation resides, is not the domain in which the group or user accounts reside, choose another from the List Names From field.

4. In the Names field, select the groups or users and click the Add button.

5. Click the OK button. This adds the groups or users to the Users and Groups window in the left window.

6. Select the group or user and choose Assign LUs from the Users menu to display the Assign User LU/Pool Sessions dialog box.

7. In the Available LU and Pools field, select the LUs and pools to assign to the account and click the OK button.

Note

Before you can assign permission to an LU or LU pool, you must create one. Creating an LU is discussed in the previous sections, and creating an LU pool is discussed in the following section.

USING LOGICAL UNIT (LU) POOLS

An LU pool is a collection of logical units grouped into a single entity. It is similar to a group account in that it contains multiple user accounts grouped into a single entity. Both offer easier management of resources, but LU pools offer additional benefits as well:

◆ Efficient resource management: Most installations find that not every user is accessing the same resource at the same time. So it is possible to support 50 users with only 25 LUs if you group all the LUs into a single pool and assign all 50 users to this LU pool. As long as you do not have more than 25 simultaneous users, you'll never run out of LUs.

◆ Fault tolerance: An LU pool can contain LUs from more than one SNA Server. As long as one server is available with LUs in this pool, your users can continue to access them without interruption. This can be very useful when you need to perform maintenance or in case of a server failure.

◆ Load balancing: You can use an LU pool to balance the load on a particular server, which increases perceived user performance. When you use an LU pool with LUs from multiple servers, the individual load is balanced among these servers based on the number of connected users.

You can create a 3270 terminal/printer, LUA, or downstream pool by opening the LU Pools window and then choosing Pools | New Pool to display the New Pool dialog box. Then enter a unique name for the pool in the Pool Name field, enter a description in the Comment field, and choose the type of pool to create in the LU Type field. If you specified 3270 for the LU type, choose a display mode in the 3270 Display Mode field. Then just click the OK button.

After you create the pool, you have to assign logical units to it. Select the pool and choose Pools | Assign LUs to display the Assign Pool LUs dialog box. This is just a matter of selecting the individual LUs in the Available LUs field and clicking the OK button to assign the LUs to the pool.

Tip

Don't forget that before your users can actually use the LU pool, you must assign the appropriate permissions as described in the preceding section.

MANAGING THE SNA SERVER SERVICES

By default, the SNA Server Services are configured to be inactive at system startup. This means that before your users can use an LU, you have to start the appropriate server or individual connection. This is accomplished by choosing the server or connection in the Servers and Connections window and choosing Services | Start Service. Stopping a server or connection follows the same methodology, but you should choose Services | Stop Service instead.

Any connection configured with On Server Startup activation will be automatically activated when you start the appropriate server. Connections that use the On Demand activation setting are activated as required when a user attempts a connection. Any connection configured with the By Administrator activation requires manually starting or stopping the connection as specified earlier.

Tip

You can provide additional fault tolerance and ease of administration by configuring SNA Server to start up when NT Server starts. Just set the SNA Server service to automatic, rather than manual, in the Control Panel Services applet. You can do the same for the NVAlert and NVRunCmd (NetView Alert and Run Command services). Do not configure the SnaNtMn service to Automatic, however, or it will fail to

> start. SNA Server automatically starts this service for any connection that is configured to use it.

CONFIGURING SNA ADMINISTRATOR

Configuring SNA Server only consists of two choices. You can configure the display options by choosing Options | Preferences, which is pretty self-explanatory, or Options | Server Broadcasts, which requires a bit of discussion. This choice displays the Server Broadcasts dialog box, as shown in Figure 32.7.

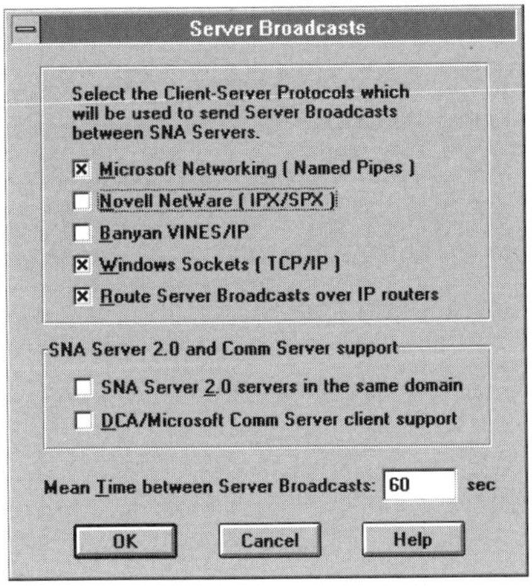

*Figure 32.7.
Configuring SNA
Server broad-
casts.*

In the Select the Client-Server Protocols Which Will Be Used to Send Server Broadcasts Between SNA Servers section, you can choose from the protocols you have installed and configured SNA Server to use. For efficiency, use a single protocol for server broadcasts if you can. If all your installations support TCP/IP, for example, use just TCP/IP. But if you have some servers configured for TCP/IP and some for IPX/SPX, be sure to enable both these protocols so that the installations can communicate between themselves. If you will be using non-TCP/IP protocols over a WAN, you should enable the Route Server Broadcasts over IP Routers checkbox. If you do not, the server broadcasts will fail to propagate across the routers.

Tip

> Before you do decide to enable the Route Server Broadcasts over IP Routers, check with your network administrators (if your company has a separate network administration group) because this option relies on the TCP/IP capability to encapsulate NetBIOS requests.

> Sometimes, this may not be considered the best option because it can utilize a high percentage of network bandwidth. Your network administrators may have a better alternative.

In the SNA Server 2.0 and Comm Server Support group, you should disable the SNA Server 2.0 Servers in the Same Domain checkbox unless you have SNA Server 2.0 installations in the same domain. This option can seriously degrade SNA Server 2.x performance because it requires server broadcasts be sent once a minute. It also uses a significant portion of your network bandwidth that could be used for more productive requirements. If you have any DCA/Microsoft clients, you should enable the DCA/Microsoft Comm Server Client Support checkbox. You also should make sure that you have enabled Microsoft Networking as an available transport protocol because these applications require NetBEUI.

If you are not supporting SNA Server 2.0 installations, you can specify how often SNA Server broadcasts set the time, in seconds, in the Mean Time between Server Broadcasts field. This value ranges from 45 to 65535, with a default of 60. The default is a good choice because broadcast messages are not guaranteed to be received by the client and this will compensate for lost messages. If your network is not error prone, however, and your servers are not overburdened, then you can increase this value and lower the network bandwidth requirement.

SECURING SNA SERVER

Now that you have spent so much time configuring SNA Server, you should spend a little more time to protect your investment. This is very important and should not be overlooked in your effort to provide a service to your network clients. Spend just a little more time to restrict the modifications that are possible to just a few administrators by following these steps:

1. Choose Permissions from the Security menu to display the SNA Domain Permissions dialog box.

2. Click the Remove button to remove the default Everyone group (which has full control of SNA Server Administrator).

3. Click the Add button to display the Add Users and Groups dialog box.

4. Choose the group you want to allow full administration of your SNA Server domain (such as Domain Admins) in the Names field. If you want to choose a user account instead of a group account, first click the Show Users button. If the user or group is not in the current domain, choose the correct domain from the List Names From drop-down listbox.

Note

> If you have not already created a group for SNA Server administration, it is a good idea to do so in User Manager for Domains. This group can be assigned permission to administer SNA Server and to limit the damage that could be caused by unfamiliar domain administrators (Domain Admins).

5. Choose the access control setting of Full Control in the Type of Access drop-down listbox, and click the OK button.

6. Click the OK button once again, and you have secured access to your SNA Server domain.

Tip

> You can further restrict access to groups or users by selecting them and assigning a different type of access. This could be No Access, which prevents them from using SNA Server Administrator; Read, which provides the capability to see the configuration but not change it; Read/Write, which provides the capability to read and modify the configuration but not change permissions; and Full Control, which provides complete access.

Tip

> It is a good idea to use the Security|Auditing option to enable auditing of your SNA Server configuration if you will be providing access to several users. In this way, you can determine who did what in case of a user error—not so much to assign blame, but instead to determine who needs additional tutoring in their duties.

USING THE SNA TRACE UTILITY

If you are encountering problems with SNA Server, you might want to look into the SNA Server Trace utility. This utility is located in your Microsoft SNA Server Program Manager group. It provides two basic options for you:

◆ It can be used to send trace messages to the event log, which makes them easier to read.

◆ It can send detailed trace messages to trace files (`*.TRC`) in the TRACES directory of your SNA Server root installation directory (generally, `C:\SNA\TRACES`).

To use the SNA Server Trace utility, follow these steps:

1. Launch the SNA Server Trace utility. The SNA Server Trace Options dialog box appears, as shown in Figure 32.8.

Figure 32.8.
The SNA Server
Trace Options
dialog box.

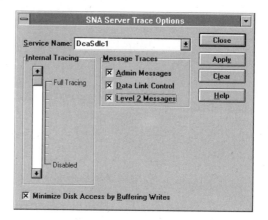

2. In the Service Name drop-down listbox, specify the service to trace.
3. In the Message Traces group, choose what messages to trace. This varies based on the selected service and may be any of the following:

   ◆ Admin Messages: Messages between SNA Server Administrator, SnaBase, and SnaServer (PU 2.1 node).
   ◆ 3270 Messages: Messages between 3270 applications.
   ◆ Data Link Control: Messages between SnaServer (PU 2.1 node) and the link services.
   ◆ SNA Formats: DLC messages in SNA Server formats.
   ◆ LU 6.2 Messages: Messages between SnaServer (PU 2.1 node) and the APPC dynamic link library.
   ◆ Level 2 Messages: Messages specific to the ISO Level 2 model.

4. If you have specified the SNA applications as the selected service, you can trace API messages, which can be any of the following:

   ◆ APPC API: Activity between APPC applications and the APP dynamic link library.
   ◆ CPI-API: Activity between the CPI-C applications and the CPI-C dynamic link library.
   ◆ LUA API: Activity between the LUA applications and the LUA dynamic link library.
   ◆ CSV API: Activity between the CSV applications and the CSV dynamic link library.

5. If you have a support provider on the line, such as Microsoft Product Service Support, you may need to enable the Internal Tracing option by moving the slider to the requested level. This is not normally useful to administrators.

6. To enhance performance, leave the Minimize Disk Access by Buffering Writes checkbox enabled, but if you are attempting to determine the cause of a system crash, disable this option so that the trace logs will be more current (if the system crashes, information in the buffer will be lost).

7. Repeat these steps for each service to trace.

8. Click the Apply button and then click the Close button.

Note

Although the trace files might be helpful in some situations, you most likely will require some help from a network guru in order to interpret the data. Most times the information obtained from the trace utility is only used by Microsoft technical support personnel to resolve an otherwise unresolvable problem.

SUMMARY

In this chapter, you explored some of the basic requirements for configuring your SNA Server installations to support your clients' access to your SNA-compatible mainframe. The key feature to remember is that before you can use a link service, you must define the connection, set up the connection, and then configure any advanced properties. After the connection is created, you must assign logical units. And, finally, you must assign permissions to groups or users to access the logical units. Permissions should be based on groups rather than individual users.

You can use Logical Unit pools to offer increased resource efficiency, fault tolerance, and increased performance. And before you walk away from your SNA installation, be sure to safeguard it by assigning specific security to determine just who can use the SNA Server Administrator to configure the installation.

In the next chapter, you will look into optimizing your SNA Server installation. Some of the topics you will consider include how to choose the right server platform and server models. You'll also learn how to configure your base Windows NT Server platform, and then you will look into specific SNA Server configuration choices to improve performance.

32

MANAGING YOUR SNA SERVER GATEWAY

- Examining Server
  Optimization

- Tuning SNA Server

CHAPTER 33

Optimizing SNA Server

After SNA Server is up and running, you naturally will consider how you can make it perform better. Then again, you might not. A lot depends on your network clients' requirements. Because you are a busy network administrator (aren't we all?) and your job is to serve your network clients as best you can, it follows that their needs will determine your goals. You might be thinking that if your network clients are happy, then why should you make any changes. After all, the number one rule of a network administrator is don't fix what isn't broken, right? This type of philosophy is a defensive one, however, and it means that you are always playing catch-up while you try to put out the immediate fires. I prefer to choose a proactive methodology and to solve potential problems before they become noticeable to my network clients. This has proven to be a good methodology because it provides a basis for a smooth-running network, and it is really nice to be able to tell your colleagues at your weekly meetings that everything is under control and working fine.

Of course, you cannot do this properly unless you also understand the limitations imposed upon you by your choice of a hardware platform and server configuration. You also need to understand the limitations of SNA Server and, in particular, how you can tell when SNA Server is bogging down and what you can do to improve the situation. This chapter examines these topics. It starts with a look at how you can optimize your server platform within these limitations, and then moves on to how you can optimize SNA Server performance. The key to this entire discussion is the choices you make, the choices you have already made, or the choices that have already been made for you concerning your SNA Server implementation.

EXAMINING SERVER OPTIMIZATION

When you build a house to live in, the first item on the agenda is to build a solid foundation. This foundation then supports the framework that carries the load for your house. If the foundation is poorly built, then the framework that supports the house may collapse. This leaves you sleeping in the rain, if you are lucky enough to survive the collapse. When you look at the BackOffice components, you can think of Windows NT Server as the foundation and various operating modes as rooms within the house. You can consider the individual BackOffice components—which include Mail/Exchange, SQL Server, Systems Management Server, and SNA Server—as the furnishings within the rooms. Each piece of furniture places a load on the room's floor, which in turn places a load on the framework and foundation of the house. It takes careful planning to make sure the framework or foundation is not overloaded. So, in keeping with this architectural analogy, the first concern in getting SNA Server to perform well is to choose a foundation or, in your case, to pick a server platform. After you decide this, it is time to build your rooms by choosing the right server model to implement.

Choosing the Right Server Platform

As much as I would like to give you a single recommendation for the foundation to build your house on, in all honesty, I can't do this. Not because I don't want to, but because the technology changes too rapidly. The platform that is fastest today might not be the fastest tomorrow. If you are looking for the fastest possible computer to use for SNA Server, I suggest that you rely on your vendor to show you proof of the platform's performance, and then shop around a bit more to see whether the vendor's claims are legitimate. Your choice for a platform that will support SNA Server today falls into two camps. There is the Intel and compatible group, and then there is the RISC group, which includes the MIPS, PowerPC, and Alpha processors.

There are really only two problems with the RISC choice, but if you can overcome them, then these platforms can serve you well. The first problem is device drivers. Without the proper device driver, your peripherals will not work with Windows NT or SNA Server. This is likely to be a short-term problem because device drivers are being ported to these platforms. The more serious problem is your choice of peripherals to support SNA Server. If you are planning to use an SDLC or X.25/QLLC adapter, you probably will not have much of a problem. On the other hand, if you are looking to use a DFT, TwinAx, or Channel adapter, you probably will find that a device driver is lacking or that your hardware platform cannot support it. Most DFT adapters require interrupt 2 in order to function properly, for example, and the current RISC platforms do not support peripherals that require this interrupt.

These problems do not occur on the Intel processor platforms, which is one reason why I tend to lean toward their recommendation. I do suggest that you be careful, though, in choosing a compatible Pentium processor from AMD or Cyrix—not because these processors do not perform their function, but because Windows NT was not specifically designed for them. In most cases, these compatible processors work fine for Windows 3.x, OS/2, or UNIX, but I have seen a few quirks with Windows 95 and would not be surprised to see them with Windows NT as well.

Note

The new Pentium Pro recently introduced by Intel is a very fast processor. For 32-bit code, it performs as well as or exceeds many of the RISC platforms. And because the BackOffice components are 32-bit code, it should make a good high-end server platform for NT and SNA Server.

Regardless of your processor choice for your server platform, you should consider a few tips to improve performance:

◆ Choose a multiprocessing platform or one that can be expanded to support multiple processors. SNA Server, like most of the rest of the BackOffice components, is very processor intensive. An additional CPU can offer performance benefits.

◆ Choose the fastest possible I/O expansion bus. The PCI bus is one of the best out there, and it makes a good backbone for your disk subsystem, video subsystem, and network subsystem. But these three choices often fill up the available PCI bus slots, leaving you with ISA slots for the rest of your peripherals. You can do better by choosing EISA as your secondary bus. This gives you compatibility with existing ISA components, yet enables you to use 32-bit bus mastering peripherals as well.

◆ Choose the fastest possible network adapter. There are two reasons to use the fastest network adapter possible on your server. First, SNA Server uses a Windows NT Server domain controller to authenticate users prior to giving them access to an SNA Server session. Second, SNA-to-SNA (or APPN/APPC) connections can be improved. Both of these can generate a lot of traffic on the network, so if all your servers are on a high-speed backbone, they can take advantage of this to improve the authentication and SNA Server performance.

◆ Choose a fast disk subsystem. If you designate your server just for SNA Server and supply enough physical RAM to prevent paging, then your disk subsystem is not as critical. If you do not have sufficient RAM to prevent paging, however, or you use your server for other needs besides SNA Server, then a fast disk subsystem becomes critical. A fast wide SCSI subsystem is a good choice and is preferred over EIDE/IDE subsystems.

◆ Don't skimp on system memory. Nothing is more critical to your performance than physical memory. You should have at least 32MB, and if you can, use 64MB or more of RAM. The exact amount you need varies based on the load you place on SNA Server. To learn more about this, you should refer to Chapter 13, "Tuning Your Server," in the section "Finding Memory Bottlenecks" to help you find exactly how much RAM you need.

Tip

Chapter 12, "Getting the Most from Your Microsoft Network," includes more specific information on choosing a platform for Windows NT Server. This chapter describes the various server platforms, I/O expansion bus, disk subsystems, software configuration, and various hardware options.

CHOOSING THE RIGHT SERVER MODEL

When you install SNA Server, you can use a primary domain controller, a backup domain controller, or a server as the base platform. Each of these has performance trade-offs, as summarized in Table 33.1, that you should consider before you install SNA Server. In any case, if you limit your server for use only by SNA Server, rather than using it for more than one BackOffice component, you will achieve better overall performance.

TABLE 33.1. SERVER MODEL PERFORMANCE TRADE-OFFS.

Windows NT Server Model	Pro	Con
Primary domain controller	Useful for organizations with a limited number of servers. Increases SNA Server authentication performance, thereby lowering network traffic slightly.	Decreases general performance of the server, impacts user/group replication, lowers its capability to authenticate users, and decreases overall SNA Server performance.
Backup domain controller	Provides increased SNA Server user authentication performance. Lowers network authentication traffic. Best used for periodic connections.	Decreases general performance of the server, lowers its capability to authenticate users, and decreases overall SNA Server performance.
Server	Provides the most processor time for SNA Server and can increase performance. Best used for consistent SNA Server connections.	Requires a primary or backup domain controller to authenticate SNA Server users, which increases network traffic.

As you can see from Table 33.1, the best platform for SNA Server is Windows NT Server operating in server mode, dedicated specifically to SNA Server. This mode does not perform any network authentication or maintain an account database, so it is a superior base platform because it can provide more processor time to SNA Server. Because it does not include a user database, however, all user authentication must be performed by a primary or backup domain controller. This increases the network traffic for each SNA Server session. This is not a problem if all your servers are on a high-speed network backbone and if your primary or backup domain controllers can handle the increased authentication load. For these reasons, this platform serves best for long-term SNA Server sessions.

For short-term sessions, in which a user logs on and off rapidly from SNA Server and his mainframe connection, the best platform is a backup domain controller dedicated to SNA Server. This decreases the user wait time to be authenticated for the SNA Server session and decreases the network traffic for user authentication. Due to the increased load SNA Server places on the backup domain controller, however, its capability to authenticate other network users may be diminished. This may increase the wait time for your network clients to be authenticated, and therefore require you to add an additional backup domain controller to compensate.

The worst possible choice is to use your primary domain controller as your SNA Server platform. A primary domain controller is the heart of your network. It is responsible for maintaining your entire user account database. Any account administration occurs on this copy of the database. Any changes must be replicated from the primary domain controller to your backup domain controllers. Any increased processor load, such as by SNA Server or other BackOffice components, impacts your entire network—and, generally, not for the better. There are really only three reasons why I would recommend this. First, if you have no other choice. Second, if you are building a development platform for testing custom code. And finally, if you have a network with fewer than 50 users, it offers acceptable performance.

CONFIGURING YOUR SERVER AS A BASE PLATFORM FOR SNA SERVER

The final step in configuring your base platform is to tune the basic network configuration and to set your process priorities. These steps should be completed before using Performance Monitor to tweak the best possible performance, as described in Chapter 13. The first step in this process is to choose a network model to increase SNA Server's network throughput. This is accomplished by configuring the Server service in the Network Control Panel applet.

You can follow these steps:

1. Open the Control Panel Network applet. The Network Settings dialog box appears.

2. In the Installed Network Software field, double-click on the Server entry. Or, highlight the server entry and click the Configure button to display the Server dialog box.

3. Select the Maximize Throughput for Network Applications radio button. This allocates additional nonpageable memory for use as network buffers and increases the performance of your client/server application.

4. Click the OK button. Then click the OK button in the Network Settings dialog box. Do not restart your computer as prompted at this time.

After you configure the network to increase the throughput of your client/server applications, it is time to set your process priorities. This can be accomplished by following these steps:

1. Open the Control Panel System applet. The System dialog box appears.

2. Click the Tasking button to display the Tasking dialog box.

3. Select the Foreground and Background Applications Equally Responsive radio button. This provides equal processor time to all processes in the system.

Tip

By setting all processes to be equally responsive, you increase the performance of all background processes at the expense of foreground applications. This can make the computer difficult to use for centralized administration. If you will be using this computer for additional tasks, select the Foreground Application More Responsive Than Background option. This still increases the performance of your background applications, of which SNA Server is one, and increases the performance of your foreground application to a point where it is usable.

4. Click the OK button, and then click the OK button in the System dialog box. Restart your computer as prompted in order for the changes to be put into effect.

Tuning SNA Server

Tuning SNA Server for maximum performance with the Performance Monitor is not an easy task. Before you even begin this process, optimize your base platform as described in Chapter 13. Then you can work at tuning for optimum SNA Server performance. Keep in mind, though, that performance tuning is always going to uncover another bottleneck when you solve one bottleneck. If you add another processor to increase processor performance, for example, then most likely, you will find that the disk subsystem becomes a bottleneck. In the next section, you will look at the SNA Server performance object counter, which you can use to determine the load on your server in an effort to tweak the maximum possible performance.

You should keep some additional concerns in mind:

◆ Processor activity: Windows NT Server requires more processor power than other network file servers. And each additional service you add to this base increases the load on the processor. You should monitor your processor activity to make sure that it stays below 80 percent usage. Slight peaks of 100 percent are okay; however, a constant usage of 80 percent or higher is an indication that more processing power is required for optimum performance.

◆ Memory activity: If you are paging to disk at all, then you do not have sufficient memory for maximum performance. This is not a problem unless you are attempting to get the best possible performance from SNA Server. If you do want the best, however, then you should never even see the disk light in an active state. With sufficient physical memory, SNA Server and any required supporting services and buffers can be completely resident in system memory.

Note

Keep in mind that each process, or thread, requires additional system resources. Each SNA Server connection requires additional resources as well. So as additional connections come online, additional resources are required to maintain the same level of performance. If you are paging to disk, then you are wasting processor cycles that could be used to service your client requests. If maximum throughput is your goal, then no other single component can increase your performance as much as adding sufficient memory to keep all your processes resident in physical memory.

◆ Disk activity: If you do not have sufficient physical RAM, then your disk subsystem becomes a bottleneck as your server pages to/from your paging file. A slow disk subsystem can drag your system to its knees.

◆ Network activity: Considering that all of your SNA Server clients pass data through one network card, and then SNA Server passes this data through your SNA network adapter card, you can understand that your network adapter's capability to pass data is going to impact your SNA Server performance. You should monitor your network activity to see how much of your bandwidth is in use and prepare to split your network into additional segments if required. You will look into this subject a bit more in the following section.

Tip

In order to properly maintain your SNA Server installations you'll also need to be kept in the loop regarding modifications to the network topology. What I mean here is that if your mainframe administrators plan to make any changes, they should notify you first. You should also be informed of any software additions—such as those planned by your SNA application development group—or any modifications planned for your SNA clients—such as a new version of their connectivity software.

LOAD BALANCING SNA SERVER

Load balancing is a means of splitting the load on a particular service or peripheral. This section focuses primarily on network activity. This includes both your network adapters and your SNA adapters. Both of these impact your ability to service your SNA Server clients. The things to look out for follow:

◆ Network bandwidth: If your network is using 50 percent of your network bandwidth on an Ethernet network, you should consider splitting the network into multiple segments. If you do not split the segment, you most likely will encounter additional network collisions. This increases the error rate and decreases network throughput.

Tip

If you are using TCP/IP as your primary network protocol and reach 50 percent network bandwidth utilization, then you can use two network adapters on your server, with each adapter having a different TCP/IP address, and split the single segment into two separate segments. You can even use Windows NT's capability to internally route the two physical segments to create a single logical segment.

◆ SNA bandwidth: Your capacity to transfer data to and from your SNA-compatible mainframe is limited by the bandwidth of your SNA Server adapter and the performance capabilities of your SNA-compatible mainframe. When your adapter is the limiting factor, you can add adapters to increase the data-carrying capacity. If your SNA-compatible mainframe is a bottleneck, then adding additional adapters will not help. Your only choice in this matter is to add additional mainframe capacity through additional hardware on your mainframe.

◆ Network protocols: Although you can bind all your network protocols to a single network adapter, you will realize increased performance by using a single adapter per protocol.

USING THE SNA SERVER PERFORMANCE MONITOR COUNTERS

As with most products that you add to Windows NT Server, SNA Server also includes performance object counters you can use to determine its activity. Table 33.2 summarizes the available object counters you can use to monitor the activity of your SNA Server installation. You must realize that performance is relative to your hardware platform, however. To determine your capacity, you should start by monitoring your system in an idle state to gain a feel for its base capacity. Then, as time goes by, and you add users to your system, you can determine SNA Server's capability to handle the additional load.

TABLE 33.2. SNA SERVER PERFORMANCE MONITOR OBJECT TYPES AND OBJECT COUNTERS.

Performance Object	Object Counters	Description
SNA Adapter SnaAdapterName	Adapter Failures	Number of times since startup that a network adapter has encountered an error condition.
SNA Adapter SnaAdapterName	Connection Failures	Number of times since startup that a connection has encountered an error condition.
SNA Adapter SnaAdapterName	Data Bytes Received/Sec	Number of data bytes received per second.
SNA Adapter SnaAdapterName	Data Bytes Transmitted/Sec	Number of data bytes transmitted per second.

33

Performance Object	Object Counters	Description
SNA Adapter SnaAdapterName	Frames Received/Sec	Number of data frames received per second. A frame is an information structure recognized by one of the various protocols related to SNA. Frames contain multiple bytes of data.
SNA Adapter SnaAdapterName	Frames Transmitted/Sec	Number of data frames transmitted per second.
SNA Adapter SnaAdapterName	Successful Connects	Number of times since startup that a successful connection has been made.
SNA Adapter SnaAdapterName	Throughput Bytes/ Sec	Total number of bytes flowing through the SNA Server per second. This includes both incoming and outgoing bytes, and is a good indicator of how heavily your SNA Server is loaded.
SNA Adapter SnaAdapterName	Throughput Frames/Sec	Total number of data frames flowing through the SNA Server per second. This includes both incoming and outgoing frames, and is a good indicator of how heavily your SNA Server is loaded.
SNA Logical Unit Sessions	Data Bytes Received/Sec	Number of data bytes received per second.
SNA Logical Unit Sessions	Data Bytes Transmitted/Sec	Number of data bytes transmitted per second.

continues

TABLE 33.2. CONTINUED

Performance Object	Object Counters	Description
SNA Logical Unit Sessions	Throughput Bytes/Sec	Total number of bytes flowing through the SNA Server per second. This includes both incoming and outgoing bytes, and is a good indicator of how heavily your SNA Server is loaded.

Note

SnaAdapterName is used as a generic name to replace the specific SNA Server adapter. If you have installed an SNA Server SDLC adapter, for example, then the name you see in the Performance Monitor object type is SnaSdlc1.

Tip

Instead of being concerned with byte-oriented counters when looking to optimize performance for your SNA Server clients, use the frame-oriented counters. Most SNA Server traffic is frame-based, rather than byte-based, and these counters give you a more realistic performance curve to use.

SUMMARY

This chapter's primary concern was to help you optimize SNA Server's performance. First, you need to choose the right platform to build the foundation for your SNA Server installation. The best overall choice you can make for maximum performance and compatibility with existing SNA adapters is to choose a multiprocessor-capable platform with an Intel processor (preferably a Pentium or Pentium Pro). Then choose the right server mode. If your domain controllers can handle the additional authentication requirements, then you should install SNA Server on a Windows NT Server platform operating in server mode. Otherwise, use a backup domain controller dedicated to SNA Server.

After you pick the best possible platform, you can turn your eye toward configuring the software. Configure your server to optimize your network throughput and set your process priorities so that your foreground and background processes receive equal processor time.

When considering hardware upgrades, adding physical RAM is the best solution to increasing overall system-related performance. Then consider using multiple network adapters to increase your network capacity and using multiple SNA adapters to increase your SNA data-carrying capacity.

When looking to use Performance Monitor to fine-tune your SNA Server installation, rely on the frame-based performance object counters for the most realistic view of SNA Server performance.

In the next chapter, you will look at issues specific to your Windows NT clients. This includes troubleshooting network adapter configuration and authentication problems, supporting SQL Server client access, installing and configuring the ODBC utilities, troubleshooting SQL connection problems, and installing the Microsoft Mail client.

- Windows NT Clients

- Windows 95 Clients

- Windows for
  Workgroups 3.11,
  Windows 3.x, and
  MS-DOS Clients

- Macintosh and UNIX
  Clients

P A R T VII

Client Connectivity

- Solving Basic
  Network-Related
  Problems

- Supporting SQL
  Server Access

- Installing the
  Microsoft Mail Client

CHAPTER 34

Windows NT Clients

Supporting your Windows NT Server or Windows NT Workstation clients on your network is generally an easy task because the basic Windows NT platform is more stable than your MS-DOS, Windows, Windows for Workgroups, and Windows 95 platforms. You can experience some basic network problems or basic connectivity problems with some of the Microsoft BackOffice client utilities, however. That is what this chapter is about: how to find and solve these problems.

This discussion starts with basic network-related problems. This generally amounts to authentication problems and resource access problems. Next, you'll learn about the problems caused by the configuration of your client components. A good part of this is related to installation, so this chapter covers the installation of the various SQL Server client utilities and those you can use for troubleshooting client connections to SQL Server. You'll also learn about the installation of the Microsoft Mail client.

SOLVING BASIC NETWORK-RELATED PROBLEMS

Many of the problems you will encounter with your Windows NT clients are network related. Most of them are caused by a failing network adapter, an improperly configured network adapter, or a network transport-related problem. After you have a working network adapter, you can have other problems that fall into two groups: basic authentication problems, in which the domain controller cannot be found to grant your user access to the network; or basic connectivity problems, in which your users cannot access a particular shared resource. In the following sections, I share the techniques I have garnered over time for finding and solving these problems.

BASIC NETWORK TROUBLESHOOTING

The first indication that you have a network-related problem is a message that cannot be authenticated, so Windows NT used cached information to authenticate you and log you on to the system. I'll be the first one to agree that using cached information is a good thing, simply because you must be authenticated in order to log on to a Windows NT computer. If you cannot be authenticated by the system and cannot use a prior authentication, you can't log on to the system to solve the problem.

Note

The capability to use cached information is possible only if you have logged on successfully at least once before the failure occurs.

On a Windows NT Server domain controller, a failure to be authenticated is a serious problem. If it occurs during the initial logon after the system is installed, you are unable to log on to correct the problem. This is one reason why I suggest that you always install the MS Loopback adapter when you install Windows NT Server. This way, you always will be able to log on to the system, even if your network adapter completely fails.

On a Windows NT Workstation or a Windows NT Server operating in server mode, you always can log on using the local (Workgroup) account database. Just change the From entry in the Logon dialog box from your domain name to your computer name. Then you can use the Administrator account you created when you installed Windows NT Workstation—at least you can if you remember the administrator password.

If you can't remember the password and you have no cached authentication information to use, your only recourse is to solve the problem in a blind fashion. You can replace the network card. Try the repair process. Copy the system event log to a disk (if the file system is a FAT partition) and read it on another NT computer to find the cause of the failure. Or you can delete and reinstall the Windows NT Server or Windows NT Workstation.

USING THE EVENTLOG VIEWER TO TROUBLESHOOT YOUR NETWORK PROBLEMS

Assuming that you can log on to the system, what can you do to find the problem? Well, your first step should be to look at the system event log. The first thing you should know about the system event log is that you should ignore the errors you see at the top of the log. Most of these error messages are cascade error messages—the original error caused all the other failure messages to occur. Look at Figure 34.1, for example. This is a copy of my event log on my portable computer (a WinBook XP) without an attached network adapter (a Xircom PE3 parallel port adapter).

In Figure 34.1, all the messages between the top of the log (aside from the Service Control Manager message) and the highlighted entry are caused by the Xircom adapter. The first message is

```
Xcspe31 : The Xircom Pocket Ethernet II adapter was not found connected to
the configured parallel port.
```

The last error message is

```
The server could not bind to the transport \Device\Nbf_Xcspe31.
```

Between these messages, you will find several error messages relating to transports not being able to bind to the adapter, logon authentication error messages, and general server error messages. These messages vary, based on your particular configuration and the type of network error. But the place to start to determine the cause is at the beginning. This is right before the highlighted EventLog entry in Figure 34.1. Start at this point and work your way back to determine the root cause. Generally, the first error message you find will be the problem you have to solve. In most cases, this will be a network adapter failure; this leads to the next topic: how to find problems and what to do to solve them.

Figure 34.1.
A sample network
adapter cascade
failure.

Date	Time	Source	Category	Event	User	Computer
8/16/95	11:23:29 PM	Service Control Mar	None	7026	N/A	WINBOO
8/16/95	11:23:21 PM	Server	None	2504	N/A	WINBOO
8/16/95	11:23:18 PM	Srv	None	2012	N/A	WINBOO
8/16/95	11:23:17 PM	Srv	None	2012	N/A	WINBOO
8/16/95	11:23:17 PM	Srv	None	2012	N/A	WINBOO
8/16/95	11:23:16 PM	Srv	None	2012	N/A	WINBOO
8/16/95	11:23:16 PM	Srv	None	2012	N/A	WINBOO
8/16/95	11:23:09 PM	NETLOGON	None	5719	N/A	WINBOO
8/16/95	11:22:51 PM	Nwlnklpx	None	9005	N/A	WINBOO
8/16/95	11:22:51 PM	Nwlnklpx	None	9006	N/A	WINBOO
8/16/95	11:22:51 PM	Nbf	None	9005	N/A	WINBOO
8/16/95	11:22:51 PM	Nbf	None	9006	N/A	WINBOO
8/16/95	11:22:49 PM	Service Control Mar	None	7000	N/A	WINBOO
8/16/95	11:22:49 PM	Xcspe3	None	3	N/A	WINBOO
8/16/95	11:22:47 PM	EventLog	None	6005	N/A	WINBOO
8/14/95	11:00:24 PM	Rdr	None	3012	N/A	WINBOO
8/14/95	10:57:52 PM	Xcspe3	None	15	N/A	WINBOO
8/14/95	10:57:50 PM	EventLog	None	6005	N/A	WINBOO
8/14/95	6:43:25 AM	Rdr	None	3012	N/A	WINBOO
8/14/95	6:24:09 AM	Xcspe3	None	15	N/A	WINBOO
8/14/95	6:24:07 AM	EventLog	None	6005	N/A	WINBOO
8/14/95	6:21:23 AM	Rdr	None	3013	N/A	WINBOO
8/14/95	6:15:16 AM	Xcspe3	None	15	N/A	WINBOO
8/14/95	6:15:14 AM	EventLog	None	6005	N/A	WINBOO
8/14/95	6:13:06 AM	BROWSER	None	8033	N/A	WINBOO
8/14/95	6:13:06 AM	BROWSER	None	8033	N/A	WINBOO

FINDING AND SOLVING NETWORK ADAPTER PROBLEMS

Network adapter failures generally are caused by a physically related problem or a resource conflict. This discussion is concerned with resource conflicts, but you shouldn't overlook obvious physical problems. You might be surprised by how many connectivity problems are caused by the network user plugging the 10BASE-T network cable into the phone jack rather than the data jack, for example. Sometimes these same users use a phone cable to connect their network adapter to the data jack. And, as you probably know, a phone cable cannot support the required bandwidth required for data transmission. These cables may look similar to the uninitiated but shouldn't to a network troubleshooter.

Tip

While you are considering cable-related problems, don't overlook termination-related items for a thin Ethernet-based network adapter, or even mixing the input and output cables for a fiber-optic (FDDI)-based network adapter.

Another item to consider is whether your network cabling closet also includes your phone lines, and you just had the phone company service this closet. This is a good indication that the network client connectivity problem is related to this phone company service call and that you should start with a look at the cabling connections. Perhaps the user's network connection has been disconnected accidentally. If an entire group of users suddenly has a problem after a service call, most likely your concentrator or router was disconnected or disabled. Although these are fairly obvious items to consider, I mention them because sometimes the obvious solutions often are overlooked in the haste to solve the problem. Sometimes it can be difficult when you have your supervisor looking over your shoulder and watching your every move.

After you consider the obvious cable-related problems, it's time to look at some of the network adapter resource conflicts that can occur. When considering your resource conflict, the first thing you should ask the user is what has changed on his system since it last worked. Did he add a sound card? A new modem? Or other hardware? Or perhaps he changed some BIOS setting to try to tweak out the last bit of performance on his system. Be sure to ask the user, but do it gently. Many users are afraid to admit their errors. When you ask, be sure to inform them that you are not looking to assign blame, just to solve the problem. Also assure them that you can keep any information just between the two of you. This can get the user to open up, which can provide you with the clues you need to get him up and running in a minimum amount of time.

If you can't find any clues, the first item to consider is a resource allocation problem. Determining this can be easy or difficult, depending on your network adapters. If you have a software-configurable network adapter, just run the configuration utility to determine the resources required by the adapter. If you do not have a software-configurable adapter and no utility you can use to determine the resource requirements, then you must open up the case to examine the adapter configuration. Before you get drastic and open up the case, however, it's a good idea to try to use the network configuration utility to perform a network adapter test. If that is not possible, you can use a network client installation disk, which you can create with the Network Client Administrator application. You can use this disk to connect to the network and then, if it succeeds, the network adapter is functioning properly. If it doesn't succeed, the network adapter is malfunctioning, or you may have a resource conflict.

Resource conflicts generally fall into four categories: an interrupt conflict, an I/O (input/output) port conflict, a DMA (direct memory access) conflict, or a memory conflict. For each of these problems, there are a few things you can do to try to isolate the conflict.

Interrupt conflicts are the most common problem, but they are also the easiest to solve. This is particularly true because there are only 16 interrupts, although not all of these are available. Table 34.1 lists the available interrupts and their uses. If your network adapter is using one of the reserved interrupts or one that is rarely available, there is a good chance that you have found your problem. If not, then you may have an I/O conflict.

TABLE 34.1. HARDWARE INTERRUPTS ON INTEL PLATFORMS.

Interrupt	Availability	Description
0	No	System timer.
1	No	Keyboard.
2	No	Programmable Interrupt Controller cascade.
3	Rarely	Used by COM2/COM4 or as the default for some network adapters, such as those from 3Com.
4	Rarely	Used by COM1/COM3 and almost every system that has at least a single serial port. If you do not have any serial ports, this interrupt should be available.
5	Yes	Often available, but some sound cards or 8-bit SCSI cards require this interrupt. The 8-bit Future Domain or Trantor SCSI adapters, for example, use this as the default setting.
6	No	Floppy controller support.
7	Rarely	Used by LPT1 and, once again, it is rare for a system not to have at least one parallel port. If the port is not in use, however, it can be disabled so that this interrupt is free to be used by other devices.
8	No	Used by the system clock.

Interrupt	Availability	Description
9	Yes	Often available. If you have a device configured to use IRQ 2, however, it will be reflected (cascaded) to this IRQ, making IRQ 9 unavailable.
10	Yes	Often available. This is my favorite IRQ for use by network adapters.
11	Yes	Often available. It also is the default for most 16- and 32-bit SCSI adapters, however.
12	Yes	Often available unless the system has a PS/2 mouse port built into the motherboard.
13	No	Used by the math coprocessor or software emulation.
14	Rarely	If the system has an ST-506–compatible disk controller (MFM, RLL, IDE, EIDE, or ESDI), this interrupt is used. If the system is SCSI-based, however, this IRQ often is available.
15	Yes	Often available for use because there is no industry-wide usage of this IRQ for default adapter settings. If you have an EIDE controller that supports four EIDE disk drives, then it may use this interrupt, however.

34

WINDOWS NT CLIENTS

I/O conflicts are more difficult to diagnose, but if your Windows NT computer still is working, you can try to use WinMSD.EXE (Windows NT Diagnostics, located in the Administrators Tools Program Manager group) to help you solve your problem. Run the application and click the IRQ/Port Status button. The Interrupts/Ports dialog box appears, as shown in Figure 34.2. This dialog box can be useful in isolating interrupt conflicts as well; however, not every interrupt or I/O port used by the system is listed. Those that are in use by installable device drivers are listed, though. This is where you should start your comparison. Table 34.2 provides a summary of commonly used I/O ports where you should be able to isolate a potential conflict. Table 34.2 should help you isolate the problem. Just keep in mind that most manufacturer I/O port summaries include only a starting I/O address; they rarely include the complete I/O range. So it is possible to have an I/O overlap, where one I/O port range starts inside an existing I/O range.

Figure 34.2.
The Windows NT
Diagnostics
Interrupts/Ports
dialog box.

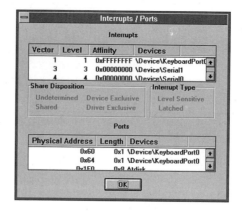

TABLE 34.2. INPUT/OUTPUT PORTS ON INTEL PLATFORMS.

I/O Port	Availability	Description
0000h—000Fh	No	Direct Memory Access (DMA) controller
0020h—0021h	No	Programmable interrupt controller
0040h—0043h	No	System timer
0060h—0060h	No	Keyboard
0061h—0061h	No	System speaker
0064h—0064h	No	Keyboard
0070h—0071h	No	System CMOS/real-time clock
0081h—0083h	No	Direct Memory Access (DMA) controller
0087h—0087h	No	Direct Memory Access (DMA) controller
0089h—008Bh	No	Direct Memory Access (DMA) controller
008Fh—008Fh	No	Direct Memory Access (DMA) controller
00A0h—00A1h	No	Programmable interrupt controller
00C0h—00DFh	No	Direct Memory Access (DMA) controller
00F0h—00FFh	No	Math coprocessor
0170h—0177h	No	Used by ST-506 and compatible hard disk controllers
01F0h—01F7h	Rarely	Used by ST-506 and compatible hard disk controllers
0201h—0201h	Rarely	Gameport joystick port
0220h—022Fh	Rarely	SoundBlaster and compatible sound card
02E8h—02EFh	Rarely	Communications port (COM4)

I/O Port	Availability	Description
02F8h—02FFh	Rarely	Communications port (COM2)
0300h—030Fh	Rarely	Commonly used by network adapters
0330h—033Fh	Rarely	Adaptec SCSI controller or SoundBlaster Pro MIDI Interface
0376h—0376h	Rarely	Used by ST-506 and compatible hard disk controllers
0378h—037Ah	No	Printer port (LPT1)
0388h—038Bh	Rarely	Adlib (including SoundBlaster) and compatible MIDI cards
03B0h—03BBh	No	Video controller
03C0h—03DFh	No	Video controller
03E0h—03E1h	Often	Unless you have a PCMCIA controller such as in a portable computer
03F2h—03F5h	No	Standard floppy disk controller
03F6h—03F6h	Rarely	Used by ST-506 and compatible hard disk controllers
03E8h—03EFh	Rarely	Communications port (COM3)
03F8h—03FFh	Rarely	Communications port (COM1)

Tip

If you have a Plug-and-Play BIOS, such as those commonly used in computers on a PCI expansion bus, take a look at the BIOS settings. Some PCI components can have their interrupt assigned by the BIOS. This can override the Plug-and-Play capability to dynamically assign an interrupt. It also can cause problems with Windows NT's capability to detect or change an interrupt assignment for a network adapter.

This same principle of isolating a resource conflict can be applied to direct memory access (DMA) channel-related problems and memory buffer conflicts. Tables 34.3 and 34.4 list some of the more common DMA channel assignments and memory address assignments. Pay particular attention to the DMA assignments. I've seen several problems associated with network adapters, sound cards, and SCSI adapters. It is a terrible thing to watch a hard disk get scrambled when your sound card plays a .WAV file or you access the network.

TABLE 34.3. DIRECT MEMORY ACCESS CHANNELS ON INTEL PLATFORMS.

DMA Channel	Availability	Description
0	Rarely	Often used for memory refresh, although if you have a computer that uses a hidden refresh option, this channel generally is available.
1	Yes	Often used by sound cards, but otherwise available.
2	No	Used by the floppy controller.
3	Yes	Often used by sound cards or other 8-bit adapters.
4	No	Cascade DMA channel.
5	Yes	Often available; this is also the default, however, for most 16- and 32-bit SCSI adapters.
6	Yes	No standard usage.
7	Yes	Often available, but sometimes used by 16- and 32-bit sound cards.

TABLE 34.4. MEMORY ADDRESS USAGE ON INTEL PLATFORMS.

Memory Address	Availability	Description
A000h—AFFFh	No	VGA video frame buffer default.
B000h—B7FFh	No	Monochrome video frame buffer default.
B800h—BFFFh	Often	Used by some high-color video cards in resolutions greater than 800×600.
C000h—C7FFh	No	Video ROM default.
C800h—CFFFh	Yes	No standard usage.
D000h—DFFFh	Yes	No standard usage.
E000h—E000h	Often	This area generally is available except on a PS/2 or other computers with an extended BIOS; if you have a Plug-and-Play (PnP) or extended 128KB BIOS, this area is unavailable.
F000h—FFFFh	No	System ROM default.

Tip

When looking for a problem associated with a memory buffer, be sure to start with the BIOS settings. The BIOS can be used to shadow (copy from RAM to ROM) a memory location. And if it just so happens that this address range is shadowed, then the network adapter will be unable to use it. I've seen similar problems caused by shadowing a SCSI or network adapter's ROM as well.

There is one other item not directly related to the items mentioned so far that still can cause network adapter failure: the speed of your expansion bus. The ISA standard defines the bus speed as a maximum of 8MHz, but many users push this speed to 10MHz, 12MHz, or even higher. This can cause some peripherals to fail or to operate in an unpredictable manner. And although this configuration may work under MS-DOS, Windows, Windows for Workgroups, or Windows 95, it may not work under Windows NT. When you are looking for problems, don't assume that, because the configuration works under another operating system, it also works under Windows NT. I've never seen another operating system that places as much of a strain on the hardware as Windows NT. Comparisons of Windows NT and other operating systems just are not valid, and you should not make the assumption that they are valid during your troubleshooting.

TROUBLESHOOTING AUTHENTICATION PROBLEMS

Authentication problems fall into two basic groups. You can have a failure to be authenticated by the domain controller during a logon sequence, or an authentication failure while attempting to access a shared resource on the domain. You also can have a protocol-related failure, but that is a little outside the scope of this chapter.

Authentication failures not caused by a failed network adapter often are caused by one of the following reasons:

◆ No computer account: If you have a Windows NT client that is a member of the domain but you have no computer account on the domain controller, you have no trusted connection between your Windows NT client and the domain controller. This means that you cannot be authenticated (or logged on) by the domain controller. A similar problem can occur if your Windows NT client changes from a domain to a workgroup and then attempts to join the domain again. Even though a computer account still exists on the domain controller, it cannot be reused. Instead, a new computer account must be created, although it can have the same name. This is because computer accounts are like user or group accounts in that they have an assigned security identifier (SID). This SID is stored in the computer

34

WINDOWS NT CLIENTS

account on the domain controller and in the Registry of the Windows NT client. If a user moves from a domain to a workgroup or from one domain to another domain, however, the SID is reassigned based on the new configuration.

◆ No user account: This is an obvious problem, but it sometimes is overlooked. Generally, this problem is caused by the lack of a user account on the domain controller or because the user misspelled the user account name or the password. You can find similar problems if the user account has the Password Must Be Changed at Next Logon option enabled or if the account has been locked out due to repeated attempts to log on to the system with an invalid password.

◆ A trust relationship: If your Windows NT client is a member of a workgroup, be sure that you do not have any two-way trust relationships established on the domain to which your client needs access. In this situation, your Windows NT client will not be able to establish a trusted connection to the domain, even though the user has a valid user account. It is quite similar to the No Computer Account situation mentioned earlier. On a domain with no trust relationships or a one-way trust relationship (from the domain, the user needs access to a higher domain used for administrative purposes), a workgroup computer can access the domain resources by mapping the local user account to a user account on the domain. When two-way trust relationships are involved, however, this user account mapping does not take place.

Authentication problems related to accessing shared resources generally are caused by a permission-related problem. If a user needs to access a shared directory but receives an Access denied message, for example, it is definitely a permission-related problem. The same problem can occur for printer access or named pipe access. To solve these kinds of problems, you should check the client permissions in the following order:

◆ Group membership: Check to make sure that the user account is a member of the group you used to assign permissions to access the shared resource.

◆ Share permissions: Check the shared resource to be sure that the group has the appropriate permission to access the sharepoint. You also should make sure that the user is not a member of any group that has the No Access permission assigned. If a user is a member of a group that has the No Access permission assigned, then this group assignment overrides any other group share level permission for the user.

Suppose that you have a printer called HP_Laser. The user is assigned to the group LaserPrinter, which has print permission assigned to it for the printer. The user also is a member of the ColorPrinter group, which has the No Access permission assigned for the printer, however. The user therefore will be unable to print to the HP_Laser print queue.

◆ Directory and file permissions: If the sharepoint can be accessed but the user cannot access directories and files, this is an indication that the user account is not a member of the appropriate group. Or, this might indicate that the user is a member of a group that has the No Access permission assigned.

◆ Cached account information: Did you know that Windows NT also caches group account information when accessing a shared resource? If you find that a logged-on user is not a member of a group with the appropriate permissions to access the shared resource, and then you add this user to the group, the user still will be unable to access the shared resource. What do you do? Just have the user log off and then log back on again. This flushes the cached information, and when the user attempts to access the resource this time, access should be granted to the resource.

Tip

In some cases, the solution is a bit more drastic and instead of just logging off and then back on again, you might have to shut down and restart the computer to flush an internal cache.

Supporting SQL Server Access

Providing your Windows NT clients access to SQL Server for Windows NT requires that you install the appropriate client drivers. Some of these drivers may be installed automatically by your application but, in some cases, these are older drivers that need to be updated to work properly under Windows NT. Then there is the issue of supporting your Windows on Windows (WOW) applications as well as your Windows NT applications. Both these applications have specific utilities and drivers and, although you should be able to support your 16-bit applications executing on the WOW layer under Windows NT, you might experience problems with some applications. If you experience such a problem, install the 16-bit drivers as well; in most cases, this solves the problem. This is really what this discussion is about: how to install and configure these utilities to provide application connectivity and a bit of troubleshooting technique.

Installing the SQL Client Utilities

Before you can use any of the 32-bit client utilities (such as the SQL Client Configuration utility, SQL Object Manager, SQL Administrator, ISQL/W, or SQL Security Manager), you have to install them. Unlike with the 16-bit utilities, you do not have a separate set of installation disks. Instead, you have to use the original installation medium—generally, a CD-ROM.

To install the 32-bit SQL Client utilities, follow these steps:

1. Connect to a sharepoint where you have copied the SQL Server for Windows NT CD-ROM installation directory. This will be I386 for Intel processors, MIPS for MIPS processors, or Alpha for Alpha processors.

2. Run the installation program (SETUP.EXE). The Welcome dialog box appears.

3. Click the Continue button to continue the installation. In the next dialog box that appears, enter your name and company name. Then click the Continue button. In the confirmation dialog box that appears, click the Continue button if the information displayed is correct, or click the Change button if it is incorrect and follow the prompts.

4. In the SQL Server Setup for Windows NT – Options dialog box, enable the Install Utilities Only checkbox. Then click the Continue button. The Install Client Utilities dialog box appears.

5. Select the client utilities to be installed and the location for the utilities. Then click the Continue button. Your files are copied to the location you specified, and a Program Manager group is created. A prompt appears, telling you to restart your computer.

6. Restart your computer.

You can use the SQL Client Configuration utility to specify the default network library. Or you can use it to specify several different connections that use different network libraries.

Note

One of the interesting aspects of SQL Server for Windows NT is that the SQL Server can respond to a broadcast request from the client so that no default configuration has to be created before you can use the client utilities. Not all applications are capable of connecting without a default configuration, however, so it is best to use the client configuration to specify your connections.

To specify the default configuration, follow these steps:

1. Launch the SQL Client Configuration Utility.

2. Select your default network library from the Default Network drop-down listbox. This can be Named Pipes, Banyan VINES, NWLink IPX/SPX, or TCP/IP Sockets.

3. Click the Done button.

To specify multiple connections for multiple servers or multiple network transports, follow these steps:

1. Launch the SQL Client Configuration utility.

2. Click the Advanced button. The Advanced Client Options dialog box appears, as shown in Figure 34.3.

Figure 34.3.
The Advanced
Client Options
dialog box.

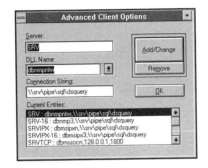

3. In the Server field, enter the name to be used by your applications to connect to a specific SQL Server installation. This name can be the same as your SQL Server computer name but does not have to be. It can be any name you choose.

4. In the DLL Name drop-down listbox, specify the network library to use.

Note

The NetBEUI network library is DBNMP3 for 16-bit applications and DBNMPNTW for 32-bit applications. For the Banyan VINES transport protocol, specify DBMSVIN3 for 16-bit applications and DBMSVINN for 32-bit applications. For the IPX/SPX transport protocol, specify DBMSSPX3 for 16-bit applications and DBMSIPXN for 32-bit applications. And if you are using TCP/IP as your transport protocol, specify DBMSSOC3 for 16-bit applications and DBMSSOCN for 32-bit applications.

5. In the Connection String field, specify the appropriate connection type to be used. This will be ServerName\pipe\sql\pipe (default) for named pipes over NetBEUI or IPX/SPX, a StreetTalk name for Banyan VINES, or an IP Address,Socket, for the TPC/IP protocol.

6. Click the Add/Change button to place the entry in the Current Entries drop-down listbox. Repeat these steps for each source to be created.

Note

Notice in Figure 34.3 that I have already filled out the fields and have created multiple sources—some for 16-bit client access and some for 32-bit client access. The only difference between the 16-bit and 32-bit clients is the server name and the DLL name. The multiple sources are really for use by the ODBC-32 applet. By creating multiple server names, I can specify different server names (such as SRV for 32-bit access using named pipes over NetBEUI or SRV-16 for named pipes over NetBEUI for my 16-bit applications) and keep the network address and network library set to the default setting. This can ease your management tasks by providing a consistent interface for your network clients to use.

USING OPEN DATABASE CONNECTIVITY

Many people, including myself, prefer to use the Open Database Connectivity (ODBC) drivers to access SQL Server because these drivers provide an additional layer between your application and the data source. A data source is an application server such as SQL Server or a data file such as a dBASE file. And with ODBC drivers, you can change your data source just by selecting another driver. This means that the application does not have to be changed in order to be run locally. Instead, all you have to do is export the database from your SQL Server to a supported file format on your hard disk. This can enable your sales staff, for example, to run the same application, such as an inventory program, on their portable computers while they are on the road just as they do when they are in the office.

Tip

Although you also can use the ODBC drivers for applications designed to upload or manipulate data on your SQL Server, you will find that the additional layer provided by the ODBC drivers slows down data access. If performance is the ultimate goal, you should use the DB-LIB APIs in your application. The ODBC drivers ultimately use these same APIs, and if you write your application to use these from the beginning, you can obtain significant performance improvement.

Note

The DB-LIB driver (DBNMPWNT.DLL) installed on your system by the ODBC Utility installation program and used by the SQL Server ODBC driver supports only named pipes on the NetBEUI transport protocol. If you are using IPX/SPX or TCP/IP as your network transport, you will have to install the other DB-LIB drivers, as described in the "Installing the SQL Client Utilities" section, and then configure the ODBC driver to use the appropriate DB-LIB driver, as explained in the following section, "Creating a Data Source for Use by Your Applications."

INSTALLING THE ODBC UTILITIES

To install the ODBC utilities and SQL Server driver, follow these steps:

1. Insert the SQL Server ODBC Utilities disk into drive A. Alternatively, you can connect to a sharepoint where these utilities have been copied.
2. Change to the 32i subdirectory and run the Setup program (SETUP.EXE). This installs the 32-bit version of the ODBC driver. The 16-bit version is in the root directory.

Note

The ODBC 2.0 drivers included in the 32i subdirectory can support 16-bit ODBC-compliant applications running under Windows NT on the Windows on Windows (WOW) layer, so you should not have to install both versions of the utilities unless you experience problems.

3. When prompted, click the Continue button. The Install Drivers dialog box appears.
4. Select the SQL Server entry and click the OK button. The Data Sources dialog box appears.

Note

Clicking the Advanced button in the Install Drivers dialog box displays the Advanced Installation Options dialog box. Here, you can specify version-checking, driver-manager, and translator options. In most cases, these options do not need to be changed. In case you are curious, you can click the Versions button to check the installed versions of the drivers installed on your system.

5. Click the Close button to complete the installation, unless you also want to create a data source. In that case, click the Add button and then follow the steps described in the following section.

CREATING A DATA SOURCE FOR USE BY YOUR APPLICATIONS

You can create a new data source from the ODBC-32 Control Panel applet. When you launch the applet, the dialog box shown in Figure 34.4 appears.

Figure 34.4.
The ODBC Data
Sources dialog
box.

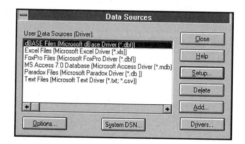

You can click the Options button to provide a trace facility so that you can trace the ODBC calls made on your system for troubleshooting. In the ODBC Options dialog box that appears, you can enable or disable the trace facility and specify a file to contain this trace information.

You can click the System DSN button to install and configure data sources that can be used by all users of the system. Clicking this button displays a System Data Source dialog box, which looks the same as the ODBC Data Sources dialog box. Adding a system data source follows the same actions as the following procedure. The only difference is that data sources configured from this dialog box can be accessed by all users in the ODBC Data Sources dialog box, whereas the following procedure creates data sources for just the current user.

To create a data source, follow these steps:

1. Launch the ODBC-32 Control Panel applet to display the Data Sources dialog box.
2. Click the Add button. The Add Data Source dialog box appears.
3. Select the SQL Server entry and click the OK button. The ODBC SQL Server Setup dialog box appears.
4. Click the Options button to expand the dialog box.
5. In the Data Source Name field, enter a name that will be displayed in your ODBC compliant application Open Data source dialog box.

6. In the Description field, enter a comment for the data source.

7. In the Server drop-down listbox, enter the name of your SQL Server. This varies for each support platform. If you will be using a SQL Server database on a Banyan VINES server, enter the Banyan StreetTalk name—for example, `BanyanSrv@Production@DB`.

   If you will be using a SQL Server database on a Novell NetWare server, specify the SQL Server name registered in the NetWare bindery. This name is specified when you install SQL Server on the NetWare server. If you install SQL Server on a Windows NT Server with just IPX/SPX as the transport protocol, then you also will specify a name to be used by your Novell clients. This name, which may be different than the name of your Windows NT Server, should be specified as the server name.

   For a SQL Server database on a UNIX server, specify an alias name. This name is not really used; it is just a placeholder. On a Windows NT Server using TCP/IP as the only transport protocol, however, specify the computer name in the Server drop-down listbox.

8. In the Network Address field, specify the name of the SQL Server address to use. For SQL Server for Windows NT, this is a named pipe and is usually `\\ServerName\pipe\sql\query`, where `ServerName` is the computer name of your server. If you specified a different name for the pipe during the installation, specify that name in the Network Address field.

   If you specify Default, the default driver library is used for your specified server.

   If you are using SQL Server on a Banyan VINES server, specify the StreetTalk name for the SQL Server address.

   If you are using SQL Server on a Novell NetWare server or SQL Server on a Windows NT Server using IPX/SPX as the only transport protocol, specify Default to use the same name as that in the Server drop-down listbox. If you want to use a different SQL Server installation, specify a different name in the Network Address field.

   If your SQL Server installation is on a UNIX server or a Windows NT Server with TCP/IP as the network transport protocol, specify an IP address and socket. These items are specified during the SQL Server installation and appear in the form of Address,Socket—for example, 128.0.0.1,1800.

9. In the Network Library field, specify the DB-LIB dynamic library to be used for your connection. If you specify Default, the network library specified in the SQL Client Configuration utility for your server name is used.

Note

The NetBEUI network library is DBNMP3 for 16-bit applications and DBNMPNTW for 32-bit applications. For the Banyan VINES transport protocol, specify DBMSVIN3 for 16-bit applications and DBMSVINN for 32-bit applications. For the IPX/SPX transport protocol, specify DBMSSPX3 for 16-bit applications and DBMSIPXN for 32-bit applications. If you are using TCP/IP as your transport protocol, specify DBMSSOC3 for 16-bit applications and DBMSSOCN for 32-bit applications.

10. In the Database Name field, specify the SQL Server database to use. This name is case-sensitive, so be sure to specify the correct name and case.

11. If you have installed the optional languages on the SQL Server (version 4.2 or later), you can specify an alternative language driver to use in the Language Name drop-down listbox.

12. The Generate Stored Procedure for Prepared Statement option is a performance option to create stored procedures (precompiled procedures) on the SQL Server, which are used by the ODBC drivers. Leave this checkbox enabled unless you are supporting multiple versions of ODBC and are having problems.

13. The Fast Connect Option checkbox normally is disabled by default, but for transaction-oriented applications, this option can be enabled to increase performance. Normally, each time an ODBC application connects, the ODBC drivers execute informational queries that retrieve information required to implement metadata support, including the retrieval of user-defined data types.

14. The Convert OEM to ANSI Characters option normally is disabled and is used to provide a code page translator between your client application and the SQL Server database. If you have a nonstandard code page, you can specify an alternative by clicking the Select button.

15. Click the OK button to add the new data source. Repeat these steps for each data source to add.

TROUBLESHOOTING SQL SERVER CONNECTION PROBLEMS

When troubleshooting SQL Server connection problems, the first item is to determine whether it is a network problem or a SQL Server problem. You can use the MAKEPIPE/READPIPE programs to determine this. MAKEPIPE.EXE will create a named pipe and wait for a client to connect. READPIPE.EXE is the client side of this application and attempts to connect to the named pipe created by MAKEPIPE. If it succeeds, it sends a command to close the pipe. The syntax for MAKEPIPE follows:

```
makepipe [/h] [/w] [/ppipe]
```

The switches for this command are:

- /h: Displays a usage summary.
- /w: Specifies the wait time in seconds between read and write operations. The default is 0 seconds.
- /p: Specifies the pipe name to use. The default pipe name is abc.

The syntax for READPIPE follows:

```
readpipe [/h] [/n<iter>] [/{q¦t}] [/w] [/s<Server>] [/p]<pipe>] [/d<Data>]
```

The syntax for the READPIPE command is this:

- /h: Displays a usage summary.
- /n: Specifies the number of iterations to perform. The default is 1 iteration.
- /q: Specifies how to query for incoming data. If this switch is not specified, the application reads the pipe and waits for data to be sent. Otherwise, it polls repeatedly.
- /t: Specifies to use transact-named pipes. This option overrides polling.
- /w: Specifies the wait time in seconds to pause during the polling operation. The default is to wait for 0 seconds.
- /s: Specifies the server name. If no pipe name is supplied, the application uses a local pipe name.
- /p: Specifies the pipe name to use. The default pipe name is abc. This pipe name must be the same as the pipe name specified on the MAKEPIPE command line.
- /d: Specifies the data string to be sent. The default string is shutdown.

If your test succeeds in connecting to the named pipe, your network is functioning properly. This means that you have a connection-related problem based on your client configuration, or you have a permission-related problem. You can perform client configuration testing with any of the Microsoft SQL Server client utilities. I generally use ISQL/W. With this application, you can specify to use the name specified in your SQL Client Configuration utility, or you can use a name from the network browse list (when you specify the server to connect to). If you cannot connect from the name specified in the SQL Server Client Configuration utility but can connect from the name specified in the browse list, then the problem is in the connection string specified in the Client Configuration utility.

34

WINDOWS NT CLIENTS

If you cannot connect with either name, then there is a good chance you have an access permission problem. This is fairly easy to test, depending on which mode you have your SQL Server configured to use. It can be one of three modes:

◆ Integrated: Uses the domain database to assign permissions.

◆ Standard: Uses only the user accounts specified with the SQL Server Administrator.

◆ Mixed: Supports both methods.

If you are using the integrated configuration, try to use a domain Administrator account and password to connect. If you are using the standard or mixed configuration, use the System Administrator (sa) account. If either of these works, then the user account you previously specified to connect to SQL Server with is the problem. In this case, use the SQL Security Manager to check the permissions for the user account if using the integrated or mixed model, or SQL Administrator if using the standard model.

INSTALLING THE MICROSOFT MAIL CLIENT

Installing the Microsoft 32-bit mail client is quite easy, because the first time you run it, the application prompts you to create a new postoffice or connect to an existing postoffice. You should choose to connect to an existing postoffice, of course. And all you need to know to successfully connect is the name of the sharepoint that contains your workgroup postoffice. The default name is always ServerName\WGPO, where ServerName is the name of the server where you created the shared directory. If you specified a different name when you created the workgroup postoffice (as discussed in Chapter 8, "Additional Administrative Tools"), use that sharepoint name instead. After you are connected successfully, you are asked whether you already have a mailbox. If you do, then you need to specify this mailbox and password to access it. If not, you are prompted to create one. That's all there is to it. Unless...

And there's always an unless with software installation, isn't there? The area to look at here is compatibility problems with existing 16-bit applications. If you migrated any of your existing 16-bit mail configurations during your installation, for example, then the 32-bit mail client generates an error message for each 16-bit DLL that it attempts to load. And this could be a significant number of error messages. Error messages occur because, when you migrated your settings to Windows NT, this information was placed in the HKEY_CURRENT_USER\Software\Mail subkey in the Registry. And this key is the same key used by the 32-bit mail client to store its configuration information. There are two solutions. First, you can delete all the Registry keys contained within the subkey but leave just the key HKEY_CURRENT_USER\Software\Mail\Microsoft Mail. Then you can reinstall the 32-bit mail client. At this point, it reinitializes itself and prompts you for any required information. After the setup succeeds, you can run the application without further incident. Second, you can browse through each key and remove any reference to the 16-bit DLLs—more troublesome, but still acceptable.

Even though you have deleted any 16-bit configuration information from the Registry, this does not mean that you cannot still use the 16-bit applications. These applications still can access their original .INI files instead of the information contained in the Registry, because Windows NT provides a mechanism to pass these profile API requests to a .INI if the requested key cannot be found in the Registry.

SUMMARY

This chapter focused on basic network troubleshooting topics for your Windows NT clients and discussed the installation of the SQL Server client utilities. Special attention was applied to configuring the system with the SQL Client Configuration utility, to provide a basis for you to install multiple data sources with the ODBC-32 Control Panel applet. You also learned about the basic installation and configuration of the Microsoft 32-bit mail client.

The next chapter discusses some of the same issues described in this chapter but specifically how they apply to your Windows 95 clients.

- Solving Basic
  Network-Related
  Problems

- Looking At Windows
  95 Boot Options

CHAPTER 35

Windows 95 Clients

Windows 95 is Microsoft's premiere replacement operating system for the current estimated 60 million computers running MS-DOS, Windows, or Windows for Workgroups. It has some unique capabilities and can offer your network clients a great deal of functionality. It even can make your life as a network administrator easier in some respects. On the other hand, any new operating system has unique compatibility problems with the existing software base, and this could make your life as a network administrator quite troublesome. So the first thing you should keep in mind is to go slowly with the upgrade process. Don't make a mass migration until you have installed Windows 95 on several computers and tested them thoroughly for compatibility with your hardware and installed software base.

Tip

> If your client workstations are capable of running Windows NT 3.51 and you do not have any software products that will not operate on Windows NT 3.51, you might want to consider migrating to Windows NT instead of Windows 95. Although Windows 95 offers more compatibility for legacy applications and applications that require direct access to the hardware, it is a hybrid operating system. It still has many 16-bit system components, even though it supports 32-bit Win32 applications. As such, it cannot offer the robustness and security provided by Windows NT.

Windows 95 supports a variety of network operating systems right out of the box. This includes Microsoft Windows NT–based networks in a workgroup (peer-to-peer) or domain based. You even can mix the two. Along with this, you can install network software to connect to a Novell NetWare file server as a network client, and even share your client resources with any other Novell NetWare server or client. You can even install both the Microsoft network support and the Novell network support simultaneously. What you cannot do is have both of these network clients configured to share files and printers simultaneously. Only one of these client drivers can support file or print sharing to other network clients.

Along with support for Microsoft and Novell networks, Windows 95 includes client network drivers for Banyan VINES, FTP Software's NFS, and SunSoft PC-NFS. And if your network is not on this list, then you can install the same network drivers you currently are using with your Windows 3.1 or Windows for Workgroups 3.11 clients. In fact, during the installation of Windows 95, it autodetects and, in some cases, upgrades your existing network drivers. You should consider how these drivers will impact your client connectivity and resource usage, however, because many of these drivers are 16-bit (real-mode) drivers. And mixing 16-bit (real-mode) and 32-bit (protected-mode) drivers can cause complications.

Tip

Windows 95 includes a file describing some of the specific network-related problems and solutions you might encounter while upgrading your Windows 3.x installations to Windows 95. This file is called `network.txt` and is located in the root installation directory (generally, `C:\WINDOWS`).

Problems also can occur when you mix network-transport protocols. The initial version of Windows 95 includes support for the Microsoft NetBEUI, IPX/SPX compatible, TCP/IP, and DLC protocols. It also includes support for the Novell NetWare IPX ODI, IBM's DLC protocol, Digital Equipment Corporation (DEC) Pathworks, Banyan VINES Ethernet or token ring protocols, and SunSoft's PC-NFS protocol. Some of these are 32-bit, such as the NDIS 3.0 drivers, whereas others are 16-bit, such as the NDIS 2.0 and ODI drivers. Although mixing these different protocols can give you simultaneous access to different networks, it also can cause you some severe grief. Sometimes when you use multiple network drivers, for example, your clients can connect to one network but find that they fail to connect to the other. Or you can add an additional network transport protocol to a current network driver but suddenly find that you cannot be authenticated by your server or that you fail to connect to a resource.

This chapter is all about client connectivity and the problems you might experience. It starts with a basic discussion of the hardware-related problems and solutions unique to Windows 95, and then moves on to some of the software configuration related possibilities.

Note

Supporting your SQL Server applications on Windows 95 follows the same basic principles as outlined in Chapter 34, "Windows NT Clients," in the section "Supporting SQL Server Access."

SOLVING BASIC NETWORK-RELATED PROBLEMS

Most of your network-related problems will be caused by a hardware conflict of some type or an incorrect software configuration. The starting point for a hardware-related problem should be a look at Chapter 34's section, "Finding and Solving Network Adapter Problems." This section describes the basic hardware trouble-shooting topics. But, of course, there is more to it than what is covered in the last

35

chapter; this chapter talks about Windows 95 rather than Windows NT. And Windows 95 still includes an expanded memory manager, upper memory support, Plug and Play, and PCMCIA support—all of which can cause you problems if they are not working properly.

ISOLATING A HARDWARE RESOURCE CONFLICT

This chapter (just like the preceding chapter) begins with a look at resource conflicts simply because a hardware resource conflict is the most common cause of a network adapter failure. The first step you should take in isolating the hardware failure is to use the Control Panel system applet. Just click the Device Manager tab to display the Device Manager page, as shown in Figure 35.1. This page displays all the installed hardware that Windows 95 recognized and has a device driver installed to support the associated hardware.

Figure 35.1.
The Device
Manager page of
the Control Panel
system applet.

If a device is not working properly, the device tree is expanded automatically and displays a small informational icon next to it. In such a case, just select the device and click the Properties button to display the device properties General page, as shown in Figure 35.2. This page displays a message in the Device Status box, indicating the current operating status. If the message is "This device is working properly," then the cause is generally a software-related problem, such as an incorrectly configured network protocol driver.

Figure 35.2.
The General page
of the Device
Manager dialog
box.

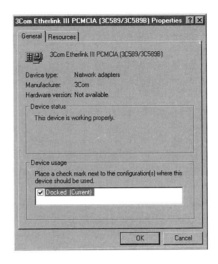

If you installed Windows with Microsoft TCP/IP as the only network protocol, for example, then in order to assign the initial IP address, you have to follow these steps:

1. Execute the Control Panel Network applet to display the Network dialog box's Configuration page.
2. If you have a DHCP Server on the network, just close the Network applet by clicking the OK button. This updates the IP address, which is obtained from the DHCP server.

Tip

> If you do not display the Control Panel applet at least once, you are not assigned a valid IP address. The default address you are assigned is generally 127.0.0.1, which is used for loopback testing. So although you will be able to ping yourself and it may appear that the TCP/IP protocol is configured properly, you will be unable to ping any external network resource. This also means that you will be unable to be authenticated by your domain controller or to connect to any shared resources.

3. If you do not have a DHCP Server on the network, then select the TCP/IP protocol bound to your network adapter and click the Properties button to display the TCP/IP Properties dialog box. The IP Address page should be displayed.
4. In the IP Address page, enable the Specify an IP Address radio button. Then enter an IP address and subnet mask.

5. Select the Gateway tab to specify your network gateways.

6. Select the DNS Configuration tab. Click on the Enable DNS radio button; enter the host name, domain name, and IP addresses of your domain name servers in the DNS Search Order field and click the Add button for each DNS server to add.

7. Click the OK button to return to the Network dialog box's Configuration page to configure your next TCP/IP bindings if you have more than one installed network adapter, such as the dial-up adapter used for remote access connections. After you complete all your network configurations, click the OK button to confirm the changes.

The other possibility is a hardware-related error, and if this is the case, then an error message is displayed in the Device Status field. To reconfigure the device, select the Resources tab to display the Resources page, as shown in Figure 35.3. If you have a resource conflict, such as an I/O, an interrupt, a DMA, or a memory conflict, it is displayed in the Conflicting Device List drop-down listbox. (At least it is if Windows 95 has recognized the conflict, but this may not always be possible.) Windows 95 displays a resource conflict only for MS-DOS and Windows device drivers that registered a resource usage in a manner that Windows 95 was able to detect. And that's where the catch is; if Windows 95 cannot detect a resource that is in use, it may configure another device to use it and cause a device failure.

Figure 35.3.
The Resources
page of the Device
Properties dialog
box.

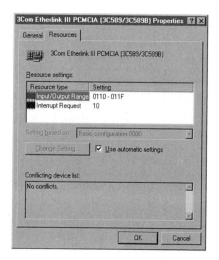

Let me give you an example that occurred on one of my systems. This particular system is using a peripheral adapter that combines a sound card, fax/modem card, and CD-ROM card. It requires up to four separate interrupts, three DMA channels, and a minimum of three base I/O registers, depending on the options enabled. And although some of the resources were recognized as in use, the interrupt reserved for the MIDI support was not. This caused my PCMCIA network adapter to fail because it was assigned the same interrupt. So how do you solve such a problem? Well, it is not very difficult to resolve and can follow one of two patterns. You can configure the device to use a different resource than that assigned to it by Windows 95 or you can inform Windows 95 that the resource is in use by reserving it.

To change a resource from the setting assigned to it by Windows 95, follow these steps:

1. Launch the Control Panel system applet to display the System Properties dialog box and then select the Device Manager tab.

2. Expand the tree for the device type you want to change. To change a network card's allocated resource, for example, expand the Network Adapter tree.

3. Select the device and click the Properties button. The device properties General page appears.

4. Select the Resources tab to display the Resources page, as shown in Figure 35.3.

5. Clear the checkbox for Use Automatic Settings. This enables you to change a resource setting from that assigned by Windows 95 for a Plug and Play device.

6. Select a resource in the Resource Settings field under the Resource Type column and click the Change Setting button. A resource edit box appears where you can change the resource assignment. Repeat this step for each resource you want to modify.

7. Now it is just a matter of clicking the OK button in each dialog box to return you to the System Properties dialog box. Then just click the OK button once more and Windows 95 prompts you to restart your machine for the new settings to take effect.

Before you reserve any system resources, it is a good idea to determine what resources are already in use. Click the Properties button for the Computer device in the System Properties dialog box to display the Computer Properties dialog box, as shown in Figure 35.4. On the View Resources page, you can select the Interrupt Request (IRQ), Input/Output (I/O), Direct Memory Access (DMA), or Memory radio button to display the resources that are in use.

35

WINDOWS 95 CLIENTS

Figure 35.4.
The View
Resources page
of the Computer
Properties dialog
box.

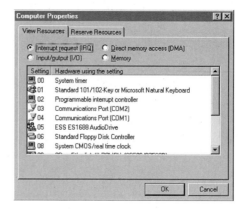

After you examine the resources in use, you can reserve resources by selecting the Reserve Resources tab. Then choose Interrupt Request (IRQ) to reserve a hardware interrupt, Input/Output (I/O) to reserve an I/O range, Direct Memory Access (DMA) to reserve a DMA channel, or Memory to reserve a memory range. For each of these types, just click the Add button to display an Edit Resource dialog box, where you can specify the resource to reserve.

Warning

Do not reserve a resource that is in use by a system device, such as the interrupt for the hard disk, because the device may not be operable under Windows 95. If such a problem occurs, immediately reboot the system and press the F5 key after you see the `Starting Windows 95` message to start Windows 95 in safe mode. In safe mode, you can reconfigure the system and undo the change you made.

ISOLATING A SOFTWARE RESOURCE CONFLICT

You may experience additional problems specifically related to Plug and Play network adapters, PCMCIA network adapters, or parallel port network adapters; these may seem like a hardware problem but, in reality, they are software-configuration problems. Or you may experience problems with your network client drivers and/or network transport protocols that also are software related. This section takes a look at a few of these situations to give you an idea of what to look for and how to solve such problems. This chapter starts with the hardware-related problems that you might encounter, and then moves on to the network driver-related problems.

Consider your network adapter configuration as the first item to look at if you have a software configurable or Plug and Play network adapter. In a software configurable network adapter, such as those from 3Com, run the softset utility from MS-DOS (when you see the Starting Windows 95 prompt, press F8 and select Command Prompt Only) and verify that the I/O port is the same as the one you selected for your network adapter configuration and that the interrupt is not used by any other device. Also, if you use a DMA channel or upper memory address, verify that these are free as well. Then make sure that you excluded the memory address, if used on your network adapter, from your EMM386.EXE device driver line in the config.sys file. If you have a network adapter that uses the D000-D3FF address, for example, your EMM386.EXE entry will look like the following:

```
DEVICE=C:\WINDOWS\COMMAND\EMM386.EXE X=D000-D3FF
```

If this area is not excluded, then you may have a memory conflict as the network driver attempts to access the network adapter. If you are using an NDIS driver, generally Windows 95 makes the appropriate exclusion internally. But if you use a 16-bit network driver, particularly one that binds to the network adapter before the 32-bit components load, then the memory exclusion must be included on your expanded memory manager device line or the network device driver fails to bind to the adapter. If the exclusion does not include the entire network adapter buffer, then the network driver may bind to the adapter but cause unexpected results. I have seen authentication failures occur with a Windows NT Server, for example, but normal authentication on a LAN Manager for UNIX with a partially excluded memory buffer.

A similar problem can occur for a Plug and Play network adapter when you load a 16-bit network driver. Even more confusing to troubleshoot is when you load a 16-bit network driver successfully, but then find that you cannot successfully use a 32-bit NDIS 3.1 transport protocol on the same Plug and Play network adapter. There is a reason for this and a solution as well, however. When you load a 16-bit network driver and it binds to your Plug and Play network adapter, it generally disables the Plug and Play functionality. So when Windows 95 loads and attempts to load the 32-bit Plug and Play network adapter driver, the driver fails to load because the network adapter no longer can be found or configured. This causes the 32-bit network transport drivers to fail to bind to the adapter. The solution to this problem is to use the software-configuration disk that shipped with your adapter to configure the adapter to function in non-Plug and Play mode, and then to remove the network adapter from the Device Manager page of the Control Panel system applet. After you accomplish these steps, you can run the Add New Hardware Control Panel Wizard to find your adapter and install an appropriate device driver. Then you should be able to add and use a 32-bit network transport protocol in addition to your existing 16-bit network driver.

35

Note

Not all 16-bit network drivers support multiple network transport protocols being bound to the same physical adapter. The Microsoft NDIS and Novell ODI drivers generally support multiple network transport protocols, and if your network driver supports one of these specifications, you should make use of it if you expect to successfully bind 16-bit and 32-bit transport protocols. For what it is worth, I have had the greatest success in this area with the Microsoft NDIS drivers—a 2.0 (real-mode), a 3.1 (protected-mode), or both simultaneously.

In today's ever-expanding world, you will find more and more people using portable computers in the business marketplace. Portable computers commonly are used by your sales staff when they are in the office or on the road. Temporary help, such as consultants, also often use portable computers. And even company executives make use of portable computers while in the office or at home. These computers often use PCMCIA network adapters to connect to the network. With Windows 95, you will find the built-in PCMCIA support to be a blessing or a curse, depending on your PCMCIA adapters.

Let me explain a bit more to bring this into perspective. Windows 95 includes 32-bit PCMCIA drivers for PCMCIA chipsets from Cirrus Logic, Compaq, Databook, Intel, Maxtor, SCM Swapbox, Vandem, VLSI, and a generic PCIC or compatible PCMCIA chipset. If you have one of these and supported 32-bit PCMCIA drivers for your PCMCIA cards, things should be in good shape. But all your PCMCIA cards must have 32-bit drivers—not just some in order to make life easy for you. And this is because you absolutely cannot simultaneously install the 16-bit (real-mode) and 32-bit (protected-mode) PCMCIA drivers. If you do, neither will work and generally Windows 95 will fail to load. This makes sense when you consider that there is only one PCMCIA controller, and both of these drivers want full control of the device.

Tip

If you have an HP Omnibook portable computer, you will find a PCMCIA driver in the \DRIVERS\PCMCIA\HP subdirectory of the Windows 95 CD-ROM. To install it, run the Control Panel Add New Hardware applet. When prompted, select No to have Windows 95 detect your hardware, and then click the Next button. Then select PCMCIA Socket as the hardware type and click the Next button to continue. Next, click the Have Disk button. When the Install From Disk dialog box appears, enter the path to the HP PCMCIA chipset driver and click the OK button. Then, when prompted, select the driver for the PCMCIA chipset and click the OK button to install the driver. After you reboot the system, you will be able to run the Control Panel PC-CARD Wizard to remove the 16-bit PCMCIA drivers and enable the 32-bit PCMCIA driver you just installed.

So what can you do about a conflict arising from mixing 16-bit and 32-bit PCMCIA drivers? There are several possible solutions. You can look for a new 32-bit device driver for your PCMCIA adapter from the manufacturer, or you can replace the adapter with a Windows 95 supported adapter. Or you can just use the 16-bit PCMCIA drivers that shipped with your computer, although not all 16-bit drivers will work with Windows 95, so this option is of limited use. And if you use a 16-bit driver, you also have to use a 16-bit network driver (NDIS 2.0 or ODI) in order to connect to the network. Another option is to configure Windows 95 to use a multiboot MS-DOS menu and multiple configurations, so that one option will use the 16-bit PCMCIA drivers and the other configuration will use the 32-bit PCMCIA drivers. Then, your clients can choose the configuration that best suits their needs. This section explores these options one at a time.

Note

If you want to use a real-mode driver (NDIS 2.0, ODI, or other 16-bit network driver) to connect to your network, in most cases, you also will be forced to use the 16-bit PCMCIA drivers or a real-mode PCMCIA enabler for your network adapter. This is because the network adapter cannot be configured until after the 32-bit PCMCIA drivers are loaded. This process occurs after the 16-bit network driver attempts to load.

The best solution is to find a 32-bit device driver for your PCMCIA network adapter because the protected mode PCMCIA chipset drivers provide complete Plug and Play support and do not use any conventional memory as do the real-mode PCMCIA drivers. You can find additional drivers from Microsoft as they become available from the following sources:

◆ Microsoft Network: Every Windows 95 computer has the potential to connect to the Microsoft Network. All you need to do is install the software and subscribe to the service. And I heartily suggest that you do so. On the Microsoft Network, you can choose to select the Windows 95 Files area to look for updated drivers, stop by the Portable Computers forum (GO PortComp), which is maintained by yours truly, or check out the various hardware manufacturers in the Computers and Software Category Hardware subfolder. As drivers become available from the manufacturers, I will be placing them in my forum in the Portable Computers File library in the Updates and Patches subfolder.

◆ CompuServe: Check out the Windows Driver library (`GO WDL`) for updated drivers.

◆ Internet: You can find updated drivers in Microsoft's FTP site (`ftp.microsoft.com` in the Products\Windows\Windows95 area) or on the World Wide Web (`http://www.msn.com`).

◆ Microsoft Download Service: Microsoft maintains a BBS, which is available at (206) 936-6735. If you have problems connecting or need additional information, you can call Microsoft at (800) 936-4200.

The next item is to consider replacing your network adapter with a Windows 95 supported adapter. And although I am not fond of this solution, sometimes it is required if you want to obtain the maximum performance and usage for your portable computer users. In some rare cases, a hardware upgrade is available from the manufacturer. Take, for example, the D-Link Corporation's DE650 PCMCIA network adapter. The early model was never designed for Plug and Play and is not supported by the Windows 95 32-bit drivers. You might be able to obtain from the manufacturer an updated version of this adapter that is supported, however. A member in my Portable Computers forum was able to obtain this upgrade from the manufacturer for about $60, and you might want to consider the same possibility for your unsupported adapters.

If you need to set up multiple configurations for your users so that you can use the 16-bit or 32-bit PCMCIA drivers, you can follow these basic steps:

1. First make sure that your current configuration has the 16-bit PCMCIA drivers installed on your system and that these are the active drivers. Normally, when you install Windows 95, this is the default configuration until you run the PC-CARD Wizard to replace the drivers with the 32-bit counterparts.

2. Copy your current `config.sys` to `config.pcm`, your `system.ini` to `system.pcm` and `system.w95`, and your `win.ini` to `win.pcm` and `win.w95`, although you may not need to use the `win.ini` file. To determine whether you really need to copy it, load it up in Notepad and check your `load=` and `run=` command lines. If you have a PCMCIA driver here, then you need to make a copy of the file.

3. Launch the Control Panel system applet. Select the Hardware Profiles tab to display the Hardware Profiles page in the System Properties dialog box.

4. Select the profile you want to copy. If you have a docking station that can be detected by Windows 95, you may have more than one profile displayed. Generally, these are called Docked and Undocked.

Tip

If you have a docking station that Windows 95 cannot detect, you can carry out the following steps to create a configuration for it. The only difference between a detected and nondetected docking station is that normally, Windows 95 automatically uses the correct hardware profile. If it cannot detect the docking station, however, you need to manually select it from a list during system startup.

5. Click the Copy button and supply a new name for the profile—perhaps something like Undocked-16. Do the same for the docked profile if you will be using the 16-bit drivers there as well.

6. Restart your computer. During the startup, you see a message that Windows 95 cannot determine which profile to use and that you should select it from the list.

7. Select the profile you want to use with 32-bit PCMCIA support.

8. Launch the Control Panel PC-CARD applet. The first time this runs, it offers you the chance to enable 32-bit PCMCIA support. Enable the checkbox and step through the Wizard.

9. When prompted to restart the system, do so. Be sure to power off the system as recommended. Repeat steps 6 through 9 for the Docked 32-bit PCMCIA configuration if you will be using it as well.

10. After restarting the system, launch the System Editor (SYSEDIT.EXE) to edit your config.sys, autoexec.bat, system.ini, and win.ini files. Alternatively, you can use Notepad to edit these files.

11. Create a multiboot MS-DOS configuration. This requires that you edit the config.sys and autoexec.bat files.

A default multiboot configuration for Windows 95 looks something like this for your config.sys file:

```
[Menu]
MenuItem=Docked, Docked configuration with 32-bit PCMCIA
MenuItem=Docked-16, Docked configuration with 16-bit PCMCIA
MenuItem=UnDocked, Undocked configuration with 32-bit PCMCIA
MenuItem=UnDocked-16, Undocked configuration with 16-bit PCMCIA
MenuDefault=UnDocked,3

[COMMON]
DOS=UMB
DOS=HIGH
DEVICE=C:\WIN95\HIMEM.SYS

[Docked]
INCLUDE=32-bit
```

35

```
[Undocked]
INCLUDE=32-bit

[Docked-16]
INCLUDE=16-bit
INCLUDE=PCMCIA

[UnDocked-16]
INCLUDE=16-bit
INCLUDE=PCMCIA

[32-bit]
DEVICE=C:\WIN95\EMM386.EXE NOEMS
DEVICEHIGH=C:\WIN95\SETVER.EXE

[16-bit]
REM - Exclusion needed for 16-bit PCMCIA adapters
DEVICE=C:\WIN95\EMM386.EXE NOEMS X=D000-DFFF
DEVICEHIGH=C:\WIN95\SETVER.EXE

[PCMCIA]
Place your real-mode PCMCIA drivers here!
```

And your `Autoexec.bat` file would look something like this:

```
@ECHO OFF
PROMPT $p$g
PATH=C:\WIN95;C:\WIN95\COMMAND;C:\;C:\DOS;C:\MOUSE
SET TEMP=C:\TEMP
GOTO %CONFIG%

:Docked
copy c:\windows\system.w95 c:\windows\system.ini /y
GOTO EXIT

:UnDocked
copy c:\windows\system.w95 c:\windows\system.ini /y
GOTO EXIT

:Docked-16
copy c:\windows\system.pcm c:\windows\system.ini /y
Place any network drivers or other real-mode drivers here!
GOTO EXIT

:UnDocked-16
copy c:\windows\system.pcm c:\windows\system.ini /y
Place any network drivers or other real-mode drivers here!

GOTO EXIT
:EXIT
```

Note

You do not necessarily have to copy the .INI files, unless you still want to enable modem resume, modem sleep, and optional PCMCIA sound-event notifications provided by the PCMCIA Windows 3.x drivers.

> And, in some cases, these Windows 3.x drivers fail to load anyway. Only testing with the specific drivers can tell you for sure whether they are needed and if they offer any additional functionality.

12. Reboot your system and select the startup profile you want to use. You will not see the MS-DOS menu if you used the same names for the menu items as the profile names, as I have done here. Because the names are the same, Windows 95 just boots using the menu item with the same name as the profile. Only if your profile names are different from your menu item names will you see two distinct menus.

Before you finish up this section on PCMCIA support, you should examine two other potential troublesome spots. First, your 32-bit PCMCIA normally picks a memory address range to use for PCMCIA support. If you need to change it, you can do so by running the Control Panel PC-CARD applet and selecting the Global Settings tab. Second, your users should get used to stopping a network card before removing it. This prevents data loss. To stop a PCMCIA network card, double-click on the PCMCIA icon on the Taskbar. Then choose the PCMCIA card and click the Stop button.

LOOKING AT WINDOWS 95 BOOT OPTIONS

One of the more interesting configuration options for Windows 95 is configuring the various components to load. Windows 95 uses several switches in the MS-DOS.SYS file, located in the root directory of the boot drive, to control these components. These switches are divided into two sections: the [Paths] section, which describes the Windows 95 directories required to boot the operating system, and the [Options] section, which describes the various configuration switches. The switch syntax is SwitchName=SwitchValue. Table 35.1 lists the switches provided in MS-DOS.SYS.

TABLE 35.1. THE WINDOWS 95 BOOT CONFIGURATION OPTIONS.

Option	Description
	[PATHS]
HostWinBootDrv	Defines the boot drive. For example, HostWinBootDrv=c.
WinBootDir	Defines the Windows 95 boot directory that contains the startup files. For example, WinBootDir=c:\windows.

continues

Windows 95 Clients — 35

TABLE 35.1. CONTINUED

Option	Description
WinDir	Defines the Windows 95 installation directory specified during the installation. Generally, WinDir=c:\windows.
	[OPTIONS]
BootDelay	Specifies the time, in seconds, to delay booting the operating system. This is provided to give the user time to press F8 after the Starting Windows 95 message is displayed and to choose an alternative startup option. The default is 2 seconds. If BootKeys=0, this option is disabled.
BootFailSafe	Enables safe-mode system startup. The default is 0, which disables this setting. Setting this value to 1 enables an automatic safe boot.
BootGUI	Enables (1) or disables (0) the automatic loading of the Windows GUI. The default is 1.
BootKeys	Enables (1) or disables (0) the startup option keys. These are F4 for booting your previous version of MS-DOS, F5 for SafeBoot, F6 for SafeBoot with Network support, or F8 for menu selections (Command Prompt Only, SafeBoot, Step by Step Confirmation, and so on). The default is 1.
BootMenu	Automates the display of the boot menu when set to 1, or requires the user to press F8 to see the menu when set to 0 (the default).
BootMenuDefault	Sets the default menu selection. The default is 3 for a computer without any network support or 4 for a computer with installed network support.
BootMenuDelay	Specifies the time, in seconds, to display the startup menu before booting the default selection. The default is 30 seconds.

Option	Description
BootMulti	Enables (1) or disables (0) the multiboot capability. A value of 1 enables the prior version of MS-DOS to be loaded after the user presses F4. The default is 1.
BootWarn	Enables (1) or disables (0) the warning message to be displayed during a SafeBoot. The default is 1.
BootWin	Enables (1) or disables (0) setting Windows 95 as the default operating system to boot. The default is 1.
DblSpace	Enables (1) or disables (0) the automatic loading of DBLSPACE.BIN to support DoubleSpace compressed drives. The default is 1.
DoubleBuffer	Enables (1) or disables (0) loading the double buffering driver for a SCSI controller. The default is 1. Note: If a SCSI controller is detected and Windows 95 determines that this driver is not needed, it is disabled.
DrvSpace	Enables (1) or disables (0) the automatic loading of DRVSPACE.BIN to support DriveSpace compressed drives. The default is 1.
LoadTop	Enables (1) or disables (0) the loading of COMMAND.COM or DRVSPACE.BIN at the top of the 640KB memory area. If you are using Novell NetWare drivers or other software that makes assumptions about specific memory locations for software components, disable this setting. The default is 1.
Logo	Enables (1) or disables (0) the Windows 95 logo at system startup. The default is 1.
Network	Enables (1) or disables (0) SafeMode with networking support (F6) as a menu choice. The default is 1 for computers with network support installed or 0 for computers with no network.

35

WINDOWS 95 CLIENTS

SUMMARY

This chapter's primary concern was detecting and resolving network adapter resource conflicts specific to Windows 95. Hardware resource conflict solutions were illustrated with the Control Panel system applets to inform you how to determine the resources in use and how to change a conflicting resource for a particular adapter.

This chapter also discussed some of the specific problems you might encounter with Windows 95 and Plug and Play network adapters. And it placed special attention on portable computers and PCMCIA options. In the PCMCIA discussion, you also learned how to create multiple profiles and use the Windows 95 capability to autodetect the appropriate MS-DOS configuration so that you can configure a computer to use 16-bit or 32-bit configurations.

The next chapter looks at some of the same types of problems you might encounter with your Windows for Workgroups, Windows 3.x, and MS-DOS network clients.

CHAPTER 36

Windows for Workgroups 3.11, Windows 3.x, and MS-DOS Clients

Even though Windows NT and Windows 95 are available for use as network clients, not everyone will make use of them. In some cases, the network client hardware platforms do not have enough horsepower to support Windows NT or enough memory to support Windows 95 effectively. In other cases, the company is playing a conservative role, and company policy is limiting the migration path, or there just is not enough money in the budget to upgrade everyone. And so you have to make do with what you have and continue to support an older operating system, even though you know there is something better out there.

Note

When it comes time to choose a version of Windows to run on a computer, I generally make my determination based on the amount of physical memory installed on the computer. The processor speed is not nearly as important as the amount of physical memory. Insufficient physical memory means more paging to disk, and even the fastest processor can make Windows unusable if it is constantly paging to disk. I recommend that you run only MS-DOS or Windows 3.1 in standard mode on a computer with less than 2MB of RAM. If you have between 2MB and 4MB of RAM, then Windows 3.1 running in enhanced mode is a good choice. If you have between 6MB and 8MB, then Windows 95 is a good choice. If you have more than 8MB (at least 12MB), Windows NT Workstation is the way to go. Keep in mind that all these recommendations assume that you have sufficient hard disk free space and other hardware requirements for the operating system.

This chapter discusses some of the basic connectivity support issues involved in maintaining these older operating systems. It starts with a look at MS-DOS because it is the foundation that both Windows 3.x and Windows for Workgroups 3.11 use to build on. It then moves on to explore specific issues with Windows 3.x and Windows for Workgroups.

SOLVING BASIC NETWORK-RELATED PROBLEMS

When I have to find a reason that an MS-DOS, Windows 3.x, or Windows for Workgroups network client cannot connect to the network, I generally find that the cause is a resource conflict. And most of the time, this resource conflict is caused by a memory manager. The rest of the time, it seems that a true hardware resource conflict exists or that there is a software configuration problem. This section focuses on these issues. You will learn how to determine what the problem is and how to solve it.

MS-DOS CONNECTIVITY

The very first possibility to pop into my head when it comes to MS-DOS connectivity problems is that the problem is a memory-management conflict—particularly if the network adapter was working but now has failed. It doesn't have to be a network buffer memory address conflict, however. It could be caused by loading a driver into upper memory, the driver making certain assumptions about its operating characteristics, and thereby failing. Or it could be caused by loading an operating system component into upper memory, such as your files, buffers, or file control blocks. It doesn't really matter what the cause is, as long as you can solve it. And solving a memory-related problem follows a few basic steps.

The first thing to do is to determine whether the initial cause is memory manager-related. The easiest way is to just comment out the memory manager in the config.sys file and reboot the computer. If the problem then disappears, you have a definite memory manager problem, and you need to determine the type of problem.

To determine whether you have just an upper memory area conflict, follow these steps:

1. Exclude the entire A000–FFFF memory range in your memory manager and reboot. If the problem then goes away, you probably have a simple memory conflict, which is solved easily, although it is a bit time-consuming.

2. Change your memory exclusion from A000–FFFF to A000–CFFF and reboot. If the problem goes away, then you have a memory address conflict in the A000-CFFF range.

3. If the problem does not go away, change your memory exclusion to D000–FFFF and reboot. If the problem goes away, then you have a memory address conflict in the D000–FFFF range.

If the problem went away in step 2 or step 3, then the next step is to subdivide your exclusion once more. As an example, try to exclude A000-B7FF instead of A000-CFFF. If that fails, try B800-CFFF. If that works, continue the process of halving the memory exclusion until you reach a multiple of 4KB that continues to work properly. This will be x000–x1FF for a 4KB exclusion, for example, x000–x7FF for a 32KB exclusion, and x000–xFFF for a 64KB exclusion, where x is A, B, C, D, E, or F for the appropriate 64KB page in the upper memory area.

Tip

One of the weird memory address conflicts I have encountered is a conflict with a network adapter's reserved boot ROM address. A network boot ROM is used to boot a workstation from a network drive rather than a local hard disk. Some network adapters, such as some of the Intel models, reserve an address range for the network boot ROM, even if no ROM is installed. If you do not exclude this area, then the network connectivity can be a bit spurious. You might be able to connect to a LAN Manager server and access resources without problems, for example, but fail to be authenticated by a Windows NT Server or to access resources on a Windows NT domain. You can locate this reserved address by using your Softset utility that shipped with the network adapter.

If excluding a memory address did not solve the problem, but commenting out the memory manager did work, you probably have an operating system component being loaded into upper memory that is causing your network driver to fail, or you have a driver loaded into upper memory that is causing the problem. To determine whether the problem is caused by loading a driver into upper memory, just remove the statements prefacing the device drivers that load the driver into upper memory. For the MS-DOS drivers, for example, change DEVICEHIGH=DeviceDriver to DEVICE=DeviceDriver; for QEMM, change QemmRootPath\LOADHI.SYS DEVICE=DeviceDriver to DEVICE=DeviceDriver, where QemmRootPath is the QEMM installation directory. Do the same for the autoexec.bat file by removing the LOADHIGH or LH (for MS-DOS upper memory support) statements in front of any of your drivers.

If you are using QEMM, comment out the following drivers if they are installed in the config.sys:

DOSDATA.SYS   Loads MS-DOS components (files, buffers, and so on) into upper memory

DOS-UP.SYS   Loads additional MS-DOS system components into upper memory

ST-DBL.SYS   Stealths the MS-DOS DoubleSpace compression driver by swapping it in and out of the EMS page frame

ST-DSPC.SYS   Stealths the MS-DOS DriveSpace compression driver by swapping it in and out of the EMS page frame

Note Other memory managers have similar functionality provided by different drivers, and you should refer to your documentation to find the exact driver names to comment out.

If you are using QEMM or another third-party memory manager, you also should consider problems that can occur from shadowing a ROM or using the stealth features. Shadowing a ROM is the process of copying the memory contained in the ROM to system RAM and remapping the address to the new location to increase performance. Stealthing is the process of mapping RAM into the same location as a system ROM to be used as an upper memory area for loading device drivers. When you stealth a ROM, the memory address is mapped twice. It is mapped once for access from system services, in which case the ROM mapping is used, although this also could have been copied to RAM. It also is mapped once for access as an upper memory address. You also can stealth the MS-DOS compression drivers, which creates an additional set of mappings: one for software that accesses the EMS page frame; and one for MS-DOS to access the stealth compression driver, which shares the same address as the EMS page frame. Any of these items can cause you problems, and you should remove them one at a time to determine the cause of the problem.

Tip

You should consider a little problem that can throw you off track when removing these configuration switches from your memory manager. As you remove a switch, it affects the amount of upper memory available, which means that a device driver may fail to load high. If the driver that fails to load into upper memory is the cause of the problem, it will seem as if the configuration switch you removed solved the problem. But it might not have, because the next time you maximize your upper memory area, the same driver may be loaded into upper memory and the problem may recur. This is why I suggest that you try this step last, rather than first.

If you do not have an upper memory conflict, then the problem generally falls into a resource conflict category. This could be an interrupt, I/O, or DMA conflict. The tables in Chapter 34, "Windows NT Clients," can help you isolate the conflict. And while you are considering hardware conflicts, don't forget to check the network cabling. Many times, a 10B-T cable can be placed into the phone jack instead of the data jack by your user. Or the network adapter can be configured to use a 10B-2 transceiver type instead of the 10B-T transceiver it is actually using. And take a close look at the cable used to connect the network adapter to the data jack. It might be a phone cable instead of a real network cable with RJ-45 connectors. You might be surprised at some of the things your network users do when they decide to reorganize their office space. And don't forget to take your own network patch cable to connect the network adapter to the data jack. Your user might just have damaged the patch cord by rolling over it continuously with his office chair.

Tip

The protocol.ini file contains the resources currently allocated for use by the network adapter driver. If you change the network adapter configuration, you also must change the resource assignments in this file.

The final item I consider is the network driver configuration. If you are using a LAN Manager client driver to connect to your Windows NT domain, I suggest that you get rid of it unless you absolutely must continue to use it. Windows NT Server includes the Network Client Administrator in the Network Tools Program Manager group, which you can use to create installation disks to install the Network Client v3.0 client drivers. The Network Client v3.0 can work with any existing NDIS 2.0 network adapter driver and includes support for the NetBEUI, NWLink, and TCP/IP protocols. The TCP/IP protocol supports DHCP and WINS, which can make your life as an administrator quite a bit easier.

Consider also your network transport bindings if you are using multiple network transports. The default installation includes both the NetBEUI and NWLink transports, for example, with IPX/SPX being the default transport. Sometimes this can cause you additional problems, however. If you have bridges installed on your network to create a single logical network, try to use only the NetBEUI protocol. See if you can connect with it. Or, if you have routers instead of bridges, try the NWLink protocol.

Finally, if your network is TCP/IP-based, forget about the NetBEUI and NWLink protocols and use just the TCP/IP protocol. See if you can ping yourself (PING ComputerName) to see whether the software is installed correctly and working. When you get a return, if it is working correctly, check the IP address. If it is in the 127.0.0.x range, then the software is not configured properly. Either a DHCP server cannot be found on the network, or your routers might not support DHCP and are filtering out the relevant packets. In the first case, you need to check your Windows NT Server domain controllers to verify that the DHCP service is running. In the second case, you need to check your documentation for the router to determine what packet types it may be filtering. You also can take a look at Chapter 9, "Using DHCP, WINS, and DNS," which might offer some additional insight. As a temporary measure, you can assign a permanent IP address for the computer by running the Setup program located in the Network Client v3.0 directory (generally, C:\NET).

Tip

The Network Client v3.0 includes a diagnostics capability. The first time you execute the command NET DIAG, it looks for another computer that is acting as the diagnostic server. If it cannot find a diagnostic server, it prompts you to become the diagnostic server. This syntax for executing the command follows:

```
NET DIAG /NAMES /STATUS
```

Here, you can use /NAMES to specify the name of another diagnostic server to avoid potential collisions with other diagnostic servers and clients. You can use /STATUS to get configuration information from another computer.

Looking At the Network Client V3.0

The Microsoft Network Client v3.0 ships with Windows NT Server and is located in the \CLIENTS\MSCLIENT subdirectory of the CD-ROM. You can use the Network Client Administrator tool, located in your Network Tools Program Manager group, to create installation disks. You later can use these disks to install the Network Client v3.0 on your client computers. If you have a network adapter that is not included in the supported network adapter list, you should check the \CLIENTS\WDL\NETWORK subdirectory on the CD-ROM to see whether your network adapter is listed. If so, just copy the entire set of files to an additional floppy disk and, when prompted for a network adapter in the Network Client v3.0 Setup program, specify Other. You are then prompted to insert your OEM disk to copy the appropriate network drivers. You can use this same mechanism with any OEM driver—even those that are not included on the Windows NT Server CD-ROM—as long as it includes an NDIS 2.0 (real-mode) network driver.

Before you install the Network Client v3.0 on all your MS-DOS clients, however, you should be aware of a few limitations:

◆ Intel 8088 processors: If you have an older IBM XT or compatible computer with an Intel 8088 processor, you cannot use the full redirector. During the setup, you must change from the default Full Redirector setting to the Basic Redirector setting. This prevents you from accessing SQL Server because this requires the full redirector. The Setup program also might pause for up to five minutes on a computer with an 8088 processor. If this occurs, do not restart your machine—just wait for the Setup program to continue.

◆ Minimum free memory: The Network Client v3.0 Setup program requires a minimum of 429KB of free conventional memory. If you have too many terminate-and-stay-resident (TSR) programs loaded or existing network drivers that leave you with less than 429KB free, you must remove the drivers or unload the TSR programs before you run the Setup program.

◆ NWLink protocol: The NWLink protocol included in the Network Client v3.0 does not support SPX. It only supports IPX. If you have software that uses Novell's SPX protocol, it will not work with the Network Client v3.0. You should use your existing Novell network drivers instead.

◆ DLC protocol: If you install the DLC protocol, then you also must manually edit your autoexec.bat file. Make sure that the first network line (before your drivers) is NET INITIALIZE /dynamic and the last network line (after all your drivers but before the NET START command) is NETBIND.

◆ Browsing for resources: The Network Client v3.0 does not include a browse master. Therefore, in order to browse for network resources, you must have a Windows for Workgroups, Windows 95, Windows NT Workstation, or Windows NT Server computer accessible from the client and operating as a browse master.

Note

Even without a browse master accessible from the client, you still can connect to shared network resources. You just need to know the resource name and its location. To connect to a shared CD-ROM drive (with the share name of CD-ROM) on a server (called SRV), for example, use this command:

```
NET USE DriveLetter: \\SRV\CD-ROM
```

where DriveLetter is an MS-DOS drive letter (F:, for example).

◆ Remote Access Software: Windows NT Server also includes the Remote Access Software 1.1a client, which you can use to connect to a Windows NT Server, Windows NT Workstation, Windows 95, or Windows for Workgroups computer running the RAS server. Do not use the RAS Setup program to install the software, however, if you also have installed the Network Client v3.0. Instead, use the Network Client v3.0 Setup program. Just select the Microsoft Remote Network Access Driver from the list of supported adapters. Then choose Listed Options Are Correct and follow the prompts. After exiting the Setup program, run the RASCOPY.BAT program to copy the RAS support files. After you install the software, change to the RAS subdirectory (generally, C:\NET\RAS) and run the Setup program there to configure your modem settings. If you decide to remove RAS, use the Network Client v3.0 Setup program to remove the Microsoft Remote

Network Access driver; do not use the Setup program in the RAS subdirectory.

◆ TCP/IP: There are a few quirks with the TCP/IP protocol for the Network Client v3.0. The Network Client v3.0 does not support DNS resolution using WINS or WINS resolution using DNS, perform as a WINS Proxy Agent, or register its computer name with the WINS server, for example. You may experience other minor differences as well.

◆ Domain authentication: In order to be authenticated by a LAN Manager or Windows NT Server computer, your Network Client v3.0 client must be using the full redirector.

Note

If you are using TCP/IP and you have a router between your server and the client, you need to add an entry in the client LMHOST file. The format follows:

```
###.###.###.### ComputerName #DOM:DomainName
```

Here, ###.###.###.### is the server's TCP/IP IP address, ComputerName is the name of the server, and DomainName is the name of the domain. For a Network Client v3.0 client to be authenticated by my server (called SRV) in the WORK domain, for example, the entry would be

```
128.0.0.1 SRV #DOM:WORK
```

You also will be required to add the Network Client v3.0 client's IP address to the server's LMHOST file or manually register the client's computer name with your WINS server with the WINS Manager.

The Network Client v3.0 also uses some components that were migrated from the Windows for Workgroups drivers. You therefore will find that, along with the common entries in the protocol.ini file (such as adapter configuration settings), you also will find a copy of WFWSYS.CFG and entries in a system.ini file. The WFWSYS.CFG file is unique to each installation, but you can use the ADMINCFG program (located on your Windows for Workgroups installation disks or in the \CLIENTS\WFW\NETSETUP subdirectory on your Windows NT Server CD-ROM) to configure some of the security-related settings (such as password caching, validated logons, and so on).

Note

ADMINCFG is a Windows program, not an MS-DOS program, so you need a copy of Windows for Workgroups on the client installation to change the WFWSYS.CFG file. Or, you can copy it to a disk and modify it from another machine running Windows for Workgroups and having access to the ADMINCFG.EXE program. For more information on the ADMINCFG program, see the section "Windows for Workgroups 3.11 Connectivity," later in this chapter.

The specific entries in the system.ini file that apply to the Network Client v3.0 are under the [Network] section. Table 36.1 lists these entries.

TABLE 36.1. NETWORK CLIENT V3.0 CONFIGURATION OPTIONS.

Option	Specifies
autologon	Whether the Network Client v3.0 client automatically prompts you to log on when it starts. Values can be Yes or No. The default is Yes.
computername	The name of your computer that will be used for all NETBIOS name resolution.
lanroot	The installation directory of the Network Client v3.0 client.
username	The default user name to be supplied during a logon attempt.
workgroup	The name of your workgroup. This name can be different from your domain name but, for simplicity, it should be the same name.
reconnect	Whether to restore previous network connections after a successful logon. Values can be Yes or No. The default is Yes.
dospophotkey	The key to press (including the Ctrl+Alt keys) to launch the pop-up interface. The default key is N, meaning that you press Ctrl+Alt+N to launch the pop-up interface.
lmlogon	Whether Network Client v3.0 prompts you for a domain logon when you log on. Values can be 1 (enabled) or 0 (disabled). The default is determined during your software installation. If you make no changes, it is disabled (0).
logondomain	The name of the Windows NT Server or LAN Manager domain to log on to.
preferredredir	Which redirector to use when you load the network drivers with the NET START command. Values can be

Option	Specifies
	Basic, Full, Netbind, Popup, NetBEUI, or Workstation. The default is Full, unless changed during the software installation. Normally, the values are only Full or Basic, as determined by the Setup program. But you can specify any of the alternatives. Netbind only binds the protocol and network drivers, Popup loads the pop-up interface, NetBEUI loads the NetBEUI protocol, and Workstation loads the Workstation service and prompts you to log on.
filesharing	Specifies that the workstation can share directories on the network (on), or cannot share directories (off).
printsharing	Specifies that the workstation can share a locally attached printer on the network (on), or cannot share directories (off).
Maxconnections	Specifies the maximum number of connections to support.
autostart	The redirector that is in use. If you installed a network adapter during Setup and chose the Run Network Client Logon option, the autostart entry lists the redirector (Basic, Full, Netbind, Popup, NetBEUI, or Workstation). If you installed no network adapter or chose the Do Not Run Network Client option, then the autostart entry has no value, but the NET START command still appears in your autoexec.bat file.

You also will find two additional sections in the system.ini file. These include the [network drivers] and [Password Lists] sections, which include the NDIS network adapter and protocol drivers to load, and the user password list files.

WINDOWS 3.1 CONNECTIVITY

If you still are using Windows 3.x as your client operating system, then most problems that occur will be related to your MS-DOS configuration. And that is where you should start your troubleshooting efforts. Begin with booting just MS-DOS and the network drivers and log on to the network. If that is successful, then it is time to look at some of the Windows 3.x-specific issues. If it fails, you first must resolve the MS-DOS problems before you can continue. This section assumes that your MS-DOS configuration is working properly.

Note

If you are installing a new installation of Windows 3.x and you already have installed the Network Client v3.0, you should specify the Network Type as LAN Manager 2.1. This installs the appropriate Windows 3.x drivers for you to use in order to connect to your network resources.

Tip

If you want to set up a shared copy of Windows 3.x to use for all your network clients, then connect to the network with a Network Client v3.0 boot disk. Connect to a sharepoint where you want the shared copy to be installed. And then run the Windows Setup program in administrative mode (setup/a) on a client workstation to copy all the files to the shared directory on the server. Your network clients can then connect to this shared directory and run the network installation (setup/a) to install the configuration and required boot files on their local computer.

Once more, the first item to consider when troubleshooting your network configuration under Windows 3.x when running in enhanced mode is—you guessed it—an upper memory conflict. This is most often a conflict with your network adapter's memory buffer. And depending on the expanded memory manager you use, it may or may not automatically exclude the memory addresses you specified on the memory manager's command line in the `config.sys` file. So how can you tell if you really have a memory conflict? Well, you can try the following procedure.

Comment out your memory manager in your `config.sys` file and reboot the system. Then start Windows. If the problem still exists, then you have a different problem. It could be a driver problem, a corrupted file, a hardware conflict, or something similar. Try the following steps:

◆ Run a virus utility to check for infected files. If you do not have a third-party utility, such as McAfee SCAN, use MSAV (the Microsoft Anti-Virus utility). If you find infected Windows files, clean your installation. Or, from a clean boot disk, repartition, reformat, and reinstall everything.

◆ Run a disk utility to check for cross-linked or corrupted files. If you do not have a third-party utility, such as Norton Disk Doctor, use ScanDisk. If you do not have a recent version of MS-DOS with ScanDisk, use `CHKDSK/F`. If you find corrupted Windows files, reinstall Windows.

◆ Check your hardware configuration for conflicts. If you have a sound card or other device that uses a driver that can reconfigure the card through software, make sure that these settings are correct and do not conflict with the network adapter.

If commenting out your memory manager did solve the problem, then uncomment your memory manager and reboot the system. Then check to see whether you have a memory conflict only with Windows in enhanced mode by starting Windows 3.x in standard mode. You do this by using the command-line switches /s or /2 (for example, WIN/S). If, at this point, everything is working, but when you start Windows in enhanced mode (WIN or WIN/3) it fails, I can almost guarantee that you have an upper memory conflict. If this is the case, you can take the following actions:

◆ Begin your testing by adding the line EMMExclude=A000-FFFF to your system.ini file in the [386Enh] section. Then try to run Windows in enhanced mode once again.

◆ If this works, start subdividing the exclusion. Change A000-FFFF to D000-FFFF and try again. If that works, break it up again to D000-E7FF and try it again.

◆ If it failed, try the A000-CFFF range. If that works, break it up again to A000-B7FF and try it again.

◆ After you find the memory-range half that solves your problem, keep lowering the exclusion range by half until the problem recurs. At this point, start adding increments of 4KB until the problem no longer occurs. You now can be assured that you have found your problem area and excluded it from use by Windows.

If you do not have a memory conflict, then you may have a problem caused by one of the Windows 3.x internal network configuration settings. You can modify the defaults by adding or changing the entries in your system.ini file in the [386Enh] section. These entries include the following:

◆ NetDMASize: If your network adapter uses a DMA channel to transfer data, then you may have to increase the size of the buffer that Windows allocates. The value entered here should be a multiple of 4 for best performance. The default is 0 for ISA (standard AT or compatible) computers and 32 for MCA (Microchannel). It would be a rare occurrence to need a DMA buffer of more than 64KB.

◆ NetHeapSize: Specifies the size of the internal data buffer used for network transfers. The default is 12 (KB) and modifications should be made in increments of 4. If you want to increase your buffer to 32KB, for example, change this value to 32.

Tip

> You also can use the `NetHeapSize` parameter in standard mode. Just place the key word below the `[standard]` section. The default buffer size is 8KB for standard mode operation.

◆ NetAsyncFallback: Specifies the Windows attempt to save a failing asynchronous NETBIOS request. Generally, if the buffer allocated is too small, Windows fails the request. If this value is set to On, Windows attempts to save the request by allocating a buffer in local memory and preventing any other applications from running until the request is received or the time-out specified in NetAsyncTimeout is reached. Values can be On or Off. The default is Off.

◆ NetAsyncTimeout: Specifies the time, in seconds, for Windows to enter a critical section and wait for an asynchronous NETBIOS request to be received. The default is 5.0 seconds. You can enter any value and include a decimal.

◆ NoWaitNetIO: Specifies that synchronous NETBIOS requests be converted to asynchronous NETBIOS requests, which can improve performance but could cause computability problems. Values can be On or Off. The default is On.

◆ TimerCriticalSection: Specifies the time, in milliseconds, for Windows to enter a critical section and wait when an application uses a timer interrupt. Some network software fails if this setting is not used. The default is 0 for a LAN Manager, and for a Windows NT Server–based network, the default value is 10,000.

◆ InDOSPolling: Prevents Windows from running other applications when a memory-resident application (usually, a TSR or network driver) has the InDOS flag set. This flag is used by applications that have to be in a critical section when performing an INT21h (most of the MS-DOS functionality is an INT21h API) operation. Values can be On or Off. The default is Off.

◆ Int28Critical: Specifies that Windows maintain a critical section for software that uses the INT28h interface. Some network virtual device drivers perform internal task switching on this software interrupt, and may hang the real-mode network software. Values can be On or Off. The default is On, and you should make sure that it stays that way.

◆ UniqueDOSPSP: Specifies that all MS-DOS virtual machines (VMs) use a unique program segment prefix (PSP). Many network drivers use the PSP to identify the VM that requested the network data. The values can be On or Off. The default is On for a LAN Manager or MS-NET-compatible network and Off for all others.

◆ PSPIncrement: Specifies the offset (in increments of 16 bytes) to ensure that the PSP for each VM is unique. The range is from 2 to 64, with a default of 2. For LAN Manager networks, the default is 5.

WINDOWS FOR WORKGROUPS 3.11 CONNECTIVITY

When you start looking at Windows for Workgroups 3.11 (WFW)-related network problems, things can become a little trickier. And this is because WFW can use both real-mode NDIS 2.0 network drivers and protected mode (NDIS 3.0) network drivers. It also can support multiple 16-bit network transport protocol stacks, multiple 32-bit network transport protocol stacks, or both simultaneously. This can complicate things, but I prefer to use this as my network operating system (when the choice is one of Windows 3.x or WFW) simply because it outperforms Windows 3.x.

This is because WFW builds on the 32-bit disk access features provided in Windows 3.1 and includes protected-mode drivers for accessing the FAT file system (VFAT), caching I/O requests (VCACHE), and 32-bit network adapter drivers and transport protocols. All these protected-mode drivers mean that WFW is faster and more stable than Windows 3.1. Because the network drivers used are generally protected-mode drivers, there is less conventional memory overhead. This means that you can run MS-DOS applications that previously would not run because of the lack of conventional memory used by your network client drivers.

Troubleshooting network connectivity on a Windows for Workgroups computer consists of two separate possibilities. You troubleshoot your real-mode or your protected-mode drivers, but not both simultaneously. For the most part, you will be dealing with protected-mode drivers because these offer the greatest performance. But not every transport protocol is available in a protected-mode version. The Data Link Control (DLC) protocol, for example, is available only in a real-mode driver, and it is used to access IBM mainframes or to control a network-capable HP printer.

Now look at this situation from the beginning, which is always a good place to start in your troubleshooting. If you are using both NDIS 2.0 and NDIS 3.0 drivers and are experiencing a connectivity problem, you first should determine which component is having the problem. Start with these steps:

◆ Boot the system, but do not start Windows for Workgroups. Instead, issue a NET LOGON command to log on to the network. If you can log on successfully and access resources on the network, your problem probably is related to your protected-mode drivers.

◆ Before you make this assumption, however, start Windows for Workgroups. You receive a message stating that the real-mode drivers already were started, which prevents your NDIS 3.0 drivers from being loaded. You can ignore this message for now. Just check to see whether your network connectivity is working properly. If it works and you can access shared resources, then you do have a problem with your NDIS 3.0 drivers.

◆ The next step is to determine which driver is causing the problem. This is best done by removing the NDIS 2.0 support with the Network Setup applet. After you remove all the real-mode drivers, restart the computer. If the problem goes away, you have an interaction problem with your real-mode and protected-mode drivers. So the simple fix is only to use the protected-mode (NDIS 3.0) drivers. But sometimes this is not a viable method because you may have to use a real-mode protocol and drivers as well, in which case you may have to use just the real-mode drivers.

Tip

> Sometimes the interaction problem is caused by loading the NDIS 2.0 drivers into upper memory blocks. You can use the LoadHigh switch to disable loading of the NDIS 2.0 drivers into upper memory and force them to load into conventional memory by adding the entry to your system.ini file. This switch is discussed a little later in this section, along with other switches that might prove useful.

◆ Next, look at your NDIS 3.0 protocol settings. Select a single protocol to use. I suggest starting with NetBEUI if your network supports it as your only protocol. After restarting your computer, see if your network connectivity is working properly. Perform this step for each protocol you use to verify that each works properly.

◆ Begin mixing your protocols. Add an additional protocol, such as the IPX/SPX-compatible protocol, and restart your computer. Confirm that the network works properly. Repeat this for each additional protocol you have installed. But only use two protocols (maximum) at a time. The idea here is to find the two protocols that conflict with each other so that you can determine your alternatives.

◆ Finally, you can mix all your protocols after you have identified the conflicting pair. At this point, it is a matter of isolating the conflict and attempting to solve it via configuration settings in the [Network] section of your system.ini file. Some of these settings are discussed later in this section. You might need to disable DirectHosting support, for example.

◆ You might have to install another network adapter and bind the conflicting protocol to use only that network adapter to resolve the problem and continue to provide support for all the required protocols.

Tip

As an alternative to installing multiple network adapters, you might want to consider a move to Windows 95. Windows 95 uses the NDIS 3.1 specification, which is just different enough that it might enable you to use the multiple protocols without problems. I have experienced authentication-related problems with the NetBEUI and NWLink protocols on my WFW configuration, for example, but when I migrated it to Windows 95, the problem disappeared completely.

After you identify the conflicting protocol, you should attempt to resolve it first by configuring it via the Drivers dialog box. Select the protocol and then click the Settings button. In the dialog box that appears, you can select the packet type, number of sockets, and other options for the NWLink protocol. For TCP/IP, you might want to disable DHCP and WINS support and manually allocate an IP address, allocate a gateway address, and configure the computer for DNS resolution. The idea is to eliminate possible causes and, optionally, to find a solution that works until you can resolve the underlying problem.

The most common failure is an authentication failure in which you cannot access the domain controller to be authenticated during a logon sequence, which also means that you have no access to the domain's shared resources. Generally, I only see this with protected-mode protocols when you have more than one protocol installed. The default is to install the NWLink (IPX/SPX-compatible) protocol and the NetBEUI protocol, with NWLink as the default. This can be good or bad, depending on which version of Windows NT Server you are using and sometimes even which service pack you have installed.

The good part includes the fact that NWLink is routable, whereas NetBEUI is only bridgeable. And routers are usually more efficient than bridges. The bad part is that the default setting for Windows NT Server is to use automatic detection of the Ethernet packet types; believe it or not, this can cause you more problems than it solves. If you leave this setting as is and use NWLink on your WFW client, you probably will see authentication failures on Windows NT Server 3.51. The solution is to change the packet type to 802.3 with the Windows NT Control Panel Network applet. You also should set the WFW clients to use the 802.3 packet in the Network Setup applet.

Note

Automatic packet detection can be further complicated by networks that have mixed Windows NT Workstations, Windows for Workgroups computers, and Novell NetWare servers. To avoid potential problems, make sure that you select a single packet type to use.

Tip

> In a mixed Novell and Microsoft network, you also should configure the NWLink settings to assign a unique network number to each Windows NT Server. This can prevent additional connection-related problems.

Windows for Workgroups includes several .ini-specific settings used to control the behavior of the network components. The primary entries are in the `system.ini` file in the `[Network]` section and include the following:

◆ AutoLogon: Specifies whether to automatically prompt you to log on when WFW starts. Values can be Yes or No; the default is Yes. If you have a blank password, you are not prompted to log on.

◆ ComputerName: The name of your computer, which is used for all NETBIOS name resolution and is specified during the installation.

◆ UserName: The default user name to be supplied during a logon attempt.

◆ Workgroup: The name of your workgroup. This name can be different from your domain name but, for simplicity, it should be the same name. The only time you would want to use different names is if you want to subsegment your shared resources during browsing. If you have a lot of computers in the same domain, for example, all the computers are listed under this domain, but if you also have your WFW computers configured to use different workgroup names, they also can be found in the browse list for the workgroup. Essentially, the computers are in two browse lists, but the workgroup browse list is easier to use in order to find the shared resource because it is smaller.

◆ Reconnect: Specifies whether to restore previous network connections after a successful logon. Values can be Yes or No; the default is Yes.

◆ Reshare: Specifies whether to restore previous shared resources when the operating system is restarted. You do not have to be logged on to the system in order for the resources to be shared. Values can be Yes or No; the default is Yes.

◆ LMLogon: Specifies whether to prompt you for a domain logon when you log on. Values can be 1 (enabled) or 0 (disabled). The default is 0. You can change this setting in the Control Panel Network applet. Just click the Logon button to display a dialog box to enable domain logon via a checkbox.

◆ LMAnnounce: Specifies whether the WFW computer is made visible to LAN Manager computers in the browse lists. The value can be Yes or No; the default is No.

◆ LogonDomain: Specifies the name of the Windows NT Server or LAN Manager domain to log on to. You can change this setting in the Control Panel Network applet. Just click the Logon button to display a dialog box to specify the name of the domain to log on to and enable the Logon to Domain checkbox.

◆ AutoStart: Determines the redirector used by the real-mode (NDIS 2.0) network components when you start the network before booting WFW—if you issue a NET LOGON command, for example. Values can be Basic, Full, Netbind, Popup, NetBEUI, or Workstation. The default is Full. Netbind only binds the protocol and network drivers, Popup loads the pop-up interface, NetBEUI loads the NetBEUI protocol, and Workstation loads the Workstation service and prompts you to log on.

◆ LoadHigh: Loads NDIS 2.0 drivers into upper memory blocks. This item is installed only if you also have real-mode (NDIS 2.0) drivers installed on your system. The value can be Yes or No; the default is Yes.

◆ EnableSharing: Specifies whether local resources are shared on the network. The value can be Yes or No. You can set the default by using the Network Setup applet in the Network group.

◆ NoSharingControl: Disables the user's capability to change the EnableSharing entry via the Network Setup applet. The value can be 0 (disable user control) or 1 (enable user control). There is no default because this entry must be added manually to the system.ini file.

◆ FileSharing: Specifies whether to share directories on the local computer. The value can be Yes or No. You can set the default by using the Network Setup applet File and Print Sharing dialog box.

◆ PrintSharing: Specifies whether to share directories on the local computer. The value can be Yes or No. You can set the default by using the Network Setup applet File and Print Sharing dialog box.

◆ LogonDisconnected: Specifies whether to connect to a previously connected resource and to make sure that it is available for use. Or, it just specifies to include the resource connection and to physically connect to it only when used. This is referred to as a ghosted connection. The value can be Yes or No. The default is No to enable ghosted connections. You can change this setting in the Control Panel Network applet via the Logon button.

◆ Comment: Specifies a description to be displayed in the browse list. You can change it in the Network Control Panel applet.

◆ LogonValidated: Used internally to verify that a user was logged on to the domain. When the user logs off, this setting is used again to make sure that the connections are disconnected properly, which prevents the next user

36

Windows for Workgroups 3.11

from making use of any previous connections. The value can be Yes or No. The default is Yes if validated by a domain server or No if not validated by a domain server.

◆ StartMessaging: Specifies whether to load the messenger service (provided by WinPopUp). The value can be Yes or No; the default is No. You can change this setting in the Control Panel Network applet via the Logon button.

◆ LoadNetDDE: Specifies whether to load Network DDE support at system startup. The value can be Yes or No; the default is Yes.

◆ DomainLogonMessage: Specifies whether a message is displayed after a successful logon to the domain. The value can be Yes or No; the default is Yes. You can change this setting in the Control Panel Network applet via the Logon button.

◆ CacheThisPassword: Specifies whether to cache passwords in the local user's password file. The value can be Yes or No. The default is specified by the last user who logged on and changed the Save This Password in Your Password File checkbox.

◆ MaintainServerList: Specifies the possibility of your computer becoming a master or backup browse master. Values can be Auto, Yes, or No. If set to Auto, the computer queries the network for a master browser. If no master browser is available, this computer becomes the master browser. If set to Yes, this computer always maintains a browse list and becomes the master browser if the original master browser goes offline. If set to No, this computer never becomes a master browser.

Note

A browse master is determined by an election (query) process. If a Windows NT Server computer is available, it has the highest priority, followed by LAN Manager servers, Windows NT Workstations, Windows 95, and finally a Windows for Workgroups computer.

◆ DirectHosting: Specifies to enable direct hosting over IPX first, and if that fails, to use hosting over NETBIOS. Some monolithic drivers (such as Novell's NETX driver) require that this setting be disabled. Values can be On or Off, and the default is On.

◆ DeferBrowsing: Disables the automatic expansion of the browse list in the Browse dialog box for directories or printers. Values can be Yes or No. The default is No, unless Remote Access is installed. You can change this setting in any Browse dialog box by setting or clearing the Always Browse checkbox.

USING THE ADMINISTRATION CONFIGURATION PROGRAM

Windows for Workgroups includes the program `ADMINCFG.EXE`, which is not installed by default. To install it, you must manually expand it from your distribution medium, or you can just copy it from the `\CLIENTS\WFW\NETSETUP` program. It can be run only on a computer that has WFW installed on it. When you run it, you are prompted for the location of the `WFWCFG.SYS` file to open. After you select the file, you may be prompted for a password. Then, the Security Settings dialog box shown in Figure 36.1 appears. You use this dialog box to disable the client workstation's capability to share directories, printers, and Clipboard pages.

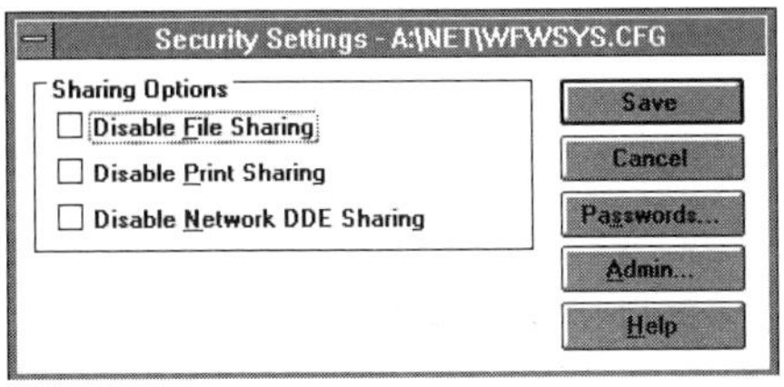

Figure 36.1.
The Security
Settings dialog
box.

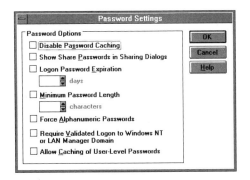

If you click the Passwords button, the Password Settings dialog box appears. (See Figure 36.2.)

Figure 36.2.
The Password
Settings dialog
box.

The Password Settings dialog box offers the following options:

◆ Disable Password Caching: Disables caching of passwords that the user has supplied during a successful connection attempt in his password file. This requires a user to specify a password for each connection every time an attempt is made to connect to a shared resource.

◆ Show Share Passwords in Sharing Dialogs: Specifies whether an asterisk (*) is displayed in the password box for each character the user enters (the default) or to display the actual password in normal text in the password box.

◆ Logon Password Expiration: Specifies a password expiration date so that the user is forced to change his password.

◆ Minimum Password Length: Specifies a minimum password length.

Note

The Logon Password Expiration and Minimum Password Length options are only useful for a workgroup. If the user is a member of a domain, it is better to set the account policies with User Manager, which applies to all users of the domain.

◆ Force Alphanumeric Passwords: Specifies that the user must use an alphanumeric password rather than all alphabetic characters. This means that there must be at least one digit in the user's password.

◆ Require Validated Logon to Windows NT or LAN Manager Domain: Specifies that only authenticated users of the domain are allowed to access shared resources on the computer. Normally, a workgroup computer allows anyone to access a shared resource if they know the password. Enabling this checkbox prevents any non-domain members from accessing the shared resources.

◆ Allow Caching of User-Level Passwords: Specifies that the password file should contain passwords for user-level (domain access) shared resources, as well as the default share-level (workgroup-only access) passwords. This option can be used to store all the passwords a user needs to access a shared resource, which can be useful for those users who just can't remember their passwords without writing them down and violating security. The only password the user needs to know is the password to open his password file, and this password is the same as the password with which the user logs on to the system.

If you click the Admin button in the Security Settings dialog box, the Administrator Settings dialog box appears, as shown in Figure 36.3.

You can specify the following settings in the Administrator Settings dialog box:

◆ Update Security Configuration: If this checkbox is enabled, you can specify a UNC path name to the location of the WFWSYS.CFG file in the Network Path field, which is used to update all connected users of a shared WFW installation. If a password is required to access the file, enter it in the Password field.

◆ Use Root Directory Only: Specifies that the user will use the settings stored in the WFWCFG.SYS file stored in the root directory of the shared installation or the WFWCFG.SYS located in a subdirectory that is the same as the computer name of the workstation. If no subdirectory is found, then the WFWCFG.SYS file located in the root directory is used.

◆ Display Error Messages: Displays security-related error messages on the client workstation.

◆ Custom Logon Banner: Displays a custom sign-on banner when the user logs on to the network. Just enter the text in the Text field.

◆ Set Password: Displays a Password dialog box where you can specify a password required to open the WFWCFG.SYS file to make any modifications. This can prevent a user from changing any settings that you specify.

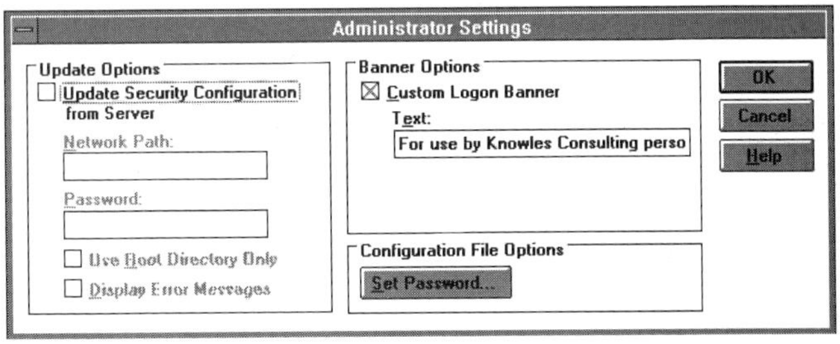

Figure 36.3.
The Administra-
tor Settings
dialog box.

SUMMARY

This chapter focused on network connectivity for your MS-DOS, Windows 3.x, and Windows for Workgroups 3.11 clients. It included some basic troubleshooting techniques for you to use to solve connectivity-related problems. It discussed using the Network Client v3.0 network client software for your MS-DOS and Windows 3.1 clients to use as their network client.

Special attention was placed on Windows for Workgroups 3.11 connectivity and troubleshooting techniques useful in your day-to-day activities. You also learned how to use the Windows for Workgroups Administration Configuration (ADMINCFG.EXE) program to specify various security-related settings for your Network Client v3.0 and Windows for Workgroups clients.

In the next chapter, you will look at some of the issues relating to Macintosh and UNIX connectivity on your Windows NT Server–based network.

- Macintosh Client Connectivity

- Installing the Microsoft UAM

- UNIX Client Connectivity

CHAPTER 37

Macintosh and UNIX Clients

One of the biggest advantages of Windows NT Server is its interoperability with other operating systems. You can integrate Windows NT Server with any MS-NET-compatible network, which is to be expected, but you also can integrate Novell networks. With the Gateway Service for NetWare, you can use your Windows NT Server to provide access to NetWare shared directories or print queues, even if your network clients do not support the IPX/SPX protocols. If you add the optional software packages, such as the File and Print Services for NetWare, your Windows NT Server can emulate a Novell NetWare Server. If you also include the Directory Services for NetWare, you can use a single logon to access not only your Microsoft network domain resources, but your NetWare network resources as well.

Support for your Macintosh networks is quite similar, except Windows NT Server includes all the tools you need to instantly support your Macintosh clients. This support is provided by the Services for Macintosh. You even can support your UNIX-based clients, although UNIX integration in the base package is not nearly as full-featured as other network-integration options. That is what this chapter is about: issues that you might encounter as a network administrator while supporting your Macintosh and UNIX clients. This chapter starts with a look at some of the more common problems with Macintosh clients, and then moves on to UNIX client connectivity problems that you might encounter.

MACINTOSH CLIENT CONNECTIVITY

Macintosh problems fall into three categories. You have authentication-related problems, directory- or file-related problems, or printer-related problems. Most of these authentication problems are correctable by installing the Microsoft UAM (Universal Authentication Module) on the client computer or removing the requirement for the Microsoft UAM in the Services for Macintosh on your Windows NT Server. Some directory- and file-related problems require more drastic action for correction on the server or, in some cases, cannot be corrected. Noncorrectable problems generally are caused by a limitation in the Macintosh operating system or a Windows NT file system limitation. When the problem is printer related, a workaround generally can be implemented on the Windows NT Server computer or the Macintosh computer, depending on how the printer is accessed.

TROUBLESHOOTING AUTHENTICATION-RELATED ISSUES

Before you can determine exactly what type of authentication problem is occurring on your network and how to solve it, you need to look at the three types of network logons that can occur. The Services for Macintosh can use a Macintosh guest account, the Windows NT Server domain Guest account, or a Windows NT domain user account.

The primary difference between the Macintosh guest account and the Windows NT domain Guest account is that any Macintosh user can connect to your Windows NT Server Macintosh Volumes using the Macintosh guest account if you have the Guests Can Use This Volume checkbox enabled (the default) for a volume. When a user connects using the guest account, no password is required. This means that there are no restrictions on who can access the volume. If you disable the Guests Can Use This Volume checkbox, however, you still can allow users to connect, but only if they have the Microsoft UAM installed and use the domain Guest account, if you have enabled it in User Manager for Domains, or if it is a specific domain user account.

Tip

Always disable the Guests Can Use This Volume checkbox on any Macintosh volume you create. You still can allow all users to connect using the domain Guest account, by publishing the Guest password. By using the domain Guest account, however, you can further restrict access to shared files to prevent network disruptions and ease your administrative duties.

Caution

Never disable the Guests Can Use This Volume checkbox on the Microsoft UAM volume, or new Macintosh clients will be unable to connect in order to install the Microsoft UAM on their computers. If you do disable this property, you will be required to distribute the Microsoft UAM on a floppy disk or other medium before your new clients can access your domain resources.

The Microsoft UAM is used to encrypt a password sent out over the network so that a hacker or a curious user with a network sniffer cannot capture a user account and password for unauthorized use. When your network clients use the Microsoft UAM to connect to your domain resources, they can be authenticated using the Macintosh guest account or any domain account, simply by choosing Guest or Registered User Generally in the UAM. To use the domain Guest account, use the Registered User option and specify Guest in the Name field and a password in the Password field, if one is required.

This process may actually vary a bit, depending on the version of the operating system used on the Macintosh client and the settings you have enabled for the

Services for Macintosh. If the Macintosh client is using a version of the operating system earlier than 7.1, the options to use the Macintosh guest account and clear text password encryption (meaning no encryption) still are available to the user via the Apple standard UAM, even if the Require Microsoft Authentication checkbox has been enabled in the MacFile Attributes dialog box on the Windows NT Server computer. If the version of the operating system is 7.1 or later, however, and the Require Microsoft Authentication checkbox is enabled, the Macintosh guest option is unavailable and only the Microsoft encrypted password option is available.

You now can see that determining why a client cannot connect can be a troublesome process, depending on how you configured the Services for Macintosh, how your Macintosh clients are configured, and what version of the Macintosh operating system they have installed. So let me help you make things simpler: Require every user to have System 7.1 or later, the Microsoft UAM installed in his AppleShare folder, and a domain user account. And on your servers running the Services for Macintosh, make sure the Require Microsoft Authentication checkbox is enabled, the domain Guest account is disabled in User Manager for Domains, and the Guests Can Use This Volume checkbox is disabled for every Macintosh volume on your server, aside from the Macintosh UAM volume. This gives you consistent user access to your shared resources by allowing any Macintosh user to obtain the Microsoft UAM from the Microsoft UAM volume, but requires a Windows NT domain user account with an encrypted password to access any shared resources.

INSTALLING THE MICROSOFT UAM

In order for your Macintosh clients to install the Microsoft UAM and abide by your network security policy, they must follow these steps:

1. On the Macintosh client, from the Macintosh Apple menu, select the Chooser, to display the Chooser dialog box.

2. Select the AppleShare icon and the zone in which the Windows NT Server running the Service for Macintosh server resides, to update the list of file servers.

3. Select the Windows NT Server from the File Server list and click the OK button. The Logon dialog box appears.

4. Select the Guest option and click the OK button. The Server dialog box appears.

5. Select the Microsoft UAM volume, disable the Checked Items Will Be Opened at System Startup Time checkbox, and click the OK button.

6. Close the Chooser dialog box.

7. On the Macintosh desktop, open the Microsoft UAM Volume folder.

8. Open the AppleShare folder.

9. Open the local computer's System folder.

10. Drag the Microsoft UAM into your System folder.

11. Close the System, AppleShare, and Microsoft UAM folders.

And that is all there is to it. You now are ready to connect to your Windows NT Server computers using your domain account. You can connect shared volumes or shared printers on the network.

Troubleshooting Directory and File-Related Issues

After you eliminate authentication-related problems by instigating a common user access policy, your access problems generally relate to one of two possibilities. Either the file in a shared environment has been renamed due to name translation, or the permissions have been set or modified, which prevents user access.

Understanding Filename Translation

When you start mixing network client access to a shared directory, you also start running into name-translation problems as users save the various files in the directory. For all intents and purposes, the file disappears. Understanding how name translation occurs can help you find these files. The basic rules follow:

◆ All Macintosh volumes must be created on an NTFS partition.

◆ A valid NTFS directory or file can contain a maximum of 255 characters if created by a Windows NT or Windows 95 client. The name can contain any character except the following:

? \ * " < > | / :

◆ A valid Macintosh directory or file can contain a maximum of 31 characters and can include any characters except a colon (:).

◆ A valid MS-DOS directory or file can contain a maximum of eight characters followed by a period and then a three-character extension. The name can contain any character except a space, including the following:

/ [ ] ; = " \ : | , *

◆ If a name is greater than the MS-DOS convention, then the name is shortened according to these basic steps:

◆ All spaces are removed.

◆ The characters are changed to uppercase.

◆ All illegal characters are dropped from the name.

◆ The first six characters of the filename are used, followed by a tilde (~) and a single digit. Then the file extension, followed by a period and the first three characters of the last part of the name, is appended to the name.

◆ If the name is not unique, based on the previous step, then the digit is incremented. If a valid name cannot be generated with a single digit, the name is truncated to five characters, followed by a tilde and two digits, followed by a three-character extension.

If the NTFS name is greater than 31 characters, the Macintosh client is able to view only the MS-DOS 8.3-compatible filename.

As you might have guessed, if a Win32 application saves a data file or renames a directory to greater than 31 characters, both your MS-DOS and Macintosh clients see a shortened version of the filename. This name can be pretty cryptic. If you have a file named `Development Project File for August 1, 1995.DOC`, for example, then your MS-DOS and Macintosh clients see `DEVELO~1.DOC`. If the original filename was `Project File 8-1-95.DOC`, however, that is also the name your Macintosh clients see, although your MS-DOS clients see `PROJEC~1.DOC`.

TROUBLESHOOTING PERMISSION PROBLEMS

You can set permissions on files with the File Manager MacFile menu option. These permissions apply only to Macintosh users. If you share a directory on your Windows NT Server as both a Macintosh volume for your Macintosh clients to access and as a regular sharepoint for your other network clients, however, you must maintain the corresponding permissions. If you don't, unpredictable results can occur.

Macintosh clients assign permissions based on three sources: owner, user/group, or everyone. For each of these sources, three permission levels may be applied, including the capability to see folders, see files, and make changes. Windows NT includes permissions based on groups or users and can include more levels than that defined for your Macintosh clients. So to maintain the appropriate permissions, keep in mind the permission settings listed in Table 37.1 and stick to the Windows NT Server subset when assigning permissions for your other network clients.

TABLE 37.1. MACINTOSH TO WINDOWS NT PERMISSION LEVELS.

Macintosh Permission	Corresponding Windows NT Permission
See Folders	Read
See Files	Read
Make Changes	Write and Delete

TROUBLESHOOTING PRINTER-RELATED ISSUES

Remember that the key to eliminating as many potential printing problems as possible begins with a simple rule: Control your access to the printer! This rule is simple in theory but sometimes difficult in practice, due to the constraints imposed upon you by your company's network policies. So, in some cases, you may have to modify this basic philosophy by allowing selected network clients to have their own local printers. If you have a shared network printer, however, that should be another story.

Begin your administrative duties by installing the printer on the network. Then create a printer on your Windows NT Server by following these steps:

1. Launch Print Manager.
2. Choose Create Printer from the Printer menu to display the Create Printer dialog box.
3. In the Printer Name field, enter a name for the printer.
4. In the Driver field, specify a printer driver to use for the printer.
5. In the Description field, enter a comment for the printer.
6. In the Print To field, select the port the printer is connected to if it is a local printer, such as LPT1.

   If the printer uses an HP Jet Direct card, choose Other, choose Hewlett-Packard Network Port, and then choose the Ethernet address for the port. If the printer is a TCP/IP printer, choose LPR Monitor and enter the IP address and printer name. If the printer is an AppleTalk printer, select Network Printer, select AppleTalk Printing Devices, and click the OK button. In Available AppleTalk Printing Devices, select the zone and the printer and click the OK button. Next, click the Settings button, which prompts you to capture the printer. Click the Yes button.

Tip

It is extremely important to capture the printer to prevent any other Macintosh user from printing directly to the printer and bypassing your security restrictions. Capturing a printer also enables you to manage the printer, such as specifying the time the printer is available for use, pausing/resuming the printer, pausing/resuming/deleting print jobs, or performing similar management duties. If, on the other hand, you do not capture a printer, your Macintosh users can connect to it and send any print jobs they want to it, and you cannot manage these particular print jobs.

7. Enable the Share This Printer checkbox. In the Share Name field, enter the MS-DOS–compatible printer name. Next, enter a comment in the Location field, specifying where this printer is physically located.

8. Click the OK button to create the printer.

After you create the printer, all your network clients can use it. This includes your MS-DOS, Windows, Windows NT, Macintosh, or even UNIX clients. And this can present another potential problem; if everyone can print to the printer, some users will abuse their network privileges by printing expensive greeting cards on your $10,000 color printer, for example. You therefore should limit access to printers of this type.

For your regular domain users, you can limit access by following these steps:

1. You can assign permissions for the printer by choosing Permission from the Security menu.

2. Specify the groups who will be able to print to or manage the printer.

3. For all other groups, you assign the No Access privilege to prevent them from using the printer.

For your Macintosh users, you can limit access by following these steps:

1. Create a user account in User Manager for Domains. Be sure to assign a password for the account, because this user account and password are required by your Macintosh users to connect to and use any printer controlled by this server.

2. For this account, assign the right logon as a service.

3. In the Control Panel Service applet, select the Print Server for Macintosh. Click the Startup button.

4. Specify the Use This Account option and specify the user account you created in step 1, along with the account password. Then click the OK button.

5. Stop and then restart the Print Service for Macintosh in order for the changes you made to be applied.

After you complete these steps, all your Macintosh users must specify the user account and password in order to connect to and use any of the printers on the computer running the Services for Macintosh with the associated user account.

Tip

The process to limit access to your printers for Macintosh users restricts all Macintosh users from printing to shared network printers on the Windows NT Server. Even for users who have a logon user account, this process should be used only for a limited number of printers. Only the printers you want to restrict access to should be so protected. All your other Windows NT Servers should use the local system account for the Print Services for Macintosh to allow any Macintosh client to connect to and use the shared network printers.

Most of the other printer-related problems you encounter with your Macintosh clients relate to printer-driver problems. The Services for Macintosh requires that a 6.x or higher LaserWriter printer driver be installed on the client. And to eliminate as many potential problems as possible, you should use the latest driver that you have personally certified for use on all your Macintosh clients. Mixing and matching drivers can cause additional complications, but do not just distribute the latest driver indiscriminately. Instead, test the driver completely before making it available. As part of your testing process, you should accumulate jobs that have caused you problems in the past so that you can test them with the newest drivers. Only after you test them should you distribute them.

UNIX CLIENT CONNECTIVITY

Windows NT Server is designed to interoperate with your UNIX-based network—not to replace it. It therefore provides only limited connectivity to your server. Specifically, your Windows NT Server can provide two basic functions to your UNIX clients. It can act as an FTP (File Transfer Protocol) server so that your UNIX clients can send and receive files, and it can act as a print server so that your UNIX clients can connect to and print to any shared printer for which they have a printer driver.

In order for your Windows NT Server to operate as an FTP Server or as a print server, you first must install these services from the Control Panel Network applet. The basic steps to accomplish this follow:

1. Launch the Control Panel Network applet.

2. Click the Add Software button.

3. Choose the TCP/IP and Related Components and click the OK button. The TCP/IP Installation Options dialog box appears.

4. Enable the checkboxes for the FTP Server Service and the TCP/IP Network Printing Support and click the Continue button.

5. Click the OK button in the Network dialog box.

   The FTP Service Configuration dialog box appears, where you can specify the following options:

◆ Maximum Connection: Specifies the maximum number of simultaneous users that can connect to your server. The default is 20, with a maximum of 50. Or, you can specify 0 to enforce no maximum connection limit.

◆ Idle Timeout: Specifies the maximum length, in minutes, the service will allow a connection that is no longer active to be used before disconnecting the user.

◆ Home Directory: Specifies the default drive and directory the user connects to.

◆ Allow Anonymous Connection: Allows users to connect using the username anonymous or FTP (which is a synonym for anonymous) and no password. The user is prompted to supply an e-mail address as the password, however. If this option is disabled, only users with valid domain accounts can connect to the FTP Server.

◆ Username: Specifies the Windows NT user account to use for users who connect using the anonymous account. This account should be configured to limit access to your server. It never should have administrative privileges, for example. I recommend that you set this option to the domain Guest account or another account with limited access rights.

◆ Password: Specifies the password to be used with the username specified in Username.

◆ Allow Only Anonymous Connections: Specifies that only an anonymous connection can be used. I highly recommend that you enable this option because the FTP Service does not encrypt passwords, and any connected user with a sniffer can find user accounts and passwords to hack into your system.

6. Restart the system after you are prompted to restart your system in order for your changes to take place.

7. After logging onto your system, you need to configure the FTP Service via the Control Panel FTP Server applet to display the FTP Server Security dialog box.

8. For each drive specified in the Partition field, specify the permissions: read or write. If no permission is specified, the user is unable to change drives. You also can use the File Manager Security | Permissions menu option to limit access to the root directory or any subdirectories for the user account you specified earlier.

9. Click the OK button for your changes to be applied.

10. Launch the Control Panel Service applet.

11. Select the TCP/IP Print Server and click the Startup button.

12. Change the Startup type to Automatic. This automatically starts the TCP/IP Print Server every time you restart your server.

13. Click the OK button. After you return to the Services dialog box, click the Start button to start the TCP/IP Print Server.

14. Now your UNIX clients can print to your shared printers by specifying the IP address of your server and the printer name of the shared printer. This name is not the same name as that defined in the Share This Printer on the Network field; instead, it is the name you specified in the Printer Properties dialog box Printer Name field.

15. Close the Services applet by clicking the OK button and close the Control Panel.

SUMMARY

This chapter discussed some of the basic issues that arise when supporting your Macintosh and UNIX clients. The primary focus was on Macintosh client connectivity, with tips on establishing policies for your Macintosh users to avoid potential problems, and configuring your Macintosh clients to use the Microsoft encryption package.

SYMBOLS

Index

D

MS-DOS clients
DOS-UP.SYS, 1042-1045
DOSDATA.SYS, 1042-1045
memory conflicts
loaded drivers,
1042-1045
resolving, 1041-1045
network problems, troubleshooting, 1041-1045
resource conflicts
network driver configura-
tions, 1044-1045
network protocols, 1044
troubleshooting,
1043-1045
ST-DBL.SYS, 1042-1045
ST-DSPC.SYS, 1042-1045
**MTA Site Configuration
Properties dialog box,
837-839**
**Multiple Access Unit
(MAU), ring topology, 12**
**multiple DHCP servers,
installation planning,
284-295**
**multiple disk subsystem,
performance options,
410-411**
**multiple master domain
model, 27-29**
implementing, 50-51
installation criteria, 27-29
network planning, 50-51
multiple network adapters
adding, 422-423
segments, 423
Windows NT Server, data
protection, 82-83
multiple network protocols
implementing, 386-387
network isolation tools,
386-387
multiple postoffices
administering (Dynamic
Drive Administrator), 827
connecting (Microsoft Mail),
822-827

**Multiple UNC Provider
(MUP), 8-9**
**Multiple UNC Router
(MUR), 8-9**
**multiport repeater, star
topology, 11**
**multiprocessing platform
(SNA Server), 984**
**multiprocessors, hardware
optimization, 733-735**

N

**name space, configuring
(Exchange Server),
836-837**
naming
Exchange Server organiza-
tion, 836-837
Microsoft Mail post-
offices, 796
SQL Object Manager,
triggers, 579-580
**NET ACCOUNTS command,
user accounts configura-
tion, 175-176**
NDIS, *see* **Network Device
Interface Specification**
**NET command, local
groups creation, 172-173**
Net Libraries
installing SQL Server,
528-529
SQL Client Configuration
utility, testing, 604-605
NET SHARE command
network sharepoints
creating, 204-205
deleting, 211
modifying, 204-205
NET USE command
network sharepoints
connecting, 214-215
disconnecting, 216
**NET USER command, user
account management,
183-184**

NetBEUI
advantages/disadvan-
tages, 19
network protocols, 19
**NetWare, Windows NT
Server migration, 117-118**
**NetWare directory, sharing
(Gateway Services for
NetWare), 129-130**
**NetWare printer, sharing
(Gateway Services for
NetWare), 130**
**NetWare server, emulating,
130-132**
**Network Adapter Card
Detection dialog box,
102-103**
network adapters
adding hardware, 419-423
cabling problems,
1001-1007
default binding order,
modifying, 419-423
Exchange Server optimiza-
tion recommendations,
867-868
graphical mode setup
(Windows NT Server),
selecting, 102
manufacturers list for SNA
Server, 901-903
Microsoft Mail, optimization
recommendations,
860-861
multiple implementation,
adding, 422-423
network protocols, 419-423
resource conflicts,
1001-1007
SMS single system optimi-
zation, 739-740
SNA Server, optimization
recommendations, 984
SNA Server requirements,
900-903
troubleshooting for Win-
dows NT clients,
1000-1013

Program Manager, selecting applications, 106
Program Properties dialog box, 708
Promote to Primary Domain Controller command (Computer menu), 153
promoting backup domain controller to primary domain controller, 153
Properties command (MacFile menu), 164
Properties dialog box, 156-158
Properties menu commands
  Connect to Server, 348
  Find All Servers, 348
  Pause Service, 348
  Service Properties, 350
  Start Service, 348
  Stop Service, 348
proprietary connections, planning, 786-787
protected mode drivers, Windows for Workgroups 3.11 clients, 1053-1058
Protocol (firewall component), 385
protocols, multiple implementation, 386-387
proxy agents
  implementing, 385-386
  network isolation tools, 385-386
publication servers and server replication, 593-594
Publishing Directories dialog box, 345
pull partners (WINS Server), 316-318
purchasing
  third party UPS replacements, 258-261
  UPS Service, 254
push partners (WINS Server), 316-318

Q - R

Queries windows (SMS Administrator), 673-674
Query Expression Properties dialog box, 713
Query Properties dialog box, 713
querying
  clients, inventory packages, 712-713
  SMS, inventory packages, 712-713
Queue menu (Microsoft Mail), 820

RAID (Redundant Array of Inexpensive Disks), hardware alternatives, 418-419
RAM (Random Access Memory)
  Exchange Server optimization recommendations, 871-872
  memory recommendations, 417-419
  memory upgrades, 417-419
  Microsoft Mail optimization recommendations, 863-864
  SMS multiple system optimization, 741-742
  SMS requirements, 683
  SMS single system optimization, 739-740
  SNA Server, optimization recommendations, 984
  SNA Server requirements, 899-903
RAS (Remote Access Service)
  acccss permissions, disabling, 391-393
  accessing Internet, 143-145
  configuring, 141-142

dial-in encryption, 391-393
encryption settings, 141
hardware requirements, 138-141
installing, 138-141
integrating with Windows NT Server, 137-138
modem settings, 140
PPP accounts, encrypting, 393
security issues, 391-393
SLIP accounts, encrypting, 393
RAS Administrator
  client connections, monitoring, 143
  client connectivity, setting, 142-143
RAS connections
  high speed modems, 61-62
  ISDN adapters, 62-65
  X.25 network, 61
RAS Server Protocol Configuration dialog box, 391
Re-sort (Microsoft Mail), 821-822
reading
  README.WRI file, 91-93
  SETUP.TXT file, 91-93
README.WRI, installation planning (Windows NT Server), 91-93
READPIPE command, SQL Server connection problems, 1016-1018
REAL (SQL Server data type), 489
real mode drivers, Windows for Workgroups 3.11 clients, 1053-1058
Rebuild (Microsoft Mail), 821-822
REBUILD agent (Mail Directory Synchronization Requestor), 825-826

Z

X

A VIACOM SERVICE

The Information SuperLibrary™

Bookstore	Search	What's New	Reference	Software	Newsletter	Company Overviews
Yellow Pages	Internet Starter Kit	HTML Workshop	Win a Free T-Shirt!	Macmillan Computer Publishing	Site Map	Talk to Us

CHECK OUT THE BOOKS IN THIS LIBRARY.

You'll find thousands of shareware files and over 1600 computer books designed for both technowizards and technophobes. You can browse through 700 sample chapters, get the latest news on the Net, and find just about anything using our massive search directories.

All Macmillan Computer Publishing books are available at your local bookstore.

We're open 24-hours a day, 365 days a year.

You don't need a card.

We don't charge fines.

And you can be as **LOUD** as you want.

The Information SuperLibrary

http://www.mcp.com/mcp/   ftp.mcp.com

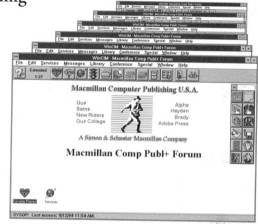

Microsoft Exchange Server Survival Guide

Pete McPhedran—Aurora Communications Exchange

Readers will learn the difference between Exchange and other groupware, such as Lotus Notes, and everything about the Exchange Server, including troubleshooting, development, and how to interact with other BackOffice components. Includes everything operators need to run an Exchange server. Teaches how to prepare, plan, and install the Exchange server. Explores ways to migrate from other mail apps, such as Microsoft Mail and CC:Mail. Covers Microsoft Exchange.

$49.99 USA　　*$70.95 CDN*
0-672-30890-8　*700 pp.*

Programming Windows NT 4 Unleashed

David Hamilton, Mickey Williams, & Griffith Kadnier

Readers get a clear understanding of the modes of operation and architecture for Windows NT. Everything—including execution models, processes, threads, DLLs, memory, controls, security, and more—is covered in precise detail. CD-ROM contains source code and completed sample programs from the book. Teaches OLE, DDE, Drag and Drop, OCX development, and the component gallery. Explores Microsoft BackOffice programming.

$59.99 USA　　*$84.95 CDN*
0-672-30905-X　*1,200 pp.*

Windows NT 4 Server Unleashed

Jason Garms

The Windows NT server has been gaining tremendous market share over Novell, and the new upgrade—which includes a Windows 95 interface—is sure to add momentum to its market drive. *Windows NT 4.0 Server Unleashed* is written to meet that growing market. It provides information on disk and file management, integrated networking, BackOffice integration, and TCP/IP protocols. CD-ROM includes source code from the book and valuable utilities. Focuses on using Windows NT as an Internet server. Covers security issues and Macintosh support.

$59.99 USA　　*$84.95 CDN*
0-672-30933-5　*1,100 pp.*

Microsoft SQL Server 6.5 Unleashed, Second Edition

David Solomon & Daniel Woodbeck, et al.

This comprehensive reference details the steps needed to plan, design, install, administer, and tune large and small databases. In many cases, the reader will use the techniques in this book to create and manage their own complex environment. CD-ROM includes source code, libraries, and administration tools. Covers programming topics, including SQL, data structures, programming constructs, stored procedures, referential integrity, large table strategies, and more. Includes updates to cover all new features of SQL Server 6.5, including the new transaction processing monitor and Internet/database connectivity through SQL Server's new Web Wizard.

$59.99 USA　　*$84.95 CDN*
0-672-30956-4　*1,200 pp.*

Windows NT 4 Web Development

Sanjaya Hettihewa

Windows NT and Microsoft's newly developed Internet Information Server are making it easier and more cost-effective to set up, manage, and administer a good Web site. Since the Windows NT environment is relatively new, there are few books on the market that adequately discusses its full potential. *Windows NT 4 Web Development* addresses that potential by providing information on all key aspects of server setup, maintenance, design, and implementation. CD-ROM contains valuable source code and powerful utilities. Teaches how to incorporate new technologies in your Web site. Covers Java, JavaScript, Internet Studio, and VBScript.

$59.99 USA $84.95 CDN
1-57521-089-4   744 pp.

Building an Intranet with Windows NT 4

Scott Zimmerman & Tim Evans

This hands-on guide teaches readers how to set up and maintain an efficient intranet with Windows NT. It comes complete with a selection of the best software for setting up a server, creating content, and for developing Intranet applications. CD-ROM includes a complete Windows NT intranet toolkit with a full-featured Web server, Web content development tools, and ready-to-use intranet applications. Includes complete specifications for several of the most popular intranet applications: group scheduling, discussions, database access, and more.

$49.99 USA $70.95 CDN
1-57521-137-8   600 pp.

Designing and Implementing Microsoft Internet Information Server 2

Arthur Knowles & Sanjaya Hettihewa

This book details the specific tasks for setting up and running a Microsoft Internet Information Server. Readers will learn troubleshooting, network design, security, and cross-platform integration procedures. Teaches security issues and how to maintain an efficient, secure network. Readers learn everything from planning to implementation. Covers Microsoft Internet Information Server 2.0.

$39.99 USA $56.95 CDN
1-57521-168-8   336 pp.

World Wide Web Database Developer's Guide

Mark Swank & Drew Kittle

Teaches readers how to quickly and professionally create a database and connect it to the Internet. Real-world database problems and solutions illustrate how to manage information. Includes HTML, Java, and the newest Netscape 2.0 features to help organize information. CD-ROM included! Explores ways to convert and present database information quickly and professionally. Readers learn how to use the latest Java and Netscape 2.0 releases. Covers the World Wide Web.

$59.99 USA $84.95 CDN
1-57521-048-7   800 pp.

Add to Your Sams Library Today with the Best Books for Programming, Operating Systems, and New Technologies

The easiest way to order is to pick up the phone and call

1-800-428-5331

between 9:00 a.m. and 5:00 p.m. EST.
For faster service please have your credit card available.

ISBN	Quantity	Description of Item	Unit Cost	Total Cost
0-672-30890-8		Microsoft Exchange Server Survival Guide (Book/CD-ROM)	$49.99	
0-672-30905-X		Programming Windows NT 4 Unleashed (Book/CD-ROM)	$59.99	
0-672-30933-5		Windows NT 4 Server Unleashed (Book/CD-ROM)	$59.99	
0-672-30956-4		Microsoft SQL Server 6.5 Unleashed, Second Edition (Book/CD-ROM)	$59.99	
1-57521-089-4		Windows NT 4 Web Development (Book/CD-ROM)	$59.99	
1-57521-137-8		Building an Intranet with Windows NT 4 (Book/CD-ROM)	$49.99	
1-57521-168-8		Designing and Implementing Microsoft Internet Information Server 2	$39.99	
1-57521-048-7		World Wide Web Database Developer's Guide (Book/CD-ROM)	$59.99	
❏ 3 ½" Disk		Shipping and Handling: See information below.		
❏ 5 ¼" Disk		TOTAL		

Shipping and Handling: $4.00 for the first book, and $1.75 for each additional book. Floppy disk: add $1.75 for shipping and handling. If you need to have it NOW, we can ship product to you in 24 hours for an additional charge of approximately $18.00, and you will receive your item overnight or in two days. Overseas shipping and handling adds $2.00 per book and $8.00 for up to three disks. Prices subject to change. Call for availability and pricing information on latest editions.

201 W. 103rd Street, Indianapolis, Indiana 46290

1-800-428-5331 — Orders   1-800-835-3202 — FAX   1-800-858-7674 — Customer Service

Book ISBN 0-672-30977-7

CD-ROM Licensing Information and Installation Instructions

By opening this package, you are agreeing to be bound by the following agreement:

Some of the software included with this product is copyrighted, in which case all rights are reserved by the respective copyright holder. You are licensed to use software copyrighted by the publisher and its licensors on a single computer. You may copy and/or modify the software as needed to facilitate your use of it on a single computer. Making copies of the software for any other purpose is a violation of the United States copyright laws.

This software is sold as is without warranty of any kind, either expressed or implied, including but not limited to the implied warranties of merchantability and fitness for a particular purpose. Neither the publisher nor its dealers or distributors assume any liability for any alleged or actual damages arising from the use of this program. (Some states do not allow for the exclusion of implied warranties, so the exclusion may not apply to you.)

By opening this package, you are agreeing to be bound by the following agreement which applies to products supplied by Northern Lights Software:

Aurora is a copyrighted product of Northern Lights Software, Ltd., and is protected by United States copyright laws and international treaty provisions. Copyright 1994, 1995, 1996. All Rights Reserved. Aurora Utilities for Sybase, Aurora Desktop, Aurora Script Manager, Aurora Distribution Viewer, and Aurora Cost Retrieval DLL are service marks of Northern Lights Software. Sybase is a trademark of Sybase, Inc.

Period of evaluation. By installing the software, it is understood that the provided software is for the purposes of evaluation only, and cannot be used beyond a period of thirty (30) days unless the software is registered. The software can be registered only by Northern Lights Software, Ltd., or its empowered agents.

The companion CD-ROM contains sample programs developed by the author, as well as third-party tools and product demos. The disc is designed to be explored with a browser program. Using Sams' Guide to the CD-ROM browser, you can view information about products and companies and install programs with a single click of the mouse. To install the browser, here's what to do:

Windows NT Installation Instructions:

1. Insert the CD-ROM disc into your CD-ROM drive.
2. From File Manager or Program Manager, choose Run from the File menu.
3. Type `<drive>\setup` and press Enter, where `<drive>` corresponds to the drive letter of your CD-ROM. If your CD-ROM is drive D, for example, type `D:\setup` and press Enter.
4. The installation creates a Program Manager group named BackOffice Administrator. To browse the CD-ROM, double-click on the Guide to the CD-ROM icon inside this Program Manager group.

Windows 95 Installation Instructions:

1. Insert the CD-ROM disc into your CD-ROM drive. If the AutoPlay feature of your Windows 95 system is enabled, the Setup program starts automatically.
2. If the Setup program does not start automatically, double-click the My Computer icon.
3. Double-click the icon representing your CD-ROM drive.
4. Double-click on the Setup.exe icon to run the installation program. Follow the instructions that appear. When Setup ends, double-click the Guide to the CD-ROM icon to begin exploring the disc.

Following installation, you can restart the Guide to the CD-ROM program by clicking the Start button, selecting Programs, and then BackOffice Administrator and Guide to the CD-ROM.

Note

The Guide to the CD-ROM program requires at least 256 colors. For best results, set your monitor to display between 256 and 64,000 colors. A screen resolution of 640×480 pixels is recommended. Adjust your monitor settings before using the CD-ROM.